MASSENET

Jules Massenet at the piano. *Autour d'une partition* (Around a Score),
by Albert Aublet, salon de 1888. Collection Roger-Viollet, Paris.

MASSENET

A CHRONICLE OF HIS LIFE AND TIMES

DEMAR IRVINE

AMADEUS PRESS
Reinhard G. Pauly, General Editor
Portland, Oregon

ISBN 0-931340-63-2
Designed and composed by Carol Odlum
Printed in Singapore

AMADEUS PRESS
(an imprint of Timber Press, Inc.)
9999 S.W. Wilshire, Suite 124
Portland, Oregon 97225

Library of Congress Cataloging-in-Publication Data

Irvine, Demar.
  Massenet : a chronicle of his life and times / Demar Irvine.
      p.   cm.
  Discography: p.
  Includes bibliographical references (p.   ) and index.
  ISBN 0-931340-63-2
  1. Massenet, Jules, 1842–1912. 2. Composers—France—Biography.
  I. Title.
  ML410.M41I8 1994
  230'.044'0922—dc20   93-24443
                                                              CIP
                                                              MN

To Greta

In remembrance of the Paris of our youth

Contents

Illustrations

Foreword

EMAR IRVINE'S MAJOR STUDY of Massenet came to my attention in an unusual way. It had occurred to me that Massenet's memoirs, *Mes souvenirs,* should be available to English-speaking readers. In checking the Massenet literature, I soon discovered that an English translation had indeed been published many years ago under the title *My Recollections* (Boston, 1919). Further investigation led me to the new French edition of *Mes souvenirs* (Paris, 1992), annotated with great care by Gérard Condé, a scholar in his own right and music editor for *Le Monde.* In Condé's bibliography, I found a surprising entry:

> Demar Irvine, *Massenet: A Chronicle of His Life and Times* (Seattle, 1974). Typewritten by the author but never published, this erudite study is the most reliable source of information about Massenet.

A surprise indeed! Irvine and I, both members and at various times officers of the American Musicological Society, have known each other for many years; yet with his characteristic modesty, he never mentioned his magnum opus to me. After locating and reading one of the precious copies he had distributed to libraries, I concluded that the time had come to publish this work, which is aptly termed a chronicle of the composer's life and times.

The audience for Massenet's operas is larger now than it was a generation ago. Moreover, many of today's readers have a keen appreciation of history, including music history, when presented in a broad cultural context, as Demar Irvine does here with consummate skill. I am delighted that this fascinating study is finally reaching a public who can give it the recognition it deserves.

REINHARD G. PAULY

Preface

WHEN *WERTHER* OPENED IN PARIS in 1893 (Massenet was not yet fifty-one), Alfred Bruneau could write in *Gil Blas*: "The composer of *Werther* is presently the most performed of French composers, hence the best known and most famous musician of our epoch. His works, so numerous and so lustrous, are in the repertoire of all the opera houses, adorn the music racks of every piano, are fixed in the memories of even the most unyielding dilettantes." Massenet had seemingly reached the pinnacle of his fame; and yet, after *Werther*, another sixteen operas would reach the stage!

The principal ingredient in Massenet's success, besides talent, was compulsive hard work. If one *waited* for inspiration, he contended, it would never come. Requiring but little sleep, he regularly arose at the crack of dawn to devote five or six hours to composition before turning to his voluminous correspondence and other routine matters of a normally action-packed day. Even on his many travels, he took his work along so as not to waste time in hotel rooms.

After *Marie-Magdeleine* and *Les Érinnyes* projected him to fame in 1873, Massenet had pushed on with *Le Roi de Lahore*, *Hérodiade*, *Manon*, *Le Cid*, and for the Exposition of 1889, *Esclarmonde*. By the time he was seventy he had completed twenty-eight operas and seen twenty-two of them produced on the stage. Another three were produced within the decade following his death—an impressive showing for a composer devoted to the lyric theater, as was Massenet.

To his contemporaries Massenet was above all a melodist who charmed his hearers with his astonishing faculty for invention and with the novelty, attractiveness, and expressive power he knew how to breathe into a musical phrase, all under the control of well-schooled craftsmanship. The accompanying harmonies were considered very elegant, very new, and often very piquant. That he had many imitators was quite apparent to those of his generation; but for his part, while Massenet assimilated, he imitated no one. Ultimately it is his orchestration that attracts attention: fresh and varied, it subserves admirably all the nuances of dramatic intent and bears the hallmark of a master.

Two months after Massenet's death in 1912, his arch rival, Saint-Saëns, penned an appraisal that was both hard and fair:

> Others speak lightly of his [Massenet's] works as "pleasing," as though this were a deprecation. But is it so reprehensible to please? . . . We admire the art of the Greeks: it was not profound. Their marble goddesses were beautiful, and their beauty suffices. . . . A master of his craft, knowing all the secrets of his art, Massenet eschewed those contortions and exaggerations which the naïve confuse with musical science. . . . He pursued the path which he himself laid out, profiting from new forms of expression imported from abroad which, moreover, he assimilated perfectly as an artist who remained completely French.[1]

That Massenet's music suited his times ought not to be held against him. No more so his financial rewards, which in the realm of serious music, have been bracketed with those of Verdi and Puccini.[2] If Massenet avoided the symphony as not suited to his particular talent, he succeeded in delighting concert audiences with descriptive orchestral suites and enhancing popular plays of the day with his incidental music. In addition, he wrote ballets, piano pieces, choral works, and well over two hundred songs.

For the present chronicle I have attempted to preserve some of the more useful (and more accurate!) elements from the Massenet literature, discounting heavily the pretty anecdotes and legends, and relying instead upon primary sources for additional factual information, some of which is here made reliably accessible for the first time. My objective, simply put, was to follow the composer around and observe how he spent the days and years of his life. The results should at least furnish a firm basis for further research.

In a broader sense, Massenet is here but the central theme for reanimating an era. Other personalities and events long since forgotten, or only half-remembered, have also been recalled and lined up onstage to play their contributory rôles. I have thus included (and tabulated in the index) the names of many singers, composers, conductors, poets, critics, and others, each of whom under more favorable circumstances might merit his or her own biography. These few clues may be of incidental use to future students of a fascinating epoch.

The present work was conceived in the summer of 1964, when my late good friend Hans Moldenhauer, of Spokane, Washington, loaned me seventy-two Massenet letters from his rich collection of composer autographs. That got me started. Seven years and two trips to Europe later, my Massenet typescript was complete. In 1974, after no publisher had expressed interest in the book, I had a hundred copies of the typescript made and bound for libraries, then put the whole matter out of mind. To my delight, it was resurrected in 1992 by Amadeus Press of Portland, Oregon.

My study of Massenet arose from the thought that he was being unduly neglected. That has changed somewhat. For example, there have been revivals of *Esclarmonde* and *Le Roi de Lahore* by Dame Joan Sutherland and Richard Bonynge, who is an expert on Massenet source materials; the Opera Theater of St. Louis presented nine very successful performances of *Cendrillon* in May and June of 1993; the Massenet Association, founded by the composer's descendant Anne Bessand-Massenet and housed at his Château Égreville (Maison de Massenet, 77620 Égreville, France), is advancing the composer's music through meetings, research, and performances; and the Massenet Society in New Jersey is planning to publish, in five volumes, new English translations of the libretti for all twenty-five of Massenet's operas. Still, to my surprise, very little has been published about this eminent and prolific composer.

Grateful acknowledgment is hereby extended to the following institutions for access to sources: Bibliothèque Nationale; Bibliothèque de l'Opéra; Bibliothèque de l'Arsenal; Archives Nationales; Archives de la Ville de Paris; Archives du Palais de Monaco; Archives de la Ville de Nice; Bibliothèque Nationale et Universitaire, Strasbourg; Badisches Generallandarchiv; University of Washington Library; Music Division, Library of Congress; the Newberry Library; the Boston Public Library; the New York Public Library; Théâtre Royal de la Monnaie; Haags Gemeentemuseum; Heugel et Cie; G. Ricordi & C.; the Moldenhauer Archive; Mairie, 9e Arrondissement. The University of Washington Library, with assistance from the University of Washington Graduate School Research Fund, was able to acquire 128 autograph letters.

Of all the persons who have helped in one way or another, I wish to thank in particular for their kindly interest and generous assistance: General Robert Massenet de Marancour; Yves L. Massenet; Pierre Bessand-Massenet; François Heugel; Signora L. Pestalozza; Franck Banchieri; Henriette Buschot; Mme M. Lang; Mme Felkay; Mlle A. Royer; Dr. I. Kecskeméti, Winfried Transfeld; Roland Chantepie; Jean Leloup; Dr. Hans Moldenhauer; F. Gerald Borch; Peter Demery; Dr. Edward N. Waters; Dr. Dallas D. Irvine; Rev. Ari Roest Crollius, S.J.; Gerri Benedikt; and Bob Salmon.

With this edition at long last in print, my special gratitude goes to Robert B. Conklin and Reinhard Pauly of the lively and forward-looking Amadeus Press for their encouragement, to Carol Odlum for her excellent contribution as editor, and to Paul Jackson for his generous loan of more than thirty vintage photographs and other memorabilia.

DEMAR IRVINE
SEATTLE, 1993

Massenet in the 1990s— A Fresh Appraisal

O VER THE PAST FIFTEEN YEARS, Massenet's image has undergone a considerable transformation in the minds of music lovers, performers, and critics alike. Perhaps it was inevitable for those works that have contributed most toward his fame—*Manon*, *Werther*, and *Thaïs*—to be somewhat slighted before it became impossible not to recognize in them that element of indestructibility common to all masterpieces. Their music seemed fragile, and their success was deemed ephemeral, like the enchantment of the feminine listeners who—sin of sins!—enjoyed them so much. We are now starting to notice that this music does hold up and is far richer and more varied (and consequently more thoroughly misunderstood) than was once believed. As we make discovery after discovery—some of them unexpected— we are beginning to realize that it is time to stop confusing the "Massenet style" with its caricature, which stemmed from distorted traditions and the routines of the theater.

Certainly Massenet's style is distinctive enough to be identified by its melodic contours. Yet its very unity displays a diversity which was cultivated by the composer and which fueled the flame of his inspiration. Now, since even the part of his output that was thought to have passed forever into eclipse has begun to be revived and recorded, it has become possible to consider the whole from a chronological standpoint and to revise certain judgments that have sprung from often biased contemporary appraisals. Until rather recently, scarcely anything except *Manon*, *Werther*, and portions of *Thaïs*, *Hérodiade*, and *Le jongleur de Notre-Dame* seemed worthy of attention; the works that preceded them were said to be awkward endeavors, and those that followed (or intervened) merely repetitive.

It should not be forgotten, however, that the success of *Werther* was far from the overnight variety. The score, completed in 1887, lay dormant for five years before it was first performed in Vienna, in German; after the 1893 French première at the Opéra-Comique, it took ten years for audiences to warm up to its somber drama. *Thaïs*, initially a failure, had to wait thirteen years for the success that it finally achieved. Without the talent and beauty that Lina Cavalieri brought to the title role in 1907, *Thaïs* would perhaps be as little known today as *Le Mage* or *Ariane*. Replaying these forgotten scores in our time does more than merely satisfy the curiosity of a few musicologists; it gives the public a chance to experience operas that were genuinely successful when first performed, works of unquestionable quality that still hold appeal for audiences—ultimately leading, perhaps, to their return to the repertoire.

Indeed, thanks to the performances at Saint-Étienne's 1990 Massenet Festival, we now know that his last opera, *Cléopâtre*, contains some beautifully novel effects and that, at the time of its composition (1912), those who accused Massenet of stylistic complacency were reproaching him for having an individual style, the one thing he was incapable of changing. Instead of noting the remarkable variations within the style they knew so well, they chose merely to dwell upon its persistence.

In fact, it can be affirmed that as early as *Marie-Magdeleine*, his first oratorio (premièred in 1873), Massenet found the lush lyricism and cajoling sweetness that were to bring him success. He would subsequently exploit it on occasion (*La Vierge*), though more often he tried to free himself from it in order to avoid lapsing into petrified mannerism and, indeed, to broaden his range of expression. Still, the development of Massenet's musical language was marked by reactionary stages; it alternately advanced and receded as it evolved—surprising at first consideration, but logical upon analysis. It could be said, for example, that the elegant neoclassicism of *Manon* (1884) provided the antidote to the grand-opera virus to which the composer had succumbed in *Le roi de Lahore* (1877) or *Hérodiade* (1881), though, paradoxically, what followed *Manon* was *Le Cid*, a work whose brilliance rings a bit hollow. After the latter's plethora of brass and stage heroics, Massenet was able to immerse himself in the psychological intimacy of *Werther*. Then came the spectacular but uneven *Esclarmonde*, that blend of Wagnerian and Meyerbeerian influences composed for the Universal Exhibition of 1889. And so the evolution continued.

With each new opera, Massenet seemed to reach a point of no return. By choosing subjects as antithetical as possible to the ones immediately preceding them, he kept himself on a jagged course, continually casting aside solutions that had become outmoded: those of *Manon* were inconceivable in *Le Cid*, those of *Le Cid* impossible in *Werther*, and so on. Amazingly, he never lost his own personality along the way—and that essential personality is what remains, in large part, to be discovered.

It is surprising to note the extent to which reliable sources for even the most basic facts about Massenet's life and works are still lacking. There are a few biographies, of course. Louis Schneider's account, written mainly during the composer's lifetime, is a veritable compendium of information, but unfortunately it brims with inaccuracies. In the autobiographical *Mes souvenirs* (My Recollections), which was written during the final months of his life, Massenet naturally presented the image of himself he wished to leave for posterity—the elusive, idealized image of a creator whose truest self was revealed in his music. Alfred Bruneau offered his *Massenet*, and there are a few other biographies; but the more recent the book, the more apt it is to mislead with secondhand information.

Though it probably adds little to our appreciation of, say, *Chérubin* to know whether its composer was the youngest in a family of eight, twelve, twenty-one, twenty-two, or twenty-three children (all figures appearing in one book or another), future biographers must sift out the truth. The same goes for most major events in Massenet's life, whether it be the year he entered the Conservatoire (1851 or 1853?); the duration of his "exile" in Chambéry, which interrupted his studies at the Conservatoire (six months or two years?); or the composition dates of his works, such as that of *Amadis* (1891, 1902, or 1910?). The answers to such questions will not affect the general public's understanding of the music, but many members of the listening audience are eager for significant information. Moreover, to combat the prejudices that sometimes prevent legitimate appreciation, and even the widespread performance, of certain works, it is necessary to examine their genesis in a critically objective manner.

Demar Irvine was the first to accomplish this important task, in the definitive study of Massenet that now, at last, appears in print. On a more modest scale, in my critical edition of *Mes souvenirs*, I too sought to elucidate the composer's life and thought. And that same elusive goal—historical truth—is currently being pursued by Patrick Gillis, whose *Catalogue raisonné de l'oeuvre de Massenet* (Catalogue of the Works of Massenet)—slated for publication in 1994—will probably challenge many details, and even the most firmly established convictions. Thus the revision of history marches on.

GÉRARD CONDÉ
PARIS, 1993

Translated by E. Thomas Glasow

Jules Massenet as a young man. Collection Lim M. Lai.

Parentage and Early Life

Jules-Émile-Frédéric Massenet was born on 12 May 1842, in the township of Montaud, near Saint-Étienne (Loire), France. His father was Alexis Massenet (1788–1863), and his mother was Éléonore-Adélaïde Royer de Marancour (1809–1875), whom Alexis had married at Albi on 9 May 1830 after the death of his first wife. The four children of this second union were Julie, Léon, Edmond, and Jules. In accordance with custom they had the right to bear the name Massenet de Marancour, or indeed Massenet Royer de Marancour. Jules, unlike his brothers, never used the matronymic; in his later public life he even preferred "Massenet" without the prenomen.

Saint-Étienne lies thirty-six miles by rail southwest of Lyon, on the Furan river, a tributary of the Loire. Sitting in the midst of the second largest coalfield in France, the city underwent a phenomenal growth in the nineteenth century. The chief industries were iron and steel, the manufacture of small arms, hardware, and ribbons. The first railway in France was built in 1829 from Saint-Étienne to Andrézieu, and a second in 1831 to Lyon.

Adjoining Saint-Étienne on the east was the township of Montaud, including the quarter near the Furan river known as La Terrasse, where the Massenets were living. Schneider published a photograph of the house as it appeared in 1908: a large stone structure of four stories, still surrounded by park and open country and not yet swallowed up by the city.[1]

At this point in his career Alexis Massenet was director of a manufactory of scythes situated at La Terrasse. His products were shown at the Paris Exposition of 1844 and won for him the decoration of Chevalier of the Légion d'Honneur. In an autobiographical sketch published in 1892, the composer recounted how his father "became an iron-master, and was the inventor of those huge hammers which, crushing steel with extraordinary power by a single blow, change bars of metal into sickles and scythes. So it was that, to the sound of heavy hammers of brass, as the ancient poet says, I was born."[2]

Beside the factory was an orchard where flowers grew in abundance. Here Jules's older brother Léon would go to play on Sundays with his school comrade Jules

Vallès. When these two met again in Paris, around 1856, Vallès came to know the younger brother Jules, and years later set down his impressions.

About 1844, the Massenet family moved into the city of Saint-Étienne, occupying for the next four years a *premier étage* apartment at No. 4 Place Marengo. Alexis entered into partnership with Messrs. Dumaine and Dorian to set up a branch factory at Pont-Salomon, near Saint-Étienne. This new enterprise did not prosper very well. By February of 1848 the family was installed in the Rue de Beaune in Paris, and Massenet père seems no longer to have been very active.

Massenet's *Souvenirs* begin, dramatically enough, with 24 February 1848— date of the abdication of Louis-Philippe as well as of little Jules's first piano lesson from his mother. That will be an appropriate point to resume the story in the next chapter. Meanwhile, a regression is in order to uncover the family background.

The name Masson is fairly common in France; a derivative—Massenet, with *o* softened to *e*—is associated with the region of the Loire. Masson is generally not equated with the occupation of stonemason (*maçon*), but evolved from Thomas, for which the hypocoristic form Thomasson suffered an aphaeresis, or dropping of the first syllable. One could say, then, that Massenet and his revered teacher Ambroise Thomas were remotely related etymologically. By a meaningless coincidence, there is a town of Masseney near Waldheim in Saxony, a few miles from Freiberg, where Massenet's father completed his training in metallurgical engineering.

The history of this particular Massenet family begins with the composer's grandfather, Jean-Pierre Massenet, who was born on 25 February 1748 at Gravelotte, in the diocese of Metz (Lorraine), and died on 28 October 1824 at Strasbourg. His papers turned up sixty-six years later in a notary's office and were deposited in the Strasbourg municipal library. Here Rodolphe Reuss examined the dossier and, in 1897, published a biography entitled *Souvenirs Alsatiques; Jean-Pierre Massenet: Cultivateur à Heiligenstein, Député du Bas-Rhin, Professeur à l'Académie de Strasbourg*. In a footnote on page 144, Reuss confessed that, although many of his readers will doubtless wonder whether the illustrious composer is a descendant of this Massenet, he has been unable to find any information on the subject.

The dossier of Jean-Pierre Massenet, the grandfather, contains a copy of his birth record but no other information until 1774, when he would have been twenty-six. He was the son of one Jean Massenet, whose occupation is given as *manoeuvre*, and of Marie-Anne Warin (who died at Metz in November 1788). To translate *manoeuvre* literally as "day laborer" seems unkind. In view of the notable achievements of many descendants (Jules Massenet was the only professional musician), perhaps the great-grandfather was a skilled mechanic.

Jean-Pierre had two brothers and a sister. His brother Joseph emigrated to Germany, respelled his name as Massenez, and founded a distinguished collateral branch of the family.* His other brother Jean, or Jacques, was for a time at Brest, probably as a carpenter or shipwright, but returned to Metz in 1786 with two crushed fingers.

---

* See Appendix 1: The Massenet Family.

Jean-Pierre obtained for him a position as driver of artillery carriages. His sister, Jeanne, married one Nicolas Campion in 1781 and moved to Le Havre.

We can only surmise how Jean-Pierre Massenet obtained an education culminating in the degrees of Doctor of Philosophy and Docteur-ès-Lettres.[3] His qualities of intellect and personality no doubt attracted influential support, as from the Mathieu family in Metz and their relatives in Strasbourg. In pre-Napoleonic times, the aristocratic families of Russia and the Baltic lands often entrusted the education of their sons and daughters to French or German preceptors and governesses. This was Jean-Pierre's occupation from sometime prior to 1774 until 1787. We pick up his trail in St. Petersburg in 1774, when he may have been preceptor for the Igelstroem family. Then, from the autumn of 1775 until 1778, Massenet was companion-tutor to Ernst Otto von Vietinghoff (1757–1780), son of a Livonian baron. The two spent some time in Strasbourg, Spa, Paris, London, and Berlin, where they parted company when Ernst Otto came of age and joined the military.

Jean-Pierre next visited the Vietinghoff family in Riga and was in St. Petersburg in 1779, but then we lose sight of him until February 1783 when he was back in Strasbourg. His dossier contains correspondence relating to a preceptorship for the youngest Vietinghoff son, Christoph Burkhard (1767–1829). The terms discussed were a five-year contract with an annual salary of two thousand francs, all expenses paid, and a gratuity of six thousand francs at the end of the tutelage. For some reason the negotiations fell through.

In 1784, Massenet was at Turin and Venice, in which latter city he met his future wife, Françoise-Hélène Mathieu. At this time, Barbara Juliana von Vietinghoff, the sister of his former charge, would have been in Venice with her husband, Baron Alexis von Krüdener. This Baroness Krüdener (1764–1824), who had literary pretensions in the Paris salons, later wandered about as a religious mystic, always welcomed because of her great wealth, and died in the Crimea when about to set up a colony for repentant sinners.

Jean-Pierre's next documented assignment was as tutor-companion to Prince Michael, son of major general Prince André Galitzin and Princess Eisabeth Yousoupoff. The Galitzins were a numerous, powerful, and distinguished Russian family. An uncle of Massenet's young charge, Prince Dmitri Galitzin, was ambassador at Vienna, dying there in 1793. To still another member of the family, Prince Nikolai Galitzin (1794–1866), Beethoven dedicated the late quartets Opp. 127, 130, and 132.

The new preceptorial duties began in Italy on 27 June 1784, and the association lasted for three years. On 10 September, Prince Michael was matriculated at the University of Leyden, together with "Pierre Jean Massenet, ex Gallicae provincia Lorraine, annos academicos habent, ephorus principis Galitzin."[4] Shortly thereafter, Massenet sent the family a bill for expenses from 27 June to 15 September amounting to 5068 florins.*

---

* Reuss, Jean-Pierre's biographer, calculated that 5068 florins would have had the purchasing power of 20,000 francs in 1897.

A year and a half later (March 1786), Massenet and Prince Michael were apparently still at Leyden. That summer the noted Dr. Cabanis, then at Geneva, cured Prince Michael of a troublesome tapeworm. Pupil and preceptor then proceeded to Lyon for several months' study of letters and art. Mesmerism engaged their attention, and they were introduced to the mysteries of a Masonic lodge. By the summer of 1787 they were in Moscow, where the prince purchased for Massenet a *calèche* and provided a French-speaking servant.

On 20 July 1787, Jean-Pierre Massenet and Françoise-Hélène Mathieu signed their marriage contract at Mitau, Courland. Massenet thereby acquired a distinguished collection of in-laws, mainly active as jurists, magistrates, or in branches of government.* He got on splendidly with his new relatives even though, as time wore on, his relations with his wife deteriorated. Indeed, in some family arguments the brothers-in-law took Jean-Pierre's side rather than Hélène's. The youngest of Massenet's new brothers-in-law was Philippe-Gaëtan Mathieu de Faviers (1761–1833), who made a brilliant career in the military service of supply—a fact of no small importance in the lives of future Massenets. He was *commissaire général* for the Army of Helvetia under General Masséna and for the Army of the Rhine under General Moreau. After the campaigns of 1805–07, Napoleon made him *ordonnateur en chef de la Grande Armée*. From 1809 he was in Spain as *intendant général* (chief commissary) for the Armée du Midi, but was retired at the Restoration when regular members of the military took over the services of supply. He was created a baron by Louis XVIII in 1817, and a peer of France by Louis-Philippe in 1832.

After their marriage at Mitau, the Massenets returned to Alsace. Jean-Pierre, now nearing forty, declined further offers for tutoring. The time had come to settle down. A new contract drawn up some months after their arrival specified what each had brought to the community property: Jean-Pierre's thirty thousand francs, and Hélène Mathieu's ten thousand francs.

On 25 June 1788, a son was born at Strasbourg and given the name Pierre-Michel-Nicolas-Alexis. At the baptism, Prince Galitzin was godfather, represented by Jacques-Christoph Jacquin, of Otrott, as proxy. It was this Alexis who, nearly fifty-four years later, was to become the father of the composer Jules Massenet.

In December 1788 the Massenets took possession of a property at Heiligenstein, which lies at the foot of the Vosges mountains near Barr, Alsace. There, on 23 August 1790, a second son was born and christened Auguste-Pierre-Charles. This time the godfather was Pierre-Charles Mathieu, *avocat* of the Parlement de Metz, represented by the same Monsieur Jacquin as proxy. In the sequel, Auguste Massenet entered the service of the grand duke of Baden, in 1809, as lieutenant of the grenadiers of the guard. He was gravely wounded before Strasbourg on 5 July 1815 and died four days later.

Jean-Pierre Massenet apparently lived through the Revolution and the Terror quietly enough. In August 1791 he was elected as one of nine deputies to represent

---

* See Appendix 1: The Massenet Family.

the Département du Bas-Rhin at the Legislative Assembly in Paris. There are no speeches or other signs of activity on record. After leaving the Assembly he was, for a time, inspector of primary schools. In 1796, Massenet was called to the École Centrale du Bas-Rhin as professor of history. His son Alexis attended the same school as a student of mineralogy.

By November of 1805, Jean-Pierre and Hélène reached a parting of the ways and divided their community property. Mme Massenet then resided with her sons, chiefly at Stützheim on a property purchased from her brother Jacques Mathieu. For a time she was at Freiberg in Saxony with Alexis, who there completed his training at the famous school of mines. Gaëtan Mathieu-Faviers (then in Berlin with the Grande Armée) wrote to Jean-Pierre on 24 December 1808 that he planned to go to Dresden, and perhaps even to Freiberg, where he supposed he "would still find Alexis and his mother."[5]

The next word from Gaëtan to "Mon cher Massenet" was in a letter from Madrid dated 14 October 1809. He arranges to discharge Mme Massenet's debts and settles upon his nephew Auguste Massenet an annuity of six hundred francs. Gaëtan has intervened with the authorities regarding a professorship for Jean-Pierre at the university [which did not materialize until 1812]. Alexis, finished at Freiberg, has been employed by a mining company to inspect the Guadalcanal mine in Andalusia. The mine is unapproachable because of the Spanish guerillas in the mountains, but Alexis has kept busy in the office and even made some money in a speculative venture.[6]

On 19 October 1812, Jean-Pierre Massenet was appointed professor of history in the faculty of letters and sciences of the Académie de Strasbourg. Later, because retirement pensions had been abolished, a special arrangement was made (18 May 1819) whereby he was to retain his title of professor and salary of fifteen hundred francs provided he "give lectures as often as the state of his health would permit." The main burden of his duties was taken over by an adjunct, who would inherit the professorship upon Massenet's definitive retirement. During his last years Jean-Pierre Massenet resided at 9 Quai des Bateliers. He died on 28 October 1824, and there were 150 invitations to the funeral.

In July 1812 Alexis Massenet is mentioned as "deputy of the imperial army of the South at the mines of Almaden."[7] It is known that he served under Marshal Soult, duke of Dalmatia, as staff-officer with the rank of captain. The drama of Napoleon's retreat from Moscow tends to eclipse our interest in the Peninsular War with England. The duke of Wellington had landed at Lisbon on 22 April 1809, and within a month the French had evacuated Portugal. But it was not until 12 August 1812 that Wellington entered Madrid. He tenaciously pursued his purpose, and with the Battle of Toulouse, 10–12 April 1814, the French were defeated. On 11 April, Napoleon abdicated.

With the cessation of hostilities, the pro-Napoleonic Alexis, not wishing to serve the Restoration, resigned his commission and took up a career in the metallurgical industry. He was briefly at Albi, then settled in Toulouse on the Rue des Amidonniers. His affairs prospered, and in 1816, at Toulouse, he married Sophie de

Jaegerschmidt, whose family had migrated from Sweden to Baden several generations previously.

Of the eight children born to Alexis and Sophie, at least three reached maturity and can be identified: Alfred, Auguste, and Camille. Shortly after Napoleon's Hundred Days and Waterloo (18 June 1815), Hélène Massenet had sold her property at Stützheim; soon she left Alsace and joined her son at Toulouse. She must have taken a lively interest in her grandchildren, no doubt instilling in them the proud traditions of the Mathieu family by recounting many a story and anecdote. Alfred Massenet (1819–1851), who never married, served in the military and was retired for reasons of health at some time prior to his decease. Auguste Massenet (1821–1892) served in the navy and was later captain of an ocean liner, perhaps on a South American run. In any case, his half-brother Léon Massenet de Marancour published in 1883 a traveler's guide to Madeira, Teneriffe, San Vicente, Dakar, Pernambuco, Bahia, Rio de Janeiro, Montevideo, and Buenos Aires. Camille Massenet (1822–1901), while a student at the École Polytechnique, was present at the entombment of Napoleon's remains at the Invalides in 1840. He eventually became a colonel of engineers, specializing in pontoon bridges, and was decorated with the high rank of Officier of the Légion d'Honneur.

Space prohibits recounting further exploits of descendants of Alexis and Sophie Massenet. If there is a pattern, it is that the sons were typically trained as engineers and entered careers as army officers, in several instances rising to the rank of general. An administrative talent appears predominant—if not with the military or naval establishment, then in branches of government or in industry. Occasionally there is another specialist in mining engineering. Or there is Alexis's grandson, Louis-Marie Massenet (1863–1905), who died in the Andes while heading an important survey expedition of the French Geographic Service.

Sophie de Jaegerschmidt died in childbirth in 1829. It can be readily understood that Alexis could not leave his children for long without a mother. On 9 May 1830, he married Éléonore-Adélaïde Royer de Marancour, at Albi, capital of the département of the Tarn, some twenty-four miles northeast of Toulouse.

Mlle Royer de Marancour was born at Metz in 1809, daughter of Edmé-Raphaël Royer de Marancour (1772–1844), a *commissaire des guerres* under the First Empire, who in 1807 had married a Prussian lady, Caroline Schroer, while in Berlin serving as commissary for the Legrand Division. (It will be remembered that Gaëtan Mathieu-Faviers was also in Berlin at about this time.) Monsieur Royer de Marancour, a man of position and substance in Metz, provided his daughter with every advantage, including excellent training in piano. As a young girl, after the Restoration, Éléonore was presented to the Duchesse d'Angoulême (1778–1851) who, as the first child of Louis XVI and Marie-Antoinette, was known as Marie-Thérèse de France. It is said that the acquaintance was more than casual and that the duchess took a close interest in Éléonore's upbringing. Certainly the memoirs of the duchess, involving her escape from the Temple, the long years of exile, and all that followed, are an enthralling story in themselves. Little wonder that the composer Massenet, long after, was attracted to the subject for a *drame musical* set in 1792–93, which he called *Thérèse*. Like the ending of some other tragic opera, Marie-Thérèse of France, her husband the Duc d'Angoulême, and his father Charles X, ended their days in exile. They were entombed in a Franciscan cloister near Gorizia, in the then Austrian crown-land of Görz-Gradisca—a fruitful plain shut in by mountains northerly from Trieste.

For some years Alexis and his young wife remained in Toulouse, where their children Julie, Léon, and Edmond were born. They then moved to La Terrasse, near Saint-Étienne. It was there that Alexis's mother, Françoise-Hélène, died on 18 October 1840 at the age of eighty-three. A year and a half later, in the same house, Jules Massenet came into the world.

We shall meet Jules's sister and brothers again as the chronicle progresses. For the present, let it suffice to say that Julie Massenet (1832–1905) married the painter Paul Cavaillé in 1853. Léon Massenet de Marancour (1834–1886) remained unmarried and became a journalist and globe-trotter. In the Bibliothèque Nationale one finds half a dozen of his publications, besides the traveler's guide to South America already mentioned and his *Confessions d'un commis-voyageur* of 1865. Edmond Massenet de Marancour (1837–1929) entered a military career and became a general, as did his eldest son Robert Massenet de Marancour, who, in keeping with the times, rose to the rank of general in the new branch of aviation.

Paris;
Chambéry

WITH A DRAMATIC FLOURISH, Massenet's *Souvenirs* begin on 24 February 1848—date of the abdication of Louis-Philippe of the House of Orléans, who had reigned for the material interests of France, the greater good of the House of Orléans, and the prosperity of the middle classes. Louis-Philippe had survived eight attempts upon his life and endured a clamorous opposition from monarchists, Bonapartists, leftist republicans, and the newer anarchist and socialist movements. One focal issue was electoral reform: a mere 200,000 Frenchmen were allowed to vote. At last, on 22–23 February, the people of Paris rose in arms and quickly won over the police, the national guard, and even the regular troops. The Citizen King, deserted by his courtiers, quietly escaped to England as "Mr. Smith."

The Massenet family was living at this time in the Rue de Beaune, a street on the Left Bank that emerges at the Quai Voltaire along the Seine. Perhaps the house was at No. 1, for the Massenets had a view from their apartment windows of the Jardin des Tuileries. In those days the Tuileries Palace was still standing, embraced between the now open arms of the westernmost wings of the Louvre. The Massenet apartment was a ringside seat for revolution. Indeed, on one occasion in that historic February when Madame Massenet and her sons had to cross the Tuileries gardens, they found themselves pinned down by cross fire, flat on their stomachs for several hours.

If Jules was born, as he poetically put it, to the sound of heavy metallurgical hammers, then he was introduced to music, by his own account, to the sound of small-arms fire. For in February of 1848 he received his first piano lesson from his mother. Madame Massenet was an accomplished pianist who also composed a little. As long as her husband was prosperous, her talents were no doubt considered among the social graces. But it is strongly hinted that the Massenets had now lost whatever means they formerly had and that Madame Massenet contributed to their income by giving piano lessons.

The family would have consisted of the father, Alexis (age sixty); the mother, Éléonore (thirty-eight); Julie (fifteen); Léon (thirteen); Edmond (twelve); and Jules (who would turn six in May). The sons of Alexis by his first marriage had left the parental nest to take up their military or naval careers. Éléonore had no doubt reached the firm resolve that her youngest son, Jules, should devote his life to the arts rather than to engineering or the military.

While studying diligently with his mother, Jules also attended the Lycée Saint-Louis—a longish walk to the Rue de la Harpe, where Baron Haussmann would later make a corner between the new Boulevard Saint-Michel and the Rue de Vaugirard. The dates of his attendance are vague. He withdrew, perhaps, when he was about thirteen. But the classical education offered was solid enough to be of permanent value. We are told that Jules was for a time quite interested in astronomy. Had he not become a musician, he would have liked to be an artist. This, no doubt, an afterthought occasioned by his association with artists as a youth and young man.

On his way home from the Lycée, did Jules sometimes take a detour and linger in the Jardin du Luxembourg? Did he gaze at the placards outside the Théâtre de l'Odéon? Did he wander into Saint-Sulpice to hear the organ, or sit on the steps of the seminary to admire the view of the square? It was this great seminary of the diocese of Paris (closed in 1906) that Ernest Renan had quitted in 1845, abandoning all thoughts of a career in the church. The seminary scene in *Manon* comes to mind. And in the last years of his life Massenet returned to this charming district, occupying an apartment in the Rue de Vaugirard just across from the Luxembourg.

Jules presented himself for the entrance examination at the Conservatoire on 10 January 1853.[*] According to his biographer Schneider, he played the finale of Beethoven's sonata "Opus 29" astonishingly well.[†] Just which of the three finales Massenet performed is not made clear; one rather suspects it was the bouncing E-flat major of Opus 31, No. 3. In the usual summary fashion, the director's report for the quarter, January–March 1853, merely lists under new students: "Massenet, age 10 years, 7 months, admitted to a piano class."[1]

At this time Jules was rather delicate and not very tall. In a drawing by Cham he is shown seated on five or six folios of music, with hands in the air barely reaching the keyboard. This is, of course, one of Cham's humorous exaggerations. His caricatures in *Le Charivari* and *Le Monde illustré*, and in published albums, delightfully document the small happenings of daily life during the Second Empire. Cham, son of the Marquis de Noé, was a friend of the Massenets and often came to spend an evening with them.

---

[*] Massenet may also have been examined on 9 Oct. 1851, as stated in the *Souvenirs*, but he was not admitted at that time.

[†] The three sonatas of Beethoven's Op. 31 had also circulated, since Cappi's Viennese edition of 1805, as "Op. 29."

The Conservatoire was then at the corner of the Rue du Faubourg Poissonnière and the Rue Bergère.* During the 1850s this prestigious school of the musical and dramatic arts admitted about 60 percent of those who applied; during the 1852–53 school year, 509 students were enrolled, including 295 men and 214 women. Daniel-François-Esprit Auber had assumed the directorship in 1842, following Cherubini's retirement. Auber's *Masaniello, ou la Muette de Portici* had won for him a place in the Académie des Beaux-Arts in 1829 as successor to Gossec. Auber's real forte was a kind of lightweight but sophisticated and musicianly *opéra comique*, which he turned out at the rate of almost one a year from 1811 until 1869. His *Fra Diavolo* (1830) held its place at the Opéra-Comique until the end of the century.

When Massenet entered the Conservatoire, there were four professors of composition: the Neapolitan Michele Enrico Carafa, whose operas had achieved an extraordinary popularity in Paris in the 1820s; Aimé-Ambroise-Simon Leborne, a pupil of Cherubini and recipient of the 1820 Prix de Rome; Jacques-François-Fromental-Élie Halévy, the eminent Jewish composer of *La Juive* (1835) and a dozen subsequent operas; and Adolphe Adam, whose *Le Postillon de Longjumeau* (1836), ballet *Giselle* (1841), and others, had gained for him a European reputation. Classes in harmony were offered by Bienaimé, Reber, Elwart, and Bazin. Solfège was taught by Tariot, Savard, and (for women) Goblin. Berlioz, assistant curator of the library since 1839, had been appointed librarian on 1 January 1852.

Male piano students could enter the class of either Laurent or Marmontel. We shall soon meet fifty-six-year-old Laurent, who was Massenet's teacher. His confrere, Antoine-François Marmontel (1796–1867), a native of Clermont-Ferrand, had won first prize in piano in 1832. In 1837 he was engaged to teach solfège at the Conservatoire, and in 1848 he fell heir to the piano professorship vacated by his teacher Zimmermann.† Marmontel achieved a considerable reputation by training a long list of career pianists, though he is now best remembered for having taught Bizet and Debussy.

Female piano students could choose between that elegant idol of the salons, Henri Herz, and Mme Louise Farrenc.‡ Violinists might study with Joseph Massart, Jean-Delphin Alard, or Narcisse Girard, successor to Habeneck as conductor of the Concerts du Conservatoire. For the cellists there was Auguste-Joseph Franchomme. One of the more permanent figures at the Conservatoire was François Benoist, professor of organ from 1819 until he was pensioned off in 1872 to make room for his pupil and successor César Franck.

---

* In 1911 the Conservatoire moved to the Rue de Madrid; its former site is now occupied by a branch office of the Postes, Télégraphes, et Téléphones.

† Pierre Zimmermann (1785–1853) taught the young prodigy Alkan, Ambroise Thomas, César Franck, and numerous others. His three daughters married persons of note: Anne Zimmermann married Charles Gounod in 1852. Juliette, a sculptress, married the painter Édouard Dubufe (1820–1883); fate would have it that their granddaughter would marry a grandson of Massenet. Berthe Zimmermann married the architect Jean-Marie-Baptiste Pigny (1821–1881).

‡ Louise Farrenc (1804–1875) published, in collaboration with Édouard Fétis, an extensive anthology, *Trésor des pianistes*, 20 vols., 1861–72.

Considering the importance of opera, it is not surprising to find seven teachers of singing at this time. The Italians were Filippo Galli, Marco Bordogni, and Michele Giuliani. Galli, at first a tenor, had changed after an illness into a great basso cantante noted for his success in Rossini's *La Gazza ladra*. The tenor Bordogni made his debut at La Scala in 1813 and is said to have taught Henriette Sontag, who made a sensation in Paris in 1826 as Rosina. Giuliani has somehow escaped mention in the reference works. Then there were three native Parisian singing teachers. Louis-Antoine-Éléonor Ponchard sang at the Opéra-Comique between 1812 and 1837 and was the first operatic tenor to be decorated with the Légion d'Honneur. Auguste-Mathieu Panseron, though not a career singer, was an excellent teacher; a Prix de Rome of 1813, he had studied the style of the old Italian singing masters, was accompanist at the Opéra-Comique, and wrote graceful French romances as well as solfeggi for training the voice. Mme Laure-Cinthie Montalant Damoureau had been favored by Rossini with important rôles in *Le Siège de Corinthe* and *Moïse*. Finally, there was Louis-Benoit-Alphonse Révial, from Toulouse, about whom little information is available.

Massenet entered Laurent's piano class and, at the same time, Savard's class in solfège. Adolphe-François Laurent (1796–1867) had worked for the service of supply in the Ministry of War from the age of seventeen until 1822, when he won a first prize in piano. He was a cavalry officer for a time, but from 1828 he taught at the Conservatoire. Massenet apparently benefited from his instruction and developed a certain loyalty and devotion for his teacher. Augustin Savard (1814–1881), though unable to inspiré Massenet to prize-winning accomplishment in solfège, was to prove beneficial a few years later as a private coach for harmony.

At the end of the school year, in July 1853, seventeen male students tried for the prizes in solfège. Eleven made some kind of showing: two first prizes, one second prize, three *premier accessits*, two *deuxième accessits*, and three *troisième accessits*, among which Massenet was ranked last. He continued in Savard's class for another two years but was unable to better his mark.

During the 1853–54 school year, Massenet continued his classical studies at the Lycée Saint-Louis along with his work at the Conservatoire. On 26 November 1853, his sister Julie, then twenty-one, married the painter Pierre-Paul Cavaillé. Cavaillé, a native of Lauzerte (Tarn-et-Garonne) and a pupil of Picot, became known a little later for his portraits and historical scenes. His portrait of Mlle de Lapommeraye, of the Opéra, was exhibited in the Salon of 1859 along with a canvas on the death of the Duc de Montmorency. His painting *The Death of Abel* dates from 1866. Julie Cavaillé-Massenet was also a painter in her own right, exhibiting in the Salons from 1865 to 1881, mostly portraits of women and children.

Early in December of 1853, the prizes earned in July at the Conservatoire were formally distributed. Massenet understandably took some pride in his heavy bronze medal for solfège, inscribed with "Conservatoire Impérial de Musique et de Déclamation."

The following summer—July 1854—Massenet earned a *troisième accessit* in piano. After the usual long delay, the medals were distributed on 24 December 1854 at half past twelve.[2] *L'Enfance du Christ* by Berlioz, having been first performed on 10 December, was given again on this Christmas Eve. The *Souvenirs* recount how young Jules sneaked in. Evading his mother's watchful eye, he joined some companions who were singing in the children's chorus, and under their protection he gained entrance to the wonderful world of backstage.

Alexis Massenet, now sixty-six, was beginning to feel the infirmities of his years; his physician advised him to try the treatment at Aix-les-Bains, in Savoy. This watering place, situated on the beautiful Lac du Bourget, is noted for the restorative powers of its sulphurous waters in cases of rheumatism and gout. Actually the family settled at Chambéry, nine miles south of Aix-les-Bains, where it is said they found relatives or friends to welcome them. There was apparently first an exploratory visit in September 1854, followed by a definitive *déménagement* in January 1855. A touching letter, in Jules's hand, is dated "Chambéry, 12 September 1854."[3] He writes to a companion, "Dear Adolphe," that he has been gone from Paris now for two weeks, and that he does not expect to return until he is fifteen [i.e., 1857]. He then expects to return alone to celebrate the triumph of his teacher Laurent by winning a first prize in piano. He comments that the region where he is appears grandiose, solitary, and verdant, and conveys his respects to his addressee's father, mother, and dear sisters. As to the identity of "Adolphe," we shall meet no less than three likely prospects in the piano trials of 1856.

The performance of *L'Enfance du Christ* alluded to would place the family domicile in Paris as late as December 1854. But in the quarterly report of the Conservatoire it is noted that Massenet, age 12 years 8 months (i.e., January 1855), has left the Conservatoire for the provinces. His absence was short-lived: in October 1855 he was readmitted to the piano class.[4]

During the 1855–56 school year, then, Massenet was living with Paul and Julie Cavaillé, at the corner of the Rue Condorcet and the Rue Rochechouart, near the foot of Montmartre. Toward the end of the year, he was practicing madly in the hope of winning a prize. The account given years later (1882) by Jules Vallès, though vague about the date, fits nicely into the period of May to July 1856.[5] As a writer, Vallès became known for his sketches of threadbare bohemians and street life in Paris, as in *Les Réfractaires* (1865) and *La Rue* (1866). His most ambitious work was an autobiographical trilogy, *Jacques Vingtras* (1879–86). One day, quite by accident, Vallès ran into his old school comrade Massenet from Saint-Étienne days. This could only have been Léon, already fired with literary ambitions. The two decided to collaborate on a burlesque to be entitled *L'Écureuil du déshonneur* (literally, "The Squirrel of Dishonor"). Léon knew an actor. What an opportunity! The two young optimists needed only to channel their ebullient wit into a suitable farce in order to score a great success in the theater—or so they thought. For two months they got together every evening, after first visiting the brasserie des Martyrs, to concoct the scenario and dialogue. The locale for these efforts was a studio loaned by a close relative, obviously Paul Cavaillé, where they set up field beds when they needed to catch some sleep. But promptly at nine o'clock in the morning, Massenet's younger brother would arrive to begin his piano practice. At the sound of his footsteps on the stairs, the collaborators would quickly hide the evening's work on their burlesque, along with the bottle of cognac that furnished inspiration for the difficult scenes. Vallès described this younger brother (i.e., Jules) as about fourteen or fifteen, with long blond hair and deep, penetrating eyes. Teenager though he was, he intimidated the two collaborators with his meticulous punctuality and the furious energy with which he attacked his instrument. Needless to say, "The Squirrel of Dishonor" never reached the stage.

In the piano trials of July 1856, Massenet received a *premier accessit*. This was not bad, in view of the competition. First prize went to Joseph-Louis Diémer (1843–1919), a pupil of Marmontel. Diémer became a career pianist and, indeed, succeeded to Marmontel's professorship in 1887. It was Diémer who played the harpsichord offstage in Massenet's *Thérèse* (1907) and first performed his piano concerto (1903). The second prize went to Émile Paladilhe (1844–1926), who went on to the Prix de Rome in 1860 and was rather well known in France at the turn of the century as a composer. Of the three *premier accessits*, Jean-Joseph-Benoît Pujol was ranked first, Massenet second, and Émile-Adolphe Canoby third. Pujol was twenty-one, and Canoby was a year older than Massenet. Two *deuxième accessits* were given out: to Adolphe-Jacob-Isaac David, five months younger than Massenet, and to Adolphe-Marcellin Truy, who was three and a half years older. The "Dear Adolphe" letter of the previous September might well have been addressed to either Canoby or David, or even to the somewhat older Truy. A more remote possibility is Adolphe-Léopold Danhauser, seven years older, whom we shall meet in 1862. A lone *troisième accessit* in piano went to Théodore Dubois, not quite nineteen. Before long he would make a clean sweep of first prizes, winning the Prix de Rome in 1861.

Though precise documentation is lacking, we may assume that the fifteen months from July 1856 to fall 1857 were spent at Chambéry. In the *Souvenirs*, it is referred to as "two long years." Massenet, who liked to compress things dramatically, probably added together the nine-months' absence of 1855 with the longer period involving the 1856–57 school year. In any case, the time spent at Chambéry was not without profit. Classical studies were continued, alternating with the furious practice of scales, arpeggios, sixths, and thirds befitting the best preparation for virtuosity. His hair was worn long, in keeping with the virtuoso-image of the times.

Quite by accident, Jules came across some pieces by Schumann, who was still little known in France. He delighted in playing them for the local provincials, who were not yet accustomed to such "detestable false notes." There was also ample opportunity for pleasant walks around Chambéry, where some of the neighboring peaks range up to four or five thousand feet. A favorite outing was to the Dent du Nivolet with its splendid panorama. There was also Les Charmettes, where Jean-Jacques Rousseau had found happiness for a time as the guest of Mme de Warens.

In the quarterly roll of students who entered or left the Conservatoire, Massenet's name does not appear between the time of his readmission in October 1855 and his final *sortie*, in 1863, with the Prix de Rome. A *lauréat* (the title made legitimate by even an *accessit* in piano) had the privilege of being absent for a reasonable time without being removed from the rolls.

The Prix de Rome

W E MUST ASSUME THAT MASSENET rejoined Laurent's piano class in the fall of 1857 and that he was again living with the Cavaillés. Émile Paladilhe had won the first prize in piano that year, and Ernest Guiraud, another Marmontel pupil, would win it in 1858. Massenet's turn would come in 1859. The scanty documentation for these two years can be quickly pieced together.

On 16 September 1858, the sixteen-year-old Massenet figured in a concert at Tournai, an ancient Belgian town straddling the Escaut (the French name for the river Scheldt). One of his friends at the Conservatoire, Alphonse Hermann, was from Tournai. During his visit, Jules stayed with Alphonse in the Rue Perdue just behind the church of St Quentin. The "grand concert," as it was called in the account given a fortnight later in the *Courrier de l'Escaut*, began at 7:30 P.M., admission three francs, and was a great success. Hermann's collaborators were Mme Guillery, of the Paris Opéra; Monsieur Lotto, violinist; and Monsieur Massenet, pianist. The three young men were identified as *lauréats* of the Paris Conservatoire. The provincial reviewer remarked that the young pianist seemed timid before the audience, but addressed his instrument with power and a sure technique, drawing sounds that reached the spectators full of purity and vigor. Sometimes, said the reviewer, lapsing into rhetoric, it was as though little pearls were dropping into a crystal cup.

By now Jules had a few private piano pupils and, of far more lasting consequence, had begun his apprenticeship in the theater. He seems to have started out playing the triangle in the orchestra of the Gymnase in the Boulevard de Bonne-Nouvelle, a block or so from the Conservatoire. A few months later he moved to the Théâtre-Lyrique as timpanist. Here he played three nights a week at 2.50 francs per night, thus adding 7.50 francs to his weekly income. It is said that he retained this position right up to the time he won the Prix de Rome.

In old Paris, there was a cluster of theaters in the district now dominated by the Place de la République, which did not assume its present grand form until 1880. It was then called the Place du Château-d'Eau after the water-tower that once stood there. Running westerly from the Château-d'Eau was the Boulevard Saint-Martin, with two important theaters: the Théâtre de la Porte-Saint-Martin and the Théâtre de l'Ambigu-Comique. Southerly from the Château-d'Eau extended the old Boulevard du Temple, from the 1830s a fashionable promenade for socialite and demimondaine alike. Baron Haussmann's "improvements" of 1862 erased many of the old landmarks. In the 1850s, moving from north to south along the Boulevard, one came upon the following theaters: (1) Théâtre-Historique, founded in 1847 by Alexandre Dumas and renamed Théâtre-Lyrique in 1852; (2) Cirque-Olympique, or Cirque-Impérial, home of the Opéra-National from 1847 to 1851; (3) Folies-Dramatiques, or Théâtre-Déjazet; (4) Théâtre de la Gaîté; (5) Les Funambules; (6) the old Théâtre-Saqui, which was renamed Délassements-Comiques. Across from the latter, on the west side of the Boulevard, the Jardin Turc dispensed food, drink, and entertainment. In old prints one sees well-dressed promenaders and horse-drawn carriages coming and going. It was at No. 42, where he lived from 1856 to 1871, that Gustave Flaubert wrote *Madame Bovary* and *Salammbô*.

The theaters mentioned, all on the east side of the Boulevard du Temple, had stage doors that opened in back onto the old Rue des Fossés-du-Temple—so named because, in the days of Louis XIII when the city extended no further, it had been the site of a moat. For Massenet, this stage-door side was a kind of wonderland peopled with crowds of supernumeraries waiting in the dim light for their entrance cues.

The Théâtre-Lyrique provided lively competition for the Opéra-Comique. The former Théâtre-Historique had been completely refurbished; statues of Corneille and Molière were replaced by Lully and Gluck, and the doors were opened to opera on 27 September 1851 with Boisselot's *Mosquita la sorcière*. Félicien David's *La Perle du Brésil* was staged there on 22 November 1851, amassing sixty-eight performances by the end of the 1852–53 season. For the record, some other premières of this period may be noted:

Adolphe Adam, *La Poupée de Nurembourg* (one act), 21 February 1852
Adolphe Adam, *Si j'étais roi*, 4 September 1852
Albert Grisar, *Les amours du diable*, 11 March 1853
Ferdinand Poise, *Bonsoir, Voisin* (one act), 18 September 1853
Adolphe Adam, *Le bijou perdu*, 6 October 1853
Antoine-Louis Clapisson, *La promise* ("historiette provençale"), 16 March 1854
Ernest Reyer, *Maître Wolfram* (one act), 20 May 1854
Halévy, *Jaguarita l'Indienne*, 14 May 1855
Clapisson, *La Fanchonnette*, 1 May 1856
Louis-Aimé Maillart, *Les dragons de Villars*, 19 September 1856
Victor Massé, *La Reine Topaze*, 27 December 1856
Charles Gounod, *Le médecin malgré lui*, 15 January 1858
Gounod, *Faust*, 19 March 1859
Gounod, *Philémon et Baucis*, 18 February 1860
Maillart, *Les pêcheurs de Catane*, 19 December 1860
Reyer, *La statue*, 11 April 1861
Louis-Pierre Deffès, *Le café du roi* (one act), 16 November 1861

Charles Gounod. Courtesy Paul Jackson.

The turnover in management was rapid at first. Edmond Seveste was succeeded in 1854 by Émile Perrin, who was replaced by Pellegrin in 1856. During 1856–60, Léon Carvalho was manager, and the Théâtre-Lyrique attained its first real heyday. His wife, Mme Miolan-Carvalho, was a principal attraction as dramatic soprano. In 1860, the directorship went to Charles Réty.

Staples of the repertoire included Grétry's *Richard Coeur-de-Lion*, Mozart's *Le mariage de Figaro*, Rossini's *Le barbier de Séville*, and the Castil-Blaze version of Weber's *Der Freischütz* known as *Robin des bois*. Weber's *Euryanthe*, in a new French translation by Leuven and Saint-Georges, was produced on 1 November 1857. There were also such works as Adam's *Le roi d'Yvetot* and *La reine d'un jour*, Thomas's *Le panier fleuri*, Hérold's *Marie*, and Auber's *La sirène*.

In the *Souvenirs*, special mention is made of *Faust*, in which the rôle of Marguerite was created by Mme Miolan-Carvalho. Deloffre conducted, and Massenet was proud to sit in such a fine orchestra. Gounod, then forty, managed the rehearsals from onstage, and Jules, while counting rests, had ample opportunity to engage in hero worship. Later in life they became good friends and colleagues in the Académie des Beaux-Arts. Another work mentioned is Reyer's *La statue* (whose première was attended by Bizet); Massenet thought it a superb score and a tremendous success. Curiously, the *Souvenirs* make no mention of another significant event: the restoration of Gluck's *Orphée* by Berlioz, with Pauline Viardot in the title rôle. By crossing the Italian and French versions of 1764 and 1774, Berlioz sought to establish the true Gluck style. Staged on 18 November 1859, this version attained 124 performances in two seasons.

"In the summer of 1859," as he wrote long afterwards (1898), Victorin de Joncières first encountered Massenet at the Café Charles in the Rue des Poissonniers, Montmartre.[1] From the account given, it must have been May, June, or early July. Son of a journalist, Joncières had first studied painting, then switched to music. He wanted to have an orchestral work performed, and he was advised to try the amateur orchestra that played on Fridays, as a special attraction, at the Café Charles. The conductor, with the imposing name of Claude-Marie-Mécène Marié de l'Isle, was a portly little man of forty-eight, with graying hair and an alert, piercing glance behind his gold-rimmed spectacles. After winning first prize in double-bass playing at the Conservatoire in 1830, Marié had played for a while in theater orchestras. He then turned to singing, making his debut at the Paris Opéra in 1840 as Eléazar in *La Juive*. Furthermore, he had fathered and trained three talented singers: Paola, Irma, and Marie-Célestine. The latter, married at fifteen to a sculptor named Galli, is best known as Galli-Marié (1840–1905), creator of the rôles of Mignon (1866), Carmen (1875), and in between, Lazarille in Massenet's *Don César de Bazan* (1872).[*]

Joncières, then, was welcomed at the Café Charles and assigned at once to the bass drum and tambour, alongside an adolescent named Massenet at the timpani. The modest orchestra, making up in enthusiasm what it lacked in skill, ran through some favorite overtures such as *La Gazza ladra*, and the two percussionists struck up an acquaintance. Massenet, it seems, had written a *Marche religieuse*, which he hoped the orchestra would play on some festive occasion at the church of Saint-Pierre de Montmartre. It was furthermore his ambition to have his one-act operetta, *Les deux boursiers*, performed at the École Lyrique de la Tour-d'Auvergne. Apparently neither work ever reached a performance, though it was not like Massenet to throw things away; their substance may have appeared metamorphosed in some later works. The *Souvenirs* mention that at about this time Massenet gave lessons in solfège and piano at a "poor little school in the neighborhood," which leads us to hypothesize a music school in the Rue de la Tour-d'Auvergne, just a few steps from the Cavaillé apartment. Joncières serves further as witness that, at about this time, Massenet was playing timpani three nights a week in a theater and, while awaiting the piano prize, was serving as accompanist to the tenor Gustave Roger.[†]

Six and a half years after entering Laurent's piano class, Massenet at last achieved his goal: a first prize in piano. The jury heard the thirteen male contestants

---

[*] In reference works, Galli-Marié has sometimes been confused with her niece, whom she trained: Jeanne Beugnon, known as Jeanne Marié de l'Isle (1872–1926).

on 26 July 1859. The set piece was Ferdinand Hiller's Concerto in F minor—the one dedicated to Moscheles.[*] As the performers awaited their turn in the foyer of the Conservatoire concert hall, Massenet, eleventh on the list, suffered agonies of suspense. Then, having played his stint, he rushed home to recount the experience to his sister, only to find that she had gone to hear the contest. In rushing back again to the Conservatoire, Jules bumped into his boon companion Alphonse Duvernoy, who informed him that Monsieur Auber had announced the jury's decision.[†] Still rushing about, Massenet then went to Laurent's place. Although the master was at lunch with some generals, he welcomed his pupil and presented him with a touching memento of his esteem: a full score of *Le Nozze di Figaro* that Laurent himself had received, along with his first prize in piano, back in 1822. Laurent's flattering inscription included the admonition: "Go on as you have begun and you will be a great artist."

The prizes were distributed on 4 August 1859.[‡] The discourse was given by Jules Pelletier, secretary general of the Ministre d'État. He took the occasion briefly to eulogize Auguste-Mathieu Panseron, professor of singing since 1835, who had just died on 29 July. Pelletier then went on to deplore the cruel mutilation, in a grievous accident, of the celebrated artist Gustave Roger, who might at least take some consolation in the widespread sympathy aroused by his condition. This Roger we shall meet again shortly, when Massenet makes the acquaintance of Wagner.

The distribution of prizes was followed by the usual concert, this time with an orchestra directed by Pasdeloup. We must remember that the Conservatoire trained actors and actresses as well as musicians—hence the inclusion of scenes from Racine and Monvel, presented by young *lauréats* in tragedy and comedy.

1. Weber, Overture to *Oberon*

2. Pixis, Duo for two pianos
   > Mlle Mongin (first prize, women)
   > M. Massenet (first prize, men)

3. Meyerbeer Air from *Robert le diable*
   > Mlle Litschner (first prize, singing)

4. Rode, fragments from the Fourth Violin Concerto
   > Magnin (first prize, violin)

---

† From page 18: Victorin de Joncières (*recte* Félix-Ludger Rossignol, 1839–1901) reached the operatic stage two months before Massenet: his *Sardanapale*, with Christine Nilsson, was given at the Théâtre-Lyrique on 8 Feb. 1867. He continued both as a composer and pro-Wagner music critic. Whether his symphonic ode, *La Mer* (1881), was known to Debussy is perhaps beside the point.

* The twenty-seven women who competed in piano in 1859 would have had their own jury, scheduler, and set piece.

† Second prize went to Albert Lavignac (1846–1916), who became a noted music educator, writer, and editor-in-chief of a monumental *Encyclopédie de la musique*. As for Victor-Alphonse Duvernoy (1842–1907), he had already won his first prize in piano (1855) and would have a full career as performer, composer, teacher, and music critic.

‡ In 1858, at the instigation of Camille Doucet, then head of the Bureau of Theaters, the long wait until November or December had been abolished in favor of a speedier award of the prizes.

5. Auber, Air from *La muette de Portici*
    Peschard (first prize, singing)
6. Racine, fragments from *Phèdre*, Act IV
    Mlle Schmit (Phèdre)
    Mlle Rousseil (Oenone)
    Maubant (Thésée)
7. Monvel, *L'Amant bourru*, Act I, Scenes 3 and 4
    Mlle Cellier (la Marquise)
    Léautaud (Morinzer)
    Worms (De Pienne)
    Malard (Saint-Germain)
8. Verdi, fragments from *Le Trouvère*, Act IV
    Mlle Gillièss (Léonore)
    Roudil (le comte de Luna)
    Peschard (Manrique)
    Maubant (un soldat)[2]

A comment or two, to satisfy the curious: Who was Johann Peter Pixis (1788–1874)? His name was once bracketed with Liszt, Chopin, Herz, Czerny, and Thalberg as among the six greatest European pianists, and in his heyday his works figured constantly on concert programs.[3] As for Marie-Louise Mongin, she later taught privately in Paris, and in 1870 she married L.-A. Coedès. Aurélie Litschner, Hungarian by birth, later became Mme de Fère, and it is thought that she founded a school of music in Brooklyn, perhaps in 1872. And did Racine's *Phèdre* make an impression upon the young Massenet? He would later write an overture, and still later incidental music for this tragedy.

Even with a first prize in piano, the world is not yet necessarily one's oyster. At some time—unspecified—Massenet was offered a post as pianist in one of the large cafés in Belleville. Prior to its incorporation into Paris in 1860, Belleville was an independent working-class village beyond the old Barrière de Belleville, where there is today a Métro station. Chronicles of old Paris mention the two cabarets of Desnoyers and Heinsselain, which were the starting point for the annual Descente de la Courtille, a lively but disreputable procession on Ash Wednesday that proceeded down the Rue du Faubourg-du-Temple to the Place du Château-d'Eau and the fashionable Boulevard du Temple. Massenet's café remains anonymous, though he thought it was "the first café" to provide music for its customers. The salary of thirty francs per month was welcome.

It was presumably in the fall of 1859 that Massenet entered classes at the Conservatoire with Bazin in harmony and Benoist in organ, which was rather like running up two blind alleys at once. Bazin's teaching was not at all to his liking, and Massenet left the class after only a month (though perhaps, as some say, Bazin bluntly told him to get out). The organ study suggests that Massenet had in mind a salaried church position; he may have envied Saint-Saëns, who only the year before had been appointed organist at the Madeleine. But nothing ever came of it, not even the least *accessit*, and he gave it up after a while.

The fiasco with Bazin's class led Massenet to a sensible resolution regarding his theoretical training. He sought out his former solfège teacher, who had meanwhile published a *Cours complet d'harmonie* (1853) and who, indeed, advanced to professor of harmony in 1866. Savard provided the effective coaching needed.* "Every evening," according to the *Souvenirs* (which appears doubtful in view of his other commitments!), he would walk all the way from Montmartre to Savard's place in the Rue de la Vieille-Estrapade, behind the Panthéon. By ten o'clock he was ready to start for home, full of the good advice imparted by the simple but learned teacher. At ten francs per lesson, Massenet ended up owing Savard three hundred francs. But the kindly Savard subcontracted to Jules the task of making an orchestral arrangement of a military-band accompaniment to one of Adolphe Adam's masses—a task, by coincidence, worth exactly three hundred francs; thus the score was evened. In any case, Massenet was prepared to enter Reber's harmony class on 17 January 1860.

Meanwhile, Massenet was useful as an accompanist to the tenor Roger. Gustave-Hippolyte Roger (1815–1879) had won first prizes in singing and in *opéra comique* in 1837. Immediately engaged for the Opéra-Comique, he made his debut there on 16 February 1838, as Georges in Halévy's *L'Éclair*. An intelligent and gifted singer of distinguished appearance, Roger soon became the favorite tenor of Parisian audiences. He was later called to the Opéra where, on 16 April 1849, he created a sensation opposite Pauline Viardot in *Le Prophète*. On 27 July 1859, Roger's gun burst when he was out shooting, mangling his right arm so badly that it had to be amputated. He tried to carry on bravely with a prosthetic arm, but his operatic career was no longer the same. From 1868 until his death in 1879, he was professor of singing at the Conservatoire.

Roger owned a sumptuous estate, the château Plessis-Trévise, east of Paris at Villiers-sur-Marne, near the Bois du Plessis-Trévise. Here Massenet had the occasion to meet Wagner, late in 1859 or at the beginning of 1860. Wagner had arrived in Paris in the fall of 1859 with ambitious plans. It will be recalled that three concerts of his works were given on successive Wednesdays early in 1860 at the Salle Ventadour: on 25 January, and on 1 and 8 February. But Wagner really hoped to conquer Paris with a production of *Tannhäuser*, for which a suitable French translation was needed. He turned to Roger, who had sung in Germany and possessed a good working knowledge of the German language.

Massenet later recalled the circumstances of the meeting.[4] Wagner stayed for ten days at Plessis-Trévise, occupying the Chinese Room (so called because of its bamboo furniture) next to Massenet's room. Wagner played for Roger from a copy of *Tannhäuser* in which Edmond Roche's translation had been written with ink.

---

* In the sequel, the teacher's son—Maurice-Emmanuel-Augustin Savard—studied composition with Massenet, won the Prix de Rome in 1886, and became director of the Lyon Conservatoire.

Massenet was impressed by Wagner's playing ("like a musician, not at all like a pianist"), by his knowledge of French, and by his impatience with Roche's wording. In the end, we know that Wagner lost patience with Roger as well. When *Tannhäuser* was finally given on 13 May 1861, at the Opéra in the Rue Le Peletier, it was in a French version by Charles Nuitter.

At Plessis-Trévise, after his daily stint with the translation, Wagner would take lonely walks in the neighborhood and reappear only at dinner time, when he was usually silent and contemplative, though a few times he broke out into almost feverish monologues on the subject of his great expectations in Paris. After ten days, wrote Massenet, the guest departed and a new guest appeared: Gounod. What a contrast!

Just at this time Massenet substituted for six months as timpanist with the orchestra of the Théâtre-Italien, housed in the Salle Ventadour. He thus participated in the rehearsals for Wagner's three concerts. The orchestra was split into two factions, with Massenet on the side of the pro-Wagnerites, deeply moved (even to the point of tears) by this new music. He considered the concerts a success, and *Lohengrin* in particular (i.e., the Prelude, Bridal Procession, and third-act Prelude) made a lasting impression upon him.

The visitor to modern Paris can readily find the site of the Salle Ventadour by turning off the Avenue de l'Opéra a few steps down the Rue des Petits-Champs. There, in the midst of what would otherwise be a quiet square, stands a fine old building (now the Banque de France). Situated on the axis of the Rues Méhul and Monsigny, it is flanked on either side by the Rues Marsollier and Dalayrac, the street names recalling favorite composers of the Opéra-Comique when, during 1829–32, its performances were given at the Salle Ventadour. From 1841 until 1878, this was the home of the Théâtre-Italien, where the Parisian public could hear opera in the Italian language. Nearby, through an entrance in the Rue Dalayrac, one reaches the Passage de Choiseul—a kind of narrow glass-covered mall within a complex of buildings, where one can shop at the little stalls. In nineteenth-century Paris there were many such *passages*, in strategic locations, usually near a theater. They were a boon to the pedestrian in inclement weather, and at least one—the Passage des Panoramas, off the Boulevard Montmartre—offered the modest (but then spectacular) diversion of viewing the "panoramas." Even today, in the Passage de Choiseul one comes upon the stage door of the Bouffes-Parisiens, which fronts on the Rue Monsigny.

While thumping the kettledrums at the Théâtre-Italien, Massenet had occasion to hear some of the noted Italian singers of the day: the tragediennes Penco and Frezzolini, Graziani, the tenor Mario, the buffo Zucchini, and the baritone Enrico Delle Sedie, later professor of singing at the Conservatoire. Conscientiously retuning his timpani as indicated in the music, Massenet often discovered that he was out of tune with the rest of the orchestra. A colleague, wiser in the traditions of the Théâtre-Italien, advised that he just leave them in D and A: the arias were constantly transposed to suit the singers, and anyway, no one would be offended!

On 17 January 1860, Jules was admitted to Reber's harmony class. Napoléon-Henri Reber (1807–1880), conservative in taste, was first successful in chamber music (he was called "the Boccherini of our time"), and he continued with stage works in the old *opéra comique* tradition, freshened up with modern orchestration. In the eyes of the establishment he represented a wholesome influence vis-à-vis the disturbing trend toward noise and bombast among some of the other French and Italian composers. While the success of Reber's *Le Père Gaillard* (1852) was still fresh in people's minds, he was elected to the Academy of Fine Arts.[*] Professor of harmony since 1851, he inherited Halévy's composition class in 1862. His *Traité d'harmonie* (1862), which went through several editions, no doubt reflects the kind of instruction Massenet received.

In July 1860, twelve students undertook the trials in harmony. Jules's exercises—a given bass, and a given melody—are still preserved in the Bibliothèque Nationale. The first prize, however, went to Justin Perrot; the second prize to Émile Girard. Massenet received a *premièr accessit*, and a *deuxième accessit* went to Victor-Marie-Léon Godefroy. Arthur Pougin (1834–1921), a prolific writer on music and himself at one time a student in Reber's harmony class, published an extensive memoir on Massenet in 1912.[5] He there reported that Reber is supposed to have said to young Jules: "My dear boy, you should have had a first prize; but you didn't get it, which is a pity. The essential thing, for you, is not to waste any time. Do not remain here, where there is nothing more for you to do, but enroll at once in a class in composition." This makes a pretty speech to be retold long afterward. Actually, the "at once" dragged out for a year; Massenet did not enter Ambroise Thomas's composition class until the fall of 1861. In the interim, it is at least conceivable that he continued in Reber's harmony class during the 1860–61 school year, and that Reber, convinced there was "nothing more" for him to do (a polite phrase that can be taken two ways), discouraged him from again attempting a prize in harmony.

In September of 1860, Massenet visited the Hennequin family at Guînes, a town five miles inland from Calais. Louis and Sophie Hennequin were proprietors of a private school catering exclusively to children of English families. Massenet had met their daughter, Emma Hennequin (1843–1898), at the Paris Conservatoire. Family tradition has it that they were for a time engaged to be married; in any case, they carried on a steady correspondence up to the time of her death. Mlle Hennequin was a talented soprano and an excellent pianist. With the collaboration of Massenet and the violinist Darchicourt, she gave a concert at Guînes on 23 September 1860.[†]

Musical events in Paris early in 1861 included more Verdi and at least a brief sampling of Wagner. Verdi was by then, of course, well known to the Parisian public,

---

[*] The Institute of France comprises five academies, election to which is a signal public honor. The Academy of Fine Arts promotes music as well as painting and sculpture. The fixed number of seats means that election is only possible when a previous member dies. (Refer also to page 105.)

[†] In 1869, Emma Hennequin married a Norwegian; their son Gaston Borch (1871–1926) studied with Massenet at the Conservatoire and was active as an orchestral cellist, conductor, and composer.

despite the fiasco of *Les Vêpres siciliennes* (Opéra, 13 June 1855). The Salle Ventadour had resounded to the original Italian of *Il Trovatore* (1854),* *La Traviata* (1856), and *Rigoletto* (1857), and on 13 January 1861, *Un Ballo in maschera* appeared at the Théâtre-Italien (Auber's opera of 1833 on the same subject, *Gustave III, ou le bal masqué*, had quietly expired at the Opéra in 1859). Massenet later paid tribute to Verdi as "the immortal creator of so many masterpieces," and surely his knowledge of Verdi's scores dates from his youth. Then, on 13 March 1861, *Tannhäuser* was staged at the Opéra, only to be withdrawn by Wagner after the third performance. It was immediately made the butt of several parodies. The French pronunciation—Tann-ho-ZEHR—was caricatured at the Théâtre-Déjazet on 30 March in the two-act spoof *Panne-aux-Airs* (loosely: "a weak rôle that puts on fancy airs"), text by Clairville and music by F. E. Barbier. At the Variétés on 6 April, a more elaborate parody in three acts, *Ya-Mein-Herr, Cacophonie de l'Avenir*, was produced by the writers Clairville, A. Delacour, and L. Thiboust (with some new airs by V. Chéri). Such were the topics of conversation in those days.

Of more immediate interest for 1861 was Massenet's first publication, a *Grande Fantaisie de Concert sur le Pardon de Ploërmel de Meyerbeer, pour le piano*. This work was issued by Brandus et S. Dufour, then at 103 Rue Richelieu, with the dedication "À mon cher maître, Monsieur A. Laurent."[6] Running to nineteen pages, the fantasy covers the gamut of improvisational variations one would expect in a bravura piece of those times and displays Massenet's technical equipment as a pianist. There are nine discernible sections, ranging in length and weight from the opening eight-measure adagio largamente in B minor to the final tempo di marcia in B major, with bravura passages including alternating octaves. The middle portions tend towards andante or andantino, with a suitable complement of measured trills, an occasional chromatic run or cadenza prestissimo, and even a glissando on the black keys. The style may be forgiven; after all, it was the most likely sort of thing to get published.

By the fall of 1861, Massenet felt sufficiently independent to occupy an attic lodging of his own at No. 5, Rue de Ménilmontant.† This location was convenient to his work at the Théâtre-Lyrique. His neighbors on the same floor were some clowns from the nearby Cirque Napoléon. Besides accommodating the ever-popular circus performances, the Cirque Napoléon (from 1873, Cirque d'Hiver) was the scene of Pasdeloup's famous Sunday popular concerts, inaugurated on 27 October 1861. When the hall became oppressively warm, the third-floor casement windows were opened, and the sounds of the orchestra drifted up to Massenet's attic room. From his lofty perch he applauded his gods: Wagner and Berlioz.

On 2 November 1861, Jules entered the composition class of Ambroise Thomas. The relationship was congenial: Massenet always thought of his *Maître* with

---

* Also in French, as Le Trouvère, Opéra, 12 Jan. 1857.

† Renamed Rue Oberkampf in 1864.

Ambroise Thomas and autographed card. Photography by Reutlinger. Courtesy Paul Jackson.

reverence and devotion. Thomas (1811–1896), born at Metz, was a Lorrainer like Massenet's own grandfathers. Prix de Rome of 1832, he was the seventh of Lesueur's pupils to attain this honor.* By 1860, Thomas had produced sixteen operas and two ballets, well suited to French tastes and characterized by honest workmanship and competent orchestration. *Le Caïde* (1849), for example, was an extravagant comedy laid in Egypt, and *Psyché* (1857) dramatized a Greek myth in a way somewhat com parable to Gounod's *Sapho* of 1851. Thomas's more lasting works were still to come: *Mignon* (1866) and *Hamlet* (1868). Thereafter, the strong new currents in French music, together with his position as director of the Conservatoire, inevitably left Thomas stranded as a "conservative" of the old school. Withal, or perhaps therefore, three of his Prix de Rome pupils made the Institut (Massenet, Théodore Dubois, Charles Lenepveu), and others (such as Bourgault-Ducoudray, Sieg, Lefebvre, and Salvayre) were locally well known until the next wave of progress swept them into oblivion.

---

* Of the dozen Prix de Rome pupils of Jean-François Lesueur (1760–1837), the best known are Berlioz (1830) and Gounod (1839). Others deserving passing mention as minor celebrities during Massenet's career were Eugène Prévost (1831), Antoine Elwart (1834), Ernest Boulanger (1835), Xavier Boisselot (1836), and Louis Besozzi (1837).

It seems remarkable not only that Massenet was encouraged to try for the Prix de Rome some six months after entering the composition class but that he succeeded in obtaining an honorable mention. Preliminary trials eliminated all but a select group of candidates, who were then confined to cell-like mansard rooms at the Institut where they ate, slept, and worked until the task was completed. The text for the prize cantata was *Louise de Mézières* by Édouard Monnais, and the *entrée en loge* was set for Saturday morning, 17 May 1862. The journalist Charles Formentin had the foresight to jot down, before they were effaced, Massenet's scribblings on the wall of his little cubicle. At first: "Rien. Absolument rien. Toujours rien." (No ideas.) By 23 May, though still feeling impuissant, he had finished the duo and started the cantabile for the third time. On 2 June he dozed until a quarter past nine, then recommenced his introduction. By 10 June, at eleven o'clock, he had finished.

When the cantatas were performed for the jury, Massenet (listed as a pupil of Thomas and Reber) received an honorable mention. The Premier Grand Prix, with its trip to Rome, went to Louis-Albert Bourgault-Ducoudray (1840–1910), who had already produced an opera three years previously at his home town of Nantes. Bourgault-Ducoudray later became professor of music history at the Conservatoire. Second prize was awarded to Adolphe-Léopold Danhauser (1835–1896), a pupil of Halévy, Reber, and François Bazin. For thirty years, from 1866, Danhauser taught solfège at the Conservatoire; the several volumes of his *Solfège des solfèges* were long a pièce de résistance for students.

After the trials in composition, there was still the concours in counterpoint and fugue, for which six candidates appeared in 1862. Jules took second prize. First prize went to one Jean-Léon Roques, later accompanist at the Bouffes-Parisiens, conductor, and organist at St-Pierre-de-Chaillot. A single *premier accessit* was awarded to Édouard Wachmann, born in Bucharest in 1838.

The distribution of prizes on 4 August 1862 included a discourse by Comte Walewsky, Ministre d'État, and the usual musical program. It is to be hoped that Massenet attended. Along with fragments from Meyerbeer, Halévy, and Adam, he would have heard an excerpt from Henri Herz's Fifth Piano Concerto played by Mlle Trautmann, first prize in piano. Marie-Christine Trautmann became a famous concert pianist, and married Alfred Jaëll, another noted pianist.

On 3 November 1862, Massenet appeared in another concert at Guînes with Emma Hennequin and Darchicourt. Much later, a street in Guînes was named after him, and the journals duly mentioned that "Massenet played here."

The time arrived for all young men born in 1842 to report for military service. Massenet's mother appeared before the authorities at Nice on 12 December 1862. The parents' domicile was given as 13 Rue Gioffredo, Nice, and Jules's address as 5 Rue de Ménilmontant, Paris. It was noted that Jules already had three brothers in the service of their country, which exempted him from military duty.[7] A fortnight later, on 1 January 1863, his father died.

For the Prix de Rome competition of 1863, five aspirants went into seclusion at four in the afternoon on Saturday, 16 May, to set the cantata text *David Rizzio* by Gustave Chouquet. The place to work was provided by the Institut, but each contestant had to pay for his own meals and for the rental of a piano. Massenet had saved up for this occasion and pawned his gold watch, memento of his first communion, to be sure of his meals. But he lacked the exorbitant price of twenty francs for piano rental and had to make do without. This left him defenseless and distracted, to be sure, with four close neighbors each pounding upon a piano and singing at the top of his lungs. Somehow he got through the task; on 8 June 1863, after three weeks and two days, he left his cell. Formentin, who took note of the graffiti on the walls, gave us Massenet's pun: "When does David Rizzio resemble a cracked casserole? At the end of the duo, when he says 'Je fuis.'" (Je fuis: "I flee," also "I leak.")

After the cantata came the concours in fugue, and this time Jules won first prize. When the cantatas were performed for the jury, Massenet had the advantage of three excellent singers, all from the Opéra: Mme Van de Heuvel-Duprez, the tenor Gustave Roger, and Marc Bonnehée. He was awarded the Premier Grand Prix. Second prize went to Titus-Charles Constantin (b. 1835), who became a conductor, and Gustave-Raphaël Ruiz (b. 1840) received an honorable mention. Danhauser, winner of second prize the previous year, did not even place this time; he found employment for a time as inspector of singing instruction for the common schools of Paris. The fifth contestant was Théodore-César Salomé (1834–1896), later organist at the Trinité, *maître de chapelle* at the Lycée Saint-Louis, and professor at the Collège Rollin.

When the prizes were distributed on 3 August 1863, the usual musical program was prefaced with a discourse by M. le maréchal Vaillant, Ministre de la Maison de l'Empereur et des Beaux-Arts. As the third number on the program, the winner of the first prize in violin, Édouard Colonne, played what was designated as De Bériot's "Solo de violon en la mineur." Within ten years Colonne would have his own orchestra, founded with the backing of the music publisher Hartmann, and Massenet's *Marie-Magdeleine* would be among the first works performed.

In November, Massenet completed his first orchestral work. The autograph is preserved in the Bibliothèque Nationale: "Ouverture en sol. Partition orchestre. Classe de Mr Ambroise Thomas." At the end, on page 67, is the annotation: "Paris, 29 novembre 1863. Jules Massenet."

CHAPTER 4

The Villa Medici

ACCORDING TO THE *SOUVENIRS*, the Prix de Rome winners, now pensioners, set out "on the day after Christmas" to pay the traditional formal calls on members of the Institut. This would have been a formidable task, considering that the five sections of the Académie des Beaux-Arts would comprise, at full strength, forty members. No doubt some friends went along, for there were three full carriages winding into every quarter of Paris on the appointed rounds.

The other prize winners for 1863 were the painters Layraud and Monchablon, the sculptor Bourgeois, the architect Brune, and the engraver Chaplain. If Massenet was indeed present, and if they did call upon the musicians of the Institut, these would have been Auber, Carafa, Thomas, Reber, Clapisson, and Berlioz. To avoid having to make a speech, most of the Academicians sent out word that they were not at home. The architect Hittorff, it is said, shouted quite audibly from his bedroom to his servant: "Tell them I'm not in!" But, by the rules of the game, merely touching base was enough to fulfill the obligation.

The stipend of Prix de Rome pensioners is usually mentioned as 3000 francs annually for five years. Schneider, however, states that the annual *traitement* was 2310 francs, with an additional allowance of 1200 francs for subsistence (*indemnité de table*). In any case, upon leaving Paris each received 600 francs for the expenses of the journey. The artists usually spent the full five years in Rome; architects, three years in Rome and two in Athens; musicians, two years in Rome, one in Germany, and two in Paris. Incidental travel during tenure, for broadening experience, was of course encouraged.

On the appointed day, the heavy diligence was to leave Paris from the Rue Notre-Dame-des-Champs. The pensioners crowded into the cheapest places at the rear, where they would be exposed to all the dust of the road. In the old days, the professors would come to see their pupils off. It is told how the painter Couder came to take leave of his pupil. Couder, one must remember, was favored by Louis-Philippe because his drawing was "correct," his coloring "satisfactory," and his price inexpensive! His touching last admonition: "Above all, don't forget my style!"

Actually, Massenet missed all this hustle and bustle. He had gone on ahead. Perhaps when he wrote his *Souvenirs* the lively accounts of his fellow pensioners, retold many times, made him feel as though he himself had lived through the events.

To have arrived in Rome on Sunday, 24 January, after thirty-six days of travel (as he reported to Thomas), Massenet would have left Paris on Saturday, 19 December, or perhaps Sunday, 20 December. He stopped first at Nice, where his father was buried in the Cimetière du Château. New Year's Day was spent with his mother, now living at Bordighera. One can imagine the reunion between Éléonore, now fifty-four, whose husband had been laid to rest one year ago, and Jules, all fresh and rosy with success and standing on the threshold of a career.

On 3 January Jules rejoined his companions, who were waiting for him in their carriage on the Corniche road. Brune, the architect, acted as treasurer for the group, so that they could enjoy easy living without straining their budget. By eight that evening they stopped at Loano, still forty-seven miles short of Genoa. Setting foot upon Italian soil should have been an occasion for rhapsodies over picturesque landscapes and the scent of mimosa and lemon blossoms. Actually, the weather turned bitterly cold, and in some places in northern Italy the travelers encountered three feet of snow on the ground.[1]

Withal, the sense of liberation from the cramped routine of Paris was invigorating. During two days at Genoa the chief attraction was the Campo Santo—that cemetery so rich in marble monuments. At Milan they stared in wonderment at the cathedral and made the pilgrimage to the monastery-turned-cavalry-barrack to view Leonardo da Vinci's *Last Supper*. The Austrian soldiers, they noted, had cut a door in the central panel of the picture. At Verona they naturally went to see the tomb of Juliet. Vicenza, Padua, and Venice were on their itinerary, as were Pisa and Florence. In all, Massenet reported to Ambroise Thomas, sixteen cities were visited. Baedeker's guidebooks were too expensive, but somehow the young pensioners managed to find and immerse themselves in a wealth of art works and landmarks. Italy of the 1860s made a profound and stirring impression upon Massenet at every turn.

Ordinarily, the travelers would have entered Rome by the Ponte Molle, greeted with a boisterous welcome from the resident pensioners of the Villa Medici. Instead, as a final picturesque flourish to their journey, they took a steamer from Livorno to Civitavecchia, Massenet sucking oranges all the way as a precaution. The train from Civitavecchia brought them to Rome around three o'clock in the afternoon on Sunday, 24 January, taking the "old guard" by surprise. (A letter from Florence announcing their plans had not yet arrived.) A special dinner was hastily prepared, well seasoned with practical jokes on *les nouveaux affreux*. Massenet was handed a bell and sent to summon the boarders. In the unfamiliar grounds, now shrouded in darkness, he promptly fell into a fountain.

The next day, the dining hall was transformed into a bandit's den. The servants, instead of wearing the green livery of Napoleon III, were got up as rough characters. From time to time dishes and bottles were sent flying. The newcomers were seated at an artfully soiled and wine-spattered table under the proud, disdainful scrutiny of their seniors. Art was discussed in outrageous mock-serious terms to the general refrain that here, while the food was simple, all lived in brotherly harmony. Amidst the hubbub and ragging, Massenet, eyes lowered in embarrassment, saw carved in the pine table the name Hérold—memento of 1813 when the future composer of *Le Pré aux clercs* had arrived at the Villa Medici. Later, as a climax to the initiation, the newcomers were taken for a little "walk." In those days the ruins of ancient Rome were still a jumbled wilderness, the weed-grown Forum a favored browsing place for goats by day and a hunting ground for stray cats by night. By stealthy design, Massenet suddenly found himself deserted and alone in the vast Colosseum. The cold, pitch-dark January night disclosed no egress; only in the light of dawn did a shivering, exhausted Prix de Rome find his way back to the Villa Medici, somewhat cleansed of any feelings of self-importance.

The Monte Pincio, once the site of the luxurious gardens of the fabulously wealthy general Lucullus and later the scene of Messalina's orgies, received its name from the palace of the Pincius family, erected there under the Roman Empire. The Villa Medici, originally built in 1540 for Cardinal Ricci da Pontepulciano, came about 1600 into the possession of Cardinal Alessandro de' Medici, and after being in the hands of the grand dukes of Tuscany, was taken over by the French in 1801 to house the Académie de Rome. The Pincio gardens, laid out by Valadier under Napoleon in 1809–14, were in the nineteenth century a favorite promenade and meeting place of society, on foot or in their carriages, during the two hours before sunset, when music was played. Indeed, we must recall that in those days other prominent hills of Rome were still occupied by villas of the nobility, surrounded by handsome gardens. The Eternal City was not yet the capital of Italy.

From the window of Massenet's room, all of Rome lay spread out in a panorama, with the outlines of St. Peter's dome and the Vatican in the distance. Just vacated by Théodore Dubois, who had left the Villa Medici to travel, it was the same room once occupied by Ambroise Thomas. Actually a vast salon, as only the Romans built them, it took some arranging of furniture to avoid an impression of emptiness. Jules had a grand piano installed at once, and heaped up piles of music paper and scores on his worktable in anticipation of the serious endeavors he was now free to pursue. On the Friday after his arrival he wrote a long letter to Ambroise Thomas recounting his adventures. Before getting down to solid work, he wrote, he wanted to spend some time in getting to know Rome. His teacher is to convey his greetings to Constantin, Chauvet, Sieg, and all the rest of the class.

For a time, Massenet missed the companionship of other musicians: there was no one with whom to talk shop or to play over new four-hand pieces at the piano.[2] Théodore Dubois, Prix de Rome of 1861, had put in his statutory two years and left. Bourgault-Ducoudray, who had come the year before, was reserved and did not mix too frequently with the other pensioners. By way of compensation, Jules got along splendidly with the artists of the Villa Medici, making many lasting friendships. They all assembled at least twice a day for meals in the *salle à manger*, where hung the portraits of all the Grand Prix winners since the foundation of the French Academy in Rome. Soon (1865) Layraud's portrait of Massenet was to be added. One friend was Alexandre Falguière, painter, sculptor, and admirer of the early Florentine Renaissance, with whom Jules would travel to Naples later in the year. Another was Charles-Auguste-Émile Duran, known as Carolus-Duran, who later became a distinguished society portraitist and maintained his friendship with Massenet through the years.

The director of the French Academy in Rome was the painter Victor Schnetz (1787–1870), a man of congenial disposition and gruff humor who was deservedly popular with the students. His private life was simple enough, and yet he was quite capable of fulfilling the representative functions of his position. Schnetz's early paintings were quite coloristic, but with success and maturity he became more academic. He was, in fact, director of the École des Beaux-Arts in Paris for several years before assuming the directorship of the Académie de Rome, and in 1853 he started a second tour of duty in that post. Schnetz, who loved the countryside around Rome and had been fond of sketching the Sabine brigands, was full of anecdotes. His Sunday evening salon, open to all the students, was frequented by the high society of Rome, and persons of eminence passing through were likely to show up, happy to find at the Villa Medici a little corner of French territory.

Jules was much impressed by his first Roman Carnival, which to a proper Parisian seemed like a wild bacchanalian revelry. For the main procession, a large car was constructed by the Villa Medici architects and decorated by the sculptors. As the students rode upon this gorgeous creation, they threw confetti and flowers at the Roman beauties crowded onto their balconies along the Corso and were rewarded with bewitching smiles. With the coming of Ash Wednesday (10 February), thoughts would again turn to serious work. We can imagine Massenet at his piano, or bent over his writing table, or simply meditating on his next artistic creation, wrapped in a "dressing gown" consisting of a worn-out overcoat. Only later did he acquire the traditional red *robe de chambre*.

The first *envoi* from Rome was normally expected to be a *Messe solennelle*, and the second, an opera in French or Italian. By the first week in March, Jules had sketched the Kyrie and Gloria of his projected Mass. He had by now even found a violin teacher, with whom he also played Beethoven sonatas.[3] He wrote to Thomas that he planned to leave on 6 March for a little excursion to Tivoli, Subiaco, and Albano; he and his companions would proceed by carriage, on horseback, or on foot, as the mood struck them, and they would return by way of Frascati. The woods of Subiaco proved to be a romantic spot. This region of the Sabine hills, some thirty miles east of Rome, was the cradle of the Benedictine order. Here were the three cloisters of Santa Scholastica and the Sagro Speco (sacred grotto) of Saint Benedict. As the wanderers passed through the woods, Massenet's ear caught a melody played by a shepherd on his *zampogna* (rustic bagpipe), and he jotted it down on a bit of paper obtained from a Benedictine monk in the nearby abbey. These few notes became the opening theme of the women at the fountain in *Marie-Magdeleine*, which he was already turning over in his mind as a sacred drama. Chaplain, who was busy sketching all the while, left a graphic document: Massenet seated on a donkey jotting down his theme. The sketch was dated 7 March 1864.[4]

Among the visitors to Rome at this time was the painter Flandrin, who especially asked to meet the pensioners. Hippolyte Flandrin (1809–1864), a pupil of Ingres, had first come to the Villa Medici in 1833, together with Ambroise Thomas; he was now famous for his religious paintings for churches. Before entering the Academy to which he was returning after so many years, he first dipped his fingers into a little fountain and crossed himself as though entering a holy place. A few days later he was dead. It was a sorrowful group that cut wreaths of laurel from the villa gardens and laid them on his bier in the church of San Luigi de' Francesi.

Flandrin's death fell on Monday of Holy Week (21 March), and now the usual papal ceremonies had to be omitted because of the illness of Pius IX. But Massenet attended services at the Sistine Chapel and at St. Peter's, finding the music impressive even though his fellow pensioners were less than enthusiastic. He had meanwhile discovered in Rome an excellent music lending library run by one Lansberg. Here he could borrow the masses of Palestrina, Lasso, Allegri, and others, to study prior to their performance, thus redoubling his pleasure.[5]

In such a conducive atmosphere, Jules rushed ahead with his Mass. By mid-April he had finished the Credo, but he found the composition unusually fatiguing. In the end the Mass was abandoned. Completed in May, it was put into a drawer to rest in the hope that he might return to it a few months later with fresh vision. But when that time came his mind was crowded with fresh projects.[6]

One morning in March, the reserved Bourgault-Ducoudray had finally paid Massenet a visit. They played bits of Bach Passions, which Bourgault had not known before. Early in April, Bourgault left to join his family at Naples, expecting to return to Rome only for the three summer months to write his *envoi*. This information was volunteered by Massenet in a letter to Ambroise Thomas of 16 April, where he also noted that the next Prix de Rome competition would be beginning in a couple of weeks and sent his regards to Monsieur Chouquet.[*]

Further letters to Thomas (23 April and 26 May) afford insight into Massenet's autodidactic training in Rome. He again praises Lansberg's lending library, which supports his hope to return to Paris a better musician. He has discovered a whole new world: the music of Beethoven, Handel, Bach, Mozart, Haydn, Weber, Mendelssohn, and untold operas and symphonies. He plays through all these scores, fortifying both his fingers and his memory. As for classic piano schooling, he relies upon Bach and, especially, Beethoven.

---

[*] Gustave Chouquet (1819–1886) taught in New York during 1840–56, and later, in Paris, wrote musical articles for periodicals and an excellent history of French opera. He contributed to the first edition of *Grove's Dictionary* and established a catalogue of instruments in the museum of the Conservatoire, of which he was curator from 1871. Besides *David Rizzio*, Chouquet provided texts for three of Massenet's early songs and several of his choral works.

On 6 July he wrote from Palestrina, whence he expected to return to Rome in three or four days. He described the *campagna*, thanked Thomas for getting Chauvet to write, and mentioned that he had just finished a quintet for strings. There is a veiled reference to the "strange news" about Saint-Saëns that deserves some clarification here. Saint-Saëns had tried for the Prix de Rome, without success, as early as 1852. From 1861 he was piano professor at the École Niedermeyer (where Fauré, Gigout, and Messager were among his pupils), but he yearned to write for the stage. Still only twenty-eight, Saint-Saëns resolved to compete once again for the Prix de Rome in 1864. Just at this moment (for the years 1864 to 1871) an imperial decree removed the task of judging the cantatas from the jurisdiction of the mixed membership of the whole Académie des Beaux-Arts and assigned it to a special jury. The result was interesting, if not "strange." Besides the Grand Prix, which went to Charles-Victor Sieg, no other prizes were awarded.*

Another footnote to music history is perhaps implied in Massenet's correspondence of 1864. In April he mentioned to Thomas that he had heard of an opera competition. Not having a suitable poem for his second *envoi*, Massenet wondered if he should try the text (not specified) prescribed for this contest. But in a postscript of 6 July he remarked that the concours of the Théâtre-Lyrique [of which Carvalho was then manager] appeared to be nothing much; he had expected something quite different. By coincidence, it was just at this time that Auber is supposed to have "persuaded" Carvalho to commission *Le Timbre d'argent* from Saint-Saëns. Whether commissioned or entered in a contest, the work did not reach the stage of the Théâtre-Lyrique until 23 February 1877.

In July, Massenet and his companions, Falguière and Chaplain, started off for Naples, where they arrived on the twenty-fifth. It was customary for pensioners of the Villa Medici to lodge on the fifth floor of the Casa Combi, overlooking the broad quay of Santa Lucia. Here they took possession of a vast room with three beds and a convenient balcony where items of apparel could be hung to dry in the Neapolitan manner. Meals were taken mostly on the quay Santa Lucia, beside the sea, the delectable abundance of seafood washed down with Capri wine. The comrades had provided themselves in Rome with comfortable travel outfits of white flannel with blue stripes. In Naples these costumes aroused suspicion, being similar to uniforms worn by local convicts. In youthful fun, the three completed the impersonation by parading to the local café dragging imaginary balls and chains on their right legs.

Long hours were spent in the Museo Borbonico enthusing over the collections of antiquities from Herculaneum, Pompeii, Stabae, and Cumae. The more he saw, the more Jules admired those bronzes, marbles, and frescoes, recalling tragic memo-

---

* In contrast to previous years, when there was usually a Premier Grand Prix (two in 1854, none in 1856), a Second Grand Prix (two in 1854, 1856, and 1861), and often an honorable mention besides. This pattern was resumed in 1872, when the Académie des Beaux-Arts resumed jurisdiction. Meanwhile, during 1864–71, the special jury seems to have been more conservative: only a Grand Prix was awarded (none in 1867), with rarely a second prize (1868, 1870), or an accessit (1871).

ries of antiquity. He was reminded of an *Alceste* or *Orphée* of Gluck. Indeed, his impressionable mind searched for music in those excavated masterpieces: in the Pompeian Medea, Ceres, the satyrs and bacchantes. What ravishing music must have animated them thus to orgiastic dance!

After the Naples collections, the tourists were eager to visit Pompeii. But there, for lack of a parasol, the searing heat was debilitating. There were too many guards standing about, and the place closed too early when, in reality, it would have all been at its best toward sundown for effects of light, shade, and color. Thus wrote Massenet to Ambroise Thomas on 3 August; but he added that he was very happy with "this divine country." He had brought along music paper, but had not touched it. He was feeling fine, but missed his piano.

As dutiful tourists, the comrades climbed Mount Vesuvius, scorching their shoes in the process. They walked along the Bay of Naples to Castelammare and Sorrento. At Sorrento they were impressed with the orange trees, and they visited the birthplace of Torquato Tasso, which they found in a run-down condition with only a simple bust to commemorate the great poet. Further along, on the Gulf of Salerno, they pondered the destiny of Amalfi, once powerful and populous but long since sunk to the status of just a large village. During the night's repose some new associates joined the party, necessitating shaven heads as a remedy, which made for an even greater resemblance to convicts.

The trip to Capri on an orange-laden boat lasted from four o'clock in the morning until ten at night, thanks to a storm that overtook them en route. With an effort, one can imagine the beauties of Capri before it had begun to be overrun by swarms of tourists. The then small, picturesque towns of Capri and Anacapri; the Blue Grotto; the dominating Monte Solaro rising from the sea, with its ruined castle and superb view of the whole Bay of Naples: it all must have seemed like some magnificent dream to Jules and his comrades. Inspired, Massenet now began to jot down page after page of sketches, which he intended to work up later into compositions. Nine years later he was to return to Capri on holiday, after the success of *Marie-Magdeleine* in Paris.

By October the travelers were back in Rome, whence Massenet sent Ambroise Thomas a detailed report on 8 October. He is again incessantly at his piano, and he dreams and talks only of Handel, Bach, and many others, too. He has started the habit of copying out musical passages that particularly strike him. In this way he is accumulating an anthology of choice fragments from all the classic composers. The process of copying, or of making a piano reduction, helps with analysis. Besides, when memory falters he will have a dependable reference at hand. He has been enjoying some pieces by Schumann, and he is making a systematic study of organ music. The Mass of last spring has been laid aside; instead, he is planning a Requiem with organ accompaniment. He wants it to be redolent of the good, solid style of Bach preludes.

Jules also enjoyed talking with Charles Renaud de Vilbac, organist at Saint-Eugène in Paris, who was in Rome for a recital at SS. Trinità de' Monti on the afternoon of 11 October. Vilbac, himself a Prix de Rome of 1844, advised him to write a new Mass and a Te Deum; but Massenet preferred the plan of submitting as his first *envoi* a Requiem and a symphony. Meanwhile, his friend Bourgault-Ducoudray was busy with his second *envoi*: a French opera, *Meo Patacca*, after a poem by Berneri.

The first song by Massenet of which we have any record emerged in October of 1864: *L'Improvisatore—rimembranza del Trastevere*, to a poem by G. Zaffira. By the end of November he had almost finished his Requiem, set for four-part chorus and four soli, with organ accompaniment. In the Dies Irae, Confutatis, and Offertory, cellos and basses were added. As he wrote to Sophie Hennequin, he had wanted to do "a serious work, a religious work worthy of being written in memory of my poor and beloved father. It will be my first important work, and could I make a better choice?" Never, he wrote to Thomas, had he had so much pleasure and interest as for this work. And yet he was later on the point of abandoning it when a timely word from Thomas encouraged him to persist.[7]

We may here anticipate the report sent in by Victor Schnetz under the heading "Works executed by the pensioners during the year 1864, exhibited in April 1885, and sent to Paris on the 13th July following." (The exhibit was of works by the artists.) Regarding Massenet, the report stated that the compositions to be submitted were a *Messe de Requiem* and an *Ouverture orchestre*. Under remarks: "M. Massenet, not yet having completed his work for the period of the *envoi*, will have it sent to Paris at the same time as the painting by Ulmann."[8] It developed that Ulmann was not to leave for Paris until the end of August 1865, at which time he was enjoined to place Massenet's compositions directly into the hands of Ambroise Thomas. As for the overture, this could have been none other than the *Ouverture en sol*, fortunately left over in the portfolio from November 1863.

Charles Garnier was in Rome for a few days in November 1864, dining every evening with the pensioners of the Villa Medici.[9] Garnier had recently achieved instant fame when his plan for the new Paris opera house was adopted. As a Prix de Rome of 1848 in architecture, he felt the urge, like so many others, to revisit the old scene, where he could project some measure of inspiration to an oncoming generation while basking in their adulation.

On Sunday, 27 November, Bourgault got up a garden party to which came twenty men and women from the Trastevere, all in costumes of the early 1800s.[10] The weather was splendid. No doubt the colorful group moved about on the long terrace with its dolphin fountain, in view of the main façade of the Villa Medici with the crouching lions on its porch and the motto blazoned over its entrance: À NAPOLEON LE GRAND—LES ARTS RECONNAISSANS. On one side of the terrace were the formal gardens, on the other side the *bosco*—that romantic natural woods with its little paths and, all hidden, the sixty-one steps leading up to a hexagonal temple with a magnificent view of Rome. The party wound up in a brilliantly lighted sculptor's studio, where six musicians with mandolins and guitars provided music for the costumed dancers. As the ultimate in informality (in those decorous times), the spectators so far "forgot themselves" as to join in the saltarella. Massenet had received Bourgault's permission to bring as guests Monsieur and Madame Gosselin, with whom he had often dined and passed the evening. In return, Bourgault went along with Massenet to the Gosselins' for dinner on the Tuesday following. Massenet, a devotee of four-hand piano arrangements, found in Mme Gosselin an able partner for playing symphonies.

On 23 December 1864, a farewell dinner was given for Bourgault, who left Rome and the Academy the next day. On Christmas Eve, a group of pensioners went on a tour of midnight masses at the various churches of Rome, including San Giovanni in Laterano and Santa Maria Maggiore. Massenet was deeply moved by the simple devotion of the crowds of men and women packed into the churches and kneeling on the beautiful mosaic pavements. Shepherds brought their cows, goats, sheep, and pigs into the public square before the church to recall the scene in the manger, and as if to receive the Savior's benediction.

The next day, according to the *Souvenirs*, Massenet first saw his future wife. He was on the long flight of steps leading to the church of Santa Maria in Aracoeli, on the Capitoline hill, when two fashionable foreigners—in this case Frenchwomen—passed by. He was especially charmed by the younger of the two and was delighted, shortly thereafter, to meet them at one of Liszt's gatherings and learn that they were mother and daughter from Paris. The young lady in question was identified in subsequent letters as Mlle Ninon de Sainte-Marie and as Mlle Orry de Sainte-Marie. She was an excellent musician, a charming pianist, and furthermore a "ravissante jeune fille." She had studied in Paris with the Dutch pianist Ernest Lübeck.[11] In Rome she seems to have continued her piano study with one Liegt, though an account published in 1904 identified her teacher as Giovanni Sgambati (1843–1914), a pupil of Liszt, who attained some distinction as a composer.[12]

The family party had obviously come to Rome to spend the winter. Besides Ninon, there were her mother (whose full name we never learn); her brother, the painter Abel Orry de Sainte-Marie (1839–1886); and the latter's wife. We are never introduced to Ninon's father, though it is assumed that her parents moved in society. Her birth record was destroyed in the fire at the Hôtel-de-Ville in 1871, but the marriage documents of 1866 give the legal name as Louise Constance de Gressy and indicate that she was born in the Ninth Arrondissement of Paris on 25 June 1841.[*]

Liszt was then living in the monastery of the Madonna del Rosario, on the Monte Mario.[†] No doubt he played in Schnetz's salon and would have been friendly with Massenet, as with all young musicians. "Liszt was at my house yesterday," wrote

---

[*] Madame Massenet died at Égreville on 8 June 1938. The tomb in the little cemetery there bears the inscription: "Louise Constance Massenet, née De Gressy. Née à Paris, 1841. Décédée à Égreville, 1938."

[†] Liszt entered the third order of St. Francis of Assisi on 25 Apr. 1865 and was thereafter known as the Abbé Liszt. The Monte Mario is a hill north of St. Peter's where Mario Mellini owned a villa in the fifteenth century.

Massenet to Sophie Hennequin on 29 November 1864; in discussing a song that Jules had just written to a poem of Alfred de Musset, Liszt commented that "the composer could, in these intimate melodies, express even the most hidden feelings of his heart."[13]

During 1865—his second year at the Villa Medici—music flowed freely from Massenet's pen. It is said that he sketched an opera, *Esméralda*, drawn from Victor Hugo's novel of 1831, *Notre-Dame de Paris*. Did Massenet in his lending library come across Alberto Mazzucato's score of 1838? Or Vincenzo Battista's of 1851? Both had been successful Italian operas. For a beginner like Massenet, it was quite usual to acquire practice by resetting some previously used libretto. As long ago as 1836, Louise Bertin, daughter of the proprietor of the *Journal des Débats*, had produced *La Esméralda* at the Paris Opéra. By coincidence parts of this work were revived in concert form on 6 July 1865. Perhaps word of this caused Massenet, who was easily discouraged, to abandon his project.

Much that was sketched or completed at Rome has been lost; or rather it was typically reworked and absorbed into later compositions. From January to June, Massenet sketched a symphony, then abandoned it.[*] Sketches for a symphonic suite, *Pompéia* (no doubt made with the impressions of Pompeii fresh in mind), were probably not worked up and orchestrated until early in 1866. There must have been a trio, for in a letter to Julie Cavaillé (11 March 1865) Massenet mentioned that he was writing a *second* trio. He hoped to have it performed at a soirée of the Princess Czartoryska, by her and the Prince de Chimay. He would dedicate the work, however, to Mlle Ninon de Sainte-Marie, who could perform it with her cousin Jules Armingaud and the cellist Léon Jacquard. Massenet also sketched an *opéra comique*, *Noureddin*, and an Italian opera, *Valéria*.[†]

Why, then, in writing to Ambroise Thomas, did Jules appear so dejected and discouraged? Thus (1 April 1865), he apologized for three months of silence and confessed to a lack of confidence in his work. The Requiem has lain dormant for months, but now he is revising it and hopes to finish it by Easter [16 April]. By 27 June his self-effacement becomes querulous: fifteen months in Rome, and what has he accomplished? Forty pages of a Requiem, which he is still afraid to send in. He bemoans having left Paris with too little experience; he should have had two more years of solid study with Thomas. He even suggests reentering the composition class upon his return. He is flailing about in desperation for a project for a second *envoi*. Should he try to reset Émile Augier's *Sapho*, or Halévy's *Guitarrero*? He has seen neither the libretto nor the music for either.[‡]

---

[*] Letter to Thomas, 27 June 1865. See also Dec. 1871, when a symphony was tried over by Pasdeloup but not publicly performed.

[†] Sketches in the Bibliothèque Nationale. Noureddin, incidentally, is the name of a personage in Félicien David's *Lalla-Roukh*, staged at the Opéra-Comique on 12 May 1862.

[‡] *Sapho*, music by Gounod, was first staged on 16 Apr. 1851; *Guitarrero*, on 21 Jan. 1841.

Throughout his life, Massenet was never to be released entirely from his moments of melancholy and doubt. Later, to be sure, he worried over the conditions of a performance, or whether a work was going to come off, or whether success was slipping from his grasp. "Oh why," he once wrote to his publisher in desperation, "did I ever compose that *Thaïs*!"[14] He was also often merely sad—*triste*—with no very obvious reason. But in the Rome period the signs of dejection that appear—and they are not too serious—seem to reflect the heavy responsibility a young man in his position must have felt. It is the agony of ambition, anxious to be up and doing, yet with no tangible accomplishments to point to. It is the indecision of a creative talent as yet untried by fire.

There was, after all, one solid and comforting source of strength. "My piano," he wrote, "is my resource, my consolation. I work at it with care."[15] He worked on the Chopin études but depended most upon Beethoven and Bach. He took an interest in the musical training of his nephew, François Cavaillé, now about ten. A letter to his sister Julie (11 March 1865) contained detailed advice: How poorly directed were those years of study with Laurent, and how difficult to make up for the misspent effort! One should never touch Goria or Rouellen but live instead with Mozart. Later Haydn, Bach above all, and Beethoven—these are the daily bread of the artist.

Massenet's friendship with the Gosselins continued; it was Mme Gosselin who introduced him to the salon of Princess Czartoryska, also frequented by the Prince de Chimay, a violinist, and his wife, an able pianist. There was also much playing of four-hand music with various "French ladies," but most of all with Ninon. Between them they exhausted the available symphonic literature: Mozart, Haydn, Beethoven, Mendelssohn, Schumann. Jules's former classmate Sieg, four years older, was now in residence; the two of them gadded about Rome together and went to musical soirées. Sieg, too, was drafted for four-hand playing, and it is on record that they went through Beethoven's Ninth Symphony.[16]

Early in March there was an especially pleasant outing, by carriage, to Ostia and the Castel Fusano with its lovely pine woods. All the Sainte-Maries were along, as well as another painter friend, Firmin Girard. As the artists sketched, Massenet jotted down a few measures of a Larghetto. Surely the picturesque scenery must have added to his awareness of a growing romantic attachment for Ninon. It was "one of the most pleasant days" of his entire sojourn in Rome. In the best novelistic tradition, it has been asserted that Ninon's family at first raised objections to a marriage. This seems a bit contrived. They welcomed him as a son-in-law a year and a half later, which seems hardly an unduly protracted engagement.

A letter to Thomas of 14 August 1865 helps to set certain matters straight. Massenet was glad to hear that Charles Lenepveu had won the Prix de Rome. Ulmann, he wrote, will leave for France on the twenty-fifth or thirtieth, bringing Massenet's *Messe de Requiem* and *Ouverture symphonique* for Thomas to see and criticize.[*] With

---

[*] Ulmann (b. 1829), Prix de Rome of 1859 in painting, had completed his five years in Rome.

time beginning to run short, he is thinking of his second *envoi* and would like to do a symphony with chorus, in three parts, on the subject of Pompeii. He also plans a Mass—short and intimate, with emphasis on the voices but using an organ and divided strings to provide the diversity of an orchestra. It is doubtful that the Mass was written, though the idea of divided strings was indeed used in the first music for *Les Érinnyes*, performed in 1873. As for Pompeii, it probably got momentarily pushed aside for another project.

A few days later, Massenet was off for an outing to Terni and Papigno with Firmin Girard and some other friends. Then, toward the first of September, he arrived in Venice for a stay of two months. The first few days were devoted to sightseeing. But he rented a good Pleyel upright, practiced his Bach and Beethoven, and even ordered some "rare" Beethoven sonatas from Trieste—rare because unheard of in Venice! He noted down the strangely beautiful Austrian trumpet calls when the gates were closed for the night, and used the motif years later in the fourth act of *Le Cid*.

Writing to Thomas on 26 September, Massenet mentioned having composed some songs to Gautier texts. Now at long last, for the past week, he had been at work on his *Symphonie d'envoi*. When he next wrote, on 21 October, the composition was already finished and needed only to be copied out later in Rome. The writing had been most pleasurable, and he now felt the urge to do something larger, if only he had a poem.

The "symphony" was duly noted, the following year, in the report of the new director of the Academy in Rome, Robert Fleury, who had by then replaced Schnetz.[17] Massenet, in lieu of the usual French or Italian opera, had submitted: "Symphonie (en fa) en 4 parties. Grande partition, orchestre." The description neatly fits the *Première Suite d'orchestre*. When Pasdeloup performed the suite for the second time, in 1868, there was a sharp exchange between Albert Wolff in *Le Figaro*, who called it a symphony, and Massenet, who insisted it was a suite. Though the *Symphonie d'envoi* cannot be expunged from the record, it seems only fair to give the composer the last word and to enter the work in his catalogue as the first suite.

Two songs can be associated with Venice: the setting of Victor Hugo's *Nouvel chanson sur un vieil air*, and of Alfred de Musset's *Souvenir de Venise*. His mind much relieved, Massenet planned to remain there until 5 or 6 November, then return slowly to Rome by way of Padua, Vicenza, Verona, Mantua, Parma, Florence (several days), Siena, Pisa, Assisi, Perugia, Viterbo, Orvieto.[18]

On 17 December 1865, Massenet took final leave of his comrades at the Villa Medici. His trunk was packed with clothing and souvenirs of Italy and sent on its way. There were a last sad dinner at the large table in the dining hall, a last look at the December sunset over Rome from the window of the room he would no longer occupy, and that evening, the final warm embraces beside the train in the Stazione dei Termini. The next day he was in Florence for a lingering farewell to its art treasures and landmarks. After another stop at Pisa, he took the diligence along the picturesque Mediterranean coast via Spezia to Genoa. The train carried him from

Genoa to Paris, away from sunny Italy to the gray skies of the Île-de-France. He was welcomed at the home of his sister Julie, and with the ten francs left in his pocket, he purchased an umbrella.[*]

---

[*] The official biographer, Schneider (who surely knew better!), hinted that Massenet at this time visited "all the principal cities of Germany, stayed at Pesth for several months," and apparently having somehow got married in Rome, "returned with Mme Massenet to Paris."[!] Caveat lector!

1866

Back in Paris; Marriage

T HE PRIX DE ROME CARRIED a stipend for five years, of which only two had expired. Massenet could therefore count upon a steady three thousand francs per year through 1868.* Theoretically, at least, this would tide him over until other more permanent sources of income could be established. In the Paris of those days, the young composer, or literary writer, would try to get an opera or play produced; if he achieved a hit, the door would be opened to further opportunities, leading perhaps eventually to substantial royalties and a measure of renown and independence. But this was not the easiest of games to play. It would require both patience and influential friends. Meanwhile, a young composer could give piano lessons, keep on writing to improve his craft, get performances where he could, and if the reviews were at all favorable, gradually build an image with the public.

So, then, Massenet paid a call at the Ministry of Finance to collect his allowance for the first quarter of 1866. He was now installed in a room on the fifth floor at 14 Rue Taitbout. Ninon and her parents occupied an apartment nearby, at 51 Rue Laffitte. The two streets run more or less parallel, converging at the Boulevard des Italiens where, at 2 Rue Taitbout, was Tortoni's restaurant — a favorite Parisian rendezvous from 1804 until its demise in 1894. The Rue Laffitte had its share of associations. No. 1 was the house of Sir Richard Wallace, who inherited the priceless art collection of the fourth Marquis of Hertford upon the latter's death in 1870. Sir Richard's granddaughter, Georgette Wallace, would one day be a noted interpreter of Massenet's late operas under the stage name of Lucy Arbell. The buildings at 19, 21, and 23 Rue Laffitte housed the Rothschild bank and residences of Baron James de

---

* Ambroise Thomas, as professor of composition, received an annual salary of 2500 francs. (The pianist Marmontel, at sixty, received only 1600 francs!) Admittedly, Conservatoire salaries of this magnitude were merely incidental to other sources of income: composers drew royalties from their operas, and performers earned fees for concerts and private lessons, or even salaries from concurrent positions elsewhere.

Rothschild, Edmond de Rothschild, and Baron Gustave de Rothschild. Eventually Massenet would be on speaking terms with some of the Rothschilds.

Parallel with the Rue Laffitte, to the east, was the then shorter Rue Le Peletier, not yet broken through by the Boulevard Haussmann. No. 16 Rue Le Peletier, at the corner of the Rue Pinon (now Rue Rossini), was the home of the Paris Opéra from 16 August 1821 until the building burned down on the night of 28/29 October 1873.[*] Considered one of the best halls in Paris, for both proportions and acoustics, the Opéra in the Rue Le Peletier had been built by the architect Debret at a cost of 2,300,000 francs. The site had been a spacious garden belonging to the mansion of the Duc de Choiseul. The mansion, or *hôtel*, was kept to house the theater services, with its entrance on the Rue Grange-Batelière (now Rue Drouot). For the opera hall, they had saved all they could of the columns, cornices, and trimmings of the demolished theater in the Rue Richelieu. The stage was 33 meters wide, including the wings, and 30 meters deep. The proscenium was 12.60 meters wide and 13.80 meters high. However, the dressing rooms were small and the corridors dark. The *foyer de danse* was just an oblong room, poorly lit. The theater was really not well constructed, and Castil-Blaze in 1855 had warned of the fire hazard in that mass of wood and plaster. Operas and ballets were given on Monday, Wednesday, Friday, and occasionally on Sunday. In 1866, seats booked in advance (*en location*) were priced: orchestra, twelve francs; parterre, seven francs; amphitheater stalls, fifteen francs; baignoires, twelve francs; loges, first to fifth levels, from fourteen to three francs, depending upon location. Ladies were not admitted to the *fauteuils d'orchestre*. Tickets purchased at the door were a little less: the gallery gods who stood in line had access to the fourth and fifth levels for two and a half francs.

This, then, was the Opéra in the Rue Le Peletier as Massenet would have known it in his youth. None of his works were to be performed there. Already in 1861, before Massenet had even entered Thomas's composition class, ground had been broken for the new opera house, which came to be known as the Palais Garnier. Of the 160 plans submitted in competition, Charles Garnier's plan was selected and adopted on 2 June 1861. Excavation began in July. When they had dug down eight meters, they ran into a veritable subterranean river, and had to go six meters deeper for solid terrain. The first stone was laid on 21 July 1862, and the following year masonry began to appear above ground level. The façade was unveiled on 15 August 1867, but some years were still to elapse before the final formal inauguration of the new Opéra, 5 January 1875.

---

[*] The Opéra had previously occupied (from 1794) a theater in the Rue de Richelieu, across from the Bibliothèque Nationale, a site now given over to the charming Place Louvois. When the Duc de Berry was assassinated there (13 Feb. 1820) the building was immediately demolished. While awaiting the construction of a new theater in the Rue Le Peletier, the opera company moved to the Salle Favart, and also gave a few concerts in the hall at No. 8 Rue Louvois, which had been built in 1791 by Brogniart.

Léo Delibes. Courtesy Paul Jackson.

Besides the Théâtre-Italien in the Salle Ventadour, and the Théâtre-Lyrique,[*] there was still the ever-popular Opéra-Comique, where in 1866 the price of a seat ranged from nine francs down to one franc. The Salle Favart, as it was called, was but a few steps off the Boulevard des Italiens, nestled between the Rues Marivaux and Favart and facing the tiny Place Boïeldieu. An Italian troupe occupied the original Salle Favart until it burned down on 13 January 1838 (after the final scene of *Don Giovanni*). Crosnier, director of the Opéra-Comique (which had been playing in a succession of other theaters), obtained possession of the site. A new Salle Favart was constructed, and the Opéra-Comique opened there, on 16 May 1840, with Hérold's *Le Pré aux clercs*. Following Crosnier there had been a succession of other directors, but it was Adolphe de Leuven who was in charge from 1862 until 1874, at first in association with Eugène Ritt and later with Camille Du Locle. Leuven would shortly be giving Massenet his first chance at the lyric stage.

The French genre of *opéra comique*, incidentally, must not be equated with comic opera. Its roots go back to the classics of the eighteenth century: Grétry, Monsigny, Philidor. Subsequent generations of librettists and composers leaned toward more serious subjects of a romantic, historical, or even realistic nature. Despite changing musical styles in the nineteenth century, the term *opéra comique* persisted, as in the case of Bizet's *Carmen*, Delibes's *Lakmé*, or Massenet's *Manon*. As the

---

[*] In Oct. 1862, the Théâtre-Lyrique had moved to a theater in the Place du Châtelet, where it remained until May 1870. Carvalho was director during 1862–68.

century wore on other designations were indeed tried out, such as *drame lyrique* (drama set to music), *comédie lyrique, conte lyrique,* or even *roman musical* (Charpentier's *Louise*). For lighter musical fare, the Parisian public turned to the many other theaters offering *opérette, opéra bouffe,* or *vaudeville*.

Only two performances are on record for Massenet in 1866—both orchestral works. At No. 18 in the Rue Cadet (in the general vicinity of the modern Folies-Bergère) was a café, Le Casino, that boasted an orchestra led by the cornetist-conductor Joseph Arban. Here, on Saturday, 24 February, the four movements of Massenet's *Pompéia* were given a public hearing, even evoking critical notice in the *Revue et gazette musicale*. The reviewer noted certain characteristics of Berlioz: a vigorous hand, with a horror of commonplaces. The work was assessed as descriptive, following a program step by step, now grandiose, now naïve, sometimes exaggerated in expression, but withal genuine in its conception. Most notable of all was the skill in orchestration, surprising in so young a composer, who was no doubt guided more by feeling and instinct than by experience.[1] *Pompéia* thereupon disappears from view, to be swallowed up eventually in the music for *Les Érinnyes*.

In July 1866, *Deux fantaisies* for orchestra were played at the Concerts des Champs-Élysées. Again the effect was assessed as descriptive music à la Berlioz. The first of these pieces, *Une noce flamande,* was a scene for orchestra and chorus to a poem by Gustave Chouquet. A male chorus comes in with "Attendons tous le gai cortège, les fiancés qui vont s'unir"; there is a *Marche nuptiale,* the chiming of carillons, and finally a robust *Walzer* with such vigorous touches as ascending chromatic scales, down-bows at the frog, and the closing refrain: "Il n'est, vous savez, de noce flamande sans un long festin, sans valse allemande." The second fantasy, *Le Retour d'une caravane: Marche,* was furnished with a long argument ("It was toward evening . . . Everyone welcomes them . . ."); again we have descriptive music with a certain flair for orchestration to be expected in an alert young French composer of those times.

Massenet's further collaboration with Gustave Chouquet brought good fortune. An Alleluia for mixed voices, without accompaniment, won first prize in the 1866 competition of the City of Paris. Lightning struck again in 1868, when *Le Moulin,* for four-part male chorus, won another City of Paris prize.

One day, while riding atop a Parisian horse-drawn omnibus, Massenet fell into conversation with a fellow passenger who turned out to be the poet Armand Silvestre. They quickly became good friends. Massenet looked at once into Silvestre's *Rimes neuves et vieilles* (1862) and composed a song cycle, *Poème d'avril*. Armed with a letter of introduction from Ernest Reyer, to whom the work was dedicated, Massenet approached the publisher Antoine Choudens.[*] But Choudens, grown rich from

---

[*] Antoine Choudens (d. 1888) had been in business since 1844; his son Paul de Choudens (1850–1925) carried on the business after his father's death, and also wrote opera librettos.

things like Gounod's *Faust*, ushered him out of his office without even bothering to look at the manuscript. A similar reception awaited him at the firms of Flaxland and Brandus.[*] Then, quite unexpectedly, he was accosted by a tall, fair young man with a kindly, intelligent face, who informed Massenet that he had recently opened a music store at 19 Boulevard de la Madeleine, that he knew who he was, and that he was ready to publish anything he liked. Thus began the association with Georges Hart-mann, who became Massenet's principal publisher until 1891, when he sold his business to Heugel.[†]

Massenet's melodies suited the tastes of the times and became quite popular. Thus, in Alphonse Daudet's novel of Second Empire society, *Le Nabab* (1877), the heroine Mme Jenkins sits at her piano and deciphers the latest song of a fashionable young composer:

> Que l'heure est donc brève
> Qu'on passe en aimant!
> C'est moins qu'un moment,
> Un peu plus qu'un rêve.
>
> (*Poème d'avril*, No. 6)

Much of Massenet's time was now occupied with dashing about Paris giving piano lessons at the homes of his pupils. He is supposed to have said that to give a music lesson required only three phrases: "Bonjour, Mademoiselle!" (Good day, Miss), "Un peu moins vite, s'il vous plaît" (Not quite so fast, if you please), and at the conclusion, "Mes hommages, je vous prie, à Madame votre mère" (My respects, I beg of you, to Madame your mother). For which he received two francs—enough for fiacre fare, except that one would ride the omnibus instead. Biographers used to sniff at such activity as ill-paid drudgery. Why? For young composers it is excellent public relations! Today's pupil will be tomorrow's purchaser of piano music and songs or of tickets to the opera. Fame, like calumny, spreads more quickly by word of mouth than by any other means.

The kindly Ambroise Thomas continued to look after his young protégé. He introduced Massenet to his wealthy friends, at whose musical soirées young Jules performed and, in the process, learned to judge the tastes and preferences of an elite

---

[*] Gustave-Alexandre Flaxland (1821–1895) took over Grue's business in 1847, and was established at 4 Place de la Madeleine. In June 1869, he was bought out by Durand, Schoenewerk et Cie. Flaxland did publish a set of three four-hand piano pieces by Massenet in 1867. Gemmy Brandus (1823–1873), in the Rue Richelieu, had taken over Schlesinger's business in 1846; he was the proprietor of Meyerbeer's works.

[†] Georges Hartmann (d. 1900) seems to have been connected with publishing in Germany, but came to Paris and became a naturalized citizen. At some time in the 1870s he moved his business to 60 Rue Neuve-St-Augustin, renumbered in the 1880s as 20 Rue Daunou. The earliest copy seen of *Poème d'avril* was engraved and printed by C. G. Böder of Leipzig and bears Hartmann's plate no. 211. Inasmuch as publication dates were seldom imprinted on the music, it is difficult to establish an accurate chronology; Heugel et Cie do not have Hartmann's publication schedule in their archives.

society. The songs in particular, of which he eventually wrote well over two hundred, suggest that the environment of the salon was one of the composer's natural habitats. At one such gathering Massenet saw Léo Delibes for the first time, and was a little jealous of the latter's fine way with a ladies' chorus. After all, Delibes was only six years older, yet he had already produced a dozen operettas and was now assistant chorus master at the Opéra. Perhaps in a competitive spirit, Massenet tried his hand at some choral works over the next year or two; one of these (presumably *Le Moulin*) he had the satisfaction of hearing performed by a four-hundred-voice male chorus.

In the summer of 1866 Massenet fell ill. Cholera visited Paris regularly during the decade 1865–75, and so the neighbors in the Rue Taitbout were afraid to look in on the sick man. But word somehow reached Ambroise Thomas, and he not only came but brought his own doctor, who happened also to be physician to the emperor. Such fine attention no doubt contributed to a speedy recovery, whereupon Massenet completed ten piano pieces and sold them to Girod for the handsome sum of two hundred francs.[*]

The great event of 1866 was Massenet's marriage to Louise Constance de Gressy. On 6 October they appeared at the headquarters of the Ninth Arrondissement to make the civil arrangements. Jules-Émile-Frédéric Massenet is entered in the record as living with his mother at 14 Rue Taitbout, while Mademoiselle De Gressy's address is given as 51 Rue Laffitte. On the following Monday, 8 October, the formal ceremony was held in the little church of Avon, near Fontainebleau. Among the witnesses who signed were the painter Abel Orry (the bride's brother) and the "widow Orry."[†] Present but not signing as formal witness was the bride's cousin, the eminent violinist Jules Armingaud.[‡] The wedding ceremony was enlivened by a flock of sparrows that flew in through a broken window and chirped a descant to the kindly words of the good curé Potier. Afterwards they walked in the lovely woods. The October sunshine highlighted the variegated foliage and stimulated the birds to song. Already Massenet's head began to hum with all the love songs he would write in a lifetime. A

---

[*] Étienne Girod (d. 1880) had acquired Launer's business in 1854. There was also an Augustin-Célestin Girod who, however, died in 1865. The *Dix pièces de genre* for piano appeared in 1867 with the imprint G. et A. Girod. In 1868, four songs appeared with E. et A. Girod, 16 Boulevard Montmartre. From 1880 the business was carried on by Étienne's widow as Veuve Girod. The would-be historian of music publishing must collect and collate plate numbers and search for elusive biographical information. Cecil Hopkinson's monumental *Dictionary of Parisian Music Publishers, 1700–1950* provides an excellent starting point.

[†] We are thus confronted with a confusing cumulation of names: Orry, Sainte-Marie, and De Gressy. In such matters, Massenet's heirs maintain a stony silence.

[‡] Jules Armingaud (1820–1900) was born at Bayonne, near Biarritz. At nineteen he was refused admission to the Paris Conservatoire as too advanced. He played in the Opéra orchestra and, in 1855, founded a famous string quartet (with Édouard Lalo, Mas, and Léon Jacquard) to which winds were later added to form the Société Classique. It is said that he introduced Beethoven quartets into Paris musical circles. Armingaud's *Modulations* (1895) is a book given over entirely to witty sayings, from one-liners to developed anecdotes. It represents the kind of mot juste with which French conversation sparkled at the fin de siècle.

week's honeymoon was spent at the seashore, where the young composer busily corrected proofs for the *Poème d'avril.*

It was a happy marriage that was to endure for forty-six years, until Massenet's death. Their only child was Juliette, born on 31 March 1868. As time went on, Massenet had to travel a great deal to supervise rehearsals of his operas, conduct concerts, or simply put in an appearance on important occasions. Or Madame Massenet would go off on vacation, or to a health resort, leaving her husband to concentrate upon some new work. Such brief absences only strengthened the ties that bound the family together. As for domiciles, they always had a Paris apartment and a summer place not too far from Paris. Besides, the Massenets often traveled together—to the seashore or the mountains, and in later years, to the south of France for the winter months. From a wife's point of view Massenet must have been an ideal husband: kindly to the point of never wanting to hurt anyone's feelings; a ready and witty conversationalist with a twinkle in his eye; and while an obsessive worker, never too busy to attend to the nuances of sociability.

With increasing fame, Massenet jealously guarded the privacy of his personal and family life. From the evidence available, we must conclude that he enjoyed a rare domestic serenity and happiness and that he wanted to encase it in a protective covering. Like most successful men, Massenet had his detractors who, not content with belittling his artistic aims, made frontal attacks upon his character or perpetuated sly innuendos regarding his personal deportment. The conscientious biographer must dismiss all hearsay evidence as rubbish. Thus, Massenet's supposed "affairs" with named correspondents—typically prima donnas—are probably sheer fabrications of mischievous minds. The tone and substance of his letters, written by a sensitive artist in another day and age, can be readily misinterpreted by the inexperienced or ill-informed. That the man had a warm heart we can be sure, and also that he was friendly and urbane. But as far as we are concerned here, his only mistress was the lyric theater, to which he was utterly devoted.

La Grand' Tante;
The Franco-Prussian War

W
HEN THE YOUNG COUPLE RETURNED from their brief honeymoon they installed themselves in the cheerful, spacious apartment of the wife's parents. Soon Ambroise Thomas sent word that there was a chance to submit a one-act work for performance at the Opéra-Comique.

As one of the conditions for receiving a government subsidy, the Opéra-Comique was supposed to produce annually a one-act opera by a Prix de Rome winner. The requirement was not difficult to circumvent. In fact, there was a sizable accumulation of young composers back from Rome and impatiently awaiting a commission. Since 1862, Adolphe de Leuven had been director of the Opéra-Comique in association with Eugène Ritt. He was perhaps now in a good mood, having produced a hit with Thomas's *Mignon* (17 November 1866). As a courtesy, De Leuven would have asked each of the professors of composition—Carafa, Bazin, and Thomas—to suggest which of their pupils should be approached. The offer of a production was made not only to Massenet, on Thomas's recommendation, but also to Jean Conte, a pupil of Carafa and Prix de Rome as long ago as 1855, and to Samuel David, a pupil of Halévy and Basin, and Prix de Rome of 1858. The industrious Massenet simply finished well ahead of Conte and David, thereby gaining priority.

The libretto for *La Grand' Tante* was concocted by Jules Adenis and Charles Grandvallet. Grandvallet need not detain us, but Jules Adenis deserves passing mention as the author, in collaboration, of a wide variety of *comedies*, *vaudevilles*, and *opéras comiques* librettos. Together with Saint-Georges he provided the text for Bizet's *La jolie fille de Perth* (Théâtre-Lyrique, 27 April 1867).

————————◆————————

The story of *La Grand' Tante* is economical enough for a curtain raiser, requiring only three characters. Guy de Kerdrel, a young marquis stationed in Africa as cavalry

Victor Capoul and Marie Heilbron. Courtesy Paul Jackson.

sergeant, returns to France expecting to inherit the château of his deceased great-uncle. His great-aunt, Alice de Kerdrel, turns out to be a charming girl of twenty whom the old gentleman had married on his deathbed. As might be expected, tender feelings are aroused in the young man's heart. His original plan—to sell the château as quickly as possible—now seems less urgent. There is, to be sure, the matter of the unsigned will. Guy forges a signature, only to have such incriminating evidence of a serious misdeed torn up by Alice. Then an earlier and valid will is dredged up, in which the elderly miser disinherited his "ne'er do well" great nephew in favor of the young widow. After a combat of mutual generosity, the girl accedes to the prayers of the young man, who has discovered that one way to gain both a fortune and a lovely bride is to marry your great-aunt. The third person in the cast is the female servant, La Chevrette—a rôle assigned to Caroline Girard, a spirited singer and actress whom one critic called a "devil in skirts."

◆

    Rehearsals got under way. Alice was to be played by Marie Roze, who had carried off first prizes in singing and in *opéra comique* in 1865 and been engaged at once for the Opéra-Comique. Guy de Kerdrel was to be no less than Victor Capoul, the tenor who charmed habitués of the Opéra-Comique from 1861 to 1870 before he moved on to a wider audience in London, New York, and elsewhere.[*] At the last minute the casting was upset: Marie Roze was taken away and replaced by a "seventeen-year-old beginner," Marie Heilbron. The latter had studied at the Brussels Conservatoire and with Duprez in Paris, making her debut in 1866 at the Théâtre-

---

[*] Victor Capoul (1839–1924) taught singing in New York, 1892–97, and was later stage manager at the Paris Opéra, 1901–07.

Lyrique in *La Fille du régiment*. After further experience in the provinces, she had made her official debut at the Opéra-Comique in Meyerbeer's *L'Étoile du nord*. It was this "beginner," then, who sang Alice de Kerdrel and who, seventeen years later, would create the rôle of Manon.

By an ironic coincidence, Massenet's first stage production served as curtain raiser for a work by the same Bazin who had once ejected him from harmony class. François Bazin's three-act *opéra comique*, *Le Voyage en Chine*, first given on 9 December 1865, had turned out to be his most successful work.[*] At the première of *La Grand' Tante*, on 3 April 1867, there were two "incidents" which, far from marring the performance, contributed to the audience's delight. The scene was laid in Brittany, and the tenor Capoul was to make his first entrance out of the stormy night with the words: "What a country! What a wilderness! Not a soul in sight!" And then, catching sight of Mlle Girard: "Thank God! At last a human face!" But Mlle Girard, occupied with some bit of stage business, had at this crucial moment turned her posterior. The anecdote is as old as show business, guaranteed to produce howls of merriment. In the wings, Jules Adenis is supposed to have turned to Massenet with: "Listen. What a splendid start! The audience is amused." The other incident (also hoary in the annals of the theater) is supposed to have occurred at the end of the piece. It was customary not to mention the authors' names until the close of the première. We can visualize the scene: the manager advances to center stage and clears his throat. "Mesdames, Messieurs, it is a pleasure to announce the authorship of the work you have just enjoyed." At that moment the theater cat walked serenely onstage; the laughter drowned out the announcement, so that the public would have to read the names on the posters for the *second* performance.

The reviewers clucked their tongues at the inane libretto but accorded sufficient notice to the music to feed the young composer's ego for several days. Noted with brief commentary were Mlle Girard's song "Les Filles de La Rochelle," the romance "File, corvette agile," the tenor aria "Allons, camarade," and the duos "Fée, ange ou femme" and "L'amour que je rêve." Johannes Weber's phrase (*Le Temps*) sounds a little too pat, like a favorite cliché: "His melodies are distinguished and charming, and flow without effort." More noteworthy are the repeated references to the orchestration. Ernest Reyer (*Journal des Débats*) found "a considerable skill in the management of the orchestra," while for Eugène Tarbé (*Le Figaro*) "all of the orchestral part is treated with a masterly hand and does not reveal a single instance of inexperience." For Gustave Bertrand (*Le Ménestrel*) there was, in fact, too much orchestration: "The young artist does not treat the voices with as much skill as the instruments; the ritornellos burst with activity; the accompaniments, with their

---

[*] Revived as late as 1899 and 1906. *Le Voyage en Chine* owed its success to a lively and entertaining libretto by Eugène Labiche and A. Delacour. A stubborn Breton refuses his daughter's hand in marriage. The suitor entices his would-be father-in-law onto his boat, then takes off on a "voyage to China" (all the while in sight of Cherbourg), until the daughter is delivered as "ransom" for returning to terra firma.

multiple dialogues and indiscreet replies, crowd the singers. If [the composer] would calm this excessive zeal, by pruning away a little of this luxuriant busywork, there would remain a singular and congenial talent." Eugène Tarbé, in perhaps the most flattering of compliments, wrote that Massenet's score "does not seem like the work of a beginner. . . . Sheer instinct has replaced, for the composer, that which one ordinarily learns only after repeated attempts: the art of writing for the stage."[1]

La Grand' Tante rode along on the double bill for a total of seventeen performances in 1867. It was apparently never revived, and the orchestra score was lost in the fire at the Opéra-Comique in 1887. The piano-vocal score was published by Girod, with a dedication to Ambroise Thomas. Years later, Massenet remarked to a young composer that for La Grand' Tante he received a shoddy royalty of only 1 percent for each performance.[2] By then his works were drawing 10 percent. Still, whenever he went to collect, he would invariably ask: "Is that all?"

Meanwhile, amidst the final preparations for his stage debut, Massenet had achieved a hearing before the concert public. On Sunday, 24 March 1867, Pasdeloup presented the Première Suite d'orchestre at one of his Concerts Populaires de Musique Classique. How this came about is recounted in touching detail in the Souvenirs. Massenet went regularly to Versailles to give music lessons to a family there. One day, en route, he was caught in a heavy shower and waited it out in the station. Pasdeloup was there, in the same predicament. Pasdeloup had never spoken to Massenet, but now he struck up a conversation. If, perchance, Massenet had written something for orchestra while at Rome, he would like to see it. (His cordiality was doubtless influenced by the acceptance of La Grand' Tante at the Opéra-Comique!) The score of the suite composed at Venice was sent to Pasdeloup that same week. Then one day Massenet ran into a cellist from Pasdeloup's orchestra, who recounted that they had just read through a remarkable suite but that the composer's name was not on the parts. The description, of course, left no doubt. Massenet rushed home to break the good news to his wife and mother-in-law. At the concert he sat in the third balcony, apparently separate from his family and friends who no doubt turned out in force.

Albert Wolff's unkind review in Le Figaro related to another performance of the suite by Pasdeloup, on 2 February 1868. The matter may just as well be disposed of here. The suite consists of four movements: (1) Pastorale et fugue; (2) Variations; (3) Nocturne; (4) Marche et Strette. The leisurely, melodious opening pastorale leads into an allegro in fugal style that still reeks of contrapuntal studies. The variations are mostly andantino quasi allegretto but, for the last few pages, move into allegro vivace assai. The Nocturne is competently descriptive. The vigorous finale, in F minor, unleashes considerable energy but subsides at the end to a cyclical return of the pastoral theme, in F major. The effects of all that four-hand playing of classical symphonies (through Schumann) are evident; still, the composer's real bent would lie more toward descriptive music.

In his review, Albert Wolff remarked that a small "accident" had to be recorded. The score of a very young composer had somehow wandered into Pasdeloup's program between some overtures by Mozart and Mendelssohn and had become the victim of its own temerity. The public, he said, welcomed the unfortunate little thing with such coldness that after ten minutes their noses were frozen. The "victim" was carried to the nearest pharmacy, where first aid was administered, so that by a quarter past four young Massenet could bring the poor wounded creation home again. "A fragment of a symphony would have been enough. The opening pastorale had its small *succès d'estime*. But when, toward the end, the storm broke out with bass drum and piccolo, the latchkeys joined in."*

Théodore Dubois wrote a long letter to Wolff, accusing him of exercising his wit to please the public ("Ah! that Wolff is really quite droll!") while totally discouraging all young composers. Dubois is unfamiliar with the suite, and cannot judge of its merits. But Wolff, as a responsible critic, if displeased, should have produced some frank and valid criticism based on genuine artistic considerations, with an analysis of the pieces and a reasoned explanation of their shortcomings. With French politeness, Dubois prefers to think that Wolff had no evil intention but was merely carried away by a moment of euphoric humor that he might later regret. The fantasy about the pharmacy, and so on, was not in very good taste, which was surprising in one whose critical talent is ordinarily so distinguished.

Massenet, too, wrote a letter to Wolff (the only time he engaged in polemics of this sort), and the columns of *Le Figaro* provided at least a brief moment of publicity. The work reviewed, he wrote, was a suite and not a "symphony." (Apparently a touchy point; Massenet would forever renounce any attempt to produce a symphony.) Witty persons, like imbeciles, are subject to error. For example, it was *not* the first occasion when the suite (not a symphony) was heard; Pasdeloup had probably included it in the program because of its excellent reception the previous year. "Two years ago, Monsieur, I was in Rome, where young composers live in admiration of the wonderful things of the past, and in ignorance of the *foule des petits agréments* (loosely: mess of agreeable fripperies) that await them upon their return to Paris."[3]

Ultimately, after the Franco-Prussian War, the *Première Suite* was supplanted by a half dozen other suites that held their place more readily in the concert hall. They were all more or less exercises in descriptive orchestration, a kind of "preparation" for the operatic theater to which Massenet would devote himself so wholeheartedly after *Hérodiade*.

Paris in 1860, after the annexation of the faubourgs, counted a population of a million and a half, which would rise by 1900 to two and a half million. The half-century was punctuated with a series of international expositions, each larger and more elaborate than the last: in 1855, 1867, 1878, 1889, and 1900. The Exposition Universelle of 1867 was a kind of frenetic festival, a premature wake over the remains of Louis Napoleon's empire. Amidst widespread disaffection with the regime, there was yet an illusive confidence in some quarters, including the army, that France was still the strong master of her own destiny. The grand exhibition in the Champ-de-Mars,

---

* A reference to the old-fashioned hardware house keys, with a hole in the end, which made excellent whistles for expressing disapproval.

intended as a potent symbol of prosperity, served as a magnet to draw all the world to the French capital. King Wilhelm and Queen Augusta of Prussia came, as did Counts Bismarck and Moltke. The Sultan Abdul-Aziz of Turkey put in an appearance, and Tsar Alexander II escaped an assassin's bullets while riding with Louis Napoleon in the Bois de Boulogne. In all, fifty-seven reigning monarchs contributed their pomp and circumstance to the passing show.

Business bloomed and the theaters prospered. The Exposition was set to open on 1 April, and as we have seen, two days later Massenet made his debut at the Opéra-Comique. On 12 April, Offenbach's *La Grande Duchesse de Gérolstein* began its run at the Variétés. The star, Hortense Schneider, was courted and idolized by all the eminent visitors to Paris. When her carriage was stopped at the Exposition gate reserved for royalty, she simply insisted that she *was* the Grand Duchess of Gerolstein and gained admittance. Two weeks later (27 April), Gounod's *Roméo et Juliette*, destined to become a staple of the French repertoire, opened at the Théâtre-Lyrique.

On 3 August 1867, the Ministry of Beaux-Arts opened three opera competitions: works were to be submitted suitable for the Opéra, the Théâtre-Lyrique, and the Opéra-Comique. For the Opéra, the winning libretto was *La Coupe du roi de Thulé*, in three acts, by Louis Gallet and Édouard Blau. Among the musical settings submitted, the jury wavered for a time between Massenet's entry and that of Eugenio Diaz de la Peña, finally awarding Diaz first place and mentioning Massenet for second place. Ernest Guiraud was rated third, and Grat-Norbert Barthe fourth; Bizet's entry received no mention.[4] Diaz had to wait long enough for a performance at the Opéra where, from 10 January 1873, his work was given twenty-one times and was considered the best of his three operas. Massenet's "thousand pages of orchestration" for *La Coupe du roi de Thulé* served for three decades as a well from which he drew many a passage for subsequent works.[*]

Massenet did not enter the Théâtre-Lyrique competition for which the composer could have a free choice of libretto. The winner was Jules Philipot, with *La Magnifique*. Émile-Adolphe Canoby's *La Coupe et les lèvres* placed second, and Édouard Lalo's *La Conjuration de Fiesco* was allotted third place.[5]

The Opéra-Comique competition actually opened on 30 August 1867 and was to close on 30 April 1868. But because Saint-Georges was late with his libretto for *Le Florentin*, the closing date was extended to 30 July 1868. Fifty-three scores were submitted, with first place going to Charles Lenepveu, a pupil of Thomas and Prix de Rome winner of 1865. (Massenet is said to have placed third.) Like Diaz, Lenepveu had a long wait: when the Opéra-Comique finally staged *Le Florentin* on 25 February 1874, it was a failure.[6]

---

[*] "Shortly after" [?], according to the *Souvenirs*, Saint-Saëns wrote to Weimar to see if *La Coupe du roi de Thulé* could be performed there: "Events, however, decreed otherwise." After Massenet's death, Saint-Saëns recounted that he had obtained access to the theater at Weimar for one of Massenet's works [not specified] after *Samson et Dalila* was staged there [2 Dec. 1877], but Massenet had received the idea with "glacial coldness." (*L'Echo de Paris*, 1912; quoted in Alfred Bruneau, *Massenet*, 1935, p. 86.)

There was also a cantata competition for a musical setting of Romain Cornut's *Les Noces de Prométhée*, with a carrot attached. The winner was to receive a medal, to be sure; but in lieu of a cash prize, each performance of the cantata was to carry a five-thousand-franc royalty. By simply neglecting to perform the cantata, the sponsors avoided having to dispense any real cash. Saint-Saëns, the winner, quickly found this out. All told, there were 103 entries. It is said that the runners-up were Guiraud, Massenet, and Weckerlin, and that Bizet's entry was among the top fifteen.[7]

Finally, a prize of ten thousand francs was offered for a hymn, suitable for performance on international occasions. No doubt Massenet would have tried for this juicy plum, but he would have been buried among 823 entries and hence probably secretive about the outcome.

Each year, to commemorate the birthday anniversary of Napoleon Bonaparte, it was customary to perform a special cantata at each of the Paris opera houses. For the Théâtre-Lyrique, on 15 August 1867, the cantata was Massenet's *Paix et Liberté*.[8] The score, of which Massenet kept no copy, was taken to the Opéra-Comique; there it burned in the fire of 1887.[9]

Meanwhile, Gustave Flaxland, who had turned down the *Poème d'avril*, was glad in 1867 to publish Massenet's "first suite" of four-hand piano pieces: (1) Andante; (2) Allegretto quasi allegro; (3) Andante. For those who think of Massenet in terms of the Elegy or the Meditation from *Thaïs*, his piano music—whether for two or four hands—may come as something of a pleasant surprise. It does not, of course, partake of the rich coloristic palette of a Debussy or Ravel; neither does it drip with romantic syrup. On the whole rather classic in tone, the piano music represents an intimate little world of Massenet, with its own charming moments.

On 2 February 1868, the first orchestral suite was again played by Pasdeloup, eliciting Albert Wolff's caustic humor as we have already seen. No other significant performances have come to light for that year. The great event was the birth of Juliette on 31 March.[*] By 7 July, Massenet had finished *Le Florentin*. In a letter of that date (written from Marlotte, where he was doubtless staying with his wife's brother Abel Orry), he gave careful instructions to Paul Cavaillé for delivering the package in "the competition for the Opéra-Comique." In these situations, the composer often resorted to every possible subterfuge to avoid recognition, apparently assuming that what the jury didn't know wouldn't hurt them.[†] Cavaillé is to carry the package to the office of the director general of theaters, make sure it is the proper place to submit

---

[*] The public record of Massenet's life is so secretive that this fact had to be deduced from an annotation in the score of *Werther*. On page 31 of Act I, Massenet wrote the date Thurs., 31 Mar. 1887, morning, and "19 ans de Juliette."

[†] The score would be identified only by a motto: an accompanying sealed envelope bearing the motto contained within the composer's name and address. In 1880 a series of such envelopes came into the hands of Ernest Lévine, who published the list in the *Moniteur universel* with the hope of discovering the names of some contestants from a bygone competition. Massenet wrote to him that if he would open No. 30, "Dieu seul est grand," he would find inside "M. Massenet, 51 rue Laffitte, Paris."[10]

manuscripts, and then quickly decamp without leaving any traces. Massenet himself, he says, would have been too readily recognized by "ces messieurs." He is not entirely happy with what he has produced, still dreams of orchestral effects he might have used, and hopes that this "nightmare" will vanish when Cavaillé disposes of it as indicated. He sends a kiss to Mama and Julie; no doubt the mother was now living with the Cavaillés.[11]

More mystifying is a letter to Paul Poirson (who later wrote, with Louis Gallet, the libretto for Gounod's *Cinq-Mars*):

> Saturday in September '68
>
> The music is finished, and will be ready to be played for Mlle Granier on Monday at 1:30. If you make an appointment at her place, make sure that no one is present but you and me and our diva. . . . I kept my word, didn't I?
> Tout à vous,
>
> J. Massenet
>
> P.S. If you would like to hear the rest of the work, I shall await you tomorrow, Sunday, at 10 or 10:30. At 11 o'clock I have to go out.[12]

"Our diva" could only have been sixteen-year-old Jeanne Granier, who became a smashing hit in Charles Lecocq's *Giroflé-Girofla* at the Renaissance in 1874 and was a great star of operetta until she turned to spoken drama. I have been unable to identify the music that was here "finished." But the connection is interesting in the light of Massenet's *L'Adorable Bel-Boul* of 1873, in which Jeanne Granier performed.

After the success of *Poème d'avril*, Massenet drew upon Armand Silvestre for another song cycle, the romantically melancholy *Poème du souvenir*. The work was dedicated to a wealthy American lady, Mrs. Charles Moulton, who had been impressed by the earlier cycle. Further, E. et A. Girod published *Quatre mélodies*, of which "L'Esclave" was dedicated to Mrs. Moulton, "Portrait d'une infant" to Mme Ulysse Trélat, and "La Vie d'une rose" to Mme Miolan-Carvalho.

In 1869 Massenet dashed off the spritely *Sérénade de Zanetto*, which became quite a hit. The lyrics were from François Coppée's charming one-act trifle *Le Passant*, which had opened at the Odéon on 14 January 1868 and became an instant raving success. With no plot and only two characters, Coppée's little play touched a sentimental nerve in the Parisian public. A Renaissance Florentine lady, Sylvia (played by Mme Marie-Léonide Agar), is serenaded by a strolling boy troubadour, Zanetto (played by Sarah Bernhardt). That was all. But what an opportunity for Sarah![13] Like the rest of the world, Massenet followed Bernhardt's career with interest, and their paths would cross again.

Hartmann also published three *Chants intimes*, to poems by Gustave Chouquet, and *Sonnet* (Georges Pradel), opening with "Les grands bois s'éveillaient." Noteworthy in many of the early songs is the recurrence of certain favorite images: the woods, roses, April, the state of the atmosphere (the air is . . .). The bittersweet brevity of love affairs was an appealing poetic theme, and the beloved is often addressed as "Mignonne" (darling). In contrast, another, more lively class of songs draws upon the local color of Spain, Italy, or Provence.

Jules Ruelle was responsible for a libretto on *Manfred* (after Byron), which Massenet seems to have worked on in 1869 but left unfinished. Perhaps he abandoned it for a more tempting project: *Méduse*, a three-act libretto by Michel Carré of the famous Barbier-Carré team that had put together so many successful opera texts, including the recently staged *Hamlet* of Ambroise Thomas. Naturally it was Thomas who introduced his young protégé to Michel Carré, no doubt coaxing him to do something nice for this promising young man. Massenet worked at the score from the summer of 1869 through the winter and into the next spring. He was to play the work over for Opéra director Émile Perrin when, alas, war broke out. *Méduse* was shelved for all time; or rather, it was probably picked apart and used elsewhere.

Charles-Louis-Napoléon Bonaparte (1808–1873), though born in Paris, had been raised in exile. Educated in Switzerland and Augsburg, he had acquired a marked German accent and indeed was almost a stranger to French ways when, in his fortieth year, he at last entered the mainstream of French politics. More a man of letters than a practical politician, he delighted in elaborating the Napoleonic ideas as a kind of theorist in statesmanship. Eventually he hypnotized his countrymen into approving by plebiscite his coronation, on 2 December 1852, as ruling monarch of the Second Empire. As empress he selected the Spanish countess Eugénie-Marie de Montijo (1826–1920), a great beauty but deficient in political sagacity. The wedding was held with great pomp at Notre-Dame on 30 January 1853.

Louis Napoleon fancied himself as a mediator, or if need be and the occasion were opportune, an upholder of the right. He joined England in the Crimean War (1854–56) against Russia, then helped the Italians in their struggle for unity, defeating the Austrians in 1859 at Magenta and Solferino. Eugénie's favorite color, a purplish shade of red, was promptly renamed "magenta." Lombardy was ceded to the Italians, and Savoy and Nice to France. Prussia and Austria joined forces in 1864 for the Schleswig-Holstein affair, but were at each other's throats two years later because of Bismarck's policies. When the Austrians were trounced at Königgrätz (Sadowa), Louis Napoleon attempted to mediate a settlement (at the same time putting in a claim for Rhenish Bavaria and the Saar), but he was rebuffed. An attempt to purchase Luxembourg from Holland fell through because of Bismarck's objections.

When Émile Ollivier was called by Louis Napoleon in January 1870 to head a new constitutional government, he announced in his opening speech to the Chambers that "peace was never more assured than now." The cliché has a familiar ring! Certainly Eugénie and her circle were eager for a war that would raise France by humbling Prussia. The fever of war has been known to unite a country divided within itself, and even to enhance the prestige of leaders who are bunglingly impotent in the face of domestic problems. French arsenals were bulging with efficient new small arms, and the military seemed to be in excellent shape.

The Bourbon queen of Spain, Isabella, had been deposed by revolution in 1868, and that country sought a new ruler. After secret negotiations, the Spanish government informed the French ambassador on 2 July 1870 of the coming election of Prince Leopold of Hohenzollern-Sigmaringen, who had married the sister of the king of Portugal. France was roused to a fury of indignation: no Hohenzollern could be tolerated on her southern borders. The candidature was withdrawn, but France pressed Wilhelm of Prussia for a firm promise that no member of the House of Hohenzollern would ever in the future accept the Spanish throne. At one point, on 13 July, Wilhelm refused further to see the French ambassador Benedetti; the incident was interpreted by the war party in France as a humiliating insult. French troops were hastily sent to the front, and on 19 July France declared war on Prussia.

On 28 July, Louis Napoleon left for the front, proceeding to Metz. The plan was to cross the Rhine and drive a wedge between north and south Germany to the Elbe, after which friendly assistance was expected from Austria and Italy. But the French war machine was no match for the expertise of Moltke and his colleagues. Early in August the Germans laid siege to Strasbourg and overran Lorraine. On 18 August there was a bloody battle near Gravelotte—the birthplace of Massenet's grandfather. Metz was besieged, and the emperor and most of the French army were bottled up in Sedan, which capitulated on 2 September.

Six weeks had sufficed to crush the French empire, leaving a French republic to agonize for another five months. The Germans proceeded with the siege of Paris, which lasted from 19 September 1870 until the capitulation on 28 January 1871. There was less injury to the city than might have been expected. Only after the acceptance of peace terms did the Germans march into Paris, on 2 March. They left the next day.

Meanwhile, on 18 January 1871 in the Hall of Mirrors at Versailles, Wilhelm III, seventh king of Prussia, had been crowned Wilhelm I, Kaiser of the Second German Reich. By the peace of Frankfurt in May, Germany received Alsace and the German-speaking part of Lorraine as far as Metz. An indemnity of five billion francs imposed upon France was paid off with surprising promptness, so that by the autumn of 1873 the last German troops were withdrawn.

After Sedan, the provisional government moved from Bordeaux to Versailles. The Parisian populace, led by Red Republicans, suspecting some iniquitous plot to establish a reactionary monarchy, drove the government troops out of the city and established the Commune of 27 March. Then came the second siege of Paris, this time by the French army. When, on 20 May, Marshal MacMahon succeeded in entering the city, the Communists proceeded the next day to set fire to the chief buildings. The Tuileries Palace, Hôtel-de-Ville, and other landmarks were destroyed, and for a time the fire threatened to destroy the whole city. The Théâtre-Lyrique in the Place du Châtelet, closed during the past year, was partially destroyed.

The horror inspired by the Commune drove the wealthy classes from Paris. Pessimists thought the former prestige of the capital was forever ruined. But throughout its history French civilization has been remarkably resilient. By the autumn of 1873, most of the private houses that were burned had been rebuilt and the salvageable monuments restored. The streets and public places were again as splendid and gay as in the best days of the empire.

Of his war experiences Massenet later wrote:

In 1870—a dismal date for my poor country—the Prussian cannons, answering those of Mont Valérien [a fort defending Paris], often lugubriously punctuated the fragments that I tried to write during the short moments of rest that guard duty, marching around Paris, and military exercises on the ramparts, left us. There the musician, in the physical weariness of this novel life, vainly trying to find a few moments of forgetfulness, did not altogether abdicate his rights. In the leaves of a finished score, but one which would never be brought before the public, *Méduse*, I find annotated the patriotic cries of the *Marseillaise* sung by the regiments as they passed my little house at Fontainebleau on their way to battle. And so in other fragments I can read the bitter thoughts that moved me when, having returned to Paris before it was invested, I was inspired by the woeful times that were upon us during the long winter of that terrible year.[14]

We can deduce from this letter that it was probably the pre-orchestral version of *Méduse* that Massenet was prepared to play over for Émile Perrin before the outbreak of hostilities and that during the summer he hopefully continued with the orchestration at Fontainebleau. In any case, he was shut up in Paris during the siege, serving in the national guard.

Massenet apparently left Paris, along with so many others, at the time of the Commune. The autograph of the *Sérénade d'automne* bears the date "Biarritz, 15 April 1871," while the duo *Au large* was marked "Vals, 7 May 1871."* In a letter written long after, he mentioned "Bayonne, dear city where I lived for several months after the war," adding that he had relations there: "the celebrated violinist Armingaud, who is my cousin."[15] Bayonne is five miles inland from Biarritz.

Wherever Massenet celebrated his twenty-ninth birthday, it was on that day (12 May 1871) that Auber died in Paris. Ambroise Thomas took over as director of the Conservatoire, and a few years later Massenet would join him there as professor of composition. By early June of 1871 Massenet was back at Fontainebleau where he wrote a few songs and started work on *Scènes pittoresques*, finding life "most exquisite" after the recent privations and inspired by the "sweetly peaceful branches" of the great trees of Fontainebleau.

In the midst of widespread destruction, the Opéra in the Rue Le Peletier had somehow been spared. Olivier Halanzier-Dufrénoy was made its provisional director on 1 July, and on 1 November he assumed the real directorship until 1879. The Opéra-Comique also reopened; by 7 December 1871 it had celebrated its one thousandth performance of Hérold's *Le Pré aux clercs*.

Gounod had sat out the war in England, doing his patriotic bit with *Gallia*, a sincere lamentation for the plight of his country, which was given at the opening of London's International Exposition in May. In July he returned to Paris, and on

---

* There is a Vals in Switzerland, but more probably this was Vals (Ardêche), a few miles west of the Rhône midway between Saint-Étienne and Nimes.

29 October 1871, the Concerts du Conservatoire began the season with a performance of *Gallia.* (The following month, the work was even mounted on the stage of the Opéra-Comique.) The Conservatoire concerts under Georges Hainl, principal conductor since 1864, tended to be conservative in tone. Before the end of the season Hainl would turn over his baton to his long-time assistant, Ernest Deldevez, and Charles Lamoureux would move in as *his* assistant.

Pasdeloup, who was considered more progressive, began his season on 22 October 1871, at the Cirque National.[*] Pasdeloup reserved his Tuesday morning rehearsals for reading through new works from which to make an occasional selection for the Sunday concerts. During this particular October, the twenty-year-old Vincent d'Indy went to each Tuesday rehearsal eagerly awaiting the turn of his Scherzo. There he saw various musical personages who were admitted to these otherwise closed sessions: Ernest Reyer, Bizet, Massenet, Duparc, Castillon, Camille Benoît, the publisher Hartmann, and so on. They were all interested in hearing new works, and they enjoyed ardently discussing the musical questions of the day. When the Scherzo was finally read, Bizet and Massenet, at the rear of the hall, tried desperately to guess who the composer might be. Massenet at first thought Saint-Saëns, but at the development he changed his guess to Rubinstein. At the end they asked Pasdeloup, who had forgotten the name but pointed to "that young man there." Fortunately, Alexis de Castillon was present to make the proper introductions, and Bizet and Massenet warmly congratulated their new young colleague.[16]

Massenet had good reason to attend rehearsals, for Pasdeloup gave his *Scènes hongroises* on 26 November and again on 17 December. The program of this second orchestral suite is a Hungarian wedding: (1) Entrée en forme de danse; (2) Intermède; (3) Adieux à la fiancée; (4) Cortège, Bénédiction nuptiale; Sortie de l'église. Massenet's biographer Schneider explained the work's ethnic interest with the absurd fabrication that, after Rome, Massenet had "lived in Perth for several months" and there wrote *Scènes hongroises.* We need not search far for another possible source of inspiration: the two books of Brahms's Hungarian Dances for piano, four hands, which appeared in 1869. The timing is interesting, for it was during the winter of 1869–70 that Massenet tore himself away from *Méduse* long enough to write three sets of four-hand piano pieces.[†]

After the performance of *Scènes hongroises* Arthur Pougin wrote:

> M. Massenet, whose reputation is beginning to be solidly established, is above all a colorist: he manages the orchestra with an ease and refinement which Berlioz might have admired, and he succeeds in being picturesque even where his ideas are not striking, which is exceptional. There are some quite nice things and some real finds in this second suite, whose program is a Hungarian wedding and where the special features of Magyar music are

---

[*] Opened as Cirque Napoléon on 11 Dec. 1852; renamed Cirque National on 4 Sept. 1870; from 1873 called Cirque d'Hiver.

[†] Six Danses; three Marches; two Berceuses.

perfectly compatible with the nature of the composer's talent. Originality is already much less cherchée than in the previous works; M. Massenet is close to having found his way, and to having passed through the phase where the composer necessarily imitates someone. We await his first symphony; and without doubt we shall not have long to wait, for encouragement—and success—have not been lacking for him thus far.[17]

Two days after the second performance, Massenet wrote to his friend the pianist-composer Paul Lacombe in Carcassonne, apologizing for not replying sooner to his letter of the previous autumn:

Here one leads a life that is senseless, hustled, often enough fruitless, which means that for three months I have not written a single additional measure to the piece that was in progress at the time of my departure from my tranquil little house in Fontainebleau. First the lessons which keep me quite engaged, then the noises, the conversations, the soirées, the conferences regarding projects (which never lead anywhere but take up one's time), the rehearsals which turn your head inside out, the emotions over performances which take away what little brain you have left: all this will indicate why, the days having only twenty-four hours, I was unable to find ten minutes to have the great pleasure of writing to you. And I do not as yet count for anything in the artistic world; I am a nobody, and already I let myself get so used up!

The Suite (or *Scènes hongroises*) played by Pasdeloup on 26 October [read 26 November] is nothing but an orchestral arrangement of four pieces for four hands which you know, and which are in the three collections (Danses, Berceuses, and Marches). I have had the pieces forming the Suite re-engraved, with the changes and in the order of their execution at the concert. The first performance was very good, and the press quite friendly. But the second performance of Sunday, 17 December, was much better: the second piece had to be given twice, and the rest was strongly applauded. I ought to be very happy, and yet I am not at all. For this is not the kind of music I would want to see esteemed. I do not value very highly this suite of little pieces. Withal, as orchestration there are some effects that are sometimes diverting and that come out with boldness and clarity. The instrumentation of these pieces is not in the coloring that is usual to my orchestration; the picturesque excels in this suite.

Pasdeloup had them try over my symphony (the one of which I gave you a small idea once at your place). But I am afraid of it, and I prefer to let things rest for this winter, unless my overture to *Méduse* is given, which is something rather solid and sure, for the orchestra, and quickly learned.[18]

The letter was dated 19 December 1871, and signed "J. Massenet, 38 rue Malesherbes"—our first documentation for this domicile in Paris, where he remained until late in 1879.

Arthur Pougin has shed light on the symphony, which has disappeared from Massenet's oeuvre. In 1875, after the performance of the third suite, Pougin asked Massenet why he did not write a real symphony, and received the reply:

Massenet's *carte de visite* with the address 38 rue Malesherbes.
The message is to librettist Louis Gallet. Courtesy Paul Jackson.

I tried it once, but succeeded too poorly to imagine that the desire would ever return. I wrote a regular symphony during the siege of Paris; later, I asked M. Pasdeloup to try it over with his orchestra, and I saw that I had taken a completely wrong path. So I renounced having it performed. My symphony, written almost entirely in minor, sounded utterly mournful and disconsolate. I cannot assert, however, that the thoughts that oppressed us during those painful times had no effect upon my spirit; the work was bad because it was bound to be. Besides, I do not believe I have the temperament of a symphonist: to write a good symphony it is not a question of having lots of ideas, but of developing them artfully, to stretch them out, to play with them as you might say, to draw out of them everything they can give. That is not my nature. On the contrary, it bores me to spin out my thought, to chop it up, to pursue it incessantly, and even to keep coming back to it. What I have to say, musically, I have to say rapidly, forcefully, concisely; my discourse is tight, nervous, and if I wanted to express myself otherwise I would not be myself. I think, therefore, that I am better suited to opera than to symphony.[19]

It was a foresighted remark for 1875. Massenet could have said "music for the stage," for as it turned out he did not disdain incidental music, or even ballet. His first project for a ballet, probably in 1872, turned out to be a blind alley. Massenet had made the acquaintance of Émile Bergerat, who later married Théophile Gautier's daughter and who left us a delightful four volumes of *Souvenirs d'un enfant de Paris*. The two of them paid a call on the now somewhat elderly Gautier, and found him sitting in a large armchair surrounded by his three cats. Massenet was always fond of cats, and this was enough to break the ice with Gautier at once. It was Bergerat's idea to induce his future father-in-law to dash off the scenario for a ballet, for which Massenet would supply the music and thus, as collaborator with a great name, gain entrance to the Opéra. Gautier outlined two subjects on the spot: the Erlking's Daughter (which Massenet rejected in deference to Schubert) and the Rat Catcher—*Le Preneur des rats.* The latter subject seemed appealing, but it is not clear how much, if any, of the music was written. Halanzier, of the Opéra, vetoed the idea apparently sight unseen, for it was only on a later occasion that Halanzier is supposed to have spoken to Massenet for the first time.

Don César de Bazan; Les Érinnyes; Marie-Magdeleine

MASSENET WAS NOW APPROACHING his thirtieth birthday. He was still giving music lessons and would continue to do so right up to *Hérodiade*. He had obtained a few public performances, and his vocal and piano pieces circulated among amateurs. He was known, but scarcely more so than many another struggling composer in Paris. Of the eight operas he had started, sketched, or completed, only *La Grand' Tante* had reached the stage, and that was a mere curtain raiser. Within little more than a year Massenet's reputation would receive a considerable boost, thanks partly to *Don César de Bazan*, more so to the music for *Les Érinnyes*, and most of all because of *Marie-Magdeleine*, which established his fame.

Through the years, a kind of mythology grew up around *Marie-Magdeleine*. Some biographers flatly stated that it was composed at Rome or in 1866. Such flights of fancy overlook one small detail: whatever sketches Massenet brought back from Rome (even including the *zampogna* melody from the woods of Subiaco), *Marie-Magdeleine* could not have been written without the services of a librettist. Actually, the plan for the work was conceived by Massenet's publisher Hartmann, who engaged Louis Gallet to put it into verse. Massenet apparently began to write the music in the autumn of 1871, finishing it in January 1872.[1]

With *Marie-Magdeleine* completed, the next step was to find someone willing to perform it. Pasdeloup, who had programmed various concert pieces by Massenet, seemed the likely person to approach. On 13 March, Hartmann brought his protégé to the conductor's house at 18 Boulevard Bonne-Nouvelle for a reading. Jules-Étienne Pasdeloup (1819–1887) had studied piano with both Laurent and Zimmermann; in 1851 he had organized a concert society for bringing young Conservatoire artists before the public, and ten years later, he had founded the successful Concerts

Populaires. He was a short, thickset man with broad shoulders and a short neck; the blue-eyed face of a blond Hercules was adorned with a great fawn-colored beard streaked with gray. Massenet once called him a "singular phenomenon"—frank, even brutal, but at bottom an excellent nature.

On that evening of 13 March, Massenet and Hartmann were kept waiting while the famous conductor heard two young girls who were seeking an engagement. Then he motioned Massenet to the piano, installing himself in an easy chair with the asthmatic sighs of a distracted listener. As Massenet played and sang, a stubborn oaken log in the fireplace persisted in emitting more smoke than flame. While the poor composer almost choked, Pasdeloup kept springing up to open the window, letting the smoke circulate out onto the boulevard in exchange for drafts of cold air. When the reading was finished, around nine o'clock, Pasdeloup in all probability made no comment beyond: "Well, gentlemen, it is way past dinner time; I need detain you no further." Legend has it, however, that to Hartmann, who tarried to ask the conductor's confidential opinion, he exploded: "Perform it? Never! It is ridiculous, absurd. Why, Méryem sings 'I hear the footsteps of Christ!' Confound it, one does not hear the footsteps of Christ!" And that settled the matter.[2] Massenet, crushed, skipped his own dinner and cried all night—or so goes the legend.

So, then, Marie-Magdeleine was not performed in 1872 but had to wait a year for Colonne and the Concert National, founded with Hartmann's backing. Meanwhile, on 26 March 1872, an *Introduction et variations* was performed by Armingaud's Société Classique. Written for string quartet, double bass, flute, oboe, clarinet, horn, and bassoon, the work can no longer be found.

Three of Massenet's colleagues had works staged at the Opéra-Comique that season, without much success. Émile Paladilhe, who had preceded Massenet by three years as Prix de Rome, produced *Le Passant*, text by Coppée, on 24 April. It folded after three performances. On 22 May, Bizet's *Djamileh* was given, and it lasted for eleven nights. The libretto, by Louis Gallet, was founded on Alfred de Musset's *Namouna*. Then, on 12 June, there appeared Saint-Saëns's *La Princesse jaune*, with text by Gallet, which attained five performances. The Opéra-Comique closed for the summer on 30 June.

Massenet again spent the summer at Fontainebleau, where Ninon's parents had a villa. The spot is pointed out today as 64 Avenue Roosevelt, where there is a plaque. In his correspondence Massenet usually simply put "Fontainebleau," though occasionally "46 avenue du Chemin-de-Fer." There, in June, he completed the song cycle *Poème pastoral*. Called "Scenes from Florian and from Armand Silvestre," it resembled a kind of rural cantata, for the first and last of the six pieces require a three-part chorus. Hartmann got up a handsome thirty-two-page edition, with an etching by Abel Orry. Song No. 5, "Crépuscule," seems the ultimate in sheer simplicity of structure for any song; and yet its repetitious melody has a certain haunting Massenet quality that made it one of the favorites of the cycle.

On 1 October 1872, Alphonse Daudet's drama *L'Arlésienne* opened at the Théâtre du Vaudeville for a run of twenty-one performances. The incidental music was, of course, by Bizet. Author and composer were distressed by the indifference of the general public, but the appreciation of a few perceptive individuals sustained and comforted them. The ill manners of the opening-night audience drew from the drama critic Auguste Vitu the sharp comment that Bizet had written an overture and some entr'actes that "deserve more attention than was accorded them." Massenet, who attended the première, and went again two weeks later, wrote a warm letter to Bizet predicting the success of the orchestral suite that was to be extracted from the music.[3]

On 3 October, Corneille's tragedy Le Cid, having been out of the repertoire for ten years, was revived at the Comédie-Française. The fact is worth mentioning because Massenet, like many other composers, tended to pluck his opera subjects from among those already tried and proven on the dramatic stage. His opera, Le Cid, was still thirteen years in the future, but the seed of an idea planted today bears fruit tomorrow. We find, too, that the classic fairy tales of Charles Perrault (1628–1703) provided, over a period of years, many an entertaining play for Parisian audiences. Thus, on 5 September 1872, there opened at the Théâtre des Menus-Plaisirs a féerie in twelve scenes entitled Les Contes de Perrault, by Oswald and Lemonnier. Massenet's librettists would later draw upon Perrault for Cinderella (Cendrillon, 1899) and, indirectly, for Griselda (Grisélidis, 1901).

At the moment Massenet was busy with a more timely project: Don César de Bazan. Victor Hugo's old (1838) poetic drama of seventeenth-century Spain, Ruy Blas, had been revived yet again at the Odéon on 16 January 1872. Sarah Bernhardt's performance as the queen of Spain projected her to stardom, and the play was the hit of the season.[4] Ruy Blas, a valet with the grand manner, impersonates at the Spanish Court the impoverished noble and rakish rascal Don César de Bazan, who had "disappeared" for opportune reasons, The parodists, sensing a splendid opening, had brought out on 13 April at the Folies-Dramatiques a four-act "musical buffoonery" entitled Le Ruy-Blas d'en face, in which the principal character was transformed into a street singer.

After the last season's run of failures at the Opéra-Comique, Camille du Locle, now the principal manager, was in the market for a new work with a better chance of success, provided it could be put together fast—in a few weeks. Adolphe-Philippe d'Ennery and Jules Chantepie concocted the necessary libretto, Don César de Bazan, drawing upon a play of the same title (by D'Ennery and Dumanoir) produced back in 1844. Du Locle offered the libretto to the Prix de Rome winners Jules Duprato and Samuel David, both of whom turned it down. Massenet was then approached.

The group that gathered at Hartmann's, for all their yearning to break into the theater, shared a certain cynical distrust of the opéra comique as genre. They picked to pieces the heritage of Grétry, Philidor, Monsigny, Dalayrac, Isouard, Berton, Boïeldieu, Hérold, Halévy, Auber, and utterly disdained the run-of-the-mill "fabricators of opera" of the nineteenth century. To throw together an opéra comique, they sneered, required only a few set formulas, and the more hasty the workmanship the better. It was in this spirit that Massenet accepted the assignment. He agreed to the hurry-up job, retired to the country to write, and was back in a few weeks with the three acts so that rehearsals and production details could proceed while he prepared the orchestration.

On 30 November 1872, *Don César de Bazan* had its première. It lasted for only thirteen performances—an unlucky number, equated with failure. Its cloak-and-dagger qualities and local color were not lasting virtues.

Don César de Bazan (sung by the baritone Jacques Bouhy), an impoverished Spanish grandee, lives an adventurous life but is noble at heart. He fights a duel during Holy Week to save a young boy, Lazarille (Marie Galli-Marié), from the brutalities of a captain. But there is a royal edict against duelling: those caught at it are to be shot, except that if caught during Holy Week they are to be hanged. Don César is arrested and condemned.

Don César is visited in prison by his old friend Don José de Santarem (sung by Neveu), who conceals the fact that he is now first minister to Charles II, king of Spain. Don José is in love with the queen who, however, refuses to take a lover unless the king first be proven unfaithful to her. Charles II (Paul Lhérie) is in love with the beautiful street singer Maritana (Mme Priola) but cannot approach her because of her low social station. Don José's plan is to have Maritana married to Don César an hour before his execution, raising her to the status of Countess de Bazan. He does not disclose his plan but merely promises benefits if his suggestion is followed: for Maritana, riches and honor; for Don César, commutation of his sentence from hanging to death by gunfire and assurance that the boy Lazarille will be looked after.

The marriage takes place in the prison. Maritana's face is veiled so that she can neither see nor be seen. The execution follows immediately. The young widow (who does not know she is a widow) is taken to the palace of San Fernando to acquire the fine manners suitable for a noble lady. They tell her that her husband will be returning soon from exile. But it is the king who visits her, saying he is Don César. Maritana says she does not love him. Charles II is about to use force when the real Don César arrives. Lazarille, it seems, had removed the balls from the muskets! Don César refuses to fight with the king. He surprises Don José at the feet of the queen and kills him. Charles makes him governor of Granada, where he goes to live happily with his beautiful bride.

The three principal singers survived to sing another day: on 3 March 1875, Galli-Marié would sing Carmen opposite Lhérie's Don José and Bouhy's Escamillo! The orchestra score of *Don César de Bazan* was destroyed when the Salle Favart burned down in 1887. But the work rose like a phoenix from the ashes. Hartmann had published a piano-vocal score; from this Massenet made up a new version, adding several numbers, and this was given at Geneva on 20 January 1888. Provincial theaters took up the opera, which even reached a few capitals: Antwerp, Brussels, Lisbon, Paris (Gaîté-Lyrique, 12 May 1912). Meanwhile, the *Sevillana* flourished among casino orchestras at various watering places. Over a decade later, Massenet would do somewhat better with yet another Spanish subject in *Le Cid*.

About the time Massenet was no doubt beginning to regret his hasty "fabrication" of *Don César de Bazan,* another French composer scored his first real success in the concert hall. On 8 December 1872, Pasdeloup presented Édouard Lalo's *Divertissement pour orchestre,* of which Massenet subsequently made a piano reduction. An excellent violinist-violist, Lalo was associated for a time with Armingaud and the cellist Léon Jacquard in their musical soirées. He had not attracted much attention with his songs and chamber music, and although his score of *Fiesque* had won third place in the competition of 1867 for the Théâtre-Lyrique, untoward circumstances prevented its performance, leaving the composer disheartened. Fortunately Lalo decided to try the orchestral field: after the *Divertissement,* he achieved a sensation when Sarasate played his violin concerto (18 January 1874) and *Symphonie espagnole* (7 February 1875). The opera *Le Roi d'Ys* (7 May 1888) further served to establish Lalo as a noteworthy talent on the French musical scene.

Massenet's next assignment came from Félix Duquesnel, director of the Odéon. Some incidental music was needed for Leconte de Lisle's *Les Érinnyes*. At Hartmann's insistence, Duquesnel called Massenet to his office, explained the situation, and read over several scenes. The young composer was delighted with the play and agreed to provide some music. Despite the December snow, he hurried to Fontainebleau and shut himself up to compose. The task was accomplished in short order, and Massenet found time to attend some of the rehearsals, of which Leconte de Lisle personally took charge. In the *Souvenirs* Massenet remembered the author as a fervent admirer of Wagner and of Daudet.

Les Érinnyes opened at the Odéon on 6 January 1873. It will be recalled that Leconte de Lisle was the leader of the Parnassians, a group of poets who reacted against Romanticism and sought to represent in poetry the scientific and positivist spirit of their times. Influenced by the Hellenist Louis Ménard, Leconte de Lisle had sought inspiration in an erudite contemplation of antiquity, as in the *Poèmes antiques* of 1852. His *Les Érinnyes* (The Furies) was based on the *Oresteia* of Aeschylus, and sought to capture in French verse the heightened expression of ancient tragedy. There were Greek choruses—men and women of Argos, Choephorae, and assorted apparitions—to round out the action with commentary. Clytemnestra, Agamemnon, Elektra, Orestes, and Cassandra are the principals, but Aegisthus is kept offstage.

◄◦►

The drama opens with the Furies pacing up and down at dawn before the palace of Pelops, and the rest of the first act deals with Agamemnon's return to Argos after the

Trojan War and his murder by his queen and her paramour. In the second act, Elektra mourns her father's death and is surprised and overjoyed at the return of her brother Orestes, who avenges his father by slaying Aegisthus and Clytemnestra. Elektra flees in horror, and at the final curtain the Furies close in upon Orestes.

———————————— •◆• ————————————

Massenet's music in the 1873 version (conducted by Colonne) was modest in scope; according to Arthur Pougin it consisted mainly of an introduction, two *intermèdes*, and a melodrama. The composer had been allowed forty musicians. Not wanting to disperse his forces among the standard instrumentation, he decided upon a full string choir of thirty-six players, to which he added kettledrums and three trombones for the Furies: Alecto, Tisiphone, and Magaera. The music in general was considered "very interesting," but the melodrama accompanying Elektra's pouring of the libations over her father's grave attracted special attention with its poignant, dolorous muted solo cello. The French heart has ever been susceptible to a bittersweet retrospective melody, and Louis Gallet soon set appropriate words to this one ("O doux printemps d'autrefois, vertes saisons, vous avez fuis pour toujours!").

When *Les Érinnyes* was revived at the Théâtre-Lyrique de la Gaîté on 15 May 1876, the incidental music had undergone a considerable metamorphosis. The score was expanded to include the full orchestra (also with players offstage), choruses were set to music, melodramas added, and some ballet numbers inserted. Meanwhile, on 9 February 1873 (and again on 16 February), Pasdeloup performed a suite entitled *Musique pour une pièce antique*, designated as Massenet's "third suite for orchestra." The movements were listed as: (1) Prélude; (2) Marche religieuse; (3) Entr'acte; (4) Air de danse des Saturnales. It is difficult to reconstruct which portions were drawn from *Les Érinnyes* and whether portions of *Pompéia* were involved. In view of the later expansion of the incidental music for *Les Érinnyes*, this suite was withdrawn and the designation "third suite" eventually allotted to the *Scènes dramatiques* of 1875.

On 18 January 1873, Adolphe Adam's indestructible *Le Châlet* reached its one thousandth performance at the Opéra-Comique. Adam had died in 1856, ceding his place in the Institut to Berlioz, but his music lived on. Our grandparents loved its elegant grace and fetching rhythms, so typical of the more homely musical atmosphere of the nineteenth century. On the lighter side, a spectacularly successful composer was Charles Lecocq (1832–1918), whose *La Fille de Madame Angot* opened at the Folies-Dramatiques on 21 February 1873 and ran for five hundred nights up to 27 December 1874. By then his *Giroflé-Girofla* had hit the boards (Brussels, 21 March 1874; Paris, Renaissance, 12 November 1874), and it became a tug-of-war in popularity between these two sparkling operettas.[*] One of Lecocq's earlier efforts was

———————————————————————————————

* The star of *Giroflé-Girofla* at the Renaissance was Jeanne Granier, who went on to further triumphs in Lecocq's *La Petite mariée* (1875), *La Marjolaine* (1877), and particularly *Le Petit duc* (1878), which ran for three hundred nights with Granier, in male garb, conquering the hearts of Paris. The diva was much admired by the Prince of Wales, later Edward VII.

linked by coincidence with Bizet. In the summer of 1856, Offenbach had launched a competition for a setting of *Le Docteur Miracle*, text by Léon Battu and Ludovic Halévy. The upshot of it was that the scores submitted by Lecocq and Bizet were adjudged of equal merit, and the prize of twelve hundred francs was divided between them. Both versions, with the same libretto and cast but different music, were given alternately at the Bouffes-Parisiens in 1857. Each received eleven performances. The following year Lecocq produced his first real hit with *Fleur-de-Thé*.

Massenet himself was caught up in this gay Parisian spirit, but his *L'Adorable Bel-Boul* was privately performed and subsequently destroyed, so that we can only guess at his handling of operetta. Considering his reputation as a gamin among close friends, it was probably a witty and hilarious bit of froth. While they were rehearsing *Marie-Magdeleine*, and needing diversion, Louis Gallet got up a libretto with a Turkish flavor involving such personages as Zaï-Za, Ali-Bazar, and Sidi-Toupi. Massenet went along with alacrity, dashing off the music for each number almost as soon as he saw the verses. The work was tried out first in March at a soirée given by Mme Gustave Dreyfus, and then performed on 17 April at a private club known as the Union Artistique, or Cercle des Mirlitons. Jeanne Granier played Zaï-Za, and the rest of the modest cast comprised Mlles Wertheimber and Dartaux, and Mssrs. Boussenot and Dreyfus. Years later Gallet still remembered little snatches of the music, and regretted that Massenet had destroyed the score. He advised his correspondent to get Massenet aside sometime, and beg him to give a confidential rendition of the part that went:

Elle a la jambe assez bien faite,	(Her legs are shapely things to view;
Une, du moins, car l'autre, hélas!	Well, one at least — alas, its mate,
Courte comme une soeur cadette,	The "younger sister" of the two,
La fait boiter à chaque pas.	Produces quite a hobbling gait.
Elle est mince comme une gaule	She is as slender as a pole . . .)
. . . etc.[5]	

Needless to say, there was nothing wrong with Jeanne Granier's legs or her figure.

The Mirlitons' Club, incidentally, had come into existence in 1860 to provide a place where the artistic and social worlds might mingle. The idea was considered eccentric at the time. Certain young men of fashion, wearied of the eternal talk of horse-racing in the club drawing rooms, set up a snug and quiet retreat in the Rue de Choiseul where they could discuss literature, art, and music with some choice artistic spirits who had been gathered about them to help while away the boresome two or three hours before dinner, or an hour or so after midnight when coming from the theater or some fashionable musical party. The guiding spirit in this undertaking was the Comte d'Esmond, who was warmly supported by such personages as General de Gramont, the Marquis de Vogüé, Prince Poniatowski, Prince Polignac, and many others. From the start it was agreed that membership should be open to working artists and men of letters. A committee for painting arranged exhibitions that were great social events, both in the Rue de Choiseul and later when the club moved to the Place Vendôme. There were also committees for literature and for music. The club rooms offered a quiet game of billiards, piquet, or bezique—or a turn at baccarat for those so inclined—and free *coco* (liquorice-water) was furnished to the members. Among the musicians who early joined the circle were Auber, Gounod, Halévy, Membrée, and Liszt. It is worth noting that in 1861, the first year of the club's active existence, Auber was president of the music committee, of which Wagner was a member. This throws light on Princess Metternich's vehement defense of *Tannhäuser*, since her husband was Wagner's colleague and friend on the committee. By 1888 the club had over two thousand members. Working artists as a rule were too busy to be steady patrons, but they did drop in occasionally—at tea time or after dinner—and found a congenial place to exchange thoughts with one another or with the patrons of art who were the club's mainstay.[6]

In the early 1870s the musicians were more likely to spend their free time at Hartmann's, whose shop was a handy meeting place close to the *grands boulevards* and just a few steps from the fashionable church of the Madeleine, where Saint-Saëns loved to improvise at the organ over which he had presided since 1858. At 19 Boulevard de la Madeleine, Hartmann's outwardly unimposing music store was surrounded by elegant shops. Inside, the premises stretched out like some vast hallway. At the end, in back, was a kind of salon where composers often gathered to talk or argue about current musical events and all sorts of artistic matters. It was like a little musical club under Hartmann's auspices. Georges Hartmann, as music publisher, was devoted to the cause of young French composers; he discovered or adopted Bizet, César Franck, Édouard Lalo, Ernest Reyer, Saint-Saëns, and many others.[*]

Among the frequenters of Hartmann's back room around 1873 was Arthur Pougin, music critic and prolific writer on musical subjects. Pougin later recalled some of the names in the group.[7] There was Théodore Dubois, who had produced *Les Sept paroles du Christ* on Good Friday, 1867, at Sainte-Clothilde—César Franck's church. Unable as yet to break into the larger opera houses, Dubois nevertheless produced *La Guzla de l'Émir* at the Athénée on 30 April 1873. Émile Paladilhe had reached the stage of the Opéra-Comique with *Le Passant*, even if it was not exactly a success. Paladilhe was actually doing better with songs, of which *La Mandolinata* was especially popular. Ernest Guiraud had produced several operas, and Pasdeloup had played his second orchestral suite on 28 January 1872. Guiraud was now readying a ballet, *Gretna-Green*. In a few years he would become a professor at the Conservatoire, where he would have the honor of being Debussy's teacher. Léo Delibes had made a great hit with the ballet *Coppélia* (Opéra, 25 May 1870) and was now about to bring out the very successful *Le Roi l'a dit* (Opéra-Comique, 24 May 1873).

The group was saddened by the premature death on 5 March 1873 of the

---

[*] Not later than 1879, Hartmann moved his business to 60 Rue Neuve Saint-Augustin, a location that was renumbered three years later as 20 Rue Daunou.

thirty-four-year-old vicomte Alexis de Castillon, who had abandoned a military career for the cultural life. One of César Franck's most promising pupils, he was cut off by consumption before his career was fully underway. He was respected by his comrades, particularly for chamber music and songs. And yet, by one of those ironies of music history, Castillon's piano concerto was hissed by the audience when played by Saint-Saëns at a Pasdeloup concert on 10 March 1872.

There were still others: Charles Lefebvre, a pupil of Thomas and Prix de Rome of 1870, returned to Paris in 1873 after tours of Greece and the Orient. A respectable career lay ahead of him, as also for Benjamin Godard, whose opera, symphonies, orchestral suites, and songs are now all but forgotten. There was the blond Irish beauty, Augusta Holmès, a piano prodigy who tried her wings with the Psalm *In Exitu* in 1873 and later undertook serious study with César Franck. Paul Lacombe would sometimes come up from Carcassonne. Son of a wealthy family, a good pianist, an esthete who expressed himself in prose and poetry and collected works of art, Lacombe admired Chopin and Bizet and was, indeed, a good friend of many noted French composers of his era. Some 150 of his own compositions, mostly instrumental, are too much of the nineteenth century to be appreciated in our own times.

These, then, were among Massenet's lifelong friends. One still comes upon letters he wrote to them, or upon a mention of his sadness when one or another of them died. Massenet himself is pictured by Pougin at that time as a kind of leader of the group, *rieur et un peu gamin*—inclined to mockery and poking fun, and a bit of a brat. Withal, he seems to have been respected for a certain precocious musical skill already demonstrated, and perhaps for the drive and industry that the others must have sensed as a dormant potential beneath a lighthearted exterior.

Massenet must have remembered Pauline Viardot from the old days at the Théâtre-Lyrique when she sang Orphée. Their paths now crossed again. Viardot had retired from the opera stage in 1863 and gone to live in Baden Baden. She still sang in concerts, however; on 3 March 1870, at Jena, she gave the première performance of the Brahms Alto Rhapsody, based on Goethe's *Harzreise im Winter*, with Ernst Naumann conducting. She also composed little operettas for which the librettos were supplied by her devoted admirer, the Russian novelist Turgeniev. Both Mme Viardot and Turgeniev returned to Paris in 1871.[*]

One evening Massenet was invited to Mme Viardot's for dinner. As might be expected, he was asked to play a little music. *Marie-Magdeleine*, so coldly rejected by Pasdeloup not long ago, was still running through his head, and so he played and sang portions of it. Mme Viardot, quite taken with the music, assured the young composer that not only would *Marie-Magdeleine* be performed, but that she would sing the part of Méryem. It has been said that when Hartmann heard this he determined to found the Concert National, to spite Pasdeloup. In any event, a series of six

---

[*] On 1 Oct. 1871, Pauline Viardot was appointed professor of singing at the Conservatoire, resigning exactly four years later.

concerts was planned for March and April of 1873, and it was arranged with Duquesnel to use the Odéon, whose large hall was very favorable for music. Édouard Colonne was to conduct, and naturally the programs were to be devoted largely to composers of the Hartmann circle. The Concert National lasted for two seasons, after which Hartmann withdrew. Colonne then founded the Association Artistique du Châtelet, which soon became firmly established and was familiarly known as the Concerts Colonne.

On 2 March 1873, the Concert National gave its first concert, which included Bizet's *Petite Suite* for orchestra. The fifth and sixth concerts were given over to sacred music. On Maundy Thursday, 10 April, the first half of the program comprised vocal works by Rossini, Saint-Saëns, Lalo, and Mme de Grandval—a viscountess known for her one-act operas and a Mass. The second half of the program brought a rather unfortunate rendition of César Franck's *Rédemption*, during which many of the audience walked out. Part of the fault lay with the composer; subsequently, upon the advice of some of his more devoted pupils, Franck would thoroughly revise *Rédemption*, giving it the more effective form in which it is known today.

The concert on Good Friday, 11 April, was devoted entirely to Massenet's *Marie-Magdeleine*, which had been carefully prepared. The work created a sensation. Pauline Viardot sang the rôle of Méryem, as she had promised; Jésus was sung by the tenor Jules-Alexandre Bosquin, of the Opéra, and Marthe by Mlle Vidal. Louis Gallet and Massenet eschewed the grandeur and prestige of the traditional oratorio (omitting, as the public noted, the usual dry fugues and contrapuntal ensembles) in favor of a new realism with Oriental coloring. *Marie-Magdeleine* is actually a sacred drama, in three acts and four scenes, and it was indeed later adapted for the operatic stage.

––––––––––––––––– ◂◦▸ –––––––––––––––––

Act I, "Mary of Magdala at the Fountain," suggests an oasis on the outskirts of the town of Magdala, where the townspeople promenade in the cool of the evening, women come to fetch fresh water at the well, and the courtesans of Magdala seek partners for the night's entertainment. Mary Magdalene (Méryem) is among these, but she expresses remorse for her errant ways and hopes for a new peace promised by a stranger, who she hopes will reappear at this very place. Judas counsels her to give up doubts and sadness and return to the kind of womanly love that brings earthly rewards. The chorus confirms that she cannot escape her destiny as a courtesan. Jesus now joins the group and chides the lying Pharisees and hypocritical women for presuming to turn a repentant sinner aside from the road to salvation. Méryem falls to her knees, but He bids her arise. The crowd is impressed by His spiritual power. Jesus tells Méryem to return home and await His visit.

Act II, "Jesus at the home of the Magdalene," is an audacious rewriting of Scripture, to say the least, but the realistic intent is handled with a delicacy that avoids offensiveness. Méryem's sumptuous apartment is filled with flowers and perfumes to welcome the coming visitor. Martha, Méryem's sister, admonishes the servant girls to be quiet, for the expected guest is not like those others who enjoy seductive songs and bantering talk. More powerful than any earthly king, He comes crowned with light and bringing, in His Father's name, true love and forgiveness. But Judas appears first, protesting to Martha his love for Jesus but arguing that an unseemly visit to the Magdalene will be turned to evil account by the Pharisees. Martha resolutely replies that nothing can tarnish His reputation and that Judas speaks like a traitor. Jesus is welcomed with a simple but touching Alleluia by the two sisters. Martha goes to prepare the supper, while Jesus and Méryem sing an extended duo in which she is made to feel confident in her salvation. The Disciples arrive. The fateful words are said: "One among you will betray me," and all join in prayer.

Act III comprises two scenes, "Golgotha" and "The Tomb of Jesus." The first scene suggests Jesus on the cross between the two thieves. An elaborate chorus of insults is broken momentarily by "Father, forgive them, for they know not what they do." The Magdalene approaches the cross and sings a poignant aria of grief that seems to reflect Massenet's study of Bach and Gluck. At the ninth hour Jesus emits a terrible cry, and it is over. In the garden of Joseph of Arimathea, Méryem and the Holy Women come at daybreak to mourn at the tomb. They are joined by a chorus of Disciples and Christians who witness the Resurrection and affirm His glory.

To understand the realism of *Marie-Magdeleine* it helps to bear in mind the sensation created by Ernest Renan's *La Vie de Jésus*, published in 1863. Renan's close study of the Scriptures in Hebrew had led him to question some of the tenets of orthodox revealed religion and to abandon his preparations for the priesthood. He became a distinguished Semitic scholar, went to Palestine with an archaeological expedition, and visited the scenes of the Gospel story. In *La Vie de Jésus* he attempted to paint the landscape, the costumes, and the manners of the times in a richness of color that is often touched with sentimentality. His interest was toward the biographical and psychological; he viewed the ancient miracles as natural incidents that somehow became distorted in the telling and were subject to a rationalistic explanation. *La Vie de Jésus* disturbed the conservatives and cost Renan his professorship in Hebrew at the College de France. But his enchanting, lyrical picture of a carpenter's son growing to maturity amid the flowers of the Galilean countryside made a profound impression and unquestionably influenced the interpretation of Biblical subjects in the arts.

After the première of *Marie-Magdeleine*, "Phémius" (i.e., Saint-Saëns) wrote in *La Renaissance littéraire* that this was the boldest attempt by a composer in Paris since *L'Enfance du Christ* of Berlioz. However, because Massenet is no Berlioz, there will be no lack of persons to congratulate him for it.

> Berlioz was not versed in this now fashionable art of equilibration that permits having friends in both camps. It was one of the ambitions of Berlioz to displease certain persons, in which it must be admitted he fully succeeded. The Muse of Massenet is not so haughty. She is a virtuous Muse who does

Hector Berlioz. Courtesy Paul Jackson.

nothing against her conscience, but she likes to please and gladly puts flowers in her hair. Let him who is without sin cast the first stone! It is a capital error to assume, as some have done, that it is a novelty to give the oratorio a dramatic form. Handel's oratorios, prototypal for the genre, differ in no way from his operas; the exception proves the rule. . . . What is new is the realistic aspect of the work of Gallet and Massenet. They have gained in oriental coloring and its many affectations; they have lost the traditional grandeur and prestige. The public, always looking for dainties, sides with them.

Massenet's music is original without being outlandish, and diverting without being frivolous: this is more than enough to assure success. Upon examination one discovers, not without astonishment, that it derives from Gounod without sounding at all like him. It is basically Gounod, but condensed, refined, and crystallized. Massenet is to Gounod as Schumann is to Mendelssohn. What is captivating about *Marie-Magdeleine* is the felicitous way in which the composer has rendered sentiments requiring the utmost tactfulness. A mere breath would have tarnished the love of Jesus and Mary Magdalene: Massenet has maintained all of its ideal purity. The gentlemen who concoct melodies could not have done that.[8]

For Ernest Reyer, in the *Journal des Débats*, the concert series at the Odéon would have justified itself had it done nothing else but make known *Marie-Magdeleine*:

Here is certainly a remarkable work, charming in its coloring and exquisite in form. If one does not find throughout the same clear indications of individuality, if one can find fault with the austerity of style, at least one could not ask for more from the composer in the way of skillful writing, finesse, and artfulness in the handling of the orchestra. . . . *Marie-Magdeleine* is the work of an artist of both talent and conviction. The poetic qualities of this admirable legend were not this time lost upon some vulgar or unbelieving soul. . . . The opening of the fourth scene, Mary Magdalene and the Holy Women at the tomb of Jesus, is a sublime inspiration. Listen to what these holy women sing and you will weep along with them, for I tell you in all truth that there does not exist any music more tender and touching, more persuasive and unadulterated.[9]

The day after *Marie-Magdeleine* the Massenets set off for Italy, going straight to Naples. Among the mail that caught up with them there was a warm letter of congratulation from Ambroise Thomas. Massenet's head was in the clouds as he read and reread the laudatory epistles of his friends. Between times he pointed out to Ninon the landmarks he remembered from his previous visit of almost nine years ago. The whole trip was a kind of delayed honeymoon, to make up for the scant visit to the seashore in 1866. Naturally, they spent a week at Capri.

Oscar Browning, who was staying at the Hotel Tiberio, left us a vignette of Capri:[*]

One of our companions in the hotel was the French composer, Massenet, who has since become famous. On the night before our departure he gave a ball to the native population, in which nothing was danced but the Tarantella. The ballroom was the courtyard of the hotel, lighted by torches; the guests sat round beating tambourines, three or four of them at a time, and the dancers performed their evolutions in the center. The refreshments were the wine of the country supplied *ad libitum*, but it was not intoxicating. The dancers were of all ages, from little children who could scarcely toddle to a very aged couple, who were celebrating, I presume, their golden or their diamond wedding, the lady attired in a robe which she had worn on her wedding day.

The dance lasted from six in the evening until midnight, and at last after repeated invitations, I was induced to try my fortune with the belle of the island, a strapping young lady named Mariuccia. Recalling my Scotch experience, I tried a hoolichan with her, but she whirled me around as Hercules whirled round Lychas. The next morning she came up smiling, and insisted on carrying my very large portmanteau, full of clothes, down to the harbour on her head, without touching it with her hands, and absolutely refused to receive payment for her services.[10]

---

[*] Oscar Browning, M.A., then assistant master at Eton, was later lecturer in history at King's College, Cambridge. An ardent traveler who tramped through the Alps in the 1860s when they were still a wilderness, Browning had come on this trip with some companions to investigate the excavations near Naples, ending up at Capri.

The Massenets left Capri on a boat that sailed at dawn on 27 April, stayed a few days at Sorrento, and on 2 May arrived in Rome "just as the Angelus was sounding," as Massenet wrote to Thomas. They put up at the Hotel Minerva, on the Piazza della Minerva next to the Pantheon. They no doubt looked at the high-water mark, reminder of the flood of 1870, on the exterior wall of Santa Maria sopra Minerva. Hébert at once sent an invitation to luncheon the next day at the Villa Medici.* Massenet enjoyed visiting the old scene. After the luncheon in the director's salon, attended also by a few students, Hébert asked to hear some passages from *Marie-Magdeleine*, the account of whose success had already reached him. The following day, 4 May, Massenet joined the students for lunch and had the fine emotion of again sitting in the familiar dining hall where his portrait still hung on the wall, along with those of all the other Grand Prix winners. After lunch they strolled in the garden and looked in at a studio where the sculptor Mercié was working on his *Gloria victis*, soon to be awarded a medal of honor by the Salon.†

Back at 38 Rue Malesherbes by mid-May, Massenet supposedly became absorbed in a new opera libretto by Jules Adenis, *Les Templiers*. After composing the first two acts he began to have serious doubts; the historical situations, though interesting, seemed too reminiscent of Meyerbeer. Hartmann's adverse reaction must have been violent indeed if, as claimed, Massenet ruefully tore into bits the two hundred pages completed. The *Souvenirs*, at this point, fall into the trap of overdramatization.‡ We are supposed to picture Massenet, after the fizzling out of *Les Templiers*, as in "serious trouble"—an opera composer without a libretto, a fish out of water. In a kind of trance his feet were guided to Louis Gallet (who had furnished *Marie-Magdeleine*), and Gallet promptly came up with the idea for *Le Roi de Lahore*. The fly in the ointment is that the score of *Le Roi de Lahore* was later clearly marked "Paris, the years 1872, 1873, 1874, 1875, 1876, January 1877." (The overture was completed in February 1877.) Just how *Les Templiers* fits in is not clear. Perhaps, in a moment of infidelity to Gallet's prior project, Massenet did indeed flirt with Jules Adenis over *Les Templiers*. Or else the whole incident belongs in an earlier year.**

In any case, *Le Roi de Lahore* was a long time in the making. Gallet, with an eye

---

* Ernest Hébert (1817–1908), the noted painter, was at this time director of the Académie de France in Rome. He was a close friend of Gounod from their Prix de Rome days, when Ingres was director at the Villa Medici.

† Antoine Mercié (1845–1916) was one of those academic sculptors who, like Falguière, admired the Florentine Renaissance. He did a stone group, *Justice*, for the Hôtel-de-Ville (rebuilt 1874–82) and the statue of Napoleon in the costume of a Roman emperor that adorns the top of the Vendôme Column.

‡ Compare the statement: "I had hardly got back to No. 46 rue du Général Foy, where I lived for thirty years," which neatly excises seven or eight years of residence at 38 Rue Malesherbes!

**In the sequel, an opera *Les Templiers*, with text by Jules Adenis, Armand Silvestre, and L. Bonnemère, and music by Henry-Charles Litolff, was staged at Brussels on 25 Jan. 1886. Litolff, a piano virtuoso and composer, married the daughter of a Braunschweig music publisher and started the once famous *Collection Litolff* with its cheap and accurate editions of the best music.

to the future, very probably submitted at least the scenario at about the time Massenet was setting *Marie-Magdeleine*. But then the composer was distracted by the sudden call to write *Don César de Bazan* and by *Les Érinnyes*, the success of *Marie-Magdeleine*, and the vacation in Italy. When he did come back to *Le Roi de Lahore*, he had his eye on the Opéra. He had learned his lesson: just quickly throwing together a little *opéra comique* is not likely to lead anywhere. The idea of sustained, industrious work—starting at the crack of dawn—was at last borne home. We can truly say that Massenet's career began in earnest with *Le Roi de Lahore*.

There was a contretemps: on the night of 28/29 October 1873, the hall of the Opéra in the Rue Le Peletier burned down. The twenty-eighth, a Tuesday, was an off-night with no performance. From eight-thirty in the evening the baritone Numa Auguez rehearsed some scenes with Mme Rivet, and they left without noticing anything unusual. At 11:25 the watchman came running down from the stage crying "fire!" A blaze had somehow started among the sets stored offstage on the "garden side" (*le côté jardin*)—the side to the left as viewed by spectators in the theater.[*] Smoke was soon pouring from the windows in the Rue Rossini at the corner of the Rue Le Peletier. The steam-driven fire engines arrived, and Colonel Charreyon of the *sapeurs-pompiers* took charge. By a quarter of one, it was deemed advisable to start clearing furniture and other movables from the administrative buildings in the Rue Drouot. As it developed, these buildings remained relatively unharmed. By two o'clock the entire hall of the theater was in flames, and at two-thirty the roof gave way and fell partly into the Rue Rossini. By four what was left of the fire was under control. Thus, in a little over four hours, the traditions and associations of fifty years were swept away. An enumeration of the sets destroyed reads like an inventory of the current repertoire of the Opéra: those for Meyerbeer's *Les Huguenots, Le Prophète,* and *L'Africaine,* Halévy's *La Juive,* Donizetti's *La Favorite,* Verdi's *Le Trouvère,* Mozart's *Don Juan;* Weber's *Le Freischütz* (in the Pacini-Berlioz version); Delibes's *La Source* and *Coppélia;* Guiraud's *Gretna-Green;* Thomas's *Hamlet;* Eugenio Diaz's *La Coupe du roi de Thulé;* and Gounod's *Faust,* which had entered the Opéra repertoire on 3 March 1869 and attained its one hundredth performance there on 12 November 1871. *Jeanne d'Arc,* by Auguste Mermet, was ready but had not yet been given. To compensate for his disappointment, Massenet had the honor of seeing his work mounted as the first *new* opera at the Salle Garnier (5 April 1876).

Opéra director Halanzier now had to find a temporary home, for the Palais Garnier was not yet ready. He arranged with Strakosch and Merelli, directors of the Théâtre-Italien, the use of the Salle Ventadour on an alternating basis. Those gentlemen, having Halanzier over a barrel, charged him a stiff rent of 240,000 francs per year—twice the amount they themselves had to pay for their lease. Here the Opéra managed to get along quite nicely during 1874.

---

[*] The opposite side of the stage was called the "court side" (*le côté cour*).

The Légion d'Honneur

O N 19 FEBRUARY 1874, *MARIE-MAGDELEINE* was again given at the Odéon,[*] and three days later Colonne played Massenet's new overture, *Phèdre*. Pasdeloup had asked Massenet, Bizet, and Ernest Guiraud each to write an overture for performance at the Concerts Populaires during the winter of 1874. Bizet's *Patrie*, which he dedicated to Massenet, achieved a popular success, while Guiraud's *Artevelde* seems to have been quickly forgotten. As for *Phèdre*, we can only guess at Massenet's motivation in turning the work over to Colonne; perhaps Hartmann exerted pressure, or perhaps the wound inflicted by Pasdeloup over *Marie-Magdeleine* had not yet entirely healed. *Phèdre* was, of course, inspired by Racine's tragedy. The overture begins with a melancholy andante in G minor that recalls the Mendelssohn of *Antigone*, and this is followed by an impetuous allegro suggesting the furious amorousness of Phèdre. Massenet tried out several mottos to be put at the head of the score, and settled upon Phèdre's lines:

Ce n'est plus une ardeur
    dans mes veines cachée,
C'est Venus toute entière
    à sa proie attachée.
	(In my blood 'tis no longer
	    mere ardor that reigns,
	It is Venus herself
	    who is clawing my veins.)

The available evidence would indicate that the third, fourth, and fifth orchestral suites belong to 1874. Massenet no doubt realized that *Le Roi de Lahore* would occupy him for some time; meanwhile, concert performances would keep his name before the public. The fifth suite, *Scènes napolitaines*, was assigned by Séré to 1864, and by Schneider even to 1863. This is pushing the Massenet legend too far. With a lively imagination, one might assume that because of the Italian subject it *must* have been written in Italy, just as it was assumed that the second suite, *Scènes hongroises*,

---

[*] With Pauline Gueymard as Méryem. Mme Gueymard sang Léonore in Verdi's *Le Trouvère* when it was first given at the Opéra (12 Jan. 1857) in the French version by Émilien Pacini. Among her other rôles was the Queen in Thomas's *Hamlet*, for which she sang the 100th performance, 23 Mar. 1874 (Salle Ventadour), and the 110th performance, 31 Mar. 1875 (Salle Garnier).

must have been written in Hungary. But there *was* no sojourn in Budapest. And Schneider, astonished at the daring qualities of a score written by "a student of the Villa Medici" in 1863, forgets that this was the year in which Massenet won his prize—not the year in which he set foot on Italian soil. On 1 April 1865, Massenet confessed to Thomas that he had done no orchestration since the overture of 1863. Then he embarked upon his "symphony" (i.e., first suite), and probably even *Pompéia* was hastily orchestrated after his return to Paris.

The suites can best be straightened out by considering the order of their appearance in concerts. After the *Première Suite d'orchestre* and the *Scènes hongroises*, the pieces related to *Les Érinnyes* were billed as a "third suite" in 1873. By 1874, the fourth suite, *Scènes pittoresques*, was ready. By October 1874, a fifth suite was also ready; but by the time it reached a performance in 1875, Massenet had withdrawn the former "third suite" and assigned the number to the *Scènes dramatiques*. The *Scènes napolitaines* then came trailing along as the fifth suite when performed in 1876.

On 22 March 1874, the fourth suite, *Scènes pittoresques*, was given at the Châtelet. This could only mean Colonne; apparently he had already moved from the Odéon. The work was a great success with the public, as might be expected from the titles of the four movements: (1) Marche; (2) Air de ballet; (3) Angélus; (4) Fête bohème. The march was considered captivating; the air de ballet featured a cello melody that was later metamorphosed into the song, "Nuit d'Espagne"; the Angelus, of course, had horns sounding the evening bells; and the Bohemian festival brought a vigorous polonaise.

In keeping with Lent (Easter fell on 5 April 1874), the Opéra-Comique presented *Marie-Magdeleine* as oratorio on 24 March, with Mme Miolan-Carvalho as Méryem. Colonne conducted the six performances, on 24, 26, 28, 31 March and 4, 9 April. By presenting religious works, Du Locle hoped to bolster the sagging income of the Opéra-Comique, as was made clear two months later when he had Verdi in to conduct seven performances of the Manzoni Requiem, as matinées on 9, 11, 12, 15, 18, and 20 June, and in an evening performance on the twenty-second. Verdi's soloists were Teresina Stolz, Maria Waldmann, Angelo Masini, and Capponi, sure to draw a crowd. The much needed revenues were thus brought in, leading a journalist to remark: "It is funny, it took a requiem to restore the Opéra-Comique to life!"[*]

For the performances of *Marie-Magdeleine*, the second timpanist happened to be Vincent d'Indy. D'Indy admired Wagner and Liszt, and only the previous summer had made a pious musical pilgrimage to Weimar, Dresden, Vienna, Salzburg, and Munich. Massenet and D'Indy were still good friends, and the latter found passages to admire in *Marie-Magdeleine*. But before long he would develop a strong aversion to Massenet's art. The gospel he ultimately preached was that there is no god but

---

[*] Verdi again conducted his Requiem at the Opéra-Comique in 1875: at two matinées on 19 and 21 Apr. and in evening performance on 23, 27, 29 Apr. and 1, 4 May, with Stolz, Waldmann, Masini, and Medini as soloists.

César Franck, and Vincent d'Indy is his prophet. While it would be unfair to say that this warped his judgment (for each man's judgment is his own affair), one must question his reporting of historical facts in his writings. D'Indy's own special talent seems to have been in the field of the larger instrumental forms. His opera *Fervaal* (1897), along Wagnerian lines, attained thirteen performances at the Opéra-Comique in 1898 and ten performances at the Opéra in 1912–13—hardly a smashing success!

Massenet spent the summer of 1874 at Fontainebleau. A letter to Édouard Blau of 6 June reflects his good humor in two French puns: he writes from "Fontaine-blau," and in a postscript says "*Le Roi de Lahore* s'avance—hors s'avance! hors s'avance!"[1] From this we gather that he was making good progress on the new opera. "Has Diaz now left you in the lurch," queries Massenet, "in favor of Ruelle's *Manfred*?" This has a familiar ring: Édouard Blau and Louis Gallet had written the text for *La Coupe du roi de Thulé*, which had won for Diaz a prize in 1867; and Massenet himself had toyed with *Manfred* and then dropped it. Blau and Gallet had now almost finished a new libretto, *Medgé*. Massenet wanted to be the first to have a look at it, and he planned a rendezvous in Paris for the evening of Saturday, 4 July, for that purpose. Nothing came of it.* Massenet's next and more productive contact with Blau would be over *Le Cid*, still some years off.

During July and August Massenet found time to work at a fifth orchestral suite, *Scènes dramatiques*, which would later undergo some alterations and become known as the third suite. He had Shakespeare in mind, and the original layout of the movements was:

1. Le Tempête (Ariel et les esprits), forty pages of music.
2. Le Sommeil de Desdémone, seven pages.
3. Ronde nocturne dans le jardin de Juliette, seven pages.
4. Macbeth (Les sorciers; Le festin; L'apparition; Couronnement du Roi Malcolm; Fanfares), thirty-eight pages.

"Macbeth" was completed first, on 25 July at 10 A.M., then "The Tempest," on 5 August at 9 A.M. The times of day reflect Massenet's habit of getting a very early start, so that by mid-morning he had several solid working hours behind him. "Desdemona's Dream," finished at 3:30 P.M. on 6 August, required perhaps only that one day's work for the seven pages involved.

A letter of 30 August thanked an unknown gentleman for conveying an invitation—presumably to a soirée—at the home one Comtesse de Chambrun.[2] Massenet remarks in a postscript that he does not even know the Countess's address. This may be taken as evidence that Massenet, as a successful composer, was being invited into the salons of society. The Comte de Chambrun, incidentally, was a dashing cavalry officer who at one time stood for election to the Chamber on a Royalist ticket. But he also campaigned fearlessly in the working-class quarters of Paris, hotbeds of socialism, picking up many votes there. Tough slaughterhouse workers followed him

---

* An opera, *Medgé*, music by Spiro Samara, was performed in Rome in 1888.

around, to see that he came to no harm, and he was wined and dined in cheap bistros with toasts of "Vive le Roi!"

September was spent at Uriage-les-Bains, a charming little watering place twelve kilometers east of Grenoble. Here Massenet quickly composed seven *Improvisations* for piano. These little pieces are quite pianistic, not very difficult to play, and suggest that the composer was consciously presenting a variety of styles, though nothing as elaborate as études. There is no romantic schmaltz, and indeed the pieces give an enlightening sidelight on Massenet's musical mind at work. He then worked up No. 7 to provide the still-missing third movement of the *Scènes dramatiques*, a kind of entr'acte entitled "Rondo nocturne dans le jardin de Juliette." The scoring was completed at Fontainebleau on 2 October.

On 4 October 1874, in the Ringtheater at Vienna, the Komische Oper produced—of all things!—*Don César de Bazan*. As far as is known, Massenet did not attend. He would have to wait for *Le Roi de Lahore* to attract any real attention abroad.

In Paris, the Opéra-Comique and the Opéra (temporarily at the Salle Ventadour) carried on as usual. The Théâtre-Italien expired in 1878; thereafter there were at best only occasional "Italian seasons" in other theaters. The Théâtre-Lyrique had closed its doors on 31 May 1870, and after the serious damage to the hall in 1871, had simply not reopened. Sporadic attempts were made through the years to continue the old Théâtre-Lyrique tradition in other theaters such as the Gaîté (under Vizentini, 1876–77, or the Isola brothers, 1903–04 and 1907–14), the Château-d'Eau (Leroy, 1879), and the Renaissance (Milliaud brothers, 1899–1900). Other entrepreneurs would rent a hall for a few performances, or for a season, to provide *opéra populaire* with a wider appeal—this in addition to the steady diet of *opérettes*, *opéras bouffes*, and *vaudevilles* involving such theaters as the Bouffes-Parisiens, Folies-Dramatiques, Fantaisies-Parisiens, Nouveautés, and so on.

At some unspecified time in 1874, one of the undertakings of a semi-popular nature at the Théâtre du Châtelet announced a coming ballet entitled *Les Filles du feu*, with scenario by Louis Gallet and music by Massenet. This was apparently only a project, for as yet not even the slightest musical sketches have come to light. The Châtelet did produce, on 4 April 1874, an *opéra féerique* in three acts and twelve scenes by Henry Litolff entitled *La Belle au bois dormant* (Sleeping Beauty). The spectacle, with libretto by Clairville and Busnach, more or less followed the account given by the father of French fairy tales, Charles Perrault. Whether or not Massenet saw the work, it surely went over the mill wheel of Paris conversation. Twenty-five years later (1899), Massenet would produce *Cendrillon*, likewise drawn from Perrault.

We cannot take leave of the year 1874 without a passing reference to science fiction. Jules Verne (1828–1905) began by turning out comedies, opera librettos, and similar hack work. But then he caught the spirit of the new scientific realism, and struck a new vein in fiction that quickly gained for him a worldwide reputation. There were such stories as *Five Weeks in a Balloon* (1863), *A Voyage to the Center of the Earth* (1864), *From the Earth to the Moon* (1865), *20,000 Leagues Under the Sea* (1870), *Around the World in 80 Days* (1872), and *Michel Strogoff* (1876). On 8 November 1874, *Le Tour du monde en 80 jours* opened in a dramatized version, in five acts and fifteen scenes, at the Théâtre Porte-Saint-Martin. Of course everyone rushed to see the exploits of Philéas Fogg and Passepartout. As one critic wrote:

> We live in a scientific era. The nineteenth century will go down in history as the century of steam and electricity, just as the fifteenth century is remembered for the discovery of America and of printing. The books of Jules Verne are known to all; no one has surpassed him in popularizing the problems of the physical sciences, in putting cosmology into novels, and arousing a passionate interest in geography.[3]

Le Tour du monde played to full houses. It was periodically revived, and eventually it would reach its apotheosis on the motion-picture screen. For the stage version, Jules Verne had the collaboration of that old pro Adolphe d'Ennery, who had enthralled audiences with *The Mysteries of Old Paris* (1865) and *The Two Orphans*, the latter of which had opened at the same Porte-Saint-Martin on 29 January 1874. ("A very great and very legitimate success," wrote Auguste Vitu, who went on to give a long account of the sisters Henriette and Louise who arrived in Paris from Normandy.) Jules Verne and D'Ennery would collaborate again to dramatize *Michel Strogoff* in 1880, and upon that occasion Massenet would furnish some incidental music.

The year 1874 will be remembered, too, for the birth of impressionism in art. A group of thirty young artists—including Monet, Degas, Renoir, Sisley, Pissarro, Berthe Morisot, and Cézanne—organized their first exhibition on the premises of Nadar, a noted photographer. Claude Monet showed five of his works, one of which happened to be called *Impression: Soleil levant*. Against this the critics directed their most witty and amusing derision, so that the term "Impressionist" came to be applied to the whole group. This the artists did not mind. For them, impressionism had nothing to do with the subjective thoughts of the artist, his memories, or his dreams. Rather, it was a technical question of putting paint on canvas as they looked at their subject matter with pure objective vision, seeking to capture the impression of light, shade, and color according to the season, time of day, weather, mood of the sun, and point of view. A second Impressionist exhibit was held in 1876, and before long the new luminous style came to be accepted even for the Salon showings.

The Palais Garnier was formally inaugurated as the new home of the Opéra on 5 January 1875. It was a gala affair, attended by the elite of the political, intellectual, and social worlds. Conspicuous by his presence was the president of the Republic, Marie-Edmé-Patrice-Maurice de MacMahon, descendant of Irish forebears, who had won the baton of Marshal of France and the dignity of Duc de Magenta in the Italian campaign of 1859. The Lord Mayor of London came, as did young King Alfonso XII of Spain. At 8:10 the director of the Opéra, Olivier Halanzier-Dufrénoy, struck the traditional three blows signaling the opening of the performance. As usual with such special occasions, there was a mixed program. The great Viennese soprano Gabrielle

Krauss, who had been a favorite at the Théâtre-Italien during 1867–71, now made her debut at the Opéra in an act from *La Juive*. There was also a scene from *Les Huguenots* and the ballet *La Source*. The program would also have included an act from *Faust* and an act from *Hamlet*, excepting that Christine Nilsson was piqued over some question of precedence and refused to appear.

The hall was lighted with gas, for electricity was considered too risky in those fire-conscious times. As a concession to technology, a system of battery-powered signal bells had been installed to facilitate internal communication. The auditorium was eventually equipped with electric lighting in 1881, but for stage lighting the innovation had to wait until 1887. The Opéra had lost many stage sets in the fire of 1873, and in any case, the new and wider stage meant starting over from the standpoint of scenic design. Thus, although the regular company comprised some forty artists with a repertoire of some sixty works, the house could not be expected all at once to provide a full gamut of offerings. The doors were opened to the general public on 8 January with *La Juive*, to which were added during the first year *La Favorite*, *Guillaume Tell, Hamlet, Les Huguenots, Faust, Don Juan*, and the ballets *La Source* and *Coppélia*. The public came in droves, from Paris, the provinces, and abroad, to satisfy their curiosity over the new opera house and set foot on the famous grand staircase. Halanzier, though he received a government subvention, managed the Opéra as entrepreneur on a business basis, and despite heavy start-up expenses realized a handsome profit. When members of the Assembly grumbled and considered reducing the subsidy, or even asking the director to split the profits, Halanzier replied that he also assumed the risks and, under other and adverse conditions, might just as easily have ruined himself financially.

Ernest Deldevez had conducted at the gala inauguration. He was concurrently conductor of the Concerts du Conservatoire where, on Sunday, 10 January 1875, the audience listened to Beethoven's "Pastoral" Symphony, portions of the Credo from Bach's B Minor Mass, the *Scènes dramatiques* of Massenet, a vocal selection from Lully's *Alceste*, and the overture to Weber's *Oberon*. Massenet's suite was played again on 17 January, and a few weeks later Pasdeloup included it in one of his programs. Auguste Vitu wrote that, of the four pieces, "Le Sommeil de Desdémone" was applauded most, and with reason. On the whole, he felt that "these episodes of picturesque music showed more skill than originality, and deserved merely the *succès d'estime* they received."[4] In a note dated 14 July 1875, appended to the autograph score, Massenet designated the work as the "third orchestral suite," with the less picturesque titles: (1) Prélude et divertissement; (2) Mélodrame; (3) Scène finale. The "Ronde nocturne" was thereby deleted.

On 4 February 1875, a drama in five acts entitled *Manon Lescaut*, by Théodore Barrière and Marc Fournier, was revived at the Théâtre du Vaudeville. Perhaps Massenet made a mental note of the play and its impact upon the public. When, a few years later, he hit upon the subject of Manon for an opera, the idea was surely not just dug up out of a vacuum. This particular play had first been produced at the Gymnase in 1851, when Massenet was nine years old. The authors drew, of course, upon the

Abbé Prévost's famous psychological-analytical-sentimental novel in which the Chevalier des Grieux is dragged to the lowest depths by his infatuation for an unworthy young woman. Massenet could hardly be expected to have known Halévy's ballet *Manon Lescaut* (Opéra, 3 May 1830), with scenario by Eugène Scribe. But as a student at the Conservatoire he no doubt saw the *opéra comique* (1856) by the director, Auber, with libretto by the same Scribe.[*]

Bizet's *Carmen* was staged at the Opéra-Comique on 3 March 1875. Massenet, of course, attended the première, At two o'clock in the morning he dashed off a note to Bizet expressing his happiness over the work, which he considered a "great success."[5] By the end of the year *Carmen* had attained forty-eight performances, but then it was dropped from the repertoire. The forty-ninth performance had to wait until 21 April 1883. Then the opera really caught on, reaching its one hundredth on 22 December 1883, its five hundredth on 21 October 1891. The librettists for *Carmen*, Henri Meilhac and Ludovic Halévy (nephew of the composer of *La Juive*), had proven their worth as a high-powered writing team for some of Offenbach's best hits. Before long Meilhac would be involved with *Manon*.

Charles Lamoureux (1834–1899) had done well enough as a violinist, playing in the orchestras of the Opéra and Concerts du Conservatoire and cultivating the best of chamber music. But he yearned to do bigger things, especially after traveling to Germany and England where he heard grand concerts of the masterpieces of Bach, Handel, and Mendelssohn. At length, taking the Sacred Harmonic Society of London as a model, he founded the Société de l'Harmonie Sacrée. The first festival was given on 19 December 1873, at the Cirque d'Été,[†] with an excellent performance of the *Messiah*. This was followed the next year by the *Saint Matthew Passion* and *Judas Maccabaeus*, and Lamoureux was thereby established as a conductor of merit. Besides doing famous masterpieces, Lamoureux was interested in new or unknown works. Accordingly, on 18 March 1875, he produced at the Cirque d'Été Massenet's *Ève*, a "mystère" in three parts with text by Louis Gallet. The rôle of Eve was sung by Mme Brunet-Lafleur, not yet thirty, who would in 1890 marry Charles Lamoureux. Adam was Jean Lassalle, already at twenty-seven a valued member of the Opéra company, while the rôle of the Narrator was entrusted to M. Prunet.

---

[*] Further, on a mixed program given as a benefit at the Opéra-Comique on 30 Jan. 1882, the moving Act III, Scene 2, of Auber's *Manon Lescaut* was presented, with Mlle Isaac and Fürst, and had to be repeated on 1 Feb. Soubies and Malherbe (1893, 335–336) seem to take it for granted that Massenet knew the Auber score and purposely reshaped the ending of his own *Manon* to improve the dramatic effect.

[†] Near the Rond-Point des Champs-Élysées. Known also at various times as the Cirque de l'Impératrice and the Cirque des Champs-Élysées. The building was erected in 1841 by the architect Hittorff for Franconi's circus. With six thousand seats, it was the scene of equestrian feats, the daring skill of acrobats, antics of famous clowns, and other attractions of the European-style circus. In the winter months, the "Summer Circus" proved an ideal place for drawing large crowds to musical events. The only trace that remains today is the name of a nearby street, the Rue du Cirque.

Ève, it was generally agreed, was less exalted in inspiration than *Marie-Magdeleine*. As usual, the orchestration was praised; but the handling of the subject was considered by critics to be sensuous, indeed voluptuous, and we find the first serious accusations of an effeminate treatment bordering sometimes on the banal. Withal, the work pleased, and drew full houses at subsequent performances.

--------------◄○►--------------

The first part opens with a chorus suggesting the splendors of nature surrounding the sleeping Adam, who awakens to find that he has a new companion in Eden. There is a chaste duo, and the Narrator explains how Adam and Eve innocently and happily mingle with the other living creatures. Further descriptive writing suggests all the wonders of an unspoiled paradise. In the second part Eve, separated from Adam, is gradually seduced by the Voices of the Night to an irrepressible desire for the boundless power, love, and triumph that the tree of knowledge has to offer. An orchestral interlude introduces the third part, where the Spirits of the Abyss exhort Adam and Eve to experience the pleasures of love. Adam, at first hesitant, at last gives in; soloists and chorus join in expressing the new ingredient of tender passion in Eden. In an epilogue, the divine malediction is proclaimed by the Narrator, and the Dies Irae undergoes a variety of musical transformations. Adam and Eve, enraptured at having discovered each other, scarcely listen.

--------------•◆•--------------

Though admittedly lacking the qualities of Massenet's best, *Ève* has its interesting coloristic passages and moments of freshness and amiable charm.

An appropriate anecdote is preserved in the *Souvenirs*. Massenet had already begun to avoid the excitement of premières, and he waited out the first performance of *Ève* at a nearby café. At each break his friend Paul Taffanel, the first flutist, would run across the street to convey the comforting news. After the last part, he said that all went well, the audience had left, and Massenet should come to thank Lamoureux. It was a ruse; once inside, Massenet was pushed onto the stage before an audience that was still there, applauding and waving their hats and handkerchiefs. Shyness was indeed a part of his makeup if, as it is said, he was "furious" at the deception and bounced back offstage more quickly than he had arrived.

As Wednesday of Holy Week drew to a close—24 March 1875—Éléonore-Adélaïde Royer de Marancour, *rentière*, age sixty-six, widow of Alexis Massenet, expired at a quarter to midnight in her domicile at 45 Rue Notre-Dame-des-Champs. Thus states the official record of the Ninth Arrondissement. The loss of his mother was naturally painful to Massenet. It is regrettable that in the *Souvenirs* the facts were rearranged to make them subservient to the "success" of *Ève*. There the maidservant frantically searches for Massenet on, we are led to suppose, the evening of 18 March; when at last she finds him at the door of the concert hall, they rush home in a fiacre into the arms of the sobbing sister, Julie, who exclaims: "Mama is dead—at ten o'clock this evening." The account is rather typical of the outward show, for the public record, often encountered in the literature on Massenet.

At some undetermined time during the following weeks, Ninon's mother also died. The following summer at Fontainebleau was clouded with mourning. But life must go on. There was some new incidental music for *Un Drame sous Philippe II*, which opened at the Odéon on 14 April 1875. This historical play, which marked the stage debut of Georges de Porto-Riche, was welcomed as a brilliant and merited success. The real reputation of Porto-Riche, however, dates from 1889 onward, when he became known as the innovator of the so-called théâtre de l'amour with dramas of psychological analysis on the relations of men and women in love. Massenet's music for *Un Drame sous Philippe II* was apparently of no great consequence: a *Sarabande espagnole du seizième siècle* for small orchestra was published, and there is mention of a Pavan; the rest has disappeared. At any rate, the composer was involved with classic forms and with a Spanish subject—a kind of preliminary study toward *Le Cid* of much later.

The city of Caen, once the favorite residence of William the Conqueror, drew Massenet for an Auber festival on 3 June 1875. Long famous for its stone quarries and lace manufacturers, Caen lies in that part of Normandy between Le Havre and Cherbourg known as the Calvados. Although Auber, born here on 29 January 1782, in later years became utterly attached to Paris, his native city nevertheless continued to honor him. Upon this occasion Pasdeloup came, bringing Mme Fourche-Madier of the Opéra and the same baritone, Jacques Bouhy, who had created the title rôle in *Don César de Bazan* and Escamillo in *Carmen*. The violinist Pablo de Sarasate came; perhaps he played Lalo's *Symphonie espagnole*, which he had introduced with such success at a Pasdeloup concert of 9 February 1875. Ernest Reyer came to hear the overture to his *Sigurd*, the opera that would have to wait until 1884 for a stage production at Brussels. When the work was finally mounted at the Paris Opéra in 1885, Reyer boycotted the performances for two years because of the "absurd cuts" that had been made.

Massenet attended the Caen festival because various fragments from *Marie-Magdeleine* and *Ève* were presented. He apparently also sat on the jury for some local competition. But, feeling that he was coming down with the "Roman fever," he left for Fontainebleau as soon as convenient. This is explained a week later in a letter regretting nonacceptance of a gracious invitation.[6] Perhaps he was indeed mildly ill. But as time went on, Massenet would grasp at any excuse, or manufacture an excuse, to put off insistent persons who would like to encroach upon his time.

As the curtain fell on the thirty-third performance of *Carmen*, Bizet lay on his deathbed in the pretty little village of Bougival, where one of the meanders of the Seine makes an elbow west of Paris. He died shortly after midnight on 3 June, and thus was one of France's most promising composers cut off in his thirty-seventh year. The funeral service was held on Saturday, 5 June, at the church of La Trinité. It is said that four thousand people came, including the entire Opéra-Comique troupe.

Pasdeloup, back from Caen, brought his orchestra to play selections from Bizet's works. Pallbearers were Gounod, Ambroise Thomas, Camille Doucet, and Camille du Locle, director of the Opéra-Comique. Among the mourners were Bizet's father, his librettist Ludovic Halévy, and his close friends Guiraud, Massenet, Paladilhe, and the pianist Élie-Miriam Delaborde. Bizet was laid to rest temporarily in the Montmartre Cemetery, and his monument will now be found in the Avenue de la Chapelle at Père Lachaise.

Massenet returned to Fontainebleau with a heavy heart to resume work on Le Roi de Lahore. It was a hot and enervating summer, with moments of exhaustion and depression. The Souvenirs recount how on one occasion Massenet permitted himself to fall asleep. The creative mind often accomplishes its best work in a somnolent condition, freed from outer tensions. As in a dream, Massenet saw his third act, the Paradise of Indra, played on the stage of the Opéra. On that day and the days following, he quickly sketched out the solution to his problem that he had grasped in a flash of intuition. Massenet's method was first to commit entirely to memory the libretto of the opera upon which he was working. In this way his mind, whether consciously or unconsciously, could occupy itself with the inventive process at any hour of the day or night. The system, seemingly miraculous to the layman, is quite elementary for any artist thoroughly immersed in his work.

A letter of 29 June to Julie refers to family matters. From the content, it appears that since the death of Massenet's mother her apartment had been closed up. He advises Julie to act in concert with their brother Edmond: give notice at once to the concierge; take the keys and open up the poor little abandoned dwelling; dispose of the furniture in whatever way seems suitable; and above all take precautions of health. This last injunction suggests that the apartment may have been in quarantine. Massenet pleads that he cannot come to Paris before late July or August. He is busy with a large orchestral work promised to Durand by 4 July;* he has to go to Limoges to judge a contest of orphéons (male choral societies); and there is always Le Roi de Lahore to take up his time.[7]

One week later (6 July), still at Fontainebleau, Massenet addressed a chatty letter to Charles Lamoureux. He recalls the time, which seems so long ago, when they would get together over cups of chocolate and tartines at "salle no. 4, rear, first floor." (Was it to discuss Ève?) Armingaud, who is staying at Fontainebleau at the moment, has described the "remarkable" caricatures that Lamoureux likes to draw. Massenet regrets not having been invited to the Rouen festival and sends respectful greetings to the conductor's wife and daughter, with a promise of a little album of piano pieces for the latter. He inquires solicitously after the health of Lamoureux's mother. In all, a model letter for keeping one's channels of communication open.[8]

Massenet was next "agreeably surprised" at being asked to serve on a jury at the

---

* By a process of elimination, we can surmise that the Première Suite d'orchestre was meant; Massenet was perhaps at long last readying it for publication.

Conservatoire on 19–20 July. In a letter presumably addressed to Émile Réty, secretary of the Conservatoire, Massenet explained that he was taking his wife to the seaside but would be delighted to come on Tuesday, the twentieth, at a quarter to twelve.[9] This was perhaps a temporary arrangement to compensate for Bizet's death. The *comité d'examen* for composition, counterpoint, and fugue had consisted of six members who, with their dates of tenure, were: (1) Bizet, 1871–75; (2) Duprato, 1871–92; (3) Elwart, 1871–77; (4) Barberry, 1872–79; (5) Benoist, 1872–78; (6) Saint-Saëns, 1871–78. In December 1875 Massenet was officially appointed to Seat 1, a position he retained until he became professor of composition in 1878.

On 31 October 1875, the eve of All-Souls' Day, Colonne opened his season with a concert devoted to the memory of Georges Bizet. The first part of the program comprised Beethoven's Seventh, the interlude from Gluck's *Orphée*, and Saint-Saëns's Fourth Piano Concerto. After the intermission there was Massenet's *Lamento* for orchestra, written for this occasion. A poem by Louis Gallet in memory of Bizet was then read with much feeling by Galli-Marié, to the muted accompaniment of the Adagietto from *L'Arlésienne*.

Another and happier special occasion can be recorded for November. Back in April, when *Un Drame sous Philippe II* was drawing capacity houses, the director of the Odéon kept his eyes fixed with alarm on the galleries, which were bending under the unaccustomed weight. The hall was ripe for renovation. From the beginning of June the workmen had taken over, and by 19 November 1875, the Odéon was ready for a gala reopening. As usual on such occasions, various stars contributed their talents to a mixed program of favorite scenes from the repertoire. There was an act from *Le Misanthrope* and an act from *Othello*; Sarah Bernhardt of the Comédie-Française appeared as Jean-Marie; and four singers, including Mme Brunet-Lafleur, provided a musical *intermède*. As a climax, they had coaxed the operetta star Jeanne Granier to appear as Musette in Act I of the Barrière-Mürger *La Vie de Bohème*. This was the occasion for the diva to present a new song of Musette, "La Jeunesse et l'amour," with words by Henri Meilhac and music by Massenet. The orchestration, running to five pages, is now in the Bibliothèque Nationale.

The winter and spring of 1875–76 were spent in Paris, with the orchestration of *Le Roi de Lahore* proceeding steadily. Although we must make some allowance for rhetorical exaggeration, the typical Massenet day, as described in the *Souvenirs*, would seem to fit this period of his life. He would arise at four and work steadily until noon. [Toward the end of this work period he undoubtedly took care of his correspondence.] Six hours of the afternoon were given over to music lessons. This would not have left much time for the midday meal, nor for Hartmann's, where he surely still dropped in quite frequently.] The evenings were often spent at the homes of his pupils' parents, where they made music and he was entertained [and no doubt lionized]. The wording of the *Souvenirs* seems obviously intended to emphasize Massenet's dependence upon music lessons for income.

Some time in February 1876, another work in lighter vein was given at the

Cercle de l'Union Artistique. Entitled *Berengère et Anatole*, with text by Henri Meil-hac and Paul Poirson, this is identified as a *saynète*, which may be variously described as a Spanish farce or a musical comedietta for two persons. The composer, Flori-mond Ronger, better known as Hervé, had popularized this genre as long ago as 1855–56 at the Folies-Concertantes. *Berengère et Anatole* was also given at the Renais-sance, once only, on 15 October 1876. The occasion was a benefit for the theater's régisseur, P. Callais, and Jeanne Granier took part. The work was called an *opérette* in one act, and the libretto was attributed to "Poirson and Grémont."[10]

Among the successive attempts to revive the old Théâtre-Lyrique may be re-corded the so-called Opéra-National-Lyrique, which occupied the Théâtre de la Gaîté during 1876–77 under the direction of Albert Vizentini. The new undertaking opened on 5 May 1876 with the opera *Dimitri* by Victorien de Joncières, whom we previously met at the Café Charles in 1859. Adolphe Jullien devoted ten pages to a critique of the work in his *Musiciens d'aujourd'hui*.[11] In five acts, with book by H. de Bornier and Armand Silvestre, the subject was drawn from Schiller's *Demetrius* and is better known to us in Mussorgsky's *Boris Godunov*.

Ten days later (15 May), the Opéra-National-Lyrique revived Leconte de Lisle's *Les Érinnyes*, with artists from the Odéon and with Massenet's now expanded incidental music, for a total of four performances. Howard Lee Nostrand, in his monograph on the treatment of antiquity on the French stage during 1840–1900, de-votes five pages to a consideration of the importance of the play.[12] By 1891 its success at the Odéon was judged by contemporary criticism to be due as much to the music of Massenet and the conducting of Lamoureux as to the drama itself. In 1887, and again in 1897, *Les Érinnyes* was given in the outdoor summer theater at Orange.

The summer of 1876 was spent at Fontainebleau, with occasional trips to Paris. The orchestration of *Le Roi de Lahore* must have been nearing completion, though the overture (written last) bears the date "February 1877." On 26 July 1876, the now thirty-four-year old Massenet was awarded the distinction of the Légion d'Honneur. According to the *Souvenirs*, the news first reached him as follows: He went to Paris on 26 July [*sic*] to discuss some matters with Hartmann. Not finding him, he dropped in at the Conservatoire to pass the time. They were just taking a break in the midst of a violin competition. Massenet went into the office of Ambroise Thomas to pay his respects, and the latter greeted him with "They gave you the cross yesterday." Whereupon Émile Réty, the Conservatoire secretary, removed the red ribbon from his own buttonhole and transferred it to Massenet's lapel. The moist kisses of Thomas, French fashion, completed the impromptu accolade. We can only imagine Ninon's reaction when her husband came home with the red ribbon in his buttonhole.

By coincidence (or by dramatic compression!), it was on this same day that Massenet was stopped on the corner of the Rue de la Paix by Halanzier—the very one who had refused the ballet *Le Preneur des rats* in 1872. But Halanzier was now all cor-diality, inviting Massenet to come to his place the next morning with the score of *Le Roi de Lahore*. Halanzier lived in a sumptuous apartment at 18 Place Vendôme, and

Massenet, together with the librettist Louis Gallet, arrived there promptly at nine for the reading. The work was accepted for the Opéra and went into rehearsal in October. *Le Roi de Lahore*, incidentally, was to be the third new work created at the Palais Garnier, having been preceded by Mermet's *Jeanne d'Arc* (5 April 1876) and Delibes's ballet *Sylvia* (14 June 1876).

During September, Ninon and Juliette went off on vacation to the Dauphiné. Massenet, tied up with affairs in Paris, ran down briefly to Fontainebleau to welcome them back at the beginning of October.[13] Another event of future significance for Massenet was the staging at the Comédie-Française, on 26 September 1876, of *Rome vaincue*, a five-act tragedy in verse by Alexandre Parodi. Sarah Bernhardt created the rôle of Posthumia, and the subject matter is similar to that of Spontini's *La Vestale* of 1807. Nostrand has commented that the drama was a brilliant success, reaching a tenth printed edition in the same year.[14] Years after, Massenet drew upon the play for his opera *Roma*, given at Monte-Carlo in 1912. Parodi, incidentally, was born in Greece of Italian parentage, but his commentators have noted that he was French by vocation and free choice.

By October, Massenet was reinstalled in the apartment at 38 Rue Malesherbes, and rehearsals of *Le Roi de Lahore* got under way. But six months would drag by before the première. As the year drew to a close, Massenet could look back with some satisfaction upon his progress and steal a glance at the red ribbon in his lapel. At some time during 1876—I have been unable to determine the exact dates—the *Scènes napolitaines* was given by both Pasdeloup and Colonne. This fifth orchestral suite comprises three movements: (1) La Danse; (2) La Procession et L'Improvisateur; (3) La Fête. The rhythm of the first movement seems to have pleased.

A few songs may be assigned to 1876. The cycle *Poème d'octobre*, in a reflective mood with rather simple accompaniments, depends for its effect upon the projection of the sentiment in Paul Collin's six poems. *Si tu veux, Mignonne* has springtime as its theme, and the setting of Georges Boyer's poem is convincing. In *La Veillée du petit Jésus* ("It is midnight, the stable is dark"), words by André Theuriet, Massenet succeeds admirably in capturing the spirit of Noël in pastoral rhythm. In our mind's eye, let us hope that he composed this on Christmas Eve. The mood is gentler than the children's Noël in *Werther*, of later date.

Le Roi de Lahore;
The Conservatoire;
The Institut

O N 31 JANUARY 1877, MASSENET wrote to Colonne excusing himself for not having sooner thanked the conductor for a "perfect" performance of *Les Érinnyes*. He had been quite ill for ten days but was now almost back on his feet. Consequently, he had been unable to look in on the rehearsals at the Opéra and had also missed the première of Saint-Saëns's *La Jeunesse d'Hercule*.[1]

Massenet had provided more incidental music for Paul Déroulède's five-act drama in verse, *L'Hetman*, which opened at the Odéon on 2 February. The scene is laid around 1646 in the reign of Ladislas IV of Poland, and the action deals with an uprising of cossacks against their Polish oppressors. One would have thought, wrote one reviewer, that the very idea of a cossack drama with names like Froll-Gheraz, Stenko, Rogaviane, Mosi, Chmoul, Mikla, and Chmelniecki (the *hetman*, or cossack leader) would have been repulsive to habitués of the theater. But the drama achieved, in fact, a complete success before packed houses filled with the elite of Parisian society. The reviewer mentioned several patriotic songs in Act II (the Cossack camp): "Et toi, sabre de bataille," "Laboureur d'hommes, travaille," "Sème la rouge semaille," and "D'où la liberté croîtra." Massenet's music seems to have been lost, with the exception of a brief fanfare preserved in the Bibliothèque Nationale.* Some years later (1886) Massenet wrote a *Chant de guerre cosaque* to a poem by Hélène Vacaresco.

While awaiting the première of *Le Roi de Lahore*, Massenet had an opportunity to observe how some of his colleagues were faring on Paris stages. Saint-Saëns's *Le Timbre d'argent* (The Silver Bell) was at long last staged at the Théâtre-Lyrique de la

---

* Paul Déroulède (1846–1914), author-poet-politician, later supported the revisionist government of General Boulanger (1837–1891) and was leader of the anti-Dreyfus forces. In 1900, Déroulède was himself found guilty of plotting against the Republic and sentenced to exile.

Camille Saint-Saëns. Courtesy Paul Jackson.

Gaîté on 23 February 1877. There were eighteen performances, and then the work sank into oblivion. Even so, in April Saint-Saëns gave up his post as organist at the Madeleine; concert fees, royalties, and a legacy from a friend had made him independent. His major frustration was *Samson et Dalila:* staged at Weimar under Liszt's protection (2 December 1877), it would not reach Paris for another thirteen years (Théâtre Éden, 31 October 1890; Opéra, 23 November 1892).

Edmond Audran (1840–1901) was less frustrated. From 1861 he lived at Marseille, producing there some operas of a lighter nature. His *Le Grand Mogul* was given at Marseille on 24 February 1877 and proved to be his first great success. He promptly moved to Paris where, in the 1880s and 1890s, he turned out a series of highly successful operettas, many of which were also popular in England. Thus, *La Mascotte* of 1880 played seventeen hundred times in Paris alone up to 1897.

On 5 April 1877, the Opéra-Comique gave Gounod's *Cinq-Mars*, book by Louis Gallet and Paul Poirson, based on Alfred de Vigny's novel of 1826 dealing with a conspiracy against Cardinal Richelieu headed by the Marquis de Cinq-Mars, a favorite of Louis XIII. The opera was not very successful. Nor was Gounod's *Polyeucte* that followed (Opéra, 7 October 1878). His *Le Tribut de Zamora* (Opéra, 1 April 1881) ran up fifty performances in four years and then disappeared. *Sapho* (1851), as

Grand staircase of the Palais Garnier, new home of the Paris Opéra, *Le Monde Illustré*, 1875. Courtesy Reinhard Pauly.

revised for the Opéra (2 April 1884), expired after twenty-eight performances. Thus Gounod had to be content with *Faust, Mireille,* and *Roméo et Juliette.*

For the successful long run, operetta was the thing. On 19 April 1877, the Folies-Dramatiques mounted *Les Cloches de Corneville* by Robert Planquette. This was one of the most successful operettas of the 1870s, reaching its one thousandth performance at the Folies-Dramatiques on 18 October 1886. The work was popular in England as *The Chimes of Normandy,* and Planquette went on to other successes such as *Rip van Winkle* (1882), *Nell Gwynne* (1884), and *Mam'zelle Quat' sous* (1897). His *Panurge* (1895) is interesting for the fact that one of Massenet's posthumous operas treated this subject.

At last, on 27 April 1877, *Le Roi de Lahore* had its première at the Opéra. The staging, scenery, and costumes were opulent (the costumes alone cost 200,000 francs); the interpretation was excellent, the occasion elegant. Maréchal MacMahon, president of the Republic, sat in one loge and the emperor Don Pedro II of Brazil in another. Massenet had outdone himself with the orchestration (which included saxophones), and some thought the work noisy. As is usual with new halls, critics had complained about the acoustics of the Palais Garnier since its opening. But Massenet received a note a day or so later from none other than the architect, Charles Garnier, who found *Le Roi de Lahore* admirable and wondered if it was the hall that made it come through so well. Ernest Reyer summed up the work as a happy synthesis of three schools: French, Italian, and German—meaning Berlioz and Gounod, Verdi, and Wagner.[2]

The performance of a five-act work at the Opéra was considered a significant achievement for a thirty-five-year-old composer. In a very real sense, *Le Roi de Lahore* marked Massenet's true stage debut and point of departure for a career as a dramatic composer. Within the context of its times, the work was a sincere and honest effort, powerful and colorful in impact and displaying skillful management of dramatic and scenic resources.[3]

--------------------◄○►--------------------

The libretto, by Louis Gallet, was based on a tale of India reported by several French travelers. The people of Lahore have come to the temple of Indra to implore divine protection against the invading Muslims. The high priest Timour offers encouragement. Scindia, the minister of King Alim, is enamored of his own niece Sita, a priestess of the temple, and he asks Timour to release her from her vows. When Timour refuses, Scindia reveals that Sita has been meeting an unknown young man. The high priest determines to investigate. The scene changes to Indra's sanctuary in the temple, where Sita and the other priestesses are assembled. Scindia manages to draw from her an admission of her interest in the young stranger. When she refuses to renounce him, Scindia calls in the priests and accuses her of sacrilege. They demand that she intone the evening prayer, which has been the young man's cue to appear, and they hope thus to entrap him. Sita is unwilling, but before they can beat her into submission a secret door opens; the young man appears and is at once recognized as King Alim. Alim confesses his love for Sita and requests her hand in marriage. But Timour now announces that the king's sacrilege must be expiated by his leading his troops against the Muslims. Scindia, thwarted in his hopeless love, plots to arrange an ambush to kill the king.

The second act is in the camp of Alim in the Thôl desert. Sita has followed and pitched her tent nearby. As the scene opens she impatiently awaits Alim's return from battle. But his troops have been routed, and the perfidious Scindia talks them over to his side with the intent of usurping the throne. Alim has been mortally wounded, and dies in Sita's arms.

The colorful third act is set in the Paradise of Indra, with its choruses of happy spirits and the celestial dances of the Apsâras. The soul of Alim arrives and makes obéisance before the god Indra. But amidst all this glory Alim's soul is not happy. The god gently questions him: Alim misses the earth, and above all Sita. Indra takes pity. He will restore Alim to life upon earth for as long as Sita shall live—not in his former royal state, but as the humblest of men. Alim is overjoyed.

Alim awakens to find himself back in Lahore, lying on the steps of the royal palace. The celestial music still rings in his ears, but he is elated to be back on earth. Crowds assemble in preparation for the coronation of Scindia. The latter comes by on his way to Sita, whom he hopes to persuade now to accept him. But what appears to be a vengeful ghost bars his way. To the crowd, Alim seems only a madman who may be killed for his insolence. Timour and the other priests contend that it is a visionary inspired by a god: in claiming Sita he is merely reaffirming the prior claim of the god whom Sita serves.

Scindia, disregarding the pronouncement of the high priest, forces Sita into marriage. The fifth act opens as she has fled the nuptial chamber and taken refuge in the sanctuary of Indra. Timour admits Alim to the sanctuary, and the lovers are reunited. But they are in reality trapped, for the place is guarded and Scindia arrives to threaten them. At last the desperate Sita stabs herself with a dagger. By Indra's decree, Alim also again becomes a spirit when she expires. The welcoming voices of a celestial choir assure the pair of a happy eternity together, while the foiled Scindia must contemplate the apotheosis of those whom he had persecuted

---

At the première, Ernest Deldevez conducted a cast comprising Joséphine de Reszk (Sita), Marius Salomon (Alim), Jean Lassalle (Scindia), Auguste Boudouresque (Timour), and Menu (Indra). *Le Roi de Lahore* was given thirty times at the Opéra during 1877, eleven times in 1878, and seventeen times in 1879. The work also caught on abroad, laying the groundwork for Massenet's international reputation. Within five years of its Paris première, *Le Roi de Lahore* had been given at Turin, Budapest, Munich, London, Buenos Aires, Rio de Janeiro, St. Petersburg, Prague, and Madrid. This could hardly have been the case had not Giulio Ricordi taken an interest in the work and arranged for an Italian translation by the remarkable man of letters Angelo Zanardini.

Giulio Ricordi (1840–1912) was a member of the music-publishing dynasty founded by Giovanni Ricordi, who had learned music engraving at Breitkopf and Härtel's in Leipzig and returned to Milan to open a music shop. There, from 1808, he published works that at first he himself engraved. Giovanni's son Tito (1811–1888) succeeded to the business, and under his management it became the largest music-publishing firm in Italy. From 1845 he issued the *Gazetta musicale*, an influential music journal. Tito's son Giulio was close to Massenet's own age; a trained musician, he was active in the affairs of the firm, whose management he took over entirely in 1887.

Giulio Ricordi heard *Le Roi de Lahore* at the Paris Opéra, was impressed, and arranged with Hartmann for its production in Italy. The first of Massenet's letters preserved in the archives of G. Ricordi & C. is actually dated 15 April 1877, some twelve days before the première. Massenet said he was "profoundly moved" by some compliment and remarked that it would be a joy to see Milan again, which suggests that he had been invited there for a conference. Ricordi had discussed Massenet with Arrigo Boito, composer of *Mefistofele*, distinguished novelist, and future librettist for Verdi's *Otello* and *Falstaff*, and also with Franco Faccio, conductor at La Scala who, after the death of Angelo Mariani, was considered by some to be the best conductor in Italy.* Massenet was "particularly touched" that their opinion was favorable.[4]

With *Le Roi de Lahore* launched at the Opéra, Massenet soon began work on his next oratorio, *La Vierge*. But the coming year was to be a busy one; his *légende sacrée* would not be finished until the summer of 1878, nor performed until 1880. The librettist was Charles Grandmougin, who worked during the daytime in the library of the Ministère de la Guerre and, around 1876, also wrote music criticism for *La Vie littéraire.*[†]

On 9 May 1877, Massenet wrote to Mme Borch that they were leaving in a few days for the mountains of the Grande Chartreuse.[5] This was wishful thinking, for the trip was postponed. On 8 June he wrote from Fontainebleau to "Mon cher Maître" (Ambroise Thomas) that they were going to the mountains for the sake of Juliette's health; their trunks were all packed and at the station, and they did not expect to return until October.[6] But then on 25 June, Massenet's brother-in-law Paul Cavaillé died in Paris at the age of fifty. Some further letters of 21 and 22 July were still dated at Fontainebleau.[7] At last, on 24 July, a letter from Uriage-les-Bains (not far from the Grande Chartreuse) indicated that the Massenets were en route to Switzerland.[8] But in characteristic fashion Massenet had to dash back to Fontainebleau, whence he wrote to Ricordi on 11 and 20 August.[9]

The Massenets arrived at St. Moritz on 29 August, putting up at the Hotel Victoria.[10] Several letters to Ricordi followed in rapid succession. Massenet has to be back in Paris around 22 September but plans to visit Milan for a day or two along the way. He is rewriting portions of *Le Roi de Lahore* and needs to see his manuscript with Zanardini's translation to make some adjustments. At the hotel he has met Count Greppi from Milan, and also Baron Gunzbourg. On 2 September he arose with rheumatic pains, probably the result of an excursion into the mountains. On 4 September, after another excursion, his rheumatism is better, and he hopes that a little touch of Italy will soon restore him completely. By 10 September the Massenets have moved to the Quellenhof at Ragatz; the rawer high altitude of St. Moritz was not good for Juliette (age nine), and the doctor advised the change. Massenet is delighted with the proofs of "our score" (i.e., now *Il Re di Lahore*), and his letters discuss a multitude of details.[11]

The visit to Italy must be pieced together from a letter of 30 September written from Fontainebleau.[12] The short visit with Giulio Ricordi was around 25 September, for they parted on Wednesday the twenty-sixth. The rendezvous was at the Ricordi villa on Lake Como, the beauties of which made a profound impression. The Massenets met Ricordi's wife, Giuditta; their daughter, Ginetta (a delightful playmate for Juliette); and the two boys, Tito and Manuel. On the way back to Fontainebleau, as

---

* Faccio's own opera of 1865 on the subject of Hamlet was to a book by Boito; it was assailed at the time as "Wagnerian."

† Grandmougin later provided the libretto for César Franck's opera *Hulda* (after Björnson's play), at which Franck worked off and on during 1881–85 but which was first performed posthumously at Monte-Carlo on 4 Mar. 1894.

the train stopped in the station at Turin, Massenet had a few words with Giovanni Depanis, director of the Teatro Regio there. *Il Re di Lahore* would have its Italian première at Turin the following February.*

By the end of October the Massenets were again installed in their Paris apartment at 38 Rue Malesherbes. There was a brief trip to Angers to conduct *Les Érinnyes*, and then on 5 November *Le Roi de Lahore* reopened at the Opéra after its three-months' rest. Despite the distracting political situation (Broglie's resignation as prime minister under pressure from Gambetta), the public's attendance and response were gratifying.

For *Il Re di Lahore*, Massenet had seen and corrected the proofs of the vocal score (September) and full score (October), but the orchestral and choral parts dragged on through November.[13] The composer marveled at the careful workmanship of Ricordi's engravers. On 10 December, Hartmann sent over a copy of the published score, which he had just received from Ricordi. Massenet wondered what was to be the fate of "these 356 pages." Certain critics in Turin, it was rumored, were hostile toward Depanis and hence toward *Il Re di Lahore*, even before it was performed. Another elegantly bound copy of the Italian edition was sent to Halanzier, director of the Paris Opéra.[14]

A letter to Ricordi of 22 December anticipates Massenet's next major project with an appended query: "... and Hérodiade?" The question alluded to the first rough outline, or scenario, which Massenet was still eagerly awaiting on Christmas Eve. (It arrived early in January.) As a Christmas offering Ricordi sent a package of delectable foodstuffs, about which Massenet raved in a letter of 29 December. There was *pannetone*, that Milanese cousin of *Kugelhopf*, and of the superb Gorgonzola cheese he wrote: "I kneel before it! And only after Hartmann shed tears did I allow him to have a little piece." Massenet was known for his sweet tooth, and the nougats were enough "to turn a hermit into a gourmet."[15]

On 9 January 1878, Massenet acknowledged receiving Zanardini's brief preliminary scenario for *Erodiade*, which appeared very promising. In the same letter he made known his wishes regarding a concert suite to be extracted from *Le Roi de Lahore*, to consist of: (1) Overture, (2) Divertissement sur les esclaves persanes, (3) Entr'acte, and (4) Cortège. The variations on the "Mélodie hindoue" can be performed at concerts as a separate piece, as can the "Marche céleste," which requires a chorus.[16]

Another letter (of 17 January) is of passing documentary interest. Maestro Pedrotti† had asked for metronome markings, and these had already been put into a

---

* Further letters of October to Ricordi deal with the advance preparations for *Il Re di Lahore*. Thus, on 9 Oct., Massenet called special attention to the need for E-flat contralto and B-flat tenor saxophones in Act III only, whereas in Act III and Act IV, Scene 2, a contrabass saxophone in B-flat is required. For Acts II and III the *jeu de timbres* is described ("bars of steel which are hit with little hammers"), and the seven pitches required in the score are specified.

† Carlo Pedrotti (1817–1893), conductor at the Teatro Regio in Turin; also, since 1865, director of the Turin Conservatory. In 1882, Pedrotti became director of the Liceo Rossini at Pesaro.

score sent to Ricordi. For the coming première of *Il Re di Lahore* at Turin, Massenet wonders if he should plan on fifteen to twenty days altogether, including travel time and visits to Turin and Rome. This would be the most he could manage during the Paris winter season, what with "le Conservatoire, mes cours et mes leçons."[17] The inclusion of "mes cours" suggests that Massenet was filling in for the ailing François Bazin, who died on 2 July. The official appointment to succeed Bazin as professor of composition was dated 7 October 1878. "Mes leçons," of course, referred to the private lessons that Massenet still gave up to the time of *Hérodiade.*

There are letters from Paris dated 1 February and 20 February; in the interim, Massenet went to Italy with Hartmann, who paid the travel expenses.* One might wonder why *Il Re di Lahore* was produced at Turin and not at La Scala in Milan. The principal music-publishing houses of Milan were Ricordi, Lucca, and Sonzogno. Ricordi was the proprietor of Verdi's operas and, in general, took a patriotic tone in pushing Italian works. One of Ricordi's engravers, Francesco Lucca, had defected and set up a rival firm, now run by his widow Giovannina, who held the Italian rights for Wagner. This explains the anti-Wagner stance of the *Gazetta musicale,* the house organ of Ricordi. (Ultimately, Giulio Ricordi's grand coup was to acquire the firm of Lucca, Wagner and all.) The third member of the triangle was Edoardo Sonzogno, whose specialty was the Italian rights for the French repertoire, notably Thomas's *Mignon* and *Hamlet.* Proprietor of the newspaper *Il Secolo,* Sonzogno later (1894) established his own theater in Milan, the Teatro Lirico Internazionale. His real prosperity began with the acquisition of Bizet's *Carmen* and Massenet's *Manon.*

The Milan triumvirate were not above crossing over into rival territory, and the struggle for La Scala was uppermost in their minds. Thus, the Lucca catalogue included *Faust, L'Africaine,* and *La Juive.* Sonzogno stole a march on Ricordi by obtaining proprietorship of the extremely popular *Cavalleria rusticana* and *Pagliacci.* In 1877, La Scala was out of sorts with Ricordi and inclined to favor Lucca. This firm arranged to import Gounod's *Cinq-Mars* for La Scala (18 January 1878), where it was a failure. Meanwhile, Giulio Ricordi had received word of *Le Roi de Lahore* in Paris, made haste to get it, and searched about for a theater. A timely visit from Giovanni Depanis, director of the Teatro Regio at Turin (who had also gone to Paris to hear *Le Roi de Lahore*), settled the matter.

So, then, Massenet and Hartmann arrived at Turin early in February for the last rehearsals. The theater had done itself proud in the matter of décor and costumes. The cast included Giuseppe Fancelli (Alim), Eleonora Mecocci (Nair),† Giuseppe Mendioroz (Scindia), Enrico Dondi (Timur), and Gaetano Roveri (Indra). At rehearsal the conductor, Pedrotti, kept turning to Massenet with: "Are you satisfied? I am so much." After the première on 13 February 1878, Massenet answered

---

* While they were away, *Narcisse,* a cantata—or rather an *idylle antique* for soli, chorus, and orchestra—was performed on 11 Feb. by the choral society bearing the name of its founder, Guillot de Sainbris.

† The character Sita was renamed Nair; "sito" suggests an offensive odor in Italian.

twenty curtain calls, thanking the public with his characteristic gestures: placing his hands on his heart, then extending them broadly and throwing kisses. The splendor of the production and its reception were considered an honor for both the theater and the city. The success was celebrated with a banquet at the Albergo d'Europa, attended by the mayor of Turin; Massenet, moved by all this, promised Turin his next opera, *Erodiade*. The promise was not kept; by the time *Hérodiade* was ready for Italy, it went to La Scala (1882). Turin had to wait until 1910!

Back in Paris, Massenet basked in his first success abroad.[*] Halanzier, impressed by the dispatches, resolved to continue *Le Roi de Lahore* at the Opéra during the Exposition of 1878. Writing to Ricordi on 20 February, Massenet inquired how "that excellent maestro Cagnoni" had fared at Turin and mentioned his own anxiety over a coming production at Rouen.[†] A few days later he felt indisposed and had to cancel a trip to Liège, where an excellent performance of *Les Érinnyes* was given.[18]

On 3 March 1878, at the Concerts du Châtelet, Colonne presented the Massenet suite drawn from *Le Roi de Lahore*. It was warmly received, and the dance of the Persian slaves had to be played twice. On the same program was Gade's *La Fille du Roi des Aulnes* (The Erl King's Daughter, Op. 30), for which the soloists were Mme Brunet-Lafleur and Lassalle. The public found that work monotonous and lacking in color but heartily applauded excerpts from Schumann's *Manfred*. Two weeks later, 17 March, Colonne gave Berlioz's Requiem.

Massenet and Hartmann set off again for Italy, this time for Rome where *Il Re di Lahore* was given at the Teatro Apollo on Friday, 22 March 1878.[‡] The first performance was a great success: one newspaper reported that Massenet had to appear twenty times in response to the applause, while a rival newspaper claimed exactly twenty-five curtain calls. There was a celebration afterward at the Hôtel de Rome; indeed, the next morning Massenet received a note from an old friend, Camille du Locle, complaining that the serenading and toasting had kept him awake!

Sunday, 24 March, was a full day. In the morning Massenet attended an audience with the newly enthroned Pope Leo XIII.[**] The numerous persons who had been admitted kneeled in rows on both sides of the grand salon. Prompted by a

---

[*] *Il Re di Lahore* was given twenty times at Turin that season and was rapidly taken up by other Italian theaters.

[†] Antonio Cagnoni (1828–1896), alas, had brought out a new opera *Francesca da Rimini* at Turin a few days after Massenet's triumphal première there. The subject did not suit Cagnoni's talent, better exemplified in his other operas such as *Don Bucefalo* (1847) and *Papa Martín* (1871).

[‡] The Teatro Apollo, on the Tiber across from the Castello Sant' Angelo (Hadrian's Tomb), was inaugurated on 26 Dec. 1796 on the site of the former Teatro Tor di Nona, which had burned down on 26 Jan. 1781. Vincenzo Jacovacci was director of the Apollo from 1839 until his death in Apr. 1881. The theater was torn down in 1889 to make room for the Lungo Tevere Tordinona, for flood control of the Tiber. The last performance there was Thomas's *Amleto* (Hamlet) on 31 Jan. 1888.

[**] The eighty-five-year-old Pius IX died on 7 Feb. His successor, Cardinal Pecci, was proclaimed Pope on 20 Feb. and installed, as Leo XIII, in the Chair of Saint Peter on 3 Mar.

chamberlain as to their identities, the Pope gave his benediction and spoke a few words to each. To Massenet, he conveyed his good wishes for the composer's art.[*]

After leaving the Vatican, Massenet went at eleven o'clock to the Quirinal Palace, where the Marchese di Villamarina presented him to Queen Margherita. The queen asked to be excused for not attending the opera, as the family was in mourning for the late king.[†] Massenet satisfied her curiosity by playing fragments of *Le Roi de Lahore* at the piano, and he left feeling deeply touched by her graciousness. He then paid a visit to Menotti Garibaldi, to whom he had a letter of introduction, and later was presented to Prince Massimo of the oldest Roman nobility.

That evening Massenet again attended *Il Re di Lahore*, and afterward he went for supper to the house of the French ambassador, the Duc de Montebello. Here, at the request of the duchess, he again played excerpts from the opera. Massenet later recalled that, since the duchess smoked, he too smoked many cigarettes while he played. When his eyes drifted upward with the smoke, he had occasion to admire the fine Carracci ceiling.

Between times, during his stay in Rome, Massenet revisited the Villa Medici and also attended the *prova generale* (final rehearsal) of a Mass by Seménow.[‡] This last bit of information is provided by the *Osservatore Romano*, which notes that the Mass was a marvelous success when attended by the elite of Roman society on the Sunday morning in the chapel of the Oblate Sisters at Tor de' Specchi.[19] By Tuesday, 26 March, *L'Opinione* observed that "il maestro Massenet" had left Rome.[**]

The next two months were spent in Paris. A letter to Ricordi (30 March) reflects Massenet's gratification at his warm reception in Italy; he wonders when he will again see "that dear and beautiful country where I was welcomed as I would wish to be in France." Martucci, visiting in Paris, paid him a call on 17 April, which he returned on the nineteenth.[††] Drafted to serve on the jury for the Prix Cressent, Massenet found himself involved with reading through the forty-nine scores submitted. On 21 April he wrote impatiently to Delibes that he had been through the first twenty scores and was waiting already three weeks to have the rest of them sent to him.[20] The upshot of it was that the jury (Massenet, Guiraud, Delibes, Dubois, Lenepveu, Eu-

---

[*] Pope Leo XIII also held an audience on Thurs., 21 Mar.—the date mentioned in the *Souvenirs*. There is, however, no list of the persons who attended, and dates given in the *Souvenirs* cannot always be trusted. It is there stated that the audience with the Pope was followed immediately by a visit to the queen, which can be documented for Sun., 24 Mar.

[†] Victor Emmanuel II of Italy died on 9 Jan. 1878 and was succeeded by his son Umberto I, born in 1844 and assassinated in 1900.

[‡] Hofmeister's catalogue for 1880–85 lists a *Meese mélodique* for soli, chorus, and organ by N. de Seménow as having been published by Le Beau of Paris.

[**] And went on to say that "Sunday, he had the honor of being admitted to present his respectful homage to Her Majesty the queen."

[††] Giuseppe Martucci (1856–1909) had been appointed professor at the Naples Conservatory in 1874, toured as a pianist, and was also active as a conductor. It was Martucci who conducted the Italian première of *Tristan* at Bologna, 2 June 1882. As a composer (two symphonies, a piano concerto, chamber music), he more or less followed the ideals of Wagner and Liszt.

gène Gautier, H. de Lapommeraye, Leuven, and Cormon) did not want to award a prize; but the Minister of Beaux-Arts, giving in to pressure from the newspapers, took it upon himself to honor the contestant ranking highest on the jury's list. This was Samuel Rousseau, whose *Dianora* (text by Chantepie) was staged on 22 December 1879, lasting through only five performances.[*]

At the Concerts du Conservatoire, the concert pair for 19 April (Good Friday) and 21 April (Easter) included the first part of *Ève*, "La Naissance de la Femme," with Mme Brunet-Lafleur and Lassalle. Sharing the program of this *concert spirituel* were Beethoven's Seventh and *Coriolanus* Overture, a Handel organ concerto with Alexandre Guilmant at the organ, a choral Cantique by Halévy, and Mendelssohn's Psalm 98 for double chorus.

The Exposition Universelle of 1878 opened on 1 May. One of its chief attractions was the new Palais du Trocadéro, designed in Oriental style by Gabriel Davioud and Jules Bourdais. The palace consisted of a circular central edifice, with minarets 230 feet high and curved wings ending in pavilions that extended on either side to an overall length of 383 yards. The chief front was toward the Seine, with a park sloping down to the river. Across the Pont d'Iéna, on the Left Bank, was the Champ-de-Mars, with the Palais de l'Exposition proper and its surrounding temporary exhibits. (The Eiffel Tower, of course, would not make its appearance until the Exposition of 1889.)

The Trocadéro Palace contained a large hall with organ (Salle des Fêtes) seating forty-seven hundred, and a smaller hall (Salle des Conférences) with five hundred seats. As its contribution to the Exposition, the French government planned for the Salle des Fêtes ten grand official concerts with orchestra, twelve organ recitals, four concerts of choral societies, and four concerts of wind-bands. For the Salle des Conférences, there were to be sixteen chamber-music concerts. A commission was appointed to select the most important French works since 1830 for performance by an orchestra of 150 and, as needed, a chorus of 200, all to be conducted by Edouard Colonne. The commission divided itself into five subjuries as follows:

1. Thomas (chairman), Franck, Guiraud, Vaucorbeil, Samuel David
2. Reber (chairman), Blanc, Delibes, Joncières, Saint-Saëns
3. Bazin (chairman), Deldevez, Guilmant, Membrée, Poise, Salomon
4. Reyer (chairman), Cohen, Deffès, Nibelle, Massenet, Gouzien
5. Gounod (chairman), Bourgault-Ducoudray, Dubois, Lajarte, Pessard, Lascoux

---

[*] Cressent, a wealthy amateur who died in 1870, had left 100,000 francs to establish a triennial competition for an *opéra comique*. The first competition, opened in 1874 and judged in 1875, awarded the Prix Cressent to William Chaumet for his one-act *Bathyle* (text by Édouard Blau), staged at the Opéra-Comique on 4 May 1877, and given nine times. The prize for the second competition of 1877–78 went to Rousseau, as indicated. In the third and fourth competitions, the winners were Georges Hüe, *Les Pantins* (text by Montagne), two acts, staged 22 Dec. 1881 and given ten times, and Edmond Missa, *Juge et partie* (text by Jules Adenis), staged 17 Nov. 1887. For *Les Pantins*, the critics could not resist the obvious pun on the librettist's name: "In this case, the mountain labored and brought forth a mouse."

A hundred works by seventy composers having been submitted, the selection was narrowed down to ten works for the grand concerts. Some writers complained of musical politics—a conspiracy to foist upon the public the works of unknowns instead of, say, more appropriate things by Massenet Saint-Saëns, Guiraud, Gounod, and Delibes.

Besides the "official" concerts, the Salle des Fêtes was available for other groups, both French and foreign. Thus in September 1878 there were three concerts of Russian music. Gilmore's band also put in an appearance.[*] As we shall see in a moment, of special interest to Massenet was the rivalry between the orchestras of La Scala and Turin, which gave concerts at the Trocadéro in June and July.

In a letter to Ricordi of 13 May 1878, Massenet mentions that the Italian exhibits at the Exposition are splendid. He needs rest and calm "after the recent fatigues of a Paris winter; Juliette [now ten] needs the air of either St. Moritz or the seaside, and since the seaside is closer he is inclined to go there.[21] On 20 May he wrote a letter of condolence to Emma Borch on the loss of her brother Albert Hennequin, violinist in the Opéra-Comique orchestra, who had just died at the age of twenty-one. He was leaving Paris the next day and planned to be away "until November."[22]

Wherever they were on 25 May, Juliette's health was a little better, and they were enjoying the place of their sojourn despite the rainy weather. From mid-June, the Massenets were back at Fontainebleau: "I came here because of a very serious family matter," he wrote to Ricordi on 17 June. A week later Massenet was concerned over the health of his wife and daughter, who appeared pale and weak.[23]

Massenet was in Paris on 29 June to hear Franco Faccio conduct the La Scala orchestra at the Trocadéro. It was a "great, great success," with twelve thousand francs in receipts, whereas the French concerts did well to take in three thousand francs. In writing to Ricordi the next day, Massenet remarked that Tuesday [2 July] would be Faccio's last concert, and then would come Pedrotti. He has given Faccio the manuscript "changes" for coming performances of *Il Re di Lahore* in Italy.[24]

The Turin orchestra, with 120 players conducted by Carlo Pedrotti, gave four concerts at the Trocadéro on 6, 9, 11, and 14 July. The first concert, on a Saturday afternoon, was attended by President MacMahon, Gounod, Massenet, Offenbach, and Arthur Sullivan.[†] The second and fourth concerts included the overture, barcarolle, and triumphal march from Luigi Mancinelli's incidental music to Pietro Cossa's drama *Cleopatra*. Massenet was pleased at the warm reception given this work, which

---

[*] Patrick Gilmore (1829–1892), born in Ireland, went to Canada with a military band, then settled in Boston where he organized his own band. An army bandmaster during the Civil War, he later (1869 and 1872) arranged monster festivals at Boston which he called "Peace Jubilees." He then moved to New York, where he organized a band that became widely known through its concert tours in the U.S. and Canada.

[†] Gilbert and Sullivan's *H.M.S. Pinafore* had opened on 25 May 1878 in London, where it had a run of seven hundred performances.

he considered well orchestrated.[*]

In a letter of 31 July 1878, Massenet is touched by all that Ricordi is doing to promote Il Re di Lahore in Italy. He is agreeable to plans for a coming trip to Italy, for which Ricordi will provide expenses. At the moment, however, his health is down; he has taken to his bed with a serious cold resulting from his attendance at the Trocadéro. His wife and daughter are leaving the next day for Chur and St. Moritz, but Massenet will remain at Fontainebleau until he feels better [and also to work on the orchestration of La Vierge, completed on 22 August]. On 18 August he thanked Ricordi for his telegram regarding the opening of Il Re di Lahore at Vicenza; had he felt better he "would have gone to Vicenza to thank all those valiant collaborators." Massenet had telegraphed fifty-nine words to Mancinelli [who apparently conducted], and this "did not express one-fourth of my feeling and gratitude." In Paris Le Roi de Lahore is playing at the Opéra to good Exposition audiences. The fortieth performance was on Friday [16 August], and Massenet gloats over the receipts of 21,935 francs for the Saturday performance [17 August], "the largest receipts since the opening of the new opera house."[25]

Ricordi was apparently trying to induce Massenet to come to Italy for an extended stay, holding out the temptations of a pleasant vacation. He could combine an appearance at Vicenza, before Il Re di Lahore closed there, with the opening at Bologna. But Massenet resists; the dates are not definite enough, and they are too far apart. He can only spare two weeks, for he is busy with corrections on La Vierge ("my life is taken up with the engravers, the copyists"), which he hopes to have performed during the coming season. [La Vierge would have to wait until 1880.] He reiterates that he expects travel expenses for the opening at Bologna.[26]

The travel plans were at last crystallized in a letter to Ricordi of 13 September. Massenet planned to leave at a quarter past eleven on Wednesday, 18 September, changing at Milan for the train to Como and taking the boat from there to the Villa d'Este. He supposed that his wife and daughter would arrive from St. Moritz before him and that he would be too late for dinner on the nineteenth. Meanwhile, "yesterday at 3:00 P.M.," at Hartmann's, Corti and Lassalle signed contracts for a performance of Le Roi at La Scala on 20 January [1879]. If when they meet, Massenet continues, he talks night and day to Ricordi about Erodiade, his friend should be indulgent and try to put up with it. Hartmann is to make the arrangements regarding the libretto, and Massenet cannot give himself "heart and soul" to the music until he knows that the contractual agreement regarding the libretto is in order.[27]

Thirty miles north of Milan one comes upon Lake Como, which stretches northward for another thirty miles into the mountains. The beauty of the surrounding scenery and the salubrity of the climate have long made the Lago di Como one of

---

[*] If the Trocadéro concerts by the Turin orchestra were an artistic success (and notable for their representation of Italian composers), the financial results were ruinous, for the mammoth hall was scarcely half-filled. The orchestra then proceeded to Lyon, where two concerts were given in the Grand Théâtre on 16 and 17 July.

the most celebrated of Italian lakes. Numerous villages dot its banks where, in the old days, were scattered the gay villas of the Milanese aristocracy, surrounded by luxuriant gardens and vineyards, with wooded hills rising above. Liszt and the Countess d'Agoult paused here to admire the scenery, and it was at Como that their second daughter, Cosima, was born on 18 December 1837.

The city of Como lies at the southern tip of the lake. Assuming that Massenet arrived here as planned on 19 September 1878, he would have taken one of the frequent boats to the village of Cernobbio, two and one-half miles up the lake on the west bank. Here he presumably stopped, or at least was entertained, at the Grand Hotel Villa d'Este et Reine d'Angleterre, which had been opened as recently as 1873 as a luxury hotel.

The place has a romantic history. Long ago, at the mouth of a mountain stream called the Garrovo, some nuns had built the cloister of Sant'Andrea; by the mid-sixteenth century it was abandoned in ruins. Cardinal Tolomeo Gallio purchased the property and in 1568 asked the architect Pellegrino Pellegrini to build for him a country house in keeping with his wealth and position. The Villa Garrovo, as it was called, was embellished with decorations in Renaissance style and had a formal Italian garden. The Cardinal's nephew Tolomeo, duke of Alvito, inherited the property, which remained with his descendants until sold in 1782 to the Marquis Don Bartolomeo Calderara. The marquis, at a somewhat advanced age, had married a Vittoria Peluso, more familiarly known in the corps de ballet of La Scala as La Pelusina. Widowed, Donna Vittoria soon married a handsome youngish general, Domenico Pino, and the Villa became famous for its receptions and entertainments.

In 1815, the Villa was purchased by Caroline of Brunswick, Princess of Wales, who renamed it Villa d'Este after one Guelfo d'Este, a remote ancestor of both the House of Brunswick and the reigning English House of Hanover. Extensive alterations were made to the property, including the building of a theater in the left wing of the villa. Concerts, comedies, and tragedies were given, and there was a constant coming and going of artists and visitors from far afield.[*] Eventually the luxurious property became too great a burden for private ownership, and in 1873 a company was formed to convert the Villa d'Este into a luxury hotel.

Across the lake from the Villa d'Este was the village of Blevio, where the Villa Ricordi was situated. Not far away was the Villa Taglioni, where Marie Taglioni, the great dancing star of Paris and other capitals, had lived for a time after her retirement in 1847. The Villa Ferranti had belonged to Giuditta Pasta, who created the title rôles in Donizetti's *Anna Bolena* (1830) and Bellini's *La Sonnambula* (1831) and who died here on 1 April 1865.

---

[*] The unhappy Caroline, spied upon and accused of imprudent conduct by her husband the Prince of Wales, was refused admission to his coronation as George IV on 19 July 1821 and died nineteen days later. The villa then passed successively to Prince Torlonia (Caroline's Roman banker, to whom she was in debt), to Prince Domenico Orsini, and in 1834 to Baron Ippolito Gaetano Ciani, who made it a center of patriotic activity for the Risorgimento.

The *Souvenirs* state that the Massenets were invited by Giulio Ricordi "to spend the month of August at the Villa d'Este." In reality, as we have seen, Massenet did not even plan to arrive at Lake Como until 19 September, and his wife and daughter did not leave St. Moritz until 13 September. The "month of August" was thrown in to make it appear that Massenet was present (he was not!) at a performance of *Il Re di Lahore* at Vicenza on 15 August. Having opened this Pandora's box, the *Souvenirs* had to extend the two weeks' trip to Italy into a "prolonged stay" in order to account for the opening of *Il Re di Lahore* at the Teatro Comunale, Bologna, on 3 October.

In all likelihood, the Massenets simply spent a week or so as guests at the Villa Ricordi, where they enjoyed the company of Ricordi's wife and children, and met Arrigo Boito and the young singer Marie Van Zandt.* The *Souvenirs* then jump to the Hotel Bella Venezia in Milan, where Ricordi brought the poet Zanardini to read to Massenet the scenario for *Erodiade*. It seems plausible that during the first days of October, on the road from Lake Como to Bologna, he stopped over in Milan for the express purpose of discussing matters with Zanardini.

On 1 October 1878, Massenet was appointed professor of counterpoint, fugue, and composition at the Conservatoire to fill the vacancy created by Bazin's death. He was to remain in this position for eighteen years, and we can review his activity as a teacher a little later. He met his class on Tuesdays and Fridays at half past one. We know that from 1880 onward his salary remained fixed at three thousand francs per annum.[28] In 1878, the other professors of composition were Reber and Massé.†

The appointment was hailed by the younger generation as the dawn of a new era, the opening of the Conservatoire to new ideas. It was Massenet, not yet thirty-five, who had forced open the doors of the staid Opéra with *Le Roi de Lahore*. Bazin had represented austere tradition, mere grammar and syntax. Reber was assessed as a reactionary whose mind was closed to progress. Massé, gravely ill, rarely met his classes. Massenet had none of the shriveled dryness of his colleagues, it was said, but from the start made friends with his students, treating them not as children but as individual personalities, each requiring guidance in its own particular direction. He discussed and analyzed the music of the masters, while at the same time preparing his students in practical ways for the Prix de Rome competitions. It was a joy to at-

---

* There is no tradition that "Massenet stayed here" at the Villa d'Este; perhaps one day careful scrutiny of the hotel's archives will reveal the facts, confirming or discrediting the statement in the *Souvenirs* that Boito "was also [*sic*] a guest at the Villa d'Este." Boito did indeed stop there on other occasions. Marie Van Zandt, just turning seventeen, was the daughter of the American singer Jennie Van Zandt and was preparing for her stage debut the following year at Turin as Zerlina in *Don Giovanni*. She would soon be a star at the Paris Opéra-Comique, creating the title rôle in Delibes's *Lakmé* in 1883.

† Henri Reber (1807–1880) was appointed professor of harmony in 1851, then succeeded Halévy as professor of composition in 1862. Victor Massé (1822–1884) succeeded Leborne as professor of composition in 1866 and resigned in 1880. When Ambroise Thomas was elevated to the directorship in 1871, no successor for composition was appointed, though it is noteworthy that Jules-Laurent Duprato (1827–1892) was advanced from *agrégé* to professor of harmony in that year.

tend his classes, for he made them into a kind of conversation containing both substance and originality.

César Franck's organ class seems to have been awkwardly scheduled at the same hour, even though students were sometimes enrolled in both classes. Occasionally Franck would find his classroom quite empty, and then he would open the door to his colleague's classroom and attempt to entice some of his organ students away from Massenet's fascinating discourse.[29] The two were always on friendly terms, though undoubtedly Massenet was concerned lest his composition students, beyond learning to play the organ, be pulled into the orbit of Franck's general influence.

The death of Bazin had also left vacant a chair in the Académie des Beaux-Arts, for which Massenet was persuaded by Ambroise Thomas to announce his candidacy. Election day was fixed for Saturday, 30 November 1878. There were, of course, many candidates for the vacancy, the foremost being Saint-Saëns.

The Institut de France, prestigious symbol of French culture, was established in 1795 to provide a great national association for the promotion of the arts and sciences. Some of the constituent academies had already had a long and distinguished history. After 1832 the Institut comprised: (1) the Académie Française (founded 1635); (2) the Académie des Inscriptions et Belles-Lettres (founded 1663); (3) the Académie des Sciences (founded 1666); (4) the Académie des Beaux-Arts (founded 1795); and (5) the Académie des Sciences Morales et Politiques (founded 1795).

The Académie des Beaux-Arts comprised forty chairs (*fauteuils*) divided into five sections: painting (fourteen chairs); sculpture (eight); architecture (eight); engraving (four); and music (six). Once elected to the Académie by a vote of its members, the individual retained his chair for life, being concurrently a member of the Institut.[*] To be elected, besides securing the necessary votes, a man must be twenty-five, French, and a resident of Paris.

In addition to its forty chairs for regular members, the Académie des Beaux-Arts had honorary chairs for men of distinction—ten for *membres libres* (Frenchmen who had made a notable contribution as patrons or connoisseurs)[†] and ten for *associés étrangers*.[‡] Furthermore, the music section was allowed its quota of six foreign *correspondants*.[**]

In 1878, the six chairs of the music section were occupied by (1) Gounod;

---

[*] A chair could also become vacant when a member was elevated to one of the six posts of permanent secretary to the Institut. This happened, for example, in 1854 when Halévy was made a secretary and his chair in the Académie des Beaux-Arts was filled by Clapisson.

[†] As for example Baron Haussmann, elected in 1867, and the Barons Alphonse and Edmond de Rothschild, elected in 1885 and 1906, respectively.

[‡] The foreign associateships of the Académie des Beaux-Arts were occasionally extended to composers, as for example, Haydn (elected 1801); Salieri (1805); Rossini (1823); Meyerbeer (1834); Verdi (1864); Brahms (1896); and Boito (1910).

[**]Among some thirty foreign correspondents for music during the nineteenth century may be mentioned Liszt (1881), Grieg (1891), and Tchaikovsky (1892). Max Bruch (1898) and Humperdinck (1908) were ejected from membership by action of the Académie on 5 December 1914.

(2) Reber; (3) Victor Massé; (4) Ambroise Thomas; (5) Reyer; (6) vacant through the death of Bazin.* Thirty-four members of the Académie des Beaux Arts assembled on Saturday, 30 November, at three o'clock, to fill the vacancy. On the first ballot the votes ran thirteen for Saint-Saëns, twelve for Massenet, six for Ernest Boulanger, two for Edmond Membrée, and one for Jules-Laurent Duprato. On the second ballot, the friends of Saint-Saëns stood firm, while six of the previously scattered votes were switched to make the tally eighteen for Massenet, thirteen for Saint-Saëns, and three for Boulanger. Gounod, Reber, Massé, and Reyer had held out obstinately for Saint-Saëns. Ambroise Thomas, of course, favored Massenet. It was therefore the votes of seventeen of the twenty-nine painters, sculptors, architects, and engravers that elected Massenet.

Some further details were recounted in the *Souvenirs*. Massenet spent that Saturday, as usual, giving lessons in various parts of Paris. Between five and six o'clock, he told Hartmann, he would be at the home of a pupil at 11 Rue Blanche, and Hartmann said that he would come there and ring twice if Massenet were elected to the Institut. Sure enough, the pupil's rendition of Stephen Heller's *Promenades d'un solitaire* was interrupted by two sharp rings, and the servant rushed in to announce that "two gentlemen have come to embrace your professor." When Massenet reached home he found waiting to congratulate him four members of the Institut, painters Ernest Meissoner and Alexandre Cabanel and architects Hector Lefuel and Théodore Ballu. Meissoner carried a report of the sitting of the Académie showing the results of the two ballots. Massenet gallantly sent off a telegram to Saint-Saëns: "My dear colleague, the Institut has just committed a grave injustice." To which Saint-Saëns, bitterly disappointed, is said to have replied: "I entirely agree with you."[30]

A fortnight later Massenet, in formal attire with white tie, was introduced as a new member to the Académie des Beaux Arts by its permanent secretary, Count Delaborde. Thereafter he was privileged to attend the sessions, dressed in the academician's dark green uniform with black breeches, and to draw the academician's annual salary of fifteen hundred francs.

Meanwhile, on 14 November 1878, Massenet began the song cycle *Poème d'amour* to poems by Paul Robiquet, which he would not complete until toward the end of the following year. The autograph of one of the songs, "La nuit sans doute était trop belle," bears the marginal comment: "Paris. First composition written on my table-piano, the first day. Thursday, 14 November 1878. Rue Malesherbes. Cold. Snow." This was a special piano that looked like an ordinary table, covered with green leather bordered with a narrow gold band. The lowering of a little board disclosed

---

* From about 1850 on, the occupants of the six chairs for music were as follows: (1) Clapisson, 1854–66; Gounod, 1866–93; Théodore Dubois, elected 1894. (2) Reber, 1853–80; Saint-Saëns, elected 1881. (3) Auber, 1829–71; Massé, 1872–84; Delibes, 1884–91; Guiraud, 1891–92; Paladilhe, elected 1892. (4) Thomas, 1851–96; Lenepveu, 1896–1910. (5) Berlioz, 1856–69; Félicien David, 1869–76; Reyer, 1876–1909; Fauré elected 1909. (6) Carafa, 1837–72; Bazin, 1873–78; Massenet, 1878–1912; Charpentier, elected 1912.

the keyboard of a Pleyel piano, cleverly concealed. It was to become a favorite companion of his labors. On 26 November, Massenet wrote to Ricordi that he had started *Erodiade*.[31]

The enterprising Albert Vizentini got up a music festival for the Hippodrome for 17 December 1878. Though complaining of the cold, snow, and distance ("away out of town, clear at the end of the Champs-Élysées"), some fifteen thousand spectators turned out—or perhaps it was twenty thousand, as some claimed.[*] At a cost of fifty thousand francs, a platform had been installed over the arena, with innumerable little gas heaters to take off the chill. "Tout Paris" came, with Mme de MacMahon in the loge of honor. The acoustics were good, and it was reported that the orchestra sounded brilliant. Vizentini conducted the "dead composers" (as one critic put it), while Gounod, Saint-Saëns, and Massenet conducted their own works. Massenet had programmed the "Paradise of Indra" from *Le Roi de Lahore*. At rehearsals only the usual full orchestra was employed, but for the grand soirée Massenet had secretly summoned a whole array of extra brass instruments for special effect. As Alfred Bruneau remarked with apparent satisfaction, Saint-Saëns was furious at this trick—the more so as "he managed the baton very awkwardly," while Massenet had an "enchanting, persuasive, and irresistible talent as conductor." [32] In fairness be it said that all three composers were recalled to loud acclaim. There was to be a second Hippodrome festival the following month.

As might be expected, Massenet wrote to Ricordi on 26 December that he had been in bed for two days with a serious cold. He hoped, however, to recover in time to conduct at the second Hippodrome concert. Time flies, he wrote. In scarcely a month he must be in Milan for rehearsals of the singers, chorus, and ballet. Ricordi is to remind the management of La Scala that travel expenses have been promised. He has received a charming letter from Barbarani at Venice, who says that La Fossa [Amalia Fossa, soprano] will remain there. This was apparently a reference to a coming opening of *Il Re di Lahore* at Venice, for which Massenet was convinced that careful preparations were being made.[33]

As the year 1878 closed, Massenet could have had little inkling of what the second half of his life would hold in store. And yet, now in his thirty-seventh year, he already had much to be thankful for: reputation and honors for which many had had to wait much longer. Financial success would come a little later.

---

[*] The Hippodrome de l'Alma was in use from 1877 until 1892. The site was not far from the Place de l'Alma, between the Avenue de l'Alma (now George V) and Avenue Joséphine (now Marceau). The Hippodrome boasted a glassed-over roof that could be partly opened in fine weather. Besides an oval track, eighty-four by forty-eight meters, there was a central arena thirteen meters in diameter. Six thousand spectators could be seated comfortably, and besides there was a vast promenade extending around the bleachers where additional throngs could stand or walk about.

1879–1881

Hérodiade

O N 1 JANUARY 1879, MASSENET wrote to Ricordi, having previously sent New Year's greetings by telegram. He discusses details for *Il Re di Lahore*, and says that plans for the coming trip to Italy will be crystallized in a few days. This time his wife and daughter will not accompany him. Ricordi had obviously sent a package of goodies: the cheese was bewondered, the marzipan "Bologna sausage" was delicious, and the *pannetone* had by now quite disappeared.[1]

The second Hippodrome festival was held on 9 January. Writing to Ricordi the next day, Massenet claimed that there were twenty-five thousand spectators, six hundred musicians, and over sixty thousand francs in receipts.[2] The third act of *Le Roi de Lahore* was again given, and this time Delibes and Joncières appeared on the program.* Noël and Stoullig, in *Les Annales du théâtre et de la musique*, had this to say:

> What was needed was some noisy works, and above all some composers put on exhibition; the public adores that. Nothing entertains them so much as seeing the composers at work on the podium. To contemplate the curling moustache of Joncières, the long hair of Massenet, and Léo Delibes's *barbe de sapeur:* this is what interests them far more than to hear the works of these star composers. Massenet triumphed again, and the applause following the performance of the Incantation scene—encored, as it was the last time— rose to a delirium. His *Le Roi de Lahore* had certainly had a brilliant return engagement at the Opéra, and the season of Hippodrome concerts will surely not close without a request for still a third performance of the third act of this opera. Perhaps there is something in the orchestration of M. Massenet that is adapted better than any other to the acoustics of this hall of iron and glass: in any case, up to now no music had produced as much effect as that of the young master.

Further concerts were given at the Hippodrome on 25 January and 11 February, and the season closed with a Berlioz festival on 8 March 1879.

---

* Delibes with fragments from *Sylvia*. Joncières conducted the chorus of cossacks and the polonaise from his *Dimitri*, and the prelude to *La Reine Berthe*.

Massenet's journey to Milan was roundabout, by way of Vienna and Budapest. He left Paris on 11 January and was presumably back in Paris by 8 February, when his leave from the Conservatoire expired. On 13 January he wrote to Ricordi from the Grand Hotel in Vienna, mentioning that he was traveling with "one of my best friends, whom you know," Armand Gouzien, editor of the *Journal de musique* in Paris.[3] They were definitely in Budapest 16–20 January. Massenet attended a dress rehearsal of *Le Roi de Lahore* (in a Hungarian translation by K. Abrányi), and Baron Frigyes Podmaniczky, intendant of the National Theater, gave a luncheon in his honor. He visited Liszt and also Mme Soldes, actress of the Népszinház (People's Theatre), where he attended a performance of *Niniche*. On 25 January 1879 *Le Roi de Lahore* opened in Budapest, and Liszt attended the first performance.[4] But Massenet had already hurried on to Italy, planning to arrive at Venice on 21 January.[5] In Milan, he looked in on the final rehearsals at La Scala and renewed acquaintance with his circle of Italian friends.

Il Re di Lahore opened at La Scala on 6 February 1879 and attained twenty performances—a good showing, considering that Verdi's *Don Carlo* had twenty-one performances that season, and Giovanni Pacini's *Saffo* fifteen. The cast included Francesco Tamagno (Alim), Anna d'Angeri (Nair), Édouard de Reszke as guest (Timur and Indra), Jean Lassalle and then Giuseppe Kaschmann (Scindia), and Montalba (Kaled).

The long trip and the excitement were exhausting, so that Massenet reached Paris in an ailing condition. He wrote to Ricordi on 13 February that he was only now arising from his sickbed. His wife and daughter were glad to see him again and to hear of his experiences.[6]

An interlude in the life of Tchaikovsky may be interjected here, though he did not meet Massenet until 1889. Tchaikovsky had spent December of 1878 at the Villa Bonciani in Florence, in precarious proximity to Mme von Meck at the Villa Oppenheim.* He touched briefly at Paris in early January before going on to Clarens, Switzerland. Here he started to compose *The Maid of Orleans* (completed fifty-two days later in Paris, on 5 March). On 18 February 1879 he again arrived in Paris, staying until mid-March. On 25 February he went alone to a Colonne concert to hear Berlioz's *Faust*, one of his favorite works. On 9 March Colonne programmed Tchaikovsky's symphonic poem *The Tempest* (preceded by Mendelssohn's Reformation Symphony), but the composer found himself disliking his own work, not entirely because of the bad performance.

Tchaikovsky also attended *Le Roi de Lahore* at the Opéra, and was so impressed that he bought the score. He wrote to Mme von Meck: "I know that you do not care very much for Massenet, and hitherto I, too, have not felt drawn to him. His opera,

---

* Nadezhda von Meck was a wealthy widow with eleven children. She admired Tchaikovsky's music and gave him financial support. (He dedicated to her his Fourth Symphony.) They carried on a lively correspondence but agreed never to meet in person. Being in Florence at the same time raised the risk of their accidentally running into each other.

however, has captivated me by its rare beauty of form, its simplicity and freshness of ideas and style, as well as by its wealth of melody and distinction of harmony." He went on to compare its love duet with Goldmark's *Queen of Sheba*, declaring that Massenet's music was far simpler, fresher, more beautiful, more melodious.[*]

At the Châtelet on Good Friday, 11 April, the Concert Colonne opened with Saint Saëns's *Marche héroïque* (dedicated to the memory of the painter Henri Regnault, 1843–1871), and closed with Massenet's *Ève*, sung by Mme Brunet-Lafleur and Lassalle. Ten days later Massenet wrote to Ricordi that he was working steadily and that he hoped to finish *Hérodiade* by November and to orchestrate it during the winter, so that "all will be ready for next spring."[7]

On 20 May 1879, Massenet wrote to his physician, Dr. Joseph Michel, asking for news of Mme Michel (who had perhaps been ill or traveling). His own health is "better from day to day," and he mentions the *entrée en loge* set for the following week.[†] This is the last letter I have seen marked "38 Rue Malesherbes."[8] By October the Massenets were installed in an apartment in the Rue du Général Foy.

After his visit to Hungary and meeting with Liszt, Massenet had arranged for orchestra a *Marche héroïque de Szabady*, which he dedicated to Liszt (who made a piano transcription). The occasion for the performance of this work was a grand festival at the Opéra, on 7 June 1879, for the benefit of the flood victims of Szégédin. The affair was organized by Armand Gouzien (Massenet's companion on the trip to Hungary), and the concert lasted until midnight. The program opened, naturally, with Berlioz's *Racóczy March*, and proceeded through a mishmash of vocal selections (including the quartet from *Rigoletto*), larded with such staples as Reyer's overture to *Sigurd* and Saint-Saëns's *Danse macabre*, up to the concluding Weber-Berlioz *Invitation to the Dance*. Massenet conducted his *Marche héroïque de Szabady*, which evoked 150 words of commentary by the critic Auguste Vitu. The latter was impressed by the rather bizarre and continuous syncopations and the crescendos leading to the "utmost limits of sonority, to a kind of furious baying of the bells on off-beats." It seems, went on this imaginative critic, as though one is "present at some furious battle, at the sacking of a city taken by storm," but amidst the horrors of war one feels a great sentiment of victory and the rousing voice of Hungarian patriotism. "The success of this new production of M. Massenet was considerable, and reveals the inexhaustible

---

[*] Karl Goldmark (1830–1915) brought out *Die Königin von Saba* at the Vienna Hofoper on 10 Mar. 1875; it became very popular for its brilliance and oriental flavor. By coincidence, this *Regina di Saba* opened on 1 Mar. 1879, at the Teatro Regio in Turin, where it was undoubtedly compared with *Il Re di Lahore* of the year previous. Stéphane Wolff, in his chronicle of the Paris Opéra for 1875–1961, mistakenly stated that *Le Roi de Lahore* was given there for the fifty-seventh and last time on 7 Mar. 1879. In fact, the work was given sixteen times in 1879, namely: 24, 28 Mar.; 2, 7, 16, 23, 26 Apr.; 2, 7, 14, 19 May; 30 July; 4, 13 Aug.; 5, 26 Sept. Other notable first performances of *Le Roi de Lahore* abroad were: Munich (in German), 13 May 1879; Covent Garden, London (in Italian), 28 June 1879; Buenos Aires (Italian), 26 July 1879; Rio de Janeiro (Italian), 13 Oct. 1879; Prague (Czech), 29 Oct. 1879; and Madrid (Italian), 14 Feb. 1880.

[†] The Prix de Rome winner for 1879 was Georges-Adolphe Hüe (1858–1948), a pupil of Reber.

resources of the young composer, whose powerful imagination produced that sono-rous fresco called the Paradise of Indra."[9]

On 13 June Massenet wrote that "in about a week" he would go to London, where *Il Re di Lahore* was given at Covent Garden on 28 June 1879. He was back in Paris by 2 July, and on the tenth he momentarily left "the sweet embraces of Salomé" (i.e., *Hérodiade*) to write to Ricordi. He thinks that Emma Turolla, whom he heard in London, might make a good Salomé.[10] Then, at the session of the Académie des Beaux-Arts on Saturday, 19 July, Massenet read the customary eulogy of his prede-cessor, François Bazin.

While Massenet was writing *Erodiade* for Italy, he undoubtedly kept an eye out for the main chance at the Paris Opéra. The exact genesis of the Italian and French versions seems to have been purposely muddled for the public record. However, Arthur Pougin's account, written in 1912, has the ring of conviction: "What is certain is that, after the success in Italy of *Le Roi de Lahore*, and at the request of the famous publisher Giulio Ricordi, the poet Zanardini had written the original libretto, taking as subject one of the *Trois Contes* published by Gustave Flaubert—the one entitled 'Hérodias'—and that it was for this libretto that Massenet wrote his music." Why was it not first given in Italy? "I do not know," says Pougin; "at any rate, the Italian libretto was translated into French by Paul Milliet and Henri Grémont, or rather 'adapted,' with notable changes involving important modifications in the score."[11]

Inasmuch as *Hérodiade* did not receive its première in Italy, but rather at Brus-sels (1881), the *Souvenirs* as well as most other French biographers conveniently ig-nore the work's Italian inception. Thus, according to one recent biographer, "It was one evening [no date given] when Massenet was celebrating at the Café Anglais the success of *Le Roi de Lahore* that the libretto of *Hérodiade* was handed to him."[12] If, as we have seen, Zanardini's libretto was ready no later than October or early November of 1878, nothing would have prevented Paul Milliet and Georges Hartmann (mas-querading as "Henri Grémont") from undertaking a translation almost at once. Just which performance of *Le Roi de Lahore* was being celebrated at the Café Anglais is nowhere made clear. The fiftieth would have been a logical occasion, and that fell on 7 May 1879.

The *Souvenirs* speak to this subject as follows:

> During the summer of 1879 I lived at the seashore at Pourville near Dieppe. Hartmann, my publisher, and Paul Milliet, my collaborator, spent the Sun-days with me. When I say with me, I abuse the words, for I kept company but little with these excellent friends. I was accustomed to work fifteen or sixteen hours a day, sleep six hours, and my meals and dressing took up the rest of the time. It is only through such tireless labor continued without ceasing for years that works of great power and scope can be produced.

In his letters to Ricordi of that summer, Massenet dissembled. He took care to date them always from "Paris" (where, if need be, Hartmann could always drop them into the mail to insure the proper postmark). For Ricordi's information, he "will spend the summer in Paris without budging, so as not to interrupt the train of work" (13 June). Or, because of constantly working at "our opera," he "did not leave Paris this summer" (10 September). In amusing contrast is a letter of 9 August to an unidentified friend: he is constantly running down to the sea to bathe, advancing his work by the method of one dip, eight measures, another dip, sixteen measures, and so on.[13]

With Massenet so concentrated on his work, Ninon and Juliette went off that summer on their own. They seem to have gone first to Plombières, a spa with hot springs in the Vosges that had been a favorite resort of Napoleon III. A handsome new casino had been opened in 1876; there were picturesque walks and a park in the valley where the village stands. From there they went to St. Moritz, and by early September they were back in Fontainebleau, where Massenet would go to see them from time to time.

Massenet rarely gave his own street address in his letters, so the inclusion of "38 Rue du Général Foy" on 11 October 1879 suggests that the Massenets had recently moved to the new address—perhaps on 1 October.[14] The house was renumbered as 46 around 1892, and this would be their domicile until the autumn of 1903.

A half mile northwesterly from the Madeleine, the Boulevard Malesherbes appears to be blocked by the imposing façade of the church of Saint-Augustin, built in 1860–71 by Victor Baltard in Romanesque style. Actually, the boulevard veers slightly to the left and runs on toward the Parc de Monceau, which in those days was surrounded by the handsome private houses of the very rich. Saint-Augustin's was a wealthy and fashionable parish. Juliette would one day be married in this very church. Parallel with the Boulevard Malesherbes, the Rue du Général Foy[*] extends for three long blocks from the church to the Rue de Monceau. No. 38 (later 46) is the fourth house south of the Rue de Monceau, on the east side of the street. Solid and well proportioned, with six stories and an attic, the house as well as the whole street suggests dignified affluence.[†]

Massenet continued to push ahead with *Hérodiade*. On 9 October he was invited to lunch at the home of Gustave Dreyfus, "one of our most wealthy collectors of art objects," and there he met the great Verdi baritone Francesco Pandolfini. The singer, not wanting to return to La Scala without some great new rôle, broached the subject of creating Hérode for the 1881 season. In the sequel, this did not work out. But Massenet was thinking ahead about casting: for Salomé he wanted a soprano of

---

[*] Maximilien-Sébastien Foy (1775–1825) was a Napoleonic general who served in the Peninsular campaign during the time Massenet's father was in Spain. Perhaps the two met at some time.

[†] A directory of 1888 shows the occupants of No. 38 as follows: (1) Baron V. A. Duperré, commandeur of the Légion d'Honneur; (2) Comtesse de Gourdon; (3) Comte Lang de Baumanoir; (4) Jules Massenet, chevalier of the Légion d'Honneur, member of the Institut, composer of music; (5) Nanot, commissaire-répartiteur adjoint des contributions directes; (6) Prou de Sainte-Radegonde, avocat à la cour d'appel; and (7) Triber, senator. Later (directory of 1900), Massenet had as neighbor in the same house the composer René de Boisdeffre (1838–1906).

the type of Emma Turolla, Marie Heilbron, or Emma Albani, while Hérodiade must be a dramatic mezzo-soprano.[15]

At last, on 27 December 1879, Massenet reported to Ricordi that "our *Erodiade*" was finished; now he could proceed with the orchestration. When Ricordi comes to Paris for the première of *Aïda* [it was given at the Opéra on 22 March 1880], Massenet will play through *Erodiade* for him. Then they can look forward to January 1881, which would be about the time [for the première at La Scala], would it not?[16]

On 2 January 1880, Massenet acknowledged receipt of a gift parcel from Ricordi weighing twelve kilograms. Maestro Lorati, at Mantua, had sent a nice telegram regarding the opening there of *Il Re di Lahore*.[17] Massenet then went to Lyon for rehearsals of *Le Roi de Lahore*, which was performed there on 18 January at the Théâtre Bellecour, of which Guimet was director. The performance (including Lassalle) was excellent, with brilliant *mise en scène* copied after that of La Scala, and with many orchestral players imported from Turin and Mantua. Their affection for Massenet was indeed touching when they went to the station at 6:00 A.M. in the bitter cold to see him off, reminding him of the good days of warm welcome in Italy.[18]

The orchestration of *Hérodiade* was begun on 24 January 1880 and would occupy Massenet for nearly eight months. Meanwhile, during February and March, Colonne programmed some Massenet works at the Concerts du Châtelet. On 1 February, the concert opened with Berlioz's overture *Les Francs-Juges* and closed with the *Tannhäuser* overture. In between were Saint-Saëns's Second Symphony in A minor (written in 1859), Gounod's *Hymn to Saint Cecilia*, and fragments from Massenet's *Les Érinnyes* and Delibes's *Sylvia*. The program for 8 February included a Bach concerto for three pianos (played by Delaborde, Diémer, and Saint-Saëns); an unnamed Widor composition, which the reporting critic found boring; and Massenet's *Scènes napolitaines*, which pleased, and which the critic found "delightful in their animation and orchestral verve."[19] On Good Friday, 26 March, Saint-Saëns was on hand to conduct Act III of *Samson et Dalila*, and Massenet conducted the "Marche Céleste," "Divertissement," and "Incantation" from Act III of *Le Roi de Lahore*. (The "Incantation" was encored.) Gounod having sent regrets, Colonne conducted three fragments from the *Messe de Sainte-Cécile*. But then Gounod himself appeared to conduct them when the program was repeated on Easter, 28 March. Some hinted that Gounod had at first got cold feet, cowed by the success of *Aïda* at the Opéra and fearful that Massenet's pretentious score would throw his own Mass into the shade.

Massenet hoped, at least, to attend the first performance of *Aïda* at the Opéra on 22 March.* To Vaucorbeil (director of the Opéra since 21 July 1879) he addressed a plea for two seats ("do not forget me, I beg of you"), and promised to bring around the score of *La Vierge* in a few days.[20] At the Opéra-Comique, Delibes brought out

---

* *Aïda* had been first given in Paris at the Théâtre-Italien (in Italian) on 22 Apr. 1876, with Stolz, Waldmann, Masini, and Pandolfini, and with Verdi conducting. The original French version by Camille du Locle and Charles Nuitter was then staged at the ephemeral Théâtre-Lyrique Ventadour on 1 Aug. 1878.

Gabrielle Krauss. Courtesy Paul Jackson.

his new opera *Jean de Nivelle* on 8 March 1880. The work, while containing some excellent music, was weak as opera; it ran up a hundred performances in a year and was then dropped. Massenet, writing to Delibes on 16 March, says that he will be free only the following week to spend an evening at *Jean de Nivelle*. Meanwhile, he has had the score in his composition class, and "my students, already twice, applauded and admired your music. . . . They say you have never done better."[21] A little later (25 April) Massenet asked "the composer of *Jean de Nivelle*" to use his influence with Carvalho. Specifically, Massenet's pupil Lucien Hillemacher hoped to improve his chances in the Prix de Rome trials by getting Alexandre Talazac, tenor of the Opéra-Comique, to sing in his cantata. This would require the director's permission.[22] Indeed, Hillemacher's setting of *Fingal* (text by Charles Darcourt) carried off the prize. This was the first of Massenet's Prix de Rome winners.[*]

From one of those indispensable marginal annotations (this time in the score of *Hérodiade*), we learn that Juliette, now twelve, attended her first communion on Thursday, 29 April 1880.[23] Massenet's little girl was rapidly growing up. Three years later he would write to Emma Borch that Juliette was now "a tall girl like her mother."[24]

Vaucorbeil decided to initiate some Concerts Historiques de l'Opéra, and these began on 22 May 1880 with *La Vierge*, a *légende sacrée* for soloists, chorus, and orchestra comprising four parts: (1) L'Annonciation; (2) Les Noces de Cana; (3) Le Vendredi Saint; (4) L'Assomption. Massenet conducted, and the rôle of the Virgin Mary was sung by the eminent Viennese soprano Gabrielle Krauss. There was also a second performance (29 May), but the projected third performance (for 5 June) was canceled for lack of patronage. It would probably take a Massenet renaissance of

---

[*] Lucien's brother, Paul Hillemacher (1852–1933), had won the Prix de Rome in 1876 as a pupil of François Bazin. From 1881, the brothers wrote their scores in collaboration, signing "P. L. Hillemacher," and came to be well regarded in French music. In 1905 they published a biography of Gounod.

Poster for *La Vierge*, 1880.

explosive proportions ever to resuscitate this work.* Still, Louis Schneider considered it "one of the most important oratorios of Massenet," better suited to the concert hall than the church, to be sure, but notable for its moments of expression and orchestral eloquence that are "pure Massenet."[25] For a time, the best-known fragment was the orchestral prelude to the fourth part, known as "Le Dernier sommeil de la Vierge," featuring a solo cello and muted strings.

---

* Part 4 only, "The Assumption," was given twice at the Concerts du Conservatoire early in the 1900s with Aïno Ackté. Part 1 only, "The Annunciation," was given at the Gala Massenet at the Opéra, 4 June 1942, commemorating the centenary of the composer's birth.

Massenet was steadily orchestrating *Hérodiade* in the hope of a La Scala première early in 1881. Then, in June, he read a letter Hartmann had received from Ricordi that left him "much saddened, for it seemed to show a complete disinterest in *Hérodiade*" (to Ricordi, 16 June, 1880). "Remember, dear friend," Massenet went on, "that when I was in Milan last year it was you yourself who proposed to come and hear my score, and you said that once you had heard it you would then make the arrangements with La Scala. What happened: you came to Paris without wanting to hear *Hérodiade*, which was easy enough for you since you stayed a week longer than you had intended." Evidently, he wrote, the La Scala calendar had some other work in view. Massenet would have preferred to know this right away, so as not to lose the winter season. Especially, he says, since he refused the work to London, Lyon, and Brussels, who wanted it.[26]

Massenet may have had tentative inquiries from these other theaters, but it is doubtful that he had any firm offers. He would certainly have had an eye on the Paris Opéra. Yet according to the official biographer, Louis Schneider, it was not until "the beginning of 1881" that Massenet played *Hérodiade* for Vaucorbeil, who refused it.[*] Schneider goes on to say that it was in February 1881 that Stoumon and Calabrési, of La Monnaie in Brussels, offered to stage the work. From the extant letters, we can assume that right up to the end of 1880 Massenet was still pinning his hopes on the miracle of a première at La Scala. (He was not far off, at that. *Hérodiade* opened at Brussels on 19 December 1881, and *Erodiade* at La Scala three months later on 23 February 1882.)

Historical hindsight helps to explain the situation as of the summer of 1880. La Scala did indeed have another work in view: Amilcare Ponchielli, the teacher of Mascagni and Puccini, brought out his *Il Figliuol prodigo* there on 26 December 1880, and it ran for sixteen performances that season, being considered an astonishing success.[†]

Massenet then injured his hand. But as soon as he could again take up his pen, he wrote first of all to his wife and Juliette, who had gone to the Vosges, and then to Ricordi (25 June 1880). Ricordi and Hartmann had meanwhile exchanged long letters, which the latter read to Massenet. Whatever the content, Massenet was deeply discouraged, though he seemed to realize that his depression would pass. The disagreement, if it can be called that, reached a climax by 23 July ("how can you speak of 'hostility'?"), and apparently a decision by Hartmann to "stay out of it as regards *Hérodiade* in Italy."[27] Thereafter, the Massenet-Ricordi correspondence moved along once more in the old track.

---

[*] Schneider (1926), 75. By then Vaucorbeil was committed to Gounod's *Le Tribut de Zamora* (Opéra, 1 Apr. 1881), and no doubt Thomas's *Françoise de Rimini* was on his waiting list (it was given on 14 Apr. 1882). His suggestion that the libretto of *Hérodiade* needed the attentions of a *carcassier* (professional bonesetter, or fixer-upper of librettos) may have been a hint that the name of Paul Milliet did not carry enough weight for the Opéra. Perhaps, too, he did find the story incendiary and libidinous, as has been claimed.

[†] Ponchielli's *La Gioconda* had been given at La Scala on 8 Apr. 1876, attaining four performances; revived there on 12 Feb. 1880, it ran for fourteen performances. His ballet *Le Due gemelle* was also doing well, with fifteen performances at La Scala in 1880.

At the Conservatoire, it was time for the annual trials for the various prizes. As already noted, the Premier Grand Prix de Rome went to Lucien Hillemacher. Second prize was awarded to Georges Marty, also a pupil of Massenet. Claude Debussy that year (1880) won a first prize in accompaniment, but in harmony he did not even place. The jury reviewing the essays in harmony (Thomas, Massenet, Delibes, Guiraud, Lenepveu, Paladilhe, and Taudou) took exception to Debussy's realization of the given bass of twenty-seven measures, in which they found at least a half-dozen instances of parallel fifths or octaves. Notwithstanding, Debussy was advised to enter a class in composition, not with Massenet but with Guiraud. Massenet's influence would have been pervasive enough in any case. Especially a few years later, after *Hérodiade* and *Manon*, melodies "à la Massenet" were much in vogue among the Conservatoire students. Indeed, when Debussy tried for (and won) the Prix de Rome in 1884, he consciously wrote *L'Enfant prodigue* in the manner of Massenet to impress the judges of the Institut, of whom the professional musicians constituted only a small minority.

By the end of July 1880, the eighteen-year-old Debussy had joined the household of Nadezhda von Meck at Interlaken. He was engaged to give lessons to her children during the summer and to play four hands with Mme von Meck, who described him as a brilliant pianist without depth or maturity. In August, Mme von Meck wrote to Tchaikovsky from Arcachon (a resort near Bordeaux) that Debussy "is a pupil of Massenet's in theory [?], so of course Massenet is his hero." And again from Florence in September she wrote that her little Bussyk, as she called him, "is preparing to be a composer and writes very nice little things, but it is all an echo of his professor, Massenet. He is now writing a trio, also very good, but redolent of Massenet." [28]

For at least a part of the summer of 1880 Massenet was at Pourville, a seaside resort four kilometers east of Dieppe on the English Channel. Late in June, Ninon and Juliette went to Fontainebleau, and perhaps elsewhere later, for they returned to Paris on 22 November after their "three months of vacation." Various letters to Ricordi of late July, August, and September deal with casting and other matters relating to *Hérodiade*. Thus, on 11 August, Massenet writes that he is working on the orchestration of Act IV and is correcting the proofs of the piano-vocal score. He plans to go that evening to hear Ladislas Mierzwinski in *Les Huguenots*. On 16 September, he acknowledges receipt of Acts I and II of the manuscript orchestra score; he had needed these for guidance in orchestrating Act V, Scene 2. As for the piano-vocal proofs: "How I should like to sing and play for you this entire work! But I cannot travel just now." When the task is finished he plans to rest, and "sleep until nine o'clock in the morning." [29]

The orchestration of *Hérodiade* was finished on 19 September 1880. By 22 September, all that remained was to look over the piano-vocal reduction of Act V, and then "I will have absolutely finished: Te Deum Laudamus." In Paris, Massenet writes, there is much talk of Ponchielli and Boito; he mentions *Gioconda* and *Mefistofele* as works that deserve a French translation. [30]

Jean Lassalle. Photography by Falk. Courtesy Paul Jackson.

Without news from Giulio Ricordi for several weeks, Massenet wrote to Tornaghi (of the firm of Ricordi) on 17 October, asking that they acknowledge receipt of Acts I, II, and III of the orchestra score, already sent, and promising that Hartmann would send Acts IV and V shortly.[31] Actually the last two acts were apparently not sent until mid-December. (Hartmann was probably having them copied out first.) On 19 November, upon returning from the provinces where he had to conduct some concerts (not further specified), Massenet wrote again to Giulio Ricordi: something must be decided about *Hérodiade;* he had been unable to obtain a leave for Lassalle to create Hérode in Milan; perhaps the première could be delayed while they looked for someone—the rôle was too important to entrust to just anyone.[32] Then, on 22 December 1880, Massenet wrote that he hoped to see the Italian translation before the work was engraved so that he could make the necessary musical adjustments. He broaches the subject of remuneration: their contract called for a sum of money upon delivery of the manuscript.[33] There is a hiatus in the available Massenet-Ricordi correspondence from this point until January of 1882, from which time the negotiations for *Erodiade* at La Scala moved along smoothly.

Meanwhile, the season of concerts, operas, and plays was well under way in Paris. On 17 November 1880, *Michel Strogoff* by Adolphe-Philippe d'Ennery and Jules Verne opened at the Châtelet. This was billed as a "pièce à grand spectacle" in five acts and sixteen scenes, adapted from Verne's popular adventure story of 1876. With typical Jules Verne suspense, it involved a voyage from Moscow to Irkutsk, accomplished in twenty-four days despite great obstacles and perils.[*] By way of incidental music Massenet furnished an *Air de la retraite* for fifes and drums of the Preobrazhensky grenadiers and a *Fanfare* for the chevalier-gardes.[34] On 3 December, a comedy by Victorien Sardou and Emile de Najac entitled *Divorçons* began its run at the Palais-Royal. We know that Massenet attended a performance on 23 December. A few years later he would be writing incidental music for other Sardou plays. At the Pasdeloup concert of 19 December, the young Hungarian violinist Jenö Hubay played a suite on *Le Roi de Lahore* orchestrated by Massenet himself. (On the same program Saint-Saëns played "Schubert's piano fantasy, orchestrated by Liszt," and the audience cheered the finale of *Walkyrie*.)

Relieved from the labors of *Hérodiade*, Massenet began on Monday, 20 December, the scoring of his sixth orchestral suite, *Scènes de féerie*. That evening he had "dinner at Passy with my wife and Juliette." We can perhaps surmise that this was at the home of M. and Mme Camille Claude, to whom a copy of *Le Roi de Lahore* was inscribed "Passy, 10 November 1879." Some pieces for the Conservatoire trials in cello and trumpet were dated at Passy, respectively 5 and 10 July 1880. And for 15 August 1880, an annotation in the score of *Hérodiade* reads, "Passy, noon. They are bringing a large tree to the middle of the garden." It is not a question of a Massenet domicile at Passy. Alfred Bruneau mentioned "the beloved park of a friendly and ostentatious home where, like all my comrades who were prize winners of 'the class,' I had luncheon as a reward for my showing in the Prix de Rome competition."[†]

On New Year's Day 1881, the weather was fine. If I decipher correctly the terse annotation in *Scènes de féerie*, Massenet met Grieg, called upon Ambroise Thomas with congratulations for his elevation to *grand officier* in the Légion d'Honneur, and was invited at nine to a reception at the presidential palace of the Élysée. Besides, he "worked for the first time with my beloved English lamp." On 2 January, Massenet began at five in the morning with page 28 of *Scènes de féerie* and stopped at ten with page 34—five hours for twenty measures of rather full orchestration. On 3 January was the funeral of the architect Hector Lefuel (close friend of Gounod since their days at the Villa Medici), and in the evening Juliette went to the Châtelet to see *Michel Strogoff*.

A note of 5 January to the Conservatoire librarian, the Alsatian Jean-Baptiste-Théodore Weckerlin, suggests Massenet's concern with the work of his favorite pupils. He had requested and received the manuscript orchestrated cantatas of Marty (who had won second prize in 1880) and Bruneau (who had not placed). He wants to keep them two months longer to compare with the reorchestration he is having them do. He now wants Claudius Blanc's score for the same reason.[35] Meanwhile,

---

[*] As late as 12 July 1881, Massenet wrote to the theater director requesting four tickets for some friends: "*Michel Strogoff* is still very popular, and I am pursued by requests!" (Bibliothèque Nationale). The piece was revived on 22 Aug. 1882 at the Porte-Saint-Martin and on 10 Apr. 1897 at the Châtelet, where it ran for 208 performances.

[†] Alfred Bruneau (1935), 19. In 1881 (when no first prize was awarded), both Bruneau and Paul Vidal received second prizes.

too, Massenet had a new colleague at the Conservatoire. Henri Reber had died on 24 November, and Delibes was appointed to succeed him as professor of composition.[*]

Souvenez-vous, Vierge Marie (text by Georges Boyer), for chorus and solo, organ and orchestra, was performed by Pasdeloup at the Cirque d'Hiver on 27 January 1881. On 4 February, at eight in the morning, *Scènes de féerie* was finished; the suite consists of: (1) Cortège; (2) Ballet; (3) Apparition; (4) Bacchanale. The best information I can find is that it was performed in London in March 1881 and at the Concerts du Châtelet some time in 1883.

Massenet was now occupied with the rewriting of *Hérodiade*, including the "important modifications in the score" mentioned by Pougin.[†] If we trust Schneider, it was in February of 1881 that Stoumon and Calabrési, directors of La Monnaie, offered to stage *Hérodiade* at Brussels the following season.[36] In the *Souvenirs*, it was "one day that summer" [1881] when Massenet casually met Calabrési on the Boulevard des Capucines, and the latter at once asked to put on *Hérodiade* at Brussels.

Then, suddenly, we find Massenet in Barcelona, where he stayed at the Fonda de los Quatro Naciones. In a letter of 18 April to Quinzard (who was associated with Hartmann), he tried out his Spanish with "Buenos dias caros Quinzardos!" The skies are ever so blue, but not necessarily Massenet's spirits. The "first festival" has been set for Saturday [23 April], and it looks promising. He was present for the Easter celebration [17 April], which was more like a carnival and quite impossible in Paris. As for "our Spanish friends," they are so busy that Massenet is left quite alone. He apparently planned to leave right after the mentioned festival, for if Quinzard wishes to write he must post his letter by five o'clock on Thursday at the latest.[37]

This is the only documentation I have found for a visit to Spain. Pending a better explanation, we may perhaps attribute to a lively imagination the account given in the *Souvenirs* regarding the opening motive of the ballet music for *Le Cid:* "I was in the very country of *Le Cid* at the time [no specific time or place is mentioned!], living in a modest inn. It chanced that they were celebrating a wedding and they danced all night in the lower room of the hotel. Several guitars and two flutes repeated a dance tune until they wore it out. I noted it down." We are reminded, actually, of Oscar Browning's account of the night at Capri in 1873, when "a golden or diamond wedding" was celebrated and nothing was danced but the Tarantella from six in the evening until midnight. There was also the vivid memory of Bourgault's party at the Villa Medici in 1864, when the spectators so far "forgot themselves" as to join in the saltarella to the strumming of guitars. As for the shifting of locales, René Brancour, writing in 1922, was also quite imaginative: the Austrian trumpets heard in Venice [1865] simply migrated "twenty-five years" [*sic*] later into Act IV of *Le Cid* of 1885![38]

---

[*] Reber's vacant chair in the Académie des Beaux-Arts was filled by the election of Saint-Saëns on 19 Feb. 1881.

[†] Later there was also a new Act II, Scene 1, for which the piano-vocal draft was completed on 6 Jan. 1882. (Autograph, Bibliothèque de l'Opéra.)

Massenet was probably not back in Paris in time to hear Pasdeloup's performance on 24 April 1881 of *Les Argonautes* (soli, chorus, and orchestra) by Augusta Holmès. The previous year the score had been entered in a competition of the City of Paris and received only honorable mention. By a narrow vote of eleven to nine (Massenet was on the jury) the prize had gone to Alphonse Duvernoy for *La Tempête*, performed by Colonne on 24 November 1880.

In the Prix de Rome trials of 1881, no first grand prize was awarded. Second prizes went to Alfred Bruneau and Paul Vidal, and an honorable mention to Edmond Missa—all three Massenet pupils. Alfred Bruneau (1857–1934) went on to a substantial career as composer, conductor, and music critic. In his slender volume on Massenet (issued by Delagrave in 1935), he earns respect on the very first page: besides Massenet, he admired Gounod, Saint-Saëns, Reyer, Bizet, César Franck, Lalo, and Chabrier. His sincere affection for Massenet is therefore not marred by hyperbole or the perpetration of silly legends.

Alfred Bruneau entered the Conservatoire in 1873 to study cello with Franchomme, and in 1876 won a first prize. Then, after three years in Savard's harmony class, he entered Massenet's composition class in December of 1879. The vast room in which the class was held contained a piano, a chair, and wooden stools. There were a dozen students, of whom Bruneau mentions Gabriel Pierné, Lucien Hillemacher, Georges Marty, Paul Vidal, and Ernest Chausson. There were also numerous auditors—French, Belgian, Italian, German, English—who sat on benches behind the regular students and followed in their scores Massenet's analyses. With his air of *gaminerie*, wrote Bruneau, one might have taken Massenet for an older brother, except that the red ribbon of the Légion d'Honneur in his buttonhole commanded serious respect. He then wore a short blond beard; later he kept only the moustache. He wore his hair long over a "magnificent forehead," his eyes sparkled with roguish inquisitiveness, and his gestures were supple and expressive.

The instruction was supposed to include counterpoint and fugue (in which he was quite expert),[*] but Massenet felt that he was really there for "composition." He would examine the submitted fugues rapidly, and he appointed Hillemacher as monitor to help the others over the rough spots in their counterpoint. Though Massenet analyzed symphonies, he did not push his students in this direction for their own creative efforts, nor towards sonatas, chamber music, trios, or quartets. Bruneau did not recall that any of the class ever had the idea of bringing in a sketch in any of these forms. Essentially a man of the theater (and also interested in grooming his students for the Prix de Rome cantata), Massenet would sit down at the piano and play over the lyric scenes submitted, making them sound effective, and addressing to each an indulgent and flattering remark. Bruneau insists that Massenet at no time encouraged students to imitate his style, but sought to develop the originality of each.

Those students who were being encouraged to enter the Prix de Rome compe-

---

[*] In André Gédalge's *Traité de la fugue* (1901), among the many fugue subjects set for exercises are thirteen by Massenet.

tition would be invited on Sunday mornings to the Rue du Général Foy, where they would be initiated into the mysteries of orchestration. Bruneau then volunteers an insight into his teacher's daily life. Not having a studio at home, he kept his table-piano and favorite swivel chair in his bedroom. He slept little and usually awakened before dawn, put on some comfortable robe over his nightgown, and went at once to his chair to work. It was only later, says Bruneau, that Massenet became addicted to a special red robe and skullcap that made him look like a "juvenile cardinal." Bruneau likens the chair and table-piano to the work space of some punctual and conscientious employee. For Massenet was consumed by a feverish and interminable drive: the need to write. He never leaned back to reflect, to dream, or to calm for a moment his exalted nerves.[39]

To this I might add: such were Massenet's regular *working* hours, when he put down on paper the ideas already assiduously collected (and surely reflected upon and dreamed about!) during the other hours of the day or night. His mind was accustomed to activity. Even in the midst of conversations, the subconscious part of his mind was often at work—scheming and planning the layout of a scene or searching for just the right orchestral sonorities to clothe a preliminary sketch.

October brought some innovations to the Parisian musical scene. On 15 October 1881, the hall of the Opéra was for the first time lighted by electricity, for a gala in honor of a visiting Congress of Electricity! On Sunday, 23 October, Charles Lamoureux inaugurated the Nouveaux Concerts at the Château-d'Eau. He was praised as a conductor, the undertaking was successful, and the Concerts Lamoureux (as they came to be called) continued to flourish under Camille Chevillard, Paul Paray, and others, after Lamoureux's death in 1899. Less significant was the series founded by Broustet at the Cirque des Champs-Élysées (Cirque d'Été). Édouard Broustet (1860–1895), son of a rich merchant of Toulouse, had studied piano with Camille Stamaty, Henri Ravina, and Henry Litolff, traveled abroad, and directed the Concerts Populaires de Toulouse and the Casino orchestra at Luchon. His first concert at the Cirque d'Été, on 30 October 1881, was adjudged "too ambitious," including, for example, Beethoven's Fifth Symphony.

In Brussels, the Théâtre de la Monnaie stands in the Place de la Monnaie, long ago the site of an *atelier monétaire*. The first theater at this location opened its doors in 1700 and was replaced in 1819 by another and more elegant theater.* This hall burned down on 21 January 1855 and was quickly replaced with a new theater, inaugurated on 24 March 1856.

Through the years, La Monnaie was oriented toward the French opera reper-

---

* Where Auber's *La Muette de Portici* was staged on 12 Feb. 1829, then banned for a time by the censors, then revived on 24 Aug. 1830, the birthday anniversary of William I (of Orange), King of the Netherlands. The duo "Amour sacré de la patrie," sung by the tenor Lafeuillade and the baritone Cassel, had to be repeated; Masaniello's air "Aux armes" roused the spectators to action. In the sequel, Prince Leopold of Saxe-Coburg was elected king of the Belgians, becoming head of a constitutional monarchy on 21 July 1831.

toire, though also justly proud of its stagings of French translations of Italian opera and of Wagner, with liberal attention also to Belgian composers. Stoumon and Calabrési took over the directorship of the theater on 1 September 1875, remaining on for ten years.[*] Oscar Stoumon, a composer, had been professor at the Brussels Conservatoire. Édouard Calabrési had been a conductor, notably at Liège and at New Orleans. Their principal conductor at La Monnaie was Joseph Dupont, who had also succeeded Vieuxtemps in 1873 as director of the Concerts Populaires. It fell to the lot of *Hérodiade* to be the first work by a French composer to have its world première at La Monnaie.[†]

In October of 1881 the rehearsals of *Hérodiade* began. Massenet stayed at the Hôtel de la Poste, in the Rue Fossé-aux-Loups at the corner of the Rue d'Argent. The first reading is described in the *Souvenirs:* the composer, directors, librettist, Hartmann, and cast assembled in the great public foyer, sitting on chairs arranged in a semicircle around a grand piano. The artists included Marthe Duvivier (Salomé), Blanche Deschamps (Hérodiade), Edmond Vergnet (Jean), Adolphe-Théophile Manoury (Hérode), Léon Gresse (Phanuel), and Auguste-Alfred Fontaine (Vitellius). Massenet played through the score for them, singing all the roles including the choruses, breaking off from time to time to refresh his energies at the plentiful buffet that had been laid out. In this way all involved were quickly apprised of the composer's intentions. When their turn came to approach the buffet, Massenet hinted slyly, there was not much food left!

As preparations went on, Massenet had to travel back and forth between Paris and Brussels. His friend Alphonse de Rothschild supplied him with a railway pass, and the customs officers at the border stations got to know him quite well. Ever thoughtful, Massenet sent them tickets for *Hérodiade*.

For the première, on Monday, 19 December 1881, a trainload of Parisians took the route north. Alfred Bruneau, on his first assignment as music critic, described the occasion. An effervescent crowd assembled at the Gare du Nord and stormed the train, which seemed inadequate to seat them all comfortably.[‡] The voyagers, in a gay mood, played outrageous jokes on the customs officers, then entered Belgium as though it were a conquered country (mingling strains of *La Brabanconne* with *La Marseillaise*) and proceeded to "occupy" Brussels. The triumph of *Hérodiade* was beyond their expectations, and during intermissions the corridors resounded with excitement. Afterward, all the Parisians were invited to a hospitable supper in the

---

[*] Succeeded by Dupont and Lapassida during 1885–89, Stoumon and Calabrési again became directors 1889–1900. Maurice Kufferath was appointed director in 1900.

[†] *Hérodiade* was followed, in this respect, by Reyer's *Sigurd* (1884) and *Salammbô* (1890), D'Indy's *L'Étranger* (1903), Chausson's *Le Roi Arthus* (1903), and Pierre de Bréville's *Éros vainqueur* (1910).

[‡] According to Schneider, more than four hundred Parisians made the trip to Brussels for the première. Special trains also ran from Liége, Antwerp, Ghent, and Louvain, enabling persons from those cities to return home right after the opera.

roomy salons of the newspaper *L'Indépendance belge*. Here Massenet was late in arriving, so that all began to wonder what had happened to him. Characteristically, he had tarried to express his indebtedness to the cast. At last he arrived escorting the blonde Marthe Duvivier, who had been especially applauded as Salomé.

Hérodiade was given in Brussels fifty-five times the first year. The scenario is rather different from the more familiar version of Oscar Wilde's one-act drama, *Salomé.*[*] Herod Antipas, Tetrarch of Galilee and the territories beyond the Jordan, took as his spouse the wife of his brother Philip, namely, Herodias—in French: Hérodiade. The incestuous relationship is vigorously denounced by John the Baptist. Herodias had left her own country and abandoned her daughter. Herod's political dream is a confederation of allies strong enough to throw off the Roman yoke. Still, Herod trembles before the power of Rome, as when the proconsul Vitellius arrives with a strong escort. Furthermore, Herod is distracted by a violent infatuation for Salomé, whom he adores from afar (not declaring his love until Act III, Scene 2). Salomé, of Siloam, is depicted as an essentially good girl; desolated when her mother abandoned her, she is torn between hatred for such inhuman conduct and the need for a mother's affection. Far from asking for John's head on a silver platter, she wants to die with him!

◄O►

Act I shows an exterior court of Herod's palace in Jerusalem at dawn. When merchants and chiefs from the various territories squabble over priorities, the Chaldean soothsayer Phanuel deplores such civil strife. Salomé has obeyed a voice that told her to go to Jerusalem where the Prophet preaches a new hope. "Il est doux, il est bon," she sings; when will she hear him again? As an abandoned child, alone and miserable, she had once met John, whose melodious, tender voice had calmed her heart. Herodias demands that Herod punish John; that very morning he had barred her way with the insult: "Tremble, Jezebel!" But Herod can do nothing; John is too important a person with the Jews. When John pursues Herodias right into the palace with his "Jezebel," they all flee from his malediction. Salomé, however, falls at John's feet. She loves him, which is agreeable to John so long as it is an idealized love.

Act II: Herod is stretched out on an ivory bed in his private chamber at siesta time. He cannot sleep for thinking of Salomé. The sweet, restful Oriental airs sung by slave girls are of no help; no more so their Babylonian dance. They offer a potion guaranteed to produce at least a vivid dream of Salomé. "Vision fugitive," he sings, drinks the potion, and indeed imagines that he sees Salomé. Phanuel dismisses the slaves with the remark: "Is this the man who makes an empire tremble?" According to prophecy, says the soothsayer, the people are miserable; they await a Messiah, and revolt is in the air. The scene changes before our eyes to the great square before the palace. The multitude shouts "Glory" to Herod, who has promised them liberty, and

---

[*] Written in French in 1893; produced in Paris, 1896, when Wilde was in Reading Gaol.

messengers bring news of the readiness of Herod's allies. But the sound of a Roman fanfare heralds the unexpected visit of the Roman proconsul, Vitellius, who wonders why the people appear embarrassed at his coming. As representative of Tiberius, he proclaims that the Temple of Israel will be respected. John and his followers, Salomé among them, enter singing "Hosannah!" Vitellius goes into the palace with Herodias, who has promised to allay any possible political suspicions and save face for Herod.

Act III: Herodias comes to Phanuel's apartment at night, seeking to learn what the stars hold in store. Phanuel points out Salomé entering the Temple across the square; Herodias's rival for her husband's affections is her own daughter! Scene 2: John has been imprisoned in a subterranean vault inside the Temple. Salomé comes at dawn to pray for him. Herod also comes, planning to save John as a useful ally. Seeing Salomé there, Herod declares his love for her, but she responds that she loves another. The priests and multitude enter ("Marche Sainte," "Scène religieuse," "Danse sacrée"). The priests demand that John be condemned for spreading dissent and perverting the people. The accused is brought in and interrogated by Herod, who finds insufficient grounds to condemn him. But the priests signal the Temple guards to seize John. When Salomé reveals her love for John by pleading to die with him, Herod loses interest in saving either of them.

Act IV opens in the underground crypt where John, contemplative and resigned, is ready to die for the cause of justice and liberty. Salomé comes, and he realizes that he has tender feelings for her. They embrace. The high priest interrupts with "Your hour has come!" Meanwhile (Scene 2), Vitellius and the Roman soldiers are entertained with ballets of Egyptians, Babylonians, Gauls, and Phoenicians at the palace festivities. Salomé rushes in to plead for John's life or, if that cannot be spared, the privilege of dying with him. The entrance of an executioner with a bloody sword indicates that it is too late. Salomé moves to stab Herodias with a dagger, but the latter proclaims: "I am your mother!" Whereupon the unhappy Salomé stabs herself.

———————————— •◆• ————————————

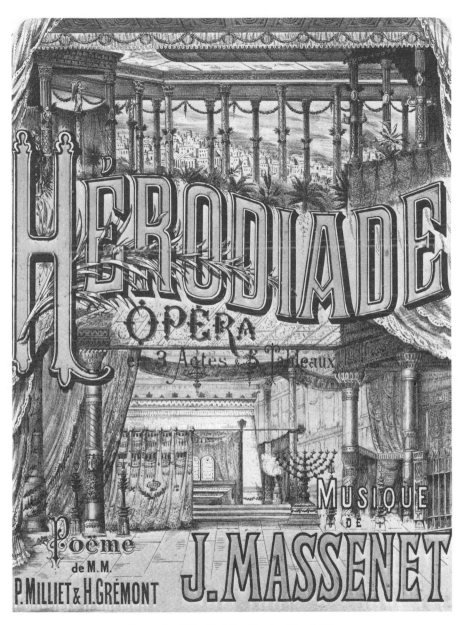

Poster for *Hérodiade* by Charles Lévy, 1881.

MANON

Poëme de M.M.
H.MEILHAC et PH.GILLE

Musique de
J.MASSENET

Poster for *Manon* by Antonin-Marie Chatinière, 1884.

1882–1884

Manon

Antoine-François Prévost (1697–1763), known as the Abbé Prévost, was born at Hesdin (Artois), some forty miles south of Calais. He was educated by the Jesuits, joined the army, and then entered the Benedictine congregation of Saint-Maur. His dual temperament, which alternately attracted him to the monastic life and the worldly, caused him to flee the austerity of the Maurist cloister in 1728. His life was then devoted to arduous literary activity, and his first long romance, entitled *Mémoires d'un homme de qualité*, appeared in 1728–31. The seventh volume of this work, *L'Histoire du chevalier des Grieux et de Manon Lescaut* (1731), was published separately two years later and, banned by the authorities, created a sensation. It was a simple, realistic account of a man consumed by overpowering passion for an unworthy woman. Des Grieux, involved in adventurous incidents, loses all sense of honor and dignity. In a revised edition of 1753, the moral and edifying element was given somewhat more emphasis.

In the nineteenth century, Scribe wrote the scenario for the ballet *Manon Lescaut* by Halévy, which was given at the Opéra on 3 May 1830, with well-merited success. In 1851, Théodore Barrière and Marc Fournier produced a dramatized version, in five acts, at the Gymnase. When this was revived at the Vaudeville on 4 February 1875, it was surely talked about, whether or not Massenet actually attended a performance. Scribe had also written a libretto for Auber, whose *Manon Lescaut* was staged at the Opéra-Comique in 1856. For the centenary of Auber's birth, selections from his operas were given at the Opéra-Comique on 30 January 1882, including Act III of *Manon Lescaut* with Mlle Isaac and the tenor Fürst. The public was much impressed, and the scene was repeated on 1 February. Massenet, by that time well started on his own *Manon*, surely took note.

The genesis of *Manon* is still somewhat obscure as to details. The *Souvenirs* simply state that "one morning in 1881" Massenet went to see Henri Meilhac in his rooms at 30 Hue Drouot. Carvalho, director of the Opéra-Comique, had asked Massenet to set Meilhac's three-act libretto of *Phoebé*, but the subject was not to the composer's liking. At their meeting, Massenet is supposed to have suggested that they try instead, not "Manon Lescaut," but simply "Manon." According to the pretty anecdote that follows, Meilhac said he would see what he could do, invited Massenet to lunch at Vachette's the next day, and there, under his napkin, Massenet found the "first two acts" of *Manon.*

Meilhac had broken up with Ludovic Halévy, and was now collaborating with Philippe Gille.* Although in the *Souvenirs* "the other three acts followed within a few days," the final shape of the libretto was not established until the summer of 1882, when Massenet insisted upon the Seminaire scene and the scene of the Hôtel de Transylvanie. The music for the first two acts was finished by May of 1882, for on a trip to Brussels at that time Massenet played over "the first acts" for the Belgian journalist Gustave Frédérix and the singer Marthe Duvivier, who was still singing Salomé in *Hérodiade.* On another trip to Brussels, in the autumn of 1882, the Seminaire scene was drafted at the Hôtel de la Poste. In any case, the work was completed and ready for a hearing with Carvalho on 12 February 1883. The orchestration was begun on 6 March 1883, and completed (except for the prelude) on 15 July 1883.

Meanwhile, to get on with the chronicle of Massenet's life, we go back to 1882. Arriving home from Brussels at five-thirty on the morning of 30 December 1881, Massenet set himself at once to answering the letters of congratulation on *Hérodiade.* It was traditional, too, to send New Year's greetings to one's friends. The correspondence with Giulio Ricordi (in which there is a gap from December 1880) resumes on 19 January 1882, and all is now rosy. If Massenet had "resisted" the idea of *Erodiade* at La Scala, it was through fear of a possible failure there and not because of lack of confidence in Ricordi. The latter has unjustly offended Hartmann, and all he needs to do is write a little note, and then get on with the arrangements. Eight Roman trumpets will be needed for La Scala, wrote Massenet, and *Erodiade* should be announced as a "grand opera-ballo."[1] Further letters discuss details of the coming production. Then, at seven o'clock on the evening of 7 February, Massenet took the train from Paris, spent a few days at Nice and Antibes, and arrived at Milan at 12:25 P.M. on Sunday, 12 February.[2] He had asked Ricordi to reserve an *entresol* room, with fireplace, at La Bella Venezia, "like the one I had in 1879."

The La Scala season had opened as usual on San Stefano (26 December 1881), this time with Rossini's *Guglielmo Tell,* which was given sixteen performances. This was followed on 15 January by Meyerbeer's *Gli Ugonotti* (thirteen times) and on 7 February by the world première of Smareglia's *Bianca di Cervia.*† The ten performances of Smareglia's opera gave way on 23 February 1882 to Massenet's *Erodiade,*

---

* Meilhac and Gille furnished the libretto for Robert Planquette's *Rip Van Winkle* which was, however, first given in an English translation in London, 13 Oct. 1882, becoming a huge success.

† Antonio Smareglia (1854–1929) was sent by his parents to Vienna to study engineering, but upon hearing the works of Beethoven, Mozart, and Wagner, he changed to music. After studying with Franco Faccio at the Milan Conservatory, he produced *Preziosa* at the Teatro dal Verme in 1879. *Bianca di Cervia* was his second opera. Hanslick, upon hearing one of his later works in Vienna, described Smareglia's music as "Italian soul and melody wedded to German science and precision." Smareglia eventually became totally blind; but having a fabulous memory, he was able to dictate his compositions to an amanuensis.

also for ten performances. The cast included Medea Borelli (Salomé), Ladislas Mierzwinski (Jokanna), Gustavo Moriami (Erode), Romano Nannetti (Fanuele), Ezio Ciampi-Cellaj (Vitellio), and Elena Teodorini, an excellent dramatic soprano who had also sung Bianca in Smareglia's opera and Valentina in *Gli Ugonotti*, as Erodiade.

It was during this trip to Milan, according to Paul Milliet, that the seed for *Werther* was planted.[3] Massenet, Hartmann, and Milliet, it seems, went together to Milan for *Erodiade*. In the train the conversation turned to Goethe and worked around to *Werther*. [This novel of romantic love had been translated into French fifteen times between 1776 and 1797; besides, Hartmann knew German fluently.] Almost casually it was agreed that Milliet should write a libretto, and the journey ended at Milan on a note of elation. [The little matter of Massenet's stopover at Nice is not mentioned!] Milliet said he went to work on the libretto, spending years polishing and repolishing it in consultation with Hartmann but not with Massenet, who was occupied with *Le Cid*.[*] The *Souvenirs* ignore any such incident, giving instead a very pretty story of a visit to Wetzlar in August of some year not specified, followed by the statement that in the summer of 1885 Massenet, Hartmann, and Milliet came to an agreement to take up the task of writing *Werther*, for which Hartmann had "improvised a scenario." We shall cross that bridge when we come to it.

On 19 March 1882, Colonne performed *Scènes alsaciennes*, the seventh orchestral suite, at the Concerts du Châtelet. Séré assigned the composition of this work to 1881, which seems about right. That summer, we may suppose, Massenet's normally busy hands were restless to write something, for he was between *Hérodiade* and *Manon*. *Scènes alsaciennes* comprises four movements of descriptive music: (1) Dimanche matin; (2) Au cabaret; (3) Sous les tilleuls; (4) Dimanche soir. For the printed score Alphonse Daudet provided a literary elaboration:

> Alsace! Alsace!
>
> Now that Alsace is walled off, there come back to me my impressions of that lost land from former times.
>
> What I happily recall is the Alsatian village on Sunday morning, at the hour of the church service; streets deserted, houses empty, with a few old folks sunning themselves before their doors; the church filled; snatches of religious chants heard in passing.
>
> And in the tavern, in the main street, with its little panes of leaded glass, garlanded with hops and roses . . .
>
> Oh . . . la! Schmidt, something to drink!
>
> And the singing of the forest rangers as they go out for shooting practice!
>
> Oh! the joyful life and the gay companions!
>
> Further along, it was still the same village, but with the great silence of the summer afternoons. And at the very end of the place, the long avenue of lindens in whose shade, hand in hand, walked a loving couple. She, gently

---

[*] Milliet published this account in 1903, *after* the death of Hartmann.

leaning toward him and murmuring softly: "Will you love me always? . . . "

Also in the evening, in the great square, what sounds, what animation! Everyone at their doors, the bands of fair young lads in the streets, and the dancing to the rhythm of the local songs.

Eight o'clock! The beat of drums, the sound of bugles. It was the evening Retreat! the French *Retraite!* . . . Alsace! Alsace!

And when in the distance was extinguished the last roll of drums, the women called their children indoors. The old men relit their big, good pipes. And to the sound of violins the serried couples recommenced their joyous dance with hastened beat.

In a letter to Ricordi of 27 March 1882, Massenet mentioned that he had been to Brussels, whence he returned "four days ago," and that he would be leaving Paris shortly to supervise the dress rehearsal of *Le Roi de Lahore* at Nantes, to conduct a festival at Angers, and so on. On 20 April he wrote again from Paris asking for the return of "my orchestra score, which I need." Although Hartmann had sent a copy of the score for the production of *Erodiade,* Massenet had also sent along his own score, asking that it be checked note for note against the copy, for he did not trust the Paris copyists.[4]

Two events of the Paris season deserve passing mention. On 3 April, Auber's *Le Domino noir* attained its one thousandth performance at the Opéra-Comique, where it had first been produced in 1837. Auber and his librettist, Scribe, were no longer among the living to celebrate the occasion. Auber's music, with its old-fashioned sweetness and charm, was gradually losing favor to the works of a newer generation. On 14 April the last opera of Ambroise Thomas, *Françoise de Rimini,* was staged at the Opéra where it was given forty-two times until 1885.

The season at Brussels closed on 2 May 1882 with the fifty-fifth performance of *Hérodiade,* which Massenet conducted. It was a splendid occasion, as Massenet wrote to Ricordi from Paris on 7 May. Further good news was that his pupil Lucien Hillemacher had just won the prize of twenty thousand francs in the musical competition of the City of Paris. Ricordi, he said, would remember "that young man whom you met at Milan" and who had "played his *Loreley* score for me one morning on your piano."[5]

Massenet's works were subjected to arrangements of various kinds at the hands of others. Thus, on 22 May, Massenet acknowledged receiving a manuscript from Louis Baerwolf of Brussels, which he turned over to Hartmann with suitable praise.[*] Two months later (July 16), he thanked his correspondent for news of the success of "your fantasy on Hérodiade," which had been performed at the Concerts de Vauxhall au Parc, Brussels.[6]

In the Prix de Rome trials of 1882, Massenet's pupils made a clean sweep with

---

[*] Later (1889), this Louis Baerwolf was archivist at La Monnaie, where Édouard Baerwolf was conductor. Édouard seems to have been at Aix-les-Bains in 1891, and he conducted a performance of *Werther* at Marseille on 17 Nov. 1894.

their settings of Guinand's *Edith*. There had been no first grand prize the previous year, and now two were awarded: to Eugène-Georges Marty and to Gabriel Pierné. Honorable mention went to Xavier Leroux. All three would soon establish a place for themselves in French music. There were, of course, trials for prizes in all the other branches of music and acting, as for example: 21 July, singing (men); 22 July, singing (women); 25 July, *opéra comique*; 29 July, opéra. Auguste Vitu preserved a little vignette for 21 July, when Massenet served on the jury at the public trials of twenty-one male singers. The baritone Hettich sang an air from *Hérodiade* and was applauded, whereupon the spectators turned toward the jury loge to give Massenet an ovation.

Far away at Bayreuth, Wagner's *Parsifal* reached the stage on 26 July 1882. The piano-vocal score had been published, and in Paris the devout Wagnerians lost no time in giving it their attention. But when a tight little group comprising Vincent d'Indy, Emmanuel Chabrier, Henri Duparc, Gabriel Fauré, and André Messager assembled to read the new work, they were embarrassed by what they considered its decadence, if not senility. Their idol had let them down. Remarked one, pointing to the Prelude: "Why, it is just bad Massenet!" In retrospect, we might take this as a left-handed compliment for Massenet.

During the summer of 1882, Henri Meilhac went to Saint-Germain-en-Laye, staying at the Pavilion Henry-Quatre right on the famous terrace with its magnificent view of Paris in the distance. The delightful paths in the forest of Saint-Germain beckoned nearby—all this but a half hour's train journey from Paris. Massenet would sometimes come calling around five o'clock, when he knew that Meilhac's daily task was finished. The two would talk and discuss *Manon*, and here the Seminaire act was decided upon, as well as the scene of the Hôtel de Transylvanie.

In August, Massenet was invited to The Hague by C. J. Brecht, musical director of the militia band, to hear a band arrangement of excerpts from *Hérodiade* made by the assistant director, D. M. H. Bolten. The group gave daily concerts at the casino (Badhuis) during the summer season. Massenet was delighted with Bolten's arrangement, and promised to speak to his publisher Hartmann.[7] As an extra bonus, Massenet was installed at the Hôtel de l'Europe in the very room where the Abbé Prévost had once worked.[*] He was deeply touched at such kind thoughtfulness. By dead reckoning, we can assume that he was working on Act III of *Manon* at this time. The days slipped by as he made excursions to the dunes of Scheveningen, walked in the park Het Bosch, or was nuzzled by the tame deer in the Koekamp.

Late in September, Massenet was at Brussels where *Hérodiade* was being readied for a reopening on 3 October with a new Salomé, Rose Caron. He again stayed at the Hôtel de la Poste, in his former ground-floor room overlooking the Rue d'Argent, and it was here that he sketched the Seminaire act (Act IV) of *Manon*.

---

[*] The hotel, built in 1659 as a lodging for visitors from Haarlem and Gouda, was pulled down in 1906 and the site (10–24 Lange Houtstraat) occupied by the Antonio Aguilar Wine Co.

In November, Julie Cavaillé, after five years of widowhood, married Comte Amédée d'Eu de Ménil de Montigny. Paris directories toward the close of the nineteenth century list various counts and countesses as well as a Baron Montigny, with addresses but without given names. But it is possible that by 1900 Julie was the Mme de Montigny, widow, of 24 Rue de Lisbonne, which is not far from the Rue du Général Foy. Massenet's *Poésie de Mytis* (1902) was dedicated "to my sister, Mme de Montigny," and Julie died on 12 January 1905, in her seventy-third year.

In a letter to Ricordi of 5 December 1882, Massenet mentioned that Edmond Vergnet (the Jean of the Brussels *Hérodiade*) had just had "a fine success at the Châtelet in *Le Roi de Lahore*," and was coming to Milan. The reference is not clear. Was *Le Roi de Lahore* actually restaged by one of the various Opéra Populaire undertakings? Or did the tenor merely sing some excerpts at a Colonne concert? No doubt Massenet thought Ricordi would be more impressed by a general statement, without the details. A week later Massenet acknowledged receipt of "the splendid score of Boito." This was undoubtedly a new edition with French translation of *Mefistofele*, for Massenet expects to discover therein still more admirable things, thanks to the translation. "I shall go to Brussels for the première," he wrote; "and you? and he?"[*] Three days later (15 December) he wrote that he had received with some surprise a telegram from Scalizi [at Naples]; Ricordi had said nothing about a coming San Carlo performance, and Massenet could not afford the luxury of a trip to Naples. He hopes that his absence would not compromise the situation.[8] *Il Re di Lahore* was given at the Teatro San Carlo, Naples, on 25 December 1882.

Upon some undetermined occasion Massenet had met the Portuguese composer Augusto Machado, who had played for him the score of *Lauriane*.[†] The opera was to be performed at Marseille early in 1883, and on Christmas of 1882 Massenet wrote to Machado wishing him success. (See page 135.) Massenet regrets that "the trips [he] must take to Russia and Germany" will deprive him of the opportunity of coming to Marseille for *Lauriane*. Regards are to be conveyed to "our friend [?] who will no doubt come from Lisbon," and greetings to "our friend Lévy."[9] It is doubtful that Massenet would have gone to St. Petersburg at this time; *Il Re di Lahore* had been given there the previous season (10 February 1882). But in any case he was in Hamburg on 20 January 1883 to conduct the first performance there of *Hérodiade*, in a German translation.

On 12 February 1883, Massenet was invited to dinner at Carvalho's in the Rue de Prony, and after dinner from nine until twelve he played through the completed score of *Manon*. The librettists Henri Meilhac and Philippe Gille were there, and of

---

[*] Boito's opera was staged as *Méphistophélès* at Brussels, 19 Jan. 1883, with Léon Gresse, Jourdain, Delaquerrière, Marthe Duvivier, and Blanche Deschamps.

[†] Augusto Machado (1845–1924) studied at Lisbon, and also in Paris with Lavignac and Danhauser. He was later director (1892–1908) of the San Carlos theater in Lisbon, and director (1894–1910) of the Lisbon Conservatory. He composed numerous operettas as well as operas, and *Lauriane* proved to be an immense success.

[Postmark]: Paris 25 Dec. 82
Bᵈ Malesherbes

Monsieur Aug. Machado
Hotel du Petit Louvre
rue Cannebière

Bouches du Rhone   Marseille

Paris Noël /82

Certes oui je me
souviens de notre entrevue et de
l'audition de votre opéra!
— donc vous allez être
représenté — que d'émotions! —
je vous souhaite le plus
brillant résultat — et si les
voyages que je dois faire en
Russie et en Allemagne
me privent de l'occasion

de vous applaudir croyez
que je serai avec vous
par la pensée que je
vous garde fidèle et
très sympathique!
— Souvenirs à notre ami
qui viendra de Lisbonne
sans doute.

— amitiés à l'ami Lévy.

J. Massenet

This letter, written on two pages in Jules Massenet's hand, is addressed to the Portuguese composer Augusto Machado, who became friends with Massenet while studying in Paris and, indeed, was influenced by Massenet's operatic style:

> I certainly do remember meeting you and hearing your opera! — now it is to be produced — how thrilling! — I wish you a splendid success — and though the trip I must take to Russia and Germany will deprive me of the opportunity to applaud you, my warm and ever-loyal thoughts will be with you! — Greetings to our friend who will no doubt come from Lisbon. — regards to our friend Lévy.

The letter refers to the première of Machado's opera *Lauriane* in Marseille, 1883. "Lévy" may have been Émile Lévy, a publisher. Courtesy Manuscript Collection, University of Washington.

Marie Heilbron as Manon.
Photography by Benque.
Courtesy Paul Jackson.

course Mme Carvalho, now fifty-five and still singing, though she would retire in a couple of years. The auditors were delighted with the new work, and Mme Carvalho embraced the composer joyfully, exclaiming that she wished she were twenty years younger. As a consolation prize, Massenet dedicated the score to her.

The search was on for a Manon. For a time Massenet thought he had found just the right person in Mme Vaillant-Couturier, who was starring in Charles Lecocq's *Le Cœur à la main* at the Nouveautés. But Brasseur, the director of Les Nouveautés, sensing a golden opportunity, was willing to release her only on condition that Massenet write a work for his theater. It is said that Jeanne Granier was also considered for the rôle.[10]

In the fairy-tale atmosphere of the *Souvenirs* all things seem to happen by chance. So it was that, just after his interview with the director of Les Nouveautés, Massenet supposedly ran into Marie Heilbron in the foyer. Heilbron had married the Vicomte Panouse and was now rich, but still felt a nostalgia for the stage. Upon hearing about *Manon* she insisted that Massenet play it for her at once, despite the midnight hour. And so he fetched the score and went to Heilbron's place in the Champs-Élysées, where he played until four-thirty in the morning. "The next day," Heilbron signed the contract with Carvalho. (Actually, the contract was signed on 28 June 1883.)[11]

Another pretty account is given in the *Souvenirs* which, however, is in character with Massenet's sentimental nature. It seems that in the Boulevard des Capucines he often saw a young flower girl selling her fragrant wares. Though smitten by her fresh, youthful appearance, out of shyness he never spoke to her. Through a kind of obsession she became the prototype of the Manon he had in his mind's eye. Indeed, it was Mme Vaillant's resemblance to this flower girl that intrigued Massenet when he first considered her for Manon.

Meanwhile, the month from 5 February to 5 March was spent in preliminary planning of the orchestration. The drawn-out labor of actual scoring began with the first scene on the night of 6/7 March and was finished at seven in the morning on 15 July 1883. The prelude was apparently completed later, with the annotation "Allevard, 21 August 1883, 6:00 A.M."

At long last Saint-Saëns reached the stage of the Paris Opéra with *Henry VIII*, given on 5 March 1883. The work was elaborately staged and featured the baritone Jean Lassalle (Henry VIII), Gabrielle Krauss (Catherine d'Aragon), and Alphonsine Richard (Anne de Boleyn). The libretto, in four acts, was by Léonce Détroyat and Armand Silvestre, and Saint-Saëns had gone to England to research the musical atmosphere of the sixteenth century. Although *Henry VIII* never reached a one hundredth performance at the Opéra, it seems gratuitous to call it a failure. The score contains some fine music, with leading motives and with overtones of Meyerbeerian style. The opera was periodically revived (from 19 July 1889, in a reduced three-act version up to its eighty-seventh performance in 1919). *Henry VIII* is mentioned here as symbolic of the subtle threads connecting the destinies of the arch rivals Massenet and Saint-Saëns. Later, as we shall see, the prince of Monaco favored impartially the music of both composers. During the Monte-Carlo season of 1908, we shall find Massenet's *Thérèse* being followed a few weeks later by Saint-Saëns's *Henry VIII*.

At the Opéra-Comique, Delibes's *Lakmé* was staged on 14 April 1883, with the young coloratura Marie Van Zandt in the title rôle and Alexandre Talazac as Gérald. A week later, 21 April, Bizet's *Carmen* was revived after its seven years in limbo. Both works became mainstays of the repertoire.

Saturday, 23 June, was the day for judging the Prix de Rome settings of *Le Gladiateur*, a cantata text by Émile Moreau. First prize went to Paul Vidal, a pupil of Massenet. There were two second prizes: one for Claude Debussy, listed as a pupil of Guiraud, and one for Charles-Olivier René-Bibard, a pupil of Delibes. The contest in fugue came later, on 9 July, and Massenet noted with satisfaction that all the winners were from his class: first prizes, Grandjany and Perroni; second prize, Missa; first accessit, Kaiser; second accessit, Schwartz.[12]

As for the orchestration of *Manon*, Massenet took it along on his travels during the last two weeks of March. On the seventeenth there was a performance of *Marie-Magdeleine* at Ghent. Then he stopped over in Brussels where, on the nineteenth, he played over from the piano-vocal sketch the last scene of *Manon* for Frédérix at Berardi's. At Lille there was a festival on the twenty-second, and by the twenty-sixth Massenet and Hartmann were at Nantes for final rehearsals of *Hérodiade*, given there on 29 March 1883. Back in Paris, Massenet conducted two excerpts from *Hérodiade* at an Alsatian festival at the Opéra on 5 April. On that day he labored over *Manon* until three in the afternoon, then stopped exhausted, noting in the score that the weather was like summer.[13]

The first act (the inn at Amiens) was completed on 10 April, and the second act begun on the eighteenth. The twenty-ninth was a full day: starting at five in the morning with "Adieu, notre petite table," Massenet pushed on with twenty-six pages of orchestration until four-thirty that afternoon, completing Act II. Act III (Cours la Reine) was begun on 3 May, which was Holy Thursday (Ascension), and that evening there was a soirée at the home of Pierre Véron, critic for Le Charivari, in honor of the satirical journal's fiftieth anniversary. By 3 June the Seminaire scene was completed, and Act IV (Hôtel de Transylvanie) was orchestrated between 7 June and 7 July. Act V (La Route du Havre) was begun on 12 July. On the national holiday, 14 July, which fell on a Saturday, Massenet began faithfully at six o'clock on page 57. Some pages later he noted that he could hear all the bands returning from the parade: "What a din! for nothing!" By seven the next morning, Sunday, the final note of Manon was orchestrated.[14]

In August, Massenet seems to have had at least a brief vacation. He put the last touches to the prelude of Manon at Allevard (near Chambéry, in Savoy) on 21 August, and may have gone to Switzerland. In writing to Ricordi in mid-July, he had expressed regret at being unable to come to Lake Como with his wife and daughter, for "it appears that Switzerland will cause a postponement of the trip to Italy." On 18 September, back in Paris, Massenet wrote a cordial letter to Gabriel Pierné at the Villa Medici, enjoining him to be "punctual with your envoi, on the precise date."[15]

Nana-Sahib, a drama in verse by Jean Richepin, opened on 20 December 1883 at the Théâtre Porte-Saint-Martin, where it attained thirty-five performances. The incidental music by Massenet, running to forty-five pages, is preserved in the Bibliothèque Nationale. Aside from a marche anglaise for fifes and drums and a "Chant of the Brahmins," the pièce de résistance is a divertissement, "Nautch Hindou," for which the composer also made a four-hand piano transcription dated at the end "31 December 1883."

The year 1884 opened auspiciously with the staging of Manon at the Opéra-Comique on 19 January. The cast included Marie Heilbron (Manon), Alexandre Talazac (Des Grieux), Émile-Alexandre Taskin (Lescaut), and Cobalet (Comte des Grieux), with Jules Danbé as conductor.[*]

Some of the reactions may be briefly noted here. In Le Gaulois, L. de Fourcaud reminded his readers that the musical theater had outgrown the old genre of opéra comique with its airs, ensembles, and choruses strung together by dialogue. Nowadays it was a question of lyric drama, or lyric comedy, or perhaps operetta. Manon does not seem to be any of these. While recognizing in places the hallmarks of an eminent artist, Fourcaud was disappointed at a certain confusion and disunity in the work. Others, to be sure, might not share his view, as witness the warm reception

---

[*] Manon was given seventy-eight times in 1884, and ten times in 1885. Revived on 12 Oct. 1891, with Sibyl Sanderson, the work then remained in the repertoire.

accorded the second, fourth, and fifth acts. Edmond Stoullig noted that *Manon* was heatedly discussed because of its "novel tendencies," namely, the inclusion of "dialogue" without arresting the symphonic drama in the orchestra. In *Le Figaro*, B. Jouvin observed that Massenet sought a close alliance between the orchestra and the voices on the stage. The *origins* of this style came straight from Germany; the *originality* of the composer consisted in the spontaneous gushing forth of his creative nature, fortified by consummate craftsmanship and an incomparable manner of writing. And from Ernest Reyer: "Do you know what bewilders you a little in *Manon*? It is the orchestra that murmurs such pretty phrases, in mezzotint, veiled, almost elusive, while accompanying the dialogue—that dialogue of which you imagine you do not quite catch the sense because you do not hear it out in the open. That is an invention of Monsieur Massenet, a procedure of melodrama applied to the opéra-comique, and I find this invention successful and superlatively expressed. You no longer have dialogue in its simple, prosaic form; neither do you have recitative, which gave to works of *demi-caractère* (and sometimes without *caractère*) the allures of grand opera." [16]

Victor Maurel was at this time offering a season of Italian opera at the former Théâtre des Nations in the Place du Châtelet. After a skimpy eleven days of rehearsals, *Hérodiade*, in the Italian version, was mounted on 1 February 1884, reaching Paris for the first time. The cast included Mme Fidès-Devriès (Salomé), Tremelli (Hérodiade), Jean de Reszke (Jean), Maurel (Hérode), Édouard de Reszke (Phanuel), and Villani (Vitellius). The season was a financial disaster, but at any rate the tenth and last performance of *Hérodiade*, on 13 March, featured all three De Reszkes, with Joséphine as Salomé.

At the funeral of Eugène Rouher, on 8 February, Talazac sang a piece specially composed by Massenet for the occasion.[*]

The available backgrounds for the genesis of *Le Cid* may be interpolated here. The exploits of the Castilian noble, Rodrigo Diaz de Bivar (ca. 1040–1099), took hold on the popular imagination and were considerably embroidered with extravagant inventions by the *trobadores* of the century following his death. A youthful victory in single combat against a Navarrese champion gained him the title of Campeador. Alfonso VI, of Leon and Castile, banished him from the kingdom in 1081, and Rodrigo became an independent condottiere of his own troops. Amidst the rivalry of various Moorish kings, he allied himself with Moctadir, king of Saragossa, and made himself master of Valencia in 1094. Rodrigo was called by his Moorish vassals "Sid-i" (my lord), which was translated as "mio Cid." Upon his death, it is said that his widow had his embalmed body placed on a throne in the church of San Pedro de Cardeña, near Burgos, where it sat for ten years. Guilhem de Castro's play of 1621, *Las*

---

[*] The piece was apparently destroyed or reused elsewhere. The French statesman Eugène Rouher (1814–1884) had risen to the position of Minister of State under Napoleon III, for whose system he was one of the chief apologists.

Victor Maurel, shown here as Don Giovanni, portrayed Hérode when the Italian version of *Hérodiade* was first staged in Paris. Photograpy by Dupont. Courtesy Paul Jackson.

Mocedades del Cid, dealt with his subject's youth, "mocedades" being loosely equivalent to youthful adventures, or wild oats. Corneille knew of Castro's play when he wrote his own tragedy *Le Cid*, produced in 1637.

Prior to 1870, Victorien Sardou had offered a libretto for *Le Cid* to François-Auguste Gevaert, who, however, abandoned it and indeed gave up composing to devote his energies to the directorship of the Brussels Conservatoire and to his work as musicologist. Further, Louis Maillart, best known for his popular *Dragons de Villars*, was at one time offered a libretto by Auguste Maquet on *Le Cid Campréador*, intended for the Opéra, but Maillart died in 1871 without ever completing the project.[17] Raymond de Rigné thought that the libretto for Massenet's *Le Cid* dated back to as early as 1878. That was the year of Gounod's *Polyeucte*, also after Corneille. In a letter to Emma Borch dated 5 June 1885, we find the interesting statement that Massenet had been "busy for nearly three years" with *Le Cid*, and that the writing of *Manon* had been a kind of restful distraction in relation to the larger work.[18]

If we believe the *Souvenirs*, Massenet was at loose ends after finishing *Manon* [i.e., during the autumn of 1883?] and plagued Hartmann to find him a new libretto. The latter calmly pulled from his desk *Le Cid*, by Louis Gallet and Édouard Blau. Massenet later asked D'Ennery to interpolate the scene where Chimène discovers that Rodrigue is her father's murderer (Act II, Scene 2) and the scene where Rodrigue invokes the apparition of St. James of Compostella (Act III, Scene 2).

As for the actual composition, the *Souvenirs* provide a clue: "I continued my work on *Le Cid* wherever I happened to be, as the performance of *Manon* took me to the provincial theaters, where they alternated it with *Hérodiade* both in France and abroad." Thus we know that *Manon* was given at Lille on 8 March and at Brussels on 15 March 1884. The *Souvenirs* go on to say that Massenet "wrote the ballet music [Act II] for *Le Cid* at Marseille during a rather long stay there" and to give a description of his room at the Hôtel Beauveau—the room once occupied by Paganini and also by Alfred de Musset and George Sand. It is on record that Massenet conducted a performance of *Manon* at Marseille on 4 April 1884. The next definitive word we have is a remark in a letter more than fourteen months later (23 June 1885) that the orchestral score of *Le Cid* had been engraved.[19] This seems like a normal schedule for the composition and orchestration of the work.

While Massenet was at Marseille, Gounod's oratorio *La Rédemption* was performed in Paris, on 3 April 1884. Sketched in 1868 but not completed until 1881, this work had been given at the Birmingham Festival in 1882. It would be followed shortly by *Mors et Vita* (Birmingham, 1885; Paris, 22 May 1886). Perhaps, as has been suggested, Gounod turned to religious music at this time in search of the kind of success enjoyed by Berlioz's *Enfance du Christ* and Massenet's *Marie-Magdeleine*. Certainly, since *Roméo et Juliette*, his operas had not been faring too well. *Polyeucte* (1878), despite its Barbier-Carré libretto after Corneille, barely lasted six months at the Opéra. *Sapho*, originally in three acts (1851), was revived in a four-act version at the Opéra on 2 April 1884 but expired after twenty-nine performances. *Le Tribut de Zamora* (Opéra, 1 April 1881) would in turn give up the ghost after two final performances in 1885.

Plagued with the competition from Colonne and Lamoureux, Pasdeloup closed his Concerts Populaires in April of 1884. Thus ended an institution familiar to Massenet from his youth. A grand festival benefit was held for Pasdeloup at the Trocadéro on 31 May, with proceeds of nearly 100,000 francs. Instead of retiring as he should have, Pasdeloup conducted concerts at Monte-Carlo in the winter of 1885, and for the Paris season of 1886–87, he started a new monthly series with the old title. He died at Fontainebleau on 13 August 1887 from the effects of paralysis.

Massenet seems to have remained in Paris through July of 1884, no doubt slaving away at *Le Cid* while his wife and daughter went afield for fresh air. The memoirs of Mathilde Marchesi provide a little vignette from this period. Mme Marchesi, after a successful concert career, had established herself as a singing teacher first in Vienna, then in Paris. Her daughter, Blanche Marchesi, also became a noted singer and teacher. On 30 May 1884, Mme Marchesi held a large reception at her house in the Rue Phalsbourg, near the Parc de Monceau. The musical program was entirely vocal, featuring the Vicomtess de Trédern, Emma Nevada, Blanche Marchesi, and the tenor Mouliérat of the Opéra-Comique. Gounod, Saint-Saëns, Delibes, and Massenet accompanied their own works, while Mme Marchesi's pupils sang the choruses. Emma Calvé was also studying with Marchesi at this time, for her voice needed retraining after her debut of 1882 at Brussels as Marguerite in *Faust*. Calvé would create the rôle of Anita in Massenet's *La Navarraise* in 1894.

For the Prix de Rome trials of 1884, the cantata text was *L'Enfant prodigue*, by Guinand. Performed in public on 27 June, the works were judged by the twenty-eight members of the Académie des Beaux-Arts who were present and voting. The efforts of Massenet's pupils Edmond Missa and Henri-Charles Kaiser were dismissed, though Xavier Leroux earned a second prize, as did Delibes's pupil Charles-Olivier René-Bibard. The overwhelming majority, twenty-two votes, went to Claude Debussy, whose interpreters were Rose Caron, Ernest Van Dyck, and Alexandre Taskin. Debussy himself accompanied at the piano, assisted in places by his friend René Chansarel.[*] In later years Debussy was irritated by the popularity of the too obviously derivative "Air de Lia."

On 9 August, Massenet wrote from Thun, Switzerland, that he had been working like mad for a week on the third act of *Le Cid*, putting in nine or ten hours a day and going out only in the evening. And here he was supposed to be resting up from his recent labors in Paris! The weather was very warm despite the nearness of the lake and pine woods.[20]

By early October Massenet was back in Paris, ready to plunge again into the round of labors and social engagements. Schneider recounts with gusto a tale of "one evening in October," when three men assembled in a private dining room at the luxurious Café Anglais: Duquesnel, director of the Odéon at the time of *Les Érinnyes* and now director of the Théâtre Porte-Saint-Martin; the dramatist Victorien Sardou; and Massenet. Some bits of incidental music were needed for Sardou's new play *Théodora*, and Duquesnel had promised to procure Massenet, counting on his gratitude for past favors at the Odéon. As they worked their way through various courses worthy of Brillat-Savarin, Sardou unfolded his drama of the courtesan empress of old Byzantium. Massenet seemed rather silent and preoccupied and far less active with his fork than his gourmet companions. The talk turned to other things (Massenet still silent), but then the composer went to the piano with which the room was fortunately equipped and played straight off the Chanson de Théodora just as it ought to sound. There followed a hymn of triumph and a psalm of the dead, and voilà! the music was ready.[21] Writing it down and orchestrating was a mere matter of a few of those early-morning work sessions.

---

[*] Léon Vallas, in identifying the influences upon Debussy at this time, singled out Guiraud, Gounod, and Lalo, plus the timely appearance on the Paris musical scene of *Manon* and *Hérodiade*. (*Claude Debussy et son temps*, 1932, p. 38.)

Théodora opened on 26 December 1884, with Sarah Bernhardt (who was now forty), and is said to have grossed 2,500,000 francs by the end of its initial run. In the sequel, the subject was reworked as a libretto by Paul Ferrier,[*] and the opera *Théodora* by Xavier Leroux was given at Monte-Carlo on 19 March 1907.

On 24 December, Massenet wrote to Ricordi praising a new almanac he had brought out and remarking, "I rarely hear from you."[22] They continued good friends through the years, as is attested by various letters right down to 1912. But, interestingly enough, when *Il Cid* reached the stage of La Scala in 1890, it was the property (for Italy) of Ricordi's rival Edoardo Sonzogno!

---

[*] Paul Ferrier (1843–1920) made French translations of Puccini's *La Bohème*, *Tosca*, and *Madama Butterfly* at the Opéra-Comique in 1898, 1903, and 1906 respectively.

1885–1888

Le Cid

URING THE WINTER AND SPRING of 1885, along with his teaching and the preoccupations of the Paris season, Massenet pushed ahead with the orchestration of *Le Cid*. Besides, he made brief trips to the provinces for *Manon* and *Hérodiade* ("un peu partout," as he wrote to Ricordi), apparently conducting some of the first performances.[1] *Manon* was given at Geneva on 7 March and at Nantes on 11 March, though I have not found any documentation for Massenet's presence. He was at Bordeaux for *Hérodiade* (given 23 April 1885), and he conducted *Hérodiade* at Marseille on 12 May.

On 26 April, *Ève* was given again at the Cirque d'Été, where it had first been heard ten years before. A few days later Massenet requested tickets for a revival of Daudet's *L'Arlésienne* with Bizet's incidental music.[2]

From the correspondence we learn that, as of 5 June, *Le Cid* was "almost finished," and by 23 June the orchestra score had been engraved.[3] On 17 July, still in Paris, Massenet thanked Ricordi for sending the score of *Isora di Provenza* by Luigi Mancinelli, of which he wrote: "C'est brave, c'est nouveau, c'est personnel—cela me ravit. Voilà une musique bien moderne."[4]

In the Prix de Rome trials for 1885, Massenet's pupils made a good showing: first prize, Xavier Leroux; second prize, Augustin Savard fils, the son of Massenet's former solfège teacher. One of Guiraud's pupils, André Gédalge, was given honorable mention.

From the ninth to the twentieth of August, a group of nearly forty Frenchmen, including writers and artists, visited Hungary at the invitation of their Hungarian colleagues who had visited Paris in 1883. Armand Gouzien and Mario Proth were the leaders of the French delegation, while the head of the welcoming Hungarian delegation was Ferenc Pulszky.[*] The Hungarian government was not involved, and the reception and programs remained exclusively of a social-literary nature. Massenet obviously enjoyed this trip. The group took the Orient Express by way of Munich, spending most of the night in the dining car in animated conversation. Massenet was impressed throughout by the youthful vigor of Ferdinand de Lesseps, who had built the Suez Canal and was now almost eighty.

At Budapest, a gala performance was given at the Royal Theater on 11 August, with Delibes's *Coppélia* and Massenet's *Scènes pittoresques* and portions of *Hérodiade*. Amidst cries of "éljen" (hurrah!) Massenet went to the podium for *Hérodiade*, only to find that they had put on the stand the score of *Coppélia;* he was forced to conduct from memory. When Delibes's turn came, what else but that he found on the stand the score of *Hérodiade!* At the banquet that followed, where the noble Hungarian wines flowed freely, the two took their revenge: Massenet spoke for Delibes, and vice versa. When toasts were proposed, Massenet lauded Franz Liszt, to whom Hungary had given birth. Later, when Liszt read about this in the Hungarian *Gazette*, he sent Massenet a note of thanks (dated Weimar, 26 August 1885).

The guests spent four days in Budapest, then left for a week's tour of the country with visits to Dobsina, Poprád, the High Tatra, Kassa, Arad, Szentes, Mezőhegyes, and Szeged. Throughout their visit the Frenchmen were received with special celebrations and demonstrations of sympathy. Among the ceremonies was the laying of wreaths at the statue of the Hungarian poet Sándor Petőti (1823–1849) and at the memorial for the martyrs of Arad.[*]

Manon reopened at the Opéra-Comique on 25 November, with Heilbron still in the title rôle. She sang nine more performances by the end of 1885, then, the following year, she died at Nice at the age of thirty-five. In sorrow, it is said, Massenet withdrew *Manon* from the Opéra-Comique, where it was not heard again until 1891 with Sibyl Sanderson.

---

[*] From page 144: I am indebted to Dr. István Kecskeméti, of the National Széchényi Library, Budapest, for supplying names from *Pesti Napló* of 10 Aug. 1885. **FRENCH GUESTS** Composers: Delibes, Massenet. Painters: Georges Clairin, Escalier, Toney Robert Fleury, Guérard, Robs. Journalists: Badin (secretary, *La Nouvelle Revue*), Gaston Berardi (proprietor-editor, *L'Indépendance Belge*), Émile Blavet (*Le Figaro*), Comte de Noire Fontaine (*Le Soleil*), Alfred de Loustalot (*Gazette des Beaux Arts*), Montet (*Gil Blas*), Parisel (*Événement*), Mario Proth (*Le Mot d'Ordre*), Ratisbonne (*Le Rappel*), Tresfeu (*Le Gaulois*), Young (editor, *Revue Politique et Littéraire*). Writers: François Coppée, Ulbach. Lawyers: Lebrasseur, Lenger Marlet (Court of Appeals, Brussels), Weismann. Medicine: Albert Rodin (physician), Samuel-Jean Pozzi (professor of medicine). Others: Arbey (industrialist), D'Aubray (academician), Dreyfuss, the two Duplants (one inspector general of railways, the other head of the French Council of Public Education), Ébeling (secretary, Association Internationale), Armand Gouzien, Lermina, Ferdinand Lesseps (engineer), Lichtenstein (colonel), Émile Lévy (publisher), Istvan Türr. **HUNGARIAN HOSTS**—Emil Ábrányi, Mme László Arany, Nándor Borostyáni, Károly Gerlóczy (deputy mayor of the capital), Imre Greguss, Antal Günther, Imre Huszár, Imre Ivánka, Mór Jókai, Károly Légrády, Emilia Márkus, Sándor Matlekovits, Arisztid Mátyus, Sándor Országh, Ede Paulay, Ferenc Pulszky, Károly Pulszky, Viktor Rákosi, Zsigmond Sonnenfeld, József Szábo, Attila Szemere, Count Sándor Teleky, Lajos Thalloczy, Ferenc Toldy, Antal Várady, Count Jenő Zichy.

[*] In Aug. 1849, thirteen Hungarian officers were executed here at the order of the Austrian general Baron von Haynau.

Poster for *Le Cid* by Georges Clairin, 1885.

After the customary *répétition générale*,[*] the Opéra staged the first public performance of *Le Cid* on 30 November 1885. The cast included Jean de Reszke (Rodrigue), Mme Fidès-Devriès (Chimène), Rosa Bosman (L'Infante), Édouard de Reszke
(Don Diègue), Léon Melchissédec (Le Roi), and Pol Plançon (Comte de Gormas).
President Grévy honored the occasion with his presence. Characteristically, Massenet was elsewhere; he spent the evening down the boulevard at a performance of
Manon. But he could not resist stopping by at the Opéra later to hear the news, and
was relieved to hear from Gabrielle Krauss that *Le Cid* was a triumph.

----◄◦►----

Act I opens in a room in the house of Count Gormas, in Burgos. The Count and his
friends discuss Rodrigue, who is to be knighted that same day by the King. The
Count's daughter, Chimène, loves Rodrigue and rejoices when her father approves of
their prospective union. In Scene 2, the Infanta confesses to Chimène that she, too,
loves Rodrigue, though she will forever keep buried the secret of her feelings. (While
this scene does little to advance the action, the opportunity offered for emotional expression is put to good musical use by composer.) Scene 3, the great square of Burgos,
is a brilliant and solemn scene with the chiming of bells[†] and sounds of the cathedral
organ. Rodrigue is knighted. As a further honor, Rodrigue's father, Don Diègue, is
appointed preceptor to the Infanta. This leads to a quarrel in which Don Gormas insults Don Diègue. Rodrigue, sorely tried in such a predicament, decides that honor
requires him to avenge his father. Scene 4 shows a view of Burgos at night. Rodrigue
wanders alone. When Count Gormas appears, there is a duel and the Count is mortally wounded. In the ensuing commotion, Chimène suddenly realizes that it is Rodrigue who has killed her father.

Act II, Scene 1: the square of Burgos. The scene is in vivid contrast to the tragedy that preceded. The people rejoice, the Infanta distributes alms, and there are
picturesque dances: Andalouse, Madrilène, Aubade, and Navarraise. In Scene 2,
Chimène pleads with the King for justice against Rodrigue. But the sinister call of
trumpets announces the arrival of a Moorish emissary of Boabdil, who has declared
war against the King. The King regrets the loss of his best captain, Gormas. Don
Diègue nominates his son Rodrigue as captain, and this is agreeable to all.

In Act III, Chimène, alone, deplores a destiny that has separated her from Rodrigue. Then Rodrigue comes, and the text of Corneille's famous scene is preserved
almost intact. Scene 2 shows Rodrigue's camp, where soldiers are drinking and singing. Massenet interpolates a charming Moorish Rhapsody. Rodrigue, alone, invokes
the apparition of Saint James of Compostella, who promises victory in the coming
battle. The orchestra depicts the clash of arms, and Rodrigue, filled with confidence,
rushes to the head of his troops.

---

[*] To which, incidentally, Massenet invited one of his companions of the Hungarian trip: Dr. Samuel-
Jean Pozzi (1846–1918), head of the Lourcine (later Broca) Hospital.[5]

[†] The bells were ordered from the same bell founder in Milan who supplied Boito's *Mefistofele*.[6]

Act IV, Scene 1: the palace of the King at Granada. Don Diègue, Chimène, and the Infanta are all desolated at the news that Rodrigue is dead. After they have given vent to their sorrow, Rodrigue appears, very much alive and victorious. In Scene 2, the palace of the Alhambra, there is joy among the court and the people. Chimène tries again to ask for the punishment of her father's slayer, but the words will not come out. Implored by all to relent, her love wins out, and the two lovers are united.

Auguste Vitu, writing in *Le Figaro* the next day, discerned a notable evolution in Massenet's work: whereas *Hérodiade*, for example, still contains "numbers," in *Le Cid* the only real divisions were the acts and scenes (*tableaux*). The composer, in presenting a score of such "formidable compactness," as good as warns us that it is to be considered as an indivisible whole from which individual portions cannot be detached. "Massenet was considered, with good reason, first as a master of the art of writing, then as an elegist and descriptive colorist. He revealed last evening a dramatic temperament that, up to this time, had slumbered beneath the sensuous torpor of symphonic caresses. *Le Cid* contains no orchestral painting comparable to the Paradise of Indra in *Le Roi de Lahore;* in compensation, it has Chimène's lament, the love duet, the air of Rodrigue—as pure in form as conceptions by Gluck or Mozart." Johannès Weber, in *Le Temps*, remarked that Massenet had written a true overture for *Le Cid*, which the public could not be expected to understand since they didn't listen to it. The opera must be considered as a new and important affirmation of a younger school which, however, is a school of transition. "There is no question at all here of Wagner, but simply of returning frankly, without subterfuge or shabbiness, to the principles of Gluck."[*] Louis Schneider (who was twenty-four when *Le Cid* had its première) later wrote in retrospect after *Thérèse* (1907) that while *Le Cid* was hardly a Massenet masterpiece it could well have been the masterpiece of some composer of lesser stature. Tenderness, vivid coloring, heroic qualities, and tragic passion abounded in the score, which effectively evoked a Spain of the eleventh century. While less popular than some of the other operas, *Le Cid* was "one of the finest stones in Massenet's musical edifice."[8] *Le Cid* was given steadily at the Opéra through 1891, then intermittently up to a 152nd performance in 1919.

Massenet was pleased as punch with his latest opera. Why, no less a personage than the Duc d'Aumale, Henri d'Orléans, asked the composer to use his influence to have *Le Cid* performed on 11 December, for his next turn to use his box fell on that day![†] And on 11 December Massenet wrote with obvious satisfaction to Ricordi that the receipts were averaging seven thousand francs per night for *Manon* and twenty-two thousand francs for *Le Cid*. He was leaving that evening, he wrote, for Lyon (where, in fact, *Hérodiade* was given on December 18).[9] In the sequel, the archbishop

---

[*] But Henry T. Finck, after the New York performance of 1907, thought that "the versatile Massenet evidently aimed at creating a work in the style of Meyerbeer—spectacular and effective."[7]

of Lyon, Cardinal Caverot, became alarmed at the impiety of *Hérodiade*, imposed minor excommunication upon the composer and librettist, and appealed to Leo XIII for a full excommunication. The Pope, while sustaining the archbishop, refused to increase the severity of the penalty.[10]

On 23 December 1885, *Manon* (in Italian) reached New York in a performance by the Mapleson Company at the Academy of Music, with Minnie Hauk (Manon), Ferruccio Giannini (Des Grieux), and Giuseppe Del Puente (Lescaut). Massenet was invited on several occasions to come to America, but it was a trip he was destined never to make. Thus, in October of 1884, he wrote: "There is no longer a question of going to America (at least, this winter)."[11]

On 1 January, Massenet wrote from Paris that he would be leaving soon for Vienna.[12] I have been unable to document such a journey, however, and considering his remark to Alfred Stieglitz in a letter of the twenty-ninth that "in accordance with the contracts, I can count upon the performance of *Le Cid* in Vienna in the spring,"[13] it may have been wishful thinking. There was a considerable delay, for *Le Cid* was not actually staged at the Vienna Hofoper until 22 November 1887.

A letter of 24 January to Schatté, conductor at the Odéon, mentioned that "the music" would be at Schatté's disposal at Hartmann's, where Massenet could discuss "the project" with him some day around five o'clock. Schatté wanted to arrange something of Massenet's; elsewhere, in an undated letter to a theater director, Massenet recommended some of Schatté's music as "sonorous and practical, with excellent timpani effects."[14]

We can suppose that Massenet went to Lyon for the final rehearsals of *Manon*, given there on 30 January 1886. On 23 February, the duo *Horace et Lydie* was completed in Paris. Otherwise, the documentation for 1886 is frustratingly meager.

As for the genesis of *Werther*, the chronology—or rather lack of it—in the *Souvenirs* seems purposely calculated to arouse confusion. "On Sunday, August first," goes the account, carefully omitting the year, "Hartmann and I went to hear *Parsifal* at the Wagner Theater at Bayreuth." Afterwards they went to Wetzlar, scene of Goethe's *Sorrows of the Young Werther*. As they were leaving the house where Werther's Lotte had lived, Hartmann pulled from his pocket a French translation of Goethe's romance. They repaired to a German beer hall, where Massenet pored over the book, almost shedding tears over the emotional situations depicted. But then along came *Manon* and *Le Cid*, so that the idea of writing an opera on Werther was pushed aside.

Parsifal was first given at Bayreuth on 26 July 1882—sixteen times that year.

---

† The *Souvenirs*, after quoting the Duc d'Aumale's letter, go on to reminisce over the pleasant times spent, together with colleagues of the Institut such as Léon Bonnat, Benjamin Constant, Édouard Detaille, and Gérôme, at the Château de Chantilly. Here their host, Henri d'Orléans (1822–1897), the fourth son of Louis-Philippe, received them with "charming simplicity," and his conversation was that of "an eminent man of letters, erudite but unpretentious." The Château, built in 1876–81, together with its contents of art treasures and furnishings was presented to the Institut de France in 1886, though the Duc retained the use of it until his death.

Now, if Massenet had started *Manon* in 1881 or 1882, we are expected to fall into the trap of assuming that the two attended *Parsifal* that first summer. The catch is that "August first" did not fall on Sunday in 1882 but rather in 1886! Furthermore, Lavignac in *Le Voyage artistique à Bayreuth* (1897) published very extensive (if admittedly incomplete) lists of Frenchmen present at Bayreuth each summer from 1876 through 1896. Massenet's name appears *only* in the list for 1886.[*] *Tristan* was also given that summer—for the first time at Bayreuth. To have mentioned *Tristan* in the *Souvenirs* would therefore have been a dead giveaway as to the year, whereas *Parsifal* was given alone in 1882, 1883, and 1884. This is all deliciously vague, though in none of these years did August first fall on a Sunday.

Massenet is supposed to have told Robert Charvay that "mes premières mesures [de *Werther*], je les écrivis au printemps de 1885, et je notai les dernières à la fin de l'hiver 1886 [actually, 14 March 1887]. Près de deux années de labeur!"[15] In the *Souvenirs* this becomes: "At last in the summer of 1885 . . . Hartmann, Paul Milliet . . . and I [Édouard Blau is not mentioned] came to an agreement to take up the task of writing *Werther*." Hartmann (who is praised for his fluent German and understanding of Goethe) worked up a scenario and took a room for Massenet at the Hôtel des Réservoirs (once the mansion of Mme de Pompadour) at Versailles, so that he could work in quiet and comfort, surrounded by "atmosphere."[†] The room is described as a vast apartment on the ground floor, with lofty ceilings and eighteenth-century panelings and furnishings. Massenet wrote at a table "purest Louis XV." A few steps away were the famous gardens laid out by André Le Nôtre in 1667–88.

The word "summer," in Massenet's vocabulary, could mean anything from May to September. As we have seen, August of 1885 involved the trip to Hungary, and August of 1886 the trip to Bayreuth. If Massenet did indeed begin *Werther* in the summer of 1885, his work was broken off by other distractions. Much later, he remarked that he had composed Acts II and III at Étretat.[17] I have found no documentation to confirm Massenet's presence at Étretat in 1885, though he was certainly there in September of 1886.[‡] In any case, the first draft of *Werther* was completed on 14 March 1887, and the orchestration proceeded from 15 March until its completion on 2 July of that year.

On 13 October 1886, Massenet acknowledged Ricordi's telegram relating to

---

[*] Others who went that summer were Georges Hartmann, Pierre de Bréville, Camille Chevillard, Louis Diémer, Paul Dukas, Alexandre Guilmant, Vincent d'Indy, Charles Lamoureux, Silvio Lazzari, Albéric Magnard, Georges Marty, André Messager, Paul Vidal, and over a hundred other Frenchmen, including the usual contingent of Paris journalists.

[†] Compare the remark made in a letter some years later: "Do you remember Versailles in 1886 [*sic*] and Werther?"[16]

[‡] When he composed three songs: *Chant de guerre cossaque* (Étretat, 22–23 Sept. 1886); *Séparation* (Étretat, 24 Sept. 1886); *Plus vite* (Étretat, 25 Sept. 1886). In autograph annotations, Massenet complains of the continual rain and cold, and feels ill and sad. His daughter, confined in bed with illness, at last appeared in the salon on 25 Sept., when they lit the "first fire of the autumn." By 1 Oct. they were back in Paris.

the success of a "second performance" of *Erodiade* [at Bologna?] and asked wistfully if *Le Roi de Lahore* is not going to be given again somewhere. (As a matter of fact, the novelty of *Le Roi de Lahore* seems to have worn off in the intervening years, much to Massenet's regret, for he was obviously fond of the work.) And *Le Cid*? Isn't anybody interested at all?[18] Massenet was no doubt beginning to worry about *Le Cid*. It reached its fiftieth performance at the Opéra on 8 November 1886, not quite one year after its opening. But as yet it had not been staged anywhere else, and it was to prove a laggard in this respect.

Meanwhile, Massenet was still occupied with his composition class at the Conservatoire. Some of the visiting cards and little slips of paper that he sent to the librarian when he wanted material for use in class have been preserved. Thus, on Friday, 19 November 1886, he requested Wagner's *Lohengrin*, both the piano-vocal score with French text and the orchestral score.[*] We can imagine him giving a one-man performance of the opera, elucidating the while its compositional techniques. On Tuesday, 21 December, he requested the vocal and orchestral scores of Berlioz's *L'Enfance du Christ*. Very timely, too, for the following Saturday was Christmas.[20]

The Prix de Rome for 1886, by the way, had gone to Augustin Savard, who had placed second the previous year. Second prize went this time to Henri-Charles Kaiser, also a Massenet pupil. André Gédalge, Guiraud's pupil, did somewhat better than before, attaining a Deuxième Second Grand Prix. Gédalge later composed but is chiefly remembered for his treatise on fugue (1901). As professor of counterpoint and fugue at the Paris Conservatoire (from 1905), Gédalge taught such men as Arthur Honegger, Charles Koechlin, Darius Milhaud, Maurice Ravel, and Jean-Jules Roger-Ducasse.

Sardou's *Le Crocodile* opened on 21 December 1886 at the Porte-Saint-Martin. Francisque Sarcey, drama critic of *Le Temps*, remarked that the most important thing about the première, in his opinion, was Massenet's music. He recalled to his readers that the young and illustrious *maître* had composed for *Théodora* a chorus that was quite attractive rhythmically and coloristically. This time his contribution was more substantial: an overture and some entr'actes that delighted the public. There was sufficient demand for the *Entr'acte berceuse* and the *Entr'acte nocturne* for Hartmann to issue these separately in piano arrangements. Incidentally, during 1886–92 Sardou lived in Massenet's street, at 37 Rue du Général Foy.

The year 1887 opened with the supervising of rehearsals for *Le Cid*, given at Nantes on 8 January and at Antwerp on 20 January. Returning from Antwerp, Massenet wrote to Campbell Clarke, critic for the *Daily Telegraph*, that he planned to go to Milan for the première of Verdi's *Otello* at La Scala [on 5 February]. But something upset his plan. On the ninth he wrote from Paris to Ricordi that only pressing reasons (not specified) had prevented his attending this "solennité artistique," this "fête

---

[*] On Tuesday the sixteenth, Massenet skipped class to attend a funeral at Rueil: Jean-Baptiste Jouvin, music critic for *Le Figaro* under the byline "Bénédict," had died at Rueil on 14 Nov. 1886.[19]

universelle du génie!" He thanked Ricordi for sending the score of the new Verdi masterpiece, the beauties of which he had already shown to his composition class.[21]

Biblis, a scène religieuse for mezzo-soprano, tenor, baritone, chorus, and orchestra, with text by Georges Boyer, is usually said to have first been performed at some time in 1886 by the Société des Amateurs. But in a letter to Campbell Clarke dated 25 January 1887, Massenet mentioned that "Thursday evening [i.e., 27 January] I am conducting at the Salle Grande the first performance of *Biblis*." Because of this he had to pass up an invitation and the chance to meet Joseph Joachim, "a great performer and a true musician," whose qualities Massenet admired.[22]

Manon was given at Rouen on 28 February 1887. Massenet then went to Angers for some performance (not specified), returning to Paris on the evening of 11 March.[23] On 14 March, the piano-vocal draft of *Werther* was completed. The following day the orchestration was begun, and for the next sixteen weeks the margins of its pages became a kind of diary.

The Prelude to *Werther* was begun on 15 March, then interrupted. Even the first page was redated with "retouches" on 22–23 March, and the Prelude was finished on the twenty-sixth.[*] Act I was started on 31 March and continued without too many distractions to completion on 26 April. For 31 March, two marginal notes whet our curiosity. The first, "19 ans de Juliette, et sa première réception au 'Salon' (pastel: tête d'étude)," would indicate artistic talent on Juliette's part if, indeed, her portrait study of a head was accepted for exhibition. The other, "3:30, réception de Leconte de Lisle par A. Dumas fils," notes an event presumably attended by Massenet.

From 7 to 16 April, Massenet was in Bordeaux, at the Hôtel de France, for final rehearsals of *Le Cid*, given at the Grand Théâtre on 16 April 1887. Easter (10 April) was a fine, sunny day, and on 12 April, Massenet wrote to Mme Durand-Ulbach, who had sung in *Biblis* at Paris just before he left. He had not had a chance to thank her.[25] Back in Paris on 28 April, Massenet started Act II but then put it aside for a month. He picked it up again at the same page on 26 May, with the marginal comment that the Opéra-Comique had burned down in the night.

On the evening of 25 May 1887, *Mignon* was being given in the Salle Favart when fire broke out. The theater burned completely with loss of 131 lives. A funeral was held for the victims at Notre-Dame on 30 May. Carvalho, as director, was somehow held responsible. Arrested and sentenced to six months' imprisonment and a fine of two hundred francs, he was subsequently acquitted on appeal and ultimately reinstated as director in 1891. Meanwhile, the Opéra-Comique troupe moved to the theater in the Place du Châtelet that was formerly the Théâtre-Lyrique, then Théâtre des Nations, and later Théâtre Sarah-Bernhardt. Paravey, formerly director of the Grand Théâtre, Nantes, took over the management.

---

[*] Massenet had some rehearsals of a duo (possibly *Horace et Lydie?*) on 24 and 28 Mar., involving Hettich and an unnamed lady singer, for a program of 1 Apr.[24]

Many lives were lost when the Salle Favart
burned to the ground on 25 May 1887.

It was on that eventful evening of 25 May, according to the *Souvenirs*, that Massenet read through *Werther* for Carvalho, only to have the director reject it as a subject lacking in interest and "too dismal." The date seems too contrived, and there is no marginal annotation in the score of *Werther* to help us. If anything, one wonders if the unsuccessful reading took place on 28 April, and if that could account for the lapse in attention to the scoring. Indeed, the dates stare up at us from the very same page 214: Thursday, 28 April 1887 and then Thursday, 26 May—as though in his innermost subconscious Massenet felt purged (revenged upon Carvalho?) and now ready to proceed full tilt with the orchestration.*

Although *Manon* was given at Le Havre on 2 June 1887, Massenet did not go. By 8 June the orchestration of Act II was completed, and at two that afternoon there was a grand concert at the Trocadéro for the benefit of the Opéra-Comique, with the duo from Act I of *Manon* on the program. The orchestration for Act III of *Werther* had been tentatively started on 15 May, then laid aside. Taken up again on 10 June, Scene 1 was completed on the twenty-fourth. Ninon and Juliette left for Trouville on

---

* Act I had ended on page 213, and the number 13 is still included in all numerical series (as it was for *Manon*). Massenet had not yet started the habit of putting 12, 12bis, 14, etc.

Gustave Charpentier. Courtesy Paul Jackson.

15 June, Massenet having to remain in the heat of Paris because of the Conservatoire.

Saturday, 25 June, was the date for deciding the Prix de Rome competition. First prize went to Gustave Charpentier, a pupil of Massenet. Of two second prizes, the Premier Second Grand Prix was awarded to Alfred-Georges Bachelet, a pupil of Guiraud, and the Deuxième Second Grand Prix to Camille Erlanger, a pupil of Delibes. The cantata was *Didon*, text by Lucien Augé de Lassus. Both of these runners-up would have better luck another year.

The next day, Sunday, Massenet made a fresh start on the last scene of *Werther*: La Mort de Werther (pronounced "Ver-TAIR" in French). By 30 June he was installed at Trouville with his family, at 11 Rue de la Chapelle. And on 2 July, at half past eleven, he was able to inscribe "Fin de Werther" on the last page, enclosing in a little circle the names of Ninon, Juliette, and Léon Bessand, his future son-in-law, who was also at Trouville at this time.[*]

---

[*] Trouville was one of those fashionable *bains de mer* of the Calvados, the maritime department of Normandy that also includes Deauville, Villers-sur-Mer, Houlgate, and Cabourg. In those days Baedeker called the beach at Trouville one of the most beautiful in France, and perhaps in the world, for the number, variety, and magnificence of its villas: "c'est le boulevard d'été de Paris."

Poster for Ambroise Thomas's ballet *La Tempête*,
by E. Buval with illustration by Bellenger.

July and August cannot be accounted for in greater detail. Perhaps, as stated in the *Souvenirs*, Massenet spent the summer of 1887—or rather part of it—at the Grand Hôtel in Vevey, Switzerland, as he is known to have done in 1888. The *Souvenirs* also mention a brief visit in August 1887 to Ambroise Thomas at his retreat on the island of Illiec. Thomas had bought there, it seems, "a whole group of islands." Only the most detailed maps reveal this hideaway off the north coast of Brittany (the Côtes-du-Nord). The nearest town on the mainland is Tréguier. If one put out from there on a boat, one would have to the left, the Sept Îles; to the right, the Baie d'Enfer; and dead ahead, Illiec. Biographers of Thomas may perhaps someday determine whether here, in calm, isolation, the old *maître* was working on his ballet *La Tempête* (Opéra, 26 June 1889).

By September, Massenet was back in Paris where he wrote the songs *Les belles de nuit* (2 September) and *Pensée d'automne* (24–25 September). Then he left for Frankfurt, where *Le Cid* was given on 1 October 1887. From Paris, on 4 October, he wrote a warm note of thanks to a "Cher ami" (the theater director?) for the pleasant moments spent at the Frankfurt theater and "chez vous." His thanks were to be conveyed to "our admirable Chimène."[26]

There is a note of mystery in a short letter of 14 October, presumably to Réty, the secretary of the Conservatoire: Is it really too late to enroll? The bearer is a Russian with a lovely baritone voice, and it would be a pity not to take an interest in him. He speaks but little French. [No name is given.][27] There were countless such letters of recommendation during Massenet's lifetime—for students, for singers in need of a connection, and so on. They are little testimonials of the man's goodness of heart, for in his kindly eyes those he nominates all seem to be very talented. Mostly, history has passed them by with a vague shrug: who was she? who was he?

On 24 November 1887, in the church of Saint-Augustin, Juliette was married to Léon-Charles Alloend-Bessand. It must have been a fine affair. Witnesses were Ambroise Thomas; Auguste Massenet, uncle of the bride; Louis Bessand, uncle of the bridegroom; and Paul Alloend-Bessand, the bridegroom's brother. Also signing the register were the Vicomte and Vicomtesse de La Batut, Hermine Leconte de Nouy, and two others whose names are illegible.*

The bridegroom's father, Charles-Honoré Alloend-Bessand, was a successful business man. As early as 1866 one finds his name in the Paris directory as an *essayeur de commerce* with two business establishments. By 1888 he was associated with the famous department store La Belle Jardinière near the Pont-Neuf and was already an Officier of the Légion d'Honneur and a former president of the Tribunal de Commerce de la Seine. By 1900 his name, as Bessand père in the directory, is followed by the initials for "notable commerçant," inserted only for those in the official list of the Paris chamber of commerce. Charles Bessand had married Emma Parissot, and their two sons, Léon and Paul, were also associated with La Belle Jardinière.

Juliette and her husband then pretty much disappear into the protective shell that Massenet built around his family.† During the years 1900–1905, they lived at 25 Avenue de Villiers, near the Place Malesherbes, which is just north of the Parc de Monceau. They had interesting neighbors. The *Bottin* of 1900 lists the following: No. 23, atelier of René de Saint-Marceaux, sculptor; No. 25, Bessand, *propriétaire*; No. 27, [René] de Saint-Marceaux père [sculptor, b. 1845]; No. 27bis, Ernest May, director of the Banque Internationale de Paris; and at the fourth house further along, No. 43, Guillaume Dubufe, artist painter [1853–1909], whose daughter, I assume, was later to marry Pierre Bessand-Massenet. In the *Bottin* for 1905, we note that Léon Bessand was a member of the Cercle Artistique et Littéraire and the Escholiers, while his brother Paul Bessand belonged to the Cercle Agricole and the Yacht-Club de

---

* Louis-Auguste Massenet (1821–1892), of Bordeaux, was a ship captain. Louis Bessand lived at Elbeuf, near Rouen, and near Pont-de-l'Arche where the Massenets purchased a property in 1891. Elbeuf was noted for the manufacture of fancy articles for linen-drapers' shops, and it seems entirely possible that Louis Bessand was in that line of business. The Vicomtesse de La Batut was Léon Bessand's sister, and the De Nouy were friends.

† For their three children, see Appendix 1: The Massenet Family.

France. In 1934, both appeared in *Tout-Paris*, the annual of Parisian society, with Léon Bessand living at 66 Rue de Lisbonne, one block south of the Parc de Monceau. Paul Bessand was by then an Officier of the Légion d'Honneur and is listed as the ex-director of La Belle Jardinière. Juliette died at Égreville, at the age of sixty-seven, on 7 September 1935.

On 1 January 1888, Massenet was about to go and see his friend Dr. Michel, of 3 Rue St-Philippe-du-Roule, when he learned that the doctor had gone to Cannes. Mme Massenet was also at Cannes, staying at the Hôtel Beau-Rivage near the beach. On at least one earlier occasion (1885) Massenet had requested an appointment because "I need your advice," leading us to suppose that Dr. Michel was Massenet's physician.[28]

On 20 January, *Don César de Bazan* was revived in a new version at Geneva. It seems unlikely that Massenet went to Geneva, for he wrote to Dr. Michel from Paris on 13 January, and by the twenty-eighth he was at The Hague, whence he returned to Paris only on the night of 14 February.

Tchaikovsky was in Paris from 24 February to 18 March, and Colonne performed some of his works at the Concerts du Châtelet: on Sunday, 4 March, the Serenade and the Fantasy for piano and orchestra (with Louis Diémer); and on the following Sunday, 11 March, the Violin Concerto (with Marsick), *Francesca da Rimini*, and a number of other selections. It was after lunch on 6 March that Tchaikovsky paid a number of calls, which he noted in his diary: "At Colonne's. . . . At Mackar's [the music publisher]. At Gounod's (did not find him in). At Mme Adam's. At Mme Bogomoletz's (found her in, it was her 'at home'). At Massenet's. At Mme Langé's. Le Temps. . . . Home." Massenet, in a letter to Quinzard (at Hartmann's) dated 11 March, mentioned that "Tschaïkovsky est venu me voir et m'a laissé un mot charmant," implying that Massenet was out at the time and that Tchaikovsky had written a few words on a visiting card. Quinzard was directed to send Massenet's own enclosed card around to the Hôtel Richepanse, near the Madeleine, where Tchaikovsky was staying.[29] Apparently the two did not actually meet until the following year. On 21 March 1888, *Hérodiade* was given at Toulouse, with Massenet present to look after the final rehearsals.

The trip to The Hague in February had been in connection with a performance of *Manon* in which Sibyl Sanderson had made her debut under the assumed name "Ada Palmer."* Massenet probably first met Sibyl Sanderson at some time in 1887. According to the *Souvenirs*, Massenet was invited to dine one evening with "a great American family." Sibyl Sanderson was there, too, and after dinner she took advantage of her great opportunity to sing for the *maître*, who was "astounded, stupefied, subjugated," by her Queen of the Night aria from *The Magic Flute*. Massenet took her under his wing, coached her in the rôle of Manon, and tried her out at The Hague.

---

* It is apparently impossible to fix the date, other than early in February 1888. There is documentation for Massenet's conducting the third performance, on Saturday, 11 February.[30]

Sibyl Sanderson as Manon. Photography by Benque. Courtesy Paul Jackson.

Sibyl Sanderson was born in Sacramento, California, on 7 December 1865, the daughter of Silas W. Sanderson, who was just then completing a one-year appointive term as chief justice of the Supreme Court of California.[*] When Sibyl was about sixteen (1881), her mother took her to Paris for two years of "finishing" in languages, music, and culture suitable for a debutante of the 1880s. Then, after two or three seasons of busy social activity in San Francisco, Sibyl took off again definitively for Paris.

---

[*] Judge Sanderson (b. Vermont, 1824) had moved to California in 1850, settling first at Placerville, and was elected in 1851 to the state assembly. After his year with the supreme court, he was elected justice for a ten-year term but resigned in 1870, at about which time he settled in San Francisco. Here the Sandersons moved in society, counting among their friends Senator and Mrs. George Hearst. Sibyl had three sisters: Edith, Marion, and Jennie. Judge Sanderson died in San Francisco on 24 June 1886, leaving a considerable fortune. (At the time of his death he was counselor for the Central Pacific Railroad Co.)

The statement that "in January, 1886, she entered the Paris Conservatory, where she studied under Massenet, Sbriglia, and Marchesi" cannot be confirmed.[31] Giovanni Sbriglia (1832–1916) is not listed among Conservatoire teachers; he had settled in Paris in 1878 and, like Mathilde Marchesi, presumably had his own studio: they did not *need* the Conservatoire. Marchesi, who published her memoirs in 1897 (with an introduction by Massenet), gave the following account:

> Some years ago Miss Fanny Reed, one of the most esteemed members of the American colony in Paris, presented to me one of her young country-women, the charming Sibyl Sanderson. "Your voice has not been properly brought out," I said to her, after having tried it. "I cannot take you in hand unless you consent to study at least two years with me." "Oh, that is too long, I have no time to lose," was her answer; and so we separated. Later on, Massenet took charge of the musical education of Miss Sanderson, and in due course of time he brought her out at the Opéra-Comique in *Esclarmonde*. After that opera had been sung for one hundred consecutive performances in Paris, and without taking it off the stage—an unprecedented feat—Sibyl was engaged for the Théâtre Royal de la Monnaie, at Brussels, where she was the leading prima donna for two seasons. Then Monsieur Carvalho went personally to see her, and he induced her to return to Paris to become a member of his famous company at the Opéra-Comique. She had hardly arrived in the French capital when Massenet came to my house [88 Rue Jouffroy] and begged me to take his protégée in hand, and to this I consented. For nearly two years Sibyl worked diligently under my teaching, after which period she was particularly brilliant as Manon in the beautiful opera of that name. [Here Mme Marchesi reproduces a letter of gratitude from Sibyl Sanderson dated 1 September 1892.] ... The Opéra-Comique stage formed an admirable framework for her voice, as well as for her refined and graceful acting.[32]

But to return to the genesis of *Esclarmonde:* It will be recalled that the orchestration of *Werther* was finished on 2 July 1887. Presumably shortly thereafter (the *Souvenirs* are not specific), Hartmann handed Massenet the libretto of *Esclarmonde*, by Alfred Blau and Louis de Gramont. Something new was needed for the Exposition Universelle of 1889, two years hence. Would Massenet set it—yes or no? The narrative is so arranged that Massenet can exclaim with delight, "I have the artiste for this part! I heard her yesterday! She is Mlle Sibyl Sanderson!" However, what with Sibyl's tryout at The Hague, along with other preoccupations, Massenet did not get down to serious work on *Esclarmonde* until 29 April 1888, finishing the preorchestral sketch, in an incredibly short ten weeks, by 6 July. The orchestration, begun on 16 July, was completed on 14 October 1888.[33]

The marginal annotations in the orchestral score provide an insight into that busy but pleasant summer.* On 28 July, Massenet played and sang *Esclarmonde* for

---

* The Prix de Rome for 1888 went to Camille Erlanger, a pupil of Delibes, for *Velléda*, text by Fernand Beissier. Paul Dukas, a pupil of Guiraud, was awarded second prize.

an assembled group comprising Paravey (director of the Opéra-Comique), Hartmann, the librettists Blau and Gramont, Gaudiers, Bianchini, Leroux, Mlle C. [?], Sibyl Sanderson, and Mme Massenet. Afterward Miss Sanderson was auditioned and engaged by Paravey, at the salary proposed, without further discussion. On 30 July, Massenet arrived at page "12bis" in the score. Hereafter he would avoid "13," and some say that this may have been more at his wife's urging than through any superstition of his own. On 5 August, Massenet left Paris for a month's sojourn at the Grand-Hôtel de Vevey, in Switzerland, where Sibyl and her mother were also staying. Here Sibyl received some assiduous coaching in her rôle as Esclarmonde.

Vevey (the scene of Rousseau's *Nouvelle Héloïse*) lies on the shore of Lake Geneva. The guests of the Grand-Hôtel could enjoy the shade of the large trees in the surrounding park, go swimming, embark on boat excursions from the little harbor, or go for pleasant walks in the vicinity. Massenet took up his orchestration each morning at six, so that after a few hours he was free to enjoy his vacation. Each evening from five to seven he would work with Miss Sanderson on her rôle. There is a letter of 8 August to Hartmann expressing Massenet's impatience with Baudon (whose firm did the engraving) for not delivering Act IV of *Esclarmonde* as promised. As soon as they are ready, one set of proofs is to be sent for Massenet and one for Miss Sanderson, together with the original manuscript. The third set of proofs is to be kept locked up in Hartmann's office.[34]

On 8 August the weather cleared, and the party made a promenade to Montreux, then on to Glion with its superb view of lake and mountains. Here they had dinner. On 17 August there was a visit to the Château Chillon on a rocky island close to shore beyond Montreux. Here, in former times, was the stronghold of the Dukes of Savoy, commanding the road from Burgundy to the Great Saint Bernard. The orchestration of Act II was finished by ten-thirty on the morning of 21 August, and despite some showers, there was a promenade to Hauteville and Blonay. On that day Paul Poirson arrived with his wife and son. On 25 August, Mrs. Sanderson underwent an eye operation at the hands of a Dr. Dor. On 27 August, Massenet, the Poirsons, and Sibyl Sanderson went for a drive to Clarens. On the evening of 30 August there was a "painful" scene between Massenet and Miss Sanderson. He was probably pushing her rather hard in her rôle, and she resigned. But then he persuaded her to resume it: "rôle rendu, puis repris."

On 31 August, Massenet paid a "visit to Nilsson at Vevey."[*] By 3 September, Mrs. Sanderson was able to take her first walk in the garden after her eye operation. On 6 September, a "grande promenade" to Glion with the Poirsons, their children [*sic*], and Mlle S. [Sanderson]. The last entry for Vevey was on 9 September.

From Paris on 13 September 1888, Massenet wrote to Guy Ropartz, thanking him for a volume of poems.[35] Then he went to Baden, whence he arrived back in

---

* Presumably Christine Nilsson (1843–1921), who had created Ophélie in Ambroise Thomas's *Hamlet* (Opéra, 9 March 1868) and subsequently became world famous. She gave one of her various "farewell" concerts on 20 June 1888.

Paris on the evening of the sixteenth. At four o'clock on the twenty-first, the first discussion of décors was held at the Opéra-Comique. On 25 September, dinner at the Sandersons', Rue [illegible], with Milliet. On the twenty-ninth, lunch with Poirsons, and that evening Massenet went to the Variétés to see *Le Fiacre 47*.

On 3 October, Massenet had dinner with "Rathbone, General Read, and S." [Sandersons]. This was John Meredith Read (1837–1896), American lawyer, diplomat, and writer, who during the Civil War had acted as adjutant-general of New York. During 1868–73 he was U.S. consul-general for France, and 1873–79 resident minister for Greece. It will be recalled that a "Miss Fanny Reed" [*sic*] had introduced Sibyl Sanderson to Mme Marchesi.

On 14 October 1888, the orchestration of *Esclarmonde* was finished. Schneider printed a facsimile of the final page (p. 869) showing the annotation "Je termine cet ouvrage à Paris, chez moi, 38 Rue du Général Roy, dimanche, 14 Oct: 1888 à 10 h ½ du matin. Hier, première de Jocelyn à Paris. J. Massenet." To which is added Sibyl Sanderson's signature.[36] After all, it was *her* opera. As for Benjamin Godard's *Jocelyn*, it had first been given at Brussels on 25 February 1888. The Paris performance of 13 October was at the Château d'Eau.

"My daughter is going to have a baby in a few days," wrote Massenet to Emma Borch on 2 November 1888.[37] This would have been Marie-Madeleine Bessand, his first grandchild. On 24 November he orchestrated the song *Pensée d'automne* especially for Sibyl Sanderson. Perhaps he then went to Toulouse for final rehearsals of *Manon*, given there on 12 December. The year closed with great expectations. On 17 December, Massenet brought the orchestra score of *Esclarmonde* to the Opéra-Comique. There followed twenty-two rehearsals in the foyer up to 16 February 1889; then fifty-seven stage rehearsals (including ten with orchestra) counting the *répétition générale* of 13 May 1889.[38]

Poster for *Esclarmonde* by Alfred Choubrac, 1889.

Esclarmonde;
Le Mage

T HE PARIS EXPOSITION UNIVERSELLE of 1889 was planned to open on 5 May and close on 31 October. About two hundred acres were given over to exhibits including, on the left bank, the Champ-de-Mars, Esplanade des Invalides, and Quai d'Orsay, and on the right bank, the garden of the Tro-cadéro, part of the quais, and the Palais de l'Industrie. A major attraction, of course, was the 984-foot Eiffel Tower from the top of which, on a clear day, one could see as far as Chartres. The tower was built at a cost of five million francs by the French engineer Gustave Eiffel (1832–1925), who supplied most of the capital and was given a twenty-year concession for the admission fees. The receipts for 1889 alone nearly paid for the cost.

Massenet's "contribution" to the Exposition year would be *Esclarmonde*. Meanwhile, after Geneva, *Don César de Bazan* was revived at Antwerp (15 January 1889) and at Nantes (21 April 1889). *Il Cid* was given at the Teatro Costanzi in Rome on 7 April, and *Hérodiade* at Montpellier on 24 April. In Paris, aside from *Esclarmonde*, it was a lean year, with only three performances of *Le Cid* at the Opéra.

A brief passing acquaintance with Tchaikovsky can be traced to March. Tchaikovsky was in Paris from 20 March to 9 April, his time rather fully taken up with visiting friends, attending receptions, and so on. On Sunday, 24 March, he went to the concert at the Châtelet, and noted in his diary: "Evening reception at Colonne's. Stifling. My songs. Acquaintance with Massenet." The following Sunday, 31 March, Colonne programmed the Theme and Variations from Tchaikovsky's Third Suite, and the latter noted in his diary: "At the Concerts Châtelet. With Brandukov [the cellist] in Mme Colonne's box. My composition. Success. Back stage. Diémer. Colonne. Massenet's enthusiasm." Later that day, incidentally, Tchaikovsky met Paderewski (1860–1941), heard him play, and found him a "nice person."

On 15 May 1889, *Esclarmonde* opened at the Opéra-Comique in the Place du Châtelet with Sibyl Sanderson in the title rôle. Billed as *opéra romanesque*, it did quite well, with ninety-one performances by the end of 1889 and ten more the following year, before it closed its run. The librettists, Alfred Blau and Louis de Gramont, had drawn upon the old twelfth-century metrical romance *Partenopeus de Blois*, whose story is similar to that of Cupid and Psyche with the rôles reversed. Partenopeus, transported by magic to a magnificent palace, there enjoys the love of the fair lady Melior on condition that their affair be kept literally in the dark, so that he never actually sees her. But one night he lights a lamp, with disastrous results. Only after a long series of adventures and sufferings does Partenopeus at last win the lady's hand.

Esclarmonde was Massenet's "Wagnerian" score, drawing upon a legendary subject involving the supernatural, and employing reminiscent or leading motives. Camille Bellaigue called it a combination of a small French *Tristan* and a small French *Parsifal*.[1]

--------------------◀◦▶--------------------

In the Prologue, the emperor Phorcas announces his abdication in favor of his daughter Esclarmonde. He has taught her supernatural powers, and in order to retain them, her face must remain veiled until she is twenty. On her twentieth birthday she is to become the bride of the victor in a tournament to be held at Byzantium.

Act I shows a terrace of the palace overlooking the sea. The Empress Esclarmonde longs for Roland, count of Blois, with whom she has fallen in love at first sight. Her sister Parséis suggests that she use her magic powers to bring him to her. Énéas, fiancé of Parséis, brings the news that King Cléomer has offered his daughter's hand to Roland. Esclarmonde, roused to jealousy, determines to assert her own priority. In Scene 2, the spirits find Roland hunting in the forest of Ardennes, and he boards a vessel to go to a magic island where Esclarmonde will meet him.

In Act II, Roland awakens on the magic island, welcomed by a chorus of spirits. Again momentarily falling asleep, he is awakened by the kiss of the veiled Esclarmonde. She frankly admits "Oui, je suis belle et désirable," and after a rapturous duet, the orchestra takes over where words are no longer needed. Scene 2 is in the magic palace. Roland, feeling the call of duty, must go to help King Cléomer, who is besieged by the Saracens at Blois. Esclarmonde promises to be with him every night, wherever he may be—a simple enough matter for a sorceress. But Roland must keep their secret.

At Blois (Act III), the people are suffering from the effects of the siege. King Cléomer informs them that the Saracen king Sarwégur has demanded a hundred virgins as tribute. The Saracen envoy comes to collect. But Roland, thoughtfully forearmed by Esclarmonde with a magic sword, goes out and kills Sarwégur in single combat. Scene 2 finds Roland alone in a room of the palace, impatiently awaiting the night's reunion with Esclarmonde. The bishop of Blois enters and asks him why he refuses the hand of the king's daughter Bathilde as a reward for saving the city. By threatening excommunication, the bishop worms out Roland's secret. Esclarmonde appears, and the bishop tears off her veil (thereby removing her magic powers). She reproaches Roland for his treachery, and her faithful spirits carry her away from impending capture by the chorus of priests.

In Act IV we find Phorcas in retirement in the forest of Ardennes. A Byzantine herald announces the coming tournament. Énéas and Parséis report to Phorcas that Esclarmonde has disappeared. Phorcas summons her with magic and lays before her the choice of renouncing Roland or having him put to death. Roland now finds Esclarmonde, but to save his life, she tears herself away from him. His magic sword shatters. In despair, Roland resolves to seek an honorable death in the tournament.

The Epilogue brings a happy ending. At Byzantium, Phorcas, Esclarmonde, and the court are assembled. The winner of the tournament enters with lowered visor. It is, of course, Roland. Not knowing who this strange veiled lady is, he refuses her hand. This pleases Esclarmonde, for he has after all remained true to her memory. She unveils, and there is an ecstatic reunion.

The impact of *Esclarmonde* upon Paris critics may be judged from a sampling of their reviews. Léon Kerst, of *Le Petit Journal*, remarked: "For a number of our composers the return from Bayreuth has had the effect of the road to Damascus upon St. Paul, and now they are searching for opera poems with tendencies ranging from *Lohengrin* to *Parsifal*, and passing by way of the *Ring of the Nibelung*." What does it matter, he says, as long as our composers avoid the German fog, remain French, and sing loud and clear like the Gallic cock.[2] And Victor Wilder, in *Gil Blas*: "We have to face it this time—take it as you will—the new work takes off under full sail on the impetuous flood of the music of the future." Wilder detects the Wagnerian influence in certain savage rhythms and violent sonorities that remind him of the Ride of the Valkyries, while the scene of the enchanted isle suggests *Parsifal,* but changes to *Tristan* for the love music. *Esclarmonde* is really "a symphonic drama, where typical themes or leitmotivs run through the orchestra, crossing and undergoing transformation, while the voices momentarily gain the upper hand with sudden melodious cantilenas." This premeditated and productive change of style obscures the Massenet we had learned to know—the delicate poet and amiable musician of caressing and charming grace. "In return, he has taken on a force and robustness which one would not have suspected in him. Perhaps, indeed, he has pushed things too far, and for my part I regret to find in his orchestration certain brutalities which, in my opinion, do not belong within the domain of music."[3]

Camille Bellaigue found *Esclarmonde* lacking in unity, simplicity, and eminence. "It divulges too much of instinctive or premeditated searching after effect. In the score, as in the poem, too many flowers and precious stones, too much phantasmagoria and trickery, and an almost constant dread of the natural and spontaneous.... Massenet's conception and expression of love are less refined in this work, which is more sensual than all his previous ones. This is a question of aesthetic trends.... Never yet, I believe, has anyone produced so accurate and detailed a musical description of *la manifestation physique des tendresses humaines.* (You will note that I try to express myself becomingly.) It is all noted down and gradated: the violins begin softly, then the violas answer the call for help, then the rest of the strings; the sonorities swell, the tempo becomes precipitous, and it all leads to a general climax that is terribly significant."[4] And Richard O'Monroy: "All the spectators became aroused to paroxysm. The men's eyes narrow in rapture, the ladies hide behind their fans. They shout *bis*, yes, an erotic frenzy."[5]

G. de Boisjolin, in *Le Monde artiste* of 26 May, considered *Esclarmonde* an artistic success and, at the same time, a large step forward in French musical art: "He has given us a true lyric drama. These are the theories of Wagner put to work with consummate art and craft by a French artist who possesses compositional virtuosity in the highest degree. We have often heard Massenet accused of being retrograde because he is melodious. His score of *Esclarmonde* is a successful reply to those accusations and a further proof that, where dramatic art is concerned, melody is not incompatible with the modern theories. . . . What is particularly noteworthy in this new work is that Massenet, while conserving his personal qualities, has introduced some expression that is uncommonly vigorous. Alongside those delicate musical impressions which are, as it were, the hallmark of his talent, there are passages that are energetic and singularly powerful. We do not hesitate to place the score of *Esclarmonde* in the first rank among the most interesting works of the modern school."[6]

Auguste Vitu took a rather different tack in *Le Figaro:* It seems to be Massenet's intention in *Esclarmonde* to avoid closing off his musical contours, and rather to leave each passage afloat, as it were. It is not that the composer is lacking in imagination and ideas, but these pass in a fugitive manner, one succeeding another, so that each disappears before it has fully unfolded. Vitu is reminded of the scene in Gluck where Orpheus wanders through the Elysian fields, seeking to discern among the happy shades the visage of Euridice. The composer evidently conceived his music as a running commentary upon the nuances of the poem. Vitu considers that the theory of impressionism has here been applied to music in "a series of effects, often delicate and harmonious in themselves, substituted for the broader harmoniousness of any finished and consummated form."[7]

Maurice Lefèvre's long article in *Le Monde artiste* of 19 May may be briefly paraphrased: A new work by Massenet is always an artistic event of a high order. *Esclarmonde* is a very special occasion, coming as it does a few days after the opening of the Exposition, when a cosmopolitan public has converged on Paris from the four corners of the world. Massenet's personality is by now well known, both at home and abroad. Everyone knows that "within that elegant, supple body with its fine and aristocratic inclinations there dwells a soul that is always restless, always searching further, never satisfied, and whose normal artistic state seems to be one of unfulfillment—not the unfulfillment of impotence (for the works are there to prove the contrary), but rather that of a man of talent who [as Boileau said of Molière] pleases the whole world yet is unable to please himself." Such a nature lends itself to controversy. "Thus, Massenet has his enthusiastic admirers and his violent adversaries. He moves constantly in an atmosphere of exertion. Repose is unknown to him, and whosoever comes within his orbit is inevitably swept along in the eternal gyration which constitutes his life. The fire which consumes him he communicates to all around him, friends, enemies, interpreters. When he enters a theater everything starts boiling; when he mounts the podium the orchestra prances under his baton; when he accompanies one of his works the singer discovers an ardor unknown before, and the instrument, even if it be a poor little spinet, vibrates and sings beneath his fingers. Of all the poems which he has already set to music, perhaps none was better suited to this magician than the adventures of the Byzantine sorceress. His talent needed this mixture of the *romanesque,* the *féerique,* and the *réel.*" For a week the libretto has made the rounds of the city, and the newspapers have recounted the story in great detail. As for the music, one senses that Massenet wanted to get out of beaten paths and has taken special care for newness. "Perhaps an audience less perceptive than that which attended the opening performances would have been taken by surprise at the progressions of sophisticated harmonies. Their uneasiness would not have disturbed our composer, who has written *Esclarmonde* above all to satisfy his artistic conscience, and who has thereby daringly emancipated French opera."[8]

As for Massenet's goings and comings, the rest of 1889 can be passed over quickly. No first prize was awarded for the Prix de Rome that year, nor even any first *second* prize. A Deuxième Second Grand Prix went to Alix Fournier, a pupil of Delibes, for his setting of *Sémélé,* text by Eugène Adenis. One almost wonders if Massenet had taken to neglecting his pupils. For his class on Tuesday, 29 October, he requested the orchestra scores for Beethoven's Fifth Symphony and for the overture to either *Sémiramis* or *Le Barbier de Séville.*[9]

On 27 November 1889, *Esclarmonde* was given at Brussels, where it ran for twenty-one performances with Mme Nuovina as Esclarmonde and Guillaume Ibos as Roland. I assume that Massenet went to Brussels for the final preparations. Whether he went to Montpellier for *Manon* (given 26 December), it is impossible to say. At any rate he was in Paris on Christmas Day.[10] From a letter to Paul Lacombe dated Paris, 7 January 1890, we learn that Massenet had just finished the corrections for his orchestral suite drawn from *Esclarmonde.* "What are *you* doing?" he inquires: "Your music interests me more than my own, with which I live too much." His wife and daughter send regards: "We all had dinner together yesterday, including my granddaughter!!!"[11] Paul Lacombe, pianist and composer, had just won the Prix Chartier in 1889 for chamber music. A native of Carcassonne, he was an admirer of Bizet, with whom he corresponded.

Esclarmonde attained its one hundredth performance at the Opéra-Comique on 6 February 1890, and expired soon thereafter. *Le Cid* was given three times at the Opéra during 1890, and that was it—a bad year indeed for Massenet's fortunes at the two principal Paris opera houses.[*] To be sure, *Manon* and *Hérodiade* were circulating

---

[*] See Appendix 3: Opera Performances in Paris, 1867–1915.

in the provinces and abroad. But Massenet kept his eye on the Paris barometer: his spirits soared at fair-weather signs of good box-office receipts and slumped when these fell. And *Werther,* long since finished, had not yet reached the stage.

In the meantime, Massenet had started work on *Le Mage.* After *Esclarmonde* had been launched, Hartmann opened negotiations with the poet Jean Richepin for a new libretto. They decided to try for the Opéra, and to use the subject of Zoroaster. Massenet seems to have alread planned out several scenes in the summer of 1889. The *Souvenirs* frankly admit that the music was not all newly composed: Massenet's friend Charles Malherbe "chose among my scattered papers a series of manuscripts which he indicated to me would serve in the different acts of Le Mage." *

On 1 July 1890, Massenet wrote to Florent Schmitt† from Chaullet, where "we are living, my wife and I, in an endearing and wholesome solitude."[12] But then his affairs called him back to Paris from at least the tenth to the twenty-first. In the orchestra score of *Le Mage,* the Prologue is dated Paris, 10 July 1890. On the fourteenth he wrote (apparently to the Conservatoire) that he would postpone his trip: "I cannot renounce our competition."[13] Then on Saturday the nineteenth his physician, Dr. Joseph Michel, wrote out the statement: "I certify that Monsieur J. Massenet is suffering from conjunctivitis and he would be very imprudent to leave his home." Massenet continues, on the same small sheet: "Je suis désolé! I must have caught cold yesterday. I do not know, but the doctor says that I can go out on Monday morning. Count on me for Monday, etc., but please apologize for me to *mon Maître* [Thomas]. It is difficult for me to *see* in order to read." In a postscript he explains that it is seven in the morning; he was suffering so much that he wanted to know what was the matter, and the doctor had come right away.[14]

Partly, no doubt, because there had been no first prize in 1889, two were awarded the Premier Grand Prix in 1890: Gaston Carraud, a pupil of Massenet; and Alfred Bachelet, a pupil of Guiraud. Bachelet later achieved the greater fame, notably with *Quand la cloche sonnera* (Opéra-Comique, 6 November 1922). There were also two second prizes: for Charles Lutz, pupil of Guiraud, and for Charles Silver, pupil of Massenet. Silver went on to first prize the next year.

The next event worth recording was the staging of *Manon* at the Vienna Hof-

---

* Charles Malherbe (1853–1911), musicologist, assembled a remarkable private collection of music autographs (which he bequeathed to the Conservatoire), and in 1898 he succeeded Nuitter as archivist for the Paris Opéra. A contributor to music journals and a writer of books on music, Malherbe was also coeditor with Saint-Saëns, from 1895, of the collected edition of Rameau's works brought out by Durand & Cie.

† Florent Schmitt (1870–1958) was born at Blâmont, in Lorraine, and entered the Paris Conservatoire in 1889. Having studied harmony with Dubois and Lavignac, and composition with Massenet and Fauré, he won the Prix de Rome in 1900. The letter in question is exceptionally cordial, beginning "mon cher ami" and signing off "Votre vieil ami, bien sincèrement à vous de cœur, Massenet." The eight letters we have seen from Massenet to Schmitt, ranging from 1890 to 1901, reflect Massenet's appreciation of Schmitt's talent and his readiness to put in a good word with the authorities or with publishers.

oper on 19 November 1890.[*] (The German translation was by F. Gumbert.) Massenet went to supervise the final preparations. The most noted conductor in Vienna at this time was Hans Richter (1843–1916), who was not only active at the Opera but also conducted the Philharmonic concerts during 1875–97. However, it was Jahn who was responsible for *Manon*. Wilhelm Jahn (1834–1900) had conducted from the age of twenty, first at Budapest, then Amsterdam, Prague, and Wiesbaden (1864–81). He was called to Vienna in 1881 by the then Intendant of the Hofoper, Leopold Friedrich, Freiherr von Hormann, and remained there until his retirement in 1897, when Gustav Mahler took over. Witeschnik has called Richter and Jahn the "two blond, blue-eyed, corpulent giants" and credits Jahn, despite his schoolmasterly outward appearance, with a flair for mounting operas in an ingratiating French-Viennese manner.[15] In his undertakings Jahn had solid support in the Belgian tenor Ernest Van Dyck, who from 1883 made an impression in Paris with concert appearances in Wagner rôles, sang Parsifal at Bayreuth in 1888, and was engaged by the Vienna Opera during 1888–98. (Thereafter, 1898–1904, Van Dyck sang Wagner rôles at the Metropolitan in New York.) Jahn's other mainstay was Marie Renard, who captured the hearts of the Viennese.[†] It was the success of *Manon* that drew *Werther* to Vienna for its world première in 1892. The real hits of this period in Vienna, wrote Witeschnik, were *Manon* and *Werther*, plus *Cavalleria rusticana* with Schläger as Santuzza.

To open the carnival season in Milan, *Il Cid* was staged at La Scala on 26 December 1890, with Franco Cardinali (Rodrigo) and Hariclea Darclée (Chimène).[‡] The work attained a good success, with fourteen performances, but it was not given again at La Scala after that season. Next on the bill was Mascagni's *Cavalleria rusticana* (3 January 1891, with twenty-three performances), a sensationally successful opera which had first been staged at the Costanzi in Rome the previous season (17 May 1890). Passing over Gluck's *Orfeo ed Euridice* (one performance) and Wagner's *Lohengrin* (eleven performances), two other operas of that season deserve passing mention. *Condor*, by the Brazilian composer Carlos Gomez, had its world première on 21 February 1891 and was given ten times. The other world première was Samara's *Lionella* (4 April), with only one performance. Spiro Samara (1863–1917), born at Corfu of a Greek father and an English mother, had studied composition with Delibes in Paris. He is mentioned here because, in all likelihood, his *Medgé* (Rome, 1888) employed the libretto that Massenet had rejected in 1874. Edoardo Sonzogno was the proprietor of *Il Cid*, *Cavalleria*, and *Lionella*.

---

[*] *Le Cid* had been given there on 22 November 1887 in a German translation by Max Kalbeck, noted music critic and writer of an eight-volume biography of Brahms.

[†] Marie Renard (1864–1939) was born at Graz as Marie Pölzi; she married Count Kinsky in 1900.

[‡] At La Scala there was usually only one *stagione* (season) of *carnevale e quaresima* (Carnival and Lent), opening on San Stefano (26 December) and lasting into April. In some years short seasons were added: for *primavera* (in May), as in 1889 and 1894; or for *autunno* (September, October, or even November), as in 1874, 1875, 1877; or for both, as in 1881.

Poster for *Le Mage* by Alfredo Edel, 1891.

Le Mage opened at the Paris Opéra on 16 March 1891. It was not exactly a failure, for it reached its thirty-first performance on 11 October of the same year. But it simply did not catch on, was never revived, and was apparently given on only one other stage (The Hague, 25 January 1896). Jean Richepin's libretto may be summarized as follows:

―――――――――――◄○►―――――――――――

Act I: The scene is the camp of Zarastra, a Persian general who has defeated the Touranians. We meet the high priest Amrou and his daughter Varedha, a priestess of La Djahi, goddess of love. Varedha declares her love for Zarastra, but the latter loves Anahita, queen of the Touranians, who is among the captives.

Act II, Scene 1: In the subterranean chambers of the temple of Djahi, Varedha is upset because everyone is so happy over the victory. Her father stokes the fire of her jealousy and promises vengeance for Zarastra's indifference toward his daughter. Scene 2 shows the square of the town of Balzhdi where, to the acclaim of the crowd, Zarastra brings the captives before the king of Iran and the assembled court and priests. As sole reward for his victory he requests the hand of Anahita, and this is agreeable both to his sovereign and to Anahita. But then Amrou interposes the objection that Zarastra had promised to wed Varedha. Zarastra denies any such commitment, but a false oath sworn by Amrou and the priests convinces Anahita that Zarastra has acted dishonorably, and she turns away from him. Zarastra is goaded to violent language and, as a result, is banished.

Act III: Zarastra has sought peace near a holy mountain, sacred to the god of fire, and is now venerated as a Magus. Alone, he thinks of the past but, on the whole, is content. The amorous Varedha pursues him to this spot. She tries every wile to win him and at last shakes his composure with the report that Anahita is about to marry the king of Iran. This, she is sure, will bring him running back to Bakhdi.

Act IV: In the sanctuary of the temple of Djahi, dances and invocations are offered to the goddess. The drama resumes: Anahita is unwilling to marry the king; the king persists; Anahita threatens an uprising of the Touranians; it is ordered that the wedding proceed (bringing Varedha revenge at last, incidentally); but then the Touranian soldiers overrun the place.

Act V presents the same scene in smoldering ruins. Zarastra wanders through the destruction. Among unburied dead he finds the wounded Varedha, then Anahita, with whom there is a joyous reunion. Varedha, coming to, invokes the vengeance of Djahi, and the fires again burst into flame and threaten the couple. But Zarastra, as Magus and priest of Ahma Mazda, has the power to extinguish the conflagration. He leaves the ruins with Anahita, while Varedha expires.

The cast included Edmond Vergnet (Zarastra), Caroline Fiérens (Varedha), Maria Lureau-Escalaïs (Anahita), Jean-François Delmas (Amrou), and Jean Martapoura (Le Roi d'Iran). The reviews in general disclose some, or even many, good things about the opera. But their very particularization leaves bare, by default, a lack of organic unity or any consummation of an effective personal style. Alfred Ernst found *Le Mage* superior to *Le Cid* but far below *Esclarmonde*. Victor Wilder preferred the good old Massenet image, and his sensitive ears were bruised by anything more forceful: Massenet has no rival for grace and charm; his music is truly fin de siècle, his melodies exquisitely deliquescent. But this restless soul has the ambition to be strong and powerful. However much he crashes the cymbals, blows full blast into the brasses, or thumps the bass drum, this does not constitute the grandiose eloquence one ought to expect from a real master.[16]

A. Landely, in *L'Art musical*, tried to do his critical duty by uncovering the faults of the whole. The talents of the collaborators are not well mated. Richepin is inclined toward violence, even brutality, while Massenet's talent is more tender and voluptuous. Each tried to meet the other halfway, with resulting compromises. True, the poetry is lyrical and colorful, but the drama has no genuine intent or purpose. Furthermore, the dramatist has not provided for characterization, so that the composer has no chance to bring to bear the musical psychology of which he is capable.[*] Hence, we have not a lyric drama, nor even an opera, but rather a succession of musical paintings, some exquisite, some powerful, but others uneven or meager. [Landely praises the whole of Act I.] Act II is uncomfortably reminiscent of *Aïda*, *La Favorite*, or *L'Africaine*. Acts III and V are marred by the predominance of stage spectacle. In Act III, for instance, the audience is so taken up with the thunder and lightning on stage as to miss the rather good religious musical qualities. One would need to hear the opera several times, so that after the eyes have had their fill the ears could begin to pay attention. As for the ballet of Act IV, it is not up to *Le Roi de Lahore* nor *Hérodiade*.[17]

Noël and Stoullig tried to take a positive position. The composer of *Le Mage*, trampling on the old molds, let his genius guide him without caring about those forms heretofore too exclusively sanctioned by the Opéra. Orchestra and drama cooperate symphonically; the drama marches ahead in the orchestra, intimately connected with the events on the stage.[18] This is not to say that the work is in any sense Wagnerian. Landely, in the review already cited, found no leitmotivs and, at best, only a few reminiscent phrases. But also, he admitted, there were no set pieces and no ritornellos.

We can sympathize, perhaps, with Adolphe Jullien, who had been waiting for Massenet to write the truly strong and personal work that would represent him at his best. Clearly *Le Mage* is not it, he says. Indeed, it is one of the least interesting of his operas. Massenet depends too much upon that "flowing melody, affected and sensuous, which most easily pleases audiences of our time, and he does not seem to have any other objective in mind than to elicit some *bravos* as quickly as possible." The tender duos of Anahita and Zarastra will no doubt make the rounds of the salons. But, for Jullien, the best spot in the score was the effective passage for muted brasses where Zarastra kneels at the foot of the mountain.[19]

Léon Carvalho, absent from the Opéra-Comique since the disastrous fire of 1887, was now reappointed director on 6 March 1891. We can imagine that Massenet was electrified into action. It was Carvalho who had originally produced *Manon*, and that work had not been seen at the Opéra-Comique since 1885. With Sibyl Sanderson in mind, Massenet no doubt approached Carvalho regarding a revival. According to Mathilde Marchesi, after *Esclarmonde*, Sibyl Sanderson went to La Monnaie in Brussels for two seasons—obviously 1889–91. At any rate, she wrote to Massenet in rather formal French:

---

[*] Compare Georges Servières: The Iranian king and Amrou do not even exist—they are mere puppets. Amrou's duo à la Verdi and air à la Gluck are quite out of style with the sanctuary of the goddess Djahi! (*La Musique française moderne*, 1897.)

Bruxelles
Dimanche, 29 Mars 1891

Monsieur,

Je suis de retour à Bruxelles depuis deux jours seulement. En arrivant j'ai trouvé votre mot. Je regrette beaucoup qu'il m'est impossible de quitter Bruxelles maintenant, et je ne serais pas à Paris avant juillet. Avec toutes mes excuses, veuillez, Monsieur, agréer l'expression de mes sentiments distingués.

Sibyl Sanderson[20]

It seems safe to say that Massenet had asked her to come to Paris to sing for Carvalho, with a view to a contract for the following season. As it developed, "July" was not too late—*Manon* did appear in October.

In May, Massenet went to London; *Manon, in French,* was given at Covent Garden on the nineteenth, with Sanderson as Manon and Van Dyck as Des Grieux. From London, Massenet wrote two letters to Quinzard. The first, dated 14 May, was addressed to Hartmann's shop at 20 Rue Daunou: "Forgive me, my dear friend, for writing on this scrap of paper. I don't have anything else, and I don't know how to ask for any—in English. Ten times already I have cried, 'Give me some paper!' They think I mean toilet paper! Many thanks for your warmhearted letter. I am so profoundly sad and alone, and discouraged, and unnerved. Manon goes on, Tuesday the nineteenth? I shall return to Paris immediately afterward—I am so far away!! I believe Le Mage took in for Friday and Wednesday something like eleven thousand [francs]? And they want to take it off! What does it matter to me at this moment. I am tired at heart of it all! À vous, mon cher ami, J. Massenet."[21]

To explain the second letter, we must remember that Henri Heugel acquired Hartmann's business on 16 May 1891.[*] Dated London, 19 May, it reads: "This evening Manon. I have not received any letter from Hartmann, only a telegram as short as telegrams are. I am thinking of you, of our faithful and long attachment to that firm [Hartmann's]! I can hardly wait to see you. I am without news of the details. To you, dear old friend, with all my heart, J. Massenet."[22]

In a narrow sense, Massenet had been sold like a chattel along with Hartmann's business. Music in stock was simply stamped over with the name of the new firm. Where a reprinting was needed, Hartmann's plates were used, with a new cover and other preliminary matter as needed by Heugel et Cⁱᵉ. The house organ, *Le Ménestrel* (The Minstrel), was founded by Léopold Heugel in 1833, and since 1839 the business had been located at 2bis Rue Vivienne, across the street from the rear of the Bibliothèque Nationale. "Au Ménestrel" (which appears constantly in Massenet's letters

---

[*] Heugel's father, Léopold Heugel (1815–1883), had started a music business in Paris about 1833, enlarged in 1842 by the addition of Jean-Antoine Meissonnier's assets. Henri Heugel (1844–1916) entered the business in 1865, became proprietor upon his father's death, and acquired E. Gérard et Cⁱᵉ about 1886. Upon acquiring Hartmann's business, Heugel set up a partnership with his nephew Paul-Émile Chevalier (1861–1931). Henri Heugel's successor was his son Jacques Heugel (b. 1890), and from 1947 the latter's sons François and André Heugel managed the firm.

hereafter) was synonymous with "at the firm of Heugel et Cie." In a broader sense, the change of management was, for Massenet, both timely and efficacious. He was soon on the best of terms with Henri Heugel, whom he addressed in his letters as "cher bon ami," while still preserving up to the last the respectful "vous" form. Without the conscientious professional help of his publisher, even in the most detailed matters, Massenet would have been a ship adrift without a rudder. We must bear this in mind in contemplating Massenet's material success.

On 10 July 1891, Mme Massenet purchased the property known as Le Vieux Manoir at Pont-de-l'Arche (Eure), a picturesque old Norman town twenty kilometers south of Rouen at the confluence of the Eure and the Seine. The house was less a manor than a rambling two-storied *pavillon* with white façade on the Rue Montalent (now No. 9 Rue Jean Prieur) and, on the other side, a pleasant terrace overlooking the Eure. The house once belonged to the Duchesse de Longueville, née Bourbon-Condé, daughter of a prince of Orléans; her fleurs-de-lis were still in evidence over the windows. Comfortably fitted out with period furniture, it was an ideal working place for Massenet's summers. To fetch his visiting friends from the railway station, he acquired a "prehistoric" landau upholstered in blue satin; drawn by two white horses, it served its purpose well but aroused the amusement of the townspeople.

The Prix de Rome for 1891 went to Charles Silver, a pupil of Massenet, for his setting of *L'Interdit*, text by Édouard Noël. Second prize was awarded to Delibes's pupil Alix Fournier, and an honorable mention to Guiraud's pupil François-Joseph-Camille Andrès.

In August of 1891, Massenet was at the Grand Hôtel in Vevey. Doubtless an agreement had been reached with Vienna regarding *Werther*, for now he was writing a ballet, *Le Carillon*, also for Vienna. A letter dated "Vevey, August 1891" is addressed to Monsieur Hudelèrt, Heugel's principal assistant. Massenet acknowledges receipt of music paper (much needed, for "I am working rather much, enormously!"), and also a letter from Heugel's partner, Paul Chevalier, which evokes the exclamation: "How good and kind you all are to me!" There are other details, such as "please find out Mlle Delna's address," and (because it would be useful) "send a score of *Le Mage* to Professor Leopold Ketten of the Geneva Conservatory"—all samples of the little chores an obliging publisher with secretarial staff was supposed to look after.[23]

On 11 August, he wrote to the singer Mme Durand-Ulbach regarding the *Poème d'octobre.*[*] No, it was not for a concert engagement but simply that he wanted Heugel to hear her interpretation, which he considered especially good. "This little private audition can take place rue Vivienne, where Heugel has had fitted up for me a large office, *very favorable for the voice*, and *very comfortable* as a place to work. Heugel spends with me and our collaborators at least an hour every day, toward 4:30 or 5:00. I shall be returning in a few days. I am going to St. Bernard, maybe to Zermatt among the glaciers [before returning to Paris]."[24]

---

[*] Mme Durand-Ulbach was on the roster of La Monnaie for 1889–90 and died in 1910.

From the mountains to the seashore: on 5 September Massenet was at Pourville, where he began the orchestration of the symphonic poem *Visions*. Besides the standard orchestra (with woodwinds in threes), the work calls for an offstage group comprising a soprano, solo violin, harp, and harmonium. By page 8 (12 September), Massenet was back in Paris "dans ma bibliothèque." The page numbers skip 13, running 12, 12bis, 14. *Visions* was a kind of special offering to his new publisher, for immediately upon its completion in November, Massenet inscribed the sixty-seven-page autograph "to my friend, Henri Heugel."

Visions was put aside for a time, and on 15 September the orchestration of the ballet *Le Carillon* was begun. The margins of its pages provide a running comment on events, as (page 1): "Paris, Tuesday, 15 Sep '91. Tomorrow, première of Lohengrin at the Opéra." *Lohengrin* was indeed first staged at the Paris Opéra on 16 September 1891, in a French translation by Charles Nuitter. The cast included Ernest Van Dyck (Lohengrin), Rose Caron (Elsa), Caroline Fièrens (Ortrude), Maurice Renaud (Frédéric de Telramund), and Jean-François Delmas (le Roi). Further along in the score of *Le Carillon*, he wrote,

23 September—"Today, third rehearsal on stage of Manon."

29 September—"First rehearsal with chorus."

Page 69—"Yesterday, Wednesday, 30 Sep '91, suicide of General Boulanger at the tomb of Mme de Bonnemains in Brussels."[*]

2 October—"Yesterday, dinner at the home of Mme and Mlle Sanderson. Gille, Van Dyck, Boyer [were present]."

3 October—"First rehearsal with orchestra, Manon, at 12:30 P.M."

6 October, Tuesday morning—"Beginning of classes [at the Conservatoire] Admirable weather the past two months."

7 October, Wednesday—"Choral rehearsal of Manon, at 12:30 P.M."

12 October, Monday—"At home during the première [i.e., first performance of this revival] of Manon, 8:30 P.M., anxieties."

The second performance of *Manon*—its ninetieth since the first première in 1884—was given on Thursday, 15 October 1891. On Friday evening, the 227 pages of the orchestration of *Le Carillon* were completed.

By 5 November, Massenet had again taken up *Visions*. On page 32 he designates middle C, B natural, and B-flat as the three notes required by the part for "Electrophone." The end was reached on Sunday, 8 November 1891, at "5:30 P.M., cold weather, alone, sad, all this day. Yesterday 100th of Manon at the Opéra-Comique." The cast at the one hundredth included Sibyl Sanderson (Manon), Delmas (Des Grieux), Taskin (Lescaut), and Fugère (Comte des Grieux).

---

[*] General Georges-Ernest-Jean-Marie Boulanger (1837–1891), thanks to his introduction of some timely army reforms and the appearance of a music-hall song in his praise, enjoyed a brief popularity as "the man on horseback." Then, exposed as "a tool in the hands of the royalists" and deserted by his partisans, he took his life at the tomb of his mistress, Marguerite Crouzet.

Poster for *Werther* by Eugène Grasset, 1893.

Werther

ESCLARMONDE WAS GIVEN AT BORDEAUX on 13 January 1892. Massenet was there, staying at the Hôtel du Chapon Fin, in the Rue Montesquieu, and returning to Paris on the morning of the fourteenth. Then, on Sunday the twenty-fourth, he left for Vienna.[1] There he was given a room at the famous Hotel Sacher, across the street from the stage entrance of the opera house. In the *Souvenirs* we read:

> My first call after my arrival was on Jahn, the director. That kindly, eminent master took me to the foyer where the rehearsals were to be held. It was a vast room, lighted by immense windows and provided with great chairs. A full length portrait of Emperor Franz Joseph ornamented one of the panels; there was a grand piano in the center of the room. All the artists for *Werther* were gathered around the piano when Jahn and I entered the foyer. As they saw us they rose in a body and bowed in salutation. At this touching manifestation of respectful sympathy — to which our great Van Dyck added a most affectionate embrace — I responded by bowing in my turn; and then, a little nervous and trembling all over, I sat down at the piano. The work was absolutely in shape. All the artists could sing their parts from memory. The hearty demonstrations they showered on me at intervals moved me so much that I felt tears in my eyes. At the orchestra rehearsal this emotion was renewed. The execution was perfection; the orchestra, now soft, now loud, followed the shading of the voice so that I could not shake off the enchantment.[*]

In a letter of 9 February (Tuesday), Massenet informed Heugel of general rehearsals for *Werther* on Tuesday, Wednesday, Thursday, rest on Friday, costumes Saturday. The general rehearsal open to the presswould be on Monday, 15 February. "If you leave [Paris] Saturday 13th at 6:50, you will arrive [Vienna] Sunday 14th for supper, and the next day Monday at 10:30 rehearsal."[2] And, indeed, Heugel as well as the librettist Paul Milliet were there for the Monday rehearsal.

The première of *Werther*, on 16 February 1892, was conducted by Wilhelm

---

[*] The account is in basic agreement with a report of an interview with Massenet, as published by Robert Charvay in *L'Écho de Paris*, illustrated supplement, Jan. 1893. See Solenière (1897), 50–56.

Jahn, with Ernest Van Dyck (Werther), Marie Renard (Charlotte), Ellen Brandt-Forster (Sophie), Neidle (Albert), Mayerhofer (le Bailli), Schlittenhelm (Schmidt), Félix (Johann), Noll (Brühlmann), and Carlona (Kätchen). The synopsis:

––––––––––––––––––––⊙▶––––––––––––––––––––

Act I, The Bailiff's House. Adjoining the house is a terrace and garden; in the distance the town of Wetzlar. It is "July 178 . . . ." The Bailiff is teaching his youngest children a Christmas carol, "Noël, Noël, Jésus vient de naître." His friends Schmidt and Johann stop by. Charlotte ("age 20"), the Bailiff's daughter, is ready to leave for the ball; but first she gives the children their bread and butter, as she has done since their mother died. Werther ("age 23"), also invited, is enchanted with the domestic felicity of the household. Brühlmann, Kätchen, and other couples, pass by on their way to the ball. Charlotte admonishes her sister Sophie ("age 15") to look after the children, and goes off with Werther. Albert, Charlotte's fiancé, returns after six months' absence; he wonders if he has been missed. Reassured by Sophie that Charlotte still cares, he leaves. An orchestral interlude suggests the passage of time, and Charlotte and Werther return from the ball. Charlotte recalls the virtues of her departed mother, whom she tries to replace in caring for the children. Werther declares his love, but the Bailiff interrupts with the news of Albert's return. Charlotte ("lowly and sad") admits: "Yes, the man my mother made me swear to marry. And yet, for a moment, with you, I had forgotten the oath of which they now remind me." Werther ("with an effort") concedes that she must keep her word, but "I . . . I shall die of it, Charlotte."

Act II, The Lindens. A square in Wetzlar before a church, with linden trees; three months later, a fine Sunday afternoon. Jovial songs to Bacchus from the nearby tavern blend with organ sounds from the church. Charlotte and Albert, now married, go to attend the church service. Werther has been observing them from a distance, grief-stricken that Charlotte is the wife of another. After the service, Albert approaches Werther sympathetically; he understands Werther's torment, and "to know is to forgive." The lighthearted Sophie, in high spirits, reproaches Werther for his solemn face. Alone with Charlotte, Werther is torn between moral duty to leave her forever and the sweet agony of being near her. Charlotte's sense of duty gives her the strength to assure Werther that she will not banish him forever; he should come again, in three months, at Christmas.

Act III, Charlotte and Werther. The afternoon of 24 December. Charlotte, alone, rereads Werther's letters. She is alarmed by the last letter: "Until Christmas, you said. But if I should not appear on that day, do not accuse me—weep for me!" Sophie tries to cheer her up but admits that "everyone seems gloomy since Werther went away." Charlotte, afraid, prays for strength. Werther appears; he had tried not to come but was impelled in spite of himself. He recalls the times they spent here: the harpsichord, the books, the poems of Ossian he was translating, the brace of pistols which he had often fingered. His melancholy gives way to ardor; they embrace for a brief instant, but Charlotte, regaining self-control, bids him good-bye and goes to her room. When Albert comes in, he senses that something is wrong. A servant brings him a message from Werther: "I am going far away; please lend me your pistols." At Albert's request (and his patience is at an end), Charlotte hands the pistols to the servant. Then, grasping the implications, she dons her cloak and rushes out, half knowing that she will be too late.

Act IV, Christmas Eve, and Werther's Death. In an opening tableau of falling snow, the orchestra recalls the themes of the opera. There is a pistol shot, and a curtain parts disclosing Werther's apartment. Charlotte arrives to find Werther mortally wounded. He revives, absolves her of all blame for his death, and requests her not to seek help. Werther is happy to die holding her hand. Charlotte confesses that from the start she felt a bond of strong attachment that could never be broken; she returns the kiss he had given her that afternoon. Outside, voices of children sing "Noël, Noël," and Werther expires.[*]

In such a *drame lyrique* one does not expect symphonic development of leading motives in any Wagnerian sense. Themes and motives simply reappear, in recognizable shape, accumulating significance with each recurrence. There are moments of calculated relief, as in Sophie's youthful *joie de vivre* and the gaiety of the couples on their way to the ball. Massenet delights in juxtaposition of musical styles, as in the scene of the lindens; his master stroke of theater is the poignancy of Werther's death amidst the unconcerned Christmas Eve joyousness of the rest of the world. When Charlotte and Werther return from the ball ("Il faut nous séparer, voici notre maison, c'est l'heure du sommeil"), the quietly blissful theme foreshadows a favorite device of Puccini: the melody in octaves with just enough accompaniment to keep the rhythm flowing. An example of expressive economy might be the brief motive, like a twinge of pain, that reveals its significance when Charlotte reads: "Tu m'as dit: à Noël, et j'ai crié: jamais!"

Five days after *Werther*, on 21 February 1892, Vienna saw the creation of Massenet's one-act ballet *Le Carillon*. The scenario of this *légende dansée et mimée* was by Ernest Van Dyck and Camille de Roddaz.

The scene is the market place (Grand' Place, or Groote Markt) of Courtrai, in Flanders. A prominent feature of the square is the Gothic brick belfry tower, where work is in progress on the great clock, not yet unveiled. Men and women are seated

---

[*] Goethe's own Charlotte Buff, daughter of a Wetzlar magistrate, was engaged to a man named Kestner. The prototype of Werther was apparently the young Jerusalem, who committed suicide in 1772 for unrequited love. Finck (1910) reported the strange coincidence that a grandson of Charlotte, Georg Kestner, committed suicide on the very evening of the Vienna première of Massenet's *Werther*. Further, that when the opera was first sung in Leipzig the tenor, Buff, was a grandnephew of Goethe's Charlotte.

around tables of the brasserie, while others dance. The young people offer flowers to Bertha in honor of her coming betrothal, though her fiancé has not yet been selected. (Bertha loves Master Karl, who is fabricating the great clock whose chimes are to greet the coming arrival of the Duke. Bertha's father, Rombalt, would prefer that she choose between Pit, *syndic* of the chimney sweeps, and Jef, *syndic* of the bakers' guild.) Rombalt catches Karl embracing Bertha and chases him away. Karl ascends to work on his clock.

The guilds enter to the acclaim of the crowd. Pit mimes his chimney-sweep's profession, while Jef is resplendent in baker's white. Both are introduced to Bertha by her father, but she snubs them, making fun of their pantomimes. A herald proclaims the grand entry, on the morrow, of the Duke. Karl pleads with the sheriff of Courtrai for an extension of time, but this is refused. Unless the chimes strike the hour of the Duke's arrival, Karl must go to prison. Bertha announces her choice: Karl. But her father assures Pit and Jef that, with the chimes unfinished, he is hardly likely to consent to such a marriage.

Night descends, and all retire from the scene. Alone, Karl gazes in desperation at his clock. He kneels before the statue of St. Martin, imploring aid. The statue glows with light, and the nodding head promises assistance. In a vision, the walls of the belfry tower become transparent, the clock face lights up, and angels strike the bells of the carillon. When the vision disappears, Karl places a ladder at Bertha's window and tells her of the hope his vision has brought. She comes down to join him, but they must hide from the passing night watch of good burghers, who are both inebriated and afraid of the dark. After Bertha and Karl have returned to their respective abodes, first Jef and then Pit come prowling to gaze at Bertha's window, where they discover the forgotten ladder. Rombalt comes out, aroused by their clumsy noise, but they convince him that Karl is the real culprit. To make doubly sure of Karl's failure, they propose to demolish the clock, and Rombalt supplies them with hammers. Pit and Jef ascend and disappear behind the veil to pursue their destructive task. St. Martin's statue glows, suggesting that the Saint, too, has a plan.

Dawn breaks. Cocks crow, and birds awaken. A curious crowd gradually assembles. The sheriff and his train make a pompous entry, and there is a *danse flamande*. Rombalt, Bertha, and Karl appear. Rombalt cynically renews his promise to accept Karl as son-in-law provided the carillon celebrates the Duke's arrival. The sheriff consults his watch; guards are ready to arrest Karl. Bertha, with seductive pantomime, tries to divert the sheriff's attention. Then the Carillon sounds! The veil falls away. St. Martin has transformed Jef and Pit into *jaquemarts:* there they stand as metal figures, striking in turn with their hammers the great bronze bells surmounting the clock's face. Bertha falls into Karl's arms, and Rombalt gives them his blessing. The Duke's cortège arrives, and the Duke places a golden chain around Karl's neck. The curtain falls amidst general acclamation.

The interpreters of *Le Carillon* were Mlle Cerale (Bertha), Frappart (Karl), Caron (Rombalt), Van Hamme (Pit), Price (Jef), Rumpel (l'Échevin de Courtrai), Klasz (un Héraut), and Nunziante (Philippe le Bon), and the conductor Joseph Hellmesberger, Jr., who was responsible for ballets at the Hofoper.

By 29 February, Massenet was back in Paris.[3] *Werther* was now a subject for conversation, and those of his friends who had been unable to go to Vienna no doubt importuned the composer to hear samples of the music. Thus a letter of 5 March to an unidentified friend (Hartmann?):

> Ah! my good and dear friend, I remember those sad days and that particular morning. I still see you listening to the reading of the Werther poem and my description of the mise en scène. You were so kind as to remember that morning of a so distant epoch—thank you! I owe your friends a reading of the score, and I shall keep my promise with the dearest pleasure. My son-in-law was here a moment ago, and I asked him to read to my daughter your interesting news.
>
> Cordially yours,
>
> J. Massenet.

An inscribed score will be sent to you.[4]

A few days later, Massenet thanked someone in Bayonne for news of a *Manon* performance there, conveying thanks "first to you, then to Lelong and to M. Barbe (our charming Des Grieux at The Hague, 1888), and finally to all our valiant interpreters," who, according to another letter, included Mlle Perdrelli.[5]

On 1 April 1892, Massenet began the first draft of *Thaïs*, to a libretto prepared by Louis Gallet based on the novel by Anatole France. By 15 July the draft was completed, at Neufchâtel-lès-Samur near Boulogne-sur-Mer, and he was ready to proceed with the orchestration, which would take another fifteen months.

The sad duty now devolved upon Massenet to write eulogies for two valued colleagues: Édouard Lalo died on 22 April, and Ernest Guiraud on 6 May 1892. His discourse for Lalo, presented on behalf of the Société des Auteurs et Compositeurs Dramatiques, may be found among his letters in the Bibliothèque Nationale; it is a brief, formal tribute to Lalo's French qualities, with special mention of "his last masterpiece," *Le Roi d'Ys*. The speech for Guiraud's funeral, on 10 May, was published along with other such documents by the Institut de France.

In the Prix de Rome trials, none of the settings of Édouard Adenis's poem *Amadis* was considered worthy of the grand prize. Two of Guiraud's pupils, Henri Busser and André Bloch, received second prizes; they would do better the following year. Following Guiraud's death, Charles Lenepveu was appointed to succeed him as professor of composition—officially on 1 January 1894.

Among Massenet's colleagues of the Institut were the painter-sculptor Jean-Léon Gérôme (1824–1904) and the sculptor Emmanuel Frémiet (1824–1910), the latter elected in the summer of 1892. The *Souvenirs* give a portion of a letter written to Massenet on 1 August: "I brought a little doll Thaïs to the Institut for you, and as

I was going to the country after the session and you were not there, I left it with Bonvalot and begged him to handle her carefully. . . . I return in a day or so, for on Saturday we receive Frémiet, who wishes me to thank you for voting for him. Gérôme." The "doll" was a colored statuette that Gérôme had made for the composer to keep on his table as he wrote *Thaïs*. Massenet liked to have at hand some such symbol or token of whatever opera he happened to be working on.

The *Souvenirs* make entertaining reading but are frustrating to anyone attempting to reconstruct Massenet's life chronologically. Thus after the letter just cited, the narrative jumps quite credibly to 1894, mentions that "between times I again visited Bayreuth . . . to applaud the Mastersingers of Nuremberg," and this evokes a flashback to the meeting with Wagner "in 1861" [actually, 1859 or early 1860]. *Die Meistersinger* was given at Bayreuth in the summers af 1888, 1889, and 1892. Massenet's preoccupation with *Esclarmonde* in 1888 seems to eliminate that year, leaving 1889 and 1892 as possibilities for a trip to Bayreuth. In any event, a letter fixed his position at Pont-de-l'Arche on 26 August 1892, when the Bessands with their two children came for dinner.[6]

Massenet wrote to Florent Schmitt on 1 October: "Make the most of that beautiful land, which I know so well, and come back with Legrand after a good vacation. It is raining here, a true Parisian weather. I am leaving this evening to 'celebrate' Méhul at Givet. I shall return soon, but I warn you that the classes will be in the morning. Again, thanks for your warm letter and my best regards to you and Legrand. J. Massenet."[7] The next day, at Givet in the Ardennes, there was a dedication of a Méhul statue; Massenet and Ambroise Thomas read speeches, which may be found among the published papers of the Institut de France, Académie des Beaux-Arts.

As the year drew to a close, Massenet was involved with rehearsals for *Werther* at the Opéra-Comique. It appears unlikely, therefore, that he went abroad for *Manon*, given at Hamburg on 31 October 1892 (for the first time in Germany), or for *Werther*, staged at Weimar on 13 November and at Geneva on 27 December.

Werther opened in Paris on 16 January 1893.[*] Jules Danbé conducted, and the cast comprised Marie Delna (Charlotte), Guillaume Ibos (Werther), Marie-Sophie Laisné (Sophie), Thierry (le Bailli), Max Bouvet (Albert), Barnolt (Schmidt), Artus (Johann), and Éloi de Roqueblave (Brühlmann). On the day of the première, *L'Echo de Paris* issued a special supplement devoted to Massenet and *Werther*. Robert Charvay's article, based on an interview, recounted in first-person style the genesis of *Werther* and Massenet's experiences in Vienna.[8] Charles Malherbe, in *Le Monde artiste*, reminded his readers that "the large shadow of Wagner hovers over the dramatic music of our time" but insisted that Wagner now belonged in a class with Bach and Beethoven, i.e., to be studied and admired but not copied. Massenet, in treating "one of the masterpieces of foreign literature," has achieved a clarity of style that is eminently French. Scarcely a contemporary German composer would have dared to set

---

[*] *Le Cid* was revived the same night at the Opéra and given six times during 1893; its next revival would be in 1900.

Werther—neither Goldmark, Brüll, Hofmann, Rufer, nor Kretschmer.* It is to Massenet's honor that his work was acclaimed in German-speaking Vienna.[9]

Alfred Bruneau, in *Gil Blas,* considered it unnecessary to explain Massenet's style: "The composer of *Werther* is presently the most performed of French composers, hence the best known and most famous musician of our epoch. His works, so numerous and so lustrous, are in the repertoire of all the opera houses, adorn the music racks of every piano, are fixed in the memories of even the most unyielding dilettantes. It can be said that his very special style is at this moment a mystery to no one. No need, then, to proselytize new converts."[10] Georges Street (*Le Matin*) was impressed by the composer's respect for the expressive qualities of the poem and avoidance of vocal or instrumental effects for their own sake. *Werther* is both striking and moving for its unity.[11] Charles Darcours (*Le Figaro*) received much the same impression: "Goethe has said somewhere that 'where words leave off, music begins'; in the score of *Werther* words and music are so closely allied as to seem born of one and the same inspiration."[12] Léon Kerst (*Le Petit journal*) found the German atmosphere of the drama convincingly maintained throughout, even though the musical treatment was "exclusively French."[13]

We are indebted to *L'Écho de Paris* for a candid description of Massenet at this time, in one of a series of "documented portraits" of noted persons, signed "Les Deux Aveugles" [The Two Blind Men]:[14]

"Portraits Documentés": Massenet

Description. Age: 50. Height: 1.71 meters [slightly over 5 feet, 7 inches] Hair: black, somewhat sparse. Moustache: black, *fine.* Forehead: open. Eyes: dark chestnut. Nose: *fort* [prominent]. Lips: *mince* [thin].

Personal. [Lives at] 38 Rue du Général Foy. Married; has a married daughter who cannot stand music. Lunches on very simple foods, always the same: eggs, cutlets, *beefsteaks* with potatoes; drinks Bourgogne, prefers the Romanet, which helps him to forget disagreeable letters. Afternoon: visits, rehearsals. 4.30 to 6:00 at Heugel's, where he receives. Dines. Seldom goes out evenings. Does not smoke (or very little).

Art. Has (in photo-reproductions, natural size): the Sistine Madonna of Raphaël, which remains lighted all night; Holbein's *Family Portrait* (Basle Museum); the portrait of Albrecht Dürer; Holbein's portrait of the Duchess of Connaught (London), which draws tears to his eyes (which he hides).

Sculpture. [Prefers] archaic, primitive.

Music. Ride of the Valkyries; Bacchanale from *Tannhäuser;* finale, Pastoral Symphony; passages in Gluck's *Orphée;* prefers music that lets him forget that it *is* music.

---

* Among other works, Karl Goldmark (1830–1915) was noted for *Die Königin von Saba* (Vienna, 1875); Ignaz Brüll (1846–1907) for his *Das goldene Kreuz* (Berlin, 1875); Heinrich Hofmann (1842–1902) for *Cartouche* (Berlin, 1869) and *Donna Diana* (Berlin, 1886); Edmund Kretschmer (1830–1908) for *Die Folkunger* (Dresden, 1874).

Opinions. Of Saint-Saëns: what an admirable musical dictionary! *quelle science!* Of Ambroise Thomas and Gounod: my patron saints; these one does not discuss. [Asked if he would have liked to be a painter]: it should be obvious that he thinks of painting when he writes music; believes, like René Ghil, that tones have colors. Most musical country: Austria, the Viennese. Likes to read memoirs (for their sense of reality), as *le Mémorial de Sainte-Hélène* (which moved him so very much). *Aucun jeu* [plays no games]. Never danced. Distractions: animals in the Jardin d'Acclimatisation; "I would like to kiss the muzzles of the horses, donkeys, and dogs that I meet." Favorite flower: carnation, provided it has a spicy smell. Likes the country, as a place of refuge.

Own Works. Prefers those he is *going* to write. Composes all his music in his head before writing it down; never at the piano. Usually, goes walking with the libretto in his pocket; memorizes it; and composes while walking.

Handwriting Analysis. Great vivacity of spirit, a little mischievous. Rare faculty for assimilation. Artistic temperament, but without *grandeur;* good taste, but more comprehensive than inventive. *Despotivité.* Is able admirably to conceal his thoughts beneath an exterior of the utmost frankness. Expert in flattery. Ambitious, but fearful, disturbed by doubts and despair. In love, should be excessively jealous. Tendencies toward the ideal, even toward mysticism, always in conflict with real aptitude for the practical things of life.

Lines of the palm. A hybrid spirit, half analytical, half synthesizing, expressing itself by imagery. Continuous struggle between inspiration and analysis, between inspired art and calculated art. Quick, spontaneous impressions, corrected by a judgment that is little sure of itself (pointed fingers, *noeud philosophique*). Continuous restlessness; morbid, invincible doubts; an excellent imagination for conjuring up endless subjects for alarm. Has difficulty in believing without proofs, yet applies reason poorly and judges rather from instinct. Mistrustful. Self-respect very high, pride moderate. Love for fame that is rapid and brilliant. Destiny fluctuates between success and disenchantment. Withal, a moderately happy destiny. Assured wealth (Apollo). A very long life, menaced by neurasthenia, Dangers at sea.

Werther was taken up at once in Belgium and the French provinces. The work was staged at Brussels on 24 January 1893 and at Antwerp toward the end of January, with Massenet present. February saw performances at Toulon, Toulouse, Nice, Reims, Amiens, Lyon (17 February), and Nantes (25 February); Angers followed in March. An undated letter in the Moldenhauer Archive fits in rather neatly here. We assume that it was sent to Heugel, and that (since *Werther* opened in Paris on Monday, 16 January) the "Thursday" mentioned was very likely 19 January:

Cher ami,

I replied emphatically by telegram to La Monnaie that my presence was of the utmost urgency—that they must expect me Thursday and reserve some stage rehearsals of which they could not suspect the importance. Now Nice is jeopardized, and Antwerp as well?! ah! what a mess! Would you please deliver the enclosed information as addressed—that is, *on stage* and in the *dressing room* of Mr Ibos [Werther]. Until this evening at the Ménestrel. "Soyez fort—soyez bon."

J. Massenet.

Boyer[*] announces Werther for Monday. They are taking off Le Cid—a stopgap.

A visiting card with envelope (Bibliothèque Nationale) yields further information. The cover, addressed to J. B. Weckerlin in Paris, was postmarked "Nice, Alpes Maritimes, . . . JA 93," with the actual date effaced. The card, printed "Massenet / 46, rue du Général Foy," documents the change of house number. The scrawled "en voyage, dans le Midi" with thanks for Weckerlin's congratulations, fixes the time as after the Paris première of *Werther*. Massenet can have found little relaxation at Nice, considering the oncoming performances there and at nearby Toulon and Toulouse.

The success of *Werther* by no means led Massenet to rest on his laurels. His grand slam would be 1894, with premières of three new operas in one year: *Thaïs, Le Portrait de Manon*, and *La Navarraise*. Even while working on *Thaïs*, Massenet somehow sandwiched in *Le Portrait de Manon*, for which the 284 pages of orchestration were finished in the spring of 1893. The one-act libretto—a sequel to *Manon*—was by Georges Boyer, editor of *Le Petit journal* and secretary general of the Opéra. The genesis of *La Navarraise* is clarified by a letter from Emma Calvé to Massenet which, though undated, obviously belongs to late January or early February 1893. By way of explanation: Puccini's *Manon Lescaut* was first staged at the Teatro Regio, Turin, on 1 February 1893 (and at Covent Garden on 14 May 1894). Augustus Harris, the noted London impresario, had leased Drury Lane in 1879, and moved to Covent Garden in 1888 where he brought many of the most famous singers of the day.

Cher Grand Maître,

Harris writes to me that he will be coming to Paris during the course of the week. If the little lyric drama which I spoke about pleased you, should you tell him that I would like to create it at London? Would you be ready in June? (Two small acts.) For in that case I would refuse to create Puccini's Manon, which he [Harris] mentioned to me for next year, and which he is going to hear in Italy a few days from now. I would be so happy and so proud to create one of your works over there, and to abandon, to enrage a little, those Italian *Maëstrini* who for some years seem to want to monopolize Covent Garden. Last year they gave five new works, of which not a single one was French! As soon as you have a free moment please let me know, so that you can hear the libretto, and know whether it suits you. Agréez, mon cher Maître, l'expression de mes sentiments les plus distingués.

Emma Calvé.[15]

Some inkling of Massenet's feverish activity at this time is gained from a letter he wrote to the music critic Raymond Bouyer:

---

[*] Boyer was a theater director; in a letter of 6 Jan. 1900, he was associated with Toulouse.

Paris, 6 April 1893

After three months, almost, of travels, rehearsals, premières . . . I return to Paris and find on my table the letters awaiting my return. Yours is . . . the spontaneity of your fine-spoken felicitations on the morrow after Werther. . . .

[As he reads, Massenet thinks of their last meeting on 11 January.]

J. Massenet[16]

Delibes's *Kassya* (partly orchestrated by Massenet) opened at the Opéra-Comique on 24 March 1893. After *Lakmé*, Delibes had wavered as to what direction to take next. Then Philippe Gille and Henri Meilhac had worked up a libretto in five acts after the story *Frinko Balaban* by the Austrian Leopold von Sacher-Masoch, best known for his novels of the sexual aberrations of Satanists. Convinced that this opera *Kassya* would be his masterpiece, Delibes labored at it long and carefully. When he died, not quite forty-five (16 January 1891), the piano-vocal score was finished, but the orchestration had scarcely got beyond the first act. Ernest Guiraud was asked, and agreed, to finish the orchestration, but then he resigned the task for various reasons. It fell to Massenet, Delibes's good friend, to finish *Kassya*, for which he also composed recitatives to replace the original dialogue.

Kassya lasted for only eight performances. Adolphe Jullien's review[17] informs us that during a trip along the Danube [1885?] Delibes had been intrigued by, and jotted down, his impressions of melodies and bizarre harmonies of Galician, Serbian, and Ruthenian origin. Kassya, the coquettish peasant girl of Little Russia—Jullien calls her half Mignon, half Carmen—cedes to the peasant Frinko Balaban in return for a pretty red ribbon and three strands of coral, which he bought at the fair of Kolomea. When her lover goes off for military duty, she becomes the servant-mistress of Count Zavale, who gives her a rich silk foulard and a brand-new sheepskin fur. The subject might have made a delightful one-acter, but Delibes the musician got carried away by dramatically irrelevant *hors-d'oeuvres*: choruses of brigands, recruiters, drinkers, peasants shivering with cold, peasants inflamed with rage, and so on.

On Holy Thursday, 30 March 1893, Massenet conducted *Marie-Magdeleine* at the Hippodrome in Lille. A warm letter from Carlo Pedrotti, eminent seventy-six-year-old Italian composer-conductor, will bear interpolation here. Pedrotti died six months later, on 16 October. The familiar "tu" form is used:

Pesaro, 8 April 1893

Amicone Carissimo,

Just returned from Turin, I found at Pesaro your congenial and friendly letter, and I thank you from my heart for the genuine expressions used in my regard . . . [The competition will be at Marseille, not Lyon]; naturally you shall be a member of the commission. . . . I have read your Manon Lescaut [*sic*]; what a beautiful opera, what a stupendous work!! One can say frankly that you are now the *first* composer of France—una vera gloria musicale. Addio, carissimo amico, accetta una cordialissima stretta di mano dal tuo affettuosissimo amico,

Carlo Pedrotti[18]

Sibyl Sanderson (while awaiting her grand rôle of Thaïs) appeared in Saint-Saëns's *Phryné* at the Opéra-Comique on 24 May 1893, with Lucien Fugère (Dicéphile), and Edmond Clément (Nicias). Saint-Saëns treated the subject of ancient Athens with a light hand—Jullien called it an *opérette*, citing Saint-Saëns's respect for that genre. The courtesan's rôle suited Sibyl Sanderson's temperament; indeed, she reappeared in *Phryné* as late as 11 June 1901, in the eighty-ninth performance at the Opéra-Comique, again with Fugère and Clément.

Vignette: on Sunday, 4 June, Massenet was invited to dinner at Heugel's, 58 Rue Pierre Charon. It was perhaps for the first time; in a brief telegram of acceptance Massenet said that he would come promptly at 3:30 "to get used to the emotion of this first début."[19] Two days before, he had written to Emma Borch: "I have decided to give up Chicago, where I was officially invited for four festivals. I am going to stay calmly at the country to work. Besides, I have finished a new work, *Thaïs*, and I shall have to be busy with it at the theater from September."[20]

For the Prix de Rome, 1893 was a reasonably good "Massenet year." André Bloch, pupil of Guiraud and Massenet, won the Premier Grand Prix. From Pont-de-l'Arche, on 11 July, Massenet wrote a friendly note to Bloch's father and mother expressing his confidence in the young man's future. The letter mentioned, incidentally, that "I shall be at the Conservatoire 20–28 July, and at Pourville in September."[21] A Deuxième Premier Grand Prix went to Henri Busser, a pupil of Guiraud. Busser, from Toulouse, was an excellent organist and also studied privately with Widor, Gounod, and César Franck. He continued to compose but became best known, from 1908, as conductor at the Paris Opéra. A second prize was awarded to Charles-Gaston Levadé, and an honorable mention to Jules-Henry Bouval, both Massenet pupils.

Manon attained its two-hundredth performance at the Opéra-Comique on 16 October 1893. Total receipts for the first two hundred performances amounted to 1,164,534 francs. Regarding royalties, Henri Busser has an interesting anecdote in his delightful memoirs, *De Pelléas aux Indes Galantes:* In 1897, Busser was negotiating with Carvalho for the staging of his one-act pastorale, *Daphnis et Chloé* (Opéra-Comique, 14 December 1897), and went to Massenet for advice. The latter was appalled at Carvalho's offer. Massenet had received 1 percent for *La Grand' Tante*, but now the going rate was a 12 percent royalty, of which the composer was entitled to four per cent. At this rate the composer's income from the two hundred performances of *Manon* would have been 46,000 francs—this from one theater alone!

On 17 October 1893, Massenet sent some corrected proofs to Heugel, presumably for the piano-vocal score of *Thaïs*. In the accompanying letter he says he will inform the Opéra as to the *tempi*, adding: "Thanks again for having been here yesterday evening—it was rather like reaching the end of an aria—I feel exhilarated."[22] The following Sunday (22 October) he finished the orchestration.[*]

---

[*] The ballet and scene of the Oasis were added in 1897.

Gounod died at his home in St-Cloud on 18 October, as a result of a stroke suffered the previous day. He was seventy-five. Within three weeks Tchaikovsky was dead (8 November) in St. Petersburg at fifty-three. Thus passed two prominent composers of their respective countries. For Massenet, two decades still lay ahead in which he would stage fourteen new operas.

With *Thaïs* delivered, and rehearsals not yet seriously under way, Massenet was able to get away from Paris to concentrate on *La Navarraise*. From Charles Le Gras[23] we have a vignette of the composer at Avignon, where he and Ninon stayed from 14 November until 14 or 15 December.* It was the postman who first reported that "a stranger has been several days at the Hôtel de l'Europe, who must be very rich, for he has rented the entire wing facing the Place Crillon, and he receives daily *that* much mail" (indicating an impressive amount). Actually, the Massenets occupied two of the rented rooms, leaving five vacant to avoid having neighbors. Jules found the locale suitably peaceful for his work; besides, his brother Colonel Edmond Massenet de Marancour was stationed at Avignon with his regiment of *pontonniers*. Some Provençal writers, Félix Gras and Frédéric Mistral, were invited to tea. Friendships blossomed.

Félix Gras accompanied Mme Massenet on promenades to Villeneuve or Colline des Anges and was impressed by her manner, easy and simple, yet distinguished. There was a daily tea from five to seven, with Mme Massenet as hostess, the conversation always enlivened by Massenet's inextinguishable sense of humor. He liked to hear gay Provençal stories (Mme Ville, proprietress of the hotel, was full of them), at which he laughed with delight. On 18–19 November, Massenet visited Nîmes, returning by way of Aigues-Mortes, which enchanted him. Another time, he visited Mistral at Maillane. On 25 November, as guest in the loge of M. and Mme Félix Gras, he heard Act II of *Rigoletto* in the theater, conducted by Tartanac, and was presented to the artists during the entr'acte. On 26 November, in honor of St. Cecilia, l'Harmonie Avignonaise gave an *aubade* to Massenet beneath the hotel windows, and he appeared on the balcony and thanked them. On 1 December there was a soirée at the home of Mme Roumanille (sister of Félix Gras) featuring as pianist Mlle R—— (later Mme Jandrier), and Massenet himself played fragments of *Thaïs*. On 12 December 1893, Massenet finished *La Navarraise*, and two or three days later left Avignon, headed toward Nice.

Henri Busser and the other Prix de Rome winners were traveling by easy stages to the Villa Medici. At Arles they ran into Massenet in the company of his *bonne femme*, as he called Mme Massenet. "She was," wrote Busser, "an amiable person, who showed her delight at a large bouquet of Parma violets which we offered her." Arising early the next morning, Busser met Massenet in the hall of the hotel, and received the advice from the *maître*: "Save all your mornings for composing or orchestrating, without waiting for inspiration, which, otherwise, never comes!"[24]

---

* During Massenet's absence, *Marie-Magdeleine* was given five times at the Éden theater in Paris. Derenbourg, the theater director, also offered one performance of Berlioz's *Damnation of Faust*.

CHAPTER 15

1894

Thaïs;
Le Portrait de Manon;
La Navarraise

URING 1894, WERTHER WAS GIVEN twice at the Opéra-Comique and then withdrawn. Revived for eleven performances in 1897, it was again put on the shelf. This in contrast to *Manon*, which, since the revival of 1891, remained in the repertoire of the theater, averaging some thirty performances a year during 1891–1915, ranging from lows of ten or eleven (1909, 1896) to highs of fifty-eight or forty-seven (1892, 1911). Not until 1903, under Albert Carré's directorship, did *Werther* assume a place in the repertoire; during 1903–1913 it was a close competitor of *Manon* at the Opéra-Comique. Meanwhile, *Werther* was making its way in the provinces and abroad: in 1894 it reached Chicago (29 March), New York (11 April), London (11 June), New Orleans (3 November), and Milan (1 December).

Werther was the ninth of Massenet's operas to reach the stage. A good start, perhaps. But he would go right on memorizing librettos and composing music in his head while he walked. During 1893–94, Massenet worked on *Grisélidis*, which would undergo revisions in 1898–99, and again in 1901, before achieving a première. In 1894 he took up *Cendrillon*, finishing the piano-vocal score the following year. Both works were laid aside in favor of a vehicle for Emma Calvé: *Sapho*, staged in 1897.

But to return to our chronicle. After mentioning Avignon, Félix Gras ("one of my dearest friends"), and Frédéric Mistral, the *Souvenirs* go on:

> The following winter was entirely devoted to the rehearsals of *Thaïs* at the Opéra. I said at the Opéra in spite of the fact that I wrote the work for the Opéra-Comique where Sanderson was engaged. She triumphed there in *Manon* three times a week. What made me change the theater? Sanderson was dazzled by the idea of entering the Opéra, and she signed a contract with Gailhard without even taking the mere trouble of informing Carvalho first. Heugel and I were greatly surprised when Gailhard told us that he was going

Sibyl Sanderson as Thaïs.
Courtesy Paul Jackson

to give *Thaïs* at the Opéra with Sibyl Sanderson. "You've the artist; the work will follow her!" There was nothing else for me to say. I remember, however, how bitterly Carvalho reproached us. He almost accused us of ingratitude, and God knows that I did not deserve that.

Toward the end of January, Massenet apparently went to Tournai (where he had appeared as pianist so long ago, in 1858!), and on 30 January he was at Namur, where Rachel Neyt (of La Monnaie) sang in some work not mentioned.[1] At the Opéra, the rehearsals of *Thaïs* went on, closed to outsiders. Thus, Massenet apologized to his good friend music critic Julien Torchet, no one could be admitted before the *répétition générale:* after all, he had to deny his own daughter and son-in-law, not to mention Reynaldo Hahn, who had come to the rehearsals of *Le Mage.*[2] On the evening of the dress rehearsal, Massenet quietly slipped out of Paris and went to Dieppe and Pourville.

Paul Taffanel conducted the première of *Thaïs* at the Opéra on 16 March 1894, with a cast comprising Sibyl Sanderson (Thaïs), Jean-François Delmas (Athanaël), Albert Alvarez (Nicias), Jeanne Marcy (Crobyle), Meyrianne Héglon (Myrtale), François Delpouget (Palémon), Laure Beauvais (début, as Albins), Berthe Mendes (début, as la Charmeuse), and Euzet (un Serviteur). The work was given twenty-seven times in 1894.

Anatole France's novel of 1890, from which Louis Gallet drew the libretto, was based on a tale of a courtesan turned saint in the *Golden Legend,* the compilation of lives of the saints by Jacobus de Voragine (1230–1298). In the novel, Paphnuce is a voluptuous young fourth-century Alexandrian, who is converted to Christianity and takes up a fierce asceticism in the desert of the Thebaid. For the opera, the name was changed to Athanaël. In the synopsis, I include the additions of the revised version given at the Opéra on 13 April 1898:

Poster for *Thaïs* by Manuel Orazi, 1894.

Act I. On the banks of the Nile, a gathering of Cenobites in the Thebaid desert. Athanaël, in his sleep, sees a vision of Thaïs in the theater, worshipped by the mob of enthusiasts. He resolves to go and save her. Scene 2: At the house of Nicias, a wealthy Alexandrian; a terrace overlooking the city and the sea. Nicias is a former friend of Athanaël, and one of the many lovers of Thaïs. Athanaël arrives and learns that Thaïs is expected at the house that very day. They replace Athanaël's shabby garments with suitable dress, and the attention of Thaïs is attracted to this fiery-eyed stranger. During the banquet that follows, Thaïs counsels Athanaël to give up duty and cultivate *l'amoureuse sagesse*. He preaches at her, but when she performs her dance of Venus he flees.

Act II. The house of Thaïs. Thaïs is tired and bored. Athanaël comes; he tries to persuade her to seek a better life, but she is not yet ready for salvation. Athanaël leaves, informing her that he will wait on her doorstep until dawn. The curtain falls, and an interlude *(Méditation)* suggests her reflection. Scene 2: A square of Alexandria; night. Sounds of revelry from an orgy of Nicias. Athanaël is stretched out on the doorstep of Thaïs. At dawn, Thaïs comes out. Athanaël persuades her to go to a monastery; but first, her house must be burned down with all its worldly souvenirs. Passing revelers stop to see what this apparent lunatic, Athanaël, is up to with torch in hand. Thaïs, now clad in a simple linen tunic, goes away, and Nicias throws pieces of gold to distract the now-angry mob.

Act III. An oasis. Athanaël and Thaïs pause to rest on their tiring journey to the monastery of the abbess Albine. The cortège of Albine and her white-garbed nuns appears, and Thaïs and Athanaël separate. Scene 2: Again the Thebaid desert. The Cenobites have finished their evening meal. Athanaël thinks only of Thaïs. Palémon exhorts him to calm down and seek repose. Athanaël falls asleep, only to see again the vision of Thaïs; the vision changes to announce her coming death. Athanaël awakens and rushes out to go to her. Scene 3: The monastery of Albine. Thaïs is dying. Athanaël, aroused to an appreciation of earthly love, tries to recall her to a life in which they can be together. But Thaïs dies, exclaiming: "I see God!"

———————————— • ❖ • ————————————

To paraphrase Alfred Bruneau, in *Gil Blas:* It now emerges that Massenet, in his choice of subjects, is obsessed with an *idée fixe*—the confrontation of courtesan and priest. Thaïs is a sister of Manon, Salomé, and many others, whether sainted or outcast; Athanaël is a cousin of Jean or Zarastra. The composer is more desirous of deploying his melodic and harmonic mastery, his marvelous gift for description, his virtuosic skill in writing, than in scrutinizing the differences among characters in order to express the humanity peculiar to each. As a result, it is Massenet's own musical personality that flows naturally and sincerely through the drama, without his having to stop and search for more varied means of expression. If Massenet is the central theme, the variations are in the separate operas for which he chooses different collaborators, even from the most opposing literary camps.[3] Léon Kerst *(le Petit journal)* seemed upset by Gallet's blank verse, even stopping to pun: the *ver blanc* (white worm) is destructive to agriculture; *vers blanc* (blank verse) is no less detrimental to music.[4]

Charles Darcours, in *Le Figaro*, wondered whether Massenet, who has such perfect control over what he writes, perhaps lets his inspiration flow too constantly and even too hastily. This leads to repetition of formulas from work to work. Not that this is evil, for Gounod, Schumann, and Wagner all had their personal formulas. But similarities of melodic shape sometimes verge uncomfortably upon "reminiscences" of previous operas by the same composer. In *Thaïs* there is nothing that stands out in relief. One wishes that he had stumbled occasionally, in order to recover with a burst of real effort. *Werther* contains inspired pages that momentarily transcend the tight control of craftsmanship; there are no such places in *Thaïs*. The work, originally intended for the Opéra-Comique, is not always suited to the larger scale of the Opéra. Greater breadth is possible, even with only two principal characters. Withal, there are charming moments: the entire first scene of the Cenobites and Athanaël's departure, for example—a complete little poem in itself, exquisitely coloristic.[5]

L. de Fourcaud *(Le Gaulois)* noted certain influences: traces of Gounod throughout, Verdi in the final scene, even the Ride of the Valkyries in the interlude entitled "Alexandria." Such eclecticism is not disturbing as long as the composer provides a real dramatic structure. Massenet seems more preoccupied with external impressions than with the inner core of the action. *Thaïs* is essentially a patchwork of vocal and orchestral segments, more or less ingenious, more or less successful for particular situations. It is not the edifice itself that is apparent, but rather the decorations.[6]

Le Portrait de Manon, in one act, opened at the Opéra-Comique on 8 May 1894. The now-older chevalier des Grieux was played by Lucien Fugère. Following the death of Manon, Des Grieux has retired to a provincial chateau, where he grieves over his lost love. To while away the time, he tutors his young nephew Jean, Vicomte de Morcerf (sung by Mlle Elven). Jean is in love with Aurore (Marie Laisné), ward of the chevalier's friend Tiberge (Grivot).

◄○►

As the opera opens we hear outside a merry chorus of peasants, with Aurore singing about the joys of life. Alone in his library, Des Grieux hears the singing, which reminds him of his own happier days. He looks at a portrait of Manon, a miniature treasured at the bottom of a chest, and recalls the past. Jean comes to take his lesson in Roman history. He begins bravely enough with Scipio but then starts talking of love, finally confessing that he loves Aurore. Des Grieux is stern: Aurore has neither fortune nor noble birth and is unsuited to be the wife of a Morcerf. Tiberge enters; he tries to persuade Des Grieux that young love must have its way. Left alone, Jean and Aurore are in despair and talk of dying together. Jean pursues Aurore, seeking a kiss, and in the ensuing scuffle the chest is upset and the portrait of Manon falls out. "How pretty she is!" they exclaim. Tiberge comes to fetch Aurore, and it is apparent that he has hit upon a happy idea. Des Grieux lectures Jean some more and sends him away. Aurore appears, dressed as Manon when she descended from the carriage at Amiens. Aurore, we learn, is the daughter of Lescaut, raised by Tiberge. Des Grieux melts, and there is a happy ending.

• ◆ •

A *bluette*, an ingratiating trifle, Georges Boyer's libretto permitted Massenet to express delicate sentiments and, above all, to recall with a tinge of melancholy the themes of *Manon*. Occasionally the singers lapse momentarily into speech, suggesting a light touch of melodrama rather than the *opéra comique* tradition of sustained dialogue.* Johannes Weber *(Le Temps)* was unimpressed by the technique: "A vocal piece starts; suddenly it is interrupted to permit a few spoken words. Another piece stops; you think it is finished, a personage continues speaking a little, then takes up singing for a few words."[7] Victorin de Joncières *(La Liberté)* found the little work delightful, "a veritable jewel, finely chiseled, of an exquisite grace." The history lesson was ingeniously treated; while the young scholar reads Scipio's examples of virtue

---

* Massenet experimented from time to time with mingled speech and song, employing the principle most consistently in the *Expressions lyriques*, published in 1913.

and continence, the orchestra accompanies lightly with piquant "scholarly" effect.[8]

Adolphe Jullien, in *Le Journal des Débats,* called the work an unpretentious piece, nicely turned out and easy to stage, quite suitable for small theaters of watering places and resort casinos. Carvalho knew what he was doing when he put it on a double bill with *Cavalleria rusticana.* Most of the principal motives of *Manon* reappear, and this is not disturbing. The spoken or declaimed passages are relatively few and, as in *Manon,* are accompanied by charming *babillage* in the orchestra. Jullien likes the scene between Jean and Aurore; they consider in turn, with exaggerated despair, the different modes of death (picturesquely orchestrated); although Aurore's *chanson villageoise* is somewhat mannered, Jean's declaration of love and Aurore's tender reply are entirely charming. Later, when Aurore (incarnation of Manon!) sings of the power of love in a quasi-celestial melody, accompanied by distant murmuring of the chorus, it is quite enough to cause Des Grieux to weaken and give his blessing to the young lovers.[9]

L. de Fourcaud interjected a sour note in *Le Gaulois,* recalling the fable of the son of the fairies who accepted from an evil spirit an ominous gift that endowed its recipient with the power of accomplishing all tasks speedily and of being constantly satisfied with his handiwork. Others flatter Massenet, but beneath apparent success may lurk grave miscalculations. The composer should heed the warning of the fable; then those who discern his true capabilities would take pleasure in doing him justice. But in our times the hours are racing by, and it is not a moment too soon to think more seriously about the future.[10]

Le Portrait de Manon had a moderate success, reaching its hundredth performance at the Opéra-Comique in 1901. The work was also given at Geneva (8 October 1894), Brussels (22 November 1894), Naples (15 December 1894), Antwerp (21 November 1895), Prague (28 December 1895), New York (13 December 1897), and has been occasionally revived since.

Of far greater impact was *La Navarraise,* staged by Augustus Harris at Covent Garden, London, on 20 June 1894. The cast included Emma Calvé (Anita), Alberto Alvarez (Araquil), Pol Plançon (Garrido), Charles Gilibert (Remigio), Bonnard (Ramon), and Eugène Dufriche (Bustamente). Massenet was in London by 7 June to look after rehearsals, staying at the Cavendish Hotel in Jermyn Street, cited by Baedeker as a "comfortable house for single gentlemen."[*]

La Navarraise represents Massenet's essay in the new style of *verismo,* with compressed action that is brutal and intense.[†] Designated as an *episode lyrique* in two acts, the libretto was by Jules Claretie and Henri Cain, after a story, *La Cigarette,* by Claretie.

---

[*] *Werther* was also given at Covent Garden, on 11 June.

[†] Mascagni's *Cavalleria rusticana* had reached the stage of the Opéra-Comique (Place du Châtelet) on 19 January 1892, in a French translation by Paul Milliet. Santuzza was sung by Emma Calvé, who soon thereafter appeared as Carmen.

THÉÂTRE NATIONAL ᴅᴇ L'OPÉRA-COMIQUE

Episode Lyrique en 2 Actes
de
JULES CLARETIE & HENRI CAIN

Musique de

J. MASSENET

Paris Au Ménestrel 2ᵉ⁰ Rue Vivienne HEUGEL & Cⁱᵉ Editeurs

Poster for *La Navarraise*
by Reutlinger, 1895.

The scene is a square in a Basque village, with the Pyrenees on the horizon. It is six in the evening. There are barricades in the square, and from the nearby valley arise puffs of smoke and sounds of shooting. Women pray before a Madonna. General Garrido is losing the fight with the Carlist troops under Zuccaraga. Anita (a poor orphan from Navarre) awaits the return of her fiancé, the sergeant Araquil. Soldiers file past. Anita prays. Araquil comes, and there is a tender reunion. But Araquil's father, Remigio (a rich, respected farmer) does not want his son to marry a nobody. It would be different if she had a dowry—even two thousand *douros*. For poor Anita this seems an insuperable obstacle. General Garrido brings his maps and plans tomorrow's attack. A report is brought that his troops are being beaten by Zuccaraga. If only someone would kill Zuccaraga, cries Garrido, he would give a fortune. Anita says she will do it for two thousand *douros*. As night falls, Araquil comes looking for Anita. Ramon, his captain, tells him that she has been seen looking for Zuccaraga, who is young and handsome. Perhaps she is unfaithful? There is an orchestral interlude as the soldiers sleep.

Anita returns, wild and bloody. She has killed Zuccaraga. General Garrido gives her the two thousand *douros*. Meanwhile Araquil had followed Anita's trail toward the Carlist positions and been mortally wounded. Dying, he curses Anita. Anita laughs, cries, and goes insane.

La Navarraise spread like some new kind of Massenet wildfire. By the end of the year it had been heard in Budapest, Brussels, and The Hague. In 1895 followed Nuremberg, Hamburg, Bordeaux, Stockholm, Paris (3 October), Vienna, Moscow, and New York (11 December). There was only one performance at La Scala, on 6 February 1896, though the Teatro Lirico in Milan took up the work in October of the same year. Toward the end of an impressive list of performances abroad, we find *La Navarraise* (in Finnish) accorded the honor of inaugurating the new opera house at Helsinki on 2 October 1911. At the Opéra-Comique after the first burst of enthusiasm (twenty-eight performances in 1895), the work settled down to a more modest place in the repertoire, with a one hundredth performance in 1913.

The reviews of the Paris première of 1895 made the expected comparisons with *Cavalleria rusticana* regarding dramatic realism, while still noting that *La Navarraise* was all Massenet. Alfred Bruneau, in *Le Figaro,* warned young composers not to attempt to jump onto this particular bandwagon. The impact of *Cavalleria rusticana,* fortified by "the few traces" of its influence in *La Navarraise,* might seduce lesser talents than Massenet's.[11] Eugene de Solenière *(La Critique)* thought that Massenet had done "what had to be done" and succeeded admirably. "There is not a young composer in France who is not impregnated—if only just a little—with his manner; those who confess it the least are precisely those most affected." They decry Massenet as slaves disparage their master.[12]

By 22 June Massenet was back in Paris, where he received word from Calvé:

Savoy Hotel, Victoria Embankment, London
22 June 1894

Cher grand Maître,

I did not have to do very much to achieve a success in your admirable new work. I did my best, and I hope to do still better without the "nerves" of the première. Thanks from the bottom of my heart for your good words. This is for me a very sweet and precious encouragement.

Your very sincerely devoted *Anita.*

Calvé

The Queen refused *Pagliacci* and asked for *La Navarraise. Vive* the queen![13]

(Each year, when in London, Calvé was summoned to Windsor Castle to sing for Queen Victoria.)

The Prix de Rome for 1894 was awarded to Henri Rabaud, a pupil of Massenet. Ribaud's active career as composer and conductor belongs to the chronicle of twentieth-century French music. Second prize went to Omer Letorey, and an honorable mention to Jules-Ernest-Georges Mouquet, both pupils of Théodore Dubois.

July and August 1894 were spent at Pont-de-l'Arche, and at least a part of September at Pourville. By 23 July, Massenet had finished the *entr'acte idylle* that precedes Act II of *Grisélidis.* Georgette Leblanc devoted her vacation to working with Massenet on the role of Anita for Brussels in the fall. There were periodic trips to Paris, as on 9 August for the funeral of Auguste Cain, a sculptor friend noted for his figurines of animals. On 11 August, Massenet wrote to "my eminent colleague," the

Russian conductor Aleksandr Vinogradsky, apparently in reply to a request for some of Massenet's music to be performed in Russia. Vinogradsky had given an all-Russian concert in Paris in the spring of 1894.[*]

On 16 September, Massenet wrote to Heugel from an unnamed city [Bordeaux?], where the opera being mounted [*Manon*?] was receiving a "first-rate interpretation" with "Mlle Gravière." Georgette Bréjean (born 1870) had been engaged at Bordeaux in 1890, where she married the theater director Gravière. Her second husband (1900) was the composer Charles Silver, Prix de Rome of 1891. The name of Mme Bréjean-Gravière, later Bréjean-Silver, crops up from time to time in the annals of Massenet performances. For Brussels, the composer wrote for her a bravura *Fabliau* to replace the Gavotte in *Manon*. In his letter to Heugel, Massenet was worried about attempting *Manon* at La Scala: despite the admirable acoustics, he is convinced that the work would be lost in the great hall; also, it is a mistake to restore the cuts,as they are planning to do.[14] In fact, when *Manon* appeared at La Scala on 13 January 1895, it was given only twice. Revived there in 1906, and sporadically thereafter, the work attained only fifty-six performances up to 1963.

Massenet was going "back to Pourville" the following day (17 September). In the score of *Grisélidis* is an annotation "Pourville, 29 September 1894," mentioning that "Ninon and I will leave Monday [1 October] for Pont-de-l'Arche and Paris" and expressing anxiety and "sad presentiments" regarding a revival of *Manon* planned for 17 December.[15]

On 10 October 1894, Verdi's *Otello* (French version by Boito and Camille du Locle) was staged at the Paris Opéra in the presence of President Casimir-Périer and Verdi. On that evening Verdi was accorded the highest decoration of the Legion d'Honneur: the Grand Cross. Two days later, Massenet was confined to his room with a passing illness (or so he said); he sent Ninon with visiting cards on the thirteenth to the Grand Hotel, where Ricordi was staying, and on the fourteenth he sent Ricordi a telegram conveying félicitations to Verdi and Boito and explaining that he would be unable to go out for another two or three days.[16]

Lacking precise documentation, we can only speculate as to Massenet's movements in November and December. He probably went to Brussels for *Le Portrait de Manon* (given 22 November) and *La Navarraise* with Georgette Leblanc (26 November). This would have prevented him from looking in on the final preparations for *Werther* at the Teatro Lirico in Milan, where the work was staged on 1 December. To please his friend Sonzogno, proprietor of the Teatro Lirico, Massenet no doubt attended a subsequent performance; on 18 December he wrote to a colleague that he had just arrived back in Paris from Italy.[17] It seems unlikely that he would have gone all the way to Naples for *Le Portrait de Manon* (15 December).

---

[*] For details of this concert and of two others (8 and 15 Nov. 1896), see *Iz arkhivov russkikh musykantov* (Moscow, 1962), which contains letters to Vinogradsky from Tchaikovsky, Balakirev, Rimsky-Korsakov, Auer, Massenet, Saint-Saëns, and Sibelius. Massenet wrote again (on 9 Apr. 1896), expressing regret at never having been in Russia, and reminding Vinogradsky of the "enthusiastic and profound impression" produced by his Paris concert.

Autographed portrait of Jules Massenet. Courtesy Paul Jackson.

1895-1896

Freedom from the Conservatoire

I N MILAN, DURING THE YEARS 1891 through 1893, La Scala had staged only
operas that were the property of Ricordi. In self-defense, Edoardo Sonzogno
acquired from the municipality the old Teatro della Cannobiana; the renovated hall opened as the Teatro Lirico Internazionale on 24 September 1894.
Sonzogno also obtained the contract as impresario for La Scala, so that for
two years he had a practical monopoly of Milanese operatic stages. The result was apparent in La Scala's Carnival-Lent season for 1895: works from the young Italian
school, such as Leoncavallo's *I Medici* and Mascagni's *Guglielmo Ratcliff* and *Silvano*,
and no fewer than six operas by French composers. These included Reyer's *Sigurd*
(26 December 1894, seven performances), Bizet's *I Pescatori di perle* (29 December,
three performances), Massenet's *Manon* (13 January 1895, two performances),
Saint-Saëns's *Sansone e Dalila* (17 January, fifteen performances), Paladilhe's *Patria*
(6 February, five performances), and Massenet's *Werther* (20 March, six performances). Manon was sung by Adelina Stehle, and Charlotte by Ada Adiny.

Massenet did not go to Italy at this time. He had previously expressed grave
doubts about the suitability of *Manon* for La Scala. Anyway, with Massenet performances now falling thick and fast in the provinces and abroad, he could no longer
look in on more than a few of them. On 10 January 1895, Benjamin Godard died at
Cannes; on the thirteenth, Massenet (in Paris) wrote to a friend of his sorrow over
the loss of this "camarade bien aimé."[1] On 30 January (still in Paris) he thanked
Raoul Blondel for conducting a performance of *Ève*, which Ninon had attended the
evening before.[2] A letter dated 5 February hinted that in about a month he would be
in Brussels.[3]

As the Paris season drew to a close, the Massenets were impatient to be up and
away. He wrote to André Bloch in Italy:

Paris, 23 May 1895

Mon cher ami,

The newspapers had already spoken of the success of your audition
before S. M. [Sa Majesté: the Queen of Italy]. Your letter further adds to the

pleasure which I felt over this. I am so happy to know that you are thus at work, and profiting so well from these *jours uniques* [i.e., the Italian sojourn]. You are always the same dear friend, always warm-hearted and full of thoughtful consideration for me; thanks, for I know how to appreciate these rare qualities. I am counting upon some superb pages from you when we receive your *envoi*. Was I not right in assuring you that country is admirable? And are you not well off at Ischia? Here—mud, fog, hatreds, etc. My wife and I live peaceably, observing from afar this "struggle for life"—which scarcely interests me, considering the little time remaining for the both of us to live. We are leaving for the country—we love so much the fresh air, and, in winter, the good sunshine.

From both of us, to you our *bien chers souvenirs*.

Massenet

Regards to Rabaud and to Busser.[4]

The "fresh air" was sought in Aix-les-Bains and Savoy, whence letters were sent on 29–30 May.[5] For the Prix de Rome competition, the cantata text was *Clarisse Harlowe,* by Édouard Noël. Omer Letorey, pupil of Théodore Dubois, received the first prize; second prize was awarded to Massenet's pupil Max d'Ollone.

By July 1895, Massenet was installed at Pont-de-l'Arche, ready for a summer's labors. Here he learned of the death on 10 July of Mme Miolan-Carvalho at Puys, near Dieppe. What a long time had elapsed since the old Théâtre-Lyrique, when Gounod had supervised the rehearsals of *Faust* with Mme Carvalho as Marguerite! Now both were gone.

The autograph piano-vocal score of *Cendrillon* provides some passing commentary for July and August. Halfway through Act I: "Pont-de-l'Arche, Sunday, 7 July. 3:30 [P.M.]. Fine weather. They are cutting the grass. Ninon in the garden. Calmness, happiness. One hears the bells for the close of Vespers." At the end of Act I: "16 July, 5:30 P.M. Admirable day. They are cutting, pruning, shaping in the garden. Ninon is happy." At the beginning of Act II, a reminder to include in the orchestration "lute, viola d'amore, and *flûte en cristal.*" On 23 July: "Rain all morning. The little swallow is doing well; it had something to eat, and is sleeping." There was an excursion to Dieppe and Pourville, from which they returned by 30 July.

The weather turned foul and rainy but brightened a little on 7 August for the visit of M. and Mme Heugel, Henri Cain (librettist of *Cendrillon*), with the latter's brother Georges Cain and wife. Massenet played through the new opera, by now well into the third act. Act IV was begun on 22 August and probably finished within a week or so (there is no date at the end).[*]

On 3 October 1895, *La Navarraise* opened at the Opéra-Comique, with Emma Calve (Anita), Henri Jérôme (Araquil), Max Bouvet (Garrido), Mondaud (Remigio), Ernest Carbonne (Ramon), and Hippolyte Belhomme (Bustamente). Jules Danbé

---

[*] In the orchestra score (1895–96), to lighten Massenet's labors, another hand wrote in the voice parts and words.

Emma Calvé as Anita in *La Navarraise*. Courtesy Paul Jackson.

conducted. Calvé had written to Massenet that summer (7 July) that she could manage fifteen performances, until 10 November, and that maybe Maurice Grau (of the Metropolitan Opera House) might even let her stay for ten days longer.[6] In fact, there were twenty-eight performances at the Opéra-Comique, and *La Navarraise* opened in New York with Calvé on 11 December.

    Werther was staged at Hamburg on 10 October, with Massenet present for the final rehearsals. On the way back he stopped off at Brussels, where he arrived on the tenth and wrote at once to Heugel from the Hôtel du Grand Monarque. Everything was going very well at Hamburg when he left, with careful staging entirely according to his wishes. He had told Pollini, the theater director, a little white lie: that he was going directly to Lyon. His wife met him at Brussels, and they expected to be back in Paris in forty-eight hours. Massenet hoped to see Heugel for a moment before taking off for Lyon on Monday [14 October]. For the moment, he was quite tired and needed rest.[7] On 19 October, *Le Cid* was staged at Lyon.

In the *Souvenirs*, it is simply stated that "I went to Nice to finish *Cendrillon* at the Hôtel de Suède; we were absolutely spoiled by our charming hosts, M. and Mme Roubion." On 11 December he wrote to Heugel, obviously delighted with the warm, clear, sunny South. Mme de Nuovina, living at 3 Rue Bassano, Paris, was to come and see Heugel. She had sung Esclarmonde at Brussels in 1889, and Kassya at the Opéra-Comique in 1893. With Calvé away in America, *La Navarraise* was in jeopardy without a new Anita.[8] Nuovina was also known for her Carmen and Santuzza, and occasionally Charlotte in *Werther*.

Between 18 and 30 December there were several performances of *Hérodiade* at Nice, with the fine tenor Georges Imbart de la Tour as Jean. The Massenets remained in seclusion; casual visitors to the hotel were told that they were out, or away on an excursion.[9] As of 31 December 1895, Massenet was raised to the grade of Commandeur of the Légion d'Honneur.

In January 1896, Massenet got away for ten days to Milan, where *La Navarraise* was in rehearsal at La Scala. Sonzogno had opened the season (26 December) with Saint-Saëns's *Enrico VIII* with only moderate success, so on 4 January he substituted the more popular *Sansone e Dalila*. But as the season drew on the patrons of La Scala grew impatient with Sonzogno's French repertoire. They applauded Mascagni's *Guglielmo Ratcliff,* but were lukewarm toward *La Dannazione di Faust* by Berlioz. The timing of Massenet's *La Navarraise* (6 February) could not have been worse; it was taken off after one performance. With Bizet's *Carmen* (23 February), the audience clamored for a change of tenor and baritone, and there were only two performances. *I Pescatori di perle* did not fare much better. Somehow, the remnants of the opera season were saved with Thomas's *Amleto*, Mascagni's *Zanetto*, and the world première of Umberto Giordano's *Andrea Chénier* (28 March 1896), which was a triumph. The ballet offering was better appreciated: Romualdo Marenco's *Day-Sin* (1 January), with twenty-one performances; Delibes's *Coppélia* (28 January), twelve times; and Tchaikovsky's *La Bella del bosco dormante* (11 March), twenty-four times. But Sonzogno's monopoly of La Scala was broken; the following season the house was again opened to Ricordi's properties.[*]

We are indebted to the *Souvenirs* for an account of Massenet's visit to Verdi in Genoa, on the way to Milan. Arriving at the first floor of the old Palazzo Doria (6 Via Garibaldi) where Verdi lived, Massenet made his way down a dark passage to find, tacked to a door, a simple card with the name: Verdi. His host opened the door, surprised at the unexpected visit. They chatted amicably and admired the view of the port from the terrace of Verdi's sitting room. Massenet was impressed by Verdi's tall stature, noble bearing, sincerity, and graciousness. As he picked up his luggage to leave, Massenet remarked that it contained manuscripts, which inevitably accompanied him on his travels. Whereupon Verdi briskly seized the luggage and accompa-

---

[*] At the close of the 1896 opera-ballet season, there was a series of four symphony concerts by the La Scala orchestra, 26 April to 18 May, with Arturo Toscanini conducting this group for the first time. He returned for the symphony series of 1899, 1900, 1902, and 1905.

Poster for Ambroise Thomas's opera *Françoise de Rimini* by Jules Chéret, 1882.

nied Massenet through the garden to the waiting carriage, commenting that he, too, took his work along on his journeys.

By 30 January, Massenet was back in Nice with a "violent trachitis" from the raw weather (letter to Heugel). The doctor's orders were to stay in his room, getting as much sun as possible. He had planned to be in Paris on Tuesday [4 February] for the composition class; but now, too hoarse to speak, it seemed better to prolong his stay at Nice. Heugel is asked to explain matters to Réty [secretary of the Conservatoire] and to Gédalge [his substitute for the composition class during his absence]. The delay is provoking: he will have to renounce going to Brussels for *Thaïs;* by no means does he want to break an engagement at Nancy for 7–9 March. Really, one cannot at the same time be a professor and also stage operas![10]

When Massenet returned to Paris early in February, he learned that Ambroise Thomas was gravely ill. The old man, eighty-four and not too well, had braved the cold to attend a gala at the Opéra where they played the prelude to his *Françoise de Rimini* and gave him a warm ovation. He returned from the theater to his apartment at the Conservatoire, took to his bed, and did not arise from it. He died on 12 February. At the next session of the Académie des Beaux-Arts (22 February), memorial discourses were read by Léon Bonnat, the painter, and by Massenet, Mézières, and Théodore Dubois.

The question of Massenet's relationship to the Conservatoire was not settled immediately. Shortly after Thomas's funeral he was called to the Ministry of Public Instruction and offered the directorship of the Conservatoire. Alfred Rambaud, the eminent historian, was then Minister of Public Instruction. Massenet declined, not wanting to interrupt his almost total involvement with the lyric theater. Théodore Dubois was appointed to the directorship, effective 6 May 1896. With Thomas gone, Massenet felt little further attachment to the Conservatoire and tendered his resignation as professor of composition. He may have taught his class until the end of the term or, very possibly, a substitute may have relieved him. In the *Souvenirs* we simply read: "Free at last and loosed from my chains forever, during the first days of summer my wife and I started for the mountains of Auvergne."

The appointments to replace Dubois and Massenet were effective 1 October 1896. The organ professor Charles-Marie Widor succeeded to Dubois's composition class. Gabriel Fauré, choirmaster at the Madeleine, was brought in to replace Massenet as professor of composition.[*] The third composition teacher, Charles Lenepveu, who had succeeded Guiraud in 1892, remained on until his death in 1910.

Traces of Massenet's teaching lingered on in the Prix de Rome competitions until 1900:

1896—Cantata, *Mélusine* (Fernand Beissier). First prize: Georges Mouquet (pupil of Dubois). Two second prizes: Richard d'Ivry (Dubois); Fernand Halphen (Massenet).

1897—Cantata, *Frédégonde* (Charles Morel). First prize: Max d'Ollone (Massenet and Lenepveu). Two second prizes: Bernard-Louis Crocé-Spinelli (Lenepveu); Florent Schmitt (Massenet and Fauré).

1898—Cantata, *Radegonde* (Paul Collin). No first prize. Second prize: Henri Malherbe (Massenet and Fauré).

1899—Cantata, *Callirhoé* (Eugène Adenis). Two first prizes: Charles-Gaston Levadé (Massenet and Lenepveu); Henri Malherbe (see 1898).

1900—Cantata, *Sémiramis* (Eugène and Édouard Adenis). First prize: Florent Schmitt (see 1897). *Second prize:* Joseph Kunc (Lenepveu). Honorable mention: Albert Bertelin (Widor).

During the period 1901–1910, pupils of Lenepveu carried off the most honors: eight first prizes, eleven second prizes, and two honorable mentions. Fauré's pupils took two firsts and four seconds; Widor's pupils, one first, and five seconds.

Returning to March and April 1896, we find no precise documentation for Massenet's activities. *Thaïs* was given at Brussels on 7 March, and *La Navarraise* was staged at Antwerp sometime in March. It would have been like Massenet to look in

---

[*] Fauré became organist at the Madeleine that same year (1896). In 1905, Dubois resigned as director; the post was again offered to Massenet, who again declined. Fauré was then appointed director of the Conservatoire.

on the final rehearsals. Whether or not he went south for *La Navarraise* at Montpellier (16 April) or *Le Portrait de Manon* at Toulouse (April) is not known.

According to the *Souvenirs*, "at the beginning of the preceding winter" (late 1895? early 1896?) Henri Cain had approached Heugel with the idea of an opera based an Alphonse Daudet's *Sapho* of 1884—a story of two lovers whose relationship is continually broken off and renewed. Cain (whose collaborator was Arthur Bernède) relied upon Heugel to persuade Massenet, who indeed took up the project with enthusiasm, working at it that summer.

On 1 May, Massenet was still in Paris.[11] By the twenty-seventh, he had settled down at the Hôtel Dumoulin in Néris-les-Bains (Allier). The therapeutic spa had been selected for the benefit of Ninon, who was in a run-down condition and had been advised to take an extended cure. In a long letter to Heugel, Massenet discussed the possible assignment of rôles for *Cendrillon* and was cheered by the thought that Vienna might be interested in *Grisélidis*. He urged Heugel to send a bound proof-copy to Jahn, taking care to praise the merits of the work.[12] Another letter, unfortunately undated, announced: "Herewith the uncorrected proofs of *Grisélidis*; and besides, *Cendrillon* in first proof."[*]

By 13 July (to Heugel), Massenet was beginning to worry about *Cendrillon*. Carvalho was planning a grand production of Mozart's *Don Juan* for November. It had been originally thought to stage *Cendrillon* on 15 November; now they want to push it back further and further, for one reason or another. At the end of the letter an idea occurs to Massenet: what about *Sapho*—with Calvé? It could go into rehearsal in September 1897.[13] In the sequel, *Sapho* was the first to reach the stage (1897), while *Cendrillon* had to wait until 1899, and *Grisélidis* until 1901.

For variety, the Massenets moved in August to Murat, in the mountains of the Cantal.[14] Emma Calvé wrote often; she had read the libretto of *Sapho* and was excited at the prospect of creating the rôle of Fanny. When not actively singing, as in the summers, Calvé resided at her château of Cabrières, near Agnessac (Aveyron). In an undated letter (most probably August 1896) she wrote:

Cabrières

Cher grand maître,

I learn from a letter of [Maurice] Grau that the Reszkes will sing *Le Cid* for certain in America, and that your very devoted servant will create the principal rôle! That is something that overwhelms me with joy, and I hurry to impart to you the good news! Here, I live in the midst of my goats, sheep, cows, pigs, chickens—happy as a shepherdess! My mountain smells of thyme and mint. I perfume my baths with all those good herbs of the Causses [du Tarn], and I drink milk! What more could one want, what with the

---

[*] To Heugel, no date. Paper and watermark are the same as for letters of 27 May, 4 July, and 13 July. Also on the same paper, another undated letter ("À propos: un nègre—puisque Cain me demande si cela est fait exprès") relates to *Sapho*, implying that he had begun to sketch this work. (Both in the Moldenhauer Archive.)

good sun and *le bon Dieu!* How right is Mme Massenet to love the Midi! Tell her from me that, two years from now, what with Cendrillon, Navarraise, and another work that I know well—but of which I do not dare speak as yet—the grand Maître can buy for himself three farms and three châteaux in the Aveyron. . . .

Emma Calvé

She tried to entice the Massenets for a visit, writing to Ninon:

Cabrières, 14 August 1896

Chère Madame,

Henri [Cain] just sent me the letter where the dear Maître speaks of coming to Agnessac. The poor lad knew how happy this would make me, and did not have the courage to conceal the good news. Plead his cause with the Maître! and mine, too, I beg of you! There is only a miserable inn at Agnessac. At Cabrières, you have a heart that loves you well, as you know! and who would be acting grievously toward you to permit you to go anywhere else. I can offer you a fine, gay bedroom with attached bath. We have good milk, good eggs, trout, wild game, exquisite mutton. *An excellent cook.* A perfect coachman. A good landau, well-springed, and with good, solid, *calm* horses. No park, no garden, but the mountain is ours! it is true that there are quite a few stones! Oh, mon Dieu! my poor house is quite old, my poor chateau-ferme quite rustic, we live here alone with Mlle Post. No visitors, no newspapers, no news, a *dream* as regards repose. Six hundred meters of altitude! is that enough? If the carriage fatigues you too much, we can go install ourselves for a week at the château de la Caze, built on the [river] Tarn, where the boats will convey you *gently* in the most marvelous region of the world. Isn't it true, you are going to say Yes! Yes! . . .

Emma Calvé

But the visit was put off. The illness of Calvé's father complicated matters. By 30 August, she had heard that the Massenets were leaving Murat; not knowing where to send her letter, she addressed it to Paris. "You were so close—five or six hours by train at the most. Well, your poor Sapho had no luck this year." Next year, wherever the Massenets might be, she promises to come and drag them back to her Cabrières despite all obstacles.[15]

When Massenet returned to Paris, he found an accumulation of mail awaiting him. On 18 September he wrote an amusing letter to an unidentified friend who had been to Bayreuth that summer; the pages are strewn with motives from the *Ring*. "After a short season at Néris," he wrote, "we made an excursion [Rhine motive] to the mountains of the Cantal. Now we are here in Paris, in passing—the South awaits us, *le Midi* [Siegfried's horn call]. . . . So you are in Switzerland. But will you return soon? Will we still be in Paris? [Siren call of the Rhine maidens] I do not know yet." A closing thematic flourish is "naturally for the [coming] arrival of the Tsar!"[16]

Before the Tsar arrived in Paris, Massenet slipped off to Brussels, where *Hérodiade* was to be given again and where Calabrési seemed interested in reviving *La Navarraise*. On "Sunday" (27 September or 4 October), Massenet wrote Heugel not to give the proofs of *Sapho* to the engraver just yet (piano-vocal score, orchestra score), but to await his return.[17]

The principal ceremonies welcoming Tsar Nicolas II were on 7 October, with the laying of the first stones for the Pont Alexandre III and for the coming Exposition of 1900. There were speeches, processions, visits to Notre-Dame, the Pantheon, Versailles, the porcelain factory at Sèvres, and so on. Throngs turned out to see the passing show, and the Massenets allowed their servants to absent themselves from the apartment. The *Souvenirs* report an anecdote: "We were at the house of friends overlooking the Parc Monceau. The procession had scarcely passed when we were suddenly seized with anxiety at the idea that the time was particularly propitious for burglarizing deserted apartments, and we rushed home." As they entered their apartment, they heard whispers and were thoroughly frightened: surely burglars had broken in! Actually, the servants had returned first and had admitted two good friends: Emma Calvé and Henri Cain.

Le Figaro had announced on 3 June previous that Calvé, before leaving for America, was contracted for twenty appearances as Manon at the Opéra-Comique in October and November. It was remarked that this would be the first time the "savage Carmen" and the "tragic Navarraise" would attempt this rôle of "sweetness and charm." In fact, the summary of performances for 1896 at the Opéra-Comique shows *Manon* eleven times and *La Navarraise* eleven times, suggesting that perhaps after all Calvé had more confidence in Anita.

In October 1896, *La Navarraise* was also staged at the Teatro Lirico in Milan. I have been unable to find the exact date, and unfortunately, a related letter from Massenet to Heugel was also undated.

> Cher bon ami,
>
> Before leaving [Paris], I have received from Sonzogno a telegram worded exactly as follows: "Milan, 11.25 P.M. Navarraise complete triumph Lirico. Brilliant retaliation [for the earlier fiasco at La Scala]. Nuovina great frenetically applauded all her passages encored last solo three times. Intermède warmly applauded. Six enthusiastic curtain calls end of opera. Superb performance. Orchestra admirable. Staging worthy of work. Sanderson begs me send you her best congratulations along with ours. Sonzogno."
>
> There at last the result waited for, since the month of January, thanks to Mlle de Nuovina, whom M. Carvalho does not consider worthy of the Opéra-Comique. I embrace you, joyfully,
>
> Massenet
>
> Your nephew will be happy over the good news from Milan!!!
>
> As regards the Conservatoire, I received yesterday evening a friendly letter from Dubois containing this passage: "The Minister cannot consider the idea that you will not be a member of the Conseil supérieur des études. I agree with him. It has therefore been decided to override your wishes and appoint you in spite of yourself."
>
> I replied by telegram to Dubois yesterday evening: "my dear Dubois, I

am profoundly touched by the intentions of the Minister of Public Instruction on my behalf. But I tell you again this evening—I ask absolutely that the wishes expressed in my letter be respected, and I count upon this as I do upon your friendship for me. Massenet. I am leaving Paris in an hour."

À bientôt, à bientôt, je suis toujours triste loin de chez moi et de chez vous![18]

The upshot was that Massenet was, indeed, a member of the Conseil supérieur des études musicales for 1896–1900.

On 17 November, the work that had pushed *Cendrillon* aside—Mozart's *Don Juan,* in a French version by Durdilly—made a grand entry at the Opéra-Comique with an excellent cast: Victor Maurel (Don Juan), Lucien Fugère (Léporello), Jane Marcy (Doña Anna), Jane Marignan (Doña Elvira), Marie Delna (Zerlina), Edmond Clément (Ottavio), Badiali (Mazetto), and André Gresse (le Commandeur). Jules Danbé conducted. The fiftieth performance, on 19 March 1897, had the same cast except for Mme Parentani as Zerlina and Mondaud as Don Juan. But over the long pull the Opéra-Comique could not compete with the Opéra where, on 7 November 1896, the three hundredth performance (since 1834) of *Don Juan* was celebrated.

Meanwhile, Massenet stopped briefly at Brussels, where *Don César de Bazan* was about to be revived (18 November) with Rachel Neyt. By 12 November, he was at Bordeaux for final rehearsals of *Thaïs.*[19] On the twentieth he wrote to Heugel, confidentially, that his address was Grand-Hôtel des Thermes, Dax (Landes), but that others should write in care of the theater at Bordeaux. The newspapers are buzzing with rumors of casting for *Cendrillon.* Massenet is upset: the joke has gone on too long; if *Cendrillon* cannot be settled, then it would be better to give up. Perhaps Heugel can take advantage of Carvalho's good humor over the success of *Don Juan* to press him for a decision. As it is, at least the news from the provinces is good—long live the provinces![20]

The Massenets apparently remained through December at Dax (near Biarritz)—another of those spas where Ninon could enjoy the warm therapeutic baths while Jules got on with the orchestration of *Sapho.* From letters to Heugel we glean some bits of information. Marie Van Zandt rejoined the Opéra-Comique in an appearance on 2 December, for which Massenet telegraphed good wishes. *Manon* had been given in October at the Petit Théâtre in St. Petersburg, and *La Navarraise* followed on 28 November, with Mme Nuovina. Masini, the theater director there, sent news of the work's success, and Massenet inquired of Heugel where to direct his reply, as such a "brilliant telegram" deserved a word of acknowledgment. Massenet purposely waited out, far from Paris, the sticky business (which fell to Heugel) of trying to persuade Carvalho to stage *Cendrillon.* But nothing was settled; the cast was not even decided upon. We sense that perhaps even Massenet had reservations about his own work for, in the end, he appeared resigned: "Let Carvalho do as he wishes. He has reasons for everything. Don't push him to produce a work that doubtless makes him uneasy. Since there is doubt, it would be best to let the matter drop."[21]

Sapho;
Cendrillon

ASSENET CONTINUED his modest but steady output of songs throughout his life; by the end of 1896, we count a total of 126 songs, of which 80 had been brought together into four volumes of collected *Mélodies*.* During 1897–99, Massenet wrote another 26 songs, of which 20 were collected in Volume V, issued in 1900. The songs are workmanlike settings of minor poets of the day. Adroit but unobtrusive accompaniments serve the lyric projection of the poetic text with French clarity. There are no daring harmonics à la Debussy or Ravel; the very conventionality and predictability of the songs ensured their ready acceptance in an age of musical soirées. Given a sympathetic reading, their faded resonances still evoke the feelings of a bygone era, like the pressed flowers that fall out of our grandmothers' albums.

The dedications suggest, indeed, that the songs were like little album leaves addressed to the composer's interpreters and friends. Thus, *La Chanson des lèvres* was for Georgette Leblanc, and *Chanson pour elle* for Mme Bréjean-Gravière. To Reynaldo Hahn was dedicated *Petite Mireille*; to Mme Henri Heugel, *Regard d'enfant*. And so on. The roster of dedications serves as an index of Massenet's esteem and affection for his many friends and associates, who would have been flattered at even such small attentions from the *maître*.

Speaking of soirées, four letters to Raoul Blondel of January 1897 discuss arrangements for a program set for 23 February, to include *Narcisse* and excerpts from *Esclarmonde*. Massenet would coach the principal singers—Mme Steinheil in *Narcisse* and Mlle Isabelle Astruc as Esclarmonde—while Blondel prepared the chorus. Then Mme Steinheil sent word that she had to be absent from Paris from the

---

* Vol. I appeared ca. 1875 and Vol. II ca. 1881 (Hartmann's records are no longer available). Heugel issued Vol. III in 1891 and Vol. IV in 1896.

sixteenth to the twenty-fifth, and a new date had to be set.[1] The correspondence breaks off, and we never learn the outcome. In such ways did Massenet manage to keep busy during the Paris season.

Sometimes the biographer fumbles in the dark, baffled by the ghosts of personalities long vanished. Thus, on 9 February 1897, Massenet wrote to a "Chère Madame et cher confrère" (obviously a lady composer) recommending a singer, a "great artist" named Mme Lydia Torrigi Heirotte. "Your *Songe,*" he continued, "was superb, as sung at Mapleson's by Miss Della Royen–frankly, superb." Another musical soirée! And who might have been the composer of *Songe?* Perhaps Augusta Holmès?[*] Or Gabrielle Ferrari?[†]

On 25 February 1897, *Manon* reopened at the Opéra-Comique with Gabrielle Lejeune in the title rôle; by now the work had outrun the rest of Massenet in Paris and was a staple in the repertoire. Mlle Lejeune was rewarded with a song dedication: *Première danse.*

Toward the end of March, Massenet had a happy excuse to flee to the South. On 1 April a Massenet Festival was given at Montpellier, with *Thaïs* and *La Navarraise.* On "Sunday" [28 March] he wrote to Heugel, well pleased with the excellent rehearsals and mentioning Delmas [as Athanaël].[2] This time Massenet was present at the performance, receiving a prolonged ovation.

On 14 April, Massenet heard for the first time a Mademoiselle Saverny and promised friends (who had doubtless invited him to the soirée for that purpose) to assist her toward a career. The next day he wrote a letter of recommendation to Mathilde Marchesi, who published it in her memoirs. "À propos of Monsieur Massenet," wrote Marchesi,

> I want to say that he has always shown deep interest in all young persons who were studying to be artists, whether it was for the lyric stage, for concerts, or as instrumentalists. And he has ever been a devoted friend and earnest adviser of those who came to Paris from abroad. Hundreds of instances could be cited of the unstinted help thus given them as well as to his compatriots; and this was true, too, of our other illustrious and distinguished friends Ambroise Thomas, Gounod, Delibes, and Benjamin Godard, all of whom were French composers, as they were "masters" among musicians.[3]

In May the Massenets were at Aix-les-Bains, where the composer worked on his new oratorio, *La Terre promise.* Here they were alarmed by news of the tragic fire, on 4 May 1897, at the Charity Bazaar in Paris. Juliette, along with other young society women, was involved; there were agonizing hours until a telegram brought assurance

---

* Augusta Holmès (1847–1903), French composer of Irish parentage. Example: opera *La Montagne noir,* Paris Opéra, 8 Feb. 1895.

† Gabrielle Ferrari (1851–1921), French pianist-composer. Her opera *Le Cobzar* was given at Monte-Carlo, 16 Feb. 1909.

of Juliette's safety. The Charity Bazaar was an annual event, sponsored by Paris society, to which everyone flocked. This year it was held in a building in the Rue Jean-Goujon, near the Place de l'Alma. The booths and decorations suggested a section of medieval Paris, with winding, narrow lanes. Society women were on duty as salesgirls and waitresses. One of the attractions was a motion-picture show; the crude projection machine ignited a bottle of ether that the operator was using. Within minutes the place was a screaming inferno of incinerated humanity. Many were saved, however, through the heroic efforts of working-class men in the vicinity—employees of the Hôtel du Palais, coachmen, shopkeepers, construction workers, a street sweeper. The charred bodies of 130 victims, mostly women and children, were laid out in the Palais de l'Industrie. As an aftermath, Paris was scandalized that many of the dandies and club men present had saved themselves without even trying to help the women and children. One of the fortunately rescued salesgirls was Georgette Wallace, granddaughter of Sir Richard Wallace. She was fourteen at the time. At twenty, she would make her début at the Opéra under the stage name of Lucy Arbell and would later create principal rôles in Massenet's *Ariane, Thérèse, Don Quichotte,* and *Roma.*

Two letters (5 and 17 May) were written from Aix-les-Bains to Heugel, who was on a busman's holiday in Venice with his wife and son Jacques. Massenet was glad to hear that Heugel had talked with Sonzogno, and was in general concerned with maintaining good relations with Italy. In a postscript (5 May), he wrote: "Thanks for the very interesting account for the scene of the Oasis [i.e., for *Thaïs*]. This shall be done if the Opéra still wants it? I shall get it written one of these days, n'est-ce pas?"[4]

In a letter to Julien Torchet of 17 May, Massenet mentioned that he and his wife had just returned from an excursion into the mountains of the Grande Chartreuse, which he found "wonderful" and "stirring." Torchet is to convey thanks to "our interpreter," and this could only mean Mme Nuovina, preparing to appear as Anita in *La Navarraise* at the Opéra-Comique on 26 May.[5]

Sometime in May, *Werther* was also revived at the Opéra-Comique. On 17 June, Marie Delna reappeared as Charlotte, and on 30 June the season closed with *Werther.* Charlotte Wyns sang Charlotte when the opera reopened on 9 September. The names of Delna and Wyns appear often in Massenet's correspondence among his faithful interpreters. Of the three performances of *Thaïs* at the Opéra during 1897, the one of 31 May is documented by a letter to Massenet from Delmas (who sang Athanaël).[6]

In July the Massenets were at Pourville. Gailhard came on the eighteenth, and they had a long conference regarding the insertions to be made in *Thaïs* for the Opéra the following season.[7] By 8 August, the Massenets were at Dieppe, and the Heugels were on vacation at Trouville. Massenet lamented the distance that separated them and was too busy to go to Orange, where *Les Érinnyes* was given on 2 August.[8] Back in Pourville by 26 August, Massenet expressed regret that they could not accompany the Heugels to Paris. He had promised Ninon to spend a few days in Brittany first. By the evening of 1 September, the Massenets were in Paris, and rehearsals started for *Sapho*.[9]

A noted drama critic for *Le Journal des Débats* was Jules Lemaître, who also wrote plays and stories.* A letter of 24 November 1897 from Massenet to "Chère Madame," was probably to Lemaître's wife. It was a question of tickets for the dress rehearsal of *Sapho*; these were no longer available, and indeed, the première was sold out as well. The Massenets have read with delight *La Contemporaine;* the writer is sorry to hear that "mon grand ami" is not well, hopes for frequent and better news, and signs "to your dear husband, to you Madame, with all my heart, Massenet."[10] Two days before, Massenet had sent Raymond Bouyer a ticket, "absolutely unhappy" that he had nothing better to offer than "this too modest place."[11]

Sapho opened on 27 November 1897 at the Opéra-Comique. A *pièce lyrique* in five acts, the libretto was by Henri Cain and Arthur Bernède, after Daudet's novel.[†] The love affair of Jean Gaussin and Fanny Legrand seems natural and convincing, realistic in the sense that it could have happened in the 1880s. The attractions that bring the lovers together and the conflicts that eventually pull them apart arise inevitably from the life-styles of these two human beings. The musical setting permits the action to proceed and the characterizations to unfold in a straightforward manner, without distractions or digressions.

For the première, conducted by Jules Danbé, the rôles were distributed: Emma Calvé (Fanny Legrand), Julien Leprestre (Jean Gaussin), Marc Nohel (Caoudal), Jacquet (La Borderie), Charlotte Wyns (Divonne), Léon Gresse (Césaire), Julia Guiraudon (Irène), and Michel (Cabassu). *Sapho* had a run of forty-two performances in 1897–98 but was then taken off and not revived at the Opéra-Comique until 22 January 1909.

—◁◦▷—

Act I. Paris. The drawing room of the successful sculptor Caoudal. Sounds of a costume ball emerge from the nearby studio. Jean Gaussin, straight from Provence, feels awkward and out of place at this festive party. Fanny Legrand, an artists' model with a past, is known to her friends as Sapho, having posed "without a stitch" for a well-known piece of sculpture. She draws Jean into conversation. While the others assemble for supper in the studio, she induces Jean to leave with her, obviously intent upon seducing him.

Act II. Jean's room in Paris, Rue d'Amsterdam. Jean has been installed here by

---

* Such as *Contes blancs* (1900). Lemaître's articles were collected and published as *Les Contemporains* (8 vols., 1885–1918) and *Impressions du théâtre* (11 vols., 1888–1920).

† James L. Ford noted (in 1899) that Sapho "has frequently been called Daudet's masterpiece, primarily because of its intense humanity, but also because it is a superb example of all that is best and most convincing and subtle in the mystical art of story telling." (Preface to *Sapho*, in the edition of Daudet's works published by Little, Brown, and Co., of Boston, in 1899.)

his parents to study for the examination that will admit him to the diplomatic service. The parents are about to adopt their niece Irène, now an orphan, and take her back with them to Provence. Jean's ties with his native soil are reflected in the Provençal song he likes to sing, "O Magali, ma tant amado," and he is deeply attached to his mother Divonne and to his father Césaire. He even knew Irène when they were children. They leave, and Jean takes up his books for study. Fanny comes to him; she has kept out of sight while his parents were around, but their affair is by no means over, for "when I love, it is for a long time." She has qualms of conscience, considering that Jean is from a different world, but the two are drawn passionately together as the curtain falls.

Act III. The garden of a restaurant in picturesque Ville d'Avray. It is a year later, and Jean and Fanny share many happy memories. Caoudal, La Borderie, and their friends select this very restaurant for refreshments and dinner. Jean is drawn into conversation, and Caoudal and La Borderie callously reveal Sapho's past, of which Jean was innocently unaware. He breaks off with her and leaves. Fanny is enraged at the hateful conduct of her onetime friends, and calls them all *canailles*.

Act IV. Avignon. Jean is home, sad and distracted. His mother suspects that some evil woman was the cause of his abrupt return, but she forgives him and tries to comfort him. Irène, too, offers friendly solace. Fanny appears and pleads for Jean to return to her, finally breaking his resistance. But Divonne, with a quiet show of maternal authority, waves her off.

Act V. Winter. Fanny is alone in the little home where they had lived at Ville d'Avray. Tomorrow she will leave, trying to forget and to repair her broken life. Loving Jean, still she realizes that she would not have been good for him in the long run. But Jean has broken off his home ties and comes back to Fanny. The decision is now hers. Realizing that her past will always be a gulf between them, when Jean falls asleep, momentarily happy, she quietly leaves forever.

The success of such a work obviously depends upon the abilities and popularity of the artist interpreting Fanny Legrand. The part was tailor-made to suit Calvé's voice, equally at home in the refinements of bel canto and in the cruder accents of veristic style. She was accused of overplaying her rôle, ranging from seductive lasciviousness to the grossness of a fishwife, as when Fanny curses her onetime friends at Ville d'Avray. For better or for worse, the tradition was established. When Mary Garden sang Fanny Legrand at the Manhattan Opera House in 1909, Henry T. Finck deplored a certain note of coarseness which, he thought, "one does not necessarily associate with a model who infatuates artists." Were the work to be revived in our times, what was once "contemporary" would have to be restudied as a period piece. If, as Finck admitted, the master hand of Massenet was still evident in "some effective, passionate climaxes," in music that "adapts itself to the lines and the moods," and in "subtle treatment of the orchestra," then perhaps a new Sapho will some day emerge.[12]

Mary Garden as Fanny Legrand in *Sapho*. Photography by Matzene. Courtesy Paul Jackson.

December of 1897 was clouded by two deaths: on the sixteenth, Alphonse Daudet died at fifty-seven; on the twenty-ninth, Léon Carvalho at seventy-two. One evening that autumn the Massenets had gone to dine at Daudet's, 41 Rue de l'Université, and the composer played *Sapho* for him. Daudet rarely went out but did attend the première of *Sapho*, sitting at the rear of a box; the next day Massenet received a congratulatory note from him. A great crowd assembled for Daudet's funeral at Sainte-Clothilde. After the chanting of the Dies Irae, they played the introduction to Act V of *Sapho*, entitled "Solitude." Daudet was buried at Père-Lachaise.

The tenth performance of *Sapho*, set for 20 December, had to be canceled because of Calvé's hoarseness. Carvalho gave the ticket-holders a free performance of *Le Barbier de Séville*, and they came back for *Sapho* on the twenty-seventh, when Calvé's voice was restored. Massenet decided to look in on the performance from the wings; there he saw Carvalho, obviously ill, though still in good humor and friendly. Within days, Carvalho succumbed to an apoplectic stroke, and on 31 December a grand procession conveyed him from the Madeleine to Père-Lachaise. Among the pallbearers were Roujon, director of the Beaux-Arts; Bertrand, director of the Opéra; and Massenet. At the tomb, Roujon made a simple speech. Massenet, very pale, almost sobbing, read a eulogy expressing the gratitude of composers for Carvalho's struggles in their behalf. Fugère spoke for the artists of the Opéra-Comique, Pitet for the administration, and that was all.

Albert Carré was appointed to succeed Carvalho as director of the Opéra-Comique on 13 January 1898.[*] With the inauguration of the new Salle Favart on 7 December 1898, the troupe was once more at home in its own theater, entering a new and active era. Massenet came to feel quite at home in the new hall. In 1902, Carré married the soprano Marguerite Giraud who, as Mme Marguerite Carré, achieved distinction in various Massenet rôles.

In January 1898, the Massenets headed for the Côte-d 'Azur. At Saint-Raphaël, they were informed at the hotel that the rooms they had reserved had been pre-empted by two ladies. These turned out to be Emma Calvé and a friend, also on a brief holiday. In deference to the *maître*, they changed their plans, and in a few days Calvé returned to Paris to resume *Sapho*. By the twenty-first, the Massenets were settled at the Hôtel Roubion in Nice but then went to Monte-Carlo for a few days.

At Monte-Carlo, besides the opera season in the theater adjoining the casino, there was a concert series called the Concerts Classiques, conducted by the Belgian Léon Jehin, who had formerly (1882–88) been active at La Monnaie in Brussels. The ninth concert of the current season fell on Thursday, 27 January—a date marked each year with a festival of Sainte Dévote, patron saint of Monaco. Jehin conducted Beethoven's First Symphony, and then the second part of the program was given over to Massenet, who conducted: the overture to *Phèdre*; *Le Dernier sommeil de La Vierge* (i.e., the prelude to Part 4 of *La Vierge*); two selections from *Les Érinnyes* (Danse grecque and La Troyenne regrettant sa patrie); the prelude to Act IV and two ballet numbers (Les Gauloises, Les Phéniciennes) from *Hérodiade*; *Crépuscule*; and the *Marche héroïque de Szabady*.

The next day, the twenty-eighth, Massenet had luncheon with the Princess of Monaco. This detained him so that he was unable to hear Louis Diémer's piano concert, which included "Eau courante" (from Massenet's *Deux impromptus* of 1896). The following morning the composer rushed to thank the pianist, only to learn that the Diémers had left. Before the luncheon with the Princess, Massenet had written to Heugel mentioning that the festival had been splendid and that he was delighted with a telegram from Carré: "Very pleased libretto Cendrillon. Will be glad to hear music. When are you returning? We have had two good performances of Manon." By the thirtieth, the Massenets were back in Nice.[13]

On 2 February (to Heugel): "Everything is going well here. Mme Bréjean-Gravière has been through the rôle of Sapho three times with me; she will have a great success at Bordeaux, that could not be otherwise. We are awaiting Manon and the concert at the opera before leaving Nice, and we shall return to Paris by stages. I shall

---

[*] Carré remained through 1913, then went to the Théâtre-Français, while Pierre-Barthélemy Gheusi and the brothers Émile and Vincent Isola took over the direction of the Opéra-Comique. During 1919–25, Albert Carré was associated with the Isola brothers, after which he was made honorary director.

let you know. From both of us, toutes nos grandes affections, and around the twenty-eighth we shall be back! Massenet."[14]

As a footnote to history, we mention Reynaldo Hahn's *L'Ile du rêve,* staged at the Opéra-Comique on 23 March 1898. The work was dedicated to Massenet. An *idylle polynésienne,* the libretto was attributed to Pierre Loti, Hartmann, and André Alexandre, based on *Le Mariage de Loti* of 1880 and set in Tahiti. Edmond Clément sang the rôle of Loti, and André Messager conducted. By coincidence, the ninth and last performance fell on Massenet's birthday, 12 May.

In April, Massenet went to Milan for rehearsals of *Sapho* at Sonzogno's Teatro Lirico. The Sapho was Gemma Bellincioni, whom Massenet is said to have addressed: "God bless you, dear great artist!" Bellincioni and her husband, the tenor Roberto Stagno, had created the rôles of Santuzza and Turiddu in *Cavalleria rusticana.* Verdi considered her the best of Violettas. Stagno had died in 1897; to assuage her grief, the widow devoted herself with all the more energy to her career.*

On 11 April, Massenet wrote to Heugel that the rehearsals were almost finished and that Bellincioni was excellent. "In Paris I will recount to you our little troubles, and, then, it will be with a smile. Your telegram, after the nine o'clock rehearsal of Thaïs at the Opéra, was entirely agreeable to me. But alas, what poor luck to have a work [staged] at the moment of reopening of hostilities at the Palais de Justice!"[15] Namely, *Thaïs* was revived at the Opéra on 13 April 1898, with new material. As for the law courts, the Dreyfus Affair had again stirred up public controversy. In 1894, Dreyfus had been convicted by court-martial of selling military secrets to the Germans and sent to Devil's Island. On 13 January 1898, the pro-Dreyfus newspaper *L'Aurore* published Émile Zola's famous open letter, ending with several paragraphs denouncing the army, each beginning with the words "J'accuse."

Sapho opened at the Lirico on 14 April. The next morning at eight, before leaving Milan, Massenet wrote a few lines to Ricordi from the Hôtel Belle Venise. He thanked his "cher grand ami" for the felicitations sent and recalled memories of *Le Roi de Lahore* twenty years previous.[16]

In Paris, Calvé played Sapho on 29 April, then left for London. On 14 May, *La Navarraise* was revived at the Opéra-Comique with Mme Nuovina as Anita. During the performance, when the Spanish troops entered with the flag of Spain, there was a salvo of applause. You see, Spain was at war with the United States over Cuba! On 25 May, Georgette Leblanc appeared as Sapho; though she was at a disadvantage in following Calvé so closely, the critic Edmond Stoullig remarked sympathetically that her interpretation, "quite different from that of her predecessor, earned for her a personal success as actress, singer, and woman." On 13 June 1898, Puccini's *La Vie de Bohème* reached the stage of the Opéra-Comique, scoring a great triumph and closing the season on 30 June.

---

* One of Bellincioni's last public appearances, if not the last, was as Salome in the Strauss work, at the Paris Opéra, 27 Nov. 1911. Thereafter she taught singing.

In July the Massenets were at Pourville, the Heugels at Trouville. Three letters to Heugel, only one of which is dated (27 July), are sufficiently related in subject matter to be assigned to that month. Massenet was suffering from a stubborn bronchitis, and on a "Friday evening" wrote that he had not been out for the last twelve days. He was fuming behind closed windows to see the ocean and the distant horizon, unable to go out and breathe it. "Ah! I have before me a quantity of vials of all nuances, without counting the mustard-plasters." Withal, he says that he is working, and even adds a postscript: "I am feeling better!" The Heugels were also suffering from minor ailments, and Massenet shows his concern and sympathy.[17] On 8 August, he wrote that they would leave in two or three days for Enghien-les-Bains, in search of a more effective cure.[18]

There are no clues as to what Massenet was working on that summer. Perhaps he was revising *Grisélidis.* It is tempting to apply to that work the enigmatic remarks in the "Friday evening" letter: "Cher bon ami, I believe your nephew will come to see you tomorrow at Trouville. If I could only be in his pocket! He will relate my entreaties, my desires. Don't say that you are annoyed until you hear me out. . . . I believe I have done something toward rescuing from abandonment a work that was deserving in certain respects. Help me in my projects of copying and publishing." There was to be still further revision of *Grisélidis* before its publication and performance in 1901.

Apparently restored, Massenet again wrote to Heugel from Paris on 20 August. In a week he will rejoin his wife "at the waters" and, after a few days of rest, return to Paris.[19] On 2 September another letter, with a promise to send along "a little souvenir of my vacation, for piano solo— *Valse folle.*"[20]

Albert Carré was busy getting together the repertoire for the new Salle Favart. On 23 September, Massenet spent the morning with him viewing the models for new sets and the costume designs for *Manon.* Massenet planned to attend the rehearsals, which involved several new singers.[21]

The Concerts Colonne opened their season on 23 October in the renovated Théâtre du Châtelet; it was a jubilee year, the twenty-fifth since the founding of the concerts in 1873. The second concert (30 October) had Massenet's overture to *Phèdre,* and the third concert (6 November) was devoted to Massenet, who conducted with dignity and authority. Edmond Stoullig mentioned some of the works given: the first orchestral suite; the Méditation from *Thaïs,* with the young violinist Jacques Thibaud (then 18) playing the solo; a scene from *Le Mage,* sung by Edmond Vergnet; excerpts from *Esclarmonde; L'Extase de la Vierge,* sung by Lina Pacary; and "Sous les tilleuls" from *Scènes alsaciennes.* Stoullig remarked that, during the twenty-five years, the Concerts Colonne had played Massenet more than a hundred times, with a total of twenty-five works.

Sapho was given at Geneva on 25 November 1898. In an undated letter to Heugel marked "Wednesday evening" [November 30?], Massenet reported that "*Sapho* is doing very well here; Mlle [Hedwige] Demours excellent, produces already a great effect. The casting is excellent. . . ."[22]

A grand gala marked the inauguration of the new Salle Favart on 7 December 1898. The lengthy mixed program offered bits from the favorite repertoire, conducted by André Messager and Alexandre Luigini. For variety during two entr'actes, the noted bandmaster Parès presented still more favorites with his Garde Républicaine band. Naturally, the Saint-Sulpice scene from *Manon* figured in this festive occasion, sung by Marie Thierry (Manon), Adolphe Maréchal (Des Grieux), Lucien Fugère (le Comte), and Gourdon (le Portier). Edmond Stoullig remarked that this was "not a very happy kind of program," but in any case Maréchal was applauded as Des Grieux. The following evening, 8 December, opera performances began with *Carmen*. *Lakmé* followed on the ninth, and finally *Manon* appeared in its new home on the sixteenth, with Mme Bréjean-Gravière as Manon.

At year's end, Massenet sent seasons greetings to Ricordi, with the request to convey his admiration to Puccini.[23]

The Teatro alla Scala in Milan had undergone some changes. The three seasons from 1894 to 1897 had not been very successful. Despite the warm reception for Puccini's *La Bohème* on 15 March 1897, the house was in trouble and, indeed, closed its doors to opera for twenty months from the end of that season until December 1898. The subventions by the city of Milan became a political issue; the monarchists and the wealthy insisted that the famous opera house was good for Milan, while republicans and socialists equally insisted that there were better uses for public funds than to subsidize the refined pleasures of the rich. The violinist Leandro Campanari, after a profitable sixteen years in the United States, returned to Milan and assembled an orchestra for a concert series at La Scala in November–December 1897. Another series of five concerts, conducted by Pietro Mascagni, was given in March–April 1898. Then the noted opera patron Duke Guido Visconti di Modrone came to the rescue; La Scala was reorganized on a firmer basis and entered a new and flourishing period. The old system of impresarios was abandoned. Giulio Gatti-Casazza was appointed director of La Scala with full administrative powers. He remained from 1898 until 1908, then left to go to the Metropolitan Opera House, which he directed until 1935.

The opera season 1898–99 began auspiciously on 26 December with Wagner's *I Maestri Cantori de Norimberga;* at the conductor's stand was Arturo Toscanini. Wagner was followed by Mascagni's *Iris* (19 January 1899), Meyerbeer's *Gli Ugonotti* (5 February), and Verdi's *Falstaff* (11 March). Massenet's *Il Re di Lahore*, conducted by Toscanini, opened on 25 March and was given for a total of three performances. Meanwhile, Massenet's ballet *Il Carillon* was given on 4 January and was repeated for a total of eleven performances.

No evidence has come to light that Massenet went to Milan. From some letters, we know that on 18 and 20 January he was at Brussels where *Thaïs* was being revived.[24] On 26 February he attended, in Paris, a concert got up by Mme Nora Barrès Diaz that included other singers as well as the pianist Raoul Pugno.[25]

A letter of 17 March 1899 rescues from oblivion a work by a little-known French composer. Massenet wrote: "You probably know that Puget's work is being staged with a splendor unique for the theater; everything is going splendidly for him." The reference is to Paul Puget (1848–1917), whose *Beaucoup de bruit pour rien* was given at the Opéra-Comique on 24 March. In the same letter, Massenet notes that the rehearsals for *Cendrillon* are going well and that they are ready to begin working on the stage. The music gains in actual performance, he says; the artists are delighted with their rôles and are having a good time.[26]

Cendrillon was duly staged on 24 May 1899, while Massenet rested his nerves for a few days at Enghien-les-Bains. Albert Carré did his best to transport his audiences visually to fairyland. As Louis Schneider put it, Perrault's tale, as reworked by Henri Cain and Paul Collin, was lightly dusted by Massenet with the magic powder of sounds.

Act I. At Madame de la Haltière's. A vast room, with a hearth at one side. The servants complain that their mistress is a shrew. Pandolphe de la Haltière was a good-natured widower with an adorable daughter, Lucette. Why, he asks himself, did he leave his pleasant farm and woods to marry a proud countess with a dowry and two daughters? His wife gets her way by grumbling and raging; she treats Lucette like a stepdaughter. Lucette is not even allowed to go to the ball. Really, he should one day assert himself. "This evening," Madame de la Haltière tells her daughters Noémie and Dorothée, "you will be presented to the King." She coaches them on how to act, for "the ballroom is a battlefield," and she has high hopes of snaring the Prince. Modistes, tailors, and hairdressers deck the three women out in finery, and they go off with Pandolphe. Cendrillon (as Lucette is called) is left alone; she enjoys her household chores but tires and falls asleep. The Fée, her fairy godmother, appears and summons hosts of sylphs, elves, and sprites to fit out Cendrillon in splendid attire so that she, too, can go to the ball and find happiness. They weave a robe of radiant stars, moonbeams, and rainbows. For perfume, there is a delicate love philtre, and jewels are fashioned of ladybirds, scarabs, and glowworms. When all is ready, they awaken Cendrillon and send her on her way in a tiny carriage, complete with coachman, page, and postillons. She is given a magic slipper to make her unrecognizable to her stepmother and stepsisters.

Act II. Ballroom and gardens of the King's palace. The King's son, Prince Charming, is silent and pensive, his thoughts reflected by the music of lute, viola d'amore, and crystal flute. No one can arouse him from his withdrawn mood—neither the Superintendent of Pleasures, nor the Dean of the Faculty of Doctors, nor the Prime Minister. Alone again, the Prince makes clear that he is melancholy because he has no one to love. The King enters with all the court; he urges his son to join the ball, where all the daughters of nobility are present. The Prince has only to choose and marry one of them. By way of divertissement, there is a parade of noble daughters, of their fiancés, a band of lutes, a lively Florentine dance, and a Rigodon du Roi. Pandolphe arrives with his wife and stepdaughters. The radiant Cendrillon comes to the ball, and all are amazed at her loveliness. The Prince gazes, enraptured, and speaks to her. Without giving her name, for she is only "a dream," she sings: "You are my Prince Charming; if I could have my way, I would devote my life to pleasing only you." The clock strikes twelve, and Cendrillon must flee. The dancing resumes, and the curtain falls.

Act III, Scene 1. Same as Act I. Cendrillon, out of breath, arrives home. In her haste she has lost her glass slipper. The belfry chimes "ah, vous dirais-je maman," momentarily frightening her. The others return, quarreling. Mme de la Haltière recites the list of eminent persons in her family tree as proof that she and hers deserve more recognition than mere nobodies. The women explain to Cendrillon that some unknown, dressed in poor taste, had come to the ball and had the effrontery to talk with the Prince, then fled amidst general suspicion. The Prince, they said, afterwards came to his senses, appearing not to care a fig for the unknown lady. Cendrillon is grieved to hear this. Pandolphe, suddenly courageous, sends the women packing and consoles his daughter. He resolves that they shall leave the city and return together to the farm where they were formerly happy. Cendrillon, alone, is unwilling to burden her father with her broken dream of love, and silently leaves home.

Act III, Scene 2. The abode of the Fée. A great oak in the midst of a meadow of flowering broom. In the distance, the sea. It is night. Invisible spirits sing in chorus. Other spirits report that a young girl is wandering in the darkness, and also a young man; both seem miserably unhappy. Cendrillon and Prince Charming wander in; separated by a bush, they do not see each other. They confess their love to the Good Fairy and implore her help. Each hears the other's voice, and the Prince learns his beloved's name: Lucette. The Good Fairy bids him hang his heart on the oak tree as a pledge of his good faith, permits them to be reunited, and they fall into a magic sleep.

Act IV, Scene 1. Cendrillon's terrace. Pandolphe watches over the sleeping girl. He had found her beside a brook, cold and inanimate; but now she is convalescing. Pandolphe tells her that in her dazed condition she had babbled about the court, the ball, the Prince, a great oak, and so on. Cendrillon is convinced that it was all a dream. A group of young girls comes to inquire how Lucette is feeling; she responds gaily, for it is joyous April. But Mme de la Haltière enters with advance notice of what the Herald soon announces—that this day the Prince will receive princesses from all regions of the earth in an attempt to discover the owner of the lost slipper. Cendrillon realizes that it was not a dream, after all, and invokes the aid of the Good Fairy.

Act IV, Scene 2. The Court of Honor of the King. Without his heart, the Prince is wasting away; only the lady of the glass slipper can restore it to him. The Good Fairy appears, bringing Cendrillon who gives him back his heart. Even her stepmother now calls her affectionately "my daughter." The entire cast addresses the audience: "The play is ended; we have done our best to carry you away to Fairyland!"

The first cast comprised: Julia Guiraudon (Cendrillon), Mlle Émelen (Prince

Poster for *Cendrillon* by Émile Bertrand, 1899

Charmant), Mme Bréjean-Graviére [la Fée], Mme Blanche Deschamps-Jehin (Madame de la Haltière), Lucien Fugère (Pandolphe), Jeanne Tiphaine (Noémie), Jeanne Marié de l'Isle (Dorothée), Dubose (le Roi), Troy (le Surintendant des Plaisirs), Gourdon (le Doyen de la Faculté), Gustave Huberdeau (le premier Ministre), and, as the six Spirits, Mlles Delorn, Françoise Oswald, Vilma, Craponne, Stéphane, and Fouquié. Alexandre Luigini conducted. *Cendrillon* was given forty-nine times in 1899 and twenty times in 1900.

Two views of Massenet's beloved château at Égreville. Courtesy Demar Irvine.

Without being too far wrong, Emma Calvé had suggested that, after *La Navarraise, Sapho,* and *Cendrillon,* Massenet would be able to buy for himself "three farms and three châteaux in the Aveyron." Instead, he settled for one chateau at Égreville, Seine-et-Marne, twenty miles south of Fontainebleau. The property was purchased on 1 February 1899 from the painter Étienne Berne-Bellecour, known for his spirited pictures of the Franco-Prussian War. The "Chateau Massenet," as it came to be called, dates from the time of Francis I and was originally the north wing of a larger structure, a portion of which was demolished at the beginning of the nineteenth century. The adjoining lands were ultimately increased by Massenet to 220 acres, partly given over to agriculture and partly to woodlot. The Massenets became greatly attached to this restful country place, only a few steps from the peaceful village of Égreville with its thirteenth-century church of Saint-Martin and picturesque covered market.

Various letters from June to October 1899 were dated from Égreville; it was also an easy run up to Paris by train when Massenet had to look after his affairs in the city. Thus, he wrote on 25 June to Florent Schmitt (who was trying for the Prix de Rome) that he would come on Friday, hoping that the train would not leave him stranded en route. "I expect much of you," he wrote, "as I repeatedly said when we saw each other in the class. I shall be hearing you on Friday and Saturday."[27] Saturday was the day for judging the cantatas; this time, two first prizes went to Levadé and Malherbe, and Schmitt had to wait another year for his Prix de Rome.

Armand Silvestre and Eugéne Morand, the librettists for *Grisélidis*, encouraged by the success of *Cendrillon*, asked Albert Carré for a conference together with Massenet, which was duly arranged for 22 July.[28] The Massenets were in Paris in August, despite the "odious" weather with "influenza in the air." In a letter to Heugel (8 August), Massenet remarked that "all is going well at the theater" [*Le Portrait de Manon* was revived at the Opéra-Comique on 26 September], and that "our *Thaïs* is really getting along very well at several large theaters: Lyon, Toulouse, Montpellier, etc., etc. At Algiers, *Sapho* was extraordinary, in the manner of Geneva!"[29]

By 17 August, the oratorio *La Terre promise* was finished. Massenet wrote to Heugel (8 October) that Tournai had requested the work for a festival the following March but that he would postpone his decision until plans were known in relation to the coming Paris Exposition of 1900.[30]

On 25 October, Massenet wrote to Heugel from Brussels: "Yesterday evening I went to *Thaïs*. This evening they are giving *Princesse d'Auberge* [by Jan Blockx]. Vive le Ménestrel! Then it will be *Mignon*, [Delibes's] *Le Roi l'a dit*, *Lakmé*; and *Cendrillon* in preparation. He will stay for the dress rehearsal, 31 October, but not for the actual performance, probably on 3 November.[31]

In December, Massenet swung over to Geneva, where *Cendrillon* was given on the fifteenth, and on to Milan, where the same work opened at the Lirico on the twenty-eighth. He even planned to go to Algiers for *Cendrillon* in January; but when the weather turned stormy, he and his wife did not want to make the crossing, and the trip was canceled.[32] On 2 January 1900, the following telegram caught up with him at Nice; he copied it out for Heugel, then sent the original along for Sonzogno to see:

> Lyon, 30 December
> Am happy to inform you immense success Cendrillon. Artists, orchestra, chorus, remarkable, as well as staging. Public warm, press good.
> Tournié [director, Grand-Théâtre].[33]

Meanwhile, as a fitting close to the 1900s, Massenet was advanced in December 1899 to the grade of Grand-Officier of the Légion d'Honneur.

Poster for *Grisélidis* by François Flameng, 1901.

Grisélidis

THE PIANIST ISIDOR PHILIPP, who had ample occasion to know Massenet, once reported that by 1900 the composer's royalties had amounted to 1,800,000 francs.[1] If Debussy was proud to put "Musicien français" after his name, ought we perhaps to display the ensign: "Massenet, Musicien millionaire"? Success, for some, is a dirty word. For others, it is a measure of the enjoyment its beneficiary must have brought to countless souls willing to pay the price of admission.

With the coming of the new century, Massenet was about to enter the final phase of his career—what may be called the "Monte-Carlo period." For it was Monte-Carlo that saw the premières, during 1902–1912, of *Le Jongleur de Notre-Dame, Chérubin, Thérèse, Don Quichotte,* and *Roma.* Gounod had said that the storm of Wagnerism would pass. Now, the hurricane of modernism was slowly gathering force, though in the comparative serenity of a pre–World War I era, there is no indication that Massenet even thought of looking for a tree to climb. Despite momentary setbacks, his last years were sunny and enjoyable; he basked in the warm rays of a tremendous prestige, kept always busy at his tasks, and had every reason to look back with satisfaction upon a life filled with accomplishment.

The Massenets began the New Year at Nice whence he wrote the following two letters to Heugel:[2]

> Nice, Hôtel de France
> 6 January 1900
>
> You can imagine my chagrin at reading your letter! To know that you are like that! to hear of the days of illness for both you and for Jacques! Ah, I am ready to give up everything, knowing that you are ill. And you take the trouble to tell me about our theaters! Alas, I am nursing a violent cold which keeps me awake at night and wears me out in the daytime! While M. Chevalier was at Nice, I believed it was nothing but a little sore throat. Ah, I did well not to take to the sea [for Algiers], and I say this despite the probably bad humor of M. Saugey, who, as far as he was concerned, merely had to await me peacefully in his office! The weather is horrible, the sea upset for

the past week. It rains incessantly, in torrents. Of course, as soon as I feel completely well, I intend to profit by my stay in the South in cultivating the theaters of the Midi: Montpellier, Toulouse (I wrote to M. Boyer to delay, if possible?), Pau (where Bouvet is preparing some works) — and finally I shall go to Dax where the cure will be very good for my knees. Alas, the North, the cold—all not very favorable for your friend who is quite broken-down at this moment. But it is your health that is our only thought!

Massenet

Thursday, 11 January 1900

Bon cher ami,

I am solid enough to be off, and I am going to Toulouse (Cendrillon). No need to dread a bad crossing [to go] there! I shall telegraph you an exact address so that M. Hudelèrt can have my mail forwarded. Is your health still dubious? Do you sleep? Do you eat? So many questions, which *I forbid you* to answer. I asked M. Chevalier to keep me well posted. Here, at Nice, all is ready for some good performances of *Hérodiade* and *Le Cid*. I was present yesterday at two rehearsals—on stage, and orchestra—to make the most of being there. . . .

Massenet

Now *Thyl* at Brussels—*Louise* at Paris—all that is very interesting.

Thyl Uylenspiegel, an opera in Flemish by the Belgian composer Jan Blockx, was staged at Brussels on 18 January 1900; the libretto was by Henri Cain and Lucien Solvay. *Louise*, of course, was the opera by Gustave Charpentier, to the composer's own text, first given at the Paris Opéra-Comique on 2 February 1900. Massenet wrote again to Heugel on 23 and 27 January from the Hôtel des Thermes at Dax, where he was benefiting from the warm therapeutic baths. Henri Heugel, as the publisher of *Thyl*, went to Brussels for the performance. Massenet had sent his felicitations to Blockx, and to Cain and Solvay. Regarding his own *Cendrillon*, he was informed that within three months of its opening at Brussels it attained its twenty-fifth performance there [on 25 January], with excellent box office: "This flatters me very much, alongside the triumph of Blockx, who quite naturally draws full houses." There was also good news from Bordeaux, where the twenty-first performance of *Cendrillon* filled the theater. Massenet was looking forward to the coming triumph of *Louise*, which he desired very much.[3]

Not mentioned in the letters were some performances at Marseille: *La Navarraise* on 18 January with Mme Nuovina, and *Thaïs* on 9 February with Marguerite Chambellan. Also, on 22 February 1900, *Le Portrait de Manon* was revived at the Opéra-Comique for a modest run of three performances.

As for Charpentier's *Louise*, it was indeed a triumph of the first order, attaining a total of eighty-eight performances at the Opéra-Comique in 1900, with another forty-four the following year. Massenet was surely proud and happy at the success of his former pupil; he perhaps felt a small twinge of envy, too. His own works attained eighty-four performances on Paris stages in 1900, namely: at the Opéra, *Le Cid*, sixteen times; at the Opéra-Comique, *Manon*, thirty-nine times, *Cendrillon* twenty times, and *Le Portrait de Manon*, three times; at the Odéon, *Les Érinnyes* (revived 11 January), six times.

La Terre promise was performed at the church of Saint-Eustache on 15 March 1900, with an immense chorus and orchestra conducted by Eugène D'Harcourt.* For this *oratorio biblique*, Massenet drew his text from the Bible: Deuteronomy for the first part; Joshua for the second and third parts. The theatrical qualities of *Marie-Magdeleine*, *Ève*, and *La Vierge* were eschewed in favor of something closer to the Handelian oratorio tradition. There is no Narrator; rather, the Voice that speaks is alternately soprano, baritone, or tenor, thereby acquiring a certain universality. For the first performance, the soprano part was sung by Lydia Nervil, the baritone by Jean Noté, and the tenor by twelve tenors in unison, as called for by the composer. The chorus represents Israel.

———————————◀○▶———————————

Part I, *Moab*, recalls the pact between Moses and God, who would lead him to the Promised Land. A noble theme, "Écoute, Israël," keeps recurring, transformed by modulations, and a fugal chorus, "Et lorsque nous serons en Terre promise," is noteworthy. The orchestration is effective, with touches of oriental coloring.

Part II, *Jéricho,* is devoted to the taking of that city. The orchestral prelude is a fugue in C minor. Then comes a march, interrupted seven times by resounding outbursts of seven great trumpets, which finally bring the walls down. The ensuing chorus of victory, reinforced by the great organ of Saint-Eustache, made a formidable sound.

Part III, *Chanaan*, or *La Terre promise*, begins in pastoral serenity. The Voice of the Eternal (soprano) speaks to Israel, and the chorus responds with a majestic fugue.

———————————•❖•———————————

The Paris Exposition of the Century opened in April, bringing swarms of visitors from all over the world until well into November. The showplaces were the new Grand Palais, Petit Palais, and the Pont Alexandre III linking them with the grand Esplanade des Invalides. This year, too, Line I of the Métro (Chemin der Fer Métropolitain) was opened, running from the Porte Maillot via the Champs-Élysées and the Rue de Rivoli to the Porte de Vincennes. The theaters of Paris prospered. At the Théâtre Sarah-Bernhardt, Place du Châtelet, one could see the famous actress in Edmond Rostand's new play, *L'Aiglon*, which was given no less than 237 times in 1900! At the Opéra-Comique, it was "the year of *Louise*"; but there was also *Carmen*,

---

* D'Harcourt had been a pupil of Massenet. Together with Saint-Saëns, he represented the French government at the Panama Pacific International Exposition at San Francisco in 1915, and was commissioned to report on musical conditions in the United States.

Manon, and *Mignon*. April 11 saw the première of Camille Erlanger's *Le Juif polonais*, based on the Erckmann-Chatrian novel *Conte d'Alsace*.* On May 30, Humperdinck's *Hansel et Gretel* reached the Opéra-Comique in a French version by Catulle Mendès.

Massenet's *Le Cid* had not been given at the Opéra since 1893; for the Exposition visitors it was dusted off (11 June) and given sixteen times. *Cendrillon* was revived at the Opéra-Comique on 21 July, mostly with the original cast, except that Mlle Thomson appeared for the first time as Prince Charmant.

In May, Massenet fell ill with a serious bronchitis, the course of which can be traced in three letters to Heugel. He had gone to the annual meeting of the Society of Dramatic Authors and Composers on Saturday, 28 April; afterward, he felt too ill to stop in at Heugel's shop, as he had planned. On 8 May, he still felt poorly, and admitted ("just between ourselves") that he had been imprudent in going to the meeting.[4] On Thursday, 17 May, he wrote:

> Cher bon ami,
>
> Each day I want to go out, and, at the last moment, hat in hand, I hesitate. The thermometer is not sufficiently encouraging for an old *bronchiteux* like myself. I know that they are working (very well, it seems) at the Opéra [for *Le Cid*]. However, next week I hope to be able to go out. This morning, a very courteous visit by Lascoux and Humperdinck. I was still in bed and unable to see anyone. . . .
>
> Massenet.[5]

The months of June to October were spent at Égreville, though in all likelihood Ninon would have gone away to one of her favorite spas in August or September, leaving Jules hard at work. For Sunday, 8 July, it was planned that the Heugels would run down from Paris for a visit. On 2 July, Massenet wrote: "And then it will be a joy to have you in our *modeste et vieille solitude*"—a stock phrase for describing his new place to his friends. The Heugels should be "indulgent." Young Jacques and his cousin will be intrigued by the "very rustic" countryside. "The air is brisk—very brisk; bring an overcoat for the promenade through the woods." And Massenet sends along a timetable of trains.[6] On Thursday (5 July), he implored Heugel to reconsider and cancel the trip—even at the last minute in the Gare de Lyon—if he decides the weather is unpropitious and a threat to his health. But then: "Please ask Mme Heugel to bring the camera! The carriage will be at the Égreville station awaiting their 10:11 A.M. arrival. . . . Jean, the faithful Jean, will be at the train to bring you to the modest carriage—it is no longer a question of a *carrosse* in blue satin as at Pont-de-l'Arche! . . . Remember my recommendations: a good overcoat for the morning walk through the woods—and, if it is wet or cold, don't come at all."[7]

---

* The compound name was used by two Lorrainers, Émile Erckmann (1822–1899) and Alexandre Chatrian (1826–1890). Their literary partnership dated from 1848, and their stories of Alsatian peasant life became known the world over. *Le Juif polonais* was dramatized in 1869 (known in English as *The Bells*), and two other plays were *L'Amico Fritz* (1876; set by Mascagni as *L'Amico Fritz*, Rome, 1891) and *Les Rantzau* (1882; set by Mascagni as *I Rantzau*, Florence, 1892).

Massenet enjoying "the old solitude" of his château at Égreville. Courtesy Demar Irvine.

The genesis of *Le Jongleur de Notre-Dame* lies under a cloud of supposition. After he was famous, Massenet liked to perpetuate stories that his operas were finished and waiting for a long time—even years—before they were performed. In some instances this was undoubtedly true. In other cases, it is an exaggeration. Thus, the chronology of the *Souvenirs* seems at times purposely garbled, to throw us off the scent. We have the warning of Raymond de Rigné that the account given out for *Le Jongleur de Notre-Dame* was completely distorted.

The *Souvenirs* speak to the matter as follows: Massenet became very ill at Paris. [Could refer only to May 1900.] After the cold winter, when spring came, he went to his "old home" at Égreville. He took along a large quantity of mail, as yet unopened. Among the mail was a manuscript for an opera libretto; it had been brought by hand to the Paris apartment, where the concierge was sworn not to divulge the author's name unless Massenet agreed to write the music. Massenet was intrigued by the title, "Le Jongleur de Notre-Dame, Miracle in Three Acts," and by the fact that it called for an all-male cast of principals. The credibility gap widens: "The score was finished and the time came to communicate with my unknown." The author turned out to be Maurice Léna, "the devoted friend I had known at Lyon where he held the chair of philosophy." Léna came to Égreville "on 14 August 1900." They hurried to Massenet's place, where the composer showed him, "spread out on a large table (I flatter myself it was a famous table, for it had belonged to the illustrious Diderot), the engraved piano and vocal score for *Le Jongleur de Notre-Dame.*" Léna was, of course, "choked with emotion" at the sight. Now note: "As I never had a piano at home, especially at Égreville, I was unable to satisfy my dear Léna's curiosity and let him hear the music of this or that scene." Later, as they strolled together near the hour of vespers, the happy idea occurred to Massenet to take his friend into the "old, venerable church" [Saint-Martin] and play fragments of the new work on the organ. It was only a happy idea—even the *Souvenirs* do not suggest that it was carried out.

Massenet, the *gamin*, was not above playing tricks. Raymond de Rigné certified that he *pretended* to have no piano at Égreville, mainly to discourage the importunate who would otherwise constantly be seeking auditions. The initiated were shown how the piano was cleverly concealed behind some paneling, to be moved out quite easily when needed. "Diderot's table" was actually a rather large writing desk, still preserved in the family.

Through a fortunate circumstance, the *premier manuscrit* (first draft) of *Le Jongleur de Notre-Dame* reposes in the Heugel archives, for after the orchestration, piano-vocal reduction, proofs, and all were finished, Massenet presented the first draft to Mme Heugel with an inscription. The manuscript is written on 113 pages and bears on the flyleaf: "À Madame Henri Heugel. En souvenir de la profonde et reconnaissante affection que j'ai pour votre mari, permettez-moi de vous offrir ce manuscrit, écrit dans la vieille solitude d'Égreville et terminé en Septembre 1900. Votre fervent et respectueux ami, J. Massenet. Paris, Noël 1901."* The only other date given is at the end of Act I: 2 September 1900.

A gala at the Opéra on 27 September 1900, held in honor of a Congress of Railways that was meeting in Paris, was attended by an elegant, cosmopolitan audience. The mixed program included excerpts from *Samson et Dalila, Faust*, and the ballet music from *Le Cid*. Four days later (1 October), the one hundredth performance of *Le Cid* was celebrated at the Opéra. Auguste Stoullig wrote: "After the admirable duo, in the third act, the whole hall made a spontaneous ovation to Massenet, who, much moved, had to salute the audience twice from the director's [Pedro Gailhard's] box, at the back of which he had kept himself concealed." For this occasion, the authors gave one thousand francs to the retirement fund of the Opéra, and Heugel et Cie an equal amount. In several letters just before, Massenet sought every excuse to avoid the attendant banquet.[8]

Shortly after, Massenet politely declined still another banquet. Théodore Lindenlaub, of *Le Temps*, got up a testimonial dinner in honor of Édouard Colonne for 31 October. Massenet wrote to Paul Chevalier (Heugel's nephew and partner) on 10 October: "Please thank M. Lindenlaub on my behalf for his kind words. But as

---

* [To Madame Henri Heugel. As memento of the deep and grateful affection which I have for your husband, permit me to offer you this manuscript, written in the old solitude of Égreville and finished in September 1900. Your fervent and respectful friend, J. Massenet. Paris, Christmas 1901.]

you know my antipathy toward involvement in any public manifestation, naturally attended by the press, and since my prose [i.e., a speech] is uninteresting, I desire to remain *in thought* [only] with my great friend, who cannot doubt my affection and admiration for him, *since a long time!*" He added: "I *avoided* the banquet for the hundredth of *Le Cid;* that is further evidence, I think, of my confirmed opinion of such gatherings."[9] Reynaldo Hahn has left us a vignette of the occasion: [31 October 1900] "Banquet in honor of Colonne. All the musicians [were] there. Foul cuisine. The toasts, models of false sincerity. Berlioz-Colonne, Colonne-Berlioz! The only good speech was that of Colonne himself, celebrating the memory of Pasdeloup and Lamoureux, delivered with a grand art of nuances. While someone was talking—I forget who—Fauré whispered in my ear: 'As for me, I want to propose a toast to the composers who contributed to Colonne's fame!' "[10]

As an example of Massenet's wit—in this case tragicomic—I offer the following letter to Heugel:

Égreville, 17 October 1900

Cher bon ami,

My wife is radiant over the plants—without number—which come flowing in from Nemours. We must have a conference!! How am I going to manage to purchase the necessary and sufficient acreage to plant your "follies,'" now that the [theater] directors find that I have "ceased to please"! and that they do not even bother to read before refusing! *In fine,* if I have ceased [to please], it is because I must have pleased [before] and I had a very fair weather in he theater—*formerly,* when I was not old, as today.

In tender and sad affection,

Massenet[11]

On 8 December 1900, Racine's *Phèdre* was revived at the Odéon, with incidental music by Massenet. To the overture (1873) was newly added some *musique de scène* to accompany the action, and four entr'actes: *Thésée aux enfers; Sacrifice et offrande* and *Marche athénienne* (before Act III); *Imploration à Neptune;* and *Hippolyte et Aricie.* According to Louis Schneider, the music made a much better impression than this particular interpretation of the play.

At some time in December, according to the *Souvenirs,* Massenet received a visit, at Heugel's shop, by a deputation of former Prix de Rome winners, led by Lucien Hillemacher. "He delivered to me on parchment the signatures of more than five hundred of my old pupils. The pages were bound into a thin octavo volume, luxuriously covered in Levant morocco, spangled with stars. On the fly-leaves in brilliant illumination, along with my name, were the two dates: 1878–1900."

On 6 January 1901, *Cendrillon* was staged at Marseille; Massenet attended the sixth performance, acknowledging an ovation from a box. He then settled for some weeks at the Hôtel du Cap at Antibes. On 27 January the eighty-seven-year-old Verdi died in Milan; it was as though Italy had lost a national hero. Massenet wrote to Heugel on the same day, explaining that since Marseille he was suffering from a severe grippe; it seemed too much of a risk to attend the funeral, where he would have to sit in a cold church, hat in hand—in Milan, in winter! On the other hand, in view of what Italy had done for him, he felt a certain obligation to put in an appearance. If only the funeral were scheduled a week or ten days hence, perhaps he would be well enough to go. "Well, then, for mercy's sake: send me by return mail thirty lines, such as you know how to write—thirty lines—to be read on behalf of the Society of Authors." [12]

Apparently Massenet did not go, for on 2 February he wrote that he was "still quite ailing." Mention of his presence at Antibes had got into the Nice newspapers, so that he was flooded with invitations. Horrified at the thought of the newspapers printing that "Massenet is ill," he simply let it be known that he was "not" at Antibes. Thus, *Cendrillon* was due to open at Nice on 6 February, but Massenet wrote to the theater director, Jauffret, that he expected to be "away on a trip for a week or ten days." [13]

For the *Souvenirs*, even a bad cold was expunged from the health record:

Carvalho [who died on 29 December 1897] had previously engaged me to write the music for *Grisélidis*, a work by Eugène Morand and Armand Silvestre which was much applauded at the Comédie-Française. I wrote the score at intervals between my journeys to the South and to Cap d'Antibes. Ah, that hotel on the Cap d'Antibes! That was an unusual stay. It was an old property built by Villemessant, who had christened it correctly and happily "Villa Soleil," and which he planned for journalists overtaken by poverty and age. Imagine, if you can, a large villa with white walls all purple from the fires of the bright sun of the South and surrounded by a grove of eucalyptus trees, myrtles, and laurels. It was reached by shady paths, suffused with the most fragrant perfumes, and faced the sea—that sea which rolls its clear waters from the Côte d'Azur and the Riviera along the indented shores of Italy as far as ancient Hellas, as if to carry thither on its azured waves which bathe Provence the far-off salutation of the Phocean city [Marseille]. How pleased I was with my sun-filled room, where I worked in peace and quiet and in the enjoyment of perfect health!

Further light is shed on *Grisélidis* by a letter to Heugel:

Hôtel du Cap, Antibes
5 February 1901

Cher bon ami,

(1) When on my return, I shall speak to you of the "New Grisélidis," will I be arousing your displeasure? (2) It is a question of an entire score, and I must forewarn you. (3) It was Baudon who engraved the first version; it was Roux who looked after the second version. It would therefore be to *that firm* that the third score (this is the word, alas) should be entrusted. (4) If you consent to this undertaking, which can permit the work now to appear in the theater, it would perhaps be useful, if you think so, to engage M. Roux for 10 March. (5) In May the directors of La Monnaie usually come to Paris, and I would have suggested to them to hear the score at that time—at your place?

(6) So then, the score could be re-engraved in March and April. (7) You are going to have other works more pressing and more successful than *Grisélidis*. It is absolutely for you to decide the fate of this work which will have cost me so much trouble, caused me so much chagrin, and made you expend already so much money. (8) Will you ever forgive me for the vexation I will have caused you? Fondly yours (and sadly always, in thinking of the painful end of my existence in the theater),

J. Massenet.

Did I misunderstand? It seems to me that you are feeling better; if that is only the case. News of *Manon* at Turin, Théâtre Regio: *Bis*—la Rêve, la petite table, le menuet d'orchestre, la gavotte chantée; and after St. Sulpice eight curtain calls (they even wanted the *bis* of that scene).[14]

Heugel was apparently agreeable, for on 14 February Massenet wrote: "Thanks for 'Grisélidis' (excellent projects!). Thanks also for the proofs received this morning. Maybe we shall go to finish our vacation at Cannes. I will let you know if we leave Antibes."[15] The proofs to be corrected are not further described. One would like to think, perhaps, that they were for the *Chansons des bois d'Amaranthe*, suite for soprano, contralto, tenor, and baritone, with piano accompaniment, composed sometime in 1900 and published by Heugel in 1901 with a dedication "to my daughter, Madame Léon Bessand."

Thaïs, missing from the Opéra playbills since 1898, was revived on 9 March 1901, for eleven performances. The Colonne concert for Sunday, 10 March, presented an all-Massenet program—the encored numbers are here marked *bis*:

Brumaire, overture (first performance)

Arioso "Aux troupes du Sultan," from *Le Roi de Lahore*, sung by Jean Lassalle—*bis*

Phèdre, suite (first concert performance): (1) Ouverture; (2) Thésée aux enfers; (3) Hippolyte et Aricie—*bis*; (4) Implorations à Neptune; (5) Sacrifice—Offrande—Marche Athénienne

(a) Air "O nuit! douce nuit," from *Ève,* and (b) Extase de la Vierge: "Rêve infini, divine extase," sung by Mme Auguez de Montalant

Méditation from *Thaïs* (violin solo by Valerio Oliveira)—*bis*

Chant provençal: "Mireille ne sait pas encore," sung by Jean Lassalle

Esclarmonde, suite for orchestra: (1) Évocation; (2) L'île magique; (3) Hyménée; (4) Dans la forêt[16]

Public acclaim for past accomplishments probably did not contribute too much, actually, toward feeding the composer's ego or making him happy. For the creative artist, happiness is the glow of activity in planning and carrying out each new project. The lift to the ego comes at that moment when the completed work is realized in production and proves to be a satisfactory approximation of the dream. Or disappointment sets in when the realization does not live up to the dream, proving the artist's calculations wrong. Still more depressing is the agony of waiting around for realization. *Grisélidis* and *Le Jongleur de Notre-Dame* had emerged from Massenet's workshop but were still waiting to be staged.

On his fifty-ninth birthday, 12 May 1901, Massenet was at Aix-les-Bains. A letter from Heugel must have kindled new hopes; Massenet "read and *reread*" it to Ninon, who was also deeply touched that "you have come to our help when circumstances were becoming truly discouraging—*after all my life of work*."[17] In all likelihood, the "measures" Heugel was taking related to *Grisélidis*, which came to production in November at the Opéra-Comique, followed within a few months by Nice, Algiers, and Brussels.

The fate of *Le Jongleur de Notre-Dame* was apparently also decided that summer. According to the *Souvenirs*, the autumn, winter, and spring had passed without anyone offering to stage the opera. Then Raoul Gunsbourg, director of the Théâtre de Monte-Carlo, brought word that Prince Albert of Monaco would be pleased to have a work of Massenet to put on. Indeed, the prince came in person to hear a reading of *Le Jongleur*, which Massenet gave at the elegant home of his publisher Heugel. Toward the end of the year rehearsals got under way in Paris, where Gunsbourg maintained an apartment. The way was thus cleared for a Monte-Carlo première the following February.

From June through September, Massenet was at Égreville.[*] On 23 June he wrote to Weckerlin, the erudite Conservatoire librarian, asking for help in finding some *chansons* and *airs de danse* typical of Artois, in French Flanders, from the eighteenth century. By the end of August the "two precious volumes" loaned had been "returned to the sheepfold," and Massenet thanked Weckerlin for enabling him to introduce some authentic Flemish airs into *Les Rosati*, a divertissement given in December at the Opéra-Comique.[18]

In October, rehearsals for *Grisélidis* were under way. Henri Busser, who was chorus director at the Opéra-Comique, jotted down in his diary: "28 October [1901]. Italian-style rehearsal of *Grisélidis*, with all the artists seated on stage, music in hand. Massenet, very excited, goes from one to the other, making known his suggestions. In the prologue, I conduct a small chorus in the wings, with nice effect. Messager, at the conductor's stand, a bit irritated by the goings and comings of the composer."[19]

The première was on 20 November, with the following cast: Lucienne Bréval (Grisélidis), Adolphe Maréchal (Alain), Hector Dufranne (Marquis de Saluce), Lucien Fugère (le Diable), Jeanne Tiphaine (Fiamina), Émile Jacquin (le Prieur), Gustave Huberdeau (Gondebaud), Daffeyte (Bertrade), and la petite Suzanne (Loys). *Grisélidis* was billed as a *conte lyrique* with a prologue and three acts. Armand Silvestre and Eugène Morand had prepared the libretto after their play of 1891, which in turn was drawn from Boccaccio's *Decameron*, the tale of the humble, patient Griselda.

---

* Leconte de Lisle's tragedy *Les Érinnyes*, given once before at the Opéra (12 Aug. 1900), was now given there for a second time, on 6 June 1901.

Lucienne Bréval as Grisélidis at the Opéra-Comique. Courtesy Paul Jackson.

The Prologue of the opera shows a forest in Provence of the fourteenth century. Alain, a shepherd, sings his love of the shepherdess Grisélidis. But the Marquis de Saluce catches a glimpse of her, offers marriage, and is accepted.

Act I. The oratory of the castle. Grisélidis has been married to the Marquis for several years, and they have a little son, Loys. The Marquis is summoned to fight against the Saracens. The Prior warns him of what might happen if he leaves his wife at home alone. But the Marquis is confident of her loyalty, even in spite of the Devil. The Devil appears (as in miracle plays, he is equipped with horns and tail). The Marquis defies the Fiend to do his worst, giving his wedding ring as a pledge of Grisélidis's loyalty.

Act II. A terrace before the castle; in the distance, the sea. The Devil has his own troubles, for his wife Fiamina is coquettish, wicked and evil tempered. However, she agrees to help him win the wager. Disguised as a Byzantine merchant and a Persian slave girl, the two call on Grisélidis. By way of credentials, they show the wedding ring of the Marquis; they explain that the latter has purchased this beautiful Persian, who is to be installed as mistress of the castle. The Marquis will marry her properly upon his return. Grisélidis submits meekly; she will take her son and leave. At nightfall, the Devil calls upon his spirits to fetch Alain. In a dreamlike state brought on through sorcery, Grisélidis and Alain feel attracted to one another, as in former tines. But the entrance of little Loys breaks the spell, and the Devil carries off the child.

Act III. The oratory. Grisélidis supplicates Saint Agnes for the return of her son. The Devil appears in a new disguise. He tells Grisélidis that a pirate has her son, who will be killed or sold into slavery unless she goes aboard the pirate's ship. At this very moment the Marquis returns from the Holy Land. The Devil points at Grisélidis, insinuating that she is going to a tryst with a handsome young lover. But the Marquis refuses to believe evil of his wife. Grisélidis returns without having found Loys. The Marquis and Grisélidis finally unravel the deceptions that have been played upon them. But where is Loys? They pray before the altar, which is suddenly flooded with light. The triptych opens, disclosing the child asleep at the foot of the image of Saint Agnes.

———————————————— ◆ ————————————————

Albert Carré was a true collaborator in providing an effective stage atmosphere, with the help of Jusseaume for the décors and Bianchini for the costumes. Massenet's lively scoring suited a story-telling mood freed from the heavier passions of *Hérodiade, Manon,* and *Werther.* Indeed, the chief protagonist of the piece is the Devil, who combines human frailties and frustrations with a folkish wit.

The second performance (23 November) was attended by Massenet and his wife; the composer, pleased with the large box office (ninety-five hundred francs), was prodigal with his compliments to the artists.[20] By the end of the year, *Grisélidis* had attained seventeen performances, to which another seventeen performances were added in 1902. The work was taken up at Nice, Lyon, Brussels, Milan (Lirico, 25 November 1902), and eventually reached New York (19 January 1910) and Chicago (12 January 1917).

An incident of early November deserves passing mention. Reynaldo Hahn was making a study of Mozart's *Don Giovanni,* and on 5 November Massenet wrote to Weckerlin suggesting that he be permitted to inspect the autograph in the Conservatoire library. "Reynaldo Hahn," he wrote, "is a man of the utmost refinement, combining with musicianship the qualities of a scholar and man of letters."[21] A battered copy of Hahn's *Notes: Journal d'un musicien* (1933) in the author's possession had been supplied with marginal dates in an unknown hand. Here Hahn has put: "Profound emotion this morning; spent two hours at the Conservatoire with the manuscript of Don Juan," the annotator has supplied "November 5, 1901"!

Paul Taffanel resigned as conductor of the Concerts du Conservatoire (he continued on at the Opéra), and on 12 June 1901, Georges Marty was elected to succeed him. As a tribute to his former pupil, Prix de Rome of 1882, Massenet completed in September an orchestral version of *La Chevrière*, the *petit conte rustique* previously published by Heugel (1895) for two women's voices and solo, with piano accompaniment. This new version was presented at the second Concert du Conservatoire of the season, on 7 December, along with Méhul's Symphony in G Minor, Mendelssohn's Reformation Symphony, and Mozart's *Ave Verum*. The critic Edmond Stoullig noted that the audience "graciously received" Massenet's "delicately orchestrated" little work, with Mlle Van Gelder as soloist.

On 9 December, the Salle Favart was given over to a matinée festival organized by a benevolent association known as "La Betterave," representing northern France and the Pas-de-Calais. This Fête du Nord, as it was called, presented a mixed program including: an overture with popular airs of the North, by V. de Wally; an amusing *saynète-prologue* by the president of "La Betterave," Édouard Noël; *Les Haleurs*, by Alexandre Georges, sung by the choral society of Valenciennes; Massenet's specially composed one-act ballet *Les Rosati*, danced by Jeanne Chasles and the corps de ballet of the Opéra-Comique; and finally, Gustave Charpentier's *La Muse du peuple*.

A few days later, on 14 December, there was another matinée benefit—this time for the family of Émile-Alexandre Taskin, who had created the rôle of Lescaut in *Manon* and who had died on 5 October 1897. The program, consisting of songs, individual acts from plays, and Act II of *La Navarraise*, brought in 13,002 francs.

Poster for *Le Jongleur de Notre-Dame* by Georges Rochegrosse, 1904.

Le Jongleur de Notre-Dame

G*RISÉLIDIS* CONTINUED ITS RUN at the Paris Opéra-Comique. On 22 January 1902, Lucienne Bréval drew a full house for her last appearance before departing for America. On the twenty-fourth, the twenty-two-year-old Suzanne Cesbron made her début as Grisélidis. Edmond Stoullig made the inevitable comparisons: the illustrious Bréval gave the rôle a mystical quality, as though she had stepped from the illuminated pages of some medieval missal; Cesbron, with a daintier figure and more modern allure, invested the part with a vibrant quality of warmth and intensity. Indeed, Cesbron was later noted for her portrayals of Manon and Charlotte.

The Massenets, meanwhile, had left the glacial cold of Paris for Nice, where *Griselidis* was staged on 20 January. Another small document of Massenet's generosity dates from this period: the publisher Quinzard had died in 1901, and his widow was in some financial distress; Massenet instructed Heugel to send her one hundred francs, charging it to his personal account.[1] By early February the Massenets had gone on to Monte-Carlo.

The principality of Monaco actually comprises three contiguous *communes*. There is Monaco-Ville proper, perched on a lofty rock, with the palace, adjacent gardens, and the picturesque old village-sized settlement. At the foot of the rock, facing the harbor, is the more populous La Condamine, which in turn merges into Monte-Carlo on its sloping hillside. In the early 1900s the whole principality counted some thirteen thousand permanent residents, who called themselves *monégasques*, with a large influx of winter guests from about November to April. Monte-Carlo had not amounted to much until a gambling casino was opened there in 1866. The present imposing Casino, by Charles Garnier, was inaugurated in 1878. Besides the *salles de jeu* (featuring roulette and trente-et-quarante), there were various salons for reading or conversation and a *salle des fêtes* (theater) for stage performances and concerts. For the élite fleeing colder climates, Monte-Carlo was a special paradise whose artistic, social, and sporting events were all duly reported in the columns of the weekly *Journal de Monaco*.

The Concerts Classiques, conducted by Léon Jehin, were held weekly on Thursdays at half past two, from November to April. From November through January, the theater was given over to operettas and ballet, after which the months of February and March were devoted to opera, usually on Tuesday, Thursday, and Saturday evenings. In 1902 the Monte-Carlo opera season opened on Saturday, 1 February, with Melba and Caruso in *La Bohème*, which was replaced on 12 February by *Rigoletto* with the same stars. Next came four performances of Massenet's *Le Jongleur de Notre-Dame* (18, 20, 22, and 25 February), followed by three performances of *La Damnation de Faust*, three of *Lohengrin*, and two of Drigo's ballet *La Côte d'Azur* on a double bill with *Cavalleria rusticana*. The season closed with Gounod's *Roméo et Juliette* (18, 22, and 25 March).

His Most Serene Highness Prince Albert had timed his return to Monaco for the afternoon of Friday, 31 January, when his yacht *Princesse-Alice* arrived from Marseille at the harbor of Monaco at two o'clock. He was welcomed by all the church bells of the principality, and at nine o'clock that evening the local musical societies joined forces to serenade him. Albert (1848–1922), of the House of Grimaldi, loved the sea and indeed held the honorary rank of rear admiral in the Spanish navy. Acceding to the throne of Monaco in 1889, he had been an enlightened absolute monarch, founding a modern hospital, developing schools, creating a port, and encouraging the arts. Having a scientific turn of mind, his great passion was oceanography, for which he had fitted out the schooner *Hirondelle* as early as 1885. This vessel was supplanted in 1891 by the six-hundred-ton yacht *Princesse-Alice*, followed in 1898 by the fourteen-hundred-ton *Princesse-Alice II*. It was in 1902 that Prince Albert published *La Carrière d'un navigateur*, with an account of his oceanographic expeditions.[*]

Presumably the Massenets were in Monte-Carlo in time to witness the prince's arrival and to attend the opening of the opera season. On 8 February, Massenet wrote to Heugel that it had been foggy the past week and that they would "return to the palace until Wednesday the 19th" but that they would then leave for Marseille.[2] The *Journal de Monaco* of 11 February confirms that M. and Mme Massenet were at the palace as guests of the prince and that the composer was busy with rehearsals. On Thursday, 13 February, Jehin included the orchestral suite from *Esclarmonde* in the program of his Concert Classique.

Le Jongleur de Notre-Dame had its première on Tuesday, 18 February 1902, and was considered by the reviewer Fernand Platy "not only a great success for the direction of our theater, but a fine victory for the eminent composer and for French music." Massenet was the object of continuous standing ovations. When, at the last act, Prince Albert placed upon the composer's breast the insignia of the Grand-Croix of the Order of Saint Charles, the hall set up a unanimous cry of "Vive le prince! Vive Massenet!"[†]

---

[*] He published, besides, over one hundred scientific papers, and ultimately (1911) fitted out the 1650-ton *Hirondelle II* as a superb oceanographic cruiser.

Charles Gilibert in *Le Jongleur de Notre Dame*. Courtesy Benedikt & Salmon.243

The cast was well chosen, with Adolphe Maréchal (Jean le Jongleur), Maurice Renaud (Boniface, the abbey cook), and Soulacroix (le Prieur). The monks, who were poet, painter, musician, and sculptor, were respectively played by Berquier, Juste Nivette, Grimaud, and Cuperninck. The only women's voices called for were the two angels, sung by Marguerite de Buck and Mary Girard.

––––––––––◄○►––––––––––

The scene of *Le Jongleur de Notre-Dame* is the Abbey of Cluny in the fourteenth century. Act I represents a market day in May. Peasants sell their produce, boys and girls dance, and monks go about selling indulgences. The *jongleur* arrives: Jean, who is poor and starved. The crowd calls for the "Alleluia du vin." The Prior appears at the door of the Abbey; he urges Jean to abandon his wicked ways. Then Boniface, the Abbey cook, returns with his donkey laden with good provisions for the kitchen. At this

† From page 240: Léon Jehin was made Chevalier of the order of Saint Charles at the third performance, on 22 Feb. To mark his tenth year as director of the Théâtre de Monte-Carlo, Raoul Gunsbourg was likewise made Chevalier on 27 Feb., when Berlioz's *La Damnation de Faust* opened with Melba, Jean de Reszke, Renaud, and Chalmin.

sight Jean succumbs; he enters the Abbey, but manages to smuggle in his jugglery outfit.

Act II is noteworthy as revealing Massenet's appreciation of medieval church music. Jean is now a regular inmate of the Abbey and has put on weight. Some monk musicians rehearse a motet. Then the various monks get into a dispute over the value of the different arts. But the good Boniface proclaims that Latin and the fine arts are not necessary, for the Virgin is not proud. In the "Légende de la sauge" he retells the story of the child Jesus hidden in the sage.

In Act III, Jean performs his juggler's tricks—the only art he knows—before the image of the Virgin. When the other monks catch him at it, they are scandalized. But the statue shines with a strange light, comes to life, and blesses Jean, who falls back dead.

Amidst the good humor as well as the realism of a fourteenth-century monastery (where even miracles are in character!), the obvious message is renewal of hope for the lowly. It was Massenet striking back indirectly at his critics. Here was an opera *without* a female lead, with no exotic seductions—a purely monastic exercise. Nor are fine aesthetic pretensions ("Latin and the fine arts") an absolute necessity for fulfillment; all that matters is to do *what* one can as *best* one can. The message was to come through even more clearly in the last act of *Don Quichotte*.

The Massenets left Monte-Carlo on 19 February, returning to Paris by way of Marseille. Giulio Ricordi—who published quantities of elegant salon music under the pseudonym "J. Burgmein"—sent along his latest effort, eliciting from Massenet the polite compliment: "You must tell our excellent colleague Burgmein he has again produced a positively brilliant suite. I like this music, which is so clever, so musical, and so typical of him." There is the usual nostalgic reference to the old days when Massenet felt "at home" in Ricordi's study in the Via degli Omenoni.[3]

By 7 March, Massenet was busy with rehearsals at Brussels, where *Grisélidis* was to be staged (20 March 1902). In writing to a friend, he mentioned an offer of collaboration (not further described) that he must reject: "How can one consider further projects when I don't know if I shall live long enough and keep the contractual agreements already promised for 1906–09."[4] This would have been a typical and calculated rebuff, to discourage some pretentious librettist.

On 20 March, Massenet arrived in Vienna where the one hundredth performance of *Manon* in the Austrian capital was about to be celebrated.[5] He remained for several days, then returned to Paris. Meanwhile, a special occasion at Monte-Carlo deserves mention as including a little-known Massenet work: On Saturday, 22 March 1902, the French colony sponsored a charity benefit (which took in forty-three thousand francs), with an evening of music followed by a grand ball. The first part of the program comprised vocal selections from Delibes's *Lakmé* and Gounod's *La Reine de Saba*, along with Massenet's *L'Extase de la Vierge*, sung by Princess Wrède, and *Pensée*

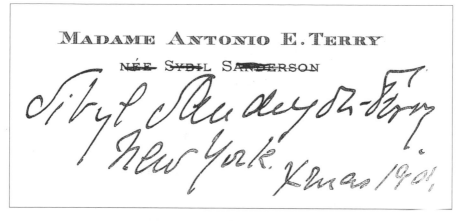

Sibyl Sanderson's autographed *carte de visite*. Courtesy Paul Jackson.

d'automne, sung by the baritone Soulacroix. Then, according to the *Journal de Monaco*, "the curtain opened on *Les Jardins de Saint-Martin*, an attractive poem by Mme Poirson [read by Mme Baretta and M. Worms, of the Comédie-Française], with orchestral accompaniment for which Massenet wrote a dainty new little score." There followed the première of *La Côte d'Azur*, a ballet with scenario by Baron de Gail and music by Drigo,[*] with principal dancers from the Russian Imperial Ballet. The grand ball began at midnight, and three hours later, a special train awaited those guests who had to get from Monte-Carlo to Nice.

Sibyl Sanderson had married Antonio Terry, a wealthy Cuban planter, on 1 December 1897 and was living quietly at her husband's château at Chenonceaux, near Tours, when a cumulation of tragedies befell. In the two years following her marriage, Sibyl suffered a paralytic stroke and lost both a daughter (shortly after birth) and her husband. A directory of 1900 listed Mme Antonio Terry as a *rentière* residing at 104 Avenue des Champs-Élysées. But the lure of the stage was irresistible, and Sanderson returned to the Opéra-Comique on 11 June 1901, in Saint-Saëns's *Phryné*. On 2 April 1902, she appeared as Manon, opposite Maréchal's Des Grieux, still drawing praise from the critics for her beauty and artistry.

Grisélidis attained its fiftieth performance on 11 April 1902, with Suzanne Cesbron in the title rôle. The next day, Henri Busser encountered Massenet in a corridor of the theater and persuaded him to go into the hall where a rehearsal of Debussy's *Pelléas et Mélisande* was in progress. He heard the last two scenes, without uttering a word. Then Debussy, noting Massenet's presence, came to greet him, and the older man expressed how deeply moved he was by this new work, "so new, so unexpected!"[6] The novelty of *Pelléas* (which premièred on 20 April 1902, with Mary

---

[*] Riccardo Drigo (1846-1930) is remembered for the *Serenade* from his ballet *I milioni d'Arlecchino* (Harlequin's Millions).

Garden) did indeed attract a curious public, and Debussy was assured a place in the repertoire.[*]

Meanwhile—as critics liked to point out in reviewing his works—Massenet's fame continued to spread abroad. At the Teatro San Carlo, Naples, *Maria Maddalena* was given as oratorio on Wednesday of Holy Week (26 March 1902), followed by a staging of *Cendrillon* on 19 April. Kroll's Opera House in Berlin welcomed performances, in French, of *La Navarraise* on 22 April and of *Manon*, on the twenty-fourth. The Manon was Vera Courtenay, the Missouri-born soprano who studied with Marchesi and was coached in her rôle by Massenet.

On 10 May 1902, Massenet again made a brief appearance as conductor. The occasion was a monster festival at the Trocadéro for the benefit of the retirement fund of Opéra-Comique personnel. The ambitious theme chosen was "The History of the Opéra-Comique Recounted by the Artists of the Opéra-Comique," and excerpts were presented from works of Grétry, Auber, Massenet, Vincent d'Indy, Charpentier, Erlanger, Pierné, and Debussy. The orchestra was conducted successively by musicians of eminence: Alfred Bruneau, Gustave Charpentier, Giannini, Alexandre Luigini, Georges Marty, André Messager, Jules Massenet, and Camille Saint-Saëns.

The month of June was spent at Égreville, with a trip to Paris on the twenty-seventh and -eighth for the adjudication of the Prix de Rome contest at the Institut. "Then, on the 30th," he wrote to an unidentified friend, "we are leaving for the waters: absolutely urgent for *ma chère femme*," thereby evading an invitation to serve as witness (for a wedding, no doubt) on 10 July.[8]

That summer of 1902, according to the *Souvenirs*, Massenet took along to Égreville a copy of Alexandre Parodi's *Rome vaincue*.[†] Massenet had known and admired Parodi, and it was perhaps the latter's death in 1901 that brought the work to mind. As he was reading it after dinner one evening, Massenet's enthusiasm was aroused, and within a few days he had sketched a musical treatment for Posthumia's scene in Act IV. But then this particular inspiration was crowded aside by other projects, so that the work on the opera *Roma* was not again seriously taken up until five years later. One of these other projects was the piano concerto, which occupied his time for about three months during 1902.

Another project was *Chérubin*. The *Souvenirs*, without giving any dates, relate that Massenet happened to see at the Théâtre-Français a three-act comedy in verse,

---

[*] The popularity rating of some of the operas given at the Opéra-Comique may be judged by the number of performances during the half-century from 1900 to 1950: 1, Bizet's *Carmen* (1,808 performances); 2, Massenet's *Manon* (1,649); 3, Massenet's *Werther* (1,126); 4, Puccini's *La Tosca* (1,043); 5, Delibes's *Lakmé* (971); 6, Mascagni's *Cavalleria rusticana* (964); 7, Puccini's *La Bohème* (962); 8, Charpentier's *Louise* (956); 9, Puccini's *Madame Butterfly* (817); 10, Offenbach's *Les Contes d'Hoffmann* (682); 11, Thomas's *Mignon* (625); 12, Gounod's *Mireille* (430); 13, Rossini's *Le Barbier de Séville* (387); 14, Massenet's *Le Jongleur de Notre-Dame* (356); 15, Debussy's *Pelléas et Mélisande* (343); 16, Lalo's *Le Roi d'Ys* (336); 17, Verdi's *La Traviata* (302).[7]

[†] *Rome vaincue* was first given at the Comédie-Française on 26 Sept. 1876, with Sarah Bernhardt as the blind grandmother, Posthumia, and the famous tragic actor Mounet-Sully as the Gallic slave Vestapor.

Le Chérubin, by Francis de Croisset; that "two days later" he asked the author's permission to use the subject; and that they came to an agreement while returning down the Champs-Élysées one rainy day, after the unveiling of the Daudet monument. Actually, *Le Chérubin* reached a *répétition générale* at the Comédie-Française in 1901 but was not produced. (The work was ultimately given at the Théâtre Fémina in 1908.) The statue of Daudet in the park of the Champs-Élysées was unveiled on 31 May 1902. One cannot always trust Massenet's chronology, but it is possible that he saw a general rehearsal of *Le Chérubin* in 1901, and he was apparently at work on Act I of his version in 1902.[*]

Chronicles of the time mention various performances of momentary interest. Vera Courtenay, after her success in Berlin, appeared as Manon at the Opéra-Comique on 4 June 1902. On 15 June, *Hérodiade* was given an open-air performance in the Roman Theater at Orange. On 20 June, *Thaïs* reappeared at the Opéra with Lucy Berthet in the title rôle and Delmas as Athanaël. *Le Jongleur de Notre-Dame* was given at Hamburg on 24 September, and *La Navarraise* at Berlin on 9 October. Massenet attended a fine performance of *Manon* at the Opéra-Comique on 16 October and afterwards congratulated the cast, which included Mary Garden as Manon, Albert Alvarez as Des Grieux, and Lucien Fugère as the Count.[10] On 5 November, *Griselda* was staged at the Teatro Lirico, Milan, and on 23 December, *Cendrillon* was sung in French at New Orleans.

---

[*] "Since April [1903] I am in Act II—but what an act! I shall bring it in October. Prior to April, I worked on Act I last year."[9]

Poster for *Chérubin* by Maurice Leloir, 1905.

Chérubin

B<small>Y NOW, MASSENET'S FORMER PUPIL</small> Reynaldo Hahn was well started on the career that would ultimately establish his reputation in France as a composer, conductor, and music critic.[*] His first opera, the Polynesian *L'Île du rêve* had attained only nine performances at the Opéra-Comique; but *La Carmélite*, staged on 16 December 1902, fared somewhat better. Emma Calvé created the rôle of Louise de la Vallière in this work. On 1 January 1903, Calvé sent New Year's greetings to Massenet, complaining of a laryngitis that forced her to abandon her rôle. She was going to the Midi to recuperate, taking along *Hérodiade* to work quietly at Salomé in preparation for Monte-Carlo.[1]

Louis Diémer introduced the Piano Concerto at a Concert du Conservatoire on 1 February 1903. Massenet had written the three-movement work as a showpiece for his good friend and had included adequate virtuosic display together with Hungarian rhythms, somewhat à la Liszt. Though repeated at a Colonne concert in October, the concerto failed to gain any permanent place in the repertoire.

At Nice, the opera director Saugey was preparing to mount *Marie-Magdeleine* on the stage. In a letter from the Villa Minerva at Monte-Carlo, Calvé wrote to Massenet: "I know that you are at Nice, very busy with rehearsals for *Marie-Magdeleine*. I do not want to pester you at this time. But as soon as you are free, I beg of you to let me know so that I can come for your precious advice on Salomé. I am working at the dear rôle very quietly while awaiting the complete recovery of my bronchi, which were overworked of late." She asked Massenet to intercede with the director to obtain two tickets for the première of *Marie-Magdeleine:* "I have such a lively desire to see this marvellous work on the stage. I hope to be able to sing it one day—not too far off."[2]

On 9 February 1903, *Marie-Magdeleine* was duly staged for the first time as *drame sacré*, with Lina Pacary (Méryem), Mlle Hendrickx (Marthe), Verdier (Jésus),

---

[*] After the liberation of Paris toward the end of World War II, Hahn was called to the directorship of the Paris Opéra (1945–46), where he revived Massenet's *Hérodiade* on 9 Mar. 1945, some weeks before Hitler committed suicide in the Berlin chancellery.

and Lequien (Judas). The work was given again in this form at Paris (1906–07), Brussels (1908), and Algiers (1910), but was not viable as opera.

On 26 February, Calvé appeared as Salomé in the first of three performances of *Hérodiade* at Monte-Carlo. The tenor (Jean) was Francesco Tamagno who, sixteen years prior, had created the title rôle in Verdi's *Otello*. Hérodiade was sung first by Blanche Deschamps-Jehin and then by Ada Adiny. Maurice Renaud, the Boniface of 1902, appeared as Hérode; René Fournets as Phanuel; and Jean Vallier as Vitellius.

Possibly Massenet looked in on rehearsals of *Grisélidis*, given at Marseille on 6 March. But he and his wife were certainly at Monte-Carlo on Saturday, 7 March 1903, for the inauguration of the Berlioz monument. The weather was fine, and at two o'clock a prestigious group assembled for the ceremony on the pleasant terrace adjoining the theater. At the center of the exedra was Léopold Bernstamm's still-veiled bust of Berlioz, which rose from a pedestal by Paul Roussel depicting in high relief the Marguerite, Faust, and Mephistophélès of *La Damnation de Faust*—all in white marble. The Berlioz family was represented by his widowed niece, Mme Chappot, with her two sons, and by two cousins, M. and Mme Michal-Ladichère. M. Combarieu spoke as delegate of the French government. Then Massenet gave a speech on behalf of the Institut, and was warmly applauded. After further speeches by M. Rivet, député for the département of Isère, and by Stéphane Jay, mayor of Grenoble, Raoul Gunsbourg handed scissors to Prince Albert, who cut the string holding the veil around the monument. To close the ceremony the orchestra played the *Symphonie triomphale*. That evening there was a gala performance of *La Damnation de Faust*, with Calvé, Tamagno, and Renaud. During the entr'actes, the audience strolled on the terrace to admire the lighting effects on the new statue and on the theater façade.[3] (Today, the stroller finds a bust of Massenet directly in front of the theater.) On Sunday there was a reception at the palace, from ten until midnight, with an elegant crowd.

Manon, a regular fixture of the Paris Opéra-Comique season, was joined in April by revivals of two other Massenet works. Calvé was to make her appearance as Anita in *La Navarraise*, but she felt indisposed, and so it was Charlotte Wyns who was warmly applauded in the rôle on 16 April 1903, supported by Maréchal and Dufranne. The impatiently awaited revival of *Werther* took place on 24 April, with Jeanne Marié de l'Isle scoring a triumph as Charlotte opposite Léon Beyle's Werther. Henri Busser noted in his diary that Massenet was "delighted with his interpreters" remarked that "this week, four of his works are billed at the Opéra-Comique—happy man!"[4]

At the Opéra, on the other hand, it was an off year for Massenet. If nothing else, at least the ballet music from *Le Cid* was included in the program of a gala affair on 2 May 1903, in honor of Edward VII. The hall was splendidly decorated. Partitions were removed so that Loges 37, 38, and 39 formed one sumptuous loge for the visiting monarch and his party. The program started off with Saint-Saëns's *Marche du Couronnement*, written for Edward's coronation the previous year, which had won for its composer the cross of Commander of the Order of Victoria. Then followed the *Ballet du Cid*, with Paul Vidal conducting. Act II of *Samson et Dalila* was given, and after an intermission, Act II of Reyer's *La Statue*. This latter work had only recently been taken up by the Opéra (6 March 1903), and the part of Margyane was sung by Aïno Ackté, the Finnish soprano who would three years later be Massenet's Méryem for the Opéra-Comique performances of *Marie-Magdeleine*.

At five o'clock on the morning of 16 May 1903, Sibyl Sanderson died in her apartment at 1 Avenue du Bois de Boulogne, where she lived with her mother. The previous November, in San Francisco, her Manon had disappointed the critics, though her performance in Gounod's *Roméo et Juliette* had been considered somewhat better. Then, after a stay at Nice, she arrived back in Paris in April with a grippe that hung on and developed into pneumonia. Near her at the end, besides her mother and sisters, Edith and Marion, was her good friend Mary Garden. The press dispatches noted that Miss Sanderson had long been active in social circles of the American colony and that many Americans as well as leaders of the theatrical world called at the apartment that afternoon to sign the register. Albert Vizentini, stage director at the Opéra-Comique, recalled her notable triumph as Esclarmonde at the Exposition of 1889 and affirmed that Sanderson had been recognized as the leading exponent of the rôles of Manon, Phryné, and Thaïs.

At the funeral service on Monday, 19 May, the church of Saint-Honoré-d'Eylau was surrounded by an overflow crowd. The casket was swamped with floral offerings, including a handsome piece from the Bohemian Club of San Francisco. An orchestra accompanied the surpliced choir, and prominent singers figured as soloists in the De Profundis and Ego Sum. The body was afterwards taken to Père Lachaise. It was reported in the press that Sibyl Sanderson had an income of twenty thousand dollars a year, under the terms of her late husband's will. This annuity, together with much jewelry and other valuables, reverted to a child of Antonio Terry by a former marriage. It was also reported that, had she lived, Sibyl Sanderson would have been married that summer to Count Paul Tolstoy, a cousin of the Russian novelist.

Jules Verne's *Michel Strogoff* was still a popular favorite at the Théâtre du Châtelet, which closed for the summer on 15 June and reopened as early as 12 August. At the Opéra-Comique, the season closed with *Manon* on 30 June. The Roman Theater at Orange was the scene of two special performances in July, for which Henri Busser conducted. Gluck's *Orphée* was given on the twelfth with a cast from Paris, and on the thirteenth Sarah Bernhardt scored a triumph in Racine's *Phèdre*, with Massenet's incidental music.

In a letter to Heugel from Égreville (July 26), Massenet did not mention his project, most likely *Chérubin*: "Since April, I am in the second act. But what an act! I shall bring it in October. Prior to April, last year [i.e., during 1902], I worked on the first act." Another letter (undated) appears to have been a follow-up: "Here are still more pages from the second act for M. Douin [the engraver]. Until Monday at the Ménestral, with the end of this act for engraving." Massenet added that he had word from Fugère regarding the rôle of Boniface [*Le Jongleur* would be staged at the Opéra-Comique the following year] and asked if *Cigale* was soon to be performed, or if it had indeed already been given.[5]

September brought more performances of *Werther* at the Opéra-Comique. Suzanne Cesbron appeared as Charlotte on the fifth. The tenor Cossira, a successful Des Grieux in the provinces and abroad, sang the rôle for the first time at the Opéra-Comique at a Saturday matinée on the nineteenth. Charlotte Wyns, about to depart for Cairo, was the Charlotte on the twenty-fifth.

In October, Massenet went to Milan for *Thaïs*, staged at the Teatro Lirico on the seventeenth. The star was the glamorous Lina Cavalieri, formerly of the Folies Bergère but now well started on an operatic career.[*] There was a dinner at the Hotel de Milan in the very rooms occupied by Verdi at the time of his death, where his grand piano and work table had been left as mementos.

At the second of Colonne's Concerts du Châtelet for the new season (25 October 1903), the program included Berlioz's *Carnaval romain* overture, Fauré's *Pelléas et Mélisande* suite, Massenet's Piano Concerto, and the Beethoven Ninth. Diémer's performance of the concerto received moderate praise from Edmond Stoullig, who thought the work rather more like a fantasy, a "new and curious incarnation of the composer of *Hérodiade* and *Werther*." The critic mentioned "an elegant Allegro and an emotion-filled Largo, leading to a picturesque Finale on Slovakian airs," disclosing Massenet's usual expert hand at orchestration.

The brothers Émile and Vincent Isola undertook a season of opera at the Gaîté, opening with *Hérodiade* (in French) on 21 October 1903. It was nearly twenty years since the work had been heard at the Théâtre des Nations. The Monte-Carlo cast of the previous winter was represented by Emma Calvé (Salomé), Maurice Renaud (Hérode), and René Fournets (Phanuel); to these were added Henri Jérôme (Jean), Lina Pacary (Hérodiade), and Weber (Vitellius). There were changes in the cast, however, as the work ran on into 1904 for a total of fifty-two performances.

Ernest Van Dyck, who had created Werther in Vienna, was at long last heard in this rôle in Paris when a gala *Werther* was given at the Opéra-Comique on 14 November. At about this time the Massenets occupied their new domicile, a mezzanine apartment at the corner of the Rue de Vaugirard and the Rue Férou.[6] The windows overlooked the Luxembourg Gardens, while the Rue Férou led directly to the Place Saint-Sulpice. The furnishings discreetly mingled a variety of periods, so that the décor was neither entirely antique nor entirely modern but graciously harmonious in the manner of the early 1900s. Along the Rue Férou was a kind of extended balcony where Massenet loved to cultivate flowers. The faithful valet, Michel, was watchdog at the door, protecting the *maître* from unwanted intrusions and expecting punctilious promptness from invited visitors. From time to time a young apprentice stationer, Roger Bénard, would deliver music paper.

There were guests in the Massenet salon on the evening of 25 November to hear Giulio Ricordi's latest composition. The next day Massenet wrote to his old

---

[*] Lina Cavalieri (1874–1944) was considered by some as "the most beautiful woman in the world"; in the Italian film of 1955, *La Donna più bella del mondo*, Gina Lollabrigida played the rôle of Cavalieri.

Lina Cavalieri. Photography by Reutlinger. Courtesy Paul Jackson.

friend of the "great success" of his achievement and pointedly mentioned the new address: 48 Rue de Vaugirard.[7]

Raymond Bouyer called in December and afterwards must have written with delight of his impressions, for Massenet responded warmly that "your note, your visit, redouble my love for my new domicile which you thus honor so much."[8] The last Sunday in December (the twenty-seventh) was "Massenet Day" at the Opéra-Comique. *Werther* was given at a matinée with Van Dyck, and in the evening Massenet appeared briefly to thank Henri Busser, who was conducting *Manon* for the first time.

A letter of 15 January 1904 indicates that the Massenets were leaving that morning for the Midi, to return in April.[9] The composer had attended some of the rehearsals of his divertissement-ballet *La Cigale*, which he found entertaining.[*] The work was given on 4 February at a matinée benefit for the Opéra-Comique retirement fund; the conglomerate program must be seen to be believed:

Mozart, *Bastien et Bastienne*

Massenet, *La Cigale*

Mme Magdeleine, in musical interpretations under hypnosis by Professor Magnin

Poetry recited by Mlle Barthet and by Coquelin *aîné*

Songs by Yvette Guilbert

A cello solo by Hollmann, playing a Molique Andante

A duo from Théodore Dubois's *Xavière*An air from Gounod's *Tasso*

An air from Charpentier's *Louise*

Charles Levadé, *Danses alsaciennes*, danced by Louise Mante and Blanche Mante

The première of *Feminissima*, a one-act pantomime by Léon Jancey, with music by Gaston Lemaire

An act from Donizetti's *Don Pasquale*

La Cigale was given an additional four times, appropriately paired with other works of the repertoire. Jeanne Chasles danced La Cigale, while Mesmaeker, a versatile singer of secondary operatic rôles, clowned the part of Mme Fourmi, rentière. Other participants were Germaine Dugué (la Pauvrette), Berthe Mary (le petit Ami), Mlle Richaume (L'Amoureux), Gina Luparia (une Cigale), and M. Delahaye (le Garçon de banque). Choreography was by Mme Mariquita, and Eugène Picheran conducted. In retelling the fable of the carefree grasshopper and the thrifty ant, Henri Cain's scenario blended comedy with pathos:

---

[*] *La Cigale* must not be confused with Edmond Audran's *La Cigale et la fourmi,* first given at the Gaîté on 30 Oct. 1886 and revived there on 10 Nov. 1904.

Poster for *La Cigale*
by Maurice Leloire, 1904

Scene 1 shows La Cigale living happily in the spring in her rustic abode. When a *pauvrette* raps at her door, Cigale gives her a mantle, bread, milk, and consolation. Mme Fourmi laughs at this generosity, and Cigale gives her the cake baking in the oven. The bill left by a bank messenger is made into curl papers. Having given everything, Cigale then gives herself to her *petit ami.*

In Scene 2 it is winter. Cigale shivers on the snowy road by moonlight. Mme Fourmi, warmly muffled up, returns from midnight mass. When Cigale knocks at her door, she refuses all aid, saying, "Well, now dance!" Two lovers pass by: it is *petit Ami* with the *pauvrette* whom Cigale had befriended. Forsaken, Cigale dies of cold in the snow. But angels surround her, and in the distance mysterious voices sing.

One of the singing angels was, in fact Julia Guiraudon, who later married Henri Cain.

Werther and *Manon* had become musical chairs for rotating artists at the Opéra-Comique. On 22 February 1904, Cossira sang Werther, with Suzanne Cesbron (Charlotte), Lucy Vauthrin (Sophie), André Allard (Albert), and Félix Vieuille (le Bailli). The next evening, the twenty-third, Frances Alda made her début as Manon. The critic Edmond Stoullig informed his readers that this "delicious twenty-two-year-old Australian" had a true Parisienne as maternal grandmother and that her aunt Mme Saville was well known to habitués of the Opéra-Comique. Alda, having sung concerts in Berlin, Dresden, Leipzig, Vienna, St. Petersburg, and London, had "arrived in Paris a month ago, not knowing a word of French." She had coached Manon for several weeks with Massenet.

Meanwhile, at Monte-Carlo, it was Saint-Saëns's turn to shine. His *Samson et Dalila* was given there, and on 14 February Raoul Pugno played one of his concertos at a Sunday concert. A charity event arranged by the Société des Bains de Mer for 18 February 1904 saw the première of Saint-Saëns's *Hélène* on a double bill with *La Navarraise*. Although Mme de Nuovina had been announced for Anita, she was replaced by Suzanne Thévenet, supported by Alvarez, Bouvet, Baer, Stuart, and Chalmin.

Henri Rabaud, former Massenet pupil, was beginning a productive career as composer and conductor; later (1920) he would succeed Fauré as director of the Paris Conservatoire. Rabaud made his début at the Opéra-Comique with *La Fille de Roland,* which Messager conducted on 16 March 1904. Massenet and Fauré attended the dress rehearsal on the fourteenth, remarking to Henri Busser that they were delighted with the musical score but found the libretto (after Henri de Bornier's play of 1874) too long and unsuitable.

Busser was to look after the rehearsals of *Le Jongleur de Notre-Dame* during Luigini's absence. On 9 April, at Heugel's, Massenet played through the score for him, and Busser confided to his diary that "it was a pleasure to see Massenet at the piano, singing and miming his opera; his youthfulness and animation are astonishing."[10]

With Fernand Halphen's *Cor fleuri* as curtain raiser, *Le Jongleur de Notre-Dame* was duly presented at the Opéra-Comique on 10 May 1904. Adolphe Maréchal, who had created the rôle at Monte-Carlo, played Jean. The rest of the cast was new: Lucien Fugère (Boniface), André Allard (le Prieur), and for the poet, painter, musician, and sculptor monks, Ernest Carbonne, Étienne Billot, Guillemat, and Huberdeau, respectively. The forty-five performances during 1904 outstripped even *Carmen* (with thirty-seven), *Manon* (twenty-nine), and *Louise* (twenty).

With *Chérubin* completed, Raoul Gunsbourg approached Massenet with a view to securing the première for Monte-Carlo the following season. On 11 June, Massenet wrote to Heugel from Égreville, enclosing some new postal-card views of the Château Massenet: "I sense your satisfaction in signing Mary Garden [to create

Chérubin]. The news of Ariane gives me a shiver of happy impatience."[11] Namely, Catulle Mendès was ready to read to the composer the text of *Ariane*. A letter of 15 June discussed tentative plans: There was to be a dinner at the president's Élysée Palace on the twenty-third, and Massenet had to attend the Institut sessions of 1 and 2 July for the Prix de Rome adjudication. If he knew for sure that between those dates the Chérubin principals [Mary Garden, Lina Cavalieri, and Marguerite Carré] would be in Paris, then he would attend the dinner and stay on. But if not, he would pass up the dinner and come only to the Ménestrel on Friday, 1 July, at four-thirty for the reading of *Ariane*.[12] It is not certain which option he took, or whether, as stated in the *Souvenirs*, the reading took place at Mendés's house. In any case, a memorandum of 9 July recorded some thoughts: Pirithoüs would be a *grand rôle* for Delmas; and a scene should be added for Proserpine.[13]

Much to Massenet's disappointment, his favorite for the Prix de Rome, Philippe Gaubert, did not even place.[14] The first-prize winner, Raymond-Jean Pech, resigned in order to get married. Second prizes were awarded to Gabriel Pierné and to Hélène-Gabrielle Fleury. By a decree of 1903, women were now admitted to the Prix de Rome competitions in all the arts.

The Opéra-Comique opened the season (with *Carmen*) on 1 September 1904, and the chronicles mention performances of *Werther* (10 September, with Charlotte Wyns and Léon Beyle) and *Manon* (17 September, with Marguerite Carré in a successful first appearance as Manon). On 1 October, the Odéon staged a three-act comedy entitled *Le Grillon du foyer*, by Ludovic de Francmesnil, after the Dickens story. The incidental music was by Massenet. At about this time, too, Jean Aicard asked for incidental music for his play *Le Manteau du roi*, which was not staged, however, until 1907.*

Still at Égreville on 15 October, Massenet wrote to Julien Torchet in appreciation of his essay on Théophile Gautier, and announced that they were going to Bourgogne to finish their vacation and would be in Paris in November.[15] By 17 November, Massenet was in Brussels for rehearsals of *Le Jongleur*. To Heugel he wrote that the cast was excellent, with Bourbon perfect as Boniface. "The weather is dreary, humid, cold, and I am coughing. Nevertheless, at rehearsals I act like a healthy man; I have been truly courageous, and I have given of myself. . . . It is only in my room, alone, that I admit to having a cold: one must not appear ill in the theater. Until Saturday after the Institut. . . . J. Massenet."[16] The Institut met on the nineteenth, and *Le Jongleur* was staged at Brussels on 25 November 1904. Geneva followed on 29 November.

---

* To Heugel, 10 Sept. 1907: "I wrote in 1904 the incidental music for this play. . . . The only copy of the score was given to him [Jean Aicard] in the autumn of 1904." (Moldenhauer Archive.)

Edmond Clément as Des Grieux in *Manon* at the Opéra-Comique. Courtesy Paul Jackson.

The five hundredth *Manon* was given at the Opéra-Comique on 13 January 1905, with Marguerite Carré (Manon), Edmond Clément (Des Grieux), Lucien Fugère (le Comte), and Delvoye (Lescaut). Massenet attended and received an ovation. According to the *Souvenirs*, his sister, Julie, died that same evening—which seems like too much of a coincidence.[*]

A few days later the Massenets left for Nice. Louis Diémer played the piano concerto at Monte-Carlo on 2 February. The next day, at Nice, Massenet wrote to "Mon cher camarade" (using the familiar *tu* with Diémer): "The result is what it always will be with you; how agreeable it is to be your collaborator!! . . . Will you remain in Nice for a few days? Sunday, day after tomorrow, if I continue to feel better, I should like so much to see you at our hotel, at whatever hour you choose."[17]

---

[*] Records of the Sixteenth Arrondissement show that Julie-Caroline Massenet (widow of Paul Cavaillé from her first marriage, and widow of Amédée d'Eu du Ménil de Montigny from her second marriage) died on 12 Jan. 1905, at 9:00 P.M., at her domicile, 6 Rue Faustin-Hélie.

By way of diversion, Massenet took a little side trip to Salon, a town of twelve thousand inhabitants between Avignon and Marseille. Here his friend Félix Abram, former president of the Conseil Général des Bouches-du-Rhône, owned the château Le Merle on the edge of the plain known as La Crau. Salon had a theater and a Cercle des Arts, where Massenet was received on 6 and 7 February. He enjoyed his visit, and later sent some music for their choral society.[18]

Prince Albert had arrived back in Monaco on Friday, 3 February. An item in the *Journal de Monaco* noted that the *rapide*, which brought him from Paris, was late; extra cars had to be added at Marseille to accommodate the large number of visitors converging on the Côte d'Azur. One of the attractions at Monte-Carlo was the première of a new Massenet opera, *Chérubin*. The dress rehearsal on 12 February was attended by an élite audience. The *Journal de Monaco* published a list of notables from the world of letters, the theater, and the arts who were present, along with the names of thirty-four critics from Paris and other European capitals.

The première of *Chérubin*, on 14 February 1905, was a benefit performance for charity, combined with the usual lottery and grand ball after the opera. Promptly at nine o'clock, Prince Albert arrived, accompanied by his aides and with M. and Mme Massenet as his personal guests. The cast was excellent, with Mary Garden (Chérubin), Margurite Carré (Nina), Lina Cavalieri (L'Ensoleillad), Blanche Deschamps Jehin (la Baronne), Mme Doux (la Comtesse), Maurice Renaud (le Philosophe), Lequien (le Comte), Nerval (le Duc), and Chalmin (le Baron).

The scene is Spain, and the plot may be taken as the further adventures of Cherubino, known to us through the *Marriage of Figaro*.

◄○►

Act I. Chérubin is no longer the timid page hesitating between the Baroness and the Countess. He is seventeen and has just been made an officer. The Count, the Duke, and the Baron are jealous of his popularity, and they take exception to his addressing verses to the Countess. The Count's ward, Nina, who has a copy of the same verses, saves the situation by saying that the madrigal was intended for her. The Philosopher (who is Chérubin's preceptor) is delighted to learn that Nina is secretly in love with Chérubin, but he is at a loss to know how Chérubin can be persuaded to reciprocate. Chérubin, in turn, is infatuated with the famous dancer L'Ensoleillad, whom he has brought from Madrid.

Act II. The officers celebrate Chérubin's promotion. A duel takes place to the sound of a gavotte, but when L'Ensoleillad enters, the Philosopher succeeds in reconciling the duelists. L'Ensoleillad appears interested in Chérubin, and the Philosopher cannot dissuade the young man from seeking involvement in what may be a dangerous adventure. Chérubin, alone, sings a love song under the dancer's window, and she melts. But the Count, the Duke, and the Baron upset matters, and the act ends in tumult.

Act III. Chérubin, with three duels on his hands, makes his will. When L'Ensoleillad prepares to continue her journey, he confesses his love, but she snubs him. He is consoled by the Philosopher. Nina had decided to enter a convent, but now Chérubin is suddenly aware of her attractions, so that there is a happy ending.

———————————— ✦ ————————————

After the Tuesday première, the opera was repeated on Thursday, Saturday, and at a Sunday matinée. The Massenets, who had been guests at the palace, left Monaco on Wednesday afternoon, the day after the première. At the Thursday Concert Classique (which they missed), the overture to *Brumaire* was included in the program.

As the Paris season advanced, Massenet was kept busy with the many chores that devolve upon a successful composer. In April, Calvé came to work with him on *Marie-Magdeleine*, which was apparently given as oratorio.[19] (Good Friday fell on 21 April in 1905.) And Massenet must have coached Marguerite Merentié in the rôle of Chimène for her début at the Opéra, on 15 May, in a revival of *Le Cid*. This work, missing from the repertoire for five years, was good for ten performances in 1905 and another six in 1906.

Chérubin was staged at the Opéra-Comique on 23 May 1905. Edmond Stoullig found Mary Garden's Chérubin full of movement, gaiety, finesse, wit, and *espièglerie gamine*, quite in contrast to her previous rôles as Mélisande and as Orlanda in Xavier Leroux's *La Reine Fiammette* of 1903. Marguerite Carré's airs as Nina were all encored. Besides Chalmin (le Baron), these were the only artists who had sung the work at Monte-Carlo. The new L'Ensoleillad, Aline Vallandri, was "a marvel of blond beauty, a brilliant soprano *joliment timbré.*"

The next evening (24 May), *Le Jongleur* was given with André Allard for the first time as Boniface. His *Romance de la sauge* was, of course, encored. By the end of 1905, Massenet could contemplate with satisfaction that no fewer than seven of his operas were played in Paris that year, for a total of 103 performances. Besides the ever-popular *Manon* and *Werther*, *Grisélidis* was resuscitated for four performances, and *Thaïs* appeared twice at the Opéra.

Théodore Dubois, now sixty-seven, wanted to retire from the directorship of the Conservatoire. As in 1896, Massenet was sounded out for the position but declined, and Gabriel Fauré received the appointment in June of 1905.

That June, Massenet was "in Provence, in the country of Mireille, in the midst of the Crau," working on *Ariane*.[20] By 31 July, back at Égreville, he had finished the orchestration of Act III. One day in August, Pedro Gailhard arrived by motor car with an architect friend to inquire how the work was progressing. At luncheon, between the hors d'oeuvres and the final cheese, Massenet expounded *Ariane*. The details of casting were settled as they strolled through the grounds, and the visitors took off in a cloud of dust along the road. Marie-Madeleine Bessand came to spend a few days at Égreville, and was delighted with a vicarious tour of Hell as her grandfather described Act IV.

The season reopened at the Opéra-Comique on 5 September 1905 with *Manon* (Marguerite Carré, Léon Beyle), and the chronicles took note of Charlotte Wyns in *Werther* (15 September), the return of Mme Bréjean-Silver as Manon (21 September), and Charlotte Wyns in the revived *Grisélidis* (23 September). On 26 September, the one hundredth *Werther* played to a full house, with Massenet present and Luigini conducting.

The orchestration of *Ariane* was finished at Égreville on 10 October, freeing the composer's mind for the next project. Jules Claretie, noted for his fine powers of observation and the dramatic qualities of his novels, prepared the libretto for *Thérèse*. Massenet had surely read Claretie's novel of some thirty years prior about the Revolutionary figure Camille Desmoulins (1760–1794) and his wife, Lucile, who had both died by the guillotine. The idea, transposed to other characters, seemed appropriate to a tragic ending for a musical drama of the Revolution.

The *Souvenirs* relate two incidents of the summer of 1905 that also contributed to the composer's psychological frame of mind for *Thérèse*. Massenet's friend Georges Cain, an expert on the history of Old Paris, invited a small party one morning to visit the former convent in the Rue de Vaugirard, where the Septembrists of 1792 had brutally massacred 120 persons. As M. Cain led the group through the intricacies of the cloister, reciting its mournful history, he stopped and pointed to a figure in white: "The ghost of Lucile Desmoulins!" But it was the singer Lucy Arbell, who had stepped aside to hide her tears of emotion. The tableau was engraved like a snapshot in the mind of Massenet, man of the theater.

Shortly thereafter, Massenet had lunch at the Italian Embassy, then in the Rue de Grenelle near the Invalides. At dessert the Countess Tornielli told the story of the residence, which once belonged to the Gallifet family. During the Terror of 1793–94, those of the family who were not guillotined escaped abroad as émigrés. When in 1798 a Gallifet wandered back to Paris, he found to his surprise that a faithful servant had successfully defended the property from confiscation. The theme of faithful guardianship, considerably transformed, provided the mainspring for the plot of *Thérèse*.

As usual, Massenet would have committed the libretto to memory, and the first clear idea for the music came to him one beautiful November afternoon as he walked in the Bois de la Cambre in Brussels, scuffling the dead leaves. Among the four or five persons with him was Lucy Arbell, who was no doubt already studying the rôle of Perséphone with the *maître*, and who would be the Thérèse at Monte-Carlo in 1907. *Chérubin* was staged at Antwerp on 23 November, and rehearsals were in progress for that work to be given at La Monnaie, Brussels, on 16 December 1905. In Paris, sometime in December, Massenet began serious work on the new opera. He must have been cheered by press accounts such as those on the return of Jeanne Marié de l'Isle as Charlotte in *Werther* (16 December) and the return of Adolphe Maréchal as Jean in *Le Jongleur* (24 December).

Poster for *Ariane* by Albert Maignan, 1906.

Ariane;
Thérèse

*I*N FEBRUARY OF 1906, the Massenets were again guests of Prince Albert at the palace of Monaco. The opera season at Monte-Carlo, as announced in the *Journal de Monaco*, comprised:

Wagner, *Tannhäuser*, 3, 10, 18 February

Spiro Samara, *Mademoiselle de Belle-Isle*, 6, 8, 11 (matinée) February

Massenet, *Le Roi de Lahore*, 13, 15, 17 February

Saint-Saëns, *L'Ancêtre*, 24 (première), 25, 27 February, 3 March

Boito, *Mefistofele*, 1, 4 (matinée), 8 (matinée) March

Bizet, *Don Procope*, 6, 10, 11, 17 March

Leoncavallo, *Paillasse* [Pagliacci], 10, 11, 17 March

Verdi, *Don Carlos*, 13, 15, 18 (matinée) March

Puccini, *La Bohéme*, 20, 22, 25 (matinée) March

A. Rubinstein, *Le Démon*, 24, 27, 29, 31 March

Massenet was well represented at the twelfth Concert Classique of the season, on Thursday, 6 February. In the first part of the program a twenty-nine-year-old cellist named Pablo Casals played the Dvořák concerto and Bruch's *Kol Nidrei*. The second half was given over to Massenet's suite *Scènes de féerie*, the songs "Si les fleurs avaient des yeux" and "Noël païen," and the overture to *Le Cid*. In writing to Heugel the next day, Massenet could think only of Lucy Arbell, who had been enthusiastically received in an air from *Le Prophète* and encored in the Massenet songs. "Day after tomorrow, a festival for me alone. I shall accompany at the piano six songs for Mlle Arbell, and the Méditation from *Thaïs* for a remarkable solo violinist of the Monte-Carlo opera." The dress rehearsal (not open to the public) of *Le Roi de Lahore* was set for two o'clock on the twelfth. Massenet was delighted with Maurice Renaud's interpretation of Scindia but, curiously enough, did not mention Geraldine Farrar as

Sita.[1] Miss Farrar had been at the Berlin Hofoper since 1901, would create the rôle of Marguarita in *L'Ancêtre*, and nine months later would make her début at the Metropolitan in Gounod's *Roméo et Juliette* (23 November 1906).

Le Roi de Lahore, then, was given on Tuesday, 13 February 1906, with the Massenets as guests in the prince's loge. According to Mata Hari's biographer, Sam Waagenaar, the famous dancer appeared in the ballet for the Paradise of Indra with Carla Zambelli's group. Puccini, who was in Monte-Carlo, sent her flowers, and Mr. Waagenaar also saw Massenet's card of felicitation in Mata Hari's scrapbook.[*] The next day (14 February), the Massenets left Monte-Carlo.

A month later (12 March), one of the Paris Trocadéro concerts was billed as a Massenet-Verdi festival, with scenes from *Manon*, *Le Cid*, and *Grisélidis*, and from Verdi's *Trouvère*, *Jérusalem*, *Aïda*, and *Rigoletto*. On Maundy Thursday (12 April) *Marie-Magdeleine* was staged as *drame sacré* at the Opéra-Comique with Aïno Ackté (Méryem), Mathilde Cocyte (Marthe), Thomas Salignac (Jésus), and Hector Dufranne (Judas), attaining twelve performances for 1906.

One beautiful spring day, Massenet went to the Bois de Boulogne to revisit the Bagatelle. Built by the Comte d'Artois in 1780, and confiscated during the Revolution to be given over to picnic parties, the little pavilion suggested the atmosphere needed for *Thérèse*. Indeed, Massenet later insisted that the scenery for the first act be a faithful reproduction. The idea appealed to Lucy Arbell, the first Thérèse, for her ancestor the Marquis of Hertford had purchased the property in 1830 and laid out the lovely gardens. Her grandfather, Sir Richard Wallace, had lived there until his death in 1890, and the Bagatelle had but recently (1904) been acquired by the City of Paris.

On 14 May, Massenet was able to obtain "for a few hours" a proof copy of *Ariane* to show to an unidentified friend ("for you alone").[2] The work was ready for rehearsal, but because of the illness of one of the principals, serious study was suspended for the summer, to be resumed at the end of September. His doings are then obscure until 28 July, when he wrote to Heugel:

"Cher docteur"! Cher bon ami!!

I am feeling better, the result of your salutory advice. For some days now at Égreville, I am resting and I am going to prepare myself in [this] quietness for those feverish days which we shall have to put in on *Ariane*. Jacques's success (which was certain—your son is uniquely intelligent) gave us the deepest pleasure. You are happy too, and you will profit well from the splendid summer residence where you are going to spend your vacation.

---

[*] Sam Waagenaar, *The Murder of Mata Hari* (London, 1964), where the date is given as 17 Feb. According to this source, during 1905 Mata Hari had danced six times at the Trocadéro, and thirty times at the most exclusive salons of Paris, including a performance at the home of Emma Calvé, accompanied on the violin by the young Georges Enesco. Waagenaar insinuated that a note written by Massenet at some time in 1906 reflected more than professional admiration for the dancer, an interpretation hardly justified by the (for Massenet) routine wording of the note.

The sixteen-year-old Jacques had probably just passed his school examination. Two weeks later Massenet wrote:

> Égreville, 11 August 1906
>
> I have had the frequent desire to write to you, and I have forbidden myself the pleasure in order to leave you in peace, at least during your precious vacation. I know that, according to your information left at the Ménestrel, everything is going splendidly with *Ariane* and with *Thérèse*. Ah, if I could go to see you in September, this would be the boon I would desire so much. For August, I have taken on an inexorable task.
>
> Tendrement à vous,
>
> J. Massenet.
>
> The days pass by too quickly; we shall be arriving, alas, at that epoque of *Ariane*—?[3]

The "inexorable task" was probably *Thérèse*, for the *Souvenirs* mention that the work was completed that summer "at the seashore." Perhaps in September the composer was indeed able to be near his friend Heugel as his labors approached an end.

Massenet had also written on 11 August to that indefatigable impresario Gabriel Astruc, who was staying at Uccle, near Brussels. Various projects were mentioned but gently put off. He would work on the ballet *Espada* next winter—it was not needed for Monte-Carlo until 1908. The Ostende projects, too, would be welcome, but later. The promised song ["La Mélodie des baisers," which Astruc published] would be forthcoming upon Massenet's return to Paris at the end of September.[4]

The rehearsals of *Ariane* at the Opéra "were resumed" (*Souvenirs*) at the end of September. It is not clear whether an urgent, undated memorandum to Heugel should be assigned to this time or to the previous June. Perhaps we can read between the lines of the *Souvenirs* a hint of some last-minute changes: "These rehearsals were in a general way to go on during the month of October, and we were to appear at the end of the month. What was said was done; rare promptness for the stage." Namely, Massenet's agonized note was written at two in the morning, after "the rehearsal of a large part of the work has just finished." He implored Heugel to stop the printing of the orchestral and piano-vocal scores: "Let us not sacrifice *Ariane* to [keeping] dates; let us rather sacrifice ourselves. To go on would be the ruin of the work's future! For pity's sake, wait, wait! Laurens must bring to me at the Opéra's copyists tomorrow, Saturday, at two o'clock, the first three acts of the full orchestra score."[5]

Another undated note to Heugel (surely later!) was in striking contrast: "Thanks, thanks! I am quite moved by your dear words. Yes, everything goes well at the Opéra. Yesterday, the fourth act for the first time with orchestra, chorus, and principals. An ovation (I mean *ovation*) for our Perséphone [Lucy Arbell] by *all* the orchestra, chorus, and artists. Mendès and Gailhard delighted."[6]

Ariane was accordingly staged on 31 October 1906, with Lucienne Bréval (Ariane), Louise Grandjean (Phèdre), Lucy Arbell (Perséphone), Lucien Muratore (Thésée), and Jean-François Delmas (Pirithoüs). Paul Vidal conducted. The poem by Catulle Mendès maybe summarized as follows:

Lucienne Bréval. Courtesy Paul Jackson.

⟨○⟩

Act I. On the island of Crete, the song of the Sirens and a chorus of Greek sailors are heard as Pirithoüs awaits his friend Thésée, who has penetrated the Labyrinth to slay the Minotaur. Ariane has furnished him the secret of the maze, and she confesses her love for Thésée to her sister Phèdre. From the rocky heights, the observers describe Thésée's feat of bravery, and the freed Athenian youths and maidens emerge. Phèdre is visibly affected by the appearance of the hero; she, too, loves him. Ariane is over-joyed when Thésée invites her to return with him to Athens. Phèdre pleads to go along so as not to be separated from her sister.Act II. On board the ship, Thésée and Ariane are immersed in their love. A tempest arises, which the jealous Phèdre hopes will engulf them all. When the storm subsides, their landfall is Naxos.

Act III. On idyllic Naxos, Pirithoüs chides Thésée for months of dawdling in-stead of fulfilling his destiny as warrior hero. When Thésée leaves for the hunt, Ariane feels rejected. Perhaps Thésée's affections have wandered, and she asks her sister Phè-dre to talk with him. But their lyrical conversation leads Phèdre and Thésée to fall into each other's arms. Ariane surprises them and faints. Restored, she laments her lot. Pirithoüs brings word that Phèdre, to vent her anger with the goddess of love, has stoned the statue of Adonis, which toppled over and killed her. The crushed body is brought back, and Thésée flees into the palace crying Phèdre's name in anguish. Ari-ane invokes the goddess Cypris, who assigns her the three Graces as guides for the descent to Hell to seek Phèdre's restoration to life.

Act IV. In Tartarus, the enthroned Perséphone, black lily in hand, dreams of the upper world. The three Graces appear, and in the ballet that follows, their charm overcomes the Furies. Perséphone is delighted to recognize in Ariane a living human form but refuses to release Phèdre. Ariane overwhelms her resistance with the gift of a basket of fresh roses. Phèdre, almost against her will, is led back to the land of the living.

Act V. On the shores of Naxos, Thésée now cries out in despair the names of both missing sisters. The captain of a war galley suggests to Pirithoüs that they abduct him by force in the hope of bringing him back to his senses. The rocks open up, and the sisters return from the nether regions, Ariane pushing Phèdre ahead as though to restore her to Thésée. Phèdre, in turn, prefers that Ariane be reunited with her husband. But when Ariane turns aside for a moment, it is Phèdre with whom Thésée embarks and leaves the shore. In the twilight, with the Sirens' song in her ears, Ariane disappears into the sea.

Massenet was obviously proud of *Ariane* and disappointed when, after sixty-one performances into 1908, the work was dropped from the Opéra repertoire. Long after his death *Ariane* was revived (with another fourteen performances) for the reopening of the Opéra, on 21 February 1937, after the fire of 1936.

The première of *Ariane* produced the usual flood of effusive congratulatory messages which by now the composer had grown to expect. Like a spoiled child, after waiting for only two days, he wrote to his journalist friend Julien Torchet: "Either you did not go to the Opéra? or the work displeased you? or I did not receive the letter which you doubtless wrote me? or? or? I ask myself why this obstinate silence to which you have never accustomed me. Your son was in a loge. The two of you were in orchestra seats. Nothing from him. Nothing from you. ????? J. Massenet."[7]

A few days later, to the pianist-composer Gabrielle Ferrari: "At last I have been able to find a free moment! What a joy for me. I shall be at your place [63 Avenue Kléber] on Friday [9 November] at 1:15. I have a rehearsal at the Ménestrel, but not until 2 o'clock. In admiration, M. Massenet."[8]

The discrepancy in signatures will be noted. I have seen only eight letters signed "M. Massenet" (*M.* for Monsieur), all from 1906–08, of which three were addressed to Gabriel Astruc. "J. Massenet" (*J.* for Jules) is by and large the most common form throughout the composer's life. Plain "Massenet" seemed to predominate during the specific period 1893–95, whereas during the last years, 1910–12, "Massenet" alternates with "J. Massenet." The letters to Ambroise Thomas were always signed "Jules Massenet."

In a letter of 2 August 1893, the composer explained: "I do not use the given name. Chance has decreed that I have a musical relative who signs Jules. To distinguish myself from him, I sign J. Massenet." (Bibliothèque de l'Opéra.) Tradition has it that on one occasion the musical relative (whose further identity I have been unable to discover) got some of Massenet's royalties by simply signing for them—enough, indeed, to make the composer furious!

Raymond de Rigné, who received numerous letters from Massenet, advanced the theory that the signature betrayed the degree of rapport or intimacy with the correspondent. Rigné had fifty letters signed "M. Massenet" and another thirty signed "J. Massenet"; only the last letters bore the simple "Massenet." This is really not enough evidence from which to draw any firm conclusions. Of more interest to a graphologist, perhaps, might be those rare occasions where calligraphic flourishes were added to the signature.

On 17 November 1906, Massenet wrote to his former pupil André Bloch: "Yes, my dear friend, I know the good news. I know from our very beloved director M. Gunsbourg that we shall be working together. It is a joy for me. . . . Until later— I will let you know at New Year's. Your old friend, J. Massenet."[9] Namely, André Bloch had been assigned to conduct Offenbach's *Myriame et Daphné* on the coming double bill with *Thérèse* at Monte-Carlo. To another former pupil, Charles Malherbe, now archivist at the Opéra, Massenet sent along in December, "to encumber you with them," the sketches for *Le Jongleur de Notre-Dame* with, on the versos, some of the sketches for *La Terre promise*.[10]

On 27 December, at a concert given at the Conservatoire, Massenet heard Florent Schmitt's fine setting of Psalm 46 (Vulgate), conducted by Henri Busser, who jotted down his impressions. Despite the "immense success," Schmitt could not be coaxed from the depths of a box to take a bow. "Massenet and Fauré," wrote Busser, "find the work very beautiful, of a rare power; to which the latter adds that Schmitt will never again attain such a choral effect."[11]

At some unspecified time in 1906 (*Souvenirs*), but at any rate after Raoul Gunsbourg had requested *Thérèse* for Monte-Carlo, Prince Albert and his chamberlain, Comte de Lamotte d'Allogny, called on the Massenets in the Rue de Vaugirard, staying for lunch. M. and Mme Jules Claretie (the librettist) and M. and Mme Henri Heugel rounded out the party. The prince sat near the piano as the composer played passages from *Thérèse*. In December, preliminary rehearsals got under way at the elegant apartment that Gunsbourg maintained in the Rue de Rivoli. Even on New Year's Eve the principals worked from eight until midnight, stopping to toast the hopes of the new year in champagne.

The Côte d'Azur offered two Massenet operas for the 1907 season: *Ariane*, staged at Nice on 1 February, and the première of *Thérèse* at Monte-Carlo on 7 February. Massenet was not very happy with the *Ariane* cast: "Ah, my heart is afflicted as I see the posters for Ariane, on the pillars, with all those different names. One must put up with it, since the contrary would have been dangerous." But otherwise Paul Chevalier, Heugel's nephew, had worked hard toward achieving a good production that will be "absolutely appropriate—for Nice!"[12]

Massenet stayed first at the Hôtel de France (Nice), and on the afternoon of Monday, 28 January, he attended the rehearsal of *Ariane*. That evening Heugel's package arrived with three copies of the printed piano-vocal score and three copies of the libretto of *Thérèse*. Massenet was delighted with the "new" look of the edition: "All is perfection, and you overwhelm us, Claretie and me! Now there is something that 'presents' the work marvelously well, and I am certain that the critics will take note of this score for which the interior would hope to deserve the exterior."[13] Indeed, when Louis Schneider published his Massenet biography the following year, he included a full-page reproduction of the cover for *Thérèse*. The chief novelty was the stark simplicity, contrasting with the elaborate *art nouveau* of earlier covers: there are the spears, oak wreaths, fasces, and liberty cap suggesting the Terror, and the dates 1792–1793.

On Wednesday, 30 January, at two o'clock, there was an orchestral rehearsal of *Thérèse* at Monte-Carlo. The artists were seated on the stage, music in hand (*à l'italienne*), but did not sing. Lucy Arbell brought her copy of the new edition, which "M. Gunsbourg never ceased admiring."[14] As Massenet entered the theater with Lucy Arbell, he met Alfred Bruneau coming from a rehearsal of his *Naïs Micoulin*, which was to have its première on 2 February. Massenet exploded: "See, *here* is your 'pale contralto'!"—referring to a slightly disparaging remark in a recent Bruneau critique. The next day he sent a note apologizing for his outburst.[15]

The *répétition générale* of *Ariane* was held at Nice on the Wednesday evening, and its première followed on Friday, 1 February. That Friday, Paderewski played at Monte-Carlo.

Thérèse was given at Monte-Carlo on 7 February 1907. The Massenets were guests at the palace and were invited to sit in the prince's loge for the première. But Massenet preferred to wait in the private salon, separated from the box by doors and hangings. The decibels of applause sufficed to penetrate this sanctum, soothing the composer's taut nerves.

The *drame musical* is redolent of lost love and lost causes:

Act I (October 1792) shows the run-down park of a château near Versailles. The Marquis Armand de Clerval, heir to the estate, left France as a royalist émigré. André Thorel, son of the former steward, bought the confiscated property at auction with the intention of someday returning it to its rightful owner. The place is crowded with memories. Here André and Armand played together as boys. Here Thérèse fell in love with Armand just before he departed. She is now married to Thorel and feels for him great honor and respect for all he has done for her, an orphan. While Thorel makes ready to leave for Paris, Thérèse remains behind to commune with her memories: "Here, the dream and tenderness. Yonder, life and duty." Armand de Clerval, in traveling cloak and on his way to the Vendée, comes wandering through the park, revisiting the home of his lost parents and reminiscing over the all too brief love he here felt for Thérèse. The two meet, and Armand redeclares his passion, but she restrains him out of duty to her husband. "Forget," she says, "forget." Armand recalls the sweet, tender melancholy minuet they danced together at the ball, so long ago.[*] "But now autumn has come," says Thérèse; "the leaves are falling, and our dreams, too, go swirling away." Thorel reenters and warmly greets his old friend, assuring him of protection and asylum.

---

[*] At the première, Louis Diémer played the harpsichord in the wings.

Act II (June 1793) is at the home of the Thorels in Paris. From the street is heard the faint roll of drums and criers hawking the latest bulletins with names of suspects. Thérèse, perturbed at the hatred and violence of the city, tries to recall the peace and quite of the countryside. Her husband suspects that she is really thinking of Armand, living incognito in their home. Thorel, who wields political power, writes a safe-conduct for Armand so that he can escape from Paris. "Soon," he tells Thérèse, "the time will come when we two can find a modest, safe retreat where I can nourish my love for you, and we shall forget and be forgotten." The concierge, Morel, brings the rumor that the Girondists have fallen from grace. Brave but anxious, Thorel takes leave of Thérèse and Armand, hoping to see them again that evening. Armand should now seek safety with his pass, but is held back by his adoration of Thérèse. He tries to persuade her to leave with him. She breaks down and consents. But Morel bursts in with news that the Girondists, including Thorel, have been arrested and are on their way to the Conciergerie. Armand departs after Thérèse has sworn to join him when he sends for her—an oath intended only to get him out of danger. For herself, only "an exquisite memory and austere duty." From the window she sees her husband being led to prison and certain death. To be with him, she cries "Vive le roi!" and the proletarian mob drags her off.

The cast included Lucy Arbell (Thérèse), Edmond Clément (Armand de Clerval), Hector Dufranne (André Thorel), and Chalmin (Morel). Léon Jehin conducted. The reviewer for the *Journal de Monaco,* after praising the work along the usual lines, noted its particular characteristics: "A further detail that honors the poet as well as the composer is that, from one end of the work to the other, the three principal personages are lovers of nature. In the midst of life's rude blows, they dream, with the greater part of their souls, of the happiness of rural solitude. Jean-Jacques Rousseau weighs upon them as, indeed, he weighed upon even the fiercest heroes of the Revolution who, during the bloodiest of times, dreamed of eclogues and bucolics."

Thérèse was given two more performances, on the ninth and twelfth. Massenet wrote to Heugel, on palace stationery:

Wednesday, 13 February 1907
7:30 [P.M.]

In half an hour we shall be thirty guests assembled in the White Salon, and then afterwards, to dinner. A grand dinner given for the interpreters of *Thérèse.* You will have heard, through the personal impressions of your nephew and the newspapers, the result of our fine performance. We leave the palace tomorrow, and after twenty-four hours spent in Monte-Carlo to complete certain errands, we shall be in Paris on Saturday. I hope to come and embrace you at the Ménestrel if the night in the sleeping-car has not totally exhausted me. . . .

J. Massenet[16]

But the Massenets' departure was postponed for several days. On the fourteenth, Louis Diémer appeared at the Concert Classique, playing the Beethoven G-Major Concerto, Liszt's Hungarian Rhapsody No. 11, his own *Caprice étude*, and Massenet's two impromptus: *Eau dormante* and *Eau courante*. On Monday the eighteenth, the International Sporting Club was the scene of a festival in honor of Massenet given by Louis Ganne with the Casino orchestra.* The *salle des fêtes* was filled, with an overflow standing outside in the corridors. Massenet was present with some friends and afterwards shook hands with all the performers and congratulated them.

Though the Massenets were no longer present, the remainder of the Monte-Carlo season was of interest for three performances of Saint-Saëns's *Le Timbre d'argent* (26, 28 February and 3 March), and for the creation of Xavier Leroux's *Théodora* (19 March), which Gabriel Fauré came to hear.

On 8 March, Gabriel Astruc wrote to Massenet regarding the ballet *Espada*, and the latter replied that they were "in agreement" as regards this project.[17] Shortly thereafter, on Maundy Thursday (28 March), *Marie-Magdeleine* was revived at the Opéra-Comique with Marguerite Carré (Méryem), Suzanne Brohly (Marthe), Léon Beyle (Jésus), and Hector Dufranne (Judas), conducted by Georges Marty. There were four performances, and then the work was shelved.

Inasmuch as Massenet's visits to Germany were glossed over or ignored by his biographers, it seems appropriate to abstract in some detail an account given in the *Journal de Monaco*. Prince Albert of Monaco arrived in Berlin on 3 April 1907, to be present at performances of the Monte-Carlo troupe for the benefit of a French hospital to be founded in Berlin. The schedule of events included:

3 April: Strauss, *Salome* (Berlin Opera)

4 April: Berlioz, *La Damnation de Faust* (Monte-Carlo troupe)

5 April: visit to the Berlin Oceanographic Museum; in the evening, Boito's *Méphisto* (Monte-Carlo) with Chaliapin

6 April: second performance, *La Damnation de Faust*

7 April: visit to the Lutheran Church; in the evening, second *Méphisto*

8 April: Bizet, *Carmen* (Berlin Opera)

9 April: Verdi, *Don Carlos*

10 April: Delibes, *Coppélia* (German performance)

11 April: Kaiser Wilhelm II bestowed upon Prince Albert the Order of the Black Eagle, highest distinction; in the evening, Leroux's *Théodora*

12 April: Strauss, *Salome* (which Saint-Saëns attended)

13 April: operatic excerpts

14 April: departure of Prince Albert

---

* Louis Ganne (1862–1923), who had studied with Massenet, César Franck, and Théodore Dubois, was also conductor for the balls at the Paris Opéra, and a very successful composer of light music.

Prince Albert was a guest at the imperial palace, and he was invited each evening to dine at the emperor's table along with two accompanying persons. Dinner was at seven so that the emperor and empress could be at the opera house precisely at eight for all the performances. On Friday, 12 April, a luncheon in honor of Prince Albert at the imperial palace was also attended by Massenet, Saint-Saëns, Grieg, Raoul Gunsbourg, and Xavier Leroux. Before lunch, the emperor gave Leroux the cross of Commander of the Crown of Prussia. After lunch, as a special favor, he showed the guests his private apartments. On the evening of the twelfth, it was the turn of Massenet and Leroux to dine at the emperor's table.

On the thirteenth, Tschirschky, the secretary of state for foreign affairs, gave a luncheon for the prince and his suite at which the emperor was present, as well as Massenet, Saint-Saëns, Gunsbourg, and Leroux. After lunch, the emperor talked for a long time with the three French composers, conferring distinctions upon Massenet and Leroux and giving his portrait to Saint-Saëns, who already held the order of Pour le Mérite. That evening at the opera an act was given from each of three works: *Samson et Dalila, Hérodiade*, and Rossini's *Barbier de Séville*. Both Massenet and Saint-Saëns received enthusiastic ovations. After the performance, Wilhelm II conferred decorations on the artists of the Monte-Carlo troupe, and Prince Albert distributed Orders of Saint-Charles.*

On 17 June 1907, *Thaïs* was revived at the Paris Opéra and remained in the repertoire each year for the rest of Massenet's life. *Ariane* was doing well, with forty performances in 1907, while the staples at the Opéra-Comique included *Manon, Werther,* and *Le Jongleur.*

Massenet had by now started *Bacchus*, for which Catulle Mendès wrote the poem as a sequel to *Ariane*. But this project was put aside to get on with the ballet *Espada*, which was surely the subject of a letter to Heugel on 1 October 1907: "The orchestra score, all ready and very clean, is at the Rue de Vaugirard. I shall give it to you upon my return [to Paris], before the twelfth. If you had any memory (but you haven't any!), you would recall that I offered you the ballet and that you had nothing to reply. You shall get only what is worthy of you, and that will be well done. Yes, I am still a hard worker, and my health, until now, is admirable: knock on wood!"[18]

In November of 1907, from far-off Vancouver Island, Emma Calvé sent congratulations to the "youthful grandfather who has just married off his pretty granddaughter."[19] Marie-Madeleine Bessand had celebrated her wedding with the young engineer René Faillot. Calvé, incidentally, planned to spend December and January in California and then embark for Japan and a world tour.

On 22 November 1907, Jean Aicard's *Le Manteau du roi* opened at the Porte-Saint-Martin theater with Massenet's incidental music. The composer was probably in Brussels, where *Ariane* was staged on the twenty-third. On the twenty-fifth, Mary

---

* Seven *Grands-Croix*, including one to Von Hülsen, Intendant of the Imperial Theaters; one *Grand-Officier*, to Winter, director of the Berlin Opera; eight *Commandeurs*, including Richard Strauss in his capacity as conductor of the Berlin Opera; three *Officiers*, including Leo Blech, likewise conductor of the Berlin Opera; and eight *Chevaliers*.

Mary Garden as *Thaïs*.
Photography by Mishkin.
Courtesy Paul Jackson.

Garden sang Thaïs at the Manhattan Opera House; the rôle, wrote the critic Henry T. Finck, "fits her personality and her art like a glove."

In December, Massenet and Heugel went off to Turin for the final rehearsals of *Ariane*, given at the Teatro Regio on the nineteenth. Tullio Serafin, acting as both conductor and stage manager, mounted the work with special care and an excellent cast, including Maria Farneti as Ariane. Two years later, Serafin would begin his long tour of duty at La Scala. While at Turin, Massenet sketched the first scene of Act III of *Bacchus*.[20]

"Les Trente Ans du Théâtre" was a benevolent society founded by Adrien Bernheim in 1901 to assist indigent retired actors and singers. Those who had worked for thirty years in the theater could count on financial aid. Besides organizing benefits at the Opéra, the Trocadéro, and so on, the society came to have the excellent side effect of presenting the best in drama and opera in the outlying districts of Paris. At one of their galas, this time on Christmas Eve of 1907 at the Opéra, the mixed program included Massenet's suite for vocal quartet, *Chansons des bois d'Amaranthe*. The soloists were Louise Grandjean, Lucy Arbell, Lucien Muratore, and Jean-François Delmas, with Massenet conducting.

In summarizing the year 1907, Edmond Stoullig reported three performances of *Scènes alsaciennes*, presumably as a ballet, though neither dates nor further particulars are given.[21]

CHAPTER 22

Bacchus

G ABRIEL ASTRUC, IN PRESSING MASSENET to write the music for *Espada*, had avoided mentioning that the scenario was by Dr. Henri de Rothschild. As late as 5 January 1908, Massenet wrote to Astruc: "M. Henri Heugel wants to draw up the contract for *Espada*, and to ascertain the name of the author of the poem. The edition of the score is supposed to be ready as soon as possible. As far as I am concerned, I make no conditions [with my publisher], but M. Heugel needs to know my collaborator's wishes in this respect."[1] The scenario, then, was attributed to "René Maugars." A month later Massenet (perhaps still ignorant of his collaborator's identity) wrote to Astruc that *Espada* had been improperly registered with the Society of Dramatic Authors and Composers: he was not entitled to two-thirds of the royalties, but only to half, with the other half going to the author or authors.[2]

The opera season at Monte-Carlo opened with Ponchielli's *La Gioconda* (1 February), and continued with Wagner's *L'Or du Rhin*. Massenet's *Thérèse* was then given, together with the new ballet *Espada*, on 13, 15, and 23 February. As the season proceeded with Italian operas, *Espada* was even paired with Puccini's *La Bohème* (12, 19, and 22 March). Lucy Arbell sang *Thérèse*, with Charles Rousselière as Armand. Happy and preoccupied, Massenet finally scribbled a note on palace stationery to Heugel on the seventeenth: "Your nephew will tell you of the success of *Thérèse* (encores, curtain calls) and of the ballet."[3]

———————————◦———————————

As for *Espada*, it is full of local color, with a bolero, a fandango, and the slow waltz of the *Espada* miming the bullfight. The scene is a *posada* near the bullring. The pretty dancer Anitra is applauded by a delirious public. She loves the toreador Alvéar and offers to dance for him alone, but he is not much interested. He prefers just to circulate, kissing the girls and teasing the women. Anitra lays the cards and predicts a great danger for Alvéar if he does not consent to be loved. So Alvéar kisses her. Trumpets announce the bullfight. Alvéar gives Anitra a rendezvous for that evening. She tries to hold him back, possessed with terrible presentiments, but Alvéar goes. Anitra is dejected, but the crowd insists that she dance. Toreadors arrive with the news that Alvéar has been killed. Nobody much cares. They want Anitra to go on dancing, which she does until she drops dead. The story is rather like Catulle Mendès's *La Femme de Tabarin* in reflecting the callousness of a populace that pays to be amused, caring nothing for the heartaches of the performers.

On his sixty-sixth birthday, 12 May, Massenet completed the score of *Bacchus* at his apartment in the Rue de Vaugirard. In July he escaped for a needed rest at the seaside, writing to Heugel:

> Villa Favorite
> St-Aubin-sur-Mer, Calvados

For you, for my wife, here is my momentary address. It is almost too cool at the seaside. Since yesterday evening I have been in the liveliest spirits. No more carriages, no more work, no more of those little things that torment my life! Quiet, laziness —such is my present life. Will it really have the salutary effect in a few days? They told me in Paris that Salvayre's piece *Solange* was a drama of the Terror. Still another one!! How "everyone" must have been relieved that *Thérèse* has not been given in Paris; what a service rendered to these coming and fortunate works! . . . M. Chevalier should be informed: manuscript and proofs of *Sapho* at 48 rue de Vaugirard on 1 August, in the morning. M. Chevalier should also please *not* mention [to anyone] that this new scene exists.[4]

Gaston Salvayre's *Solange* (Opéra-Comique, 10 March 1909) lasted for only fourteen performances. As for *Sapho*, Massenet had sought to strengthen the plot with the interpolation of a new scene for the coming season's revival.

In September of 1908, Massenet was plagued with acute rheumatic pains necessitating as much rest as possible. An apparatus was devised enabling him to write in bed, for otherwise idleness for this active soul would have been as painful as his malady. A Sunday matinée on the twenty-seventh marked the one hundredth *Jongleur* at the Opéra-Comique. Two months later, the work was staged by Oscar Hammerstein at the Manhattan Opera House (27 November 1908), with the irrepressible Mary Garden dressed as Jean (see overleaf), supported by Maurice Renaud (Boniface) and Hector Dufranne (le Prieur).

The Isola brothers had again obtained a lease of the Gaîté theater (in August 1907), where they resuscitated the spirit of the old Théâtre-Lyrique, continuing until 1914. By 16 October 1908, they got around to Massenet, staging *La Navarraise* on a double bill with Gounod's *Philémon et Baucis.** On 17 November, they offered *Le Jongleur de Notre-Dame* for the first of sixteen times. These works were followed by

---

* Given twenty-one times in 1908, *La Navarraise* was again offered six times in 1909, beginning on 23 Apr.

Mary Garden as Jean in *Le Jongleur de Notre-Dame.*
Photography by Matzene. Courtesy Paul Jackson.

Cendrillon, for a total of eighteen performances starting on 29 December. Then, on 22 January 1909, *Sapho* was revived at the Opéra-Comique with the new Act of the Letters; Marguerite Carré sang the rôle of Fanny, with Thomas Salignac as Jean.

The young poet Jeanne Dortzal reached the stage at the Théâtre Fémina on 2 February 1909 with *Perce-neige et les sept gnômes,* after the brothers Grimm. The piece was enlivened with Massenet's incidental music.

On 9 February, Massenet finished an act of *Don Quichotte* and went to his publisher's at four o'clock to keep an appointment with Catulle Mendès, the librettist for *Bacchus.* There he learned that the dead body of Mendès had been discovered early that morning in the railway tunnel of Saint-Germain. This was a severe blow; the literary authorship of works given at the Opéra carried great weight, and Massenet feared that the enemies Mendès had made through his criticism might now slaughter *Bacchus* if it came to the stage. But Heugel spoke to him firmly, as we can imply from Massenet's letter of 11 March:

> Mon bien cher et ancien ami,
>
> For the first time, this morning, I had the impression that you were angry. I count too much upon your friendship (a rare thing!) to change it by the least little cloud. I gladly abandon *Bacchus* to its fate. And this with pleasure, I repeat, if this can calm our irritations and give us back our sleep!!! ... A visit this morning from M. Stuart [régisseur of the Opéra]: courageous, energetic. I am going to the theater: *it is my duty.*[5]

Bacchus (Opéra, 5 May 1909) was perhaps the most humiliating disappointment of Massenet's career. The kindest commentary made was that the subject was too literary, too subtle, for music. The sixth and last performance was given on 19 May, and the work was apparently never again staged. The new Opéra direction, Broussan and Messager, gave the work a magnificent setting, and the *Souvenirs* apologize.

> In spite of its faults, [*Bacchus*] did not seem to warrant such an amount of abuse [in the press]. The public, however, which lets itself go in the sincerity of its feelings, showed a very comforting enthusiasm in certain parts of the work. It received the first scene of the third act, especially, with applause and numerous recalls. The ballet in the forests of India was highly appreciated. The entrance of Bacchus in his car (admirably staged) was a great success. With a little patience the good public would have triumphed over the ill will of which I had been forewarned.

The cast included Lucienne Bréval (Ariane), Lucy Arbell (la Reine Amahelly), Antoinette Laute-Brun (Kéléyi), Lucien Muratore (Bacchus), André Gresse (le Révérend), with many supernumeraries and Henri Rabaud as conductor.

––––––––––––––––◄○►––––––––––––––––

The story, developed in four acts and seven scenes, leans somewhat upon The Ramayana. When Ariane was abandoned by Thésée, she did not descend to Hades.

Bacchus loves Ariane, and takes the form of Thésée to attract her. The scene changes to India, where monks pray to Buddha. Bacchus arrives proclaiming a new religion: the joys of living. He is followed by Ariane, who is convinced that Thésée had always been of divine origin. Both are made prisoners by Queen Amahelly. But the queen is converted and falls in love with Bacchus, who agrees to marry her if she will let Ariane go free. The queen, however, has prepared a stake for Ariane, who gladly sacrifices herself.

The aim had been an opera in the grand style, "at once religious and epic." There were no doubt splendid moments, as when Queen Amahelly announces the coming of light, or when Bacchus, asked to worship the night that envelops humanity, instead exalts the light. Heugel published a variety of excerpts in piano arrangements, of which a favorite was the interlude (with the curtain down) where the apes in the Indian forests repulse the army of Bacchus. While writing this music Massenet had often visited the monkey cages in the Jardin des Plantes to study their habits.

It was not by sheer coincidence that the *Souvenirs* mentioned, with a shade of envy, the Nibelungen saga almost in the same breath with *Bacchus*. Six months before, Paul Stuart had provided the *mise en scène* for *Le Crépuscule des dieux* at the Opéra (23 October 1908), in Alfred Ernst's French version. The evening (6 May 1909) after the *Bacchus* première, *L'Or du Rhin* was heard at the Opéra with two pianos, played by Claude Debussy and Raoul Pugno. By the time the *Souvenirs* began to appear in serial form, Felix Weingartner and Artur Nikisch had each conducted a complete cycle of *L'Anneau du Nibelung* at the Opéra (June 1911).

Massenet went to Égreville to lick his wounds. He wrote to Heugel (15 June 1909): "Here, *c'est la calme* and the good smell of hay; the leaves here have a unique perfume, and I am alive, I breathe, I walk—sometimes, too, I weep."[6] Life goes on. The Heugels went to the seaside, and Massenet took time out from *Don Quichotte* to write the lively duo for soprano and baritone *"La gavotte de Puyjoli."*

The Opéra-Comique opened the new season on 1 September with *Sapho*, and Massenet attended to applaud Marguerite Carré and Salignac. At Égreville, on 8 October (to Heugel), he underscored "anniversary of my marriage—forty-three years!" and asked his publisher, should he see Broussan and Messager, to thank them for the fine performance of *Thaïs* at the Opéra.[7]

November brought news from the Manhattan Opera House in New York: *Hérodiade* (8 November 1909) was given with Lina Cavalieri (Salomé), Mme Gerville-Réache (Hérodias), Charles Dalmorès (Jean), and Maurice Renaud, who stole the show as Hérode. Then Mary Garden displayed her histrionic art in *Sapho* (17 November). Besides, the Metropolitan opened its supplementary New Theater with *Werther* (16 November); Geraldine Farrar sang Charlotte, and Alma Gluck made her operatic début as Sophie.

Jeanne Gerville-Réache
as Hérodias in *Hérodiade*.
Courtesy Benedikt & Salmon.

Geraldine Farrar
as Charlotte in *Werther*.
Courtesy Benedikt & Salmon.

Poster for *Don Quichotte* by Georges Rochegrosse, 1910.

1910

Don Quichotte

F ROM THE TRAIN that bore them off to Monte-Carlo in January of 1910, the Massenets could see the disastrous flood that inundated the Seine valley and parts of Paris. Despite difficulties (the tracks were sometimes under water), they arrived tired but safe at a sunny Côte d'Azur scented with orange blossoms.[1] When not at the palace of Monaco, they stayed in their favorite quiet apartment at the Hotel du Prince de Galles. Massenet had brought along the almost completed orchestral score of *Roma,* for which he now wrote the overture. A letter to Heugel sheds light on the genesis of *Panurge:*

Monte-Carlo
Mardi-Gras, 8 February 1910

Mardi Gras–at Nice! But here we are in silence. Your good letter interested me very much. . . . Yes, I know that our new collaborator [Maurice Boukay] is a fine literary man. . . . I prefer to wait until my return to get to know the work as a whole. It is then I shall see the future casting possibilities, the importance of the rôles, and everything. I hope there will be plenty of personages permitting some vocal ensembles, and that descriptive music will have a large orchestral part. In the second act—which seems to me the most amusing—one should not put in too much sentiment, for there is an excellent comic scene: the scene of the confession! an unrivalled scene! Yes, I can hardly wait to read those three acts that are ready, upon my return to Paris! Do you recall that Adenis has a *Panurge** with Sarah Bernhardt which, according to her, will be a success? I had asked Henri Cain for the piece (afterwards) to set to music. Adenis did not consent. So, I have no cause to reproach myself in that quarter. . . .

J. Massenet[2]

From time to time over the years Massenet had thanked Henri Heugel for advice on health matters, including, apparently, a recipe for soothing the jitters of

---

* *Les Noces de Panurge,* a comedy by Eugène and Édouard Adenis, was staged at the Théâtre Sarah-Bernhardt on 21 December 1910. Bernhardt was not a member of the cast.

opening nights. In a letter of 6 February 1910, the tables were turned, Massenet giving the advice: "I am thinking of Jacques [who had been ill]. One should not be uneasy if the condition persists; I beg of you, believe me, these maladies endure, alas, too long but they have no relation to the brain—none at all. It all comes from the stomach." And shortly thereafter: "I am glad over the news of Jacques; his pain has gone away, then, just as formerly did mine. Imagination! I took faith in that advice to calm the theater nerves, and I was cured at once!"[3]

Don Quichotte was staged at Monte-Carlo on 19 February 1910 and given five times that season. The stars were Féodor Chaliapin (Don Quichotte), Lucy Arbell (Dulcinée), and André Gresse (Sancho); Léon Jehin conducted. Henri Cain had shaped the libretto along the lines of Jacques Le Lorrain's *Le Chevalier de la longue figure* (Théâtre Victor-Hugo, 3 April 1904): Don Quichotte is not the ridiculous figure of Cervantes but an idealist who preaches good and justice. Dulcinée is desirable, elegant, rich, and much courted by the moustache-twirling coxcombs of the village of which she is one of the principal ornaments.

———————————◄○►———————————

Act I shows a village square in Spain at sundown. Dulcinée is serenaded by her admirers. When Don Quichotte and Sancho Pança arrive, the crowd makes fun of them. The Don serenades Dulcinée with a mandolin. She asks him to go fetch a pearl necklace that bandits have stolen, and he promises.

In Act II (the countryside), Don Quichotte composes verses for Dulcinée, while Sancho maintains that she is not all that worthy. The fog clears, disclosing windmills, and in the ensuing "battle" Don Quichotte is carried aloft on a sail.

Act III: In a wild and lonely place, the bandits persecute Don Quichotte, but his prayers convert them; they give up the necklace and ask his blessing.

Act IV: There is a festival in the patio of Dulcinée's house. All go in to supper, and Don Quichotte and Sancho arrive. The Don dreams of an island where he will take Dulcinée as bride. When the others return, the Don recounts his adventure. Dulcinée embraces him for returning the necklace, but when he proposes marriage she laughs.

Act V: Sancho tries to console the suffering Don Quichotte, who recounts his past, his hopes, his love, and dies invoking a star which he thinks is Dulcinée.

———————————◄◆►———————————

André Corneau, in the *Journal de Monaco*, blew hot and cold: the work was *almost* able to overcome the enormous difficulties of putting Don Quichotte in the theater. The reviewer tossed rhetorical bouquets at Massenet's colorful scoring, mainly to demonstrate that the work "can easily satisfy and fulfill the needs of the oligarchy of dilettantes and the mass of the public." The last act, however, "deserved to be greatly admired." Here, with astonishing conciseness and the simplest of means (as with the great classics), Massenet "moves us to the depths of our being, and it is

Féodor Chaliapin as Don Quichotte.
Collection James Camner.

impossible to witness the death of Don Quichotte without being impressed in the highest degree. Never had M. Massenet risen higher, and the sober eloquence of that funeral oration adds a noble, moving page to the fine pages of a composer who had the uncommon honor of being among those whom Berlioz called 'founders of musical dynasties'."[4]

In honor of the creation of *Don Quichotte*, Prince Albert gave a grand dinner on Sunday, 20 February, in the marble dining hall of the palace. The *Journal de Monaco* published the guest list, which included the principal singers, journalists, M. and Mme Henri Cain, and the Massenets, with Mme Massenet seated at the right of His Most Serene Highness. At dessert, Charles Formentin expressed the gratitude and admiration of the press for Prince Albert's encouragement of the arts, to which the prince replied over coffee in the grand salon.

"We shall leave the palace on Tuesday," Massenet wrote to Heugel on the twentieth; "perhaps I shall go to Italy."[5] Such a trip appears unlikely, for Massenet was in Paris on the twenty-fifth and at Monte-Carlo again on 1, 9, and 24 March.[6] On 1 March, he wrote to a Dr. Le Jeune that he was "about to depart for Italy for several weeks" [?] and that a proposed collaboration would be impossible: "I have, with my publisher and the theaters, a contract running to 1918; until then I can accept or undertake nothing that is not stipulated. But, if I am still alive then! it is a long way off, and I don't want to think about it! look at my birth date!!!"

That colossal palace which is the Oceanographic Museum at Monaco was formally inaugurated on 29 March 1910. At the laying of the cornerstone (25 April 1899) the German emperor had shown his lively interest by sending the Paris ambassador. From 1901, various international congresses had been held in portions of the building as these were completed or temporarily arranged. Now, completed at a cost of eight million francs, the superlative monument to Prince Albert's dedication to the sea was the scene of a solemn ceremony witnessed by high ranking officials from France, Germany, Italy, Spain, and Portugal. At half past one the crowd of guests began to assemble. The hall, except for the front rows reserved for dignitaries, was filled with academicians, scientists, and notables from the principality and its environs. At 1:55 an automobile arrived from the palace bringing Émile Loubet, ex-president of the French Republic, and Massenet in the uniform of the Institut de France, who were duly welcomed according to protocol. Another automobile brought Saint-Saëns with other officials. After the arrival of foreign dignitaries, each accompanied by his local counterpart, the prince of Monaco drew up at 2:05 in a state carriage with four black horses, heralded by trumpets and the present arms of the honor guard. As the prince entered the hall, the orchestra played the *Hymne monégasque*. When all were seated, the orchestra then played Saint-Saëns's *Ouverture de fête*, composed for the occasion. There were speeches by Prince Albert; by M. Pichon, French Minister for Foreign Affairs; by Admiral Koester, representing Germany; by Admiral Grenet of Italy; by Count Souza-Rosa, representing the king of Portugal; and by Senator Odon de Buen of Spain.

As a musical interlude, the chorus and orchestra of the Monte-Carlo Opera performed Massenet's *La Nef triomphale*, with text by Jean Aicard. Directed to the occasion were the three following lectures by Berget, Portier, and Joubin, of the Oceanographic Institute, relating to the science of oceanography and the aims of the Institute. To conclude, Léon Jehin conducted his own *Marche inaugurale* in which he had cleverly interpolated strains from the monégasque hymn. The prince (followed by almost everyone) walked through the exhibits in the various *salles*, and at five o'clock the ceremonies of departure brought the inauguration to an end. The architect, Delafortrie, had not been forgotten: somewhere in the midst of all this he was given the Légion d'Honneur by M. Pichon.

The festivities continued that evening (29 March) with a *soirée de gala* at the Monte-Carlo Opera. The Casino and grounds were brilliantly illuminated for the grand entrance of the gentlemen, who had exchanged their resplendent uniforms of the afternoon for black evening dress. The ladies were wearing their most stunning gowns and jewels. Prince Albert entered his loge at eight-thirty, accompanied by ranking foreign dignitaries; the audience stood for the *Hymne monégasque* and afterwards gave the prince a round of applause. The curtain rose, and after a graceful double curtsy, Mme Bartet read Raoul Gunsbourg's *Ode à la pensée.*

A performance of *Thérèse* followed, with Lucy Arbell (Thérèse), Charles Rousselière (Armand), and Max Bouvet (Thorel); Mme Toutain-Grün played the harpsichord offstage. The evening closed with Raoul Gunsbourg's one-act opera *Le Vieil aigle*, interpreted by the singers who had created the work at Monte-Carlo the year before: Marguerite Carré (Zina), Féodor Chaliapin (le Khan Asvab), and Charles Rousselière (Tolaïk).[*]

The next day, Wednesday, there was an official luncheon of the Commission de la Méditerranée at the Oceanographic Museum. The large hall was gaily decorated, with a place reserved for Louis Ganne's orchestra, surrounded by a profusion of green plants and flowers. The three hundred guests were distributed among six long tables; at the official table, along with the prince and ranking notables, was Camille Saint-Saëns of the Institut de France.[†] The meal was enlivened by a cantata, *Ode à l'Océanographie*, specially composed by François Bellini, former choirmaster of the Cathedral of Monaco, and performed by Léon Jehin with his opera chorus and orchestra. The Louis Ganne orchestra then took over with appropriate music:

> Saint-Saëns, Overture to *La Princesse jaune*
>
> Massenet, Méditation from *Thaïs* (R. Durot, violin)
>
> L. Ganne, *Délice*—intermezzo
>
> Delibes, Pizzicato polka from *Sylvia*
>
> Massenet, Menuet, from *Thérèse*
>
> Saint-Saëns, *Le Cygne* (H. Richet, cello)
>
> Gabriel Pierné, *Serenade*
>
> L. Ganne, *Marche Lorraine*

At dessert, the prince made a speech. M. Loubet offered a toast, and there was a long succession of speeches, winding up at three o'clock. One can readily under stand Massenet's "indisposition" in the face of such goings-on, and we can only admire the stamina of the seventy-four-year-old Saint-Saëns!

The evening of 30 March saw a grand outdoor *fête:* a kind of water ballet cantata with ships and galleys, for which the audience was seated on tribunes erected on the quay of the harbor. The theme of the entertainment was the arrival of Hercules Monoechos bringing the light of civilization to overcome obscurantism. The powerful baritone Titta Ruffo (Hercules) was equal to the occasion, and he was adequately supported by the massed efforts of a half dozen musical societies of the principality, with enthusiasts of the Étoile and Hercules Clubs manning the galleys. Naturally, fireworks were included.

We may pass over the events of Thursday (Massenet was still indisposed),

---

[*] Based on a tale by Maxim Gorky, *Le Vieil aigle* was first staged at Monte-Carlo on 13 Feb. 1909; also at the Paris Opéra, 26 June 1909.

[†] Massenet, indisposed, had kept to his room after the inauguration of the museum, thus missing *Thérèse* and other events until he reappeared on Friday.

including a morning session of the Atlantic Commission (with speeches), a luncheon for the press at the Hôtel Métropole (with speeches), and an evening lecture by Lieutenant Bourée illustrated with slides and motion pictures. As an interlude, to give the lecturer's voice a rest, there was a mixed program of vocal and instrumental music and recitations, including Massenet's *Pensée d'automne* sung by the basso Marvini.

Between the oceanographic sessions on Friday, 1 April, Prince Albert gave a grand luncheon at the palace, attended by both Massenet and Saint-Saëns, in honor of foreign delegates. An official reception that evening nominally brought to a close the solemnities connected with the inauguration of the museum. The next day (Saturday), however, the French admiral De Jonquières gave a sumptuous luncheon on board the *Patrie* in the roadstead at Villefranche. Prince Albert sat in the place of honor opposite Admiral De Jonquières, who had at his right Lucy Arbell and Saint-Saëns and at his left Mme Roux de Jonquières and Massenet. Finally, on Monday, Massenet and Saint-Saëns attended still another luncheon at the palace.

Back in Paris, Massenet received a call from Gunsbourg, who wanted a work for 1912 and was offered *Roma*. By coincidence, Maria Kousnietzoff sang Manon at the Opéra-Comique on 19 April, and it was she who was engaged to create the rôle of Fausta in *Roma*. "With her youth, fresh beauty, and superb dramatic soprano voice," enthused the *Souvenirs*, Mlle Kousnietzoff "was a feast to the eyes and . . . the prettiest and most seductive Fausta that one might wish for." No wonder! The young lady, born at Odessa in 1884, had been a ballet dancer at the St. Petersburg Opera before making her singing début at twenty-one. Later (1920) she was a film actress, and in 1927 founded the successful Opéra Russe in Paris.

In May, Massenet went to Brussels. On the ninth (Monday) he wrote from the Hôtel du Grand Monarque that he had reserved a room for Heugel for Friday. A bit of blank verse to Paul Chevalier gave his impressions: "The weather is cold / The sky is dark / My morale is gray / Paris seems to me blue / Dearly yours / Massenet."[7] On Saturday (14 May 1910), *Don Quichotte* was given by the visiting Monte-Carlo troupe, with Chaliapin.

By the end of August, surely his physicians, and probably Massenet himself, knew that his days were numbered. His health had been slowly deteriorating, though he outwardly put up a brave front. As late as 20 August he wrote to Heugel from Égreville with no mention of distress. The small talk of a composer to his publisher was embellished with comments about his country home: the trees have been growing like mad from the rains of the past year, and the old place is a true paradise at this moment. Massenet expected to see Heugel the week following.[8] Then, uneasy, he went to Paris to consult his physician, who promptly sent him to the hospital in the Rue de la Chaise for abdominal surgery.[*] It was the cancer that would carry him off two years later.

---

[*] See the letter to Heugel dated 23 Aug. 1911: "A year ago, I was at the rue de la Chaise." (Heugel archives.)

The *Souvenirs* make it all sound almost like a holiday: he was given "the best room in the place" [the salon Borghese] and received "the most admirable and devoted care" from the surgeon Professor Pierre Duval and from Dr. Richardière and Dr. Laffitte. But the next letter to Heugel gives a truer picture of the gravity of the situation:

Paris, August 31, 1910

Mon bon cher ami,

First of all, you will have heard from your nephew that I was ill—*very* ill. Now I have returned home. (I spent two weeks in the hospital in the rue de la Chaise under a different name [Monsieur Royer] because of the newspapers which, in summer, not having a great deal of nourishment, would have perhaps slipped in several lines that would be quite useless!) So, I have returned home, rue de Vaugirard, not being solid enough to go back to Égreville. I, who was supposed to go and surprise you in September at Dinard! That's finished. I am here under observation by the doctors: peritonitis averted. But that was serious for thirty-six hours. For two months I could no longer eat, nor sleep. All work impossible, my summer lost on this account, and I must remain quiet for another six weeks, unless there is a hoped-for improvement. My appetite, the pleasure of eating, and sleep have returned!!! But I take nourishment with the greatest precautions. Ah, in barely a month will take place the sessions at the Institut: one on 25 October, and on 5 November. . . . I ask you not to let anyone know what happened. I shall be well soon, and I do not want it known that I have been ill [9]

In a postscript, Massenet noted that the summer had carried off three of his friends—Berger, Bouché, of the Académie des Sciences [died 19 August]; and Charles Lenepveu [d. 16 August]—and was "close to adding my own name."

On 15 September, Massenet was well enough to deliver a discourse at the funeral of the sculptor Emmanuel Frémiet (1824–1910). The presidency of the Institut de France rotated yearly among the five Académies, so that it devolved upon Massenet to preside at the annual public session of 25 October 1910. His speech was duly published, along with the various reports and lectures given at that meeting. On 5 November, as president of the Académie des Beaux-Arts, he spoke again at the annual public session of that body.

The brothers Émile and Vincent Isola, who later (1914–25) became involved with the management of the Opéra-Comique, were still (1907–14) active in producing opera at the Théâtre-Lyrique de la Gaîté. It was here that *Don Quichotte* was staged on 29 December 1910, followed by sixty-eight performances in 1911. As at Monte-Carlo, Lucy Arbell sang Dulcinée. The Don Quichotte was the fine baritone Vanni Marcoux, whose creation of the rôle of Colonna in Henri Février's *Monna Vanna* (Opéra, 13 January 1909) had impressed Massenet. Sancho was the ever popular Lucien Fugère, now sixty-two.

Jules Massenet, late in life. Collection Roger-Viollet, Paris.

Roma

NEW YEAR'S DAY OF 1911 saw Massenet confined to bed but cheered by the many expressions of good will stimulated by the success of *Don Quichotte*. Former students left their visiting cards; flowers arrived for Mme Massenet; a bronze statuette came as a gift from Raoul Gunsbourg. It turned out to be a Massenet year in Paris, with 221 performances of nine operas at the Opéra, Opéra-Comique, and Gaîté-Lyrique.

Don Quichotte was given again at Monte-Carlo, on 18, 21, and 26 February, with Lucy Arbell, Chaliapin, and Delmas. Besides standard operatic fare, the season also saw revivals of Reyer's *Salammbô* and Dargomyzhsky's *Russalka*. Raoul Gunsbourg's *Ivan le Terrible* (premièred at Brussels on 20 October 1910) was given in March, and Saint-Saëns's *Déjanire* (of 1898) was staged for the first time as opera on 14 March, on a double bill with Marcel Bertrand's *Les Heures de l'amour* Massenet apparently avoided Monte-Carlo, for his name is nowhere mentioned in the *Journal de Monaco*. Both Saint-Saëns and Gabriel Fauré were present at a grand dinner on 13 March in honor of *Déjanire*.

On 29 March, Maria Kousnietzoff appeared as Thaïs at the Paris Opéra, with Delmas as Athanaël. The critic Adolphe Boschot hailed a "new Thaïs, full of youthful and capricious grace," who charmed the public with the power, range, brilliance, and purity of timbre of her voice. It was good, too, to see again the "always exquisite" danseuse Carlotta Zambelli.[1]

After Monte-Carlo in 1907, *Thérèse* had gone to Berlin, Geneva, Antwerp, and Lisbon. At long last, on 19 May 1911, Albert Carré staged the work at the Opéra-Comique, with Lucy Arbell (Thérèse), Edmond Clément (Armand), and Henri Albers (Thorel). On the same bill was Ravel's delightful one-act *L'Heure espagnole*. The following week, a part of the Opéra-Comique troupe left for a two months' tour of South America. Included in their repertoire of seventeen works were Massenet's *Manon*, *Werther*, *La Navarraise*, *Le Jongleur de Notre-Dame*, and *Chérubin*.

In June, two letters to Heugel from Égreville mentioned that Massenet was following his publisher's advice in taking frequent walks, which contributed to his well-being. The summer residence "has become truly very interesting . . . so vast, so beautiful." On the twenty-ninth: "I may come to Paris on Wednesday, 12 July, taking advantage of the occasion to give you the second act." The reference was to *Panurge*, further alluded to on 19 August.[2]

For the national holiday, 14 July, the Opéra opened its doors for a free matinée performance of *Thaïs* with Zina Brozia in the title rôle. Brozia was also the Salomé for *Hérodiade* at the Gaîté-Lyrique, where it opened on 30 September with Caroline Fiérens (Hérodiade), Affre (Jean), and Boulogne (Hérode). Given thirty-one times in 1911, *Hérodiade* continued at the Gaîté for an additional twenty-five performances in 1912.

The Opéra-Comique began its new season on 1 September with *Manon*, borrowing Gaston Dubois from the Opéra for Des Grieux. First appearances in Massenet rôles had become a standard audience attraction, as for Suzanne Thévenet (Charlotte, 10 September), Fernand Francell (Des Grieux, 28 September), and Nelly Martyl (Manon, 8 November). On 14 October, Edmond Stoullig noted that Lucy Arbell continued to triumph in *Thérèse*, but now with a new tenor, Sens, replacing Edmond Clément as Armand. *Thérèse* was staged at Brussels (28 October 1911), and on 8 November the Paris Opéra revived *Le Cid* for a run of five performances. Stoullig reported that the changing times had not outdated this expressive and picturesque work in the eyes of an appreciative public. Lucienne Bréval played a Chimène "full of nobility, ardor, and passion." To Dr. Raoul Blondel, Massenet wrote: "Is it possible that I receive such fine words on the morrow after that work of my precious youth!"[3]

In *L'Écho de Paris* of 11 November 1911, there appeared an introductory statement by Gérard Bauer about the forthcoming publication, in installments, of the *Souvenirs* of Massenet. Chapter 1 duly appeared on 19 November under the heading *Mes Souvenirs (pour mes petits-enfants)*, and the series continued to its conclusion in July of 1912. There are those who insist that Massenet himself wrote "not a word of it." The literary style, often flowery, indeed suggests the fine hand of a professional journalist. Selected passages sometimes correlate closely with previously published interviews or articles, implying research in newspaper files for which the composer would have scarcely had the time or patience. Still, the account achieved a first-person quality that must have required at the very least a series of interviews with whoever was responsible for the final wording. The coupling of events and impressions, often out of chronological sequence, reflects the kinds of thought association expected from a man nearing seventy, who was hurriedly sorting out the events of a distinguished career. In an undated letter to Giulio Ricordi (probably a New Year's greeting for 1912), Massenet remarked that "in the articles I am writing for *L'Écho de Paris* I recall the year 1878—the Villa d'Este—Milan!"[4] That particular installment (Chapter 15) appeared on 15 February 1912. Ricordi's reply was forwarded to Massenet at Monte-Carlo, eliciting once more the assurance: "You know that the memories of the years 1878, 1879, have remained unforgettable!"[5]

The charitable organization known as Les Trente Ans de Théâtre celebrated its tenth anniversary on 10 December 1911 with a Gala Massenet at the Opéra. The critic Edmond Stoullig thought this a jolly and elegant idea: "Massenet, a composer unanimously applauded, was it not he who was at the same time the most benevolent, the most ready to be of service, that there was? And the enthusiastic acclamations that greeted his appearance on the stage certainly were intended as testimony of general sympathy as well as a tribute of great admiration. Those were moving moments, as one saw the entire hall acclaim interminably the great composer who, his eyes wet with tears, almost trembling, sought to express with gestures his emotion and his gratitude."[6] The program comprised:

Overture, *Le Roi de Lahore*, conducted by Paul Vidal

Act V of *Don Quichotte*, with Vanni Marcoux and André Gresse, conducted by A. Amalou

Act II of *Thérèse*, with Lucy Arbell, Henri Albers, and Sens, conducted by François Ruhlmann

Méditation from *Thaïs*, with Alfred Brun, solo violin

Songs, with Massenet at the piano, sung successively by Félic Litvinne, Louise Grandjean, Meyrianne Héglon, Germaine Gallois, Francisque Delmas, Jean Noté, Lucien Fugère, and Thomas Salignac, and including *Chansons des bois d'Amaranthe*

Menuet from *Manon*, with choreography by Mme Mariquita, by four danseuses of the Comédie-Française

Two sonnets, written for the occasion by Edmond Rostand and read by Mounet-Sully of the Comédie-Française

Act III of *Manon*, with Marie Edvina and Lucien Muratore, conducted by André Messager

Act III of *Le Cid*, with Lucienne Bréval and Paul Franz

Ballet from *Thaïs*, by the corps de ballet of the Opéra

Fund-raising galas were common enough at the Opéra. On 18 December, the Aéro-Club de France sponsored an affair to found a distress fund for aviators and to erect a monument to the glory of French aviation. For the occasion Massenet wrote *Salut solennel aux aviateurs*, sung by the Association du Chant Choral. The connection was by no means farfetched. Among the many descendants of Jean-Pierre Massenet who were military officers, two were now generals: the composer's brother Edmond, and his nephew Camille. Lieutenant Robert Massenet-Royer de Marancour, Edmond's son, would soon be making his mark in aviation.[*]

---

[*] During World War I, the then Captain Massenet de Marancour was active in organizing military aviation, publishing the book *La Chasse en avion* in 1921. He later rose to the rank of general and received the Grand-Croix of the Légion d'Honneur—a distinction his uncle Jules, the composer, never quite attained. Robert, as a young student in Paris, used to visit his uncle regularly on Sundays, and recalls accompanying his parents to see Jules Massenet at Pourville, Pont-de-l'Arche, Égreville, and the Rue de Vaugirard.

Poster for *Roma* by Georges Rochegrosse, 1912.

During December, rehearsals for *Roma* got under way at Raoul Gunsbourg's in the Rue de Rivoli. Massenet, confined by illness, listened regularly by telephone from five to seven o'clock. On 4 January 1912, he wrote to Raymond Bouyer that he was quite ill, with a "passing malady, to be sure, but a cruel one."[7] In letters to Heugel, he discussed (11 January) preparations for *Roma* and (28 January) the scenery for *Panurge*, for which the designs should be ready at his return in March.[8]

On 29 January, the Massenets left Paris, and the next day were installed in the Hôtel Prince de Galles at Monte-Carlo.[9] Prince Albert sent directly an inquiry as to Massenet's health after the long journey. Cards conveying good wishes from friends piled up. To Bouyer he wrote that he was feeling quite well: the balmy southern air, the sea, the sun, were all invigorating.[10]

For the third season in a row, *Don Quichotte* was given at Monte-Carlo, still with Chaliapin. In reporting to Heugel, Massenet barely mentioned that Gunsbourg and "everybody here" considered the work an unparalleled success and went on to other matters. *Thaïs* was well received at Cairo. Albert Carré's report of receipts at the Opéra-Comique was gratifying: the *Manon* evenings have yielded maximum receipts, and a *Werther* matinée, at reduced prices, grossed seven thousand francs where one usually might expect four thousand francs.[11]

At the reading of *Roma* with orchestra, Massenet overexerted himself and caught a cold. But he was up and about again in a couple of days, feeling better than ever. The day of the dress rehearsal, he relaxed by strolling with Ninon in a picturesque olive grove, where a friendly cat welcomed them with its purring and mewing.

The première of *Roma* was on Saturday, 17 February 1912, with a distinguished cast: Maria Kousnietzoff (Fausta), Lucy Arbell (Posthumia), Julia Guiraudon (Junia), Lucien Muratore (Lentulus), Jean-François Delmas (Fabius Maximus), and Jean Noté (Vestapor).

◄○►

Act I. Lentulus arrives before the assembled Roman Senate and recounts the Roman defeat at Cannes by the armies of Hannibal. The sacred Vestal fires have gone out— an ominous sign that one of the virgins of the temple has been unfaithful to her vows, bringing down upon Rome reverses of fortune. An inquiry is to be instituted.

Act II. First the slaves are interrogated, then the Vestals. The sovereign pontiff, seeking to entrap the guilty Vestal through a subterfuge, announces the death of Lentulus. Junia, sister of Lentulus, overburdened by calamity, wants to take the blame. But it is Fausta who reveals her guilt through a show of emotion. The Gallic slave Vestapor helps Fausta and Lentulus escape.

Act III. In the sacred grove that formerly sheltered their love, Fausta and Lentulus consider their fate. Fausta is impelled by her honor as a Roman and the adoptive daughter of Fabius Maximus to surrender to authority.

Act IV. Fausta arrives in the Senate as they are considering her punishment. Learning she is to be buried alive, she dons the black veil of guilt. Her blind grandmother, Posthumia, is only vaguely aware that Fausta is in grave danger. When she kisses her granddaughter, she feels the veil and realizes the terrible truth.Act V. In the cave where Fausta is to be sealed up alive, Posthumia brings her a dagger from Fabius. When she finds that Fausta's hands are tied and useless, Posthumia herself plunges the blade into her granddaughter's heart. The crime of the Vestal now expiated, Scipio's armies celebrate their victory over the enemy.

——————————————— • ◆ • ———————————————

During the première, Massenet sat in the salon adjoining Prince Albert's loge, receiving compliments during the intermissions. At the conclusion, after enthusiastic curtain calls and offerings of flowers for the singers, all eyes turned toward the prince's loge. Albert went to fetch the composer, bringing him to the front of the loge for the public's ovation, along with a princely embrace. Afterwards, a grand ball filled the atrium of the Casino. With a momentary pause to draw the winning numbers in a lottery for charity, the festivities continued until four in the morning.

The following evening, Sunday, Massenet was guest of honor at a grand dinner in the marble dining hall of the palace.* The tables were resplendent with silver baskets filled with white cyclamen and red ranunculus. At dessert, Raoul Gunsbourg made a speech thanking Prince Albert for his enlightened protection of the sciences and arts, and congratulating Massenet on his new triumph. Massenet, deeply moved, praised Gunsbourg's splendid direction of the Monte-Carlo Opera, and subscribed to what had been said regarding the high patronage of His Most Serene Highness. The prince then responded, describing the profound impression made upon him by *Roma* and expressing the hope that the *maître* would continue for a long time to produce new works of similar artistic significance. The guests reassembled over coffee in the great salon, where Prince Albert conversed animatedly with his guests until eleven o'clock.

By Tuesday, Mardi Gras (20 February), Prince Albert had left for Corsica on his yacht, and the Massenets were back at the Hôtel Prince de Galles. In a letter to Heugel, Massenet remarked that Gabriel Fauré had been very considerate, had admired Posthumia, and had very nicely expressed his "composer's impressions" in his published review.[12] (Fauré's opera *Pénélope* was staged at Monte-Carlo a year later, on 4 March 1913.) Massenet wrote again the next day, recommending Auguste Germain's article on *Roma* in *L'Écho de Paris*. "Please send me Jérusalem," he added; "the play will not be given until 1913."[13] Namely, Heugel published in 1912 Massenet's

---

* The guest list included, besides the functionaries of the prince's household: M. and Mme Massenet, M. and Mme Henri Cain, M. and Mme Raoul Gunsbourg, M. and Mme Léon Jehin, M. and Mme Otto Lohse (conductor of La Monnaie), M. and Mme Auguste Germain (of *L'Écho de Paris*), General Townshend (of England); the singers Lucy Arbell, Lucien Muratore, Jean-François Delmas, Jean Noté; the critics Fernand Bourgeat, Charles Formentin, Louis Schneider, J. L. Croze, Albert Blavinhac, Edmond Stoullig, André Corneau, J. Prodhomme, and Jules Michel. (*Journal de Monaco*, 20 Feb. 1912.)

incidental music for Georges Rivollet's five-act drama *Jérusalem*, which was not actually given at Monte-Carlo until 17 January 1914.

In the prince's absence, the minister of state and his wife, M. and Mme Flach, opened the salons of the palace for a grand reception on Monday, 26 February. At nine-thirty, the carriages and automobiles of the five hundred invited guests began arriving, bringing all the notabilities of the principality, the élite of the foreign colony and of nearby cities. Greeted by uniformed *carabiniers*, they passed under a red velvet canopy fringed with gold to enter a palace fragrant with jardinières of flowers and branches of Japanese plum blossoms. The hall of the Council of State was transformed into a music room where, at ten o'clock, a musical program was offered: Marix Loevensohn, cellist and professor of the Berlin Hochschule, played Bach's Aria in D and a Prelude for cello alone. Mme Flora Joutard-Loevensohn, pianist, played Liszt's Polonaise in E. André Allard, of the Opéra-Comique, sang Flégier's "Les larmes" and Massenet's "Légende de la sauge," from *Le Jongleur*. Mlle Jeanne Bourdon, of the Opéra, sang Massenet's "Pleurez mes yeux," from *Le Cid*. Mlle Mariza Rozann, of La Monnaie, sang some Mussorgsky songs. Then Lucy Arbell presented Massenet's cycle of ten *Expressions lyriques*, which exploit lyric declamation along with vocal melody.* Finally, Mlle Paule Andral read poems by Jean Richepin and Henri de Fleurigny. Afterwards there was a ball, with later a supper served at little tables.

"Little by little, the dream fades away," wrote Massenet to Heugel (26 February); "all that which has been a rapture will remain only as a few lines in my memoirs!"[14] By 4 March he was back in Paris. The penultimate chapter of the *Souvenirs* closed with the words: "Here I am in Paris, on the eve of the rehearsals and first performance of *Roma* at the Opéra. I have hope. I have such admirable artists. They have already won the first battle for me. Will they not be able to triumph in the second?"

On 22 March, Massenet wrote to Ricordi:

Cher grand ami,

My memory is too profound of the joyful days—at Cernobbio, at Milan—for me to neglect the pleasure which can now still come my way! It is to you that I owe the unforgettable evenings at La Scala, 1878! You are so kind as to speak of a [new] work (distant echo of that of 1879: Erodiade). But then it is necessary for you to know that I am bound by a dreary formula that began in 1908, and will come to an end in 1920. Until then, I have no longer the right to think of a subject, a work, not provided for in the contract, where everything I am to write (until 1910—if I live?) has been decided, received, accepted, and set down. You see that my position is irreducible, and I regret

---

* According to the *Souvenirs*, it was Lucy Arbell who had suggested to Massenet the combination of the two forces of expression, singing and speaking, in one and the same voice. He had used the device earlier, though not as systematically as in these songs. Obviously, the style is quite remote from the sprechstimme of Arnold Schoenberg's *Pierrot Lunaire* of 1912.

this now since it is you, *you* who do me the joy and honor of remembering that I exist! With deepest feelings, thanks. With deepest feelings, all my kind regards,

J. Massenet.[15]

Twelve weeks later, Giulio Ricordi was dead.

For 28 March, a grand matinée had been planned for the Trocadéro as a benefit for some charitable purpose. Two months prior, Massenet had mentioned to Heugel that he was stupefied at the number of performers called for: a thousand.[16] In reply to an inquiry about the possibility of making an English translation of the *Souvenirs*, Massenet stated (31 March) that this had already been promised to H. Villiers Barnett, of Monte-Carlo, the authorized translator of Prince Albert's *La Carrière d'un navigateur*.[17]

Roma was staged at the Opéra on 24 April 1912 with the Monte-Carlo principals, excepting that Junia was sung by Jeanne Campredon. Paul Vidal conducted. Adolphe Boschot's review in *L'Echo de Paris* remarked that readers of the *Souvenirs* in the columns of that newspaper were well aware of the composer's early love for Rome. In view of the antique subject, Massenet had endowed the score of *Roma* with a classical simplicity, using a firm and sparing hand to achieve a clarity of style stripped to essentials. The accompaniment was occasionally reduced to a single line, which even then sometimes doubles the voice. For Boschot, this studied simplicity placed *Roma*, among Massenet's operas, in a position analogous to *Écho et Narcisse* in Gluck's output. Indeed, the orchestration often made one think of Gluck in a more pliant and more modern guise. The careful declamation of the text was characteristic of Massenet. The effulgent choruses were sometimes in unison, accompanied by trombones. It was perhaps no mere coincidence that, among the secondary rôles, Boschot made special mention of Mme Le Senne (la Grande Vestale); three years prior, she had made her début at the Opéra as La Haine in Gluck's *Armide*.[18]

Collectors of Massenet letters, wherever they may be, will know that many an obscure reference is clarified at once if only the date can be collated with some event in the composer's life. Thus an otherwise enigmatic letter, postmarked 25 April 1912, acquires significance on the morrow of the Paris première of *Roma*: "When a mind as eminent as yours is inclined to esteem my work, it achieves an exalted rank. How proud will be our stirring artist [Lucy Arbell] to read your account."[19]

Another gala at the Opéra, this time for the benefit of French aviation, was held on 28 April. Act III of *Werther* had Suzanne Brohly (Charlotte), Mathieu-Lutz (Sophie), Lucien Muratore (Werther), and André Allard (Albert), with André Messager conducting. Besides, there was Act II of Charles Lecocq's *La Fille de Madame Angot,* and members of the Comedie-Française presented Acts IV and V of Sophocles' *Oedipe-Roi* with Edmond Membrée's incidental music. On 3 May, the youthful *Don César de Bazan* was revived at the Trianon-Lyrique; on the eighteenth, *Don Quichotte* reached London; on the twenty-fifth, the Opéra-Comique troupe gave *Werther* in a popular matinée at the Trocadéro.

Lucien Muratore as Werther. Courtesy Paul Jackson.

At the end of May 1912, Massenet finished *Cléopâtre*.[20] We owe this information to Louis Schneider who, we can assume, was in touch with the composer's activities. According to Schneider, Henri Cain had introduced Massenet to the poet Louis Payen in January 1910, and "a few months later," Payen finished the libretto of *Cléopâtre* and Massenet set to work on it. During 1910–11, however, Massenet was occupied with *Panurge* and could scarcely have begun serious work on *Cléopâtre* before the autumn of 1911.[*] This would have given him on the order of nine months

---

[*] The assignment of *Cléopâtre* to "Paris, 14 November 1878," as in Brancour (1922, p. 183) seems untenable. Massenet did on several occasions mention Luigi Mancinelli's incidental music to Pietro Cossa's drama *Cleopatra*, apparently staged in 1877.[21]

to complete the task, indicating that he was able to maintain his accustomed pace.[*]

With *Cléopâtre*, Massenet shook a final defiant fist at the gnawing inroads of cancer; he could now go to his rest, still with a brave front toward the outer world. On 15 June, he wrote to André Bloch from Égreville, offering to intercede in some unspecified matter on behalf of his former pupil. A carefree postscript—"Bravo au Radical!"—alluded to Bloch's activity as journalist for the newspaper *Radical*.[22]

In July there was a Massenet festival at Vichy, with performances of *Roma* and a gala evening that offered portions of *Manon, Werther, Les Érinnyes, Le Grillon du foyer*, and *Thaïs*. In the last letters I have seen, the life of the theater still pulsed through Massenet's veins: July 3—"Here all is going splendidly at the theater. You have read the notice [in *Le Figaro*] about *Thérèse* at Enghien; that was unparalleled. It is raining incessantly, but I am 10.35 meters from the stage entrance and couldn't care less about the bad weather. There was a symphony concert conducted by Gaubert; the whole program *de chez nous* [Heugel publications]. A crowd such as is rare here, and an enormous success. The colossal posters in Vichy carry the heading 'Massenet Week'. . . " July 6—"This evening, second performance of *Roma* here, and Rachet tells me the tickets are selling like mad. Well, perhaps this is a good omen for the provinces. It is raining. What a beautiful theater. What an admirable orchestra . . . "[23]

The last installment of the *Souvenirs* appeared in *L'Écho de Paris* on 11 July 1912. With the heading "Pensées posthumes" (Posthumous Thoughts), the composer imagined that he had departed from this planet and could look back serenely upon all that was left behind: no more letters to answer; no more premières with their attendant discussions; no more newspapers, nor dinners to attend, nor sleepless nights. Perhaps an evening newspaper or two would mention his decease. A few friends would come to ask if the news were true, and the concierge would reply, "Alas, Monsieur went away without leaving his forwarding address." Acquaintances would exchange brief regrets over luncheon. In the theaters there would be speculation: "Now that he is dead, they will not play his works so often, will they?—Had you heard that he left still another opera?" The voice of a singer would be heard to say: "Ah, believe me, I loved him well; I always had such a success in his works." At his publishers they would weep. The immortal soul would listen to all these sounds with equanimity. As for the mortal remains, these would be sealed in a vault at Égreville, prepared long before, and in a few hours, be forgotten by the world.

The details of the last illness were later recounted by a close friend, the architect Raymond de Rigné.[24] After Vichy, Massenet stayed at Égreville until 8 August, then went to Paris to consult his doctors, who sent him to the hospital in the Rue de la Chaise. As in 1910, he was installed in the Salon Borghese. Mme Massenet remained at Égreville, and Juliette was in Switzerland with her children. His mind still full of the theater, Massenet requested music paper to start a new opera, but his nurse, Mme Long, prohibited this. He talked of Saint-Saëns, who "deserved" the Grand-Croix of

---

[*] Rigné (1921, p. 16) assigns *Panurge* to 1910–11, and *Cléopâtre* to 1911–12.

the Légion d'Honneur because he was older.[*] Saint-Saëns, he was sure, would want a grandiose funeral, whereas he, Massenet, would be content with a plain hearse and no fuss at all. Proudly he remarked that he had been embraced, right in the theater, by the prince of Monaco, but Saint-Saëns had not. To the last, the Massenets wrote to each other daily, and the composer would read and reread his wife's letters several times.

At noon on 12 August, Mme Long became concerned with the patient's weakness, and the doctor administered morphine. At four o'clock, a telegram was sent to Mme Massenet, and other members of the family were sought. The granddaughter's husband, René Faillot, one of the many Parisians who avoid the city in August, did not arrive until one-thirty the next morning. Death came to Massenet at four o'clock in the morning on Tuesday, 13 August.

Massenet had abhorred the idea of dying in a hospital. The body was therefore transferred as soon as possible to the Rue de Vaugirard. At half past five, the faithful valet Michel Châtenet set up a small bed in the master's study. Around six o'clock the ambulance arrived; during the trip Mme Long had pretended to administer oxygen, and she told them that her patient had just expired. Accordingly, at two o'clock that afternoon, the death was registered at the *mairie* of the Sixth Arrondissement as having occurred at 48 Rue de Vaugirard, the deposition being made by the composer's brother Edmond and René Faillot.

A register was set up to receive the signatures of notables who came to pay their last respects. The black-bordered death announcement, besides bearing the names of the widow, daughter, and grandchildren, was subscribed by a long list of nephews and nieces with their families. Near the end, as more distantly related through the paternal grandmother, appeared the name of Baron Henry Mathieu de Faviers.[25]

Early on Friday morning, without fanfare, the body was blessed by the vicar of Saint Sulpice and placed in a motor van for the journey to Égreville. There it remained in the little church of Saint-Martin until the following day, 17 August, when a simple funeral ceremony was held in the presence of the family and a few friends.[†] An old white horse pulled the country hearse to the picturesque little cemetery, and Massenet was laid to rest in the angle of the stone wall farthest from the entrance. The silence and peaceful rural isolation of the place bespeak a wholesome modesty and dignity.

The press, of course, took notice of France's famous composer. *Le Matin* of 14 August had the unusual display of *two* obituaries side by side: one by Alfred Bruneau and one by Debussy.[‡] It is doubtful whether, on balance, *all* the pieces in *all* the

---

[*] The honor was awarded to Saint-Saëns after Massenet's death.

[†] According to Pougin (1912), five former Massenet pupils were present: Gustave Charpentier, Reynaldo Hahn, Ernest Moret, Xavier Leroux, and Charles Silver.

[‡] Bruneau, the regular contributor, was on vacation at Villers-sur-Mer. The editor, Stéphane Lauzanne, fearing that Bruneau might not meet the press deadline, hastily asked Debussy to supply an article.

newspapers on the morrow of the composer's death would contribute much to our knowledge of Massenet. The art of fine rhetoric has a way of springing to full bloom overnight on such occasions. But as the months and years go by, further bits and pieces of the mosaic that was the deceased's career gradually come to light; with time for reflection, opinions settle into more sincere and meaningful positions.

In October, Saint-Saëns published in *L'Echo de Paris* a résumé that was both hard and fair:[26] Massenet's pupils, perhaps, appreciated him best, though they may be suspected of partiality. Others speak lightly of his works as "pleasing," as though this were a deprecation. But is it so reprehensible *to please?* One might think so, wrote Saint-Saëns, in view of all the shocking and displeasing things with which one was now confronted in all the arts, even in poetry. The horrible is considered beautiful, and the beautiful horrible. Despite all they may say, no one can prevent Massenet from being a sparkling diamond in the jewelry case of French music. No musician enjoyed so fully the public favor, excepting Auber, whom Massenet did not like, yet whom he strangely resembled in facility, fecundity, wit, and grace. Both made music that suited their times; hence their two arts are totally different. Both were accused of flattering their hearers; should one rather not say that composer and public had the same tastes, were in perfect agreement? One need not be a revolutionary, swimming against the current. Were Bach, Handel, Haydn, Mozart, or Rossini revolutionaries?

Profundity is now much in vogue, continued Saint-Saëns, and Massenet is accused of superficiality. It is true: he is not profound. But this is of no importance. As in the house of the Lord, so in Apollo's realm there are many mansions. We admire the art of the Greeks: it was not profound. Their marble goddesses are beautiful, and their beauty suffices. Are not Fragonard, La Tour, and Marivaux an honor to the French school without being profound? Each thing has its worth: the rose with its fresh colors and perfume as well as the proud oak. Should graceful things and smiles be negligible? How many I know, wrote Saint-Saëns, who affect to disdain them, and who in their hearts regret not possessing them! Art requires all kinds of artists, and none should flatter himself that he alone embraces all of art.

Massenet's melody, floating, uncertain, sometimes more like recitative than true melody, is something personal. Theoretically, Saint-Saëns ought not to like it. Yet how can one resist a Manon at the feet of Des Grieux at Saint-Sulpice? How can one reflect and analyze when one is deeply moved? A master of his craft, knowing all the secrets of his art, Massenet eschewed those contortions and exaggerations that the naïve confuse with musical science. He pursued the path he himself had laid out, profiting from new forms of expression imported from abroad which, however, he assimilated perfectly as an artist who remained completely French.

Infatuation is sometimes followed by oblivion. For Massenet, not oblivion but justice. The more ephemeral flowers on his luxuriant tree will fade away, to be sure. But the tree itself will remain. It will be a long time before we again see such a tree grow. As a final word, Saint-Saëns reminded his readers: Massenet has been much imitated; *he* imitated no one.

The End of an Era

REDERIC MASSON, OF THE ACADÉMIE FRANÇAISE, presided at the annual public session on 25 October 1912 of the five academies comprising the Institut de France. As usual on these occasions, eulogies were read for members who had died during the past year. On 26 October, the Académie des Beaux-Arts elected Gustave Charpentier to fill Massenet's vacant chair. Besides Charpentier, the music section now included Camille Saint-Saëns (elected 1881), Émile Paladilhe (1892), Théodore Dubois (1894), Gabriel Fauré (1909), and Charles-Marie Widor (1910). In memory of the close friendship between the two composers, Mme Massenet presented to Charpentier the uniform of the Institut her husband had worn.[1]

The Concerts Colonne, now conducted by Gabriel Pierné, paid tribute to Massenet in the opening concert of the season (13 October) with *Les Érinnyes* and *Marie-Magdeleine*. For 19 November, Edmond Stoullig recorded a "memorable evening" at the Opéra-Comique, where "a numerous public gave the warmest welcome" to *Le Jongleur*, with Thomas Salignac as Jean, and to *Thérèse*, with Suzanne Brohly in the title role. On 22 November, wrote Stoullig, the Opéra direction "rendered a pious homage to Massenet in reviving *Le Cid*."

At the Gaîté Lyrique, the Isola brothers revived *Don Quichotte* on 15 March 1913 for a run of eight performances, following it on 25 April with the world première of *Panurge*. To provide a sampling of Rabelais in a three-act *haulte farce musicale* was no easy task for the librettists, Georges Spitzmuller and Maurice Boukay. They invented characters and rearranged incidents in search of a plausible evening's entertainment. But if the public expected belly laughs, they were disappointed: Massenet's gentle comedy is restrained and classic, without truculence or irony. In long discussions with the librettists in 1909, the composer had argued for an archaic literary style, but was overruled because this would demand too much erudition from the spectators. The few Rabelaisian phrases retained provided no more than the whiff of garlic that seasons the leg of mutton. Scored with classic simplicity, the work lets the protagonists play their parts without any attempt at luxuriating descriptive background.

Poster for *Panurge* by Charles-Lucien Léandre, 1913.

Act I. The year is 1520. The Carnival procession passes before the tavern of Alcofibras,[*] the Hostellerie du Coq à l'Asne, in the quarter of Les Halles. Pantagruel and Panurge engage in conversation with Alcofibras. Panurge says he has just lost his wife Colombe, and doesn't know whether to laugh or cry. Pantagruel invites him to drink. Panurge is badly frightened when his "dead" wife appears; Colombe is very much alive after all. Panurge bemoans that he really has no use for a wife. Pantagruel offers to take him to a monastery where Panurge can successfully hide from Colombe.

Act II. Panurge and Pantagruel arrive at the Abbey of Thélème. The abbot, Frère Jean, explains the customs of the abbey, where there is no Lent and the monks pray to Bacchus, the nuns to Venus. Panurge is delighted with such a refuge. He makes gallant overtures to Dame Ribaude who, however, requires marriage. When Colombe puts in an appearance, Dame Ribaude offers to help in punishing Panurge. A formidable meal is served, and Panurge delivers a disputation on marriage (from Rabelais). The planned punishment is to consist in Colombe's "confession," to the monk Panurge, of multiple acts of unfaithfulness. But Panurge leaves word that he has fled such a guilty wife and gone to the Île des Lanternes.

Act III. Colombe goes straight to the Île des Lanternes, where we find her as a priestess and oracle of the temple of Bacbuc. When Panurge arrives, he is advised by Baguenaude, queen of the isle, that the oracle can perhaps furnish news of his wife. The oracle (really Colombe) answers Panurge's questions: his wife was never unfaithful; he shall see her soon on condition that he drink only when she pours and in general behaves himself. Panurge consents to the conditions. A ship brings Pantagruel and his suite, whom Panurge introduces to the charming islanders. Colombe is recognized, and all rejoice to the strains of "Vivons joyeulx et buvons frais!"[†]

Two posthumous orchestral suites were published by Heugel in 1913: *Suite parnassienne*; and *Suite théâtrale*. Both works employ poems by Maurice Léna, are scored for orchestra, chorus, and narrator, and represent a considerable departure from Massenet's earlier suites. *Suite parnassienne*, a "musical fresco" in four parts, deals with four Muses of Parnassus. *Uranie* (Astronomy) is presented in a *rêverie*, Lento sostenuto, with divisi strings and offstage violins and harp. Only at the end does the poet recite the words:

La Vierge prophétesse,	(The Virgin prophetess,
à la cime du Mont,	at the summit of the peak,
Vers le mystère immense	Has raised her beauteous face
a levé son beau front.	toward the unknown.

---

[*] François Rabelais published *Pantagruel* under the anagrammatic pseudonym Alcofibras Nasier.

[†] The cast, with some twenty rôles, included Vanni Marcoux (Panurge), Giovanni Martinelli (Pantagruel), and Lucy Arbell (Colombe).

Et dans le bleu concert	And in the blue concert
de la voûte infinie	of the infinite vault
Elle écoute vibrer	She hears the vibrations
l'Éternelle Harmonie.	of eternal harmony.)

Clio (History), with magic gesture, awakens "visions of antiquity," notably of Pompeii. In *Euterpe,* two wordless choruses hum softly in antiphony; the Poet apostrophizes Music, rising from the humble shepherd's flute to a kingdom now embracing the earth and heavens:

> Love and the Ocean form your voice profound;
> The dream of the Star is deep in your eyes.[*]

Calliope (the Epic) brings a *marche historique* in C major with many-trumpeted fanfare.

Suite théâtrale, in three parts, presents tragedy, comedy, and the dance. *La Tragédie:* even under the smiling azure skies of Hellas the sombre Melpomene first uttered her anguished sobs echoing human grief. The orchestra ranges from subdued chromatic sobbing of stopped horns through all shades of agitation and expression to a final tam-tam stroke and "Silence!" *La Comédie,* whether high comedy or low farce, or even with a tear in its eye, reflects life and thus sees all. There are some delightful scherzando moments in 9/8 time, with laughing muted trumpets. Without a break, we move to *La Danse:* to the light accompaniment of strings and harpsichord, the Poet evokes the spirit of the minuet and gavotte. The age of Vestris came and passed, as April passes.[†] The musicians then warm up to the apotheosis of the dance: "La Valse" ("very animated, voluptuous")—a vigorous testament of Massenet's powers of orchestration.[‡]

The Monte-Carlo season of 1914 paid posthumous tribute to Massenet. 14 January saw the première of Georges Rivollet's five-act drama, *Jérusalem,* with incidental music hopefully completed and published two years prior. On 23 February the memorial bust of Massenet before the theater was formally inaugurated. The participants and spectators assembled at eleven o'clock. The prince of Monaco made a speech, and M. Jacquier read the speech of the minister of public instruction, M. Viviani, who could not attend. His Most Serene Highness unveiled the monument: a lifelike bust by Bernstamm, mounted on an Ionic column with the simple inscription:

To Massenet

His Admirers 1842–1912

---

[*] Compare the last act of *Don Quichotte:* "The Star! Dulcinée!"

[†] Gaetano Apolino Balthazar Vestris danced at the Paris Opéra from 1748 until 1781; he considered that there were only three great men in Europe: Voltaire, Frederick the Great, and himself.

[‡] Compare the waltz section of *Une noce flamande* of 1866.

The ceremony was followed by luncheon, at which the sculptor was present, along with Raoul Gunsbourg and Léon Jehin.[*]

That evening saw the creation of *Cléopâtre*, with Maria Kousnietzoff (Cléopâtre), Lillian Grenville (Octavie), Mlle Carton (Charmion), Maguenat (Marc-Antoine), Charles Rousselière (Spakos), and Marvini (Ennius).[†] The genesis of the opera dated back to January of 1910, when Henri Cain introduced Massenet to Louis Payen, the librettist. The score was completed at the end of May 1912, with the title rôle intended for Lucy Arbell. When Raoul Gunsbourg proceeded with the casting for Monte-Carlo, some months after Massenet's death, he deemed it advisable to engage Kousnietzoff, much to the chagrin of Lucy Arbell, who instituted legal action but was denied exclusive rights by the court of appeal. Some 288 changes were made in Cleopatra's part to accommodate a soprano in lieu of a contralto.[‡]

Cléopâtre reflects a trend toward the classical tradition in delineating a kind of grand historical fresco with moderately simple means. The pervasive lyricism is supported by effective musical characterization; the orchestra is almost somber, hewing to the main line of the drama without the distractions of extraneous decorative effects.

------------------◄○►------------------

In the days of the second triumvirate, after Caesar's death, Octavian conquered the West while Mark Anthony pacified the East. Act I shows the camp of Marc-Antoine at Tarsus, on the banks of the Cydnus. Envoys of the Eastern powers present rich tributes, and Marc-Antoine proclaims the power of Rome and promises peace. Spakos, a freedman of Cléopâtre, brings word that the Egyptian queen will come to pay homage. Two preliminary processions, led by women of stunning beauty, lead Marc-Antoine to assume that one or the other must be Cléopâtre. But the queen's entrance is still more magnificent: on the river a gilded barge appears bearing Cléopâtre among her female attendants, like Aphrodite surrounded by nymphs. Slaves roll out a carpet. Cléopâtre, alone, approaches the tent of Marc-Antoine. She is submissive in mien, and Marc-Antoine is smitten and conquered. An envoy from Rome brings word that Marc-Antoine must return to render an account of his campaign and that, furthermore, Octavian offers the hand of his sister, Octavie, in marriage. But Marc-Antoine goes into the galley.

Act II. After several months, Marc-Antoine has finally obeyed the Senate. He is back in Rome, and this is the day he is to marry Octavie. Ennius, just back from Egypt, brings word that Cléopâtre had consoled herself with another. Marc-Antoine

---

[*] According to Schneider (1926, p. 286), the *Suite théâtrale* was performed on this occasion; the account in the *Journal de Monaco* mentions only the orchestra and chorus in Massenet's *Marche solennelle*.

[†] After the war, *Cléopâtre* was given at the Théâtre-Lyrique du Vaudeville, Paris (27 October 1919), with Mary Garden in the title rôle and Maurice Renaud as Marc-Antoine.

[‡] Schneider (1926, p. 229) mentions that Lucy Arbell sang Cléopâtre at Nantes and at Bordeaux; it was she who counted the changes.

is plunged into despair. Octavie pleads with him to let her cure his hidden sorrow, but Marc-Antoine is impelled to go to Egypt. The scene changes to a low dive in Alexandria, where Cléopâtre had come with Spakos to seek new thrills. The manager, sensing the importance af the incognito guests, offers a special attraction in the young man Adamos, who dances. The jealous Spakos tries to strangle him, but habitués of the place menace the strangers until the queen reveals her identity. As she leaves, her handmaid Charmion brings word that Marc-Antoine has returned.

In Act III, the voluptuous gardens of Cléopâtre are the scene of Lybian, Chaldean, and Scythian dances before the couch of Cléopâtre and Marc-Antoine, the latter in the robes of an Asian monarch. Cléopâtre offers to reward with a kiss any slave who will drink a poisoned cup. When Marc-Antoine expresses disgust at such depravity, she accuses him of lacking audacity. Rome's declaration of war against the Egyptian queen leaves Marc-Antoine torn between two worlds.

In Act IV, after Octavian's victory at the naval battle of Actium, Cléopâtre prepares to die. She wants to see Marc-Antoine just once more, but Spakos says she will never see him again. Marc-Antoine does arrive, but is wounded and dies. Cléopâtre takes up the basket of fruit concealing an asp.

A brief line in the *Journal de Monaco* noted that "Mme Massenet, widow of the illustrious composer, was the guest of His Most Serene Highness during the latter days of the past week," perhaps meaning March 5–7.[2] One might assume that the première of *Cléopâtre* would have been too much for her and that she attended one of the later performances.

The eighth and last volume of Massenet's *Mélodies* was published by Heugel on 19 May 1914. Half the songs in this collection had been previously published between 1893 and 1910; seven were copyrighted by Heugel in 1912, one in 1913, and two in 1914. The previous set, Volume VII, comprising songs of 1900–02, had been issued on 28 November 1912.

The end of an era was dramatically signaled by the assassination of Archduke Franz Ferdinand at Sarajevo on 28 June 1914. The world would never again be quite the same. On the French national holiday, 14 July, *Werther* was given as a free matinée at the Opéra-Comique, which then closed its doors until 6 December. In August, World War I broke out.

In the decades following Massenet's death, it was chiefly *Manon, Werther,* and *Thaïs* that maintained a place in the repertoire. The other works were by no means relegated to oblivion. Even during the war, when the Opéra-Comique reopened, *Thérèse* was revived (30 January 1915) with Lucy Arbell;[*] *Le Jongleur de Notre-Dame* was given thirteen times in 1915 (from 10 April); *Sapho* was brought back on 17 May 1916 and attained its hundredth performance (since 1897) on 24 December 1918.

---

[*] *Thérèse* was also given in London, at Covent Garden, on 22 May 1919.

Even *Scènes alsaciennes* was patriotically mounted as a ballet on 16 March 1915 and given six performances at the Opéra-Comique.

Roma appeared twice at the Paris Opéra (29 December 1917 and 8 January 1918), where *Le Cid* was revived for five performances in 1919 (from 24 September). The thousandth of *Manon* at the Opéra-Comique was celebrated on 17 June 1919. On 27 October 1919, *Cléopâtre* opened a run at the Théâtre-Lyrique du Vaudeville, with Mary Garden opposite Maurice Renaud, as Marc-Antoine.

It took *Hérodiade* exactly forty years to travel the long road from La Monnaie in Brussels to the Paris Opéra, where it was first staged on 22 December 1921, with Fanny Heldy as Salomé. The work attained its hundredth performance there in a little over four years, on 14 March 1926. One of the performances of 1921, conducted by Gustave Charpentier, was given for the benefit of a monument to the composer, a project long delayed by the intervention of the First World War. Loges were reserved for members of the Massenet family, and President Alexandre Millerand honored the occasion with his presence.

The remaining posthumous opera, *Amadis,* was staged at Monte-Carlo on 1 April 1922. The first draft of the work was apparently completed during 1889–90, between *Esclarmonde* and *Le Mage.* According to the *Souvenirs,* the score was entrusted to a friend's strongbox, "waited there in silence for twenty-one years" [?], and was being put into final shape in the summer of 1910 at the time of the composer's hospitalization. The biographer Schneider states more prosaically that Massenet returned to *Amadis* in 1901 and brought it to completion in 1902. The title rôle, says Schneider, was originally intended for Jeanne Raunay, who first appeared at the Paris Opéra in 1888 (as Uta in Reyer's *Sigurd*) and at the Opéra-Comique in 1901 (as Léonore in *Fidelio*).[3]

Amadis was billed as an *opéra légendaire* in a prologue and three acts, with text by Jules Claretie based on the early romances of *Amadis de Gaule:*

---◄O►---

The princess Élisène is the daughter of the king of Bretagne. Her twin sons, Amadis and Galaor, are the issue of her love for Périon, king of France.

In the Prologue, Élisène flees from pursuing soldiers sent to kill the two infants as representing a threat to the crown of Bretagne. Exhausted, she arrives at the foot of the Tree of the Fairies. The fairies, taking pity, offer protection. The mother gathers from the stream bed two magic stones, marked with Merlin's star, hangs them around the necks of the little princes, and dies.

The twins become separated, are raised by the fairies, and in knightly manhood are rivals. In Act I they enter a tournament, for which the prize is the hand of Floriane, daughter of old King Rambert. Floriane prefers Amadis, but it is Galaor who wins.

In Act II, Amadis has gone in shame to live in a wood as a hermit. But his love for Floriane finally impels him to return to the palace.

There (Act III) he finds that Floriane and Galaor are about to be married. He calls for a new combat, but his sword is broken. The lily branch in his hand is turned into a sword by the fairies, and he mortally wounds Galaor. Too late, they find around their necks the star-stones that identify them as brothers. Galaor forgives Amadis, whose next task will be to chase the pirates out of Bretagne.

———————————————— ◆ ————————————————

Amadis was portrayed by a soprano, Mlle Vécla, with Paul Lanteri as Galaor. The cast of the première also included Nelly Martyl (Floriane) and Gustave Huberdeau (le roi Rambert). Léon Jehin, now sixty-eight, conducted. The *Journal de Monaco* noted that Mme Massenet was a guest at the palace for several days.[*]

Later in 1922, *La Navarraise* was revived at the Opéra-Comique (21 June), and *Le Portrait de Manon* at the Théâtre-Lyrique (27 September). Even *Esclarmonde* was dusted off and staged at the Opéra: on 24 December 1923, with Fanny Heldy, and again on 11 November 1931, with Gabrielle Ritter-Ciampi.[†] The three hundredth *Thaïs* at the Opéra was celebrated on 12 January 1924, with Maria Kousnietzoff.

Lucy Arbell, now forty-two, was the Dulcinée when *Don Quichotte* at long last reached the stage of the Opéra-Comique (7 October 1924), with the veterans of the 1910 run at the Gaîté: Vanni Marcoux (Don Quichotte) and Lucien Fugère (Sancho). At The Hague, *Don César de Bazan* was staged in February 1925.

Not long after Massenet's death, a committee chaired by Gustave Charpentier had been formed to plan a suitable monument. The result of their efforts was unveiled on 21 October 1926, in the Jardin du Luxembourg, near the Rue Guynemer. The squat obelisk bears reliefs on three sides of favorite personages from Massenet's world of opera. In front, beneath the profiled head of the *maître*, stands lifelike and in the round the young but eternal image of Massenet's heroines. For the unveiling, the Paris skies wept copiously. Most of the ceremony was held in the nearby Palais, where eloquent discourses were read by Gustave Charpentier, André Rivoire, Albert Carré, and Édouard Herriot. The orchestra of the Concerts Colonne, conducted by Gabriel Pierné, played the overture to *Phèdre* and fragments from *Marie-Magdeleine* and *Les Érinnyes*.

Werther attained its thousandth performance at the Opéra-Comique on 10 October 1928, with Ninon Vallin as Charlotte. For Christmas Eve the same year, the Little Theater in London had the happy thought of producing *Cendrillon* with puppets, in English.

Jacques Rouché, director of the Opéra from 1915 to 1940, maintained the prestige of the house with new creations of opera and ballet and with important revivals. *Thaïs* and *Hérodiade* were given regularly. After the fire of 1936, the restored hall

---

[*] Prince Albert died at Paris on 26 June 1922. He was succeeded by his son, Prince Louis II (died 8 May 1949), and great-grandson Prince Rainier III.

[†] The twenty-seventh performance of *Esclarmonde* (2 June 1934) had Martial Singher as l'Éveque de Blois; Singher had made his debut at the Opéra on 21 Dec. 1930, as Athanaël in *Thaïs*.

reopened on 21 February 1937 with Massenet's *Ariane,* for a total of fourteen performances. It must have been a proud moment for Ninon, now in her ninety-sixth year. For Juliette it was too late—she had died in 1935 at the age of sixty-seven.

The composer's centennial was celebrated with a Gala Massenet at the Opéra on 4 June 1942. Included in the program were the first part (L'Annonciation) of *La Vierge* and the scene of the enchanted isle from *Esclarmonde.* That fall, *Grisélidis* was revived at the Opéra-Comique (30 October 1942).

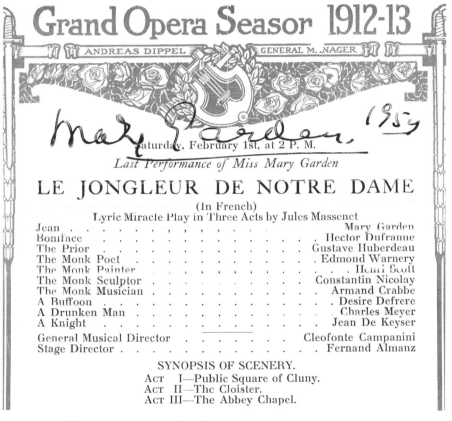

Program for Mary Garden's final performance as Jean in *Le Jongleur de Notre-Dame* at the Chicago Grand Opera, 1 February 1913. Autographed by Miss Garden in 1954. Courtesy Paul Jackson.

The Massenet Family

T
HROUGH HIS PATERNAL GRANDMOTHER, Jules Massenet was descended from the old and honorable families of Favier and Mathieu, originating in Lorraine and active in Alsace. *Jean Favier* (d. 1700) was member (from 1658) and president (from 1675) of the local parliament of Alsace, which had been established by Louis XIV. His son *François de Favier* was a member of the same provincial council during 1687–1705. François married twice: (1) Marguerite Raillot; (2) Marguerite Keller. The issue of the second marriage was five children, including *Jeanne-Françoise de Favier*. She married Alexandre Mathieu, of the parliament of Metz, which became the parliament of Alsace. Their son was *Pierre-François Mathieu*. (He occasionally signed Mathieu de Faviers.)

I *Jean Massenet* (1721– ?), the composer's great-grandfather. He married Marie-Anne Warin (or Varin), who died at Metz in November 1788. They had three sons and two daughters.

II [1] Marie Anne, 1747–1748.

[2] *Jean-Pierre*, 1748–1824, the composer's grandfather (see II, page 309).

[3] Joseph, 1750– ?, who is said to have formed a German branch of the family.

[4] Jeanne, who married Nicolas Campion and lived at Le Havre.

[5] Jean, 1756– ? (after 1818), navy worker, then carpenter.

I *Pierre-François Mathieu Favier*, the composer's great-grandfather. A member (1774–88) of the Strasbourg Chambre de Quinze, he married Elisabeth Le Chasseur (Jaeger, in German). They had four sons and four daughters:

II [1] Elisabeth, 1752–1801, married a local official who later became an artillery officer.

[2] Michel, 1753–1841, avocat-général of Strasbourg, later conseiller at Colmar.

[3] Jacques-François-Antoine, 1755–1825.

[4] *Françoise-Hélène*, 1757–1840, the composer's grandmother (married Jean-Pierre Massenet in 1787).

[5] Marie-Antoinette, 1760–1825, married Gau de Vaumerin, commissaire des guerres.

[6] Philippe-Gaëtan, 1761–1833, military administrator, first under Napoleon, then under Louis XVIII. Made a baron in 1817 and peer of France in 1832, his coat of arms authorized "Mathieu de Faviers" because the "Favier" had otherwise become extinct.

[7] Laure, 1767–1850, married Michel Thomassin, a huissier royal of Strasbourg.

[8] Louis, 1770–1842, volunteered in the army in 1791 and became a colonel in 1813.

II *Jean-Pierre Massenet*, the composer's grandfather. The son [2] of Jean Massenet (I), he was born at Flavigny and baptised at Gravelotte, near Metz, on 25 February 1748; he died at Strasbourg on 28 October 1824. In 1787, he married Françoise-Hélène Mathieu. They had two sons:

III [1] *Alexis*, 1788–1863, the composer's father (see III).

[2] Auguste-Pierre-Charles, born in Heiligenstein on 23 August 1790 and died on 9 July 1815, a lieutenant in the service of Baden. He had been gravely wounded in the battle of Leipzig, October 1813.

III *Alexis-Pierre-Michel-Nicolas Massenet*, the composer's father. Born at Strasbourg on 25 June 1788, he died at Nice on 1 January 1863. His first marriage (Toulouse, 1816) was to Sophie de Jaegerschmidt (died October 1829), of Baden. They had eight children:

[1] Edouard, 1817–1827.

[2] Alfred, 1819–1851, tradesman.

[3] Auguste, 1821–1892, navy officer, then merchant marine.

[4] Camille, 1822–1901, artillery officer.

[5] Amélie, 1824–1840.

[6] Émile, 1826–1832.

[7] Oscar, 1828–1828.

[8] Laure, 1828–1855, married a Polish doctor in St. Étienne.

His second marriage, at Albi in 1830, was to Éléonore-Adélaïde Royer de Marancour, who was born at Metz in 1809 and died in Paris on 24 March 1875. She was the daughter of Edmé-Raphaël Royer de Marancour (1772–1844), commissaire des guerres under Napoleon, and Frédéric-Caroline-Albertine Schroër. The children of this second narriage were:

[1] Julie-Caroline (see IV,).

[2] Léon-Adrien, born at Toulouse on 14 October 1834 and died in 1886, was an author and journalist.

[3] Frédéric-Auguste-Edmond (see IV, page 311).

[4] *Jules-Frédéric-Émile*, 1842–1912, the composer.

The Massenet–de Jaegerschmidt Branch

Louis Auguste Massenet, who was born at Toulouse on 30 May 1821 and died in 1892, was a sea captain. He married Louisa Cochet, and they had ten children, of whom Eugène-Ferdinand-Camille, 1848–1918, was a general; Maurice (1854–1887) was an engineer; Paul-Alexis , born in 1861, was an engineer; and Charles, born in 1870, was a government administrator.

Jacques-Camille Massenet, who was born at Boulogne on 14 November 1822 and died in 1901, was a colonel. He married Pauline Le François de Garinville, and they had four children:

V [1] Georges was inspector general of marine hydrography and Officier of the Légion d'Honneur.

[2] Amélie, 1856–1959, married Charles Vérand, general and Grand-Officier of the Légion d'Honneur.

[3] Louie-Marie, 1863–1905, was a captain for the army geographic service.

[4] André-Joseph-Emmanuel, 1864–1961, was a general and Grand-Croix, Légion d'Honneur.

The Massenet–Royer de Marancour Branch

See Alexis Massenet (III)—second marriage to Éléonore Royer de Marancour, the composer's mother.

IV [1] Julie-Caroline Massenet was born at Toulouse in 1832 and died at Paris on 12 Jan. 1905. Her first marriage, in 1853, was to Paul Cavaillé (1827–1877), artist painter. They had a daughter and two sons, François and Noël. Her second marriage, in 1882, was to Amédée Comte d'Eu du Ménil de Montigny.

IV [2] Frédéric-Auguste-Edmond Massenet de Marancour was born at Toulouse on 20 February 1837 and died in 1929. He became a general in 1894 and was a Commandeur of the Légion d'Honneur. He married Henriette Duhamel and had three sons: Robert-Henri, born 1880, a general; Jacques-Raphaël, 1881–1961, a captain and, later, an industrialist at Lyon; and Georges.

IV *Jules-Frédéric-Émile Massenet,* the composer. He was born at Montaud on 12 May 1842 and died in Paris on 3 August 1912. In 1866 he married Louise-Constance de Gressy (1841–1938). Their only child was Juliette.

V Juliette Massenet was born in Paris on 31 March 1868 and died at Égreville on 7 September 1935. In 1887, she married Léon-Charles Alloend-Bessand, a mercantile administrator. Their children were Marie-Madeleine, 1888–1974, who married engineer René Faillot in 1907; Olivier, 1890–1918; and Pierre Bessand-Massenet 1899–1985, author and historian.

Was there a German Branch?

Joseph Massenet, second son of Jean Massenet (see I [3]), is said to have been born around 1750 at Gravelot or Metz and to have died sometime before 1809. He settled at Mutterstadt, near Mannheim, as *venator* (huntsman and gamekeeper) to the Palatine Elector. There he married Anna Barbara Kunz.

Their son, Franz Joseph Massenet, was born at Mutterstadt on 18 April 1781. In 1809 he married Margaretha Kaemmerer, who was the daughter of a merchant.

Their son, Johann Ludwig Massenez,* was born at Mutterstadt in 1809. In 1838 he married Franziska Wilhelmina Behlen. At that time he was a gymnasium professor at Grünstadt, near Worms.

Their son, Joseph Ludwig Massenez, was born at Grünstadt on 26 December 1839 and died at Wiesbaden on 24 December 1923. He achieved eminence as a mining engineer.

His daughter, Hedwig Margaretha Massenez, was born at Hoerde on 4 December 1875 and married Karl Max Transfeldt (1863–1932), later a major general.

---

* The spelling of *Massenet* was probably changed to *Massenez* to avoid the German pronunciation Massen**ett.** Perhaps Germans were familiar enough with the French verb ending -*ez* to pronounce it correctly as ā.

Massenet's Birth Record
Published in Schneider (1908), 7

C E JOURD'HUI, TREIZE MAI mil huit cent quarante-deux, à cinq heures du soir,

Devant nous, adjoint du maire de la commune de Montaud, officier de l'état civil délégué, est comparu sieur Félix Nullet, âgé de trente-six ans, employé à la fabrique de faulx de la Terrasse, demeurant à Saint-Étienne, place Saint-Charles, qui nous a dit que Dame Éléonore-Adélaïde Royer de Marancourt, épouse de Monsieur Alexis-Pierre-Michel-Nicolas Massenet, âgé de cinquante-cinq ans, fabricant de faulx, demeurant en cette commune, au lieu de la Terrasse, est accouchée dans le domicile de son mari, hier à une heure du matin, d'un enfant du sexe masculin qui nous a été présenté, auquel on a donné les prénoms Jules-Émile-Frédéric.

Desquelles déclaration et présentation nous avons signé le présent acte en présence de Messieurs Martin Saurel, âgé de quarante-six ans, entrepreneur de messageries, demeurant à Saint-Étienne, rue de Paris et Charles Bessy, âgé de quarante-huit ans, teneur de livres, demeurant à Saint-Étienne, rue de la Bourse, et, après lecture faite, nous avons signé avec eux et le comparant.

Emma Calvé. Photography by Dupont. Courtesy Paul Jackson.

Opera Performances in Paris

The following tables enumerate the performances of Massenet operas in Paris opera houses during the period from 1867 to 1915.

	1867	1872	1873	1877	1878	1879	1884	1885	1886	1887	1888	1889	1890	1891	1892	1893	1894	1895	1896	TOTALS
Opéra-Comique																				
La Grand' Tante	17	—	—	—	—	—	—	—	—	—	—	—	—	—	—	—	—	—	—	17
Don César de Bazan	—	8	5	—	—	—	—	—	—	—	—	—	—	—	—	—	—	—	—	13
Manon	—	—	—	—	—	—	78	—	—	—	—	—	—	34	58	26	17	17	11	251
Esclarmonde	—	—	—	—	—	—	—	10	—	—	—	91	10	—	—	—	—	—	—	101
Werther	—	—	—	—	—	—	—	—	—	—	—	—	—	—	—	43	2	—	—	45
Le Portrait de Manon	—	—	—	—	—	—	—	—	—	—	—	—	—	—	—	—	15	6	—	21
La Navarraise	—	—	—	—	—	—	—	—	—	—	—	—	—	—	—	—	—	28	11	39
Opéra																				
Le Roi de Lahore	—	—	—	30	11	16	—	—	—	—	—	—	—	—	—	—	—	—	—	57
Le Cid	—	—	—	—	—	—	—	9	45	13	8	3	3	5	—	6	—	—	—	92
Le Mage	—	—	—	—	—	—	—	—	—	—	—	—	—	31	—	—	—	—	—	31
Thaïs	—	—	—	—	—	—	—	—	—	—	—	—	—	—	—	—	27	4	2	33
Théâtre-Italien																				
Hérodiade	—	—	—	—	—	—	9	—	—	—	—	—	—	—	—	—	—	—	—	9
TOTALS	17	8	5	30	11	16	87	19	45	13	8	94	13	70	58	75	61	55	24	709

	1897	1898	1899	1900	1901	1902	1903	1904	1905	1906	1907	1908	1909	1910	1911	1912[a]	1913	1914	1915	Totals
Opéra-Comique																				
Manon	22	20	34	39	33	30	27	29	22	31	31	41	10	41	47	36	37	23	27	580
Werther	11	—	—	—	—	—	26	4	21	22	28	35	35	38	32	38	37	22	9	358
Le Portrait de Manon	—	—	7	3	5	—	—	—	—	—	—	—	—	—	—	—	—	—	—	15
La Navarraise	8	3	13	—	3	—	3	1	—	10	—	4	—	—	11	—	13	11	—	80
Sapho	12	32	—	—	—	—	—	—	—	—	—	—	15	—	—	—	—	—	—	59
Cendrillon	—	—	49	20	—	—	1	—	—	—	—	—	—	—	—	—	—	—	—	70
Grisélidis	—	—	—	—	17	37	—	—	4	3	—	—	—	—	—	—	—	—	—	61
Jongleur	—	—	—	—	—	—	—	43	30	15	6	6	6	9	6	6	2	3	13	145
Marie-Magdeleine	—	—	—	—	—	—	—	—	—	12	3	—	—	—	—	—	—	—	—	15
Chérubin	—	—	—	—	—	—	—	—	14	—	—	—	—	—	—	—	—	—	—	14
Thérèse	—	—	—	—	—	—	—	—	—	—	—	—	—	—	12	8	—	—	2	22
Opéra																				
Le Cid	—	—	—	16	1	—	—	—	10	6	—	—	—	—	5	6	—	—	—	44
Thais	3	6	—	—	11	2	—	9	2	—	7	11	9	4	9	8	15	8	—	104
Ariane	—	—	—	—	—	—	—	—	—	19	40	2	—	—	—	—	—	—	—	61
Bacchus	—	—	—	—	—	—	—	—	—	—	—	—	5	—	—	—	—	—	—	5
Roma	—	—	—	—	—	—	—	—	—	—	—	—	—	—	—	14	—	—	—	14
Théâtre-Italien																				
Hérodiade	—	—	—	—	—	—	43	—	—	—	—	—	—	—	—	—	—	—	—	43
Gaité-Lyrique																				
Hérodiade	—	—	—	—	—	—	—	9	—	—	—	—	—	—	31	25	—	—	—	65
La Navarraise	—	—	—	—	—	—	—	—	—	—	—	21	6	—	—	—	—	—	—	27
Cendrillon	—	—	—	—	—	—	—	—	—	—	—	1	17	—	—	—	—	—	—	18
Jongleur	—	—	—	—	—	—	—	—	—	—	—	16	—	—	—	—	—	—	—	16
Don Quichotte	—	—	—	—	—	—	—	—	—	—	—	—	—	1	68	—	8	—	—	77
Panurge	—	—	—	—	—	—	—	—	—	—	—	—	—	—	—	—	15	—	—	15
Totals	56	61	103	78	70	69	100	95	103	118	115	137	103	93	221	141	127	67	51	1,908

a. Trianon-Lyrique: *Don César de Bazan* revived 3 May 1912

Geraldine Farrar as Manon. Courtesy Benedikt & Salmon.

Works of Massenet

OPERAS

COMPLETED OPERAS, WITH DATES OF FIRST PERFORMANCE

La Grand' Tante. One act. Text, Jules Adenis and Charles Grandvallet. Paris, Opéra-Comique, 3 Apr. 1867. Piano-vocal score: E. et A. Girod, [1867]. Full score lost in the fire of 1887.

Don César de Bazan. Opéra comique, four acts. Text, Adolphe-Philippe d'Ennery and Jules Chantepie. Paris, Opéra-Comique, 30 Nov. 1872. P-v score: Hartmann [1872]. Full score lost in the fire of 1887. New version: Geneva, 20 Jan. 1888.

Le Roi de Lahore. Opéra, five acts and seven scenes. Text, Louis Gallet. Paris, Opéra, 27 Apr. 1877. Autograph full score: Bibl. Opéra. P-v score: Hartmann, 1877 (full score, n.d.).

Hérodiade. Opéra, four acts and seven scenes. Text, Paul Milliet, Henri Grémont [Georges Hartmann], and Angelo Zanardini. Brussels, 19 Dec. 1881. Aut. full score: Bibl. Opéra. P-v score: Hartmann, 1881.

Manon. Opéra comique, five acts and six scenes. Text, Henri Meilhac and Philippe Gille. Paris, Opéra-Comique, 19 Jan. 1884. Aut. full score: Bibl. Opéra. P-v score: Hartmann, 1884 (full score, n.d.).

Le Cid. Opéra, four acts and ten scenes. Text, A. P. d'Ennery, Édouard Blau, and Louis Gallet. Paris, Opéra, 30 Nov. 1885. Aut. full score: Bibl. Opéra. P-v score: Hartmann, 1885.

Esclarmonde. Opéra romanesque, four acts and eight scenes. Text, Alfred Blau and Louis de Gramont. Paris, Opéra-Comique, 15 May 1889. Aut. full score: Bibl. Opéra. P-v score: Hartmann, 1889.

Le Mage. Opéra, five acts and six scenes. Text, Jean Richepin. Paris, Opéra, 16 Mar. 1891. Aut. full score: Bibl. Opéra. P-v score: Hartmann, 1891.

Werther. Drame lyrique, three acts and four scenes. Text, Édouard Blau, Paul Milliet, and Georges Hartmann. Vienna, 16 Feb. 1892 (in a German translation by Max Kalbeck). Geneva, 27 Dec. 1892 (in the original French). Aut. full score: Bibl. Opéra. Full and P-v scores: Heugel, 1892.

Thaïs. Opéra, three acts and seven scenes. Text, Louis Gallet. Paris, Opéra, 16 Mar. 1894. With ballet and Oasis scene added: Paris, Opéra, 13 Apr. 1898. Aut. full score: Bibl. Opéra. Full and p-v scores: Heugel, 1894.

Le Portrait de Manon. Opéra comique, one act. Text, Georges Boyer. Paris, Opéra-Comique, 8 May 1894. Aut. full score: Bibl. Opéra. Full and p-v scores: Heugel, 1894.

La Navarraise. Épisode lyique, two acts. Text, Jules Claretie and Henri Cain. London, Covent Garden, 20 June 1894. Paris, Opéra-Comique, 8 Oct. 1895. Aut. full score: Bibl. Opéra. Full and p-v scores: Heugel, 1894.

Sapho. Pièce lyrique, five acts. Text, Henri Cain and Arthur Bernède. Paris, Opéra-Comique, 27 Nov. 1897. Aut. full score: Bibl. Opéra. P-v score: Heugel, 1887.

Cendrillon. Conte de fées, four acts and six scenes. Text, Henri Cain. Paris, Opéra-Comique, 24 May 1899. Aut. full score: Bibl. Opéra. Full and p-v scores: Heugel, 1899.

Grisélidis. Conte lyrique, prologue and three acts. Text, Armand Silvestre and Eugene Morand. Paris, Opéra-Comique, 20 Nov. 1901. Aut. full score: Bibl. Opéra. Full and p-v scores: Heugel, 1901.

Le Jongleur de Notre-Dame. Miracle, three acts. Text, Maurice Léna. Monte Carlo, 18 Feb. 1902. Aut. full score: Bibl. Opéra. Full and p-v scores: Heugel, 1902.

Marie-Magdeleine. Drame sacré, three acts and four scenes. Text, Louis Gallet. *See under* Oratorios, 1873. First staged as opera: Nice, 9 Feb. 1903.

Chérubin. Comédie chantée, three acts. Text, Francis de Croisset [Franz Wiener] and Henri Cain. Monte Carlo, 14 Feb. 1905. Paris, Opéra-Comique, 23 May 1905. Aut. full score: Bibl. Opéra. Full and p-v scores: Heugel, 1905.

Ariane. Opéra, five acts. Text, Catulle Mendès. Paris, Opéra, 28 Oct. 1906. Aut. full and p-v scores: Bibl. Opéra. Full and p-v scores: Heugel, 1906.

Thérèse. Drame musical, two acts. Text, Jules Claretie. Monte Carlo, 7 Feb. 1907. Aut. full score: Bibl. Opéra. Full and p-v scores: Heugel, 1907.

Bacchus. Opéra, four acts and seven scenes. Text, Catulle Mendès. Paris, Opéra, 5 May 1909. Aut. full score: Bibl. Opéra. P-v score: Heugel, 1909.

Don Quichotte. Comédie héroïque, five acts. Text, Henri Cain. Monte Carlo, 19 Feb. 1910. Aut. full score: Bibl. Opéra. Full and p-v scores: Heugel, 1910.

Roma. Opéra tragique, five acts. Text, Henri Cain. Monte Carlo, 17 Feb. 1912. Aut. full score: Bibl. Opéra. Full and p-v scores: Heugel, 1912.

Panurge. Haulte farce musicale, three acts. Text, Georges Spitzmüller and Maurice Boukay [Charles-Maurice Couyba]. Paris, Théâtre-Lyrique de la Gaîté, 25 Apr. 1913. Aut. full score: Bibl. Opéra. P-v score: Heugel, 1912 (full score, 1913).

Cléopâtre. Opéra, four acts. Text, Louis Payen. Monte Carlo, 23 Feb. 1914. Aut. full score: Bibl. Opéra. P-v score: Heugel, 1914 (full score, 1915).

Amadis. Opéra légendaire, prologue and three acts. Text, Jules Claretie. Monte Carlo, 1 Apr. 1922. Aut. full score: Bibl. Opéra. P-v score; Heugel, 1913 (full score, n.d.).

UNFINISHED, LOST, DESTROYED, OR MUSIC UTILIZED ELSEWHERE

Les Deux boursiers. Operetta, one act. Written for the Théâtre de la Tour-d'Auvergne, ca. 1859. Lost?

Noureddin. Sketches for an opéra comique, ca. 1865. Bibl. Nat., Fonds du Conservatoire, Ms. 4240.

Valéria. Sketches for an Italian opera, ca. 1865. Bibl. Nat., Fonds du Conservatoire, Ms. 4241.

Esméralda. Composed at the Villa Medici, ca. 1865.

La Coupe du roi de Thulé. Opéra, three acts. Text, Louis Gallet and Édouard Blau. A set-ting of the prescribed libretto for the Paris Opéra competition of 1867. Not per-formed. Music of the second act was used for the third act of *Le Roi de Lahore* and various airs and ensembles utilized for *Les Érinnyes, Marie-Magdeleine, Éve,* and *La Vierge.*

Le Florentin. Opéra comique. Text, Jules-Henri Vernoy, Marquis de Saint-Georges. A set-ting of the prescribed libretto for the Paris Opéra-Comique competition of 1867. Finished, 1868. Not performed.

Manfred. Text, Jules-Émile Ruelle, after Byron. 1869? Unfinished.

Méduse. Opera, three acts. Text, Michel Carré père. Apparently completed (1870) but not performed.

Les Templiers. Text, Jules Adenis. Two acts completed but destroyed.

L'Adorable Bel-Boul. Fantaisie. Text, Louis Gallet. Given at the Cercle de l'Union Artis-tique (Cercle des Mirlitons), 17 Apr 1873. Destroyed.

Berengère et Anatole. Saynète. Text, Henri Meilhac and Paul Poirson. Given at the Cercle de l'Union Artistique, Feb. 1876. Also one performance only (15 Oct. 1876) at the Renaissance, at a benefit for the régisseur P. Callais. Destroyed.

Robert de France. Drame lyrique, ca. 1880.

Les Girondins. Opera, 1881.

Montalte. Listed by Séré and Schneider, without date.

BALLETS

Le Carillon. Légende dansée et mimée. Scenario, Camille de Roddaz and Ernest Van Dyck. Vienna, Hofoper, 21 Feb. 1892. Aut. full score: Bibl. Opéra. piano score: Heugel, 1892.

Les Rosati. Divertissement des roses, one act. Choreography, Mme Mariquita. Paris, Opéra-Comique, 9 Dec. 1901. Aut. full score: Bibl. Opéra. Full score (as Divertisse-ment pour orchestre): Heugel, 1902.

La Cigale. Divertissement-ballet, two acts and three tableaux. Scenario, Henri Cain. Paris, Opéra-Comique, 4 Feb. 1904. Aut. full score: Bibl. Opéra. Piano score: Heugel, 1903 (full score, 1904).

Espada. Ballet, one act. Scenario, René Maugars [Dr. Henri de Rothschild]. Monte Carlo, 13 Feb. 1908. Aut. full score: Bibl. Opéra. Piano and full scores: Heugel, 1908.

UNFINISHED OR DISCARDED

Le Preneur des rats. Project for a ballet (1872) with scenario by Théophile Gautier. Re-fused by Halanzier, director of the Opéra.

Les Filles de feu. Project for a ballet, with scenario by Louis Gallet, announced for the Théâtre d'Opéra Populaire au Châtelet (1874) but apparently not written.

INCIDENTAL MUSIC

Les Érinnyes. Tragédie antique in two parts, in verse, by Leconte de Lisle. Paris, Odéon, 6 Jan. 1873. With additions: Opéra-National-Lyrique, 15 May 1876. Full and pi-ano-vocal scores: Hartmann, n.d. (plate no. 649).

Un Drame sous Philippe II. Drama in four acts, by Georges de Porto-Riche. Paris, Odéon, 14 Apr. 1875. Sarabande espagnole (piano): Hartmann, 1875 (plate no. 858).

La Vie de Bohème. Drama in five acts (1849), by Théodore Barrière and Henry Mürger, after Mürger's novel (1848). For the reopening of the Odéon (19 Nov. 1875) after remodeling, a mixed program was given that included Act I of this play, for which Massenet wrote "La Chanson de Musette" (poem by Meilhac), with orchestra, to be interpreted by Jeanne Granier. Aut. full score: Bibl. Nat., Ms. 4304.

L'Hetman. Drama in five acts, in verse, by Paul Déroulède. Paris, Odéon, 2 Feb. 1877. Cossack songs: lost? Fanfare only (1 p.): aut. Bibl. Nat. Ms. 4242.

Notre-Dame de Paris. Drama in five acts and seventeen scenes (1850), by Paul Foucher, after Victor Hugo's novel (1831). For a performance at the Théâtre des Nations (4 June 1879), Massenet composed the air, without accompaniment, "Mon père est oyseau, ma mère est oyselle," to be sung by Esméralda (Mlle Alice Lody). Lost?

Michel Strogoff. Pièce à grand spectacle, five acts and sixteen scenes, by Adolphe-Philippe d'Ennery and Jules Verne. Paris, Châtelet, 17 Nov. 1880. Lost?

Nana-Sahib. Drama in seven scenes, in verse, by Jean Richepin. Paris, Porte-Saint-Martin, 20 Dec. 1883. Aut.: Bibl. Nat., Ms. 4288.

Théodora. Drama in five acts, by Victorien Sardou. Paris, Porte-Saint-Martin, 26 Dec. 1884. Aut.: Bibl. Nat., Ms. 4268.

Le Crocodile. Play in five acts and nine scenes, by Victorien Sardou. Paris, Porte-Saint-Martin, 12 Dec. 1886. Piano score of Entr'acte berceuse and Entr'acte nocturne: Hartmann, 1887.

Phèdre. Tragédie in five acts, by Racine (1677). Paris, Odéon, 8 Dec. 1900. Aut.: Bibl. Opéra. Full and piano scores: Heugel, 1900. For the overture, *see under* Orchestra, 1873.

Le Grillon du foyer. Comédie in three acts, by Ludovic de Francmesnil, after Charles Dickens's *Cricket on the Hearth* (1845). Paris, Odéon, 1 Oct. 1904. piano score: Heugel, 1923.

Le Manteau du roi. Drama in four acts, in verse, by Jean Aicard. Paris, Porte-Saint-Martin, 22 Oct. 1907. Lost?

Perce-Neige et les sept gnômes. Conte en vers en quatre journées, by Jeanne Dortzal. Paris, Théâtre Fémina, 2 Feb. 1909. Lost?

Jérusalem. Drama in five acts, by Georges Rivollet. Monte Carlo, 17 Jan. 1914. P-v score: Heugel, 1912.

ORCHESTRA

Ouverture en sol. Finished 29 Nov. 1863, for the composition class of Ambroise Thomas. Aut.: Bibl. Nat., Ms. 4265. The "Ouverture orchestre," which together with the "Messe de Requiem" constituted the envoi de Rome for 1864. [Transcribed and arranged by Massenet as *Ouverture de concert* for piano, 4 hands. Aut.: Bibl. Nat., Ms. 4253.]

Pompéia, suite symphonique. (1) Prélude; (2) Hymne à Éros (danse grecque); (3) Chant funèbre (choeur des funérailles); (4) Bacchanale. Presumably composed after Massenet's visit (August 1864) at Pompeii and Herculaneum. Performed by Arban's orchestra, Casino de la rue Cadet, 24 Feb. 1866. Music used in *Les Érinnyes.*

Symphonie. Sketched January–June 1865 and abandoned. Lost?

Première suite d'orchestre. (1) Pastorale et fugue; (2) Variations; (3) Nocturne; (4) Marche et strette. Composed Venice, October 1865. As Massenet's only envoi de Rome for 1865, listed in the official report as "Symphonie (en fa), en 4 parties. Grande partition, orchestre." Performed by Pasdeloup, 24 Mar. 1867. Aut.: Bibl. Nat., Ms. 4236. Full score: Durand, Schoenewerck et Cie, n.d. (plate no. 2164).

Deux fantaisies pour orchestre. (1) Une noce flamande, scène pour orchestre et choeurs (Gustave Chouquet). Finished 18 Feb. [year effaced]. Aut.: Bibl. Nat., Ms. 4266. (2) Le Retour d'une caravane. Finished 9 June 1866. Aut.: Bibl. Nat., Ms. 4258. According to Seré, both performed at a Concert des Champs-Élysées, July 1866.

Scènes hongroises, 2me suite d'orchestre. (1) Entrée en forme de danse; (2) Intermède; (3) Adieux à la fiancée; (4) Cortège, Bénédiction nuptiale, Sortie de l'église. Performed by Pasdeloup, 26 Nov. 1871. Full score: Hartmann, 1880.

Concert tzigane. Finished 20 Feb. 1873. Aut.: Bibl. Nat., Ms. 4256.

Ouverture de Phèdre. Finished 29 Dec. 1873. Aut.: Bibl. Nat., Ms. 4235. Performed by Colonne, 22 Feb. 1874. Hartmann, n.d. (plate no. 1068).

Scènes dramatiques, d'après Shakespeare, 3me suite d'orchestre. (1) La Tempête: Ariel et les esprits; (2) Le Sommeil de Desdémone; (3) Macbeth: Les Sorcières, le Festin, l'Apparition, Fanfares. Composed July–October 1874. Performed at the Concerts du Conservatoire, 10 and 17 Jan. 1875. The autograph (Bibl. Nat. Ms. 4237) shows that Massenet's original intention was to designate the work as "5me suite d'orchestre" with, as the third movement, a "Rondo nocturne dans le jardin de Juliette" (which became No. 7 of *Improvisations* for piano), and "Macbeth" in fourth place. An annotation dated "14 juillet 1875" changed the titles to: "Scènes dramatiques, 3me suite d'orchestre. [1] Prélude et divertissement; [2] Mélodrame; [3] Scène finale."

Scènes pittoresques, 4me suite d'orchestre. (1) Marche; (2) Air de ballet; (3) Angélus; (4) Fête bohème. Performed by Colonne, 22 Mar. 1874. Full score. Hartmann, 1874.

Scènes napolitaines, 5me suite d'orchestre. (1) La Danse; (2) La Procession, et l'Improvisateur; (3) La Fête. Apparently performed in 1876 by both Pasdeloup and Colonne. Full score: Hartmann, n.d. (plate no. 1092).

Sarabande espagnole du seizième siècle, pour petit orchestre. Apparently the only music published from *Un Drame sous Philippe II* (1875). Also for piano, 4 hands: Hartmann, 1875.

Lamento, pour orchestre, suite à l'occasion de la mort de G. Bizet. Performed by Colonne, 31 Oct. 1875. Lost?

Marche héroïque de Szabady, orchestration by Massenet. Composed March–April, 1879. Aut.: Bibl. Opéra. Dedicated to Liszt, who made a piano transcription. Performed at the Opéra, 7 June 1879, at a benefit for the flood victims of Szégédin, Hungary. Piano score: Hartmann, 1879. Other arrangements, including 4 hands, 8 hands.

Scènes de féerie, 6me suite d'orchestre. (1) Cortège; (2) Ballet; (3) Apparition; (4) Bacchanale. Composed Dec. 1880–Feb. 1881. Aut.: Bibl. Opéra. Performed in London, March 1881, and at the Concerts du Châtelet, 1883. Hartmann, 1882.

Scènes alsaciennes, 7me suite d'orchestre. With a program by Alphonse Daudet. (1) Dimanche matin; (2) Au cabaret; (3) Sous les tilleuls; (4) Dimanche soir. Performed by Colonne, 19 Mar. 1882. Full score: Hartmann, 1882. (Given as a ballet, Opéra-Comique, 18 Mar. 1915.)

Parade militaire, morceau de genre pour orchestre. Aut.: Bibl. Nat., Ms. 13802. Piano score: Hartmann, 1887.

Visions: poème symphonique. Composed Sept.–Nov. 1891. Aut. full score: Heugel archives.

Le Mer: Mélodie de F. Schubert, transcrite pour cor avec accompagnement d'orchestre. Full score: Millereau, 1891.

Devant la Madonne, pour petit orchestre: Souvenir de la campagne de Rome (nuit de Noël, 1864). For flute, oboe, clarinet, and strings. Heugel, 1897.

Marche solennelle. Also piano, 4 hands (by Massenet). Heugel, 1897.

Fantaisie, pour violoncelle solo et orchestre. Aut.: Bibl. Opéra. Full score: Heugel, 1897.

Brumaire, ouverture pour le drame de Ed. Noël. Performed by Colonne, 10 Mar. 1901. Piano, 4 hands (by Massenet): Heugel, 1900 (full score, 1901).

Pièces pour petit orchestre. (1) Simple phrase; (2) Cantique. For two flutes and strings. Heugel, 1901.

Concerto pour piano et orchestre. Performed by Louis Diémer, Concerts du Conservatoire, 1 Feb. 1903. Full score: Heugel, 1903.

Suite parnassienne: Fresque musicale, pour orchestre, choeurs, et déclamation, poème de Maurice Léna. (1) Uranie (l'Astronomie), Rêverie; (2) Clio (l'Histoire), Visions antiques; (3) Euterpe (la Musique), Double choeur. Full score: Heugel, 1913.

Suite théâtrale, pour orchestre, voix, et déclamation, d'aprés une ode de Maurice Léna. (1) La Tragédie; (2) La Comédie; (3) La Danse. Full score: Heugel, 1913.

PIANO

Grande Fantaisie de concert sur le Pardon de Ploërmel de Meyerbeer. Dedicated to Massenet's piano teacher, Adolphe Laurent. Brandus et S. Dufour, 1861. Copy in Bibl. Nat.

Scènes de bal. (4 hands.) Seven pieces, ending with a Marche-finale. Composed 1863? (Bizet made a two-hand arrangement for Hartmann.)

[3] *Pièces.* (4 hands.) (1) Andante; (2) Allegretto quasi allegro; (3) Andante. Published by G. Flaxland, 1867, as "Pièces pour le piano à 4 mains. Ire Suite, Op. 11" Dedicated to Saint-Saëns. Copy in Bibl. Nat. Nos. 1 and 2 were revisions of two pieces originally for cello and piano.

Dix Pièces de genre. (1) Nocturne; (2) Marche; (3) Barcarolle; (4) Rigodon; (5) Mélodie: Élégie des Érinnyes; (6) Saltarello; (7) Vieille chanson; (8) Légende; (9) Fughetta; (10) Carillon. Bibl. Nat. has: [A] "Étude du style et du rythme, 10 pièces de genre pour le piano, par J. Massenet, Op. 10." G. et A. Girod, 1867; [B] "Dix pièces de genre, nouvelle édition." ibid., 1868.

6 Dances. (4 hands.) Composed Dec. 1869–Jan. 1870. Aut.: Bibl. Nat., Ms. 4245.

3 Marches. (4 hands.) Composed Jan. 1870. Aut.: Bibl. Nat., Ms. 4246.

2 Berceuses. (4 hands.) Composed 6 Jan. 1870. Aut.: Bibl. Nat., Ms. 4244.

Le Roman d'Arlequin, pantomimes enfantins. (1) Ouverture—gigue; (2) Entrée d'Arlequin; (3) Rêverie de Colombine; (4) Sérénade d'Arlequin à Colombine; (5) Duo— finale. Dated 27 July 1871. Aut.: Bibl. Nat., Ms. 4248. Published in an *édition de luxe*, with strophes by Armand Silvestre and etchings by Henri Heyer. Hartmann, n.d. (plate no. 606). Also Hartmann, 1877.

Ma cousine, pantomime. Undated aut.: Bibl. Nat., Ms. 4252.

[*Divertissement pour orchestre*, by Édouard Lalo.] Piano reduction by Massenet. (1) Scherzo; (2) Andantino; (3) Finale. (Lalo's work was first performed at the Concerts Populaires on 8 Dec. 1872.)

[7] *Improvisations*. (1) Andantino; (2) Allegretto; (3) Triste et très lent; (4) Allegretto scherzando; (5) Andante cantabile espressivo; (6) Allegro deciso; (7) Allegretto. Dated September 1874. Aut.: Bibl. Nat., Ms. 4247. No. 7 has: "Extrait des Scènes dramatiques, No. 3, Rondo nocturne (Roméo et Juliette)." The Hartmann (1875) cover has: "Improvisations. 20 Pièces pour le piano en trois livres par J. Massenet. 1er Livre." (plate no. 751). The series was apparently not continued.

Toccata. Heugel, 1892.

Deux impromptus. (1) Eau dormante; (2) Eau courante. Heugel, 1896.

Marche solennelle. (4 hands.) Heugel, 1897. *See also under* Orchestra.

Un memento musicale. Milan: Sonzogno, [1897?].

Année passée, suite de pièces en 4 livres. (4 hands.) *1er Livre: Après-midi d'été*. (1) À l'ombre; (2) Dans les blés; (3) Grand soleil. *2me Livre: Jours d'automne*. (1) Feuilles jaunies; (2) Deux novembre; (3) Joyeuse chasse. *3me Livre: Soirs d'hiver*. (1) Noël; (2) En songeant; (3) On valsait. *4me Livre: Matins de printemps*. (1) Les premiers nids; (2) Lilas; (3) Pâques—Sortie de grand' messe. Heugel, 1897.

Valse folle. Heugel, 1898.

Valse très lente. Heugel, 1901.

Musique pour bercer les petits enfants. Heugel, 1902.

Deux pièces pour piano. (1) Papillons noirs; (2) Papillons blancs. Aut.: Bibl. Nat., Mss. 4249–4250. Heugel, 1907.

CHAMBER MUSIC

[*Quintet for strings*]. In a letter to Ambroise Thomas (6 July 1864), Massenet wrote that he had just finished a quintet for strings. Lost?

[*Second trio, for piano, violin, cello*]. (1) Première pièce; (2) Larghetto; (3) Finale en Sicilienne. No mention has been found of a first trio. A "second trio" is described as such in letters of 11 Mar. and 1 Apr. 1865.

Deux pièces, violoncelle et piano. (1) Andante; (2) (without title). Composed before 1866? Durand et Schoenewerck, 1877. See also *Pièces* for piano (1867).

Adagio religioso, violon solo et accompagnement de grand orgue avec pédales obligées. Aut.: Sept. 1867. Bibl. Nat., Ms. 4254.

Introduction et variations, pour quatuor à cordes, contrebasse, flûte, hautbois, clarinette, cor et basson. Performed by the Société Classique Armingaud, 26 Mar. 1872. Lost?

[*Quatuor à cordes*]. Composed before 1897. Lost?

Les Grands Violons du Roy Louis XV, pour 1ers et 2mes violons. Heugel, 1899.

ORATORIOS

Marie-Magdeleine. Drame sacré, three acts and four parts. Text, Louis Gallet. (I) La Magdaléenne à la fontaine; (II) Jésus chez la Magdaléenne; (III) (i) Le Golgotha; La Magdaléenne à la Croix; (ii) Le Tombeau de Jésus et la Résurrection. Performed by

Édouard Colonne and the Concert National, Odéon, Good Friday, 11 Apr. 1873 (Pauline Viardot as Méryem). P-v score: Hartmann, n.d. (plate no. 644).

Ève. Mystère, three parts. Text, Louis Gallet. Performed by Charles Lamoureux and the Société de l'Harmonie Sacrée, Cirque d'été, 18 Mar. 1875. P-v score: Hartmann, n.d. (plate no. 777).

La Vierge. Légende sacrée, four scenes. Text Charles Grandmougin. (1) L'Annonciation; (2) Les Noces de Cana; (3) Le Vendredi Saint; (4) L'Assomption. Finished 22 Aug. 1878. Performed (Massenet conducting at Concerts Historiques de l'Opéra, 22 May 1880. P-v score: Hartmann, n.d. (plate no. 1093).

La Terre promise. Oratorio biblique, three parts. Text, Massenet, after the Vulgate. (1) Moab; (2) Jéricho; (3) Chanaan. Performed at the church of Saint-Eustache, 15 Mar. 1900. Full score: Heugel, 1900.

OTHER RELIGIOUS WORKS

[Messe]. Composed March–May 1864. Lost?

Messe de Requiem. À 4 et 8 voix, avec accompagnement d'orgue, de violoncelles et de contrebasse. For four soli and four-part chorus. Cellos and basses added in the Dies Irae, Confutatis, and Offertory. Begun October 1864. This work and the "Ouverture orchestre" were sent to Paris in August 1865, as the envoi de Rome for 1864.

Ave Maris Stella. Motet à 2 voix, avec accompagnement de violon-celle ad libitum. Aut. 30 May 1880: Bibl. Nat., Ms. 4338. Hartmann, 1886.

Souvenez-vous, Vierge Marie: Prière de St. Bernard. (Memorare.) Choeur et solo, orgue et orchestre. Text, Charles Boyer. Aut. 6 Dec. 1880: Bibl. Nat., Ms. 4234. Performed by Pasdeloup, 27 Jan. 1881. Hartmann, 1881.

Pie Jésu, chant et orgue. Aut. 4 Feb. 1884: Bibl. Nat., Ms. 4339. Also with cello ad libitum: Heugel, 1893.

Biblis, scène religieuse. Mezzo-soprano, tenor, baritone, chorus, and orchestra. Text, Georges Boyer. Incipit: "La nuit emportant le mystère." Performed 27 Jan. 1887. P-v score: Hartmann, 1887.

O Salutaris. Soprano, organ, harp, and chorus. Heugel, 1894.

Panis angelicus. Voix d'homme [tenor, or baritone] et de femmes [2 soprani] et solo, ou pour voix seule (homme ou femme) [with organ accompaniment]. Heugel, 1910.

CANTATAS, CHORUSES

Louise de Mézières. Text, Édouard Monnais. Written *en loge* 17 May–10 June 1862, in competition for the Prix de Rome. The work received honorable mention. Lost?

David Rizzio. Text, Gustave Chouquet. Written *en loge* 16 May–8 June 1863, winning for Massenet the Premier Grand Prix de Rome. Only the *Ballade de David Rizzio* was published: Léon Escudier, n.d.

Alleluia. Mixed chorus, without accompaniment. Text, Gustave Chouquet. Incipit: "Sous un épais manteau de neige." First prize (1866), competition of the City of Paris. E. et A. Girod, n.d. (plate no. 5031).

Prométhée. Text, Romain Cornut. Written for one of three competitions opened by Napoleon III in 1867. (*See also* the operas *La Coupe du roi de Thulé* and *Le Florentin.*) Not performed. Music presumably utilized elsewhere.

Paix et Liberté, cantate. Performed at the Théâtre-Lyrique, 15 Aug. 1867. The manuscript (of which Massenet kept no copy) was taken to the Opéra-Comique and was there destroyed in the fire of 1887.

Narcisse. Idylle antique, for solo and chorus. Text, Paul Collin. Incipit: "O Phébus! O Phébus! tu te réveilles." Performed by the Société Guillot-Sainbris, 11 Feb. 1878. Hartmann, 1878. Also an Aut. orch. score (winter 1885–86): Bibl. Nat., Ms. 4267.

Apollon aux Muses [Apollo's Invocation]. Ode for tenor voice and orchestra. Text, Paul Collin. According to Séré, composed for England; also given Concerts du Conservatoire. A copy, revised and annotated by Massenet (Sept. 1884–Feb. 1885): Bibl. Nat., Ms. 4300. This became the great mystic scene in Act III of *Le Mage.*

La Fédérale. Marche de la Fédération des sociétés musicales de France, composée à l'occasion du centenaire de la Fédération de 1790. For unison chorus. Text, Georges Boyer. Incipit: "Au nom de la patrie et de la liberté." Hartmann, 1890.

Épithalame. Duet and unison chorus, with harpsichord accompaniment. Text, Armand Silvestre. Incipit: "Calliope blanche et seulette." In P. A. Silvestre, *Floréal* (Paris, 1891).

Les bluets. Chœur avec soli, pour 2 voix de femmes avec accompagnement de piano à 4 mains. Text, Jeanne Chaffotte. Heugel, 1899.

À la jeunesse. Chœur à 2 voix de femmes sans accompagnement. Text, Jules Combarieu. Heugel, 1904.

La Nef triomphale. Chorus and orchestra. Text, Jean Aicard. Performed at Monaco, 29 Mar. 1910. lost?

FOUR-PART MALE CHORUSES

(Author of the text is in parentheses.)

"1812" (E. Moreau). Incipit: "Salut, Moscou! Salut ville sainte!" Aut. Feb. 1860: Bibl. Opéra.

La caravane perdue. Scène chorale pour voix d'hommes (Noilhan-Lamontine). Composed 1867? Aut.: Bibl. Nat., Ms. 4257, with annotation stricken: "Morceau imposé à la division d'excellence, concours du 4 et 5 Juin 1870."

Le Moulin (Gustave Chouquet). Incipit: "Lorsque notre moulin tourne plein." E. et A. Girod, n.d. (plate no. 5032), with annotation: "Couronné au concours de la ville de Paris, 1868."

Villanelle (Jules Ruelle). Composed 1872?

Moines et Forbans (Gustave Chouquet). Incipit: "La nuit va couvrir de son voile." Hartmann, n.d. (plate no. 949). Set piece for a choral competition at Lyon, 20 May 1877.

Cantate en l'honneur du Bienheureux Jean-Gabriel Perboyre, missionnaire Lazariste. Chœur à 4 voix d'hommes et baryton solo avec ou sans accompagnement d'orgue. Composed 1879? Aut.: Bibl. Nat., Ms. 4301. Hartmann, 1890.

Le Sylphe (E. Bernier). Aut 1879: Bibl. Opéra.

Amour (Paul Milliet). Aut. 16 May 1880: Bibl. Opéra. "Écrit pour le concours international de Romans et Bourg Péage, 8–9 août 1880."

Alerte (Joseph Massiat). Ca. 1880–86?

Donnons (Georges Boyer). 1886?

Chant de concorde (Simon Salmona). 1893?

Mort a Néron! (Maurice Galerne). Heugel, 1913.

VOCAL DUOS, TRIOS, QUARTETS

Deux duos et un trio (Camille Distel). Women's voices. (1) Marine, duettino: "Viens, la voile Putine avec le vent"; (2) Joie, duetto pour deux soprani: "Un oiselet sautille et chante"; (3) Matinée d'été, trio pour voix de femmes: "Le beau matin vient de luire." Issued by Durand, Schoenewerck et Cie, 1879, in *Trois mélodies, deux duos et un trio, Op. 2* (plate no. 2650). There may have been an 1868 edition. *Joie* was published by Mme Maeyens-Couvreur in 1869. In 1880, Durand, Schoenewerck et Cie is identified as "Ancien Maison G. Flaxland."

Le soir (L. Baillet). Duo pour voix de femmes. Aut. 18–19 Apr. 1870: Bibl. Nat. Ms. 4309. Hartmann, 1872.

Au large (Louisa Seiffert). Duo pour mezzo-soprano et baryton. Aut. 7 May 1871: Bibl. Nat. Ms. 4318.

Dialogue nocturne (Armand Silvestre). Duo pour soprano et ténor. Aut. 24 July 1871: Bibl. Nat. Ms. 4320.

Rêvons, c'est l'heure (Paul Verlaine). Duo pour soprano et ténor. Aut. 26 July 1871: Bibl. Nat. Ms. 4312. Hartmann, 1872.

Salut, printemps (L. Baillet). Duo pour voix égales. Hartmann, 1879.

Horace et Lydie (Alfred de Musset, after Horace). Duo pour soprano et baryton. Aut. 23 Feb. 1886: Bibl. Nat. Ms. 4233. Heugel, 1893. In collected *Mélodies*, Vol. 4 (1896), No. 19.

Lui et elle (Thérèse Maquet). À deux voix. Deux mélodies: (1) Lui; (2) Elle. Hartmann, 1891.

Aux étoiles (Thérese Maquet). Duo ou choeur pour 2 voix de femmes. Hartmann, 1891.

Les fleurs (Jacques Normand). Duo pour soprano et baryton. Heugel, 1894. (*Mélodies*, IV, 20). Also orchestrated.

Noël. Scène chorale à 2 voix de femmes et solo, avec accompagnement de piano. Heugel, 1895.

La chevrière (Édouard Noël). Petit conte rustique pour 2 voix de femmes et solo avec accompagnement de piano. Heugel, 1895. Version with orchestra, Aut. Sept. 1901: Heugel archives.

Chansons des bois d'Amaranthe (Marc Legrand, after Redwitz). Suite for soprano, contralto, tenor, baritone, with piano accompaniment. (1) "O bon printemps" (trio); (2) "Oiseau des bois" (duo); (3) "Chères fleurs" (quartet); (4) "O ruisseau" (trio); (5) "Chantez" (quartet). Composed 1900. Heugel, 1901. Ded. "À ma fille, Madame Léon Bessand." Also orchestrated.

Poème des fleurs (Biagio Allievo, trans. by Armand Gaspuy). (1) Prelude (2 soprani, contralto); (2) L'Hymne des fleurs (contralto solo); (3) La danse des rameaux (2 soprani); (4) Chanson de mai (chorus of women's voices). Composed 1907. Heugel, 1908.

Le temps et l'amour (Ludana). Duo pour ténor et baryton. Heugel, 1907.

L'heure solitaire (Joseph Ader). Duo pour soprano et contralto. Heugel, 1908.

Immortalité (Jules Combarieu). Canon à 2 voix. Incipit: "Pour le juste, la vie n'est point ici-bas." Aut. Sept. 1909: Library of Congress. Revue musicale (supplement), 15 Oct. 1909.

La Gavotte de Puyjoli (Édouard Noël). Gavotte chantée et dansée pour soprano et baryton. Incipit: "La marquise a dit: 'Mon bon Puyjoli'." Aut. 21 June 1909: Moldenhauer Archives. Heugel, 1909. (*Mélodies*, VII, 10)

La Chanson du ruisseau (Antonin Lugnier). Choeur avec solo, pour 2 voix de femmes, Heugel, 1912.

La Vision de Loti (Édouard Noël). Poème mélodique a 4 voix: soprano, contralto, ténor et baryton. Heugel, 1912.

SONGS

In approximate chronological order.[*] Poet in parentheses; incipit in quotation marks. Roman-Arabic references (as: I, 20) are to volume and number in the collected *Mélodies*: I (ca. 1875); II (ca. 1881); III (1891); IV (1896); V (1900); VI (1903); VII (1912); VIII (1914).

1867–1869

Ballade de David Rizzio (Gustave Chouquet). "Le pâtre, à l'écho des montagnes." From the prize cantata af 1863. Léon Escudier, n.d. (plate no. 2334).

L'Improvisatore: rimembranza del Trastevere (G. Zaffira). Aut. Rome, Oct. 1864–Paris, Jan. 1870 [cf. I, 20]. Also for tenor and orchestra: aut. 28 Aug. 1872: Bibl. Nat. Ms. 4259.

Nouvelle chanson sur un vieil air (Victor Hugo). Aut. Venice, 6 Sept. 1865–Paris, 6 Mar. 1869.

Souvenir de Venise (Alfred de Musset). "À Saint Blaise, à la Zuecca." Composed 1865? Also aut. Paris, 24 Feb. 1872 [I, 16]. Also arranged for two sopranos as *À la Zuecca, chanson vénitienne* (Hartmann, n.d., plate no. 812).

"Je crains tes baisers, ô vierge charmante" (Gustave Chouquet, after Shelley). Aut. Paris, June 1866. Included in *Chants intimes* 1869. [II, 15]

Poème d'avril (Armand Silvestre). Composed 1866? Hartmann, n.d. (plate no. 211). Ded. Ernest Reyer. (1) Prélude: "Une rose frileuse" (recited); (2) Sonnet matinal: "Les étoiles effarouchées"; (3) "Voici que les grands lys"; (4) "Riez-vous?" (recited); (5) Vous aimerez demain: "Le doux printemps a bu" [I, 5]; (6) "Que l'heure est donc brève"; (7) "Sur la source elle se pencha"; (8) Complainte: "Nous nous sommes aimés trois jours."

Poème du souvenir (Armand Silvestre). Composed 1868? Hartmann, n.d. (1) À la trépassée: "Lève-toi, chère ensevelie!" [I, 8]; (2) "L'air du soir emportait"; (3) "Un souffle de parfums"; (4) "Dans l'air plein de fils de soie"; (5) "Pour qu'à l'espérance"; (6) Épitaphe: "Souvenir éternel."

Quatre mélodies. (1) L'Esclave (Théophile Gautier): "Captive et peut-être oubliée," ded. Mme Charles Moulton; (2) Sérénade aux mariés (Jules Ruelle): "Voici l'heure du

---

[*] For an alphabetical listing, see Noske (1970), 372–387.

mystère"; (3) La vie d'une rose (Jules Ruelle): "Par un beau matin," ded. Mme Miolan-Carvalho; (4) Le portrait d'une enfant (Ronsard): "Quand je vois tant de couleurs," ded. Mme Ulysse Trélat. E. et A. Girod, 1868.

Sous les branches (Armand Silvestre). "En avril sous les branches." Aut. 13 May 1868. Hartmann, 1869 [I, 10].

Trois mélodies (Camille Distel). Composed 1868? Issued by Durand, Schoenewerck et Cie, 1879, in *Trois mélodies, deux duos et un trio, Op. 2* (plate no. 2650). (1) Bonne nuit: "La terre dort au ciel pur"; (2) Le bois de pins, souvenir de Douarnenez: "L'ombre descend de leurs rameaux"; (3) Le verger, ancienne chansonnette: "Oh! combien j'aime le verger."

Chants intimes (Gustave Chouquet). (1) Déclaration (after Shelley): "Je crains tes baisers, ô vierge charmante" (*see* 1866); (2) À Mignonne: "Pour qui sera, Mignonne" (plate no. 276) [II, 18]; (3) Berceuse: "Enfant rose, fleur éclose" (plate no. 277) [III, 11]. Hartmann, 1869.

Sérénade du Passant (François Coppée). "Mignonne, voici l'avril." Hartmann, 1869 [I, 9]. Also known as *Sérénade de Zanetto*. Text from Coppée's comedy *Le Passant*.

Sonnet (Georges Pradel). "Les grands bois s'éveillaient." Hartmann, 1869 [II, 5].

1871–1875

1871–72; s*ee* Vol. I: 2, 7, 12, 18.

Poème pastoral (Scènes de Florian et d'Armand Silvestre). Aut. June 1872. Edition with etchings by Abel Orry: Hartmann, n.d. (plate no. 668). (1) Pastorale: "Voici venir le doux printemps" (choeur a 3 voix); (2) Musette (Florian): "L'autre jour sous l'ombrage" [III, 6]; (3) Aurore: "Cocorico, le coq chante"; (4) Paysage: "Arbre charmant qui me rappelle"; (5) Crépuscule: "Comme un rideau sous le blancheur"; [I, 15] (6) Adieux, à la prairie: "Adieu! adieu! bergère chérie" (1 voix et choeur à 3 voix). Nos. 2, 3, 5 also orchestrated.

Nuit d'Espagne (Lauis Gallet). "L'air est embaumé." Hartmann, 1874 [I, 6]. First entitled, *L'heure d'amour. Air de ballet des scènes pittorèsques. Prose rythmé sur une chanson serbe par Louis Gallet.* Then: *Guitare.* Unrelated to *Guitare* (Victor Hugo), 1886.

Volume I: 20 Mélodies. Hartmann, ca. 1875 (plate no. 756).

1 Élégie (Louis Gallet). "O doux printemps d'autrefois." Ded. Mme Marie Brousse. Also E. et A. Girod, 1875.

2 À Colombine: sérénade d'Arlequin (Louis Gallet). "Colombine charmante." Ded. Mme Ernest Bertrand [aut. 17 Feb. 1872]. Hartmann, 1872.

3 Les Femmes de Magdala (Louis Gallet). "Le soleil effleure la plaine." Ded. Ernest Hébert.

4 Stances de Gilbert (Laurent Gilbert). "Au banquet de la vie, infortuné." Ded. Mme Édouard Lalo.

5 Vous aimerez demain (Armand Silvestre). "Le doux printemps a bu." Ded. Mme Charles Moulton. From *Poème d'avril*, 1866.

6 Nuit d'Espagne (Louis Gallet). "L'air est embaumé." Ded. Gustave Dreyfus. *See* 1874.

7 Chant provençal (Michel Carré). "Mireille ne sais pas encore." Ded. Mme Michel Carré [aut. Fontainebleau, 23 July 1871]. Also orchestrated: aut. 4 June 1880 (Bibl. Nat. Ms. 4264).

8 A la trépassée (Armand Silvestre). "Lève-toi, chère ensevelie." Ded. Carolus Duran. From *Poème du souvenir*, 1868.

9 Sérénade du Passant (François Coppée). "Mignonne, voici l'avril." Ded. Mme Miolan-Carvalho. *See* 1869. Also orchestrated.

10 Sous les branches (Armand Silvestre). "En avril sous les branches." Ded. Marie Delessert. *See* 1868

11 "Dors, ami, dors et que les songes" (Jules Chantepie). Ded. Mme Galli Marié.

12 Il pleuvait: impromptu-mélodie (Armand Silvestre). "Il pleuvait, l'épaisseur des mousses." Ded. Mlle Antoinette Faure [aut. Fontainebleau, 8 June–2 Aug. 1871].

13 Chanson de Capri (Louis Gallet). "Connaissez-vous qui m'a charmé?" Coupure de *Don César de Bazan*. Ded. Diaz de Soria.

14 Un adieu (Armand Silvestre). "Sur ta bouche avec le désir." Ded. J. Bouhy.

15 Crépuscule (Armand Silvestre). "Comme un rideau sous la blancheur." Ded. Mlle N. Stamaty. From *Poème pastoral*, 1872.

16 Souvenir de Venise (Alfred de Musset). "À Saint Blaise, à la Zuecca." Ded. Albert Cahen. *See* 1865.

17 Sonnet païen (Armand Silvestre). "Rosa, Rosa, l'air est plus doux." Ded. Hermann Léon.

18 Sérénade d'automne (Augustine-Malvine Blanchecotte). "Non! tu n'as pas fini d'aimer." Ded. Marie Trélat [aut. Biarritz, 15 Apr. 1871].

19 Madrigal (Armand Silvestre). "Le soir frissonne au coeur des roses." Ded. J. Nicot.

20 L'Improvisateur (G. Zaffira, trans. by R. Bussine jeune). "Vois-tu là-bas sur le chemin." Ded. L. Pagans. *See L'Improvisatore*, 1864.

1876–1881

Poème d'octobre (Paul Collin). Composed 1876? Hartmann, 1070 (plate no. 1041). Ded. Ernest Hébert. Prélude: "Qu'il est doux d'éveiller"; (1) "Profitons bien des jours d'automne" [III, 13]; (2) "Hélas! les marronniers"; (3) "Qu'importe que l'hiver éteigne les clartés"; (4) "Belles frileuses qui sont nées" [II, 16]; (5) "Pareils à des oiseaux que leur aile meurtrie."
1876–77; *see* Vol. II: 1, 3, 7, 8, 20.

Poème d'amour (Paul Robiquet). Aut. Sept. 1878–Nov. 1879. Hartmann, 1880. Nos. 1-5: *Lui*, No. 6: *Elle, Lui*. (1) "Je me suis plaint aux tourtourelles"; (2) "La nuit, sans doute, était trop belle"; (3) "Ouvre tes yeux bleus" [III, 12]; (4) "Puisqu'elle a pris ma vie" [II, 19]; (5) "Pourquoi pleures-tu?" (6) Duo: "Oh! ne finis jamais, nuit clémente."

Sérénade de Molière: Musique du temps, transcrite par J. Massenet. "C'est un amant, ouvrez la porte" [II, 2]. Hartmann, 1880.

Anniversaire: Devant la maison de Th. Gautier, Octobre 1880 (Armand Silvestre). "Le poète dort: l'oiseau chante" [II, 6]. (Gautier died 23 Oct. 1872 at 32 Rue de Longchamps, Paris, 16me.)

Come into the garden, Maud (Alfred Tennyson). In: Songs from the published writings of Alfred Tennyson (Poet Laureate) set to music by various composers, edited by W. G. Cusius. London: Kegan Paul, 1880.
1880; *see also* Vol. II: 13, 17.

Les enfants (Georges Boyer). "On ne devrait faire aux enfants" [III, 1]. Aut. 22 June 1881. Hartmann, 1882. Also orchestrated: aut. 4 Aug. 1883.

Volume II: 20 Mélodies. Hartmann, ca. 1881 (plate no. 1250).

   1 "Si tu veux, Mignonne" (Georges Boyer). Hartmann, 1876. Also orchestrated: aut. 12 Dec. 1887.

   2 Sérénade de Molière. "C'est un amant, ouvrez la porte." Hartmann, 1880.

   3 Les oiselets (Jacques Normand). "Sous le brouillard léger que soulève l'aurore." Hartmann, 1877 (plate no. 877).

   4 "Loin de moi ta lèvre qui ment" (Jean Aicard).

   5 Sonnet (Georges Pradel). "Les grands bois s'éveillaient." Hartmann, 1869.

   6 Anniversaire (Armand Silvestre). "Le poète dort: l'oiseau chante." *See* 1880.

   7 Aubade (Gabriel Prévost). "Le jour parait à l'horizon." Hartmann, 1877.

   8 Le sentier perdu: idylle (Paul de Choudens). "J'ai voulu le revoir ce sentier sous les bois." Hartmann, 1877.

   9 Les alcyons (Joseph Autran). "Vos destins sont pour l'homme un étrange mystère."

 10 Narcisse à la fontaine (Paul Collin). "Enfin, elles s'en vont."

 11 "Que l'heure est donc brève" (Armand Silvestre). From *Poème d'avril*, 1866.

 12 "Souvenez-vous, Vierge Marie" (Georges Boyer). *See also under* Other Religious Works, 1880.

 13 Souhait (Jacques Normand). "Si vous étiez fleur, ô ma bien aimée." Hartmann, 1880.

 14 Néére (Michel Carré). "Au détour du chemin, ma Néére fidèle." Adapted from *Les Érinnyes* (La Troyenne regrettant la patrie perdue).

 15 Déclaration (Gustave Chouquet, after Shelley). "Je crains tes baisers, ô vierge charmante." Aut. 1866, and *Chants intimes*, 1869.

 16 Roses d'octobre (Paul Collin). "Belles frileuses qui sont nées." From *Poème d'octobre*, 1876.

 17 Le sais-tu? (Stéphan Bordèse). "N'as-tu pas vu l'hirondelle?" Hartmann, 1880.

 18 À Mignonne (Gustave Chouquet). "Pour qui sera, Mignonne." From *Chants intimes*, 1869.

 19 "Puisqu'elle a pris ma vie" (Paul Robiquet). From *Poème d'amour*, 1878–79.

 20 La veillée du petit Jésus (André Theuriet). "Il est minuit, l'étable est sombre." Composed 1876?

1882–1891

Poème d'hiver (Armand Silvestre). Hartmann, 1882. (1) "C'est au temps de la chrysanthème"; (2) "Mon coeur est plein de toi"; (3) "Noël! en voyant dans ses langes"; (4) "Tu l'as bien dit: je ne sais pas t'aimer."

"Où qui s'envole" (Paul Bourguignat). Aut. Oct. 1884.

1884; *see also* Vol. III: 7.

1886: *see* Vol. III: 5, 16, 19; Vol. IV: 9, 10, 14, 17.

Pensée d'automne (Armand Silvestre). "L'an fuit vers son déclin" [III, 17]. Aut. 25 Sept. 1887. Orchestrated for Sibyl Sanderson: aut. 24 Nov. 1888 (Bibl. Nat.).

Fleurs cueillies (Louis Bricourt). "Vous avez pris un jour une fleur, ô ma belle." Rouen: A. Klein; and Paris: G. Hartmann, 1888.

Enchantement (Jules Ruelle). "Comme un rayon qui luit" [III, 2]. Sur un air de ballet d'Hérodiade, paroles adaptées par Jules Ruelle; arrangé 1890. Hartmann, 1890. 1887–89; *see also* Vol. III: 8, 9, 18.

Rien n'est que de France (Armand Silvestre). "Où sont, sous les matins en pleurs." With accompaniment of harp or harpsichord. In P. A. Silvestre, *Floréal* (Paris, 1891).

L'âme des fleurs (Paul Delair). "Gardez les fleurs que je vous ai données." A. Quinzard, 1891 (plate no. 1).

Les mères (Georges Boyer). "Celle qui devient mère, a comme une auréole." Aut. 25 Oct. 1891. A. Quinzard, 1892 (plate no. 92). A second version: aut. 9 July 1901.

La neige (Stéphan Bordese). "L'enfant Jésus, né dans l'hiver." Durand, 1891. 1891; *see also* Vol. IV: 4, 13.

Volume III: 20 Mélodies. Heugel, 1891 (plate no. 7041).

1. Les enfants (Georges Boyer). "On ne devrait faire aux enfants." *See* 1881.
2. Enchantement (Jules Ruelle). "Comme un rayon qui luit." *See* 1890.
3. Septembre (Hélène Vacaresco). "Que les premiers jours de Septembre."
4. "Dans le sentier parmi les roses" (Jean Bertheroy).
5. Guitare (Victor Hugo). "Comment, disaient-ils, avec nos nacelles," Hartmann, 1886.
6. Musette (Florian). "L'autre jour, sous l'ombrage." From *Poème pastoral*, 1872.
7. Printemps dernier (Philiippe Gille). Aut. 6 Aug. 1884. Hartmann, 1885.
8. Marquise: menuet pour chant (Armand Silvestre). "Vous en souvenez-vous, Marquise?" Hartmann, 1888.
9. Les belles de nuit. (Thérese Maquet). "Joyeux et clair, le soleil luit." Aut. 2 Sept. 1887.
10. "Je cours après le bonheur" (Guy de Maupassant).
11. Berceuse (Gustave Chouquet). "Enfant rose, fleur éclose" From *Chants intimes*, 1869.
12. "Ouvre tes yeux bleus" (Paul Robiquet). From *Poème d'amour*, 1878–79. Also orchestrated.
13. Automne (Paul Collin). "Profitons bien des jours d'automne." From *Poème d'octobre*, 1876.
14. Le poète et le fantôme (No poet given). "Qui donc es-tu, forme légère?" Also orchestrated.
15. Beaux yeux que j'aime (Thérèse Maquet). "Il est des étoiles aux cieux."
16. Noël païen (Armand Silvestre). "Noël! Noël! sous le ciel étonné." Hartmann, 1886.
17. Pensée d'automne (Armand Silvestre). "L'an fuit vers son déclin." *See* 1887.
18. Royauté (Georges Boyer). "Le poète est roi." Aut. 6 Sept. 1889.
19. Quand on aime: sérénade (Eugène Manuel). "Quand on aime, on est tout léger." Aut. 1886. Another aut., inscribed to Georges Hartmann, 23 Apr. 1887.
20. Sonnet matinal (Armand Silvestre). "Les étoiles effarouchées." From *Poème d'avril*, 1866.

1892–1896

1892; *see* Vol. IV: 8.

1893; *see* Vol. IV: 2, 3, 12, 16, 18; Vol. VIII: 16.

Mienne! (Ernest Laroche). "De ce soir, je serai joyeux." Heugel, 1894.

Soir de printemps: déclamatorium (Gabriel Martin). Heugel, 1894.

Tristesse (P. Carrier). "Marcher dans un sentier de pierres et de roses." Heugel, 1894. 1894–95; *see also* Vol. IV: 3, 6, 11, 15.

Poème d'un soir (Georges Vanor). Heugel, 1895. (1) Antienne: "Tes yeux aux lueurs fières"; (2) Fleuramye: "J'ai bu tout le printemps sur la fleur de ton rire"; (3) Defuncta nascuntur: "Les roses se sont fermées."

Berceuse (Henri Gibout). Heugel, 1896.

Volume IV: 20 Mélodies. Heugel, 1896 (plate no. 8305).

1 L'âme des oiseaux (Hélène Vacaresco). "Le printemps a jeté sa lyre." Ded. Mme Trouard-Riolle.

2 Pensée de printemps (Armand Silvestre). "C'est l'espoir des beaux jours." Ded. Mlle Madeleine de Nocé. Heugel, 1893. Also orchestrated.

3 Je t'aime (Suzanne Bozzani). "J'ai cherché dans mon coeur." Ded. Marie Delna. Heugel, 1893. Also orchestrated.

4 Chanson andalouse: sur un air de ballet du Cid (Jules Ruelle). "Pourquoi chanter l'amoureuse ivresse?" Ded. M. Lauwers. Heugel, 1891.

5 Ave Maria: composé sur la Méditation de Thaïs. "Ave Maria, gratia plena." Heugel, 1894.

6 Hymne d'amour (Paul Desachy). "Comme un lierre grimpant s'enlace." Ded. Lucienne Bréval. Aut. 20 Mar. 1895. Heugel, 1895. Also orchestrated.

7 Devant l'infini (Émile Troillet). "Les feuilles dans les airs tourbillonnent."

8 "Ne donne pas ton coeur aux roses du chemin" (Paul Mariéton). Ded. Mme M. Japy Steinheil. Heugel, 1892.

9 Plus vite (Hélène Vacaresco). "Lorsque le vent du soir l'agite." Aut. 25 Sept. 1886 (Heugel archives).

10 Chant de guerre cosaque (Hélène Vacaresco). "Vierge, tes cheveux noirs dépassent ta ceinture." Aut. 23 Sept. 1886 (Heugel archives).

11 Sévillana: sur l'entr'acte de Don César de Bazan (Jules Ruelle). "À Séville, belles Señoras." Arranged 1895. Heugel, 1895. Also orchestrated.

12 Fourvières (Maurice Léna). "Dans la brume rêveuse." Ded. Mons. Cretin-Perny. Heugel, 1893.

13 L'éventail: vieille chanson française (Morel-Retz). "Aimable bijou de famille, éventail léger." Ded. Marguerite Vilma. Aut Apr. 1891. Heugel, 1892.

14 Séparation (Paul Mariéton). "Puisque tu ne veux pas m'attendre." Ded. Mme Charles Dettelbach. Aut. 24 Sept. 1886.

15 Elle s'en est allée (Lucien Solvay). "Là-bas, sous d'autres cieux." Ded. Mlle Rachel Neyt. Heugel, 1895.

16 Larmes maternelles (M. C. Delines, after Nekrassoff). "La guerre a fait une victime." Ded. Victor Maurel. Heugel, 1893. Also orchestrated.

17 Jour de noces (Stéphan Bordèse). "Il fait beau, le ciel nous protège." Ded. Mme Conneau. Aut. 18 Feb. 1886.

18 Départ (Guérin-Catelain). "Puisque pour moi le temps a sonné." Ded. Esther Sidner. Heugel, 1893. Also orchestrated.

19 Horace et Lydie: duo (Alfred de Musset). "Du temps où tu m'aimais, Lydie." *See under* Duos, 1886.

20 Les fleurs: duo (Jacques Normand). "Jetant leur fantaisie exquise de couleurs." Ded. Jules Diaz de Soria and his daughter. *See under* Duos, 1894.

1897–1900

Souvenance (Paul Mariéton). "J'ai vu tous les yeux qu'on aime en ce monde." Heugel, 1897.

1897; *see also* Vol. V: 11, 16, 17, 18; Vol. VII: 14; Vol. VIII: 9.

1898; *see* Vol. V: 2, 4, 9, 10, 13, 19.

Éternité (Marguerite Girard). "L'éternité! je l'ai comprise." Ded. F. Castelbon de Beaux-hostes. Béziers: Justin Robert, 1899.

Passionnément (Charles Fuster). "Tout recevoir de toi me charme." Ded. Mme M. Montégu-Montibert. Heugel, 1899.

1899; *see also* Vol. V: 1, 3, 5, 6, 7, 8, 12, 14, 15, 20; Vol. VIII: 12.

1900; *see* Vol. VI: 2, 15, 17, 18, 19, 20; Vol. VII: 3, 17.

Volume V: 20 Mélodies. Heugel, 1900 (plate no. 20,292).

1 Chanson pour bercer la misère humaine (Georges Bouver). "Le petit Jésus, en habits de neige." Ded. Gisèle Boyer. Heugel, 1899. Also orchestrated.

2 Amoureuse (Morel-Retz). "Tu voudrais lire dans mon âme." Ded. Charlotte Wyns. Heugel, 1898.

3 Première danse (Jacques Normand). "Des bons vieux airs connus." Ded. Mlle Gabrielle Lejeune. Heugel, 1899. Also orchestrated.

4 Regard d'enfant (Léon G. Pélissier). "Petit enfant, fragile et beau." Ded. Mme Henri Heugel. Heugel, 1898.

5 Petite Mireille (Bernand Beissier). "Lorsque vous dormez." Ded. Reynaldo Hahn. Heugel, 1899.

6 Pour Antoinette (Paul de Chabaleyret). "Quand je m'en vais par les sentiers." Ded. Mlle Rachel Lawney. Aut. 23 Aug. 1899.

7 Les mains (Noël Bazan). "Lorsque je regarde mes mains." Ded. Comtesse de Maupeou. Heugel, 1899.

8 "Ce sont les petits que je veux chanter" (Édouard Grieumard). Ded. Jean and Madeleine Gironce. Heugel, 1899.

9 Les âmes (Paul Demouth). "Dites-moi ce que sont les âmes." Ded. Mlle Marie-Laure Constantin. Heugel, 1898.

10 La dernière chanson (Louis Lefebvre). "Si désormais vivre ensemble." Heugel, 1898.

11 Premiers fils d'argent (Marie de Valandré). "Le soir, quand pour dormir." Ded. Mme Alice Vois. Heugel, 1897.

12 Coupe d'ivresse (H. Ernest Simoni). "Jusqu'à ta bouche, j'ai levé la coupe." Heugel, 1899.

13 Vieilles lettres (Jacques Normand). "Quand chauffant nos pieds aux tisons." Ded. Paul Séguy. Heugel, 1898.

14 Vous qui passez (Paul de Chabaleyret). "O vous qui passez, solitaire." Heugel, 1899.

15 Amours bénis (André Alexandre). "Une aube fraîche et printanière." Ded. Mme Oulmont. Heugel, 1899.

16 Pitchounette: farandole pour chant (Jacques Normand). "Pitchounette, entends-tu pas." Ded. Mlle Eléonore Blanc. Heugel, 1897. Also orchestrated.

17 À deux pleurer (J. Le Croze). "Comme vous dormiez." Ded. Croze. Aut. 20 Aug. 1897.

18 Chanson pour elle (Henri Maigrot). "Pour toi j'écris cette chanson." Ded. Mme Bréjean-Gravière. Heugel, 1897.

19 Le nid (Paul Demouth). "Si j'étais le bon Dieu." Ded. Mme M. Japy Steinheil. Heugel, 1898.

20 "Avril est là, chantant." (François Ferrand). Ded. Rose Ferrand. Heugel, 1899.

1901–1903

On dit (Jean Roux). "On dit beaucoup de choses." Heugel, 1901. Also transcribed by Massenet for piano as *Simple phrase*.

1901; *see also* Vol. VI: 8, 9, 13, 14.

Quelques chansons mauves (André Lebey). Heugel, 1902. (1) "En même temps que ton amour"; (2) "Quand nous nous sommes vus pour la première fois"; (3) "Jamais un tel bonheur."

1902; *see also* Vol. VI: 1, 3, 4, 5, 6, 7, 10, 11, 12, 16; Vol. VIII: 19.

1903; *see* Vol. VII: 2; Vol. VIII: 13.

Trois poèmes chastes. Heugel, 1903. (1) Le pauv' petit, légende (Georges Boyer): "Il était un petit enfant." (2) Vers Béthléem (Paul Le Moyne): "Ils cheminent depuis longtemps"; ded. Luc-Olivier Merson; aut. Sept. 1903; (3) La légende du baiser (Jean de Villeurs): "Un jour de fête au Paradis"; ded. Mlle Jeanne Salomon.

Vol. VI: 20 Mélodies. Heugel, 1903 (plate no. 21,704).

1 Je m'en suis allé vers l'amour (Théodore Maurer). "Pleins d'un concert de fraîches voix." Ded. J. Faure. Heugel, 1902.

2 Ce que disent les cloches (Jean de la Vingtrie). "Les cloches tintent dans l'air triste." Ded. Mme Marie Grandeau. Heugel, 1900.

3 Poésie de Mytis. "Lorsque nous serons seuls." Published in *Musica*, 1902.

4 Sainte Thérèse prie (Pierre Sylvestre). "Je le possède." Ded. Mme Rose Caron. Heugel, 1902. Also orchestrated.

5 L'heure volée (Catulle Mendès). "Sonneur qui sonnes l'heure et l'heure." Ded. F. Delmas. Heugel, 1902.

6 Extase printanière (André Alexandre). "O je t'implore à genoux." Ded. Mlle Madeleine de Nocé. Heugel, 1902.

7 L'heureuse souffrance. "Coeur, va vite, pauvre coeur." Chanson de cour Henri IV, recueillie et arrangée par Georges de Dubor. Ded. Mme M. de Laboulaye. Heugel, 1902.

8 Voix de femmes (Pierre d'Amor). "Voix des mamans, voix câlineuses." Ded. Mme Jeanne Raquet-Delmée. Heugel, 1901.

9 Mousmé (André Alexandre). "Au jardin de ma fantaisie, fleur du Japon, Mousmé jolie." Heugel, 1901.

10 Avec toi! (Julien Gruaz). "Avec ton courir dans les plaines." Ded. Robert Le Lubez. Heugel, 1902.

11 "Les amoureuses sont des folles." (Duc de Tarente). Ded. Mlle Emelen, de l'Opéra-Comique. Heugel, 1902.

12 Ave Margarita: prière d'amour (Édouard Noël). "Je te salue, ô Marguerite." Ded. Mlle Blanche Gellée. Heugel, 1902.

13 On dit (Jean Roux). "On dit beaucoup de choses." Ded. Mlle Georgette Wallace. Heugel, 1901.

14 "Le printemps visite la terre." (Jeanne Chaffotte). Ded. A. Chaffotte. Heugel, 1901.

15 Rondel de la belle au bois (Julien Gruaz). "Ouvrez vos tendres yeux." Ded. Mlle Fanchon Thompson. Heugel, 1900.

16 Sur une poésie de Van Hasselt: L'Attente. "L'azur si pur des cieux joyeux." Ded. Mme Albert Duval. Heugel, 1902.

17 Soeur d'élection (Émile Troillet). "O ma soeur d'idéal." Ded. Mlle Lilly Marguerite Bécherat. Heugel, 1900. Also arranged for orchestra as *Cantique*.

18 Mon page (Maurice de Théus). "J'ai pour page un bel escholier." Ded. Mme de Nuovina. Heugel, 1900.

19 Amoureux appel (Georges de Dubor). "Viens, ô le désiré, viens chanter avec moi." Ded. Mlle Loventz, de l'Opéra. Heugel, 1900.

20 La rivière (Camille Bruno). "Ah! la rivière chantait ainsi." Ded. Mlle Lydia Nervil. Heugel, 1900. Also orchestrated.

1904–1912

Avant la bataille [de Reichshofen] (Jean de Villeurs). Facsimile of the aut. in *Figaro illustré* (Paris: Choudens, 1904).

"Dors, Magda, si blanche et si rose." (Armand Silvestre). Ded. Louis Coquelz. Heugel, 1905.

Chanson juanesque (Félicien Champsaur). "Toujours! et, demain, plus jamais!" [VIII, 14]. As musical prelude in Champsaur's *Saisons d'amour* (Paris, Bosc, n.d.). Also Heugel, 1905.

Tes cheveux (Camille Bruno). "Tels que les brins de paille fin." Heugel, 1905.

Chant de nourrice: pour chant et déclamation (Jean Aicard). "Dors, mon petit enfant, dors." Intended for a contralto, offstage and unseen, and "the Poet," who declaims near the piano. Ded. Mme Émile Viallet. Heugel, 1905.

1905; *see also* Vol. VII: 6, 15; Vol. VIII: 15.

La mélodie des baisers (André Alexandre). "Toujours les lilas fleuriront." Gabriel Astruc, 1906.

En chantant (Georges Boyer). "Dans la familiale demeure." Ded. Mlle Lucy Arbell, de l'Opéra. Heugel, 1906.

C'est le printemps (Adrien Gillouin). "L'azur sourit, le vent tiédit." Heugel, 1906.

1906; *see also* Vol. VII: 9; Vol. VIII: 17, 20.

L'heure douce (Ernest Chabroux). "Ainsi qu'un fier guerrier." Ded. Jean Bertheroy. Heugel, 1907.

1907–08; *see* Vol. VII: 4, 7, 8, 16.

Dormons par les lys (Hélène Picard). "C'est toi qui me diras les saisons infinies." Ded. Mme Maurice Sulzbach. Heugel, 1908.

La gavotte de Puyjoli (Édouard Noël). "La marquise a dit: 'Mon bon Puyjoli' " [VII, 10]. Ded. Mme Jules Claretie. Heugel, 1909. *See also under* Duos.

Ton souvenir (Émile Feillet). "Mon coeur n'est pas dépossédé." Heugel, 1909.

Dieu créa le désert (Madeleine Grain). Heugel, 1910.

Toujours (Paul Max). Heugel, 1910.

Retour de l'oiseau (Paul Stuart). Heugel, 1911.

1909–11; *see also* Vol. VII: 1, 5, 11, 12, 13; Vol. VIII: 5.

Effusion (Henri Allorge). "C'est toi que j'aime en la nature." Ded. Muratore. Heugel, 1912.

Volume VII: 20 Mélodies. Heugel, 1912 (plate no. 25,631).

    1 La mort de la cigale (Maurice Faure). Heugel, 1911.

    2 "Oh! si les fleurs avaient des yeux." (G. Buchillot). Extracted from *Chérubin*. Heugel, 1903.

3 Au très aimé (Caroline Duer). Heugel, 1900.

4 C'est l'amour (Victor Hugo). "Oh oui! ta terre est belle." Heugel, 1908.

5 Chanson désespérée (Edmond Teulet). Heugel, 1910.

6 La marchande des rêves (Armand Silvestre). "Pour faire mes heures plus brèves." Heugel, 1905.

7 La lettre (Mme Catulle Mendès). "Je mets sur le papier luisant." Heugel, 1907.

8 Le Noël des humbles (Jean Aicard). "L'enfant est nu." Heugel, 1908.

9 Orphelines (Ludana). "Elles marchent deux par deux." Heugel, 1906.

10 La gavotte de Puyjoli (Édouard Noël). "La marquise a dit: 'Mon bon Puyjoli'." *See* 1909.

11 Rêverie sentimentale (Mathylde Peyre). "Si tu m'aimes." Heugel, 1910.

12 Rien ne passe (Lucien Monrousseau). Heugel, 1911.

13 Tout passe (Camille Bruno). Heugel, 1909.

14 Si tu l'oses (Daniel Garcia Mansilla). Heugel, 1897.

15 Les yeux clos (G. Buchillot). Heugel, 1905.

16 "Si vous vouliez bien me le dire." (Ludana). Heugel, 1907.

17 Avril est amoureux (Jacques d'Halmont). "Avril dort sous la lune blanche." Heugel, 1900. Also orchestrated.

18 Âmes obscures (Anatole France). "Tout, dans l'immuable nature." Ded. Louise Grandjean, de l'Opéra. Heugel, 1912.

19 Heure vécue (Mme M. Jacquet). "Une nuit brune d'un soir d'hiver." Ded. Mlle Marié de l'Isle. Heugel, 1912.

20 Menteuse chérie (Ludana). "Menteuse chérie, lorsque tu m'as dit." Ded. Vanni Marcoux. Heugel, 1912.

Expressions lyriques: avec déclamation rythmée. Heugel, 1913 (plate nos. 26,127–26,136).

1 Dialogue: "Pourquoi donc ne dis-tu plus rien?" (Marc Varenne).

2 Les nuages: "Les voyez-vous passer sous le ciel monotone?" (Comtesse Maurice Roch de Louvencourt).

3 En voyage: "Où donc allez-vous, Madame, sans postillon ni piqueur?" (Théodore Maurer).

4 Battements d'ailes: "Les soirs d'été si doux, voilés de crêpes bleus" (Jeanne Dortzal).

5 La dernière lettre de Werther à Charlotte: "Il faut nous séparer" (Comte R. de Gontaut Biron).

6 Comme autrefois: "J'ai revêtu, ce soir, son large manteau noir" (Jeanne Dortzal).

7 Nocturne: "Il était minuit, la bonne odeur du bois" (Jeanne Dortzal).

8 Mélancholie: "Sur les flots de la vie, suivant ce qui me tient" (Anonymous).

9 Rose de mai: "Ce n'est pas ta beauté qui m'attire" (S. Poirson).

10 Feux follets d'amour: "Mes soeurs! dans cette nuit d'étoiles" (Madeleine Grain).

Volume VIII: 20 Mélodies. Heugel, 1914 (plate no. 26,480).

1 Aube païenne (Lucien Rocha). "Quand de mon tertre en fleur." Ded. Mme Payen-Rocha. Heugel, 1913.

2 La nuit (Victor Hugo). "Parfois, lorsque tout dort." Heugel, 1914.

3 Les extases (Annie Dessierier [Jean du Clos]). "Des chants, des fleurs et du soleil." Ded. Lucy Arbell. Heugel, 1912.

4 L'amour pleure: romance de jadis (Madeleine Postel). "Le pauvre Amour est tout en larmes." Ded. Marguerite Carré. Heugel, 1912.

5 Dites-lui que je l'aime (Georges Fleury-Daunizeau). "Dites-lui que les fleurs ont ouvert leur calice." Ded. Mouliérat, de l'Opéra-Comique. Heugel, 1910.

6 Soleil couchant (Victor Hugo). "Le soleil s'est couché ce soir." Ded. J. F. Delmas. Heugel, 1912.

7 Jamais plus (Olga de Sarmento). "Dans un nuage d'or." Ded. Nova Monteire Kendall. Heugel, 1912.

8 Soir de rêve (Antonin Lugnier). "Au bosquet de ta lèvre." Heugel, 1914.

9 La chanson des lèvres (Jean Lahor). "Lèvres, ô mères du baiser." Ded. Mme Georgette Leblanc. Heugel, 1897.

10 Voix suprême (Antoinette Lafaix-Gontié). "O murmure du vent qui monte." Ded. Virginie Haussmann. Heugel, 1912.

11 Si tu m'aimes (Anne Girard-Duverne). "Si tu m'aimes, dis-le ce mot qui fait ma vie." Ded. Maria Kousnietzoff, de l'Opéra. Heugel, 1912.

12 L'ange et l'enfant (Marie Barbier). "L'ange Amabed a cueilli des roses." Ded. Marie Barbier. Heugel, 1899.

13 Au delà du rêve (Gaston Hirsch). "Où n'atteindrai-je pas?" Ded. Mlle Pierina Tamburini. Heugel, 1903.

14 Chanson juanesque (Félicien Champsaur). "Toujours! et, demain, plus jamais!" See 1905.

15 Et puis . . . : rondel (Maurice Chassang). "Vous aurez la fleur d'oranger." Ded. Mme Marthe Chassang. Heugel, 1905.

16 Être aimé (Victor Hugo). "Être aimé! tout est là, vois-tu." Heugel, 1893.

17 Ivre d'amour (after Grégoire Akhtamar). "Je suis ivre d'amour." Ded. Mme Enriqueta Basavilbaso de Catelin. Heugel, 1906.

18 Noël des fleurs (Louis Schneider). "Il pleut des iris, des jasmins, des roses." Ded. Mme Charlotte Lormont. Heugel, 1912.

19 "Ma petite mère a pleuré" (Paul Gravollet). Heugel, 1902.

20 Éveil (Alfred Gassier). "La vierge étoile est effacée." Heugel, 1906.

L'oiseau de paradis (Jules Princet). Heugel, 1913.

Parfums (Jeanne Dortzal). Heugel, 1914.

Le coffret d'ébène (Victor Jannet). Heugel, 1914.

Je mourrai plus que toi (Paul Verlaine). Heugel, 1922.

La verdadera vida: coplas (Guillot de Saix). "La la la! La vie a mal guidé mes pas." Musique de J. Massenet et Marc Berthomieu. Heugel, 1933.

TRANSCRIPTIONS, ARRANGEMENTS, ORCHESTRATIONS

Carlo Baldi. *Marche napolitaine.* Transcribed for voice (text, Pierre Barbier) and piano. Heugel, 1903.

Boccherini. *Sicilienne de Boccherini.* Transcribed for piano. Bibl. Nat. Ms. 4251. Heugel, n.d.

Léo Delibes. *Les Nymphes du bois.* Chorus (text, Charles Nuitter). Orchestrated by Massenet. Bibl. Nat. Ms. 4299.

Léo Delibes. *Kassya.* Drame lyrique, four acts. Text, Henri Meilhac and Philippe Gille. Completed and orchestrated by Massenet. Paris, Opéra-Comique, 24 Mar. 1893.

Édouard Lalo. *Divertissement pour orchestre. See under* Piano, ca. 1872.

Franz Schubert. *La Mer. See under* Orchestra, 1891.
"En avant! casquette au front" (Marc Legrand). In: J. Hemmerlé (ed.), *Chansons du blé qui lève.*
"Yamez you nou beyrez": chant béarnais. In: Pascal Lamazou (ed.), *Airs béarnais les plus populaires*, 1887.

Mary Garden as Manon. Courtesy Paul Jackson.

Bibliographical Notes

Preface (pages XIII–XV)

1. Saint-Saëns, L'Écho de Paris, 13 Oct. 1912. Given in Bruneau (1935), 91–97.

2. See Ernst Krause, Richard Strauss: The Man and His Work, translated from the German by John Coombs (London: Collet, 1964): 204–205.

Chapter 1: Parentage and Early Life (pages 1–7)

1. Louis Schneider, Massenet: l'homme, le musicien (Paris: Carteret, 1908): 8.

2. Massenet, "Autobiographical Notes by the Composer Massenet," Century Magazine 45 (Nov. 1892): 122.

3. O. Berger-Levrault, Annales des professeurs des académies et universités alsaciennes, 1523–1871 (Nancy, 1892): 160.

4. Communicated by the Keeper of the Records, Senaat der Rijksuniversiteit tu Leiden.

5. Reuss, Jean-Pierre Massenet, 118.

6. Ibid., 124–126.

7. Ibid., 142.

Chapter 2: Paris; Chambéry (pages 8–14)

1. [Paris Conservatoire], Entrées et sorties des élèves, 1842–1870. Archives Nationales, F21-1290.

2. [Paris Conservatoire], Distribution des prix, 1831–1874. Archives Nationales, F21-1305.

3. Bibliothèque Nationale, autograph letters, No. 27.

4. [Paris Conservatoire], Entrées et sorties des élèves, 1842–1870. Archives Nationales, F21-1290.

5. Jules Vallès, in Le Réveil, 11 July 1882. Quoted in Schneider (1926), 17–18.

Chapter 3: The Prix de Rome (pages 15–27)

1. Victorin de Joncières, Le Gaulois, 23 Oct. 1898. Quoted in Schneider (1926), 19–22.

2. Constant Pierre, Le Conservatoire National de Musique et de Déclamation, Paris, 1900.

3. See Harold C. Schonberg, The Great Pianists (1963), 97–98.

4. Letter [ca. 1910] to Karl Lahm, published in Opern Welt, July 1961.

5. A. Pougin, "Massenet," *Rivista musicale italiana* 19 (1912) 916–985.

6. A copy of the *Grande Fantaisie* is in the Bibliothèque Nationale .

7. Communicated by the Archives de la Ville de Nice.

Chapter 4: The Villa Medici (pages 28–40)

1. To Ambroise Thomas, Rome, 29 Jan. 1864.

2. To Ambroise Thomas, 5 Mar. 1864.

3. To Thomas, 5 Mar. 1864.

4. Reproduced in Schneider (1908), 22.

5. To Thomas, 16 and 23 Apr. 1864.

6. To Thomas, 8 Oct. 1864.

7. To Sophie Hennequin, 29 Nov. [1864]. F. Gerald Borch collection.
   To Thomas, 22 Nov. and 4 Dec. 1864.

8. Académie Impériale de France à Rome: Travaux des Sections de Gravure en taille douce et de Composition musicale pour l'année 1864. Archives Nationales, F1-607.

9. To Thomas, 22 Nov. 1864.

10. To Thomas, 4 Dec. 1864.

11. To Julie Cavaillé, 11 Mar. 1865; to Thomas, 1 Apr. 1865.

12. "Nos Portraits: M. Massenet," *Le Monde musical*, 15 May 1904.

13. To Sophie Hennequin, 29 Nov. [1864]. F. Gerald Borch collection.

14. To Henri Heugel, no date. Moldenhauer Archive.

15. To Thomas, 27 June 1865.

16. To Thomas, 1 Apr. 1865.

17. Académie Impériale de France a Rome: Travaux des Sections de Gravure en taille douce et de Composition musicale pour l'année 1865. Archives Nationales, F21-607.

18. To Thomas, 21 Oct. 1865.

Chapter 5: Back in Paris; Marriage (pages 41–47)

1. René Brancour (1922), 12.

Chapter 6: *La Grand' Tante*; The Franco-Prussian War (pages 48–62)

1. Johannès Weber, *Le Temps*, 17 Apr. 1867; Ernest Reyer, *Journal des Débats*, 18 Apr. 1867; Eugène Tarbé, *Le Figaro*, 5 Apr. 1867; quoted in Schneider (1926), 59–60. Gustave Bertrand, *Le Ménestrel*, 7 Apr. 1867; quoted in Solenière (1897), 4.

2. Henri Busser, *De Pelléas aux Indes galantes* (1955), 95.

3. Albert Wolff, *Le Figaro*, 4 Feb. 1868, quoted in José Bruyr, *Massenet* (1964), 22. Dubois, in Schneider (1926), 277–279. Massenet, ibid., 279–280; also Bibl. Nat. aut. letters, No. 23.

4. Albert Soubies and Charles Malherbe (1893), 202.

5. Ibid., 202.

6. Ibid., 202–203.

7. See Mina Curtiss, *Bizet and His World* (1958), 197.

8. Pougin, "Massenet" *Rivista musicale italiana* 19 (1912): 931.

9. Soubies and Malherbe (1893), 132.

10. To Ernest Lévine, 17 June 1880. University of Washington Library.

11. [To Paul Cavaillé], Marlotte, 7 July 1868. Quoted in Ives Leroux (1963), 8.

12. To Paul Poirson, Sat., Sept. 1868. University of Washington Library.

13. See Cornelia Otis Skinner, *Madame Sarah* (1966), 78–80.

14. "Autobiographical Notes by the Composer Massenet," *Century Magazine* 45 (Nov. 1892): 124.

15. To "Cher Monsieur" in Bayonne, dated Paris, 9 Mar. 1892. University of Washington Library.

16. Léon Vallas, *Vincent d'Indy*, Vol. 1 (1946), 99–103.

17. Quoted in Pougin, "Massenet," *Rivista musicale italiana* 19 (1912): 931–932.

18. To Paul Lacombe, 19 Dec. 1871. Bibliothèque Nationale.

19. Arthur Pougin (1912), 932.

CHAPTER 7: *DON CÉSAR DE BAZAN; LES ÉRINNYES; MARIE-MAGDELEINE* (PAGES 63–77)

1. Henry T. Finck, *Massenet and His Operas* (1910), 42, citing Julien Torchet in *La Revue du siècle*, Feb. 1890. From a letter to Emma Hennequin dated 18 Nov. 1871, it appears that Massenet was working on his "sacred drama in two parts" at that time. F. Gerald Borch collection.

2. Finck, op. cit., 42–43; Schneider (1926), 245–247, quoting Félix Dequesnel in *Le Gaulois*, 14 Mar. 1900.

3. Mina Curtiss, *Bizet and His World* (1958), 340, where Massenet's letter to Bizet of 16 Oct. 1872 is quoted.

4. See Cornelia Otis Skinner, *Madame Sarah* (1966), 99–100.

5. Louis Gallet to a music critic, 12 Sept. 1892, quoted in Schneider (1926), 266–267. Gallet, in a lapse of memory, put "1874" instead of 1873

6. Gaston Jollivet, "Art at the Mirlitons' Club, 1860–1888," *Art and Letters* (Apr. 1888): 105–120.

7. Arthur Pougin (1912), 916–917.

8. Saint-Saëns, *La Renaissance littéraire*, 12 Apr. 1873. Quoted in Solenière (1897), 104–105.

9. Ernest Reyer, *Journal des Débats*, 23 Apr. 1873. Quoted in Solenière (1897), 105–106.

10. Oscar Browning, *Memories of Sixty Years at Eton, Cambridge, and Elsewhere* (1910), 200–201.

CHAPTER 8: THE LÉGION D'HONNEUR (PAGES 78–90)

1. To Édouard Blau, 6 June 1874. University of Washington Library.

2. To "Cher Monsieur," 30 Aug. 1874. University of Washington Library.

3. Auguste Vitu, *Les Mille et une nuits du théâtre*, Série 3 [covering 1874–75]. Paris: Ollendorff, 1886.

4. Auguste Vitu, op. cit.

5. To Bizet, 4 Mar. 1875. Quoted in Mina Curtiss, *Bizet and His World*, 395–396.

6. To Mme Heuzey, 11 June 1875. University of Washington Library.

7. To Julie Cavaillé, 29 June 1875. Published in Ives Leroux, *Hommage à Massenet* (1963), 9.

8. To Lamoureux, 6 July 1875. Bibliothèque Nationale.

9. [To Émile Réty ?], 14 July 1875. Bibliothèque Nationale.

10. *Almanach des spectacles*, 1876.

11. Adolphe Jullien, *Musiciens d'aujourd'hui*, Série 2 (1894), 328–340.

12. Howard Lee Nostrand, *Le Théâtre antique et à l'antique en France de 1840 à 1900*, 109–114.

13. Letter to ? , 3 Oct. 1876. Published in Ives Leroux, *Hommage à Massenet* (1963), 10.

14. Howard Lee Nostrand, op. cit., 137.

CHAPTER 9: *LE ROI DE LAHORE*; THE CONSERVATOIRE; THE INSTITUT (PAGES 91–108)

1. To Édouard Colonne, 31 Jan. 1877. Bibliothèque Nationale.

2. Ernest Reyer, *Journal des Débats*, 10 May 1877. Quoted in Solenière (1897), 9–10.

3. Arthur Pougin, "Massenet," *Rivista musicale italiana* 19 (1912): 921–942.

4. To Giulio Ricordi, 15 Apr. 1877. Ricordi archives.

5. To Emma Hennequin, 9 May 1877. F. Gerald Borch collection.

6. To Ambroise Thomas, 8 June 1877. Bibliothèque Nationale.

7. To Ricordi, 21 July 1877. Ricordi archives.
   To a librettist, 22 July 1877. University of Washington Library.

8. To Mme Borch, 24 July 1877. F. Gerald Borch collection.

9. To Ricordi, 11 and 20 Aug. 1877. Ricordi archives.

10. To Ricordi, 30 Aug. 1877. Ricordi archives.

11. To Ricordi, 1, 2, 4, 10 Sept. 1877, Ricordi archives.

12. To Ricordi, 30 Sept. 1877. Boston Public Library.
    Also to Ricordi, 4 Oct. 1877. Ricordi archives.

13. To Ricordi, 10 Sept. [incorrectly marked "Agosto 1877"], 9 Oct., 2, 25, 27, 29 Nov. 1877, Ricordi archives.

14. To Ricordi, 10 and 15 Dec. 1877. Ricordi archives.

15. To Ricordi, 22, 24, 29 Dec. 1877 and 9 Jan. 1878. Ricordi archives.

16. To Ricordi, 9 Jan. 1878. Ricordi archives.

17. To Ricordi, 17 Jan. 1878. Ricordi archives.

18. To Ricordi, 20 and 27 Feb. 1878. Ricordi archives.

19. *Osservatore Romano*, Wed., 27 Mar. 1878.

20. To Léo Delibes, 21 Apr. [1878]. Bibliothèque Nationale. The year can be assigned by cross reference to a letter to Ricordi, dated 18 Apr. 1878, which similarly expresses the desire to get away from Paris for six months, from 20 [or 18] May.

21. To Ricordi, 13 May 1878. Ricordi archives.

22. To Emma Hennequin Borch, 20 May 1878. F. Gerald Borch collection.

23. To Ricordi, 25 May, 17 and 24 June 1878. Ricordi archives.

24. To Ricordi, 30 June 1878. Ricordi archives.

25. To Ricordi, 31 July and 18 Aug. 1878. Ricordi archives.

26. To Ricordi, 25, 29, 31 Aug. 1878. Ricordi archives.

27. To Ricordi, 13 Sept. 1878. Ricordi archives.

28. See Constant Pierre, *Le Conservatoire national de musique et de déclamation* (Paris, 1900), under "Personnel administratif et enseignant."

29. Léon Vallas, *César Franck* (London, 1951), 253–254.

30. Schneider (1926), 36. James Harding, *Saint-Saëns and His Circle* (1965), 158.

31. To Ricordi, 26 Nov. [no year; obviously 1878]. Ricordi archives.

32. Bruneau (1935), 26.

33. To Ricordi, 26 Dec. 1878. Ricordi archives.

CHAPTER 10: *HÉRODIADE* (PAGES 109–127)

1. To Ricordi, 1 Jan. 1879. Ricordi archives.

2. To Ricordi, 10 Jan. 1879. Ricordi archives.

3. To Ricordi, 13 Jan. 1879. Ricordi archives.

4. *Pesti Napló*, 15–19 and 23–24 Jan. 1879. Communicated by Dr. István Kecskeméti, National Széchényi Library, Budapest.

5. To Ricordi, 10 Jan. 1879. Ricordi archives.

6. To Ricordi, 13 Feb. 1879. Ricordi archives.

7. To Ricordi, 21 Apr. 1879. Ricordi archives.

8. To Dr. Joseph Michel, 20 May 1879. Bibliothèque Nationale.

9. Auguste Vitu, *Les Mille et une nuits du théâtre*, Série 7.

10. To Ricordi, 13 June 1879. Ricordi archives.
    To a director, 2 July 1879. University of Washington Library.
    To Ricordi, 10 July 1879. Ricordi archives.

11. Arthur Pougin, "Massenet," *Rivista musicale italiana* 19 (1912): 945.

12. José Bruyr, *Massenet: Musicien de la belle époque* (Lyon: Éditions du Sud Est, 1964), 39.

13. To Ricordi, 13 June and 10 Sept. 1879. Ricordi archives.
    To "Cher ami," 9 Aug. 1879. Bibliothèque Nationale.

14. To Ricordi, 11 Oct. 1879. Ricordi archives.

15. To Ricordi, 11 Oct. 1879. Ricordi archives.

16. To Ricordi, 27 Dec. 1879. Ricordi archives.

17. To Ricordi, 2 Jan. 1880. Ricordi archives.

18. To Ricordi, 23 Jan. 1880. Ricordi archives.

19. Noël and Stoullig, *Annales du théâtre et de la musique*, Vol. 6.

20. To "Mon cher Directeur," no date [March, 1880]. University of Washington Library.

21. To Delibes, 16 Mar. 1880. Bibliothèque Nationale.

22. To Delibes, 25 Apr. 1880. Bibliothèque Nationale.

23. See Bruneau (1935), 19.

24. To Emma Borch, 21 Feb. 1883. F. Gerald Borch collection.

25. Schneider (1926), 257–259 passim.

26. To Ricordi, 16 June 1880. Ricordi archives.

27. To Ricordi, 25 June and 23 July 1880. Ricordi archives.

28. Catherine Drinker Bowen, *Beloved Friend* (Dover, 1946), 377–379 passim.

29. To Ricordi, 11 Aug. and 16 Sept. 1880. Ricordi archives.

30. To Ricordi, 22 Sept. 1880. Ricordi archives.

31. To Tornaghi, 6 and 17 Oct. 1880, Ricordi archives.

32. To Ricordi, 19 Nov. 1880. Ricordi archives.

33. To Ricordi, 22 Dec. 1880. Ricordi archives.

34. Schneider (1926), 268.

35. To Weckerlin, 5 Jan. 1881. Bibliothèque Nationale.

36. Schneider (1926), 76.

37. To Quinzard, 18 Apr. 1881. Bibliothèque Nationale.

38. Brancour, *Massenet* (1922), 11.

39. Alfred Bruneau, *Massenet* (1935), 9–16 passim.

Chapter 11: *Manon* (pages 129–143)

1. To Ricordi, 19 Jan. 1882. Ricordi archives.

2. To Ricordi, 31 Jan., 3, 5, [9], Feb. 1882. Ricordi archives.
   To Tito Ricordi, 11 Feb. 1882. Boston Public Library.

3. Paul Milliet, in *L'Art du théâtre*, No. 31 (July 1903). Quoted at length in Schneider (1926), 118–119.

4. To Ricordi, 27 Mar. and 20 Apr. (also 19 Jan.), 1882. Ricordi archives.

5. To Ricordi, 7 May 1882. Ricordi archives.

6. To Louis Baerwolf, 22 May and 16 July 1882. Also 18 May 1891. University of Washington Library.

7. See A. N. Verveen, "Jules Massenet op Bedevaart in Den Haag," *Mens en Melodie*, Jg. 22, No. 6 (1967), 177–180.

8. To Ricordi, 5, 12, 15 Dec. 1882. Ricordi archives.

9. To Augusto Machado, 25 Dec. 1882. University of Washington Library.

10. Alfred Bruneau, *Massenet* (1935), 65.

11. Annotation in the orchestra score of *Manon*, Act IV, p. 89.

12. Annotation in the orchestra score of *Manon*, Vol. 1, p. 7.

13. Annotations in the orchestra score of *Manon*, Act I, pp. 63–203 passim.

14. Annotations in the orchestra score of *Manon*, passim.

15. To Ricordi, 19 July 1883. Ricordi archives.
    To Gabriel Pierné, 18 Sept. 1883. Bibliothèque Nationale.

16. L. de Foucaud, *Le Gaulois*, 20 Jan. 1884. Noël and Stoullig, *Les Annales du théâtre et de la musique*, 1884. B. Jouvin, *Le Figaro*, 20 Jan. 1884. Ernest Reyer, *Journal des Débats*, 26 Jan. 1884. All quoted in Solenière (1897), 22–26.

17. Albert Soubies and Charles Malherbe, *Histoire de l'Opéra-Comique: la seconde salle Favart, 1860–1887*, 77–78.

18. To Emma Borch, 5 June 1885. F. Gerald Borch collection.

19. To Ricordi, 23 June 1885. Ricordi archives.

20. To Quinzard, 9 Aug. 1884. Bibliothèque Nationale.

21. Schneider (1926), 269–271.

22. To Ricordi, 24 Dec. 1884. Ricordi archives.

CHAPTER 12: *LE CID* (PAGES 144–161)

1. To Ricordi, 12 Apr. 1885. Ricordi archives.

2. To "Mon cher Directeur" [Borel], 30 Apr. 1885. University of Washington Library.

3. To Emma Borch, 5 June 1885. F. Gerald Borch collection.
   To Ricordi, 23 June 1885. Ricordi archives.

4. To Ricordi, 17 July 1885. Ricordi archives. *Isora di Provenza* was staged at Bologna in 1884.

5. To "Cher grand Gonfalonier" [Dr. Pozzi], 19 Nov. 1885. University of Washington Library.

6. To Ricordi, 13 Sept. 1885. Ricordi archives.

7. Finck (1910), 169.

8. Auguste Vitu, *Le Figaro*, 1 Dec. 1885. Johannès Weber, *Le Temps*, 8 Dec. 1885. Both quoted in Solenière (1897), 33–34. Schneider (1908), 123–124.

9. To Ricordi, [11] Dec. 1885. Ricordi archives.

10. Schneider (1926), 78.

11. To Mme Oudinot, 27 Oct. 1884. F. Gerald Borch collection.

12. To Emma Borch, 1 Jan. 1886. F. Gerald Borch collection.

13. To Alfred Stieglitz, 29 Jan. 1886. F. Gerald Borch collection.

14. To Schatté, 24 Jan. 1886. Bibliothèque Nationale; Massenet letters, No. 41 [and cover, filed with unrelated No. 4]. To "Mon cher Directeur," no date, No. 23.

15. Robert Charvay, illustrated supplement, *L'Echo de Paris*, 15 Jan. 1893. Quoted in Schneider (1926), 120–121.

16. To Campbell Clarke, 9 Mar. 1892. F. Gerald Borch collection.

17. [To Henri Heugel], 8 Aug. 1897. Moldenhauer Archive.

18. To Ricordi, 13 Oct. 1886. Ricordi archives.

19. [To Réty], no date [15 Nov. 1886]: "Prière de préviser mes élèves que j'ai demain Mardi l'enterrement de Jouvin à Rueil." Bibliothèque Nationale, No. 19.

20. Visiting card, 19 Nov. 1886. Signed slip, 21 Dec. 1886. Bibliothèque Nationale.

21. To Campbell Clarke, 25 Jan. 1887. F. Gerald Borch collection.
    To Ricordi, 9 Feb. 1887. Ricordi archives.

22. To Campbell Clarke, 25 Jan. 1887. F. Gerald Borch collection.

23. To L. F. Revius, 12 Mar. 1887. Gemeentemuseum, The Hague.

24. To "Chère Madame," 23 Mar. 1887. Bibliothèque Nationale.

25. To Mme Durand-Ulbach, 12 Apr. 1887. University of Washington Library.

26. To "Cher ami," 4 Oct. 1887. Boston Public Library.

27. To "Cher ami," 14 Oct. 1887. Bibliothèque Nationale.

28. To Dr. Joseph Michel, 11 Apr. 1885, 8 Dec. 1887, 1 and 13 Jan. 1888. Bibliothèque Nationale.

29. To Quinzard, 11 Mar. 1888. Bibliothèque Nationale.

30. To Campbell Clarke, 14 Feb. 1888. F. Gerald Borch collection.

31. *Dictionary of American Biography*, 1935.

32. Mathilde Marchesi, *Marchesi and Music*, 1897.

33. *Esclarmonde*, first draft, Nall collection; orchestra score, Bibliothèque de l'Opéra.

34. To "Cher ami" [Hartmann], "Mercredi, Vevey" [8 Aug. 1888]. Bibliothèque Nationale.

35. To Guy Ropartz, 13 Sept. 1888. Bibliothèque Nationale.

36. Schneider (1908), 142.

37. To Emma Borch, 2 Nov. 1888. F. Gerald Borch collection.

38. Schneider (1908), 143n.

CHAPTER 13: *ESCLARMONDE; LE MAGE* (PAGES 163–175)

1. Camille Bellaigue, *L'Année musicale*, 1890. Quoted in Solenière (1897), 42.

2. Léon Kerst, *Le Petit journal*, 15 May 1889. See Solenière (1897), 47–48.

3. Victor Wilder, *Gil Blas*, 17 May 1889. See Solenière (1897), 46–47.

4. Camille Bellaigue, *L'Année musicale*, 1890. See Solenière (1897), 41-42.

5. Richard O'Monroy, *Gil Blas*, 17 May 1889. See Solenière (1897), 47.

6. G. de Boisjolin, *Le Monde artiste*, 26 May 1889. See Solenière (1897), 37–38.

7. Auguste Vitu, *Le Figaro*, 16 May 1889. See Solenière (1897), 43–44.

8. Maurice Lefèvre, *Le Monde artiste*, 19 May 1889. See Solenière (1897), 38–41.

9. Slip dated 29 Oct. 1889. Bibliothèque Nationale.

10. To Emma Borch, 25 Dec. 1889. F. Gerald Borch collection.

11. To Paul Lacombe, 7 Jan. 1890. Bibliothèque Nationale.

12. To Florent Schmitt, 1 July 1890. Bibliothèque Nationale.

13. To "Bien cher ami" [Réty?], 14 July 1890. Bibliothèque Nationale.

14. "Je certifie" and "Je suis désolé," 19 July 1890. Bibliothèque Nationale.

15. Alexander Witeschnik, *Wiener Opernkunst* (Wien: Krenn & Scheriau, 1959).

16. Alfred Ernst, *La Paix*, March 1891. Victor Wilder, *Gil Blas*, 18 Mar. 1891. See Solenière (1897), 68–71.

17. A. Landely, *L'Art musical*, 31 Mar. 1891. See Solenière (1897), 65–68.

18. Noël and Stoullig, *Annales du théâtre et de la musique*, 1891. See Solenière (1897), 71.

19. Adolphe Jullien, *Musiciens d'aujourd'hui*, 1892. See Solenière (1897), 72.

20. Sibyl Sanderson to Massenet, 29 Mar. 1891. Facsimile of the autograph in Solenière (1897), facing p. 143.

21. To Quinzard, 14 May 1891. Bibliothèque Nationale.

22. To Quinzard, 19 May 1891. Bibliothèque Nationale.

23. To Hudelèrt, Aug. 1891. University of Washington Library.

24. To Mme Durand-Ulbach, 11 Aug. 1891. University of Washington Library.

CHAPTER 14: *WERTHER* (PAGES 177–188)

1. To Henri Heugel, 13 and 24 Jan. 1892. Heugel archives.

2. To Heugel, 9 Feb. 1892. Heugel archives.

3. To Ricordi, 29 Feb. 1892. Boston Public Library.

4. "Ah! mon brave et cher ami," 5 Mar. 1892. University of Washington Library.

5. To "Cher Monsieur," 9 and 29 Mar. 1892. University of Washington Library.

6. To Emma Borch, 27 Aug. 1892. F. Gerald Borch collection.

7. To Florent Schmitt, 1 Oct. 1892. Bibliothèque Nationale.

8. Robert Charvay, *Écho de Paris*, illustrated supplement, Jan. 1893. See Solenière (1897), 50–56.

9. Charles Malherbe, *Le Monde artiste*, 22 Jan. 1893. See Solenière (1897), 57.

10. Alfred Bruneau, *Gil Blas*, 18 Jan. 1893. See Solenière (1897), 58–59.

11. Georges Street, *Le Matin*, 17 Jan. 1893. Solenière, 57–58.

12. Charles Darcours, *Le Figaro*, 17 Jan. 1893. Solenière, 58.

13. Léon Kerst, *Le Petit journal*, 17 Jan. 1893. Solenière, 58.

14. A clip may be found in the Massenet dossier in the Bibliothèque de l'Arsenal.

15. Emma Calvé to Massenet, no date. Irvine collection.

16. To Raymond Bouyer, 6 Apr. 1893. Bibliothèque Nationale.

17. Reprinted in *Musiciens d'aujourdlhui*, Série 2 (1894).

18. Pedrotti to Massenet, 8 Apr. 1893. Irvine collection.

19. To Heugel, 4 June 1893. Heugel archives.

20. To Emma Borch, 2 June 1893. F. Gerald Borch collection.

21. To André Bloch's father, 11 July 1893. University of Washington Library.

22. To Heugel, 17 Oct. 1893. University of Washington Library.

23. Charles Le Gras, "Souvenirs de Massenet à Avignon," *Les Tablettes d'Avignon et de Provence*, 17 May 1936. Clip in the Massenet dossier, Bibliothèque de l'Arsenal.

24. Busser (1955), 70–71.

CHAPTER 15: *THAÏS; LE PORTRAIT DE MANON; LA NAVARRAISE* (PAGES 189–197)

1. "Vous êtes un bon ami," Paris, 8 Jan. 1894. "Cher ami," Namur, 30 Jan. 1894. Both Library of Congress.

2. To Torchet, 10 Mar. 1894. University of Washington Library.

3. Alfred Bruneau, *Gil Blas*, 18 Mar 1894. See Solenière (1897), 76–77.

4. Léon Kerst, *Le Petit journal*, 17 Mar. 1894. Solenière, 75–76.

5. Charles Darcours, *Le Figaro*, 17 Mar. 1894. Solenière, 78–79.

6. L. de Fourcaud, *Le Gaulois*, 17 Mar. 1894. Solenière, 79–80.

7. Johannès Weber, *Le Temps*, 14 May 1894. Solenière, 84–86.

8. Victorin de Joncières, *La Liberté*, 13 May 1894. Solenière, 84.

9. Adolphe Jullien, *Journal des Débats*, 12 May 1894. Solenière, 86–87.

10. L. de Fourcaud, *Le Gaulois*, 9 May 1894. Solenière, 87.

11. Alfred Bruneau, *Le Figaro*, 4 Oct 1895. Solenière, 88–91.

12. Eugène de Solenière, *La Critique*, 20 Oct. 1895. See Solenière (1897), 93–94

13. Calvé to Massenet, 22 June 1894. Irvine collection.

14. To Heugel, 16 Sept. 1894. Boston Public Library.

15. *Grisélidis*, end of Act I. Bibliothèque de l'Opéra. Cf. Schneider (1926), 301.

16. To Ricordi, 14 Oct. 1894. Boston Public Library.

17. "Cher confrère," 18 Dec. 1894. University of Washington Library.

CHAPTER 16: FREEDOM FROM THE CONSERVATOIRE (PAGES 199–208)

1. To Théodore Massiac, 13 Jan. 1895. Bibliothèque Nationale.

2. To Raoul Blondel, Jan. 30, 1895. Bibliothèque Nationale.

3. "Vous me faîtes un gros plaisir," 5 Feb. 1895. Library of Congress.

4. To André Bloch, 23 May 1895. University of Washington Library.

5. Card to Baron and Baroness André Callamisi, 29 May 1895.
   To Raoul Blondel, 29 May 1895. Bibliothèque Nationale.
   To Emma Borch, 30 May 1895. F. Gerald Borch collection.

6. Calvé to Massenet, 7 July 1895. Irvine collection.

7. To Heugel, 10 Oct. 1895. Moldenhauer Archive.

8. To Heugel, 11 Dec. 1895. Moldenhauer Archive.

9. To Heugel, 18 Dec. 1895. University of Washington Library.
   To Heugel, 30 Dec. 1895. Heugel archives.

10. To Heugel, 30 Jan. 1896. Moldenhauer Archive.

11. To Frederick Grant Gleason, Paris, 1 May 1896. Newberry Library.

12. To Heugel, 27 May (and also 3 June) 1896. Moldenhauer Archive.

13. To Heugel, 13 July 1896. Moldenhauer Archive.

14. To Frederick Grant Gleason, 22 Aug. 1896 (postmarked Murat, Cantal). Newberry Library.

15. Calvé to Massenet, no date [August], 14 and 30 Aug. 1896. Irvine collection.

16. To "Cher ami," 18 Sept. 1896. Bibliothèque Nationale.

17. To Heugel, "Bruxelles, dimanche matin." University of Washington Library. Compare letter to Raymond Bouyer, Brussels, 30 Sept. 1896. Bibliothèque Nationale.

18. To Heugel, no date [Oct. 1896]. Moldenhauer Archive.

19. "Cher excellent ami," Bordeaux, 12 Nov. 1896. Library of Congress.

20. To Heugel, 20 Nov. 1896. Moldenhauer Archive.

21. To Heugel, 1, 2, and 6 Dec. 1896. Moldenhauer Archive.

CHAPTER 17: *SAPHO; CENDRILLON* (PAGES 209–223)

1. To Raoul Blondel, 16, 24, 24 (evening), and 26 Jan. 1897. Bibliothèque Nationale.

2. To Heugel, dimanche [28 Mar. 1897]. Moldenhauer Archive.

3. Mathilde Marchesi, *Marchesi and Music*, 291.

4. To Heugel, 5 and 17 May 1897. Moldenhauer Archive.

5. To Julien Torchet, 17 May 1897. University of Washington Library.

6. Delmas to Massenet, 4 June 1897. Moldenhauer Archive.

7. To Heugel, 19 July 1897. Moldenhauer Archive.

8. To Heugel, 8 Aug. 1897. Moldenhauer Archive.

9. To Heugel, 26 and 31 Aug. 1897. Heugel archives.

10. To "Chère Madame," 24 Nov. 1897. University of Washington Library.

11. To Raymond Bouyer, 22 Nov. 1897. Bibliothèque Nationale.

12. Henry T. Finck, *Massenet and His Operas* (1910), 118–119.

13. To Heugel, 28 Jan. 1898. Moldenhauer Archive.
    To Diémer, 30 Jan. 1898. Boston Public Library.
    See also the long letter to Heugel, 21 Jan. 1898. University of Washington Library.

14. To Heugel, 2 Feb. 1898. Moldenhauer Archive.

15. To Heugel, 11 Apr. 1898. Moldenhauer Archive.

16. To Ricordi, 15 Apr. 1898. Boston Public Library.

17. To Heugel: "Pourville, mercredi"; 27 July 1898; and "Vendredi soir." Moldenhauer Archive.

18. To Heugel, 8 Aug. 1898. Heugel archives.

19. To Heugel, 20 Aug. 1898. Heugel archives.

20. To Heugel, 2 Sept. 1898. University of Washington Library.

21. To "Cher ami," 24 Sept. 1898. Boston Public Library.

22. To Heugel, "Mercredi soir" [30 Nov. 1898?]. University of Washington Library.

23. To Ricordi, "fin de l'année 1898." Ricordi archives.

24. To Weckerlin, 18 Jan. 1899. To E. J. Pohl, 20 Jan. 1899. Bibliothèque Nationale.

25. Six letters from Nora Barrès Diaz to Massenet, from 24 Dec. 1898 to 27 Feb. 1899. Moldenhauer Archive.

26. To an unidentified correspondent, 17 Mar. 1899. University of Washington Library.

27. To Florent Schmitt, 25 June 1899. Bibliothèque Nationale.

28. To [Heugel ?], Mon., 17 July [1899]. University of Washington Library.

29. To Heugel, 8 Aug. 1899. University of Washington Library.

30. To Heugel, 8 Oct. 1899. University of Washington Library.

31. To Heugel, 25 Oct. 1899. University of Washington Library.

32. To Heugel, "Genève, mardi" [11 Dec.] 1899. University of Washington Library.
    To Heugel, Nice, 31 Dec. 1899. Heugel archives.

33. To Heugel, 2 Jan. 1900. Heugel archives.

CHAPTER 18: *GRISÉLIDIS* (PAGES 225–237)

1. Isidor Philipp, Massenet, un portrait," *Le Passe-Temps*, April 1945.

2. To Heugel, 6 and 11 Jan. 1900. Moldenhauer Archive.

3. To Heugel, "Mardi, 22 Janvier" [23 Jan. 1900] and "Samedi" [27 Jan. 1900]. University of Washington Library.

4. To Heugel, 2 May 1900. Moldenhauer Archive. "Mardi" [8 May 1900]. University of Washington Library.

5. To Heugel, 17 May 1900. University of Washington Library.

6. To Heugel, 2 July 1900. Moldenhauer Archive.

7. To Heugel, 5 July 1900. University of Washington Library.

8. To Paul Chevalier, 22 Sept. 1900. University of Washington Library.
   To Paul Chevalier, "Dimanche matin" [23 Sept. 1900]. Moldenhauer Archive.
   To Heugel, 25 Sept. 1900. Moldenhauer Archive.

9. To [Paul Chevalier], 10 Oct. [1900]. Moldenhauer Archive.

10. Reynaldo Hahn, *Notes: Journal d'un musicien* (1933), 114–115.

11. To Heugel, 17 Oct. 1900. University of Washington Library.

12. To Heugel, 27 Jan. 1901. Moldenhauer Archive.

13. To Heugel, 2 Feb. 1901. Moldenhauer Archive.

14. To Heugel, 5 Feb. 1901. Moldenhauer Archive.

15. To Heugel, 14 Feb. 1901. Moldenhauer Archive.

16. Edmond Stoullig, *Annales du théâtre et de la musique.*

17. To Heugel, 12 May 1901. Moldenhauer Archive.

18. To J. B. Weckerlin, 23 June and 31 Aug. 1901. Bibliothèque Nationale.

19. Henri Busser, *De Pelléas aux Indes galantes* (1955), 105.

20. Henri Busser, op. cit., 106.

21. To Weckerlin, 5 Nov. 1901. Bibliothèque Nationale.

CHAPTER 19: *LE JONGLEUR DE NOTRE-DAME* (PAGES 239–245)

1. Mme Quinzard to Massenet, 20 Jan. 1902, with Massenet's annotation to Heugel. Heugel archives.

2. To Heugel, 8 Feb. [1902]. Heugel archives.

3. To Ricordi, 28 Feb. 1902. Boston Public Library. The letter was addressed to Giulio Ricordi, 14 Burgonuovo, Milan.

4. To "Cher ami" [Paul Chevalier ?], 7 Mar. 1902. University of Washington Library.

5. To Heugel, 20 Mar. 1902. Heugel archives.

6. Henri Busser, *De Pelléas aux Indes galantes,* 112.

7. Statistics based on Stéphane Wolff, *Un Demi-siècle d'Opéra-Comique, 1900–1950.*

8. To "Cher ami," 14 June 1902. University of Washington Library.

9. To Heugel, 26 July 1903. Heugel archives.

10. Edmond Stoullig, *Annales du théâtre et de la musique.*

CHAPTER 20: *CHÉRUBIN* (PAGES 247–259)

1. Calvé to Massenet, 1 Jan. [1903]. Irvine collection.

2. Calvé to Massenet, no date [Jan. 1903]. Irvine collection.

3. *Journal de Monaco*, 10 Mar. 1903.

4. Henri Busser, *De Pelléas aux Indes galantes*, 127.

5. To Heugel, 26 July 1903. Heugel archives.
   To Heugel, no date ("Voici toujours quelques pages"). University of Washington Library.

6. To "Bien chère Madame et aimable confrère," 28 Oct. 1903 ("Dans un mois mon adresse sera: 48, rue de Vaugirard"). University of Washington Library.

7. To Ricordi, 26 Nov. 1903. Ricordi archives.

8. To Raymond Bouyer, 19 Dec. 1903. Bibliothèque Nationale.

9. To "Cher ami," 15 Jan. 1904. University of Washington Library.

10. Henri Busser, op. cit., 135.

11. To Heugel, 11 June 1904. Heugel archives.

12. [To Heugel], 15 June 1904. University of Washington Library.

13. [To Heugel], 9 July 1904. Moldenhauer Archive.

14. To a fellow academician, 12 July 1904. University of Washington Library.

15. To Julien Torchet, 15 Oct. 1904. Bibliothèque Nationale.

16. To Heugel, 17 Nov. 1904. Moldenhauer Archive.

17. To Diémer, 3 Feb. 1905. Boston Public Library.

18. M. Reynier, "Massenet en Provence," clip of 12 Sept. 1912, no periodical given. Bibliothèque de l'Arsenal.

19. Calvé to Massenet, 10 Mar. 1905. Irvine collection.

20. To Raymond Bouyer, June 1905. Bibliothèque Nationale.

CHAPTER 21: *ARIANE; THÉRÈSE* (PAGES 261–271)

1. To Heugel, no date [ca. 9 Feb. 1906]. Moldenhauer Archive.

2. To "Cher ami," 14 May [1906]. University of Washington Library.

3. To Heugel, 28 July and 11 Aug., 1906. Moldenhauer Archive.

4. To Gabriel Astruc, 11 Aug. 1906. Bibliothèque Nationale.

5. To Heugel, no date [1906], "2 heures du matin." University of Washington Library.

6. To Heugel, "Merci, Merci!," no date [1906]. University of Washington Library.

7. To Julien Torchet, 2 Nov. 1906. University of Washington Library.

8. To Gabrielle Ferrari, 7 Nov. 1906. University of Washington Library.

9. To André Bloch, 17 Nov. 1906. University of Washington Library.

10. To Charles Malherbe, 5 Dec. 1906. Bibliothèque Nationale.

11. Henri Busser, *De Pelléas aux Indes galantes*, 165.

12. To Heugel, 31, 1907. Moldenhauer Archive.

13. To Heugel, 28 Jan. and "Mardi matin" [Jan. 29], 1907. Moldenhauer Archive.

14. To Heugel, 31 Jan. 1907. Moldenhauer Archive.

15. Alfred Bruneau, *Massenet* (1935), 82.

16. To Heugel, 13 Feb. 1907. Moldenhauer Archive.

17. To Gabriel Astruc, 10 Mar. 1907. Bibliothèque Nationale.

18. To Heugel, 1 Oct. 1907. Moldenhauer Archive.

19. Calvé to Massenet, Nov. 1907. Irvine collection.

20. *Bacchus*, Act III, Scene 1, only, inscribed to Jacques Heugel on Christmas, 1909, with the note: "En souvenir d'un voyage en Italie avec ton père—*Ariane*, à Turin, 1908" [read 1907].

21. Edmond Stoullig, *Annales du théâtre et de la musique.*

CHAPTER 22: *BACCHUS* (PAGES 272–277)

1. To Gabriel Astruc, 5 Jan. 1908. Bibliothèque Nationale.

2. To Gabriel Astruc, 13 Feb. [1908]. Bibliothèque Nationale.

3. To Heugel, 17 Feb. 1908. University of Washington Library.

4. To Heugel, no date [July 1908]. Moldenhauer Archive.

5. To Heugel, 11 Mar. [1909]. Moldenhauer Archive.

6. To Heugel, 15 June 1909. Heugel archives.

7. To Heugel, 8 Oct. 1909. Moldenhauer Archive.

CHAPTER 23: *DON QUICHOTTE* (PAGES 279–285)

1. To Heugel, 26 Jan. 1910. University of Washington Library.

2. To Heugel, 8 Feb. 1910. University of Washington Library.

3. To Heugel, 6 Feb. 1910. Heugel archives.
   To Heugel, no date [Feb. or Mar. 1910]. University of Washington Library.

4. André Corneau, *Journal de Monaco*, 22 Feb. 1910.

5. To Heugel, 20 Feb. 1910. Heugel archives.

6. To Raoul Blondel, Paris, 25 Feb. 1910.
   To Dr. Le Jeune, Monte-Carlo, 1 Mar. 1910. University of Washington Library.
   To Heugel, Monte-Carlo, Mar. 9, 1910. Heugel archives.
   To Trémont, Monte-Carlo, 24 Mar. 1910. Irvine collection.

7. To Heugel, 9 May 1910. To Paul Chevalier, 9 May 1910. Heugel archives.

8. To Heugel, 20 Aug. 1910. Moldenhauer Archive.

9. To Heugel, 31 Aug. 1910. Heugel archives. See also Alfred Bruneau, *Massenet*, 87.

CHAPTER 24: *ROMA* (PAGES 287–298)

1. Adolphe Boschot, *L'Écho de Paris*, 31 Mar. 1911.

2. To Heugel, 22 and 29 June, 19 Aug. 1911. Heugel archives.

3. To Raoul Blondel, 10 Nov. 1911. Bibliothèque Nationale.

4. To Ricordi, no date [Jan. 1912]. Boston Public Library.

5. To Ricordi, 3 Feb. 1912. Ricordi archives.

6. Edmond Stoullig, *Annales du théâtre et de la musique.*

7. To Raymond Bouyer, 4 Jan. 1912. Bibliothèque Nationale.

8. To Heugel, 11 and 28 Jan. 1912. Heugel archives.

9. To Heugel, 31 Jan. 1912. Heugel archives.

10. To Raymond Bouyer, 1 Feb. 1912. Bibliothèque Nationale.

11. To Heugel, 5 Feb. 1912. Heugel archives.

12. To Heugel, 20 Feb. 1912. Heugel archives.

13. To Heugel, 21 Feb. 1912. Heugel archives.

14. To Heugel, 26 Feb. 1912. Heugel archives.

15. To Ricordi, 22 Mar. 1912. Boston Public Library.

16. To Heugel, 28 Jan. 1912. Heugel archives.

17. To "Cher Monsieur," 31 Mar. 1912. Heugel archives.

18. Adolphe Boschot, "Roma de Massenet," *Écho de Paris*, 25 Apr. 1912.

19. To Raoul Blondel, 25 Apr. 1912. Bibliothèque Nationale.

20. Schneider (1926), 221.

21. To Ricordi, 29 Dec. 1877; 20 June and 16 July 1878. Ricordi archives.

22. To André Bloch, 15 June 1912. University of Washington Library.

23. To Heugel, 3 and 6 July 1912. Heugel archives.

24. As preserved in a press clipping in the Bibliothèque de l'Arsenal, without date and without the name of the periodical. Internal evidence suggests the article was published after 1921.

25. A copy of the death announcement is preserved in the Massenet dossier at the Bibliothèque de l'Arsenal.

26. Saint-Saëns, *L'Écho de Paris*, 13 Oct. 1912. Given in Bruneau (1935), 91–97.

CHAPTER 25: THE END OF AN ERA (PAGES 299–307)

1. Alfred Bruneau (1935), 97.

2. *Journal de Monaco*, 10 Mar. 1914.

3. See Schneider (1926), 230–231.

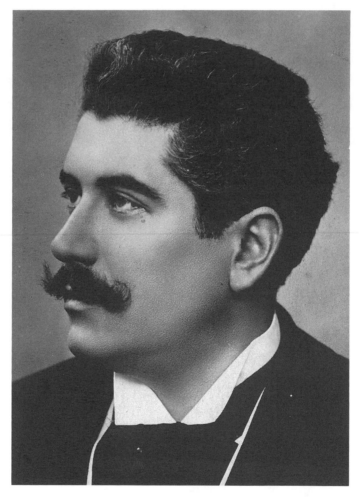

Maurice Renaud. Courtesy Paul Jackson.

Selected References
on the Life and Times of Jules Massenet

Berger-Levrault, O. *Annales des professeurs des académies et universités alsaciennes, 1523–1871.* Nancy, 1892.

Bouilhol, Eliane. *Massenet: son rôle dans l'évolution du théâtre musical.* Saint-Étienne, 1969

Brancour, René. *Massenet.* Paris, 1922. 2nd ed., 1930.

Browning, Oscar. *Memories of Sixty Years at Eton, Cambridge, and Elsewhere.* London, New York, 1910.

Bruneau, Alfred. *Massenet.* Paris, 1935.

Bruyr, Jose. *Massenet, musicien de la belle époque.* Lyon, 1964.

Busser, Henri. *De Pelléas aux Indes Galantes.* Paris, 1955.

Calvé, Emma. *My Life.* Translated by Rosamond Gilder. New York, 1922.

Chastenet, Jacques. *Histoire de la 3ème République.* 7 vols. Paris: Hachette, 1952–63.

Cinquante ans de musique française de 1874 à 1925. [Edited by] L. Rohozinski. 2 vols. Paris, 1925.

Cooper, Martin. *French Music from the Death of Berlioz to the Death of Fauré.* London, 1951.

Coquis, André. *Jules Massenet: l'homme et son oeuvre.* Paris, 1965.

Curtiss, Mina. *Bizet and His World.* New York, 1958.

Ferrare, Henri. "Massenet et Ambroise Thomas: Lettres," *Revue de Paris,* Jan–Feb 1915. Includes 20 letters dating from 1864 to 1872.

Finck, Henry T. *Massenet and His Operas.* New York, 1910.

Hahn, Reynaldo. *Notes: Journal d'un musicien.* Paris, 1933.

Harding, James. *Massenet.* London, 1970.

———. *Saint-Saëns and His Circle.* London, 1965.

Hopkinson, Cecil. *A Dictionary of Parisian Music Publishers, 1700–1950.* London, 1954.

Jullien, Adolphe. *Musiciens d'aujourd'hui.* 1ʳᵉ Série. Paris, 1892.

———. *Musiciens d'aujourd'hui.* 2ᵉ Série. Paris, 1894.

Kutsch, K. J., and Leo Riemans. *Unvergängliche Stimmen: Kleines Sängerlexikon.* Berne, 1962. 2nd ed., 1966.

Landormy, Paul, and Joseph Loisel. "L'Institut de France et le Prix de Rome," in Lavignac, *Encyclopédie de la musique et dictionnaire du Conservatoire.* 2ᵉ Partie, Vol. 6 (Paris, 1931), pp. 3479–3575. Includes brief biography and list of works for Massenet, pp. 3536–3545.

Lavignac, Albert. *Le Voyage artistique à Bayreuth*. Paris, 1897.

Leblanc, Georgette. *Souvenirs* (1895–1918). Paris, 1931.

Lehr, Ernest. "Mathieu de Faviers," in *L'Alsace noble*, Tome II, 342–344. Paris, 1870.

Leroux, Yves, editor. *Hommage à Massenet: inédits, études, témoignages, d'hier et d'aujour-d'hui, référence, bibliographie*. Fontainebleau, 1963.

Loisel, Joseph. *Manon de Massenet: étude historique et critique*. Paris, 1922.

Major, Norma. *Joan Sutherland*. Macdonald: Queen Anne Press, 1987. With Introduction by Dame Joan Sutherland.

Marchesi, Mathilde. *Marchesi and Music: Passages from the Life of a Famous Singing Teacher*. New York, London, 1897.

Massenet, Jules. "Autobiographical Notes by the Composer Massenet," *The Century Magazine*, Vol. 45, Nov. 1892, 122–126.

———. *Mes souvenirs, 1848–1912*. Paris, 1912. New edition annotated by Gérard Condé. Paris, 1992.

———. *My Recollections*. Authorized English translation of the *Souvenirs*, by H. Villiers Barnett. Boston, 1919.

[Massenet, Jean-Pierre]. *Description du Ban de la Roche*. Par Massenet et F. Walter. Strasbourg, an VI [1797–98].

Massenet de Marancour, Léon. *Les Échos du Vatican*. Paris, 1864.

———. *La Rouge et la noire*. Paris, 1864.

———. *Confessions d'un commis-voyageur*. Paris, 1865.

———. *Les Fils aux deux mères*. Drame en 5 actes dont un prologue, par MM. Henry de Kock et Léon de Marancour. [Staged Paris, Grand-Théâtre Parisien, 11 Nov. 1865.]

———. *Rien ne va plus! Banques de jeu. La Rouge et la noire. Promenade historique*. 2e édition. Paris, 1865.

———. *Les Français à Rome (Échos du Vatican)*. Nouvelle édition. Paris, 1867.

———. *Le Vrai diable à quatre: Lucifer . . . Astaroth . . . Asmodée . . . Lucifuge*. Paris, 1868.

———. *Bourbons et d'Orléans, lettre au Roi sur la fusion*. Paris, 1874.

———. *Guide pratique d'Europe au Rio de la Plata. Madère, Ténériffe, San-Vicente, Dakar, Pernambuco, Bahia, Rio-de-Janeiro, Montevideo, Buenos-Aires*. Edition française. Paris [et] Buenos-Aires: en vente à bord tous les paquebots des lignes d'Europe à la Plata, 1883.

Massenet de Marancour, Commandant Robert-Henri. *La Chasse en avion*. Paris, 1921.

Noël, Édouard, and Edmond Stoullig. *Les Annales du théâtre et de la musique*. [Published annually] Paris, 1875–95. Continued by Stoullig alone, 1897–1916.

Noske, Frits. *La Mélodie française de Berlioz à Duparc: essai de critique historique*. Paris, 1954.

———. *French Song from Berlioz to Duparc*. Revised edition of the preceding, translated by Rita Benton. New York: Dover, 1970. "Jules Massenet," 210–218, and alphabetical list of songs, 372–387.

Nostrand, Howard Lee. *Le Théâtre antique et à l'antique en France de 1840 à 1900*. Paris, 1934.

Petit Atlas pittoresque des 48 quartiers de la Ville de Paris en 1834. Par A.-M. Perrot, ingénieur (1834). Reproduit en fac-similé avec une introduction, des notes, des additions et des corrections, par Michel Fleury [et] Jeanne Pronteau. Les Éditions de Minuit. Ouvrage publié avec le concours du Centre nationale de la recherche scientifique [n.d.].

Pierre, Constant. *Le Conservatoire Nationale de Musique et de Déclamation; documents historiques et administratifs.* Paris, 1900.

Podenzani, Nino. *Villa d'Este.* Cernobbio, 1965.

Pougin, Arthur. "Massenet," *Rivista musicale italiana,* Vol. 19 (1912), 916–985.

Schneider, Louis. *Massenet: l'homme—le musicien.* [Copiously illustrated] Paris, 1908. 2nd ed. [without illustrations], 1926.

Séré, Octave [Jean Poueigh]. *Musiciens français d'aujourd'hui.* Paris, 1911. 2nd ed., 1921. Section on Massenet, with extensive bibliography and list of works.

Skinner, Cornelia Otis. *Madame Sarah.* New York, 1966. The life of Sarah Bernhardt.

Solenière, Eugène de. *Massenet: étude critique et documentaire.* Paris, 1897.

Vallas, Léon. *Claude Debussy et son temps.* Paris, 1932.

———. *Vincent d'Indy.* 2 vols. Paris, 1946–50.

———. *César Franck.* English translation by Hubert Foss. London, 1951.

Verveen, A. N. "Jules Massenet op Bedevaart in Den Haag," *Mens en Melodie,* Jg. 22, No. 6 (1967), 177–180.

Vitu, Auguste. *Les Mille et une nuits du théâtre.* 9 vols. Paris, 1884–94. Covers the period 1871–82.

Wolff, Stéphane. *Un demi-siècle d'Opéra-Comique* (1900–1950). Paris, 1953.

———. *L'Opéra au Palais Garnier* (1875–1962). Paris, 1962.

PUBLISHED VOLUMES CONTAINING SPEECHES BY MASSENET

Notice sur François Bazin, lue dans la séance du 19 juillet 1879. Institut de France, Académie des Beaux-Arts. Paris, 1879.

Funérailles de M. Guiraud, le 10 mai 1892. Discours de M. Paul Dubois et de M. Massenet. Institut de France, Académie des Beaux-Arts. Paris, 1892.

Discours prononcés à l'occasion de la cérémonie d'inauguration de la statue de Méhul, à Givet, le 2 octobre 1892. Par MM. Massenet et Ambroise Thomas. Paris, 1892.

Funérailles de M. Ambroise Thomas le 22 fevrier 1896, Discours de M. Bonnat, et discours de MM. Massenet, Mézières et Théodore Dubois. Institut de France, Académie des Beaux-Arts. Paris, 1896.

Centenaire de Hector Berlioz. Inauguration du monument élevé à Monte-Carlo, le 7 mars 1903. Discours de M. Massenet. Institut de France, Académie des Beaux-Arts. Paris, 1903.

Funérailles de M. Frémiet, le 15 septembre 1910. Discours de M. Massenet et de M. Edmond Perrier. Institut de France, Académie des Beaux-Arts. Paris, 1910.

Séance publique annuelle des cinq académies, du 25 octobre 1910. Discours du président, M. Jules Massenet . . . [etc.]. Institut de France. Paris, 1910.

Séance publique annuelle du 5 novembre 1910. Discours du président, M. Jules Massenet . . . [etc.]. Institut de France, Académie des Beaux-Arts. Paris, 1910.

Jean de Reszke. Courtesy Paul Jackson.

Selected Discography

Operas

Cendrillon
Von Stade, Welting, Gedda, Bastin
J. Rudel, Philharmonia Orchestra, Ambrosian Opera Company
CBS, M2K-35194

Cendrillon (orchestral suite from the opera)
K. Jean, Hong Kong Philharmonic Orchestra
(with *Esclarmonde*; Suite No. 1)
MARCO POLO, 8.223354

Le Cid
Bumbry, Domingo, Plishka, et al.
E. Queler, Opera Orchestra of New York
CBS, M2K-34211

Le Cid (ballet suite)
R. Bonynge, National Philharmonic Orchestra
(with Delibes *Sylvia*)
LONDON (Jubilee), 425475-2 LM2

Cléopâtre
Harries, Streiff, Olmeda, Henry, Maurette, Hacquard
Fournillier, Nouvel Orchestre de Saint-Étienne and Chorus
KOCH SCHWANN, 3-1032-2

Don Quichotte (comédie héroïque in five acts)
Crespin, Ghiaurov, Bacquier, Command
R. Bonynge, Suisse Romande Orchestra and Chorus
LONDON (Grand Opera), 430636-2 LM2

Esclarmonde
Sutherland, Tourangeau, Aragall
Bonynge, National Philharmonic
LONDON, 425651-2 LM2

Esclarmonde (orchestral suite from the opera)
> K. Jan, Hong Kong Philharmonic Orchestra
> (with *Cendrillon;* Suite No. 1)
> MARCO POLO, 8.223354

Manon
> V. de los Angeles, H. Legay, M. Dens, J. Borthayre
> Monteux, Opéra-Comique de Paris Orchestra and Chorus
> ANGEL, CDMC-63549

Manon
> G. Féraldy, J. Rogatchewsky, L. Guénot
> E. Cohen, Paris Opéra-Comique de Paris Orchestra and Chorus
> CLASSICAL COLLECTOR, FDC 2 2001

Manon
> Freni, Pavarotti, Panera
> Maag, La Scala Orchestra and Chorus
> MELODRAM, MEL-27046
> LEGATO CLASSICS, LCD-132-2
> VERONA, 27052/53

Manon
> J. Piloti, G. Aragall, V. Ganzarolli
> S. Baudo, Vienna State Opera Orchestra and Chorus
> GDS RECORDS, GDS 21044

Manon
> Sills, Gedda, Souzay, Bacquier
> Rudel, New Philharmonia Orchestra, Ambrosian Opera Chorus
> ANGEL (Studio), CDMC-69831

Manon (excerpts—three scenes)
> Favero, Di Stefano
> Guarnieri, La Scala Orchestra
> (with Verdi: *Ballo in maschera*, complete)
> GDS RECORDS, GDS 21039

Manon (extensive excerpts)
> Favero, Di Stefano, Borriello, Mainard
> Guarnieri, La Scala Orchestra
> (with Verdi: *Ballo in maschera*, complete)
> MYTO RECORDS, MCD 905.26

Manon (two tenor arias and two soprano-tenor duets)
> A. Kraus, V. Zeani
> U. Rapolo, Teatro San Carlo Orchestra
> BONGIOVANNI, GB 550/51-2

Manon (three scenes for soprano-tenor duet)
    Scotto, Kraus
    (with Gounod: *Faust*, complete)
    STANDING ROOM ONLY, SRO-811-3

Manon (three soprano-tenor duets)
    Teyte, Nash
    with orchestra
    PEARL, GEMM CD-9326

Manon–Ballet (arrangement of music from Massenet operas)
    Bonynge, Royal Opera Orchestra
    LONDON, 414585-2 LH2

Thaïs
    Esposito, Massard, et al.
    A. Wolff, Orchestre Lyrique and Chorus
    (with aria recital)
    CHANT DU MONDE, LDC-278895/96

Thaïs
    R. Kabaivanska, S. Bruscantini, N. Tagger, A. Zerbini, et al. (in Italian)
    De Fabritiis, Teatro Bellini (Catania) Orchestra and Chorus
    GOLDEN AGE OF OPERA, GAO 121/122

Werther
    Casoni, Ravaglia, Bergonzi, Trimarchi
    De Fabritiis, Naples Teatro San Carlo Orchestra and Chorus
    (with Verdi: *Forza del destino*, selections)
    MELODRAM, 27058

Werther
    V. de los Angeles, M. Meoplé, N. Gedda
    G. Prêtre, Orchestre de Paris and Chorus
    ANGEL (Studio), CDMB-63973

Werther
    Domingo, Obraztsova, Augér, Grundheber, Moll
    R. Chailly, Cologne RSO
    DEUTSCHE GRAMMOPHON, 413304-2

Werther
    Olivero Lazzari, Meletti
    Rossi, Turin Italian Radio Orchestra and Chorus
    (with Puccini arias)
    MELODRAM, MEL-27065

Werther
    Carreras, Von Stade, Allen
    Davis, Royal Opera House
    PHILIPS EMI, 416654-2 PH2

Other Works

Chansons de bois d'Amaranthe (five pieces for solo SATB voices, piano accompaniment)
American Vocal Arts Quintet
(with L. Boulanger; Brahms: *Zigeunerlieder;* Schumann: *Minnespiel*)
Titanic, TI-174

Cigale (divertissement-ballet in two acts)
R. Bonynge, National Philharmonic Orchestra
(with Tchaikovsky: *Swan Lake*)
London (Jubilee), 425413-2

Espada (ballet suite)
G. Sebastian, Paris Opera Orchestra
(with Meyerbeer: *Africaine,* excerpts; *Pardon; Prophète;* Offenbach: *Grande Duchesse*)
Forlane, UDC 16586

Fantaisie for Cello and Orchestra
M. Ostertag
R. Paternostro, Berlin RSO
(with Auber: Rondo; Popper: Concerto)
Koch-Schwann, 311039; 211039

Meditation (intermezzo for orchestra from *Thaïs*)
R. Satanowski, Warsaw National Opera Orchestra
(with Debussy: *Petite suite;* Honegger: Symphony No. 3; Ravel: *Daphnis et Chloé,* Suite No. 2)
Olympia, OCD-318

Scènes alsaciennes (seventh orchestral suite); *Scènes pittoresques* (fourth orchestral suite)
A. Wolff, Paris Conservatory Orchestra
(with Glazunov: *Seasons*)
London (Weekend Classics), 433088-2 LC

Scènes alsaciennes; Scènes hongroises
Vachey, Douai Symphony
Calliope, 1868; 4868

Song Cycles: Poème d'Avril (1866), Poème du souvenir (1868), Poème d'hiver (1882), Expressions lyriques [published 1913]
D. Top (tenor), A. Raës, piano
BNL, 112799

Songs (eleven songs)
Kruysen, with Lee
Anon, ARN-68009

Suite No. 1 for Orchestra, Op. 13
  K. Jean, Hong Kong Philharmonic Orchestra
  (with *Cendrillon; Esclarmonde*)
  MARCO POLO, 8.223354

La Vierge (oratorio—sacred drama in four parts)
  Command, Castets, Olmeda, Keller, Salmon, Hacquard
  P. Fournillier, Prague Symphony Orchestra and Choruses
  KOCH SCHWANN, 313084 K2

Index